Clusters, Networks, and Innovation in Small and Medium Scale Enterprises (SMEs)

European University Studies

Europäische Hochschulschriften
Publications Universitaires Européennes

Series V
Economics and Management

Reihe V Série V
Volks- und Betriebswirtschaft
Sciences économiques, gestion d'entreprise

Vol./Bd. 3373

PETER LANG
Frankfurt am Main · Berlin · Bern · Bruxelles · New York · Oxford · Wien

Osmund Osinachi Uzor

Clusters, Networks, and Innovation in Small and Medium Scale Enterprises (SMEs)

The Role of Productive Investment in the Development of SMEs in Nigeria

PETER LANG
Internationaler Verlag der Wissenschaften

Bibliographic Information published by the Deutsche Nationalbibliothek
The Deutsche Nationalbibliothek lists this publication in the Deutsche Nationalbibliografie; detailed bibliographic data is available in the internet at http://dnb.d-nb.de.

Zugl.: Bremen, Univ., Diss., 2009

D 46
ISSN 0531-7339
ISBN 978-3-631-60358-1

www.peterlang.de

Contents

Tables

Figures

Acknowledgement

I am very grateful to the institutions and individuals for their inputs and support in various means in making this research study a dream come through. I am really honoured to be supervised by Prof. Dr. Karl Wohlmuth and Prof. Dr. Axel Sell both at the Institute for World Economics and International Management (IWIM), University of Bremen. Both Professors provided the much needed intellectual assistance, critics, suggestions and ideas which were useful and were incorporated in the research work. My special thanks to Prof. Dr. Karl Wohlmuth for his patience, effective guidance and all the assistance he rendered to me through out the period. *"Ich bin dafür sehr danbar"*.

Many thanks to former staffs and colleagues at the IWIM, University of Bremen, Prof. Dr. Hans H. Bass, Bremen University of Applied Sciences Faculty of Business and Economics for their encouragement and cooperation. I am grateful to Dr. Uwe Staroske (Subject librarian) and Peter Mioch (Inquiries) Library of Economics, University of Bremen for their kindness and assistance in locating the necessary literature.

I am really grateful to International Office, University of Bremen, for supporting me financially through DAAD-STIBET programme. My appreciation goes to the caring Mrs Glinka of the Studentenwerk, University of Bremen, ESG, Bremen, KSG, Bremen, Ev. Jona Gemeinde in Bremen, and Mrs Elisabeth Sittig. My warmest appreciation goes to Dr. Med. Stefan and Mrs Katrin Siever of Bochum for their assistance and support during the hard times. I am grateful my friends Mr. Nicolaus Schrodter and Birthe Brandes for always standing by me. I am grateful to Dr.-Ing. Kpatcha Bayarou Frauenhofer Institute Darmstadt for his inspiration and exchange of ideas on academic issues and life in foreign country during his studies in Bremen. My thanks go to Ms. Angeline Asangire Oprong and Elvis Masley for their contributions in the proof-reading of the work especially the critical views from Ms. Oprong. I also appreciate the assistance of Tochukwu Andrew Udeh, and Okechukwu Udeh during the fieldwork.

My appreciation also to my friend Dr Reuben Alabi *(Axender von Humboldt Research Fellow, IWIM, and University of Bremen)* of Ambrose Ali University, Ekpoma, Edo State, Nigeria. Prof. Dr. John A. Ezeh (Chief), Former Dean Faculty of Business Management, University of Nigeria, Enugu Campus for their encouragement. I am grateful to the staffs of Enugu State Ministry of Industry and Commerce, Mrs T. G. Onejeme, Deputy Director of Industries, Anambra State Ministry of Commerce, Industry and Tourism; staffs of Enugu Chambers of Commerce, Industry, Mines and Agriculture; staffs of Nnewi Chambers of Commerce, Industry, Mines and Agriculture; of staffs Aba Chambers of Commerce, Industry, Mines and Agriculture; staffs of Enugu State

Nigerian Association of Small Scale Industrialist (NASSI) Secretariat, Nigerian Automobile Technician Association Nnewi Branch. I am grateful to Dr. Engr. Okonkwo former National President of NASSI for his advice. My thanks to the staffs of Central Bank of Nigeria Library, Abuja, and Federal Bureau of Statistics, Abuja, Nigeria, Nigerian Achieves Enugu and NISSER, Ibadan Nigeria.

I am grateful to my entire family: - my late father †Stephen and my mother Rhodah Uzor, my sister and her husband Mrs Esther O. Nwosu and †Rt Rev. RNC Nwosu; my brothers Godwin, Obiora, Christian, Maxwell and their wives for their unimaginable support during the period. Many thanks to Arch. Mrs Nwaneka C. Gill-Eruchalu, Barrister Peace Chiemeka Nwosu, Engr. Chike and Dr. Mrs O. Nwosu, Mr Christ and Mrs Ebele Eruchalu for their prayers. My appreciation goes to Mrs Ijeoma R. Okafor (Nee Udeh) for her valuable assistance.

I wish to thank the families that offered various support during the series of field studies in Nigeria - Sir Paul and Lady Ogechukwu Uzor Ulasi of (Otolo Village, Nnewi), Chief Barrister C. O. C. and Barrister Mrs Ebele Egumgbe (Enugu), Mr Andy E. and Mrs Nkechi Nwigwe (Lagos), Mr Charles and Mrs Eber Ola Onyegbula (Enugu), Chief Tim and Mrs Umeweni (Aba). I wish to thank my friends and relations for their support before and during the periods - Mrs Egodi Akagu (Nee Nwigwe), Mr Ben-B and Mrs Dorin Eneh, Mr Greg Ezeilo Managing Consultant/Chief Executive of Signal House Consulting Ltd, Mr. Princewell A. Udeh, and Mr Emeka B. Eneh for their valuable support. I pay tribute to those who prayed, provided spiritual and moral assistance before and during the research period but could not live to see this work materialised- †Rt. Rev. Dr. RNC Nwosu, †Chief Paul Ulasi, †Mrs K. Nwigwe, and †Mrs Elisabeth Sittig.

Dedication

To my sons

Nnaemeka Gaaniru Uzor and Nnamdi Anarazu Ernest Uzor

To my brilliant brother

Jonathan Ezike Uzor who at the age of six wanted to be a medical doctor but died a year later

To my nephew

Okechukwu Godson Chiagozie Nwosu who died from brain tumor after his final BSc. examination in accountancy at the Amadu Bello University Zaria, Nigeria.

Preface

The book presents a new approach towards the promotion of Small and Medium Enterprises (SMEs). Over the last three decades there have been controversies in development policy circles on whether Small and Medium Scale Enterprises (SMEs) in Sub-Saharan Africa (SSA) have the potential to create and sustain employment, generate income, alleviate poverty, and contribute to economic growth. The concerns were due to the worsening employment crisis in the region and increasing poverty. Although some countries have engaged in structural reforms to increase the policy space of the SMEs, progress is impeded by structural weaknesses and by increasing globalisation pressure. Several theoretical approaches with respect to promoting SMEs in the region are discussed in the book, notably the view that certain internal and external constraints are limiting the growth of SMEs, and the view that specific obstacles, such as access to finance, local and global markets, entrepreneurship and management, human resources and training, information, innovation, and access to networks and technological capability have been extensively investigated. However, the author is reaching further out with this book as a new methodological approach is used - by combining cluster, innovation, and network studies.

Although the empirical basis of this study is limited to a sub-region in Nigeria (Enugu, Anambra and Abia states), and as this is one with experience and tradition in SMEs, this study provides a new approach in understanding the dynamics and the weaknesses of SMEs in Africa which will be of use for analysis and policy reform in other African regions as well. The analytical approach is quite systematic and organised in a form that covers three operational frameworks of SMEs, notably clustering, networking and innovative activities. The methodological approach covers for these frameworks different elements of quantitative and qualitative research, and the author explains each operational framework in great detail. This approach therefore explicitly revealed the link between clustering, networking, and innovation in the promotion of the small industry sector and in the design of appropriate and adapted industrialisation strategies in Africa. The methodological approach used by Dr. O. O. Uzor can definitely be taken by other researchers as a guideline when intending to conduct a field study in small industry development in Nigeria or in any other country in Africa.

The study started by investigating the following hypotheses: firstly, there is a correlation between SME growth and employment creation and income generation; secondly, clustering of small enterprises in a defined geographical location enhances the economic performance of small enterprises; thirdly; social networks help in the reduction and elimination of the small enterprises growth constraints; fourthly, innovative activities of small enterprises are basically part of a survival strategy; and fifthly, small enterprises in Africa nonetheless have the capacity to compete. The results revealed, among others, that under favourable macroeconomic environment conditions and with access to new markets, job creation in small enterprises tends to rise. Small enterprises clusters, even with a high degree of informality characteristics, can be quite active and as well can be competitive in local markets by applying different marketing strategies to overcome external competitive pressure. Regionalisation processes and liberalisation of the market have increased trading networks of small industries across the borders of Anglo phone and Franco phone countries into a wider African sub-regional market. Innovative activity in small enterprises in sub-Saharan Africa is part of a survival strategy in an open economy. However, innovative activity in the small industry sector can be strengthened further by measures to promote human resources development and the acquisition of technological capabilities. There is a potential to overcome the character of a survival strategy in the longer term. The empirical findings also revealed several limitations in Nigerian/African SMEs similar to previous findings. The limitations include, among others, the high degree of informality, the weak institutional support, a low level of skilled labour force, a weak technological base, and the absence of linkages with large firms. The departing point is how to reduce these limitations in the current situation of globalisation pressure, and the author makes a lot of useful suggestions how this can be achieved. So the book is also a guide to policy makers on how to design new reform policies for the small industry sector in Africa.

In that context, the second part of the study focused on the relationship between productive investment and SME development. Growth in the economy depends on productive investment, and the growth of small industries depends on productive investment of the firms. Macro and micro factors are interrelated. In view of this, the author has contributed to the literature on small industries with another innovation. Hence, the Investment and SME Development (ISMED) model was developed by the author in order to address the issues relating to these limitations. The basic concept of the ISMED-model is to show why productive investment is important for SMEs and how productive investment can be accelerated by related reforms so as to contribute to SME development. The role of investment in this context is to bridge the capability gap and to increase overall performance so that the impact on the transformation of the SME sector in Nigeria and on the growth of the economy can be maximised. The model shows how investment can enhance both human and physical capital in order to increase aggregate efficiency. The aggregate effects of the investment strategies can be measured in terms of the transformation effects in the small enterprises sector and the transmission effects on the economy in general. This study by Dr. O. O. Uzor argues that the ISMED model is not strictly relevant only for Nigerian SMEs. Rather it was specifically designed for the promotion of SMEs in Africa. The model is also not restricted to any particular industrial sector, but it may be particularly relevant for the industrial sectors where the country has a comparative advantage. In such sectors the reforms along the ISMED model could produce more quickly positive results.

The third important part in the study is the review - in a very detailed form – of the Nigerian industrial policies pursued in different periods dating from 1900 to 2007. It became necessary to review the pattern of Nigeria's industrial development efforts and to show how policy shifts and reversals have led to distortions in general economic management and to poor industrial policy outcomes. As all these distortions and management failures have impeded the development of the small industry sector in Nigeria, the analysis gives guidelines for corrective action. The industrial policy objectives were ill-conceived ideas, and they were subject to frequent policy reversals. To give an example, the location of industries in Nigeria (of the so-called Industrial Core Projects/ICPs and of other public industries) has undermined the importance of linkages for small industries. These projects were rather ethnically-motivated without giving them any economic consideration. The pervasive nature of policy objectives coupled with the poor governance system made the economy to become even more volatile to domestic and external shocks.

The author has achieved not only a very detailed study of the small enterprise sector in Nigeria, but also a very complete analysis, ranging from an analysis of obstacles to firm growth to an analysis of a model for the promotion of the SMEs and an analysis of the constraints arising from the industrial policy side. The concluding argument by the author suggests that policy reforms aimed at productive investment in human capital development and infrastructure provision are needed to support sustainable development and entrepreneurial learning. It is also imperative to create an environment conducive for the transfer of know-how and providing for linkages of local SMEs with large domestic and foreign firms. Policy reforms should also continue to focus on creating stable institutions that support and enhance access to global finances.

This study is important for development policy for various reasons: Firstly, it provided a detailed analysis of the growth constraints of SMEs in Africa. Secondly, it provided detailed empirical evidence on the impact of clustering and networking and of innovative activities on SMEs in Africa. Thirdly, it provided detailed micro, meso and macro-level analyses for an industrial development model that supports productive investment and institution-building, the transformation of the SME sector, the acquisition of technological capability, and the establishment and use of linkages for SME development. Fourthly, it provided a detailed analysis on the importance of policy reforms that are aimed at a sustainable growth model for the SME sector.

As economic globalisation continues to intensify, industrial policy makers in Nigeria and development institutions in Africa should study this work carefully and design sustainable strategies on how to promote SMEs, SME clusters, SME networks, and innovative activities in SMEs in Nigeria and in other countries of Africa. The study by Dr. Uzor is a remarkable academic achievement and will influence researchers on SMEs in their endeavors. Although it is the work by an economist, the study will also give impulses to other disciplines when investigating into the development of SMEs. It is a great development task to bridge the gap between micro enterprises and large enterprises in Africa, and policy reforms for SMEs suggested by Dr. Uzor may indeed be instrumental for this.

Prof. Dr. Karl Wohlmuth
Institute for World Economics and International Management (IWIM)
Faculty of Business and Economics
University of Bremen

Chapter 1: Introduction

1.1 Research Problem

Nigerian economy has encountered prolonged Dutch Disease created by over-dependence on oil exports. Between 1970s and 1990s, the economy was supported by overvalued exchange rate primarily for imports of consumer goods. Consequently, productivity in the non-oil sectors especially the tradable goods in agricultural cash crops and in the manufacturing sector was weakened. After independence, Nigeria pursued development strategy that placed priority on certain capital-intensive industries. The policy objectives were ill conceived ideas and subject to frequent reversal. Location of the so-called Core Industrial Projects (ICPs) and other public industries were ethnic motivated without economic consideration. Investments were concentrated on final stage consumer goods that lack inter-firm linkages. The industrial capacity and the production expanded rapidly to the detriment of agricultural development. The industries were protected with high tariffs and subventions. In the course of time severe scarcity of foreign exchange and surging foreign debt compounded the economic problem. Couple with mismanagement, these strategies could not be sustained as a result of their high dependency on imported inputs hence the firms became uncompetitive and non-viable.

When oil prices collapsed in early 1980s, the country gradually slipped from a middle-income oil producing country in the 1970s and early 1980s to one of the lowest-income country in mid-1980s and 1990s[1]. In other words, a substantial improvement in income and employment could have been possible if the economy was significantly diversified away from the oil sector[2]. The consequences of over-dependence on oil ranges from risks of economic instability as a result of oil price volatility in world market, vulnerability to local conflicts on the basis of resource control as the case in Niger Delta, to the neglect of important sectors like agricultural cash crops and mining. Diversifying the economy away from oil sector and development of the private sector would have created internal shocks capable of absorbing the dilemma associated with petro-economy and can as well lead to economic upgrading. In this context, promotion of small and medium scale enterprises (SMEs) is on the premise that they support economic diversification and private sector development (PSD). The neglect of PSD during the oil boom era between 1970's and early 1980's pushed Nigeria deeper into economic recession and

---

1 The Gross National Income (GNI) per capita in 2003 was US$350 (World Bank, 2005, p. 23).

2 UNCTAD (1995) report focused on efforts made on diversification of commodity export in developing countries.

poverty when the oil prices collapsed. The relationship between PSD and poverty reduction in sub-Saharan Africa (SSA) can be inferred from two perspectives. Firstly, private sector supports development of market economy. Secondly, PSD can drive productivity growth, creation of productive jobs and higher income when subjected to good policy environment.

There have been several claims and counter claims about the potential of SMEs in SSA. Some development economic literature argues that SMEs in SSA countries possess the potential to create employment and generate income (Mead, 1998; Mead & Liedholm, 1998; Liedholm & Mead, 1998). On the other hand, SMEs in African cannot sustain employment creation rather tend to generate low income (Livingstone, 1996; Daniel and Mead, 1998). It is also argued that SMEs in Africa are isolated and lack the potential individually to improve performance or sustain competition (the missing link). The capabilities of SMEs in Africa are seen to be very weak and lack the potential to play their role in economic development and in the ongoing globalisation process (Wohlmuth, 1991, Fafchamps, 1994; Lall and Kraemer-Mbula, 2005). The aim of this study therefore is to verify these claims with respect to Nigeria. In making concluding inductions on the claims, this study therefore investigates the three SME operational structures namely clustering, networking and innovative strategy.

1.2 The Research objectives

To undertake this study, the following questions were considered: Can private sector development be the main solution to Nigeria's unemployment and poverty problems? Will human capital development act as a stimulus to the growth of private sector? To what extent can improved institutional and physical environment make the country attractive for domestic and Foreign Direct Investment (FDI)? How can the potential role of SMEs in the economy be optimised in order to impact growth? Can economic reform and sustained democracy at all levels of governance make impact on economic growth of Nigeria?

Based on these questions, the study seeks to revisit the following questions: (a) To which extent can the possible differences in production output, gross sales of small and medium scale enterprises be explained by territorially bounded external economies? (b) To what extent do information costs and transportation costs constrain the geographical availability of external economies? (c) To what extent have joint actions contributed to small enterprises performance? The study further goes to verify the claim that social networks support the small enterprises to reduce transaction costs, search costs, and contract enforcement and reaching distance market. This is followed by empirical investigation on the capabilities of small enterprises in Nigeria. In this case, the analysis is centred on the level of human capital and technological capabilities of the small enterprises. This helped in understanding the micro level of the national innovation system in terms of local technological capabilities. The background aim of this study is to evaluate the capabilities of small enterprises in Nigeria, review Nigeria's past industrial and technology policies and provide dynamic policy measures for SME development in Nigeria. The research objectives are summarised as follows:

- To establish if there are significant differences in performance between the clustered and the dispersed small enterprises.
- To show that social networks support enterprises development when the formal institution is weak and seeks ways to strengthen formal institutions for industrial development in wider perspectives.
- To investigate the strength of human capital and technological apabilities of small enterprises in Nigeria.
- To establish whether domestic investment serve as the basic instrument that drives the economic growth and FDI as the major catalyst that stimulates the economic growth as well as provide dynamic model for SME development in Nigeria.
- To review the past Nigeria's industrial policies and make policy recommendations on the promotion of SME in Nigeria based on the research findings.

1.3 Motivation of the study

This work is a reflection of author's academic and practical knowledge acquired in one of the most successful industrialised economy of the world (Germany) where SMEs and private sector play predominant role in economic development. The author's presumption is that SMEs can play an important role in Africa's poverty and unemployment problems depending on the nature of support and development environment. The presumption is shared by International Labour Organisation's (ILO) prediction that by the year 2020, vast majority of African workers will be engaged in SME activities (ILO, 1990). According to World Bank statistics, in 1995, 95 percent of industrial activities in Nigeria were found in micro and small enterprises while 2.4 percent and 2.5 percent in medium and large scale enterprises respectively (World Bank, 1995a, p. 16). Statistics further revealed that 87 percent of Nigeria's industrial activities are in small scale enterprises while 9 percent and 4 percent are in medium and large scale enterprises respectively (World Bank, 2002a, p. 138). This relative change in industrial structure demands explanation in respect to Nigeria's industrial activities. Despite decades of research on small enterprises in developing countries, there are still open questions, conflicting evidence and terms used regarding the subject. Hence, there is the need for constant updating the scientific knowledge.

During the study, the author was confronted with three challenges; firstly, the definition of SMEs. Definition of SMEs in Nigeria depends on the institutions and organisations promoting the sector. The scale used to define SMEs by Nigerian Council of Industry (NCI) did not reflect the reality on the ground in qualitative and quantitative aspects. Hence, the author considered different definitions using some parameters such as the number of employees, technology (capital and labour intensive) to aid decision making. Secondly, the problems associated with heterogeneity of the small enterprises. The heterogeneity in SMEs requires disaggregating the sector in order to identify some specific realities and thirdly, is the macroeconomic environment in which the small enterprises operate. Macroeconomic issues have to be considered in order to understand the dynamics of SMEs.

1.4 Theoretical Assumptions and Hypotheses

The main assumption of this study is that development of SME in Nigeria can be hampered by the low levels of stock of human capital especially in respect to weak technical labour force. In this case, Nigeria government has not been able to restructure its educational policy to reflect industrial needs[3]. This argument is based on the premise that the stock of human capital i.e. 'knowledge' as the new growth theory suggests, is a complimentary asset that drives economic growth[4]. The greater the stock of human capital combined with other factors, the higher the national output. Hence, the economic underdevelopment in Africa is not necessarily due to lack of technology or capital but due to low human capital development existing in the region. Technological development is a function of human development, and adaptation of new technology in local production systems depends on the type of education and the educational level of the labour force in the economy. One can therefore argue that the ability of individuals to escape from poverty trap starts from the level of educational qualification. An educated individual can apply knowledge more productively and stands a better chance of receiving higher wages compared to an uneducated one. Assuming

3 Nigeria is ranked position 154 out of 179 countries in recent UNDP human development record with Human Development Index (HDI) of 0.499 (UNDP, 2007/08, p. 231).

4 ... "No amount of savings and investment, no policy of macroeconomic fine tuning, no set of tax and spending incentives can generate sustained economic growth unless it is accompanied by the countless large and small discoveries that are required to create more value from a fixed set of natural resources" (Romer, 1993, p. 345).

that local technological capability in Nigeria is weak and needs to be upgraded, two plausible options can be considered in order to resolve the technological problem. The first are the policy measures that support an inward solution by creating measures that can facilitate local technological development. The second option is the policy measures that support a combined inward and outward solution aimed at technological leaning by improving linkages between the local firms and large Transnational Corporations (TNCs). In making deductions, it must be recognised that in the global technology market, technological inventions change faster than technological applications. Furthermore between 1987 and 1997, government expenditure on R&D expressed as a percentage of gross domestic product (GDP) in low income developing countries was 0.7 per cent (UNDP, 2007/8, p. 276). In sub-Saharan Africa (SSA) excluding South Africa, the number of researchers per million inhabitants was 81 as at 2007. SSA region excluding South Africa contributes on 0.9 per cent of world researchers[5]. In Nigeria, the average expenditure on R&D as a percentage of gross domestic products between 1987 and 1997 was 0.09 per cent (World Bank, 2001, p. 311). Based on this situation, the policy choices reflect on the balance between the capability to develop new technology and the adaptation cost by improving capabilities for linkages with the TNCs. Hence local small firms may gain by trying to catch-up through learning and imitation or may as well resolve the problem of technology the SMEs through joint-venture arrangements.

It is argued that clustering of SMEs in a particular location can can be facilitate learning or reduce the constraints faced by the small entrepreneurs. Clustering also supports the transfer of best practices effectively when small enterprises in the cluster are in direct partnership or linkage with large foreign enterprises. Moreover, policy interventions can be applied easily in a cluster of small enterprises (UNIDO, 2002). The promotion of SMEs in Nigeria has been predominantly through government sponsored loan schemes (Inang and Ukpong, 1993, p. 259; Anyanwu, 2003, p. 24; Olorunshola, 2003, p. 40). However, loan schemes were marred by alleged financial misappropriation as well as poor loan recovery rate, thus leading to waste of scarce resources. This study departs from the supply side analytical approach and focuses on dynamic factors anchored on a combination of supply and demand approach for capability improvement. Based on the above theoretical assumptions, the hypotheses of the study are:

a) There is a correlation between SME growth and employment creation and income Generation.

b) Clustering of small enterprises in a defined geographical location enhances the economic performance of small enterprises.

---

5 UNESCO Science and Technology (S&T) data update, www.uis.unesco.org/ev.php

c) Social networks help in the reduction of the small enterprises growth constraints.
d) Innovative activities of small enterprises in Nigeria are survival strategy.
e) Small enterprises in Nigeria have the capacity to compete.

1.5 Methodology

1.5.1 The Analytical Steps

This study is structured to examine and answer the questions as shown in Figure 1, that is, why are SMEs important in sub-Saharan African economy? Why are small enterprises cluster in a defined location? Why are networks and innovation very important for SMEs? Can SMEs play significant role in economic development especially in poverty reduction and wealth creation? The analytical structure is imperative because it shows clearly the procedure of the theoretical and empirical analyses. It also shows the logical steps in the investigation of the endogenous factors that limit the growth of small enterprises in the sub-Region using Nigeria as a case study. It further shows how the three operational structures of small enterprises activities can be linked in analytical work.

Clusters and networks although interwoven in concept, they are different in characteristics therefore require different analytical approach. An enterprises cluster is defined as geographical concentration of enterprises supported by institutions and self-help organisations. As against the pattern of formal localisation of industries, formation of enterprise clusters in developing countries are born of out of several constraints such as poor infrastructure and weak institutional development. Enterprises cluster formation allows small enterprises to gain some advantages which they individually are unable to achieve.

Social networks which support the competitiveness of the firms can be developed within the cluster. In general, enterprises social networks can develop not only among the Entrepreneurs within the cluster but also among those outside the clusters. Networks can be defined as observed pattern of interaction or relationships among entrepreneurs aimed at finding solutions to their common problems. The pattern of interaction can be personal or organisational depending on the level of entrepreneurship development in a given economy. Innovation is a factor that supports enterprises competitiveness. The capability to innovate depends on behavioural factors such as level of education of the entrepreneurs, acquired skills and incentives that motivate innovative activities of small enterprises.

Figure 1: Analytical Procedure of the Study

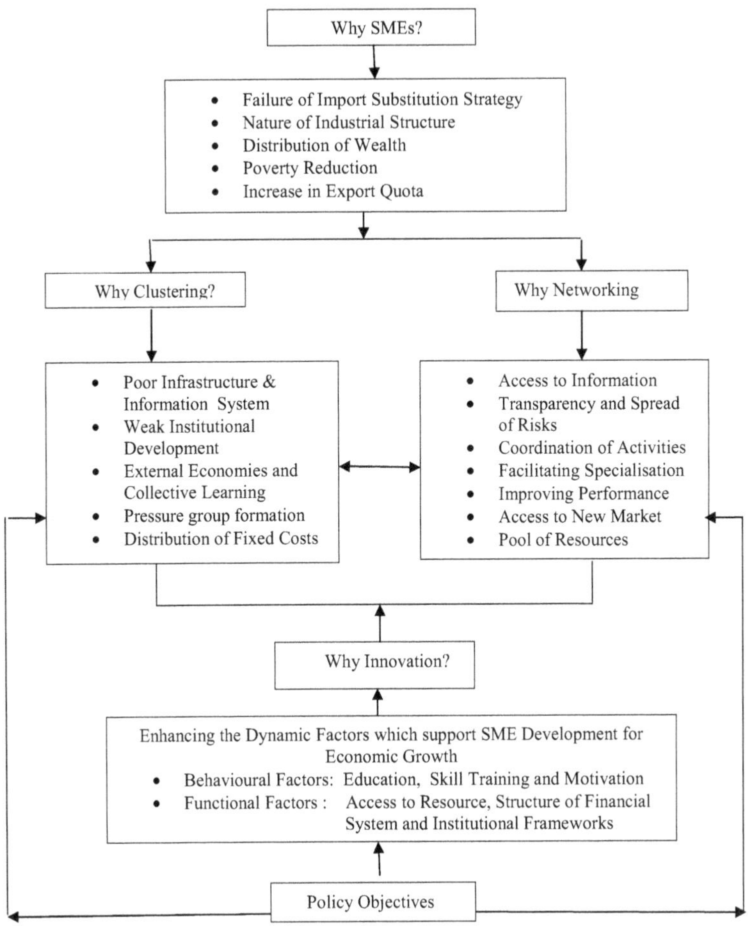

Source: Author's compilation

Functional factors such as access to resources, the structure of the financial system that promotes innovation also reflects the type of institutional framework that promotes competition hence fundamental for innovation to take place. The analysis of innovation in this study is important because the investigation focused on how small enterprises react to the changes in the World economic systems. It depicts how small enterprises compete or survive as a result of increased economic globalisation. The level of innovation discussed in the study excludes measure of inputs such as expenditure on R&D or the output such as the number of patented inventions which are common in High-Tech industries in developed economies. The study is confined to innovation in the context of enterprises reaction to the changes in market demand and/or changes in imports due to liberalisation of the market. The empirical evidence employed in the study formed the basis for development of a dynamic model for SME development in Nigeria and SSA.

1.5.2 Data collection and field survey challenges

Generally, this study is not intended to develop new theory on small enterprises, rather different assumptions and theories were evaluated under the African economic framework using Nigeria as a pivot point. The study starts by reviewing economic and social performance of Nigerian economy as well as previous poverty related reduction policies and programmes. The basic theories on promotion of small enterprises which provided the background for empirical study are reviewed. The secondary data is derived from the database of Nigerian Bureau of Statistics and Central Bank of Nigeria, the World Bank, World Development Report, World Development Indicators, International Monetary Fund (IMF), United Nations industrial Development Organisation (UNIDO), World Health Organisation (WHO), United Nations Development Programme (UNDP), United Nations Conference on Trade and Development (UNCTAD).
A combined fieldwork and surveys are used in primary data collection[6]. Integration of fieldwork and surveys within a single project opens up opportunities for mutual advantages in each of the three major phases - design, data collection and analysis (Sieber, 1982, p. 177). The use of traditional survey methods with pre set standard questionnaires only raises some questions on reliability and validity of data. Warwick (1983, pp. 278-279) argues that anthropologists have often combined observational research with survey and other quantitative approaches in field studies on the effects of rapid urbanisation

---

6 Fieldwork involves participation, interviewes and use of available records to supplement these techniques in a participating setting (Sieber, 1982, p.188). Survey sampling in field implies the use of structured interview schedules, probability samples e.t.c that are usually thought of as a participant observation study (Zelditch, Jr, 1982, p. 168).

in Africa with respect to rural and urban interdependence[7]. Gutkind (1967, p. 161) recommended not only the need to rework traditional anthropological techniques but also acceptance of research techniques of other disciplines.

As a result of ineffective channels of communication in Nigeria and educational level of interviewees, data collection entail using face to face interviews, discussions with craftsmen, entrepreneurs and their employees. To control the biasness of information, face to face interviews with private and public institutions that promote small and medium enterprises were also conducted. Observation on the business activities of the enterprise were also carried out[8]. The questions put forward to interviewees were constantly reframed or dropped or continuously regenerated, reconstructed in the process depending on the reaction of the interviewees due to sensitivity of some factors such as profits and income e.t.c.[9]. Under these changing circumstances, to generate reliable information, repeated visits were taken in order to verify and clarify information given. The author experienced multiple challenges for instance hostile and repulsive interviewees. This is presumably attributed to the fact that the previous interviews did not bring any direct personal benefit or a significant change in sectoral problems. Under this circumstance, the author employed psychological approaches in attracting the interest of the interviewees to gain confidence.

Cognitive factors such as “first instance approach”, “the micro level values” of the research and “the language” were considered to capture interviewees' attention[10]. In the first instance approach required the author to be cautious of situations subjecting the interviewees into fear, tension or suspicion[11]. Clarity and an open mind approach were required followed by detailed explanation of micro-level values of the research[12]. The author’s

---

7 There has been considerable dispute about the appropriateness of survey, methods questioning the reliability and validity of the data. Most of the critiques on survey method in developing countries come from the anthropologists that question the quality of original data that is influenced by cultural prejudice (Bulmer, 1983, p. 13). Using the words of Leach (1967, p. 82). "... the anthropologist is constantly made aware of the difficulty of fitting items of human behaviour and experience into numerical categories. It is not that the numbers are necessarily false but that they draw the enquirer’s attention away from what is of crucial significance”.

8 Field methods which do not encompass observation, interviewees and sampling are seen as narrow and inadequate (Burgess, 1982, pp. 75-78).

9 This can be referred to as adequacy of Informants for various problems in the field (Zelditch, Jr. 1982, p. 170). Different methodological approaches to field research were outlined by Burgess (1982, pp. 163-167).

10 These factors are based on researcher’s field experience.

11 Fears and suspicion are due to unexpected frequent visits of different local authorities.

12 Caution has to be taken in explaining the values of the research. Boundary of explanation is important otherwise the research will create unlimited solutions.

personal background and origin played positive role in winning the confidence of the interviewees. Interviewees were cautious in disclosing information because they were suspicious that personal interest of the researcher might have implications on his or her business interest. The researcher may pass on sensitive to potential competitor. In this case, again the open mind approach played in to reduce suspicion. Language of instruction was not the problem in this study due to the researcher's background. However, some technical jargons regarding the subject have to be simplified to the level of the interviewees because of differences in educational level and temperament of the interviewees. The ability to communicate, select and use the appropriate words which can appeal the interest of the interviewee determined the acquisition of information from the interviewees. The study used a combination of qualitative and quantitative methods in order to establish the representativeness and validity of results. The two methods supplements and complements each other especially where there are biases (Reichardt and Cook, 1979, p. 21)[13].

1.5.3 Design of Sample Representative

1.5.3.1 The Sample Procedure

The field studies cover 13 months and were carried out in three phases between 2003 and 2008 in Nigeria. The first phase took 5 months (November 2003 to April 2004). The second phase took 6 months (January and June 2005). The final phase took a period of 2 months (February and March 2008). The field studies were conducted in southeast region of Nigeria in four major cities namely: Aba, Akwa, Enugu, and Nnewi (see Appendix 1 and 2, pp. 375-376 below). Five industrial sub-sectors were covered in the study namely: wood/furniture, leather/footwear, palm kernel oil extraction, garment and light engineering. The interviews were carried out by the author and 2 assistants.

Due to extreme values in terms of size among the clusters surveyed, it was difficult to construct representative sample population from each cluster. The researcher had to consider two steps in order to construct a relatively representative sample frame for the survey. First, a percentage scale that reflected the structure of the clusters was designed in order to generate representation. Second, some assumptions were considered before developing the sample frame. The first assumption was the enterprises with more than 100

---

13 Quantitative method is associated with enumerative induction with the aim to infer a characteristic or a relationship of the variable to a parent population. The qualitative method is associated with analytic induction that is concerned with developing simple explanatory hypotheses (Brannen, 1992, pp. 5-7). Quantitative methods have to establish the frame in which qualitative interviews are carried out (Hansohm, 1992, p. 16).

workers were excluded in the sample frame because of the measure of interests and the classification of SMEs in Nigeria. The second consideration was certain criteria had to be employed to limit the number of clusters in the survey. In this case, four criteria were applied in the selection of the investigating clusters. They are a) the number of enterprises in the cluster, b) the nature of technology applied by enterprises in the clusters, c) enterprises with similar products, and c) the type of linkages. The third assumption was enterprises must be operating in a defined geographical location in order to evaluate the impact of clustering on firms. In South Eastern part of Nigeria, 8 small enterprises were identified to be in cluster formation. They are blacksmithing, women hairdressing, motor mechanics, wood/furniture, leather and footwear, garment, palm kernel oil extraction (PKO) and light engineering. Five clusters within the above enterprises were selected for the study based on the criteria stipulated above. Stratified sampling method is used because the sub-populations vary considerably. Each sub-population (stratum) was sampled independently because stratification helped to group the enterprises in the population into relatively homogeneous subgroups before making a random sampling. In sampling, few SMEs from each stratum or cluster were randomly selected to form the investigative sample. In this case, examination of parameters for each sub-domain within the population can be obtained separately as suggested by Levy and Lemeshow, (1999, p. 276).

To avoid overlapping of results, the empirical investigations were disaggregated according to subsectors. Disaggregation provided more insight into the measure of interest and the framework for comparative analysis of cluster performance as well as classification of cluster into dormant and active clusters[14]. Since there are extreme values in the cluster structure (e.g leather/-footwear and PKO), the sample population had to be constructed using a scale or percentage ratio. Table 1.1 shows the scale used in constructing the structure of survey sample. The scale is designed to yield a relatively proportional sample population such that the percentage ratio (scale) increases in an inverse proportion to the total population of the enterprises in sampled cluster. The scale is build to allow a simple two-stage cluster sampling similar to Levy and

14 An enterprise cluster is said be active if it has been able to overcome competitive pressure and had the capacity to upgrade and expand overtime, otherwise it is referred to as a dormant cluster.

Lemeshow (1999) analogue[15]. To construct the scale, the lower and upper limits of the percentage ratio to be used were determined. The lower limit reflects the cluster with the least population while the upper limit represents the cluster with the highest population among the sampled clusters. For example, to obtain the sample population for leather and footwear with highest population for about 11,535 enterprises will take a scale of 1.25 percentage ratio. The PKO with lowest population for about 100 enterprises will take a scale of 80 percentage ratios. In general, the limits are bounded in the form $\geq 5 < \infty$. It is assumed that the least possible number enterprises in a cluster are 5 firms (lower bound). The highest number of enterprises in a cluster is assumed to have a finite value. The least percentage ratio is assigned to the total population with higher value or percentage ratio. As shown in Table 1.1 above, the percentage ratio is proportional and the cluster population is classified according to proportional intervals. The highest possible percentage ratio is assigned to the cluster with lowest population of enterprises and the least possible percentage ratio is assigned to the cluster with highest population of enterprises. Table 1.1 helps to establish a representative sample that reflects the extreme values in small enterprises clusters.

Table 1.1: Structure of the scale used for survey sample design

Percentage Ratio in chosen the sample population	Total Population of Enterprises in the Cluster
0.625	≥16,000
1.25	≥8,000<16,000
2.50	≥4,000<8,000
5.00	≥2,000<4,000
10.00	≥1,000<2,000
20.00	≥500<1,000
40.00	≥250<500
80.00	≥100<250

Source: Constructed by the author based on Levyand Lemeshow (1999) analogue

15 If one city block contains ten households and another contains six households, it would not be possible to take a 30 per cent sample of households from each of the two blocks. However, if a general strategy is to have second stage sampling fractions as nearly equal as possible among the two blocks, then one would be expected to select three from the block having ten households, and two households from the block having six households, and would include scenario such as this under the general rubric of simple two-stage cluster sampling" (Levy and Lemeshow, 1999, pp. 275-6). In other words, unequal probabilities of selection can be compensated for in the succeeding stage to produce an equal probability of selection overall (Henry, 1990, p. 30).

As shown in Table 1.2, the sample population was derived by dividing the percentage ratio with 100 and multiple by the total population. The population of the enterprises in the cluster used are derived from enterprises population census conducted by previous researchers. The population of leather/footwear and Garment was derived from the cluster census conducted by Kate Meagher (2004). The population of SMEs in Nnewi light engineering was derived from Powell (2003) and compared with Nnewi chambers of Commerce and Industry data.

Table 1.2 Derivation of the Sample Population

Sector	Percentage ratio/100 Multiply by total Population	Sample Population
Leather and footwear	1.25/100 x 11,535	144
Garment	5.00/100 x 2,523	127
Wood and Furniture:	10.00/100 x 1,155	116
Light Engineering	20.00/100 x 500	100
PKO	80.00/100 x 100	80
Total		566

Source: Author's calculation

The population of the furniture and PKO was derived from the association of the enterprises and cluster census conducted by the author in Enugu. To generate the ratio of sample proportion in each cluster, each sample population is divided by the total sample population.

Table 1.3: Structure of the surveyed sample by sector and location

Location	Sector	Total Population	Sample Population	Ratio of sample proportion	Repr. Sample (Investigated)
Aba	Leather and footwear	11,535	144	0.25	36
	Garment	2,523	126	0.22	28
Enugu	Wood and Furniture	1,155	116	0.20	23
	PKO Extraction	100	80	0.14	11
Nnewi	Light Engineering	500	100	0.18	18
Total		15,813	566	1.00	116

Source: Author's field survey

The sample ratio helped to generate a fairly representative for investigation. The representative or investigated sample is derived by multiplying the ratio of sample proportion by sample population. Table 1.4 shows the structure of the enterprises investigated in the cluster by size and sector. The sample frame exhibits the dominance of micro enterprises with 0.879 per cent while small and medium enterprises are relatively small with 0.095 per cent and 0.026 per cent of the total investigative sample respectively. The enterprises are classified according to the number of employees defined by the National Association of Small and Medium scale Enterprises (NASME) in Nigeria. NASME's definition of SMEs reflected the reality on the nature and composition of Nigerian small enterprises. In each investigative sample, a simple random sampling was used to select the enterprises for interview.

Table 1.4: Structure of the enterprises investigated in the cluster by size and sector

Size	Leather/Footwear	Garment	Furniture	PKO	Light Engineering	Total
1-9	36	24	21	9	12	102 (0.879)
10-49		3	2	2	4	11 (0.095)
50-99		1			2	3 (0.026)
Total	36	28	23	11	18	116

Note: The figures in parentheses are percentage of the total

Source: Author's field survey

Table 1.5 shows different types of enterprises in the micro and small-scale footwear enterprises cluster in Aba. There are three cluster areas that make up of Aba leather/footwear enterprises cluster. They are the "Bakkasi" shoe industrial estate, which specialises on ladies shoes and leather bag production. The "Powerline" ladies shoe production unit and "Shoe-Plaza" men shoe production unit. However, the population census of the cluster did not provide disaggregated units in terms of number of enterprises in men or ladies shoe production unit.

Table 1.5: Leather/Footwear

Sector	Branch	Total	% of the Total
	Ladies shoes	24	0.67
Leather/Footwear	Men Shoes	12	0.33
Representive Sample		36	1.00

Source: Author's field survey

The production units are made up of blocks of workshops built in lines and in each area, three lines were selected randomly in order to generate the representative sample for footwear sector. They were classified as follows: Bakassi-ladies shoes (14), Power-line ladies shoes (10) Shoe-Plaza-men shoes (12). Footwear production is made up of shoemaker, shoe tailor and shoe- solo smoothing. Table 1.6 shows the production units of the garment sector. The garment enterprises are concentrated in Ngwa road area of Aba and workshops rented within the personal houses. Two production systems were identified in the sector namely: "production by order" and "production by direct market supply". The former depends on market reaction and government policy, while the latter is seasonal and requires marketing agents.

Table 1.6: Garments

Sector	Branch	Total	% of the Total
	Production by order	6	0.19
Garment	Market supply	22	0.81
Repr. Sample		28	1.00

Source: Author's field survey

Table 1.7 shows the wood/furniture enterprises selected in the sample. The wood construction units are the service providers for furniture makers and house interior designers. 1 enterprise in wood construction was selected from Ogui Carpenters Union and 6 enterprises from Enugu Timber shade. 9 furniture producers were selected from Ogui Carpenters Union while 4 were sampled from Ilukwe Carpenters Union and 3 from New Market Furniture Makers Union.

Table 1.7: Wood/Furniture

Sector	Branch	Total	% of the Total
	Wood Construction	7	0.33
Wood/furniture	Furniture	16	0.67
Repr. Sample		23	1.00

Source: Author's field survey

Table 1.8 shows the representative sample of PKO extraction enterprises in Enugu. The 11 sample of PKO extraction enterprises was selected from two of the PKO clusters in Enugu. 5 were selected from Uwani industrial estate and 6 from PKO enterprises cluster.

Table 1.8: Palm Kernel Oil (PKO) Extraction

	Sector	Total	% of the Total
Repr. Sample	PKO	11	1.00

Source: Author's field survey

Table 1.9 shows some selected branches of enterprises in Nnewi light engineering clusters. 5 branches were considered based on the measure of interests and simple random sample was used to select the enterprises. The spring manufacturing covers enterprises in different kinds of springs. Foundry covers the production of Kitchen utensils and moulding of spare parts, machine shops. The automobile technicians are service providers while the welding are the small machine producers. The automobile technicians were selected from two zones of the mechanic workshop clusters in Nnewi.

Table 1.9: Light Engineering

Sector	Branch	Total	% of the Total
	Spring manufacturing	2	0.11
	Foundry	4	0.22
Light Engineering	Machine Shops	2	0.11
	Fabrication and Welding	4	0.22
	Automobile Technicians	6	0.33
Repr. Sample		18	1.00

Source*:* Author's field survey

1.5.3.2 Selected Sample of clustered and dispersed Enterprises

Due to lack of adequate information on the variables and the characteristics of clusters such as territorially bounded concentration, two sub-sectors were used to perform regression analysis and investigate if there are significant differences in the performance of enterprises in spatially clustered areas and those operating outside the cluster.

Table 1.10: Representative sample of clustered and dispersed small enterprises by sector

	Footwear			
	Ladies shoes	Men shoes	PKO	Total No. of Sample
No. of sample	20	52	51	123

Source: Author's field survey

1.5.4 Methods of Data Analyses

The method of analyses covers different statistical and quantitative tools used to test the hypotheses. Descriptive statistical analyses were used in analysing the age of enterprises, average monthly sales and the employment creation of SMEs in Nigeria. The mean wage of employees in SMEs in South Eastern region was calculated and compared with minimum wage in public sector. This enables the research to determine the effects of income generation by SMEs in national economy. Sales turnover was used to evaluate the performance of the enterprises in clustered and dispersed enterprises in a particular period. The performance indicator was influenced by two factors, namely production volume and sales price. This is to determine analytically, if there is a positive correlation between proximity and performance of the enterprise. In this regards, correlation techniques was used to determine if the small enterprises in the cluster have higher gross sales per worker in relative and absolute terms than dispersed enterprises elsewhere, as well as if proximity has induced some cost saving effects?

Five indicators of networks on performance such as subcontracting, mode of resolving trade dispute, membership in trade association, and means of information and marketing channels were investigated. This study is not intended measure the innovativeness of small enterprises rather attempts to provide an insight into how small enterprises compete and survive in an open economy in Africa. It did not consider the traditional measure of innovative activity in terms of the measure of input such as R&D in the innovative process due to level of industrial development. The study also did not consider measure of innovative activity as a proxy measure of innovative output such as patented inventions. The measure of innovative activity considered in this study are the impact of creativity in terms of number of product designs introduced in the market and the impact of locally constructed machines in production output. Regression analysis was therefore used to model the relationship between output growth and nature of technology, labour, level of education of entrepreneurs and workers, incentives, government trade policy and innovation variables such as designs and machine designs. The central idea here is to show that innovative activity in small enterprise is a combination of factors that influence productivity growth. The anticipated productivity growth can lead to transformation effect on small enterprises and transmission effect on the economy in general.

1.6 The Study Plan

This study is divided into nine chapters. Chapter one consists of research objectives, justification of the research, methodology and the structure of the sample survey. Chapter two discusses the economic and social performance of Nigeria. It covers the poverty and inequality, health care and environmental issues in Nigeria. Chapter three highlights the theoretical conception and review of literature on small enterprises in Africa with special focus on Nigeria. Chapter four is the departing point which deals with the concept of small enterprises clusters in developing countries, followed by empirical analyses on impact and the performance of small enterprise in the cluster. Subsequently, a comparative analysis of some selected enterprises located in the cluster and those outside the cluster were performed. Chapter five provides an in depth analysis on the role of networks in small enterprises activities and their impact on small enterprises economic performance. Chapter six is concerned with the innovative activity in small enterprises using footwear and PKO enterprises as case study. The synthesis of the study is discussed in chapter seven whereby investment and SME Development (ISMED) model is proposed and analysed. In chapter eight, history of Nigerian industrial policies from 1900 to 2007 are reviewed. This is followed by a brief discussion on Nigeria technology policies. Lessons drawn from past industrial and technology policies and the outcomes of the empirical study provide the framework for policy analyses. Chapter nine concludes the study with recommendations.

Chapter 2: The Nigeria's Economic and Social Performance

2.1 Introduction

This chapter provides an insight into socio-economic background of Nigeria. It provides geographical facts about the country and brief historical background of the Nigerian people. The historical background explains the country's political economy complexity and incoherency. It analyses the country's political and economic transformation that spanned from colonial administration to the fall of the first republic as well as present socio-economic environment. The chapter explains how political institutions that began with democratic process in the late 1950s turned to anarchy and economic mismanagement. It also revealed how the country was transformed from surplus agrarian economy to food import dependent economy. The social environment in terms of quality of life, income distribution, access to education, access to health care and environmental problems were also chronologically analysed in the chapter.

2.2 The Geography and Nigeria's Political Economy

2.2.1 Geographical Facts and the People of Nigeria

The Federal Republic of Nigeria is situated between Latitudes 4° and 14° North of the Equator and Longitudes 2° 2' and 14° 30' East of the Greenwich Meridian. It covers a surface area of approximately 909,890 square kilometres with a coastline of about 853km. The surface area extended from the Gulf of Guinea on the South to the Sahara Desert on the North. Nigeria is bordered by the republic of Benin on the West, Republic of Cameroon on the East and by Republic of Chad and Republic of Niger on the North. Nigeria is made up of 36 states and 774 local government areas with Abuja as the country's capital (FBS, 2006, p. 1)[16]. Four vegetation belts, which are arranged in zones, can be distinguished from the coastal line to the interior region of the country. They are dense swamp forest, mangrove forest, savannah grassland, and the sandy areas of the southern Sahara (Coleman, 1965, p. 11; FBS, 2006, p. 1). River Niger and River Benue are the two main Rivers in Nigeria. They are intersected at Lokoja; a city at the middle of the country (see appendix, p. 375 below). Like most rivers in African countries, the Nigerian Rivers are not navigable partially due to seasonal fluctuations in water level, deposit of sand bars during dry season and poor development of river ports and inland waterways by the government (Coleman, 1965, p. 12; Olaloku, 1979, p. 1, FBS, 2006, p. 1). The climatic differences reflected the variations in rainfall across the region and fluctuation in

16 See Map of Nigeria in Appendix 1.1

rainfall across regions is also the major climatic problem of the country[17]. Nigeria has two seasonal weather conditions, the wet season that starts from April and last till November and the dry season which begins in December and ends in March. The average temperature lies between 24 ° and 27°C, but varies according to location and topography. Nigeria has a composition of about 350 ethnic groups or tribes each with a separate language but rich in culture, human and natural resources (UNDP-Lagos, 2004, p. 1). In 1933, some ancient art works were found in Nok, a rural village south of Zaria in northern Nigeria. Similar discoveries on the Plateau North of River Benue suggest that the Nok people were the earliest Nigerians. The society flourished between two and three centuries B.C. and lived around Jos Plateau region in the present middle-belt of Nigeria. The tribe was displaced following the emergence of stronger neighbours and lucrative slave trade within that period (Burns, 1969, p. 26-7). Presently, the prominent ethnic group in Northern Nigeria is the Hausa-Fulani. The Hausas lived around Southern Sahara and later migrated towards the South and settled in the territory between the river Niger on the West and Boronu settlement on the east. They are a large collection of people of different origins speaking Hamitoid language from central Sudan (Meek, 1925, p. 27). The Hausas have a long history of handicraft industry especially in production and dyeing of textiles, which have developed over time. As a result of their social interaction and commercial capability, the Hausa have mixed more freely beyond their environment than any other tribe in West Africa (Sik, 1966, p. 48). Fulani on the other hand are nomadic tribes of Barber origin but speaks Sudanese language (Sik, 1966, p. 49). During the 19th century, the Fulani gradually dominated the political power of Northern region of Nigeria with political headquarter at Sokoto. The Sokoto Caliphate was established after the Jihad, which started in 1802 under the leadership of Othman dan Fodio, a Fulani sheik (Coleman, 1965, p. 21).

In the South-West of Nigeria, a number of Yoruba empires ruled by the Obas (kings) emerged in about 11th century A.D with Ile Ife as origin of religious and political foundation of the Yoruba kingdom. The Yorubas are the largest cultural aggregation in West Africa with a history of political unity and tradition. The Yoruba myths trace their origin to Ile Ife, a town at the centre of Yorubaland where Oranyan, the mythical second King was buried (Coleman,

---

17 For example, around Jos Plateau region the annual average temperature is 14°C and 27°C while the annual average temperature in Lagos ranges between 23°C and 31°C (NBS, 2006, pp. 5-7). In the northern most part of the country, the average annual temperature is as low as 10°C and can rise to about 43°C (Olaloku, 1979, pp. 1-2). The country experiences an average rainfall of 266.5mm in the coastal areas and 190.5mm in the extreme north, resulting in water discharge of about 154 kcm3/ yr (Zabel, et al, 2001, p. 208). Statistical data shows that 33.2 per cent of land in Nigeria is arable but only 3.1 per cent is permanently cropped (World Bank, 2005, p. 131).

1965, p. 25). Other theories argue that Yoruba people migrated to the present Nigeria in the 2000 B. C. This was as a result of tribal movement set in motion by the Egyptian conquest of Arabia (Talbot, 1969, p. 276-8). Biobaku (1973, p. 26) argue that the Yoruba people migrated from the Middle East between the 7th and 10th centuries A.D. and settled at Ife formerly known as Ile Ife. Cultural indicator however shows the plausibility that Yoruba and Benin art and sculpture were derived from Nok culture (Burns, 1969, p. 26).

In the Southeast of Nigeria where Igbo is the main ethnic group had no centralised political institutions before the colonial period. The Igbos lived in small, self-contained groups of villages organised according to lineage system that did not allow social stratification. Every town or clan and family is an independent unit such that the nearest neighbours may be regarded as strangers (Basdan, 1966, p. 121). Coleman (1965, p. 28) argued that the Igbo people have more decentralised political structure than any other ethnic group in Nigeria due to natural and social factors. Firstly, the dense forest that covers the region prevented larger settlement, secondly, absence of invasions or large migration limited formation of large states or development of central political unit and thirdly, individualistic character of the people, which tended to give preference to self-achievement, prevented formation of large-scale centralised organisation. The political structure in Igbo society comprises 30 sub-tribes, 69 clans, and 500 fairly autonomous villages or village groups with institutional linkages (Coleman, 1965, p. 30). Goltzsche (1976, p. 94) revealed that institutions had evolved in Igbo society prior to colonial era. As a result of series of conflicts and wars between villages, local treaties and institutional arrangements called "Igbandu" were undertaken. Hence, free passage of goods and human movement across villages were guaranteed. This became the foundation of neo-liberalism and competitive culture across the Igbo society.

There are many other ethnic groups that make Nigeria a unique country in terms of cultural diversity. In the northern part, there are the Kanuri, Nupe, and Tiv together with about 250 other smaller tribes as well as some Yorubas living in the South-Western part of the region (Meek, 1925, p. 23). In the western part, there are the Bini (Benin Kingdom), the Ishan, and the Etsako as well as the Urobo, Isoko, Itsekiri and Ijaw, which lies within the Niger Delta region. In the eastern part of the country, there are Ibibio-Efik and the Ijaw with other nine smaller groups speaking different languages mostly in Ogoja province in the north east of Calabar (Coleman, 1965, p. 31).

2.2.2 Overview of Nigeria's Political Economy 1807- 1999

The modern economic development of Nigeria started with the abolition of slave trade by British government in 1807. Subsequently, trade shifted to palm oil and other primary commodities. The discovery of mouth of River Niger at the Bight of Biafra in 1830 allowed traders to penetrate the hinterland. Lagos was annexed as colony of Britain in 1861 and the Berlin Conference of 1885 confirmed British claim of the Niger Basin. Thereafter, Royal Niger Company was entrusted to administer the territory by the British government in 1886 (Coleman, 1965, p. 4; Fage 1969, p. 75). Between 1886 and 1990, the Royal Niger Company consolidated their position and the British interest throughout the territory. To this end, government services such as Court of Justice and Police were established with headquarter at Asaba the present capital of Delta State. This was followed by introduction of custom duties and trade licences in order to generate fund for the administration of the area (Burns, 1969, pp. 158-9). In 1900, Royal Niger Company handed over the administration of the area to British government and a high commission was subsequently established in Northern Nigeria (Coleman, 1965, p. 41)[18]. The existing administrative system in northern Nigeria then was modified and indirect rule system was introduced. The system was accepted in the Western province in 1924 after initial resistance in some parts of Yorubaland. Efforts to extend the indirect rule system to the Eastern province led to the Aba women riots of 1929. Despite the resistance, the system was accepted in Eastern province in the 1930s followed by introduction of Warrant Chiefs as well as modification of tax assessment (Coleman, 1965, p. 57). This marked the foundation of Nigeria's political economy in terms of introduction and development of monetary and fiscal systems. There was imminent need for local currency which will facilitate exchange of goods and payment of taxes and duties within the country. As currency was introduced, economic policy began to shift towards promotion of cash and food crops for export and local consumption. The wage labour system started to evolve and the agricultural sector eventually became the source of economic growth.

During the colonial period, Nigeria witnessed large expansion of cash crops for export and food crops which was supported by infrastructure development such as access road and railways construction. The construction of railway line linking the South and the North started as early as 1898. By 1932 more than 2,100 miles of railway line was completed. In 1914, Nigeria had 2,000 miles of constructed road for motor traffics. By 1926, more that 6,000 miles was constructed (Helleiner, 1966, p. 14). The missionaries on the other hand, introduced western education and health care system in the coastal and in

18 Sir Frederick Lugard (later Lord Lugard) was the first British high commissioner, who proclaimed the protectorate of Northern Nigeria.

the hinterland such that infant mortality per thousand fell drastically from 430 in 1900 to 134 in 1929 (Helleiner, 1966, p. 6). The Islamic religion and culture have already gained ground in the northern Nigeria during the period. Establishment of internal security, communication infrastructure, and introduction of common currency helped to facilitate mobility and social communication between northern and southern regions. Hence commerce, internal integration, regional interdependence and growth of money economy became effective (Forrest, 1993, p. 23; Coleman, 1965, pp. 65-67)[19].

The British colonial authority however started loosing the grip of governance after the World War II based on several factors. The early events of 1929 women riots attracted sympathy across the country, followed by considerable labour and political unrest with some section of the press raising critical views against the colonial administrative system. The situation worsened as a result of persistent inter-tribal clashes between the southerners and the northerners which were beyond police control (Burns, 1969, p. 250). The nationalism centred on sentiments for self-governance and unity of Nigeria erupted in late 1940s which later turned into active nationalist movement (Coleman, 1965, pp. 169-170). Colonial disengagement started with constitutional development and series of constitutional changes. The Richards Constitution of 1947 which marked the beginning of a new era in Nigeria's political history established the legislative organ as well as Council of Chiefs for the Northern Nigeria (Burns, 1969, p .251). The 1951 constitution further established a central legislature (House of Representative) council and Council of Ministers as principal policy making body for Nigeria. The same structure was also established in the three regions. The concept of Federalism was adopted by 1954 constitution, which granted greater autonomy to the regions and Lagos as Federal Capital Territory. The constitution also provided the modalities for the share of responsibilities between Federal and Regional government (Burns, 1969, p. 253; Forrest, 1993, p. 17). However, the Federation was very weak to the point of being confederation and the structure of federalism was a reflection of ethno linguistic background with several minority ethnic groups in each region. The political parties that emerged within the regions followed the same ethnic and cultural

19 "Systematic taxation, a common portable currency, the desire for European goods, the opportunity to pursue the profit motive, support or tolerance from the government- all these have been significant elements in the historic shift from an almost wholly subsistence economy to a predominantly money economy" (Coleman, 1965, p .66).

pattern (Zartman and Schatz, 1983, p. 2)[20]. Nigeria became political independent state in 1960 with a fundamental problem of ethnic inspired hegemonic conflicts.

The politics of the first Republic was characterised by confrontation and suspicion. There was lack of "national identity" with ethnic royalty against national interest. The minority ethnic groups were subjected to political intimidation in their respective regions and cross-destabilisation strategies by the three major ethnic political parties also gathered momentum (Kilby, 1969, p. 3; Ake, 1985, p. 11). The struggle for regional economic power heightened the tensions. The regional marketing boards, development corporations and economic policy making units became the engine for economic development with their organisational structure stronger than the newly established Federal organs. The young federation was confronted with the problem of revenue allocation provided in 1954 constitution based on the regional derivation principle. The constitution gave higher revenue allocation to the region where the export commodity was derived (Forrest, 1993, p. 21). This has been the contention in Niger Delta conflict.

The collapse of the first republic started with the outcome of the 1962 census, which gave the North an absolute majority. Political climate was polluted as the Governors of Eastern and Western Regions rejected the result. A rerun of the census in 1963 could not produce politically acceptable result but was adopted for statistical references and official use. The system collapsed in 1965 when the election results in the Western Region was allegedly manipulated. Political crises erupted followed by general strike and rebellion (Zartman and Schatz, 1983, p. 3; Forrest, 1993, p. 30; Ake, 1985, p. 13). The dreams of the fragile state floundered in January 1966 when a group of young military officers made up of Igbo ethnic group ended the parliamentary government through a military coup d'état with painful killings of some Northern political leaders. The second coup d'état in July 1966 and killings of thousands of innocent civilians of Igbo ethnic group in Northern Nigeria led to political mistrust and state of insecurity in the country (Kilby, 1969, p. 3). Consequently, a bloody three-year civil war erupted in mid-1967 between the Eastern Region (Biafra) and the rest of the country which left behind nearly one million dead.

20 1959 federal elections produced an unsustainable political party alliance at the centre. The Northern Peoples Congress (NPC), with strong base in the North and National Council of Nigerian Citizens (NCNC) with strong base in the East; formed an alliance against the Action Group (AG) with strong base in the West. This form of coalition was very unstable and could not be sustained. Such alliance was not feasible because an alliance of two strongest parties rather than two weakest parties against the strongest does not represent the balance of power theory (Zartman and Schatz, 1983, p. 2).

The political scenario in Nigeria changed after the civil war in 1970. As the military consolidated power, the country began to witness a new powerful federal civil service that was committed to the principle of federalism. The bureaucracy started to influence the economic policies, nationalisation of the economy started to surface. The creation of more states weakened the regional powers such that most economic and development policies of the states followed Federal pattern (Forrest, 1993, pp. 48-49). The sudden rise in prices of petroleum oil in international market in 1973/74 provided the Nigerian government the choice of unguided spending as a result of oil revenue windfall. The increase in oil revenue further strengthened the power of central authorities which led to budget expansion. This was followed by the creation of a strong exchange rate regime that supported cheap importation of foods and other consumer goods. In mid-1970s, Nigeria was ranked among the middle-income countries with average per capita GNP put at US$1010 in 1980 (World Bank, 1982, p. 110)[21]. This indicates an appreciable standard of living due to expanding crude oil exports and very low external debt during the period. In the late 1970s, and early 1980s the government lost control of the economy. The economy plunged into crisis when the world recession of 1980s occurred and the oil prices fell to about US$9 in 1985 and 1986. Coupled with a sharp cut in the OPEC quota, the Nigeria government's oil revenue fell from about 23 per cent of the GDP in 1980 to 13 per cent in 1985 (IMF, 1997, pp. 648-9). When the oil prices was at about US$40 per barrel, the country failed to diversify its economy or tried to escape from over dependence on petroleum exports. Consequently, Nigerian economy collapsed and left behind huge foreign and domestic debt, soaring inflation, large-scale unemployment as well as widespread corruption. The military interventions in Nigeria's politics later brought distortion in the general economic management processes. For example, the 1986 economic reform that tended to restructure the economy towards efficiency and prudent macroeconomic management was later reversed 1988/9 and later abandoned in 1993 (Bureau of Public Enterprise, 2006, p. 2). The political situation deteriorated between 1993 and 1998 following the annulment of national election results on 12th June, 1993 and increasing government violations of Human Rights. This led to censorship of the country by Commonwealth of Nations and later limited economic sanctions by International Community.

In spite of the shortcomings in Nigeria's political and economic management, Nigeria has developed the features of a modern state in a short time of its history. The country has been playing active role in regional and international politics especially in the area of conflict resolutions in Africa. More importantly, Nigeria has charted its financial institutions towards a sustainable economic growth path by consolidating the banking sector through the capital market.

21 World Bank, World Development Report 1982.

However, the ethnic, religious, class, and unresolved Niger-Delta problems as well as high incidence of corruption in public institutions especially at state and local government levels continue to pose serious problem to national unity and general economic development.

2.3 Nigeria's Economic Performance and Problems

2.3.1 The Structure of Production and Economic Growth

In the 1950s, Nigeria was an agricultural producing nation. Initially, the country was cultivating crops for local consumption and later cash crops such as cocoa, groundnut, rubber and palm products for export (Helleiner, 1966, p. 28). Between 1950 and early 1963, agriculture was the source of economic growth and the main provider of foreign exchange for Nigeria. Between 1950 and 1964, the annual GDP growth of Nigeria averaged 4.3 per cent in real terms (Kilby, 1969, p. 9)[22]. In 1950/51, the contribution of agriculture, fishry and forestry to GDP was 72.4 percent. In 1957/86, it declined to 2.5 per cent. In 1958/59, it rose to 69.0 per cent. In 1962/63, it stood at 65.0 per cent (Helleiner, 1966, p. 27). In contrast to late 1950s and early 1960s, the performance of the economy remained sluggish since 1980 in spite of several policies aimed to stimulate economic growth (see Table 2.1). The GDP rose in monetary terms from US$3,150 million in 1960 to US$11,594 in 1970 and increased drastically as a result of increase in prices of crude oil to US$98,082 million in 1980.

As indicated in Table 2.1, the GDP declined to US$28,472 million in 1990 and did not recover relative to its 1980 performance until 2005 with US$98,951million and increased to US$115,338 in 2006. In 1960, agriculture contributed 63 per cent to the GDP, and the share of agriculture to the growth consistently declined to the level of 17 per cent in 2004 but increased slightly to 23 per cent in 2005 and 2006. The discovery and production of petroleum crude oil in commercial quantities in late 1950s led to structural changes in the Nigerian economy with rapid decline in the share of agricultural output to GDP. The output of crude oil rose in 1958 from 5,000 barrels per day to 415,000 barrels per day in 1966, at an annual rate of 73.7 per cent per annum (Nafziger, 1977, p. 37). Presently the output per day rose to 1.2 million barrel. Furthermore, poor performance of agricultural export can be linked to the existing over aged cocoa trees and low yielding large wild palm trees. Long storage of groundnuts has led to poor quality condition of the product for export. This was as a result of poor transportation infrastructure which limited easy and quick

22 GDP measures the growth in output and defined as the sum of the gross value added by all residents and non residents producers in the economy plus taxes minus subsidies not included in the value of the product

facilitation of export produce. In general, wrong agricultural development policy adopted in the first National Development Plan affected agricultural output in Nigeria negatively (Tomori, 1979, p. 18, Okowa, 1985, p. 82).

On attainment of independence in 1960, the economic policy shifted to increased government investment in import replacing industries. In 1964, four industries namely cigarettes, beer, cement and textiles accounted for 40 per cent industrial output and 21 per cent of industrial employment (Kilby, 1969, p. 81). As shown in Table 2.1 above, the share of industry to GDP rose in 1960 from 11 per cent to 14 per cent in 1970. Investment in import replacing industries was further strengthened when the Organisation of Oil Producing and Exporting Countries (OPEC) increased petroleum oil prices in 1973, the share of industry to GDP growth rose in 1970 drastically from 14 per cent to 40 per cent in 1980. Hence, industry became the major contributor to GDP and accounted for 49 per cent of GDP growth in 2003 and has increased to 57 per cent since 2004. The manufacturing share accounted for a very small proportion of overall economic activities. Its share to GDP increased from 5 per cent in 1960 to 9 per cent in 1985 and 1995 and subsequently fell to 4 per cent in 2005.

Table 2.1: GDP in million US$ and the Structure of Output Expresses as % of GDP

	GDP	Sectoral Value Added as Percentage of Gross Domestic Product			
	(in M US$)	Agriculture	Industry	Manufacturing	Service
1960	3,150	63	11	5	26
1970	11,594	41	14	4	45
1980	93,082	27	40	8	32
1995	75,300	36	32	9	32
1990	28,472	33	41	6	26
1995	40,477	43	27	9	31
2000	41,085	30	46	4	25
2001	41,373	30	46	4	25
2002	43,540	37	29	4	34
2003	58,390	26	49	4	24
2004	72,053	17	57	4	27
2005	98,951	23	57	4	20
2006	115,338	23	57	n.a.	20

Key: n.a. = not available

Source: The World Bank, World Development Report 1981, p. 138; 1994, p. 166; 1996, p. 210; 1987, p. 206. The World Bank, World Development Indicators, 2001, p. 199; 1997, p. 135; 2002, p. 209; 2003, p. 191; 2004, p. 187; 2005, p. 203; 2006, p. 199; 2007, p. 195; 2008, p. 203

The service sector showed a remarkable improvement from 26 per cent in 1960 to 45 per cent in 1970 but fell to 24 per cent in 2003. Subsequently, the out put of the service sector increased by 27 per cent in 2004 but fell to 20 per cent in 2005 and 2006. Table 2.2 shows the changes in the production structure in terms of annual growth rate of GDP and sectors. The average annual growth rate of the GDP rose from 3.1 per cent between 1960 and 1970 to 4.6 per cent between 1970 and 1980. The GDP recorded the lowest annual growth rate of 1.6 per cent between 1980 and 1990 but rose to 6.0 between 2000 and 2006. The total farm output in Nigeria grew between 1960 and 1970 at an annual average negative rate of 0.4 per cent and 0.1 per cent per annum between 1970 and 1980. This suggests that relative to other sectors, per capita farm income fell considerably between 1960 and 1980. The negative growth in farm output in the said period is a reflection of change in rural labour force as resource allocation shifted to other sectors. Between 1980 and 1990, the total farm output improved at an annual average rate of 3.3 per cent and rose slightly to 3.5 per cent between 1990 and 2000. There was an improvement in agricultural sector in Nigeria between 2000 and 2006 with 5.8 per cent growth rate.

Table 2.2: Average annual growth rates of GDP, the sectors and population (in %)

	1960-1970	1970-1980	1980-1990	1990-2000	2000-2006
GDP	3.1	4.6	1.6	2.4	6.0
Agriculture	-0.4	-0.1	3.3	3.5	5.8
Industry	12.0	7.3	-1.1	1.0	5.5
Manufacturing	9.1	5.2	0.7	1.2	8.8
Service	4.9	9.6	3.7	2.9	6.5
Population	2.5	2.5	3.2	2.8	2.7*

Key: * = population growth 1990-2006

Source: (1960-1970), The World Bank, World Development Report 1981, p. 136; (1970-1980) 1993, p. 240; (1980-1990) The World Bank, World Development Indicators 2000, p. 183; (1990-2000), 2002, p. 205. (Population). The World Bank, World Development Report, 1981, p. 166; 1982, p. 142; 1992, p. 268; 2002, p. 233; 2008, p. 199

The favourable annual growth recorded from 1980 was a reflection of economic reform under Structural Adjustment Programme (SAP) of World Bank adopted in 1986. The reform measures were among others abolition of commodity marketing board and deregulation of prices and exchange rate. They also include lowering of import tariffs for agricultural inputs which brought some positive changes in agricultural productivity. The price changes encouraged farmers to improve agricultural output and exploit the chances in export markets (Adubi and Okunmadewa, 1999, p. 12). Industrial output expanded at an annual average rate of 12 per cent between 1960 and 1970 but grew at an annual average of 7.3 per cent between 1970 and 1980. However, Nigeria industrial output contracted drastically between 1980 and 1990 with negative average annual growth rate of 1.1 per cent. Between 2000 and 2006, industrial output recovered and grew at an annual rate of 5.8 per cent. As shown in Table 2.2, the manufacturing output grew at an annual average rate of 9.1 per cent between 1960 and 1970. The annual output growth rate subsequently dropped to 5.2 per cent between 1970 and 1980 and to a record lowest level of 0.7 per cent between 1980 and 1990. Between 1990 and 2000, the manufacturing output relatively grew at an annual rate of 1.2 and rose rapidly at an annual growth rate of 8.8 per cent between 2000 and 2006. Relative to a lower annual growth rate of 4.9 per cent between 1960 and 1970, the annual growth rate in the service sector rose to 9.6 per cent between 1970 and 1980[23]. However, the output fell to 3.7 per cent, 2.9 per cent between 1980 and 1990, and between 1990 and 2000 respectively. Between 2000 and 2006, the output growth in the sector increased annually by 6.5 per cent.

In general, the performance of the Nigeria's economy however depends on the price of petroleum in international market. In the 1990s, the economic growth was influenced by 1990/1991 Gulf War that pushed up the oil prices from US$15 per barrel in 1988 to US$24 per barrel in 1990 and US$20 in 1991/2 (CBN, 2003, p. 131; Katz, et al, 2004, p. 16). The increase in petroleum crude oil from 2002 also helped to induce growth in the economy. The post-SAP economic performance from 1990s shows that agricultural, industrial and manufacturing output sectors improved relatively. However, the improvement was not enough to sustain an economy which has a population growth of 2.8 per cent. Population recorded the highest annual growth rate of 3.2 per cent in the period between 1980 and 1990 but declined relatively 2.8 per cent in the period between 2000 and 2006.

2.3.2 The Structure of External Transactions

2.3.2.1 Exports of Oil and Non-Oil Commodities

Nigeria's terms of trade tripled to 15 per cent of 1974 GDP when the OPEC raised the price of petroleum crude oil in 1973 thereby making the ratio of Nigeria's export price to import price to increase rapidly (Watts and Lubeck, 1983, p. 107). As shown in table 2.3, the share of oil export to total export is between 95.5 and 98.7 per cent and will continue to dominate the Nigeria exports. In monetary terms, the value of oil export increased N950,661.4 billion in 1995 to N1,945,723.3 billion in 2000 by 104.7 per cent. It increased from N1,945,723.3 billion in 2000 to N5,752,747.7 billion in 2006 by 195.7 per cent. Between 1995 and 2006 the value of non-oil export in monetary terms improve from its lowest record of N19,492.9 billion in 1999 to N133,594.9 billion in 2006 by 585.4 per cent. Conversely the contribution of the non-oil export to

---

23 The share of food imports to total imports between 1960 and 1970 was highest by 11.0 per cent in 1970. Between 1970 and 1979 it rose to 14.8 per cent in 1979 (Ekpo, 1986).

total export (3 as % of 1) is below 10 per cent and lie only between 1.7 and 5.4 per cent. The implication is; the performance of non-oil sector in the Nigerian economy is generally weak and will not probably improve in the near future as the table indicated. The country will continue to depend on oil as the major export unless there are pro-active measures towards diversification of the economy. In spite of the measures open by SAP package for the stimulation of exports, Nigeria failed to diversify its economy in non-oil sector. Policy reversal between 1988 and 1989 in order to cushion the effect of the economic reform eroded some of the gains of the SAP (BPE Report, 2006).

Table 2.3: Nigeria Exports of Oil and Non-oil Commodities 1995-2006 (in Billion Naira)

	Total Exports (fob) in Naira Billion(1)	Oil (2)	Non-oil (3)	(2) as% of (1)	(3) as % of(1)
1995	950,661.4	927.565.3	23,096.1	97.6	2.4
1996	1,309,543.4	1,286,215.9	23,327.5	98.2	1.8
1997	1,241,662.7	1,212,499.4	29,163.3	97.6	2.4
1998	751,856.7	717,786.5	34,070.2	95.5	4.5
1999	1,188,969.8	1,169,476.9	19,492.9	98.4	1.6
2000	1,945,723.3	1,920,900.4	24,822.9	98.7	1.3
2001	1,867,953.9	1,839,945.3	28,008.6	98.5	1.5
2002	1,744,177.7	1,649,445.9	94,731.8	94.6	5.4
2003	3,087,886.4	2,993,100.0	94,776.4	96.9	3.1
2004	4,602,781.5	4,489,472.2	113,309.4	97.5	2.5
2005	6,372,052.4	6,266,096.6	105,955.8	98.3	1.7
2006	5,752,747.7	5,619,152.9	133,594.9	97.7	2.3

Source: Central Bank of Nigeria, Statistical Bulletin. Volume 17, 2006 p. 213

2.3.2.2 Import of Oil and Non-Oil Commodities

Table 2.4 shows the trend in Nigeria's total import between 1995 and 2006[24]. The value of total imports increased in monetary terms from N755.127.7 billion in 1995 to N 985,022.4 billion in 2000 by 30.4 per cent. It increased from

24 Import substitution industrialisation (ISI) strategy dominated Nigerian trade policies between 1960 and 1985. A strategy pursued to protect 'infant' industries and save foreign exchange by using different forms of import restrictive measures such as high import tariffs, import quota and import licensing. Non-tariff barriers such as import prohibitions were also applied on specific goods. To some extent, trade policies were tied to the balance of payment situation such that the number of goods listed for import licensing increases as the balance of payment becomes unfavourable. Under the SAP of 1986, some of the Nigeria's trade policies changed towards the market economy. The local currency (Naira) was devalued, foreign exchange market was rationalised and deregulation of imports and financial market were undertaken and some of the protective measures on local industries were also relaxed (Forrest, 1993, p. 213).

N985,022.4 billion in 2000 to N2,528,086.0 billion in 2006 by 156.7 per cent. The importation of petroleum oil increased from 20.6 per in 1995 to 24.5 per cent in 1999 and fell to 8.7 per cent in 2006. The imported non-oil commodities lie between 71.2 and 92.6 per cent between 1995 and 2006.

Table 2.4: Nigeria Import of Oil and Non-Oil Commodities 1995-2006 (in Billion Naira)

	Total imports (cif) in Billion Naira (1)	Oil (2)	Non-oil (3)	(2) as % of (1)	(3) as % of (1)
1995	755,127.7	155,825.9	599,301.8	20.6	79.4
1996	562,626.6	162,178.7	400,447.9	28.8	71.2
1997	845,716.6	166,902.5	678,814.1	19.7	80.3
1998	837,418.7	175,854.2	661,564.5	21.0	79.0
1999	862.515.7	211,661.8	650,853.9	24.5	75.5
2000	985,022.4	220,817.7	764,204.7	22.4	77.6
2001	1,358,180.3	237,106.8	1,121,073.5	17.5	82.5
2002	1,512,695.3	361,710.0	1,150,985.3	23.9	76.1
2003	2,080,235.3	398,922.3	1,681,313.0	19.2	80.8
2004	1,987,045.3	318,114.7	1,668,930.6	16.0	84.0
2005	2,479,322.6	182,754.8	2,296,567.7	7.4	92.6
2006	2,528,086.0	221,086.4	2,306,999.6	8.7	91.3

Source: Central Bank of Nigeria, Statistical Bulletin. Volume 17, 2006, p. 213

2.3.2.3 Balance of Payment Current Account

The current account balance explains the current position of the economy with rest of world in terms of transactions and transfers. As shown in Table 2.5 above, between 1990 and 2006, Nigeria only recorded balance of trade deficit in 1994 and 1998. The net current transfers increased from its annual average of US$668.4 million between 1990 and 1996 sub-period to annual average of US$1,480.7 million between 1997 and 2002. Between 2004 and 2006, it increased annually by US$2957.3 million. The increase in the net current transfers is a reflection of increased remittances by Nigerians in the Diaspora. The balance of payment current account was favourable between 1990 and 1992 with average surplus of US$2,819.7 million but unfavourable between 1993 and 1995 with average deficit of US$1,123 million. The highest balance of payment current account deficit of US$-4,244 was recorded in 1998 while Nigeria experienced the highest current account surplus of US$24,202million in 2005 and 2006. This could be due to rising petroleum oil prices in the world market. The external reserve improved its position from the lowest record of US$967 million in 1992 to the highest level of US$10,647 million in 2001 but fell again to US$7,415 million by 30.4 per cent in 2003 and increased rapidly from US$7,415million to US$42,735 million by 476.3 per cent in 2006.

Table 2.5: Balance of Payment Current Account (1990-2006)

Note: The trade balance was calculated by the author

	Exp. of G&S (in Mil US$	Imp. of G&S (in Mil US$)	Trade Balance	Net Income * (in mil.US$)	Net C.T (in Mil.US$)	C.A/C Bal.	Gr. Int. Res
1990	14,550	6,909	7,641	2,738	85	4,988	4,129
1991	12,264	8,986	3,279	2,631	877	1,203	4,435
1992	11,886	8,276	3,610	2,494	817	2,268	967
1993	9,908	5,937	3,971	3,335	857	-780	1,372
1994	9,879	12,504	-2,625	2,986	546	-2,079	1,649
1995	11,779	10,972	807	1,990	673	-510	1,443
1996	14,743	9,836	4,907	2,639	824	3,092	4,329
1997	15,994	14,213	1,781	3,145	1,916	552	4,075
1998	9,855	13,377	3,522	2,291	1,570	-4,243	8,709
1999	13,855	12,063	1,792	2,578	1,292	506	6,485
2000	23,047	14,124	8,923	3,287	1,348	5,636	6,485
2001	21,201	15,418	5,783	2,274	1,292	4,828	10,647
2002	17,151	15,526	1,625	2,090	1,466	1,001	7,567
2003	na	na	na	na	na	na	7,415
2004	26,993	16,064	10,929	916	2,252	12,265	17,257
2005	52,233	24,609	27,624	6,732	3,310	24,202	28,632
2006	52,233	24,609	27,624	6,732	3,310	24,202	42,735

Key: Exp. of G&S= Export of Goods and Services; Imp. of G&S = Import of Goods and Services: Net. C.T. (in M. US$) = Net Current Transfers (in Million United States Dollar); C. A/C Bal. = Current Account Balance: Gross. Int. Res. = Gross International Reserve. * All values in minus (-) i.e. income transfer of foreign expatriates, profits and dividends of foreign investors after tax.

Source: (1991 to 1994) IMF, International Finance Statistics (IFS) Yearbook, (1995-2006) The World Bank, World Development Indicators 1997, p. 211; 1998, p. 235; 1999, p. 251; 2000, p. 245; 2001, p. 787; 2002, p. 261; 2003, p. 243; 2004, p. 239; 2005, p. 255; 2006, p.251; 2007, p. 247; 2008, p. 255.

2.3.3 The Structure of Demand and Federal Government Finance

2.3.3.1 The Structure of Demand

The structure of demand consists of four major components namely private consumption, general government consumption, gross domestic investment, gross domestic savings as well as export and import of goods and services. As shown in Table 2.6, between 1990 and 1998 sub-period, the private consumption constitutes the bulk of expenditure in the economy with an annual average of 68.5 per cent of the GDP. The trend declined relatively to annual average of 51.9 per cent between 1999 and 2006. Between 1990 and 1998 sub-period, the general government consumption averaged 11.2 per cent of the GDP. It increased to an average of 21.6 per cent between 1999 and 2005 sub-period. The gross domestic investment otherwise known as gross capital formation averaged 16.6 per cent of the GDP between 1990 and 1998 but rose to 24.9 per cent between 1999 and 2006. Gross domestic savings averaged 20.1 between 1990 and 1998 but increased slightly by an annual rate of 21.9 per cent of GDP. The resource balance has experienced a negative trend as it dropped from its value of 15 per cent to the GDP to the lowest level in 1999 by -11 per cent but recorded the highest value of 19 per cent in 2005.

Table 2.6: Structure of Demand of the Nigerian Economy 1990-2006 (% of GDP)

	Private Consumption	General Gov. Consumption	Gross Domestic Investment	Gross Domestic Savings	Resource Balance
1990	59	11	15	29	+15
1991	65	13	16	23	+ 6
1992	75	6	18	23	+5
1993	63	18	15	19	+3
1994	79	10	10	11	+1
1995	69	10	18	20	+4
1996	64	11	19	na	na
1997	65	11	18	24	+5
1998	77	11	20	12	-8
1999	88	12	11	0	-11
2000	45	21	23	34	+11
2001	48	25	28	27	-1
2002	55	27	23	17	+ 6
1003	45	23	23	32	+ 9
2004	38	22	27	22	+5
2005	40	21	30	21	+19
2006	56	na	34	22	+ 12

Key: na= not available

Source: (1990-1995) World Development Report 1992, p. 234; 1993, p. 254; 1994, p. 178;1995, p. 178; 1996, p. 212; 1997, p. 238.; (1996) World Development Indicator, 1998. (1997-1999) World Development Report 1997, 1999, p. 238; 2000, p. 215; 2001, p. 227; (2000 -2006) World Development Report, 2002, p. 237; 2003, p.219;2004, p.215; 2005, p.231; 2006, p. 199; 2007, p.219; 2008, p. 227.

2.3.3.2 Federal Government Finance

The increase in oil revenue after Nigeria's civil war allowed consolidation of state ownership and unguided government spending. Oil share in Federal Government revenue rose in 1971 from 17 per cent to 71 per cent in 1973, further to 86 per cent in 1975. Subsequently, total public spending rose in 1970/73 from less than 20 per cent of GDP to 35 per cent in 1974/77 (Watts and Lubeck, 1983, p. 108). Nigeria's fiscal deficit persists in spite of the large increases in revenue. Prudent management of oil revenue became a problem in Nigeria's fiscal policy because the economic expansion policies pursued by various regimes continue to depend on real oil earnings (Forrest, 1993, p. 135). The consequences of high spending as oil prices increase are reflected in macro-economic instability. It also became a problem for government to reduce spending as oil prices and revenue decline (World Bank, 1997, p. 49; Katz, et al, 2004, p. 13)[25].

Table 2.7 above shows how government spending continues to increase with less fiscal discipline as oil revenue rapidly increased. For example, federal government revenue rose from N53,265 million in 1992 to N83,494 million in 1993 by 56.8 per cent The expenditure in the corresponding period rose by 106 per cent. This resulted to a high budget deficit financing of N107,735 million through the Central Bank and government external borrowings. The persistent budget deficit contributed to the increase in domestic and external debt, reduction of external reserve as well as adverse effect on relative prices. The fiscal balance recorded the highest deficit of N301, 402 million in 2002 but gradually contracted with highest record surplus of N117,600 million in 2006

Table 2.7: Federal Government Finance from 1990 to 2006 (in Millions of Naira)

	Curent Revenue	Expendiure	Deficit (-) or Surplus (+)	Net Balance	
				Domestic	Foreign
1990	39,033	61,149	- 22,116	27,042	1,564
1991	30,829	66,584	-30,829	32,107	274
1992	53,265	92,797	-39,532	46,716	-11,860
1993	83,494	191,229	-107,735	98,134	9,601
1994	90,623	160,894	-70,270	61,684	8,587
1995	249,768	256,521	-6,753	39,070	5,683
1996	325,144	288,095	37,049	-143,190	7,825
1997	351,262	356,262	-5,000	-60,637	13,383
1998	310,174	443,563	-133,389	103,886	16, 605
1999	662,585	947,690	-285,105	264,064	21,041
2000	597,282	701,059	-103777	103,777	n.a
2001	796,977	1,018026	-221,049	194,053	26,996
2002	716,754	1,018,156	-301,402	149,027	52,798
2003	1,023,200	1,226,000	-202,800	163,700	67
2004	1,234,600	1,377,300	-142,700	40,701	700
2005	1,660,601	1,822,018	-161,417	108,000	38,417
2006	1,826,400	1,708,800	+117,600	n.a	n.a

Key: n.a = not available

Source: IMF International Financial Statistics Yearbook, 1995 p. 590; 2003, p. 436; 2005 (December), p. 738; 2007, p. 459; 2008 (October), p. 876.

2.3.4 Macroeconomic Performance

Table 2.8 shows some selected macroeconomic indicators of Nigeria's economic performance between 1995 and 2006. Between 1995 and 2006 the GDP recorded a negative growth of -0.9 in 2002 and the highest growth rate of 10.7 per cent in 2003. The GNP per capita declined from US$260 in 1995 to US$240

25 World Bank, World Development Report, 1997.

in 1996 and improved to US$300 in 1998. Between 1998 and 2000 the GNP per capita fell to again to US$260 but increased steadily to US$350 in 2003. The GNP per capita increased between 2003 and 2006 to US$620 by 77.1 per cent. Generally, the GNP per capita performance is still very poor suggesting that the living standard of Nigerians is very poor and economy is also very weak[26]. The current account balance expressed as percentage of the GDP explains the contribution of the country's external sectors to general performance of the economy. As shown in Table 2.8, the contribution of external sector to the GDP growth declined in 1995 by 2.9 per cent but increased nearly by the same margin of 2.7 per cent in 1996. Table 2.8 shows that the external sector recorded its worst contribution to GDP growth in 1998 with negative performance of 10.3 per cent and the best performance of 24.5 per cent in 2004. The PPP purchasing power parity (PPP) GNI per capita declined from US$1220 in 1995 to US$900 in 2003 and by 26.2 per cent with lowest value of US$740 in 1998[27]. The PPP per capita increased from US$800 in 2000 to US$1,410 in 2006 by 72.3 per cent. In respect to exchange rate, Table 2.8 shows that the local currency (Naira) is gradually finding its market value against foreign hard currencies between 1999 and 2006, but the sudden rise in oil prices tend to distort its value[28]. The implication of the rising oil price is that the performance of the manufacturing sector can be weakened due to inflow of oil revenue. The official exchange rate (OER) was relatively stable between 1995 and 1998 but overvalued at N22.00 to US$1.0. It depreciated in value by 320 per cent in 1999 and further by 40 per cent between 1999 and 2003[29]. As shown in the Table, the real effective

---

26 High-income countries = Countries that have per capita GNI above US$9266 in 2000, Middle-income countries = Countries that have per capita income GNI US$756 to US$9266; Low-income countries = Countries that have per capita GNP US$ 755 and below in 2000 (Nnadozie, 2003, p. 22).

27 PPP GNI (or PPP GNP) is gross national income converted to international dollars using purchasing power parity rates. An International dollar is obtained when the exchange rates are converted by purchasing power parity to account for differences in prices between the countries. An international dollar has the same purchasing power over GNI as a U.S. dollar has in the United States (World Bank,* 2001, p. 15; Nnadozie, 2003, p. 22). * = World Bank, World Development Indicators, 2001.

28 Exchange rate is defined as the price of one currency in terms of another.

29 Official exchange rate refers to exchange rate determined by national authorities or the rate determined in the legally sanctioned exchange market. It is calculated as an annual average based on monthly averages. Real effective exchange rate is the nominal effective exchange rate divided by a price deflector or index of costs. An index of relative changes in consumer prices is used as deflator for developing countries like Nigeria. In other words, it is a measure of the value of a currency against a weighted average of several foreign currencies (World Bank*, 2001 p.293). * World Bank, World Development Indicators 2001.

exchange rate (REER) has not been stable[30]. Between 1995 and 1997, the Naira appreciated against US$ by 40.2 per cent and depreciated by 53.9 per cent between 1997 and 1999 and further appreciated by 64.3 per cent between 2000 and 2006. The fluctuation in REER depends on the movement of oil revenue. For example, the rise in government revenue from N662,585 million in 1999 to N1,023,200 million in 2003 by 54.4 per cent was due to increased oil prices. This has led to considerable appreciation of the real effective exchange rate in the same period[31]. Inflation levels declined from 75.8 per cent in 1995 to the lowest level of 6.6 in 1999 and increases to double digit of 21.0 in 2003 but dropped to 8,2 per cent in 2006.

Table 2.8: Selected Indicators of Macroeconomic Performance (1995-2006)

	Ave Annual GDPgrowth rate (%)	Average GNP per Capita (US$)	PPP GNI per capita	Current A/C Bal. (% of GDP)	Exchange Rate OER (N to US$)	REER	Inflation
1995	2.6	260	1,220	-2.9	21.90	122.2	5.8
1996	3.9	240	870	2.7	21.90	149.2	29.3
1997	3.9	280	860	0.4	21.90	171.3	8.5
1998	1.8	300	740	-10.3	21.90	155.7	10.0
1999	1.0	260	770	1.4	92.30	78.9	6.6
2000	3.8	260	800	17.0	101.70	81.0	6.9
2001	3.9	290	790	11.9	111.23	89.8	18.9
2002	-0.9	300	800	0.7	120.58	90.3	12.9
2003	10.7	350	900	6.9	129.22	104.5	14.0
2004	6.0	430	970	24.5	132.89	107.9	15.0
2005	6.3	560	1,040	18.1	127.02	123.8	17.9
2006	5.2	620	1,410	n.a	128.65	133.1	8.2

Key: GDP = Gross Domestic Product; GDC = Gross Domestic Credit; Ave. = Average; Current A/C Bal. = Current Account Balance; MCU = Manufacturing Capacity Utilisation; OER = Official Exchange Rate; REER = Real Effective Exchange Rate; Ratio of OER to PER = Ratio of Official Exchange Rate to Parallel Exchange Rate, N= Naira (local currency)

Source: World Bank, World Development Indicators, 1997, p. 203 and p. 249; 1998, p. 13, p. 174, p. 175 and p. 275; 1999, p. 12, p. 184, p. 185 and p. 291; 2000, p. 11, p. 180, p. 181 and p. 281; 2001 p. 13, p. 192, p. 193 and p. 291; 2002, p. 19, p. 202, p. 203 and p. 301; p. 2003, p.15, p. 184, p. 185 and p. 283; p. 2004, p. 15 and p. 279, p. 2005, p. 23, p. 196, p. 197 and p. 295; p. 2006, p. 22, p. 189 and p. 247; p. 2007, p. 15, p. 189 and p. 243; p. 2008, p. 15, p. 197, p. 251 (MCU and inflation rate) Central Bank of Nigeria Statistical Bulletin vol. 17 2006, p.157 and p. 177 (Current account balance, 1995-1997) IMF, International Financial Statistics Yearbook, 1999, p. 158.

30 The real effective exchange rate (REER) is the value an individual consumer will pay for an imported good at the consumer level. This price includes the tariffs and transaction costs associated with importing the good.

31 See table 2.7: Federal Government Finance p.20.

2.3.5 Nigerian International Liquidity and Aid Dependency

2.3.5.1 Nigeria's External Reserve and Debt Problems

Total external reserve minus Gold is the sum of the items in foreign reserve, reserve position in the fund, and the U.S. dollar value of SDR holdings by monetary authorities (the Central Bank). As indicated in Table 2.9 Nigerian external reserve fell from US$10,235 million in 1980 to US$1,667million in 1985 by 83.7 per cent[32]. It increased by 131.7 between 1985 and 1990 per cent, thereafter declined to US$1443 by 62.6 per cent in 1995.

Table 2.9: International Liquidity (Millions of US Dollars)

Year	Total Reserve Minus Gold	Reserve Position in the Fund	SDR
1980	10,235	370.7	132.50
1985	1,667	0.07	1.00
1990	3,864	0.07	0.8
1995	1,443	0.07	0.45
1996	4,075	0.07	0.43
1997	7,582	0.07	0.44
1998	7,101	0.07	0.52
1999	5,450	0.09	0.14
2000	9,911	0.14	0.24
2001	10,457	0.14	0.53
2002	7,331	0.14	0.11
2003	7,128	0.14	0.15
2004	16,956	na	na
2005	28,279	na	na
2006	42,298	na	na

Key: SDR= Special Drawing Rights

Source: (1980-2001) IMF, International Financial Statistics Yearbook 2002, p. 792; (2002-2003) 2004, p. 499); 2006, p. 458.

It also increased from US$1443 in 1996 to US$10,457 in 2001 by 624.7 per cent but fell by 31.8 per cent in 2003. Between 2003 and 2006, the Nigeria external reserve increased rapidly by 493.4 percentage point. However, the reserve position in the IMF Fund reduced drastically from US$370.7 million in 1980 to

32 The drastic reduction in external reserve was caused by the nature of political economy pursued between 1979 and 1983 such that large sum of the resource from oil revenue were devoted to private consumption. Private consumption took 40 per cent of total expenditure of the oil revenue between 1979 and 1981 (Gelb, 1986, p. 62-64).

US$0.14 million in 2003[33]. The special drawing right (SDRs) also fell from US$132.5 million in 1980 to US$1.0 million in 1985 and has maintained a level below US$1 million since 1990. The low reserve position in the IMF Fund and SDRs indicate that Nigeria's external reserve is not diversified[34].

2.3.5.2 Nigeria's External Debt

Nigeria's external debt escalated in the late 1970s following a sharp cut in petroleum oil prices in international market when new oil production started in the North Sea, Alaska, and Mexico. It was aggravated by the persistent balance of payments problem in 1978. As shown in Table, 2.10, by 1980, the total debt stock stood at US$8,921 million with long-term debt of US$5,368 billion. The total external debt stock rose from US$8,921 million in 1980 to US$33,439 billion in 1990 by 274.8 per cent and increased further only by 4.7 per cent in 1995. The total external debt declined from US$35,005 million in 1995 to US$29,358 million in 1999 by 16.1 per cent. It increased from US$29,358 in 1999 to 34,9963 million in 2003 by 19.1 and fell to 7,693 in 2006. Generally, the total external debt increased from US$8,921 in 1980 to US$35,890 in 2004 by 309.3 per cent[35]. Long-term debt has an original or extended maturity of more than one year and has three components namely: public and publicly guaranteed debt, private non-guaranteed loans. The long-term debt increased from US$5,368 million in 1980 to US$31,935 million in 1990 by 494.9 per cent. It averaged US$24,834.4 million between 1995 and 1999 and rose from US$22,673 in 1999 to US$31,304 in 2004 by 38.1 per cent.

---

33 A member reserve position in IMF Fund is similar to reserve assets. It comprises the reserve tranche position and creditor position under different borrowing arrangements. A reserve tranche position arises from the payment of part of a member's subscription in reserve assets and the Fund's net use of the member's currency (IFS, 2006/Feb, p. xii).

34 SDRs are unconditional reserve assets created by the IMF to supplement the existing reserve assets. SDRs are allocated to the IMF members that participate in the Fund's operations Division for SDR. The IMF cannot allocate SDRs to itself but receives them from members through various financial transactions and operations. The SDRs funds are used by members for transactions such as acquiring other member's currencies, settling financial obligations, making donations, and extending loans (IFS, 2006/Feb, p. xiii).

35 The total external debt is defined as debt owned by non-resident payable in foreign currency, goods and services. It comprises the sum of public, publicly guaranteed and privately non-guaranteed long-term debt including the use of IMF credit and short-term debt. Short-term debt includes all debt having an original maturity one year or less and interest in arrears on long-term debt.

Table 2.10: External Debt Position (in million US$) 1980, 1990-2006[36]

	Total Ext. Debt	Long Term Debt	Public & Publicly Gtd Debt	Private non Gtd Ext. Debt	IBRD Loans & IDA Credit	Use of IMF Credit	P-Debt Value % of GNP	T-Debt services % of GNP	DSR % of Exps
1980	8,921	5,368	4,271	1,097	554	0	10.1	1.9	4.2
1990	33,439	31,935	3,709	391	3,321	0	110.9	13.0	20.3
1995	35,005	29,002	28,701	301	3,489	0	132.3	na	12.3
1996	31,407	25,731	25,431	300	3,110	0	114	na	16.0
1997	28,455	22,926	22,631	295	2,783	0	72	3.8	7.8
1998	30,315	23,740	23,455	285	2,841	0	76	3.4	11.2
1999	29,358	22,673	22,423	250	2,613	0	91	2.9	6.0
2000	34,134	32,950	32,735	215	2,268	0	74	2.7	4.3
2001	31,119	29,396	29,215	181	1,958	0	81	6.7	11.5
2002	30,476	28,206	28,057	149	1,951	0	80	8.2*	8.2
2003	34,963	31,563	31,563	na	1,988	0	76	3.3*	na
2004	35,890	31,304	31,304	0	1,994	0	71	4.0	8.2
2005	22,178	20.342	20.342	0	1,859	0	34	10.2	15.8
2006	7,693	3,800	3,800	0	2,074	0	9	7.6	n.a

Key: IBRD= International Bank for Reconstruction and Development; IDA=International Development Association; IMF=International Monetary Fund; na = not available * Public and publicly guaranteed debt services % of GNP, Exps = Exports

Source: World Bank, World Development Report, 1992, p. 258, p. 264; 1993, p. 278, p. 284; World Bank, World Development Indicators, 1997, p. 219 and p. 223; 1998, p. 239, p. 243; 1999, p. 255, and p. 259; 2000, p. 249 and p. 253; 2001, p. 255 and p. 259; 2002, p. 265 and p. 269; 2003, p. 247 and p. 251; 2004, p. 243 and p. 247; 2005, p. 259 and p. 263; 2006, p. 255 and p. 259; 2007, p. 251 and p. 255; 2008, p. 345 and p.349, (Present debt value and total debt service % of GNP for 1980) The World Bank, World Development Report, 1997 p. 246.

The present debt value expressed as percentage to the GDP rose from 10.1 per cent in 1980 to 110 .9 per cent in 1990 and recorded the highest value of 132 per cent in 1995 but fell to 76per cent in 2003 and to 9 per cent in 2006. Debt burden is the problem associated with persistent rise in debt stock. The implication is that resources will no longer be channelled to poverty reduction

36 The genesis of Nigeria's debt problem was clearly analysed by Tom Forrest as follows: "...The deficit on trade account that had begun in August 1977 peaked in March 1978, just prior to the budget. The external position was maintained by borrowing of $1.7 billion in the Eurodollar market. The limits to this form of borrowing for balance of payment support were quickly reached, and the target for second loan was not met. The whole episode reveals serious deficiencies in oil policy and its coordination with macroeconomic management. Nigeria external debt started to increase sharply" (Forrest, 1993, p. 145).

programmes rather will be diverted to debt servicing[37]. The total debt service expressed as a percentage to GNP increased from 1.9 per cent in 1980 to 13 per cent in 1990 and dropped to 2.7 per cent in 2000 but rose again to a double digit of 10.2 in 2005. Despite several debt rescheduling arrangements with external creditors in 1990s, the situation failed to improve. The debt service ratio expressed as percentage to export increased from 4.1 per cent in 1980 to a highest record of 20.3 per cent in 1990. The debt service ratio subsequently declined to 4.3 per cent in 2000 but fluctuated between 11.5 and 15.8 between 2001 and 2005.

2.3.5.3 External Assistance and Aid Dependency

The total official aid received by Nigeria increased from US$250 million in 1990 to US$279 million in 1993 and declined to US$152 million in 1999[38]. It increased from US$152 million in 1999 steadily to US$318 million in 2003 and increased from US$318 million in 2003 to US$11,434 million in 2006 by 3495.6 per cent[39]. The increase in official development assistance (ODA) between 2003 and 2006 was as a result of net debt relief grant which represents the share of net ODA. Nigeria's aid per capita averaged US$3.0 per head between 1990 and 1993. It declined to US$2 per head between 1994 and 1997; and recorded the lowest value of US$1.0 between 1998 and 2001 but rose again to US$2.0 in 2003[40]. However, between 2003 and 2006, the aid per capita rose from US$2.0 to US$79.0 as a result of debt relief grant.

---

37 External debt indicators such as present debt value and debt service ratio are used to measure the degree of debt burden. Present debt value is defined as the sum of the short-term external debt plus the discounted sum of the total debt service expressed as a percentage of GNP. This shows the impact of the debt burden on the gross national income or gross national product. The debt service ratio is defined as actual debt service payment (payment of principal plus interest) as a proportion of export earnings. Debt service ratio shows severity of burden and the extent of sustainability of a country's debt service obligations.

38 Aid per capita is an index used in measuring the value of aid per head of the citizens of an aid-receiving country. It is defined as Official Development Assistance (ODA) and Official Aid from donor countries calculated by dividing the total aid received by the mid-year population estimates of that country. Total Official Aid (TOA) is defined as disbursements of loans in terms of net repayment of principal amount and grants by official agencies of the Development Assistance Committee (DAC).

39 Aid dependency is determined by percentage of aid to GNP; percentage of aid to import of goods and services or as percentage of government expenditure.

40 In comparison with other African countries, Nigeria has been receiving much less foreign aid per capita basis. The average net real official development assistance (ODA) per capita for sub- Sahara Africa countries in 2003 was US$34.0 and for Nigeria US$2.0 (The World Bank World Development Indicators, 2005 p. 351-2).

Table 2.11 shows that Nigeria's aid dependency ratio was low between 1990 and 2004. The low aid per capita in Nigeria is that donors tend to give less aid to populous countries (Devarajan, et al, 2001, p. 13). Herbst and Soludo (2001, pp. 650-1) argue that donors perceived Nigeria as a rich country based on its high oil revenue the country receive as well as flamboyant life style of Nigerian government. The recent increase can be associated to the ongoing economic reform process in Nigeria. Aid as a percentage of GNP is below 0.5 and 1.1 per cent between 1990 and 2005 but increased to 11.3 in 2006 while aid as a percentage to import ranges between 1.0 and 2.5 per cent. Between 1990 and 2004 the Aid as percentage of gross domestic investment ranged between 5.6 and 1.6. It rapidly increased from 3.6 per cent in 2004 to 45.1 per cent in 2006. This suggests that recent development assistance in Nigeria is directed more to capital investment.

Table 2.11: External Assistance/Aid Dependency of Nigerian Economy 1990 – 2006

	Total ODA (in US$million)	AID per Capita (in US$)	Aid as % of GNP	Aid as % of Import of G&S	Aid as % GDI
1990	250	3.0	0.9	2.5	5.2
1991	262	3.0	1.1	2.0	4.1
1992	258	3.0	0.9	2.3	3.7
1993	279	3.0	1.5	2.2	5.6
1994	190	2.0	0.6	1.5	3.3
1995	212	2.0	0.8	1.3	4.6
1996	191.8	2.0	0.6	1.5	3.2
1997	206.6	2.0	0.5	1.1	3.3
1998	204	1.0	0.7	1.3	2.5
1999	152	1.0	0.5	1.0	1.8
2000	185	1.0	0.5	1.0	2.0
2001	185	1.0	0.5	1.0	1.6
2002	314	2.0	0.8	1.8	3.1
2003	318	2.0	0.6	n.a	2.4
2004	573	4.0	1.0	3.3	3.6
2005	6,434	49.0	7.4	20.1	31.2
2006	1,434	79.0	11.3	n.a	45.1

Key: ODA= Official Development Assistance; G&S = Goods and Services; Govt. Exp.=Government Expenditure; GNP= Gross National Product; GDI= Gross Domestic Investment; n.a = not available

Source: The World Bank, World Development Indicators, 1997, p. 315; 1998, p. 343; 1999, p. 353; 2000, p. 343; 2001, p. 349; 2002, p. 361; 2003, p. 339; 2004, p. 335 and 2005, p. 351; 2006, p. 349; 2007, p.349 and 2008, p. 365.

2.3.6 Relative Prices Changes and Interest Rate in Nigerian Economy

2.3.6.1 Inflation Rate in Nigeria's Economy

Nigeria's monetary management remains a challenge to country as the Nigerian central bank is compelled to provide credit needed to finance the persistent federal government deficit (see Table 2.7, p. 35 above). Consequently, this has limited private borrowing as funds are diverted to deficit financing. It has also led to trade off between deficit management and inflation control by the monetary authority hence an impediment on economic development[41]. Figure 2.1 shows that inflation level was relatively under control between 1985 and 1987 but rose in 1989 by 40.9 per cent. It increased from 7.5 per cent in 1990 to 75.8 per cent in 1995[42]. Inflation level fell from 29.3 per cent in 1996 to 6.6 in 1998 but rose to 21.0 per cent in 2003. In general, Nigeria fared better in managing the inflation rate between 1997 and 2003 which averaged 12.1 per cent, and subsequently dropped to 8.2 in 2006

Figure 2.1: Inflation level in Nigeria's economy between 1985 and 2006

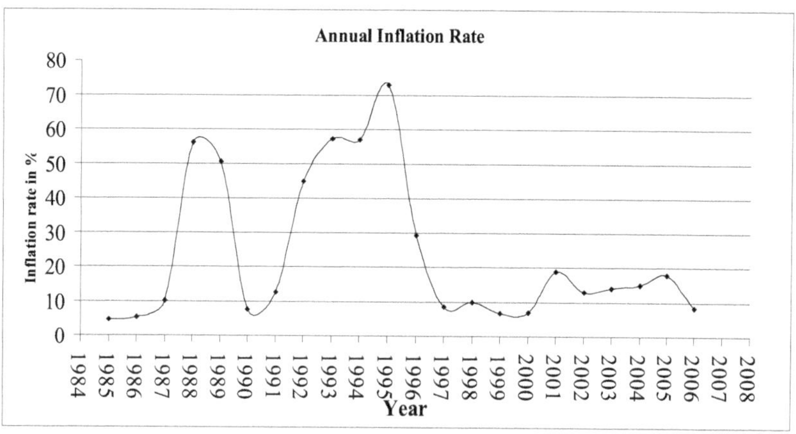

Source: Central Bank of Nigeria Statistical Bulletin, 2007, Volume 18, p. 177

---

41 Following an increased inflow of oil revenue, the effective exchange rate of the local currency (Naira) against foreign currencies appreciated, the non-oil tradable sector such as cash crops lost their competitiveness, the labour force and resources shifted away from traditional agriculture to non-tradable sector, construction, services and trading (Dutch Disease syndrome).

42 The increase in inflation level could be linked to reversal of reform policy in 1988/89 and subsequent political crises that erupted between 1993 and 1994.

2.3.6.2 Food Price Index in Nigeria

Large government expenditure can induce changes in relative price level and household resource allocation. For example, change in price of food in 1993 is a reflection of increased government expenditure in 1993. Table 2.12 shows food price index in Nigeria measured on a 1985 base year. The food price rose from 293.2 per cent in 1990 to 2,040.4 per cent in 1993. In 1995, it rose by 595.9 per cent and increased between 1995 and 2006 by 3,827.7 per cent. Based on the same argument of Zartman and Schatz, (1983, p. 16) Nigeria's national food security programme needs pro-active policy measures so that the elasticity of supply (i.e. local food production responsiveness) can respond to change in domestic demand.

Table 2.12: Food price Index (1985=100)

Year	*Food Price*
1980	40.10
1985	100.00
1990	293.20
1995	2,040.40
2000	3,923,80
2001	4,268.10
2002	5,151.50
2003	5,493.30
2004	6,318.40
2005	7,446.40
2006	8,014.10

Source: Central Bank of Nigeria, Statistical Bulletin, 2007 Vol., 18, p. 176.

2.3.6.3 Interest Rate[43]

Table 2.13 shows a wide margin between the deposit rate and lending rate in Nigeria's monetary system. It declined from 13.5 per cent in 1995/6 to 7.3 per cent in 1997/8 and rose again in 1999 to 12 per cent. The highest rate of 16.7 per cent was recorded in 2002 but subsequently declined to 10.7 per cent and 10.7 per cent in 2005 and 2006 respectively. The fluctuation in deposit rate tends to create uncertainty and psychological impact on private time deposit. Between 1995 and 1999, the lending rate was within the range of 20.2 per cent and 20.4

43 Interest rates are the price which expresses the competitive conditions that govern the loans and deposits as well as positions of the creditors and debtors in an economy. Deposit interest rate is the rate paid by commercial or similar banks for demand, time or saving deposits while the lending interest rate is the rate charged by banks on loans to prime customers. The Real interest rates are the real price of capital. They are the lending rate adjusted for inflation as measured by the GDP deflator.

per cent. It has been increasing steadily from 21.3 per cent in 2000 to 24.8 per cent in 2002. It declined again to 20.7 per cent and 17.9 per cent in 2005 and rose to 20.2 in 2006. High lending rate has three basic implications. First, the poor and small enterprises can neither borrow under such condition nor provide the lending security requirements. Secondly, such lending rate is geared towards short-term lending because the probability of default will be very high. Thirdly, loan becomes volatile when inflation is high as the case in 1995 and 1996.

Table 2.13: Interest Rate from 1995 to 2006 (% per annum)

Year	Dep. Rate	Lend. Rate	Real Int. Rate
1995	13.5	20.2	-54.4
1996	13.5	20.2	-23.6
1997	7.3	20.4	9.3
1998	7.3	20.4	8.9
1999	12.8	20.3	6.5
2000	11.7	21.3	-3.3
2001	15.3	23.4	16.4
2002	16.7	24.8	11.8
2003	14.2	20.7	-0.3
2004	13.7	19.2	-0.6
2005	10.5	17.9	-7.0
2006	10.7	20.2	8.3

Key: Dep. Rate = Deposit Rate; Lend. Rate = Lending Rate; Real Int. Rate = Real Interest Rate; na = not available

Source: World Bank, World Development Indicators 1997, p. 249; 1998, p. 275; 1999, p. 291; 2000, p. 281; 2001, p. 291; 2002, p.301; 2003, p. 283; 2004, p. 279; 2005, p. 295; 2006, p. 243; 2007, p. 239; 2008, p. 247.

2.4 Labour Force and Unemployment in Nigeria

International Labour Organisation (ILO) defines unemployed population as persons above a specified age who are available, but were not included in the labour supply for the production of goods and services. It relates to all persons not in employment who would have accepted a suitable job or started an enterprise during the reference period if the opportunity arose, and who have actively looked for ways to obtain a job or start an enterprise in the near past. The sum of the employed and the unemployed population measured for a short reference period is equivalent to the labour force, also known as the current economically active population (ILO, 2007). Unemployment and total employment indicators explain how the labour market is related to economic activity in an economy. The basic indicators are not only the national unemployment rate and total labour force but also the percentage of female labour force and labour productivity in the economy. As shown in Table 2.14, unemployed population reported in Nigeria was highest in 2000 with national unemployment rate of 4.7 per cent. The national unemployment rate fell to 2.8 per cent in 2006. The Table also shows that urban employment reached the highest level of 7.2 per cent in 2000. The rural unemployment rate dropped from 2.8 per cent in 1996 to 2.5 per cent in 1999 and rose to 3.9 per cent in 2002 and later fall to 2.6 per cent in 2004

Table 2.14: National Unemployment Rates

Year	Composite	Urban	Rural
1996	3.4	6.1	2.8
1997	3.2	6.0	2.6
1998	3.2	4.9	2.8
1999	3.1	5.8	2.5
2000	4.7	7.2	2.7
2001	4.2	4.8	3.7
2002	3.0	3.8	3.9
2003	2.9	3.2	2.7
2004	2.8	3.3	2.6

Source: Federal Bureau of Statistics 2006

Table 2.15 shows the trend in Nigeria's labour force and the annual growth rate of labour force. The labour force is defined as the supply of available labour for the production goods and services in an economy. The total labour force comprises people ages 15 and older who meet the ILO definition of the economically active population. Table 2.15 shows that Nigeria's total labour force increased from 44 million in 1995 to 50.3 million in 2000 by 14.3 per cent and increased from 50.3 million in 2000 to 54.5 million in 2003 by 8.3 per cent. However, the total labour supply declined in 2004 by 14.3 per cent and from 46.7 million in 2004 to 52.7 million in 2006 by 12.8 per cent. The ratio of female participation in total labour force declined from 36 per cent in 1995 to 34.8 per cent in 2006. This indicates that labour gender equity in Nigeria is declining rather than increasing. In the sub-periods 1980-1990 and 1990-2006, the average annual growth rate of labour force in Nigeria increased by only 1 percentage point. Table 2.15 also shows that the output per person employed remains below the benchmark or the index year of 1980 = 100. In 1990, the ratio of GDP to total employment in the Nigerian economy was 85 but increased to 93 in 2006. The implication of low productivity is that the ability of the country to create and sustain decent employment opportunities with fair and equitable remuneration will be reduced (World Bank, 2008, p. 55).

Table 2.15: Nigerian Labour Force and the Average Annual Growth Rate

Year	Total Labourforce	Female in LabourForce
1995	44.0	36.0
1996	46.0	36.0
1997	47.0	36.0
1998	48.0	36.3
1999	49.0	36.4
2000	50.3	36.5
2001	51.6	36.6
2002	52.9	36.7
2003	54.5	35.5
2004	46.7	34.8
2005	47.9	34.7
2006	52.7	34.8
	1980-2000	1990-2006
AAG of the Labour Force	2.7	2.8
	1990	2006
Labour Productivity GDP per person employed (Index: 1980 = 100)	85	93

Key: AAG= Average Annual Growth
Source: World Development Indicators 1997, p. 43; 1998, p. 51; 1999, p. 51; 2000, p. 47; 2001, p.49; 2002, p. 43; 2003, p. 43; 2004, p. 53; 2005, p. 51; 2006, p. 51; 2007, p. 45); 2008, p. 45 and p. 53.

2.5 Structure of Nigeria's Industrial Output and Manufacturing Activities in Nigeria

Monetisation of oil revenues in the 1970s in Nigeria led to rapid growth of the manufacturing sector to about 12% per annum. The share of manufacturing in GDP rose from 4% in 1970 to about 11% in 1982. Despite the expansion of the domestic manufacturing, the sector was characterised by low value added, high costs of production and poor export potential. The structural problems in the sector were concealed by the rapid increase in oil earnings (Danju and Weiss, 1997, p. 359). In response to declined oil prices, trade policy became much more restrictive during the first half of the 1980s. The Economic Stabilisation Act of 1982 was structured to impose further import restrictions in the form of an increased number of goods subject to import licences and higher import duties to some items. Such restrictions led to decline in import capacity and severe shortages of imported inputs, reduced investment, widespread plant closures and decline in capacity utilisation rates. Manufacturing output fell at an average rate of about 3% per annum from 1981 to 1986 and the index of manufacturing production declined from about 129% in 1982 to about 78% in 1986 (Danju and Weiss, 1997, p. 359).

Table 2.16 above shows the structure of Nigeria's industrial out-put comprising petroleum, mining/ quarrying and manufacturing at constant basic price in billions of Naira. As shown in Table 2.16, the contribution of crude petroleum to industrial output decline from 83.5 per cent in 1985 to 57.7 per cent in 1990 and increased to 86.3 in 1995. The decline can be linked to the fall in oil prices in world market which partly led to economic crises from mid-1990s.

Table 2.16: The structure of Nigeria's Industrial Output at 1990 constant basic price in millions of Naira

	Crude Petroleum & Natural Gas	Mining and Quarry	Manufacturing.	Total Output (Industry)	Total GDP	Non-Oil GDP
1985	72,152.0 83.5* 28.52**	951.7 1.12* 0.38*	11,307.4 13.25* 4.47** 6.25***	85,355.0 33.74**	253,013.3	180,861.3
1990	149,745.0 57.7* 31.68**	1,786.9 0.69* 0.38*	107,114.5 41.28* 22.66** 33.17***	259,514.2 54.91**	472,648.7	322,903.8
1995	93,536.70 86.3* 26.52**	831.5 0.77* 0.24*	13,167.8 12.21* 3.73** 5.08***	108,446.5 30.75**	352,646.2	259,109.5
2000	106,827.50 87.5* 25.91**	1,022.6 0.84* 0.25*	13,743.5 11.26* 3.33** 4.50***	122,061.8 29.60**	412,332.0	305,504.5
2001	112,417.40 87.3* 26.04**	1,124.84 0.88* 0.26**	114,318.76 11.8* 3.52** 35.80***	128,740.0 29.82**	431.783.1	319,365.7
2002	106,002.10 85.5* 23.46**	1,173.70 0.95* 0.26**	15,892.19 13.49* 3.70** 4.60***	123,905.9 27.43**	451.785.6	345,783.5
2003	131,336.6 87.4* 26.53**	1,238.09 0.83* 0.26**	16,776.59 11.76* 3.57** 4.61***	150,250.7 30.35**	496,007.1	363,670.5
2004	135,670.71 86.7* 25.72**	1,372.41 0.88* 0.26**	18,454.25 12.42* 3.68** 4.71***	156,486.8 29.66**	527,576.0	391,905.3

Key: * = percentage to total output (industry); ** = percentage to total gross domestic output. *** = percentage to Non-Oil gross domestic product. (Calculation of * and *** by the author)

Source: Central Bank of Nigeria, Statistical Bulletin 2007, Vol. 18, pp. 132-137

Table 2.16: Continues

	Crude Petroleum & Natural Gas	Mining and Quarry	Manufacturing	Total Output (Industry)	Total GDP	Non-Oil GDP
2005	136,345.54 *85.7** *24.33***	1,503.16 *0.95** *0.27***	20,220.45 *13.37** *3.79*** *4.75****	159,161.4 *28.39***	561,931.40	425,585.86
2006	130,193.57 *83.91** *21.85***	1,657.47 *1.07** *0.28***	22,106.58 *14.25** *3.71*** *4.75****	155,165.5 *26.04***	595,821.60	465,628.04
2007	124,285.12 *82.0** *19.58***	1,828.35 1.21* *0.29***	24,118.28 *15.91** *3.80*** *4.73****	151,563.2 *23.88***	634,656.60	510,371.46

Key: * = percentage to total output (industry); ** = percentage to total gross domestic output. *** = percentage to Non-Oil gross domestic product. (* and *** are acalculated of by the author)
Source: Central Bank of Nigeria, Statistical Bulletin 2007, Vol. 18, pp. 132-137

Between 1995 and 2005 the contribution of crude petroleum to industrial output was within the range of 86 to 87 per cent. The ratio gradually declined from 87.4 per cent in 2003 to 82.0 per cent in 2007. The contribution of crude petroleum to GDP increased from 28.52 per cent in 1985 to 31.68 per cent in 1995. Between 1995 and 2005 the share of crude petroleum to GDP growth remained between 23 to 27 per cent. The contribution of crude petroleum to GDP gradually declined from 26.53 per cent in 2003 to 19.58 per cent 2007.The share of mining and quarrying to total industrial output declined from 1.12 per cent 1985 to 0.69 per cent 1995 and rose to 1.21 per cent in 2007. The contribution of mining and quarry to Nigeria's GDP in the period between 1985 and 2007 is between 0.24 and 0.29 per cent. The contribution of manufacturing to industrial output increased from 13.25 in 1985 to 41.28 in 1990. This is reflected on GDP growth which increased from 4.47 to 22.66 per cent within the same period. The said increase can be linked to increased production in small enterprises in informal sector during the SAP. The share of manufacturing to industrial output in the period between 1995 and 2007 ranges from 11 to 16 per cent while its contribution to GDP remains at 4 per cent. The contribution of manufacturing to non-oil GDP increased from 6.25 in 1985 to 33.17 in 1995 and declined to 4.50 per cent 2000 but rose to the highest level of 35.80 in 2001subsequently falling to 4.73 in 2007. The values in Table 2.16, suggest that Nigeria's industrial sector is highly polarised in the sense that about 85 to 97 per cent of total industrial output come from petroleum sector. This implies that domestic and foreign investments in Nigeria are concentrated in the petroleum sector at the expense of the manufacturing and mining sectors. This implies that there is an urgent need to promote SMEs in Nigeria in order to strengthen manufacturing and stimulate linkage across sectors.

The contribution of industrial sector to GDP growth increased from 33.74 per cent in 1985 to 54.91 per cent in 1990 but has remained within the range of 24 and 31 per cent between 1995 and 2007. Table 2.17 shows the structure of some selected manufacturing activities in Nigeria. Table 2.17 indicates that production of consumers' goods dominate the manufacturing activities in Nigeria. As shown in the Table, between 2001 and 2007 about 23 per cent of manufacturing activities are concentrated on Food and Drinks while building materials constitutes between 22 and 23 per cent.

Table 2.17: Structure of Nigeria's manufacturing output 2001-2005 (in '000 Naira)

Product	2001	2002	2003	2004	2005
	18,609,799	18555475	18,630,545	18,598,605	18,594,875
Food and Drinks	23.11*	23.12*	23.12*	23.12*	23.35*
Electrical	1,772,761	1,766,192	1,777,454	1,772,135	1,771,927
Equipments	2.20*	2.20*	2.20*	2.20*	2.23*
	4,242,964	4,219,286	4,245,097	4,235,783	4,233,388
Vehicle Assembly	5.3*	5.26*	5.27*	2.26*	5.32*
	18,474,826	18,367,642	18,496,176	18,446,214	18,436,677
Building Materials	22.94*	22.89*	22.95*	22.93*	23.15*
Petroleum and	7,747,893	7,748,291	7,749,945	7,748,709	7,748,982
Chemical Products	9.62*	9.7*	9.62*	9.63*	9.73*
	15,114,685	15,079,944	15,129,956	15,108,196	15,106,031
Textile	18.77*	18.79*	18.77*	18.78*	18.97*
	3,838,334	3,810,718	3,835,228	3,828,094	3,024,681
Paper Conversion	4.77*	35.63*	4.76*	4.76*	3.80*
	10,721,662	10,696,643	10,726,427	10,714,910	10,712,660
Other products	13.32*	13.33*	13.31*	13.32*	13.45*
Total	80,522,924	80244191	80,590,828	80452646	79629221

Key: * = percentage to total output

Source: National Bureau of Statistics 2007 pp. 303-304

Approximately 19 per cent of the activities of activities are in textile branch while the share of petroleum and chemical products to total manufacturing activities is approximately 9 per cent. The paper conversion which includes recycling increased rapidly from 4.77 per cent in 2001 to 35.63 per cent in 2002 but subsequently fall to 3.80 in 2005. Between 2001 and 2007, production activities in electrical equipment constituted about 2.20 to 2.23 per cent of total manufacturing activities. Other manufacturing products such as footwear, sewing machines, tobacco, utensils etc. cover less than 14 per cent of the total manufacturing activities.

The performance in manufacturing activities can be reflected on the variations in the average Manufacturing Capacity Utilisation (MCU) and Index of Manufacturing Production (IMP). Capacity utilisation is the measure of the output rate that can be achieved at the minimum short-term average cost, given the existing stock of plant and factor prices. It is also defined as output level corresponding to the tangency point of short and long-run average costs. Figure 2.2 shows that the average manufacturing capacity utilisation (MCU) in Nigerian economy increased from 38.8 in 1986 after the introduction SAP to 43.8 per cent by 5 percentage point. The MCU subsequently witnessed a downward spiral to its lowest value of 30.4 per cent in 1997 by 13.4 percentage point. It gradually increased from 30.4 per cent in 1997 to 56.7 per cent in 2004 and began to slip down gradually from highest point 56.7 in 2004 to 53.3 per cent in 2006.

The IMP is an important indicator of changes in manufacturing activities. The Index measures the changes in the quantity of commodities produced by different producers. It reflects the trends in a constant basket of goods produced by establishments employing 50 or more persons[44]. As indicated in Figure 2.2, the IMP increased rapidly between 1986 and 1989 by 97.29 per cent. This suggests that there were positive changes in the quantity of commodities produced by different producers during the SAP period. However, the IMP declined from 1992 to 1998 by 27.18 and increased slightly by 10.53 percent in 2003.

In respect to trade and protection of manufacturing, the structure of tariffs indicates the level of protection in the economy or the level at which competition is stimulated in the economy. For example, the 1995-2001 tariff structure was designed to stimulate competition and efficiency by reducing tariffs on consumer goods items relative to tariffs on raw materials and intermediate and capital goods. Government's aim to reduce tariffs was to expose domestic manufacturers to import competitions (World Bank, 2002a, p. 10). The relatively higher tariffs on raw materials were aimed at encouraging investment in raw materials and intermediate goods production. The level of protection in Nigeria has reduced to a certain degree but in general, the tariffs are still high compare to world averages (World Bank, 2002a, p. 10). In 2005, the tariff binding coverage was 19.2 per cent to total imports[45]. The tariffs in respect to simple average of *ad-valorem* duties for Most Favoured Nation (MFN) principle applied in 2006 for all goods and agricultural goods were 12 and 15.6 per cent respectively while the tariffs for non-agricultural goods was 11.4 per cent (Trade Policy Review, 2005).

---

44 National Bureau of Statistics, (2003). Index of Manufacturing Production Fourth Quarter 2002, Dar es Salam Tanzania

45 The tariff binding coverage corresponds to the number of the harmonized System (HS) subheadings containing at least one bound tariff line

Figure 2.2: Manufacturing Capacity Utilisation (MCU) and Index of Manufacturing Production (IMP)

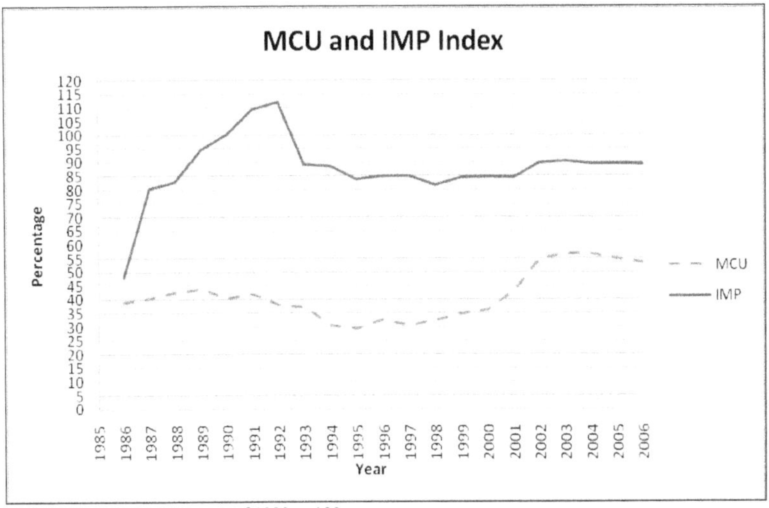

Note: IMP is at the base year of 1990 = 100
Source: Central Bank of Nigeria, Statistical Bulletin 2007, Vol. 18, p. 163 and p. 165

The weak manufacturing in Nigerian economy has several implications in the general well being and economic growth. It suggests that rate of employment in formal sector will continue to be limited. Manufacturing as source of innovative activities and entrepreneurship development will continue to be weak in Nigeria. It also suggests that poverty reduction in Nigeria will not be effective since policies have not been effectively linked the rural economic activities with the urban manufacturing activities. Furthermore, Nigeria will continue to experience the Dutch Disease syndromes as crude petroleum continues be the dominant industrial output at the expense of the manufacturing and other sector. On this note, the extent of poverty and inequality in Nigeria economy need to be analysed in order to highlight why diversification of the economy is imperative.

2.6 The Poverty and Income Inequality in Nigeria

2.6.1 Poverty in Nigeria

There is no universal definition of poverty because the term poverty is relative, complex, and multidimensional and has many perceptions (Sofo et al, 2003, p. 5). Overtime the concept has been redefined to reflect not just lack of income, but also lack of access to education, health care, good housing and other essential services. The meaning of poverty has recently been expanded to include vulnerability, isolation, social exclusion and powerlessness in terms of inability to change circumstances for good. The income poverty is the concept used to assess the poor as people living below absolute or relative poverty. One is in a state of absolute poverty when his or her income is insufficient to provide the basic needs for life. In this case, one is lacking the minimum level of financial resource to satisfy the basic needs. A person is in relative poverty when he or she cannot afford to buy a pre-specified consumption basket, which another person can afford. The World Bank (1990, p. 26) precisely define poverty as the inability to attain a minimal standard of living. Minimum standard of living refers to consumption-based demarcation which stipulates lower and upper expenditure line required to satisfy basic necessities. The income necessary to buy a minimum standard of nutrition and other necessities are within the lower poverty line. Additional amount of expenditure reflects the cost of participating in the every day social life fall within the upper poverty line (World Bank, 1990, p. 26). Income poverty is the most preferred definition in terms of determining a country's level of poverty. Table 2.18 shows that the number of rural population living below the national poverty line has declined from 49.5 per cent in 1985 to 36.4 in 1993[46].

This supports (Adubi and Okunmadewa, 1999) that SAP favoured the rural areas, as there was a boom in agricultural output due to deregulation of prices and exchange rate. The urban poverty declined by only 1.3 per cent while the national poverty declined from 43.0 per cent to 34.1 per cent in the same period. As indicated in Table 2.18, 52 per cent of the population have no access to good water sources resulting to high incidence of water born diseases in the country. The picture is discouraging when one considers Nigeria's poverty in terms of households' expenditure. The population with purchasing power below US$1.00 a day is 70.8 per cent. The poverty gap at US$1.0 a day is 34.5 per cent

46 The World Bank and Federal Office of Statistics of Nigeria used two-third mean of per capita household expenditure as basis to determine the poverty line due to absence of an official poverty line. This is the upper poverty line that determined the "poor". A one-thirds means per capita household expenditure is also used to indicate the lower poverty line, which underlined "the extreme or chronic poor" (Sofo, et al, 2003, pp. 6-7).

in 2003-survey year[47]. The poverty gap suggests that more than one third of the population cannot afford to pay out of pocket health care bills, maintain full day normal meal, send their children to school or live in standard house. Thus, indicating poor general living standard and economic hardship as rightly analysed by Obadan (1996)[48].

Furthermore, the expenditure of 92.4 per cent of the population is below US$2.00 a day and the poverty gap at US$2 a day is 59.5 per cent. The nature of Nigeria's income poverty is further reflected on the poor state of human development in the country. Human poverty is defined as the absence or denial of choices and opportunities to live a tolerable life. With respect to Nigeria, Onibokun and Kumuyi (1996) defined human poverty, as the shortage of vital resources that resulted to endurance of harsh and unbearable environment due to breakdown of economic, demographic, ecological, cultural, social system induced by bad governance. UNDP-Lagos (2004, p. 10), described poverty in Nigeria as precarious not only in terms of income poverty but also in terms of food poverty.

Table 2.18: Nigeria's Income Poverty Estimate

	1985	1992-93	1990-2004
Rural Poverty	49.5	36.4	na
Urban Poverty	31.7	30.4	na
National poverty line (in %)	43.0	34.1	34.1
Access to improved water source		2004	
Population not using improved water source (in %)		52	
International Poverty Line		1990-2005	
Population below $1 a day		70.8	
Population below $2 a day		92.4	
Poverty Gap		Survey Year 2003	
at US$1 a day		34.5	
at US$2 a day		59.5	

Source: UNDP Human Development Report, 2007/08, p. 240. Data for Rural and Urban Poverty, World Bank World Development Indicators, 2008, p. 65

As shown in Table 2.19, the number of year a new born baby will live at present mortality in Nigeria increased from 50.1 in 1998 to 51.8 in 2001 and

47 Poverty gap is the mean shortfall from poverty line expressed as a percentage of the poverty line. It reflects the depth of poverty as well as its incidence.

48 Obadan's observation epitomised the growing nature Nigeria's poverty. The intensity of poverty in Nigeria is reflected on the overcrowded settlements in major urban areas without basic social services, the nature of mass unemployment, homeless among the poorest groups, diminishing access to quality of foods and nutrition, health care and depleted educational facilities with rising trend of street begging.

subsequently fall to 43.4 in 2005 and increased slightly to 46.5 in 2005. Government efforts to maintain a long and healthy life in Nigeria increased from 0.42 in 1998 to 0.46 in 1999 and fell to 0.36 in 2005. The adult literacy rate increased from 61.1 per cent 1998 to 69.1 per cent in 2005.

Table 2.19: Nigeria's Human Poverty Estimate (1998-2005)

Variables	1998	1999	2000	2001	2002	2003	2004	2005
Life At Birth	50.1	51.5	51.7	51.8	51.6	43.4	43.4	46.5
Expectancy Index	0.42	0.46	0.44	0.45	0.44	0.31	0.31	0.36
Adult Literacy Rate								
(% age 15 and above)	61.1	62.6	63.9	65.4	66.8	66.8	na	69.1
Gross Education Enrolment Ratio	43.0	45.0	45.0	45.0	45.0	64.0	55.0	56.2
Education Index	0.55	0.57	0.58	0.59	0.59	0.66	0.63	0.52

Source: UNDP Human Development Reports, 2000, p.160; 2001, p. 143; 2002, p. 151; 2003, p. 240; 2004, p. 141; 2005, p. 221; 2006, p. 285; 2007/8, p. 231.

The education index which is derived from the combination of 2/3 of adult literacy index and 1/3 of gross enrolment index increased from 0.55 in 1998 to 66.0 in 2003 and subsequently fall to 0.52 in 2005. This suggests that government efforts to make education affordable and available are still very weak in Nigeria. The GDP index (calculated using adjusted GDP per capita (PPP US$)) of Nigeria shows a low value of 0.39, indicating that the living standard of the population is very low (UNDP 2005, p. 221). In terms of overall human development performance, Nigeria scored 0.453, rank 158th in world HDI record and 13th out of 32 countries with least human development record with HPI-1value of 38.8 per cent (UNDP, 2005, p. 221/2). The value in HPI-1 suggests that 38.8 per cent of Nigeria population have been cut off from gains of development progress[49].

The human development index measures the average achievement in a country in terms of prevision of education and services such as portable water, public-health facilities and sanitation. The achievement or performance is expressed as a value between 0 and 1 with 0 as the lowest value signifying poor performance; otherwise good performance with value of 1[50]. Table 2.20 shows the trend of Nigeria's HDI performance between 1975 and 2005. The HDI values improved from 0.321 in 1975 to 0.470 in 2005 by 46.4 per cent. Despite the improvement, the country has not been able to reach the 0.5 minimum performance benchmark of the HDI.

---

49 "HPI measures the extent of deprivation and the proportion of people in the community who are left out of progress" (UNDP, 1998, p. 25)

50 HDI is determined by a simple average of the three dimension indices HDI= 1/3(Life Expectancy Index)+ 1/3(Education Index) + 1/3(GDP Index).

Table 2.20: Nigerian Human Development Index Trends (1975-2005)

	1975	1980	1985	1990	1995	2000	2005
Values	0.321	0.378	0.391	0.411	0.432	0.445	0.470

Source: UNDP Human Development Report 2007/8, p. 236

2.6.2 Income Inequality in Nigeria

The increasing income inequalities and poverty level is continuing to be the most challenging development problem facing Nigeria's policymakers[51]. Table 2.22 shows that in 1992/3, expenditure share of the poorest 10 per cent of the population was only 1.3 per cent compare with 31.3 per cent expenditure share of the richest 10 per cent of the population. The expenditure share of the poorest 20 per cent income was 4 per cent as against 49.3 per cent share of the richest 20 per cent. In 1996/7, the inequality widened with the expenditure of poorest 10 per cent of the population accounting for only 1.6 per cent, while the share of 10 per cent richest population rose to 40.8 per cent. Table 2.21 reveals that the expenditure share of 20 per cent poorest increased by mere 0.4 per cent between 1992/3 and 1996/7 while the expenditure share of the richest 20 per cent of the population increased by 6.4 per cent in the same period.

Table 2.21: Percentage share of Expenditure in Nigeria

Survey year	Poorest 10%	Poorest 20%	Richest 20%	Richest 10%	Gini Index
1992-93	1.3	4.0	49.3	31.3	44.7
1996-97	1.6	4.4	55.7	40.8	50.6
2003	1.9	5.0	49.2	33.2	43.7

Sources: Survey Year 1992-1993, World Bank, World Development Indicators 1997 p. 55; Survey Year 1996-1997, UNDP; Human Development Report, 2005 p. 272; Survey Year 2003, UNDP; Human Development Report 2007/8, p. 337.

The 2003 survey shows that share of the poorest 10 per cent increased only by 0.3 and the poorest 20 per cent increased 0.4. By 2003, the richest 10 per cent fell by 17.6 per cent and the richest 20 per cent declined by 6.5 per cent. Nigeria's Gini Index rose from 44.7 in 1992/3 to 50.6 in 1996/7 but declined to 43.7. This indicates a less unequal size distribution of income in 1992/3 which

51 Economic development is measured by considering the components of quality of life using Physical Quality of Life Index (PQLI), human development and human outcome using Human Development Index (HDI). Income distribution is measured by the use of Gini Index. Gini index measures the extent to which the distribution of income among individuals or households within a country deviates from a perfectly equal distribution. A value of 0 represents perfect equality, a value of 1, perfect inequality. This is determined by the use of Lorenz curve.

widened by a margin of 5.9 in 1996/7 but contracted by 6.9 in 2003 survey year. The problem of income distribution is clearly portrayed by the ratio of richest to the poorest in the same percentage income group. Table 2.22 shows that in Nigeria, for every 1 per cent of the national income allocated to the 10 per cent poorest population, the 10 per cent of the richest population gets 17.9 per cent. For every 1 per cent of the national income allocated to the poorest 20 per cent of the population, the richest 20 per cent of the population gets 9.7 per cent.

Table 2.22: The ratio of income in Nigeria

Measure of Inequality	Value
The ratio of the richest 10% to the poorest 10%	17.8
The ratio of the richest 20% to the poorest 20%	9.7

Source: UNDP; Human Development Report, 2007/8 p. 337

The impact of income disparity is also reflected on the depth of inequitable in terms of access to and consumption of public goods and services, balanced diet or health care facilities. Even when the poor have access to facilities, pricing undercuts them. Table 2.23 shows the poverty in terms of health status in Nigeria and explains the depth of income inequalities in Nigeria. 20 per cent of children under the age of five in poorest quintile are exposed to malnutrition therefore would likely experience abnormal growth. 84 per cent of poorest quintile is exposed to infections while 30 per cent will be affected in richest quintile. The under-five mortality rate per 1000 children born stood at 257 as against 79 in richest quintile.

Table 2.23: The poverty in terms of the health status and Gender

Variables	Poorest quintile	Richest quintile
Prevalence of Child malnutrition (Weight for age*)	20	9
Under–five Mortality rate (per 1,000)	257	79
Child Immunization rate (Measles**)	16	71

Note: Survey year = 2003 * in %of children under age of 5. ** % of children ages 12-23 months
Source: The World Bank, World Development Indicators, 2008 p. 114

2.6.3 Health care and Economic Development in Nigeria

The Declaration of ALMA-Ata which set a goal of Health for All (HFA) by the year 2000 was adopted in Nigeria in 1978. Since then, the World Health Organisation (WHO) has made primary health care the central focus of health policy. Universal access to primary health care, health coverage, and commitment to health equity are among the cardinal principles of the health care policy (WHO, 2003, p. 107)[52]. In this contest, the first primary health care to all Nigerians was attempted in 1975 under the Basic Health Services Scheme (BHSS) (Sofo, et al, 2003). A close look at Table 2.24 shows that Nigerian's health-care system has deteriorated over the past decade. This was not only as a result of poor financing in terms of budget allocation, but also as a result of poor governance and weak policy instrument during the military administrations from early 1980s to late1990s (UNDP-Lagos, 2004) [53]. The data from World Health Organisation and World Bank, World Development Indicators revealed an alarming state of Nigerian health care. Table 2.24 shows that the Federal Government spending on health care, the total expenditure (TE) on health expressed as percentage of GDP between 1995 and 2005 was below 10 per cent with the highest TE of 5.0 per cent in 2003[54]. The picture is clearer when one compare the government and private expenditure on health between 1995 and 2000, the general government expenditure (GGE) on health was in the neighbourhood of 11 to 16 per cent of the TE on health care[55]. This increased to 30.9 per cent in 2005. As shown in Table 2.24, between 1995 and 2000, the private expenditure (PE) on health was within 84 and 89 per cent of the TE on health. It declined from 85.9 in 2000 to a lowest level of 74.4 per cent in 2002. It increased to 91.2 per cent in 2003 and fell slightly to 90.4 in 2004 and 2005. External assistance also plays an important role in Nigeria's total and public Health care financing.

---

52 There is three-tier health-care provision system in Nigeria; Federal, State, and Local Government Area (LGA). The Federal government sets policies and guidelines on health-system and controls the teaching hospitals. The states determine the policies for service provision of state hospitals for curative and preventive measures, while the local governments are responsible for the implementation and provision of primary health-care facilities (Oxfam, 2004). With high population ratio in rural areas, the local governments lack the required capacity to carry out effective primary health-care delivery in Nigeria.

53 Improving performance in health system was the central discussion of the World Health Report of 2000. Improvement of the key functions of the health care system namely: providing or delivering personal and non-personal health services, creating human and physical resources, raising revenues for the purchase of services, and transparency in overall peoples' resources as well as responsiveness to their non-medical expectations are what performance in health care system demands (WHO, 2000, p. xii).

54 Nigeria, like most developing countries national health accounting system in is very difficult as a result of low capacity and complicated compilation due to different financing sources or actors such as Federal-, state- and local governments as well as foreign assistance involved.

55 Total expenditure on health is defined as the sum of general government expenditure on health and private expenditure on health. It covers the provisions of the health services, family planning activities, nutrition activities, and emergency aid designated for health (World Bank, 2005, p. 103).

Table 2.24: Some indicators of Health Expenditure in Nigeria

Indicators	1995	1996	1997	1998	1999	2000	2001	2002	2003	2004	2005
TE on health as % of GDP	2.8	2.6	2.8	3.1	3.0	3.0	3.4	4.7	5.0	4.6	3.9
GGE on health as % of TE on health	14.5	11.7	11.7	15.4	16.0	14.1	23.2	25.6	25.5	30.4	30.9
PE on health as % of TE on health	85.5	88.3	88.3	84.6	84.0	85.9	76.8	74.4	91.2	90.4	90.4
GGE on health as % of TGE	1.7	1.3	2.1	2.3	1.7	1.7	1.9	na	n.a	n.a	3.5
ER for health as % of TE on health	na	na	1.3	1.2	3.8	7.1	7.1	6.1	5.3	5.6	4.8
ER for health as % of GGE	1.7	1.3	2$.1	2.9	3.2	3.0	na	na	n.a	n.a	n.a
Per Capita TE on health at AER US$	5.0	6.0	35.0	37.0	10.0	12.0	15.0	19.0	22.0	23.0	27.0
Per Capita GE on health at AER US$	1.0	1.0	4.0	6.0	2.0	2.0	3.0	na	n.a	n.a	n.a

Key: TE = Total Expenditure; GDP = Gross Domestic Product; GGE = General Government Expenditure; PE = Private Expenditure; TGE = Total Government Expenditure; ER = External Resources; OPE = Out-of–Pocket Expenditure; GE = Government Expenditure; AER = Average Exchange Rate; 1DR = International Dollar Rate; na = Not Available.

Source: (1995-1996) World Health Organisation, The World Health Report, 2002, p. 207 and p. 215 (1997-2001) World Health Organisation, The World Health Report, 2003, p. 175 and p. 180. (2002-2005) World Bank, World Development Indicators, 2005, p. 101 ; 2006, p. 101; 2007, p. 93; 2008, p. 95.

Data indicates that external resources (ER) for health care increased from 1.3 per cent of TE on health in 1997 to 7.1 per cent in 2000 but declined slightly to 4.8 per cent in 2005. Direct impact of external assistance on the health sector in Nigeria is reflected. The data indicates that between 1995 and 1998 the ER expressed as percentage to TE on health increased by 5.8 percentage point but fall by 2.8 percentage points between 2001 and 2005. The overall government commitment to health sector can be observed in GGE on health as a percentage of total government expenditure (TGE)[56]. With lowest budget allocation of 1.3 per cent in 1996 suggests that government has been committed in improving the health care sector in Nigeria. Furthermore, low per capita income is translated into low health spending per capita. Per capita TE on health at average exchange rate (AER) is within the range of US$5.0 and US$37.0. Per capita government expenditure (GE) on health lies between US$1 and US$6. The key implication is that out-of-pocket expenditure becomes too expensive for poor households. In other words, their access to health care will be limited when public policy allows only fees on point service (WHO, 2003, p. 120).

As shown in Table 2.25, poor financing is reflected in the low annual federal budget allocation to health sector. The annual government budget allocation to health sector between 1999 and 2003 fluctuated between 2.7 per cent and 4.7 per cent. For example, the most important input in the health system is the staff (clinical and non-clinical) responsible for delivering health services. Since health system is labour intensive, the sector therefore requires well-trained staff and medical equipment because performance enhancement in the health sector depends on knowledge, skills and motivation (WHO, 2000, p. 77).

Table 2.25: Health Services in Nigeria

Health Services	1999	2000	2001	2002	2003
Annual Federal Budget to Health (%)	4.5	2.7	3.9	4.7	4.7
Number of patients per Physician	4,479	4,529	4,675	4,722	4,769
Number of patients per Nurse	906	920	1,082	1,104	1,129
Number of patients per Bed	1,564	1,611	2,124	2,230	2,342

Source: Federal Bureau of Statistics, 2004

The collapse of health care sector in Nigeria is also as a result of brain drain attributed to poor motivation and poor institutional capacity (Sofo, et al, 2003, p. 9). Table 2.25 indicates that the number of patients per doctor in Nigeria increased from 4,479 in 1999 to 4,769 in 2003 at annual rate of 1.59 per cent. The number of patients per nurse increased from 906 in 1999 to 1,129 in 2003 at the rate of 5.94 per cent per annum. Effective health care delivery is limited when the required basic materials are poorly supplied or not available. For example, the number of patients per hospital bed increased from 1,564 in 1999

56 The GGE on health comprises the financial outlays earmarked for the enhancement of the health status of population segments. While the PE on health is defined as the sum of the expenditures comprising pre-paid plans and risk-pooling arrangements such as the outlays of private and private social insurance schemes, health maintenance organization; companies expenditure on health, non-profit organization serving households, and household out of pocket spending (WHO, 2003, pp. 141-2).

to 1,611 in 2000 and from 1,611 in 2000 to 2,124 in 2000. It averaged 2,286 patients between 2002 and 2003.

2.6.4 Interdependency of Education and Economic Development in Nigeria

2.6.4.1 Nigeria's Education Outcome

Education is a fundamental determinant of a country's economic development and growth as well as the major instrument for poverty reduction. The level of education of a country's population is an indicator of the country's socio-economic development. Literacy helps not only upgrade a person's socio-economic life, but also the power of person to understand the basic rudiment of his/her daily life. The 1990 World Conference on Education for All (EFA) set a target to reduce adult illiteracy rates in 1990 to half in 2000 (Watksins, 2000, p. 71). United Nations Millennium Development Goals (MDGs) also set a target to achieve gender parity in primary and secondary education in 2015 (World Bank, 2005, p. 43)[57]. The adult literacy rate defined as the percentage of population aged 15 and above who can read and write simple statements on their own. Several education policies in Nigeria have been initiated by various regimes. For example, in 1999, the Nigerian government initiated the Universal Basic Education (UBE) scheme. The scheme made it mandatory for every child to be educated and have free education up to junior secondary level (9th class). Despite these measures the illiteracy rate in Nigeria remain high, especially the female quota[58]. Table 2.26 shows that male adult illiteracy rate declined from 55 per cent in 1980 to 26 per cent in 2003 (representing a 19-percentage point reduction). Female adult illiteracy declined from 78 per cent in 1980 to 41 per cent in 2003 (representing a 37 percentage point reduction). Youth's illiteracy rate dropped between 1980 and 2003 by a 23-percentage point for male and a 45-percentage point for female. Generally, the number of illiterate people is still high in Nigeria. The recent human development report on Nigeria's literacy gender disparity revealed that national literacy equity in 2008 was 0.77 and 0.94 per cent for adult and youth respectively (UNDP, 2007/8, p. 336).

---

57 Cf World Bank, World Development Indicators 2005.

58 UBE programme was introduced in the country in 1999. Nigeria is a signatory to the Jomtien Conference of 1990 and endorsed the "Framework for Action to Meet Basic Learning Needs. Nigeria was actively involved in Ouagadougou (1992) "Declaration on the Education of Women and Girls" as well as Dakar Framework for Action (2002) that reaffirmed the basic learning needs of all –Education for All (EFA).

Table 2.26: Nigeria's Education Outcome (%)

	Adult illiteracy rate % aged 15 and over		Youth's illiteracy rate % aged 15-24	
Years	Male	Female	Male	Female
1980	55	78	32	58
1990	41	62	19	34
2000	28	44	10	16
2001	27	42	10	15
2002	26	41	9	13
2003	26	41	9	13
2004	na	na	na	na
2005	22	40	13	19

Note: 2002 and 2003 data were derived form Literacy outcome. (Literacy rate for male in 2002 was 74. Illiteracy rate: 100-74= 26)

Sources: The World Bank, World Development Indicators, 2000, p. 83; 2001, p. 95; 2002, p. 99; 2003, p. 89; 2004, p. 85; 2005, p. 97; 2008, p. 89.

2.6.4.2 Primary school enrolment

Primary education is very important in any economy because it represents the basic foundation of learning. Access to primary education for school-aged children is an overriding priority of national education policy because poverty reduction can be attained through schooling[59]. Table 2.27 shows the primary school enrolment of male and female of school age expressed as a percentage of total enrolment in primary schooling in Nigeria. The Table shows that between 1996 and 2006 male enrolment in primary school in Nigeria declined by 5.3 percentage points. The female enrolment increased only by 0.6 percentage points in the same period. In general, gender gap in terms of equal assess to education is still wide. Although Nigeria is a signatory to the Jomtien Education for All (EFA) goals, fluctuation in the enrolment ratio indicates that government was not committed to its objectives. Moreover, the gross enrolment rate does not imply actual school attendance because children may well enrol in their local schools, yet may not be able to attend daily classes due to poverty. The percentage of children between the age of 10 and 14 in labour force in Nigeria was 23 in 2003 (World Bank, 2005, p. 77). UNDP 2004 study revealed that the primary school completion rates in 2001 stood at 83 per cent.

Adequate supply of education facilities such as human resources, libraries, laboratories, etc can induce positive impact on education outcome. For example, the ratio of pupil per teacher is important. In case of many students, teacher may be stressed. Table, 2.27 shows that between 1996 and 2003 the number of pupils

59 In 1981 Nigeria adopted the National Policy on Education for 6-3-3-4 education system. The system comprises 6 years of primary education, 3 years of junior secondary education, 3 years senior secondary education and 4 years higher education.

to a teacher in Nigerian primary school increased from 35 in 1996 to 43 in 2003 but declined to 36 in 2005.

Table 2.27: Primary school enrolment as % total enrolment and ratio of Teacher per pupils 1996 and 2005

	1996	1997	1998	1999	2000	2001	2002	2003	2004	2005
Male	60.4	56.5	54.5	56.2	55.1	55.1	55.7	55.0	55.3	55.1
Female	44.3	43.5	40.2	43.8	43.9	43.9	42.3	44.0	44.7	44.9
Teacher per pupils	1:35	1:40	1:40	1:41	1:43	1:40	1:40	1:43	1:36	1:36

Source: Calculated from Federal Bureau of Statistics 2006 and 2007

The recent decline in teacher-pupils ratio can be related to three reasons. First, the decline can be linked to low enrolment rates or as a result of improved facilities e.g. expanded classrooms or due to increased employment of teachers. In general, a ratio of 1 to 36 is very high and suggests that primary school teachers in Nigeria are over-stretched[60]. Table 2.28 shows that the secondary school enrolment of male and female students expressed as a percentage of total enrolment in secondary schools in Nigeria. As shown in the table, between 1996 and 2006 male enrolment in secondary school in Nigeria increased by 2.2 percentage points while the female enrolment declined by the same margin. The decline in female enrolment can be linked to social norms that support early female marriage. The number of students to a teacher increased from 1 to 27 in 1996 to 1 to 40 in 2005. This suggests that government have not adjusted investment in education to reflect increased demand for secondary education by building more facilities or employing more personnel.

Table 2.28: Secondary school enrolment as % total enrolment and ratio of teacher per student

Year	Male	Female	Ratio teacher per Pupils
1996	53.1	46.9	1:27
1997	53.1	46.9	1:27
1998	55.8	44.2	1:27
1999	53.2	46.8	1:29
2000	55.1	44.9	1:31
2001	55.4	44.6	1:32
2002	55.6	44.4	1:30
2003	56.3	43.7	1:36
2004	56.4	43,6	1:40
2005	55.3	44.7	1:40

Source: Calculated from Federal Bureau of Statistics 2006 and 2007

60 This is also applicable to higher Institution. Students in tertiary institutions are faced with inadequate up-to-date equipment and resources (Oni, 1999).

2.6.4.3 Federal Government Commitment to Education

The educational system can be affected negatively when government's budget to education is limited. The share of public expenditure allocated to education shows an assessment of the priority a government assigns to education relative to other public investments. Table 2.29 shows that the total annual expenditure on education by Federal Government increased from 7.2 per cent in 1995 to 17.59 in 1997 and declined to 7.0 in 2003 but subsequently rose to 13.0 in 2008.

Table 2.29: Federal government expenditure on education

Year	% of Budget Allocation to Education.
1995	7.20
1996	12.32
1997	17.59
1998	10.27
1999	11.12
2000	8.36
2001	7.00
2002	8.00
2003	7.00
2004	12.00
2005	11.00
2006	11.08
2007	8.10
2008	13.00
Average	10.28

Source Dike 2008

This can result to general poor performance in educational outcome in terms of quality, or reduce motivation or general break down of educational system. In this respect, the percentage of GNP allocated to education explains the extent to which government resources have been translated to educational outcome. Fluctuation in education funding has the potential to affect the recurrent and capital expenditure negatively by creating uncertainty in education administration or lead to decline in capital investment in education facilities. As shown in Table 2.30 above, the share of government resource allocation to education as a percentage to GDP increased from 2.77 per cent to 6.32 in 2002 and declined drastically to 2.77 per cent in 2006. This explains the current problem in Nigeria's education system in terms infrastructure.

Table 2.30: Total education expenditure as a % of GDP

	1995	1996	1997	1998	1999	2000	2001	2002	2003	2004	2005	2006
TEE as % of GDP	2.77	2.93	2.70	5.76	3.33	3.55	2.68	6.32	3.08	2.39	2.16	2.77

Key: TEE= Total Expenditure on Education
Source: Central Bank of Nigeria Statistical Bulletin, Vol. 18, 2007

2.6.5 Environment and Economic Development in Nigeria

2.6.5.1 Trends and Inplications of Environmental Problems in Nigerian Economy

Environmental degradation such as pollution, erosion, gas flaring, oil spillages, acidification, desertification and deforestation are deteriorating at an alarming rate with a varying negative impact on Nigeria's economy as well as on the quality of life (UNDP Lagos, 2004, p. 50). The consequences of human induced degradation of environmental assets are reflected on the costs in regenerating the natural resources and loss in alternative economic opportunities. There is linkage between the environment and national development. For example, destruction of the tropical rainforest has imperilled the forest region of Nigeria with loss of arable soil and biodiversity. It is imperative that government must protect and regenerate natural resources such as forest. In 1988, government established the Federal Environmental Protection Agency (FEPA) and launched the National Policy on Environment (NPE) in 1989. In 1999, the FEPA and the Environmental Health Unit of the Ministry of Health were brought under new Federal Ministry of Environment. The duties of the FEPA included the management and monitoring of environmental standards, development of Nigeria's natural resources and the development of procedures for conducting environmental impact assessments of all development projects (Sofo, et al, 2003; UNDP, 2004, p. 50). Despite the institutional framework established, achievements relating to environmental protection and resource management have been limited. There is no articulate policy that aimed at empowering private sector initiatives of SMEs that can focus their activities on environmental protection especially in water resource management and protection of farm land in oil producing areas of Niger Delta.

Table 2.31 shows that average annual deforestation increased from 0.7 per cent between 1980 and 1990 to 0.9 between 1990 and 1995. Deforestation in Nigeria increased rapidly to 2.6 per cent between 1990 and 2000, to 3.3 between 2000 and 2003. The total annual deforestation is estimated at about 400,000 ha as against reforestation of about 1,043 ha (CBN, 2004, p. 153). This has negative inplications not only on Nigeria's wood and furniture industry, but also on the entire ecosystem. Deforestation can be linked to poverty in Nigeria because hunters who search for games often set fire onto the vegetation. Bush burning by villagers during land clearing for cultivation leads to loss of vegetation (NAP, 1997, p. 15).

Table 2.31: Some Selected Environmental Indicators

Indicators		1980-1990	1990-2000	2000-2005	
Annual Average of Deforestation		0.7	2.6	3.3	
		1980	1990	2000	2004
Total Carbon Dioxide Emissions	Per Capita (in Metric tons)	1.0	0.9	0.3	0.8
	Total (in Million) Metric Tons	68.1	36.1	40.1	113.9
Emission of organic Water Pollutants Kg per day		72,082	52,350	82,477	n.a

Source: World Bank, World Development Indicators, 1997, p. 95 and 111; 2000, p. 121; 2004, p. 141; 2005, p. 143, p. 151 and p. 159; 2008, p. 143, p. 151 and p. 159

Increased air pollution has led to increased environmental problems. The total carbon dioxide emissions declined from 68.1 million metric tonnes in 1980 to 36.1 million metric tonnes in 1990 and increased again to 40.1 million metric tonnes in 2000. It further increased to 113.9 million metric tonnes in 2004. The per capita emission fell from 1.0 metric ton in 1980 to 0.9 metric tonnes in 1990 and fell drastically to 0.3 metric tons in 2000 and increased to 0.8 in 2004. The emission of organic water pollutants declined from 72,082 kg per day in 1980 to 52,350 kg per day and rose drastically to 82,477 kg per day in 2000. This indicates that Nigeria's streams and rivers within the cities are increasingly contaminated as a result of increased refuse dumps. Other environmental problems in Nigeria include poor sanitation facilities and access to improved water sources as well as gas flaring. The proportion of the population with sustainable access to improved sanitation declined from 39 per cent in 1990 to 38 per cent in 2000. The proportion of the population with sustainable access to improved water source increased from 49 per cent in 1990 to 60 per cent in 2000 (UNDP, 2005, p. 242).

2.6.5.2 The Role of SMEs in the Environmental Management

The provision of municipal solid waste services is a costly venture and has a major problem for local authorities in developing country cities. This is because the service coverage is low, resources are insufficient, and uncontrolled dumping is widespread (World Bank, 1992, p. 54). The role of SMEs in environmental protection and management in Nigeria is very important in urban cities especially in solid waste disposal and waste water treatment. There are several important reasons why the private sector should participate in solid waste management. This is because in public service delivery, it can either be costly or inadequate. Hence, private sector participation can offer the means to enhance efficiency and competition by providing service at lower cost. This can be through application of commercial principles with greater emphasis on customer satisfaction (World Bank, 1994, p. 73). Private firms can mobilize the needed investment capital to off set the sunk costs where local public funds for investment are limited. Private firms are well situated to draw on local and international experience in waste management and introduce effective cost reducing technologies (Cointreau-Levine and Coad, 2000, p. 3). This implies that environment protection measures could be a combination of micro and macroeconomic interventions. Implementation of the measures requires also public and private sector partnership.

The growing consequences of rapid urbanisation include generation of solid waste and water pollution due to increased consumption of industrial manufactured products. Hence, the major challenge facing Nigerian urban authorities is how to manage solid wastes. Ogu (2000, p. 104) argues that despite the importance of adequate solid waste management to the urban environment in Nigeria, the performance of many city authorities is very poor. Waste management in urban areas in Nigeria can be effective and successful if the real income of the poor is improved (Ogu, 2000, p. 117). Cointreau-Levine (1994) provided four options open for private sector participation in solid waste management. The options are contracting, concessions, franchises and open competition. By contracting, SMEs can be engaged in collecting the solid waste and transfer them to large recycling or waste disposal firms based on contract arrangement. In this respect, municipal authorities must pay the SMEs for the services. Franchising in this context is the competitive process which requires private firms to deposit a performance bond with the government in order to undertake solid waste services in different parts of the city. Private firms will recover the costs of their service directly from customers and government will be responsible for regulating the prices based on the prevailing costs and economic situation. The Franchising process allows the local SMEs to form partnership venture with foreign firms who have better technological capability for their daily operations. Concessions entail a long-term contractual agreement whereby a private firm builds and runs a waste management facility. In an open competitive environmental management, a license is issued to qualified firms to compete and operate in any part of the city for the provision of municipal waste services. The implication here that local SMEs will be forced to improve their capabilities (technological and managerial) in order to enhance efficiency and be competitive in service delivery.

Increased organic water pollutants can lead to chain reactions ranging from human health hazard to productivity problems hence there is the need for public-private partnership for effective waste water treatment. Water treatment, water supply and sanitation systems are categorized as natural government monopolies due to large investments and technical systems. The sunk costs of the major infrastructure investments in the water supply and sanitation sector are significant and do not justify duplication of infrastructure. The spectrum for private sector involvement can be classified into management contracting and concession. In this respect, the option opened for SMEs can be in the service sub-contracting. SMEs can be engaged on contract basis in sewage treatment, maintenance of pipelines, consultancy of environmental management for technology based SMEs and cleaning of water ways in the cities.

2.7 Poverty Reduction Strategies in Nigeria and Industrial Development

Nigeria's poverty reduction programmes can be traced back to the nature of development policy pursed by colonial administration between 1900 and 1929. The British colonial regime viewed development of industry as the responsebility of the private sector hence emphases were laid on agricultural development and infrastructure. In order to boost rural income and export, new cash crops such as groundnut, cocoa, rubber, and cotton were introduced in the economy. This helped not only to diversify Nigeria's export base, but also to reduce dependency on oil palm products as the only source of Nigeria export earnings. By 1929, the proportion of export production accounted for about 5 to 7 per cent of the GDP. The Railway lines linking the South and the North part of the country started in 1898, by 1932 more than 2100 miles of railway line was completed (Helleiner, 1966, pp. 5-6). In 1914, Nigeria had only 2,000 miles of constructed roads for motor traffic. By 1929, more than 6,000 miles was constructed (Helleiner, 1966, p. 14). Recent record indicates that the total constructed road for both rural and urban networks in 2004 stood at 34,340.95 Kilometres (NBS, 2007, p. 309). The missionaries introduced western education and healthcare system in the hinterland such that infant mortality per thousand fell drastically from 430 in 1900 to 134 in 1929 (Helleiner, 1966, p. 14).

Prior to Nigerian independence, poverty reduction strategies were integrated in the two development plans namely -the Ten-Year Plan of Development and Welfare of 1946 to 1956, and the Economic Development Plan of 1955-1960. Investment in cocoa trees for commercial quantity was intensified in Yoruba land. Between 1925 and 1944 more than 780,000 acres of land area were planted with cocoa at annual planting rate of 30,000 to 50,000 acres per year. Production reached 100,000 between 1936/37 and 1955/56; it rose in 1956/57 to 130,000 tonnes (FAO, 1966, pp. 53-54). The volume of cocoa export increased from 9,000 tonnes in 1915 to 114,000 tonnes in 1939. Many producers responded positively to short-run price incentives by applying new technique in terms of quality control and preservation measures (Helleiner, 1966, p. 81). Palm kernel and palm oil that grew wild throughout southern Nigeria accounted for 6.4 per cent of total value of Nigeria's export by 1949. As more roads were constructed in the south, it became possible and profitable to access the product in rural areas. Increase in the harvest of palm products was possible as a result of population growth and reduced infant mortality rate. The export of palm kernel and palm oil together increased from 200,000 tonnes in 1900 to 450,000 tonnes in 1954. The newly established railway line provided the North access to western market hence the output and income of the peasant groundnut farmers in the Northern region was positively affected. The total volume of groundnut for export increased from 50,000 tonnes in 1916 to 149,000 tonnes in 1929, to 428,000 tonnes in 1954 (Helleiner, 1966, pp. 95-110).

The Pre-SAP poverty reduction policies after independent were integrated in national development plan (NDP). As shown in Table 2.32, agriculture took only 9.8 per cent of actual expenditure while non-agricultural sector took 90.2 per cent of the resource allocation between 1962 and 1968. Okowa (1985, p. 82), argues that 59 per cent of the expenditure in agricultural sector was directed to government production activities rather than promotion of small-holder activities. Resources were directed to urban development such that only rural water development got nearly 40 per cent of the resources allocated for water supply in the planned period. Resource allocation to agriculture declined by 1 percentage point between 1970 and 1974 period. Resource allocation to rural health, social welfare and electricity supply increased to 2.7, 19.0, and 10.4 percentage points respectively. Investment in rural water supply declined drastically by 24 .9 percentage points while investment in social welfare and electricity supply increased by 19.0 and 10.4 percentage points respectively.

The resource allocation to agriculture was reduced further to 6.1 per cent in the 3rd NDP but investment in rural social infrastructure improved. The actual public investment in rural health service increased to 7.2 percentage points, water resources increased to 20.0 percentage points and rural electrification increased to 23.9 percentage points while social welfare fell to 0.5 percentage points. The fourth national development plan 1981-1985 adopted an integrated approach whereby the Agricultural Development Programme (ADP) and the Accelerated Development Area (ADA) were linked together in order to facilitate greater agricultural production in the country. River Basin Development

Authorities were established and the Operation Feed the Nation replaced the Green Revolution Programme. Under the SAP measures government initiated some programmes directed towards poverty alleviation. First government created the Directorate for Food, Roads and Rural Infrastructure (DFRRI). The Agency assumed the responsibility for the provision of basic infrastructure as well as mobilising the rural producers in the form of co-operatives (Sofo et al, 2003, p. 36). The National Directorate of Employment (NDE) was established in 1986 to tackle the problem of mass unemployment especially the young school leavers (Akanji, 2002, p. 13). NDE initiated National Open Apprenticeship Scheme (NOAS) with aim to improve the traditional Apprenticeship training system in Nigeria.

Table 2.32: Some Selected Poverty reduction related programmes in pre-SAP period (1962-1980) and in %

	Agriculture (API)	Health (PPI)	Water Supply (PPI)	Social Welfare (PPI)	Electricity (PPI)
1962-1969	9.8	3.9	39.6	9.2	0.6
1970-1974	9.7	6.6	14.7	28.2*	11.0
1975-1980	6.1	13.3 (7.2)	23.6 (20.0)	0.4 (0.5)	21.9 (23.9)

Key: API = Actual Public Investment; PPI = Planned Public Investment

Note: * Comprises Labour and Social Welfare; the figures in parentheses represent actual public Investment

Source: Okowa, 1985

The apprenticeship training was supported by theoretical lessons in trade, mathematics and English on Saturdays. The programme was short-lived because the program lacks institutional support. There was no formal certificate for the graduates of the program (Boehm, 1996, p. 326). The Better Life Programme (BLP) was established in 1987 with the aim to finding solutions to the problems of the rural women such as empowerment. In 1988, the Nigerian Guinea Warm Eradication Programme (NIGEP) was inaugurated to improve the quality of life in rural areas. The NIGEP was supported by UNICEF and was under the primary health care unit of Federal Ministry of Health. The number of reported Guinea-warm cases was reduced from 650,000 in 1988 to 222,000 by end of 1992 (Obadan, 2002, p. 10). The Peoples Bank and Community Banks were also introduced in 1989. The Peoples Bank was under the Federal authority while the Community Bank was promoted under the private sector initiative. The main functions of the banks are to meet the credit needs of the small entrepreneurs in informal sector without collateral based lending modality (Obadan, 2002, p. 11; Akanji, 2002, p. 13).

In 1994 when regime changed, Nigeria witnessed radical policy reversal with strong centralised administrative structure that ended the SAP agenda. The

BLP was transformed into Family Support Programme (FSP) (UNDP, 2004, p. 30). The Petroleum (special) Trust Fund (PTF) was established and empowered to utilise the gains from increased prices in petroleum products to complete all government-abandoned projects and rehabilitate the social infrastructure. The PTF became a monopoly agency in the economy, the sole provider of the physical and social infrastructure such as road construction, transport, health, education, water supply, food and even security. In 1997, the Family Economic Advancement Programme (FEAP) was introduced. This was an economic empowerment programme designed to improve the living standard of low-income groups in the country. The aim was to support local small producers of food and services by making funds available in order to increase local production. The Federal Government further introduced the Mass Transit Programme in 1998 in order to reduce transportation and communication problem in Nigeria. A Federal Urban Mass Transit Agency was subsequently established to advise the government on issues relating urban transportation in the country. The agency later turned from advisory body to management of Federal sponsored transportation services (UNDP, 1998).

In 1999, the Federal Government of Nigeria launched a new Poverty Alleviation Programme (PAP). The document expressed three cardinal goals aimed at reducing poverty and unemployment. The basic instrument was to create effective consumer demand that can stimulate the economy, increase productivity and reduce the crime rate in the society. The policy document outlined series of goals such as providing 200,000 new jobs, creating credit delivery system for farmers, increasing adult literacy to 70 per cent, increasing health care coverage from 40 per cent to 70 per cent and immunization from 40 per cent to 100 per cent. The PAP was revised in 2001 to a National Poverty Eradication Programme (NAPEP). NAPEPs were introduced in 14 ministries with 37 core poverty alleviation institutions, agencies and programmes. The programmes were grouped into four schemes namely: Youth Employment Scheme, Rural Infrastructure Development Scheme, Welfare Services Scheme, and Natural Resource Development and Conservation Scheme (Obadan, 2002, pp. 14-16).

Considering the efforts made by different regimes, the economic and social performance of the country remains weak with low real income per capita, widening income inequality. The pro-poor interventions in post-SAP era were under Ad-hoc committee basis that lack institutional backing and were subject to dissolution as regimes changed. The sustainability of these programmes was limited due to weak collaboration with substantial Ministry such as Ministry of Economic Development or Economic Development Institutions; NGOs and the private sector. Generally, the strategies show that by error of omission, the government was running a centralised resource allocation in the middle of a capitalist economy[61]. The programmes consume significant public resources with little end result because they were politically motivated. In 2000, a new economic development strategy under the framework of National Economic Empowerment and Development Strategy (NEEDS) was conceived and focued on economic growth as fundamental instrument for poverty reduction. The NEEDS was officially lunched in 2004. The document laid much emphasis on the promotion of SMEs, targeting investment in agriculture and infrastructure development.

2.8 Summary and Conclusion

This chapter provides fundamental information on the Nigeria's economic and social development problems. The deduction as conclusion here lesson was that political institutions and governance structures were not stable before the rush for nationalism. Ten constitutional changes between 1947 and 1957 imply that the system was under pressure with little or no learning process. Regional autonomy at the early stage of development produced a scenario of ethnic based competition for political and economic dominance. Deviation from traditional development path (i.e. agricultural based development process) to public based industrialisation process made the country to lose comparative advantage on agriculture. The rapid change of the terms of trade in 1973 which was influeneced by increase in crude oil prices weakened the rural economy hence the rural labour force drifted massively to non-tradable sectors. Frequent military intervention in the politics and governance distorted the general development process. As a result, Nigeria could no longer identify its development path or readjust quickly to corrective measures to redress the past mistakes. Nigeria's income inequality and the deteriorating state of poverty are linked to poor governance during the Military era. In other words, neglect of social and production infrastructure, inadequate funding of education and poor commitment to the health care system and poor business environment led to low economic and social performance. The poverty alleviation programmes initiated by successive governments were politically motivated programmes that lacked sustainability due to poor institutional backing. The question is then, how can sustainable poverty reduction measures be achieved? In what form can growth be stimulated in order to realise a substantial reduction in poverty as well as reduction in income inequality. Private sector is the engine that drives economic development, and small and medium enterprises are considered to be the base line for a private sector development strategy. Sustainable growth can be achieved when linkages are established between the SME and the large enter-

---

61 In this context, error of omission implies not integrating the private sector initiative and neglecting the real poverty reduction measures and the target group (the poor).

prises. To achieve this, large foreign firms can be attracted when there are considerable measures on macroeconomic stability, human capital development, and institutional and physical infrastructure development.

In general, this chapter gave a detail account of the genesis and transformations of Nigeria's political economy. The chapter provided an insight into economic and social performance from 1807 to 2007. In this respect, the interdependencies of economic and social problems were analysed. Hence the chapter showed why government dominance in economic development can produce poor economic. Why government commitment in social issues such as education, health care and environment protection is very important for the economy. In general, the chapter revealed why poor empowerment of the private sectors and promotion of SMEs at early stage development led to poor realisation of poverty alleviation strategies in the country. The preceding chapter focuses on the theoretical analyses on the relationships between SMEs and economic development and growth.

Chapter 3: SMEs in Economic Development and Growth Discourse

3.1 Introduction

SMEs have assumed prime importance in SSA probably as result of concerns on job creation or change of strategy. Some countries in SSA are currently undergoing economic restructuring. As a result, there has been retrenchment and job restrictios in the public sector. The rising population growth has also mounted pressure on few job opportunities in large enterprises. The income instability in the agricultural sector and rapid population growth rate has also forced greater part of labour force in the region into informal sector. As a result, a substantial number of job seekers have turned to small enterprises as a source of livelihood (Mead, 1994, p. 1881; Daniels and Mead, 1998, p. 45). The pressing challenge governments and policy makers in sub-Saharan African countries face is how to tackle the problem of poverty in the region. The general consensus therefore is that small scale enterprises could play a substantial role in the sub-regional economic development and could as well contribute immensely in alleviating the severity of poverty in the SSA. To an extent, some of the small enterprises in the region have shown signs of an innovative potential; export capability and flexibility under unfavourable and often hostile environment. Based on these assumptions, the multilateral, regional and national development institutions such as the World Bank, ILO, IMF and African Development Bank (ADB) and the National Central Banks have acknowledged the importance of the sector in economic development. They have restructured their development policies and strategies towards promoting the private sector and designing different support programmes aimed at improving the capabilities of the SMEs in the region.

Researchers are however often confronted with many problems when investigating the economy of small enterprises in the region. For example, data regarding their contribution to GDP, changes in employment and income patterns are limited. The data is poorly structured and standardised when available. Most of the daily business activities and employment records in small enterprises are often not trapped in national statistical nets (Mead, 1994, p. 1881). Furthermore, small enterprises cover a diverse range of business activities and operate in different sectors. It is therefore imperative to disaggregating the sector into the heterogeneous groups when performing analytical work. In this regards, arguments often arise on the appropriate benchmark in classifying or grouping them into categories. Some researchers consider official registration and meeting tax obligation (Informal vs. formal) as measure in classifying small enterprises in the region. In some cases, the management pattern and technology in use are used to group the sector into (labour vs. technology) intensive categories (Tokman, 1989, p. 1069/70). Others classify them in the form of growth-oriented and innovative enterprises which are commonly found in the computer software sector in western developed economies and in new industrialising countries (NICs) of South East Asia. Most often, researchers consider size in terms of number of employees as very important measure in disaggregating the sector because it provides the appropriate framework for quantitative analysis in empirical studies.

The growth, development among SMEs and the structure of African industrial sector in general has been dubbed a scenario of "missing middle" (World Bank, 1987). African industrial structure is characterised with large number of micro enterprises at one polar end and very few number of large and modern firms on the other end (Fafchamps, 1994, p. 3). In this respect, Wohlmuth (1991, p. 7) argues that the polar structures created capability vacuum that limits industrial linkages. The production capabilities of micro and small enterprises in the region are very weak and fall outside the premise of modern production system in terms of quality and timing[62]. Livingstone (1996, p. 254) argues that the incidence of large number of micro enterprises in the region is a reflection of low purchasing power. Microenterprises are positioned to satisfy the consumption preferences of the poor households in the region. Despite the growing knowledge of these weaknesses, there has been widespread interest on the sector based on its role in economic development in developing countries (McPherson, 1996, p. 254). The support for SMEs especially the micro enterprises could be regarded as part of the strategy to increase productive employment similar to ILO report on employment, income and equity in 1972. One can also argue that it is part of income redistribution with growth strategy proposed by the Chenery, et al, 1974 for World Bank.

In line with these arguments, this chapter tries to provide theoretical explanations on why SMEs are very important and the problems the sector face in Nigeria and in sub-Saharan Africa in general. The chapter starts with theories of small enterprises and the analyses on the rationale behind the promotion of the sector from different development economic perspectives. This is followed by review of some literature on previous studies on SMEs and the analysis on why the sector failed transform or grow in Africa. This leads to discussions on the role of domestic investment and mobilisation of domestic capital for SME development in Nigeria. Theoretical analyses of the relationship between foreign direct investment (FDI) and SMEs development is also revisited. In this case,

62 The polar structure explains the problem of missing middle in African industrialisation efforts in the sense that there is problem of industrial in industrial structure in the region. The micro and small enterprises are ill equipped and lack the capacity to meet the standard required by modern large firm (Wohlmuth, 1991, p. 7; Fafchamps, 1994, p. 2).

the analysis tries to explore how linkages with multinational enterprises (MNEs) can strengthen SME development in Nigeria. The concept of corporate social responsibility (CSR) is introduced in the discussion. The analysis showed how CSR can be applied with examples to promote small enterprises development in developing countries. The analysis also tried to show the price of FDI inflow in the sense that investment climate such as better micro and macroeconomic conditions and the stock of human capital play greater role in attracting FDI. The chapter concludes with a brief introduction of our point of departure by highlighting the basic relationships between clusters, networks, innovation in SMEs development.

3.2 Definitions and theoretical conceptual of small enterprises

SMEs are relative terms used to define various small-scale business activities in the formal and informal sectors (UNIDO, 2004, p. 2). SMEs are defined using quantitative and qualitative criteria. The quantitative criteria define the arbitrary boundaries of small enterprises by showing employment capacity, level of investment capital or sales turnover. Such arbitrary boundaries provide information for statistical analysis and for the administration of small enterprise development programs (Staley and Morse, 1965, p. 2). The qualitative measures define the functional characteristics of the small enterprises such as the nature of technology, organisation and management skills.

SMEs are heterogeneous group of enterprises ranging from small workshop enterprises to medium size manufacturing enterprises as well as the service providers such as restaurants and hotels. Some are traditional handicraft and livelihood enterprises that are small by nature and common in the informal sector in developing countries. The heterogeneity of SMEs reflects the nature of labour force in terms of paid and unpaid labour, skilled and unskilled labour or technology, and labour or machine intensive enterprises. It is therefore difficult to have a universally accepted definition of SMEs. Heterogeneity characteristics however help to explain why the SMEs exist because their economic activities tend to cover diverse income groups in an economy.

The evolution of SME development can be inferred from three analytical view points. The first approach is based on Anderson's thesis on small industries in developing countries. In his work, Anderson argues that: (a) the rising agricultural output and income in the rural economy created new market opportunities for consumer and capital goods. This suggests that increase in agricultural exports in developing countries led to increased income of the rural farmer. The increased rural incomes therefore led to increased investment in inputs for agricultural production. (b) Poor infrastructure and high transportation cost in rural areas induced fragmented pattern of production in small scale units.

This implies that other set of enterprises such as trading and service sector subsequently emerged in the process. (c) Subsequent improvement in rural infrastructure and rural income growth broadened the market that induced more entry of large-scale production units (Anderson, 1982, p. 921). In this case, demand began to expand from product value to product quality.

The second explanation is centred on the work of Staley and Morse (1965, p. 2), which suggests that small enterprises emerge as a result of differentiated products that serve different income group, market segments found in modern and traditional industries. This implies that small enterprises emerge in order to exploit opportunities open in low scale economies by serving a small market segment. The third explanation relates to effect of the rapid growth of the labour force in LDCs and limited absorptive capacity of few large enterprises in the region. These groups of unemployed labour force have no alternatives rather are forced to generate their own forms of employment in order to earn income. They resort to small-scale productive activities with low-level technology, few capital requirements with little division of labour and differentiated products. This phenomenon therefore gave rise to increasing small enterprises in informal sector (Tokman, 1989, p. 1069).

In the sub-Saharan African countries, households are forced to engage in small business activities in order to sustain a living due to lack of employment opportunities. As a survival strategy, households are engaged in informal business activities where there are no better alternative opportunities to raise family income (Hart, 1970; Daniels and Mead, 1998, p. 44). In this context, Schneider-Barthold (2001, p. 331) argues that informal economic activities emerge as people search ways of surviving in difficult economic times. Empirical evidence has shown that when the economy is growing, new start-up tend to emerge; the small enterprises thrive, perform better and expand by employing additional workers (Mead and Liedholm, 1998, pp. 68-69). This suggests that improved business environment will facilitate increase in opportunities for small enterprises to expand their outputs and employment more workers. Entrepreneurs would only hire more paid staffs in a perfectly competitive market if they earned sufficiently at the point where their marginal revenue is higher than their marginal cost. This can occur only if there is signifycant growth in the economy and such employment expansion is one of the signals of enterprise's growth and represents successful economic development (Mead, 1994, p. 1882).

In developed economies, the support for SMEs is based on their unique contributions to the economy. The first assumption is the decentralising effects of certain new technologies such as numerically controlled (NC) machine tools have contributed to the reduction in the minimum efficiency scale (MES) or the level of output required exhausting scale economies (Acs and Audretsch, 1990,

p. 3). The second assumption is that increased globalisation has rendered markets more volatile in the sense that competition has become intensive due to emergence of greater number of new foreign rivals in global arena. In this respect, organisational and productive flexibility which are the competitive advantage for smaller firms than larger ones is increasingly a valuable asset in global competition (Acs and Audretsch, 1990, p. 3). The third assumption is based on the fact that composition of labour force may be a catalyst for small enterprises survival. For example, the baby boom effect entails that women have greater tendency to work in smaller firms because the flexibility in small firms is friendly to working mothers. This is not withstanding, women are increasingly emerging as entrepreneurs by engaging in self-employment and establishing their own small firms business (Brock and Evans, 1986)[63]. In this regards, many development agencies have designed series of support programmes in order to encourage women entrepreneurship. Moreover, recent deregulation movement has also contributed immensely to the viability of small enterprises. For example, the relaxation of the entry regulations in telecommunications industry has increased the opportunities for small businesses in the sector. Most importantly, the process through which entrepreneurs develop new products and processes explains how small firms in developed countries serve as sources for innovative activities, development of entrepreneurial talent and seedbed for future industrial growth (Acs and Audretsch, 1990, pp. 3-7)[64].

3.3 Literature review on SMEs in Developing Countries

In the 1970s, research on employment problems in developing countries revealed how structural imbalances led to inequalities in income and opportunities in the region. One significant problem identified in the period was the alarming rate of migration of rural labour force to urban cities. The end effect therefore was the emergence of an increasing phenomenon of employment in informal sector economy (ILO, 1972, p. 2).

Hart (1970) investigated the contribution of indigenous entrepreneurs to Ghana's development especially in job creation. The study shows that individuals engage in more than one income earning activities in order to support household income or sustain their livelihood. The author argues that a prospective entrepreneur usually raise investment capital through personal savings and support from relatives because the capital market is poorly developed. Most business activities are concentrated in service sector especially in the provision of transportation services, distribution of food items, housing or some were acting as subcontractors for government agencies. The study findings

63 Quoted in Acs and Audretsch, 1990, p. 3

64 This is based on " Schumpeter's entrepreneur" as creative destruction

indicate that high rate of illiteracy among the entrepreneurs affects entrepreneurial performance negatively. Major entrepreneurial ethics such as keeping of business records, understanding and enforcing contract agreement are grievously lacking in the system. The study recommended among others intensive investment in education in order to improve entrepreneurial skills and entrepreneurship performance.

ILO, 1972 provided comprehensive report on poverty level of small entrepreneurs in developing countries. In the report, three remarkable problems associated with the nature of employment in the region were analysed. One is poor job satisfaction in the sense that job seekers are unable to obtain the type of work or income they desired due to low level of education. The second is that the income small entrepreneurs obtain in return from their economic activities is relatively is very low. The third is concern with underutilisation and low labour productivity due to poor skill development in the region. The report laid more emphasis on the poverty level of small entrepreneurs. The major lessons from the finding suggest that improving the capability of the labour force is the best strategy to improve entrepreneurship development, labour productivity and economic performance in general.

Chenery et al (1974) work on redistribution of income stressed the need to promote small producers in order to increase employment and improve the earnings of the self-employed poor. They also argued that deliberate efforts in the form of backward and forward linkages are needed in order to strengthen the small producers in cities. This according to the authors could lead to increased income of the urban poor producers and as well improve the income opportunities for the self-employed. This argument is based the findings that poverty in underdeveloped countries is such that half of the poor are self-employed and are excluded from wage economy. Their income depends on their capacity to increase production under a favourable economic environment. The study subsequently highlighted the biased treatment the small producers face hence recommended that, capacity building in the form of training the entrepreneurs on technical and managerial matters should be the central policy strategy. The authors further recommended that macroeconomic reform especially in the areas of interest rate structure, credit allocation mechanisms, and investment on skilled enhancement should be pursued (Chenery et al, 1974, p. 145).

In the 1980s, literature shifted to problems related to growth of small producers in rural and urban economy. Schmitz's (1982) study was influenced by ILO (1972) and World Bank (1974) findings in the sense that reducing the growth constraints of small producers could have positive impact in reducing unemployment and income imbalances in the region[65]. He arguably suggests that improving the income of small producers can occur only when policy consi-

---

65 Chenery et al, 1974, for World Bank Report 1974.

derations are shifted towards reducing the growth constraints. The poor performance of the small enterprises in the developing countries was due to poor education background of the enterprises heads and workers. This is reflected on low technology base of the enterprises, poor managerial ability and high number of unskilled workers with deficiency in technical knowledge. The analysis also revealed that lack of access to market; raw materials, credit and government discrimination were among the major hurdles facing the small enterprises. Government discrimination here refers to the favours the large state owned industries enjoy with regards to access to foreign exchange, subsidized interest rates, access to credit and foreign technicians against the small producers. The study also linked the external constraints surrounding the small producers to exploitation in terms of pricing in the subcontracting arrangement with large firms.

In the same vain, Hansohm (1992) used Nyala region in Sudan as case study to investigate among other hypotheses the specific advantages of small industries. The author further investigated the claim that large firms tend to exploit small industries, and provided empirical evidence on factors constraining growth of the small industries in Africa. Hansohm findings linked internal constraints in small enterprises in the region to managerial deficiencies. Lack of access to raw materials, machinery and credit markets were identified as the major external constraints. Hansohm's findings further suggest that the hypothesis lacked statistical evidence because small industries in the region predominantly produce consumer goods. The large industries in Sudan are highly import dependant and highly subsidised hence linkages with small firms were very limited.

Anderson (1982) reviewed the role of small industries in the development processes as well as development assistance programmes designed for small industries in developing countries. The study was structured in the form of a comparative analysis reflecting the structure of employment and transformation of small manufacturing industries in selected countries in developed and developing countries. The findings revealed that in the late 1960s, most entrepreneurship activities in developing countries were households' establishments. By the1970s, most of the small enterprises in Latin America and South East Asia, Philippines, India, and Colombia have transformed from household manufacturing into small workshops and factories. On the contrary, small industries in African countries are still predominantly in household and artisan activities level (Anderson, 1982, p. 918). The poor rate of transformation among the enterprises in sub-Saharan Africa is due to weak entrepreneurial response to efficiency caused by the internal and external constraints within and around small industries in the region (Anderson, 1982, pp. 926-7).

In late 1980s and 1990s, several literature on small scale enterprises in developing countries focused extensively on informal producers and their role in the economy. Tokman (1989) analysed the genesis of informal sector and its characteristic in the economy of Latin America. The emergence of informal sector according to Tokman was partly as a result of weak technology policy initiated by the governments which failed to reflect the needs of the countries in the region. The absorptive capacity of the imported foreign technology in industries could not provide solutions to accelerated growth of labour force in the region. Furthermore, the rising inequalities in distribution of assets and factors of production in the region forced potential job seekers to generate their own forms of income earnings in informal economic activities.

In analysing the impact of informal sector in Latin America, De Soto (1989) used the phrase "the other path" to shade light on the increasing importance of the informal sector in the economies of the third world countries. De Soto's study analysed the impact of rural-urban migration in the early 1940s. It revealed how discriminatory government policies in the provision of basic amenities affected the living conditions of the poor. The first part of the study covered extensively the activities of the entrepreneurs in various sectors such as provision of shelter, trade and transportation. In the second part, he focused on the costs of remaining in informal sector and cost of moving to formal sector. The concluding part of the study highlighted the policy measures aimed at promoting institutional support and human capital development.

Levy (1991) used two sub-sectors namely leather and furniture in Sri Lanka and Tanzania respectively to examine how indigenous small and medium enterprises perceive their business environment. The impact of various constraints such as financial, regulatory, technical, marketing on their business activities was examined. In this study, entrepreneurs were asked to rank each constraint on a scale of 1-5 in order to ascertain the degree of the constraints. The outcome suggests that lack of access to finance is the major constraint small and medium scale enterprises face in both countries. Regulatory burdens (fiscal and bureaucratic) affect small enterprises business activities disproportionately. High protective trade policies in developing countries tend to limit the capacity of small enterprises to have access to imported raw materials and modern equipment. The author argues that trade policy reform and privatisation of state owned enterprises are imperative in order to support the growth of indigenous enterprises.

Mead (1994) evaluated the employment expansion in small enterprises in five sub-Saharan African countries namely Botswana, Kenya, Malawi, Swaziland and Zimbabwe. The aim of the study was to identify the patterns of growth among small enterprises and design appropriate intervention measures for poverty reduction through promotion of small enterprises. The empirical results of the study suggest that only about 1 per cent of small enterprises countries increased their labour force overtime to 10 or more workers. Most of the employment creation in the sector came through start-up. In other words, small enterprises in these countries have not been able to grow in size or transform to medium enterprises overtime.

In the late 1990s, studies on small enterprises shifted emphasis on the relationship between small enterprises and poverty alleviation. Kings (1998) examined the role and impact of SMEs on economic growth and poverty alleviation. The analysis was based on the multiple effects which donor's support programme can generate by promoting entrepreneurship in developing countries. King argues that policy intervention that aimed at increasing the productivity of small enterprises is also aimed at reducing unemployment. Such policy measure can have positive impact on poverty reduction by increasing the income earnings of the entrepreneurs and employees as output and sales increases (Kings 1998, p. 3).

Daniel and Mead (1998) used a sample of small enterprises in Kenya as case study to investigate the level of income generation in small enterprises. The study seeks to examine factors leading to income differentials in micro and small enterprises (MSEs). The result of regression analysis revealed that higher profitability was recorded among small enterprises that employ paid workers and entrepreneurs with higher level of educational qualifications. The study revealed that there are no significant differences in profit generation between rural and urban small enterprises. However, two-third of all the MSEs in the sample generates net profits less than the official minimum wage per month. The implication is that MSEs in Africa can make a significant impact in poverty reduction but in most cases, the income generated is not sufficient to move the entrepreneurs and workers out of poverty threshold. On the aggregate contribution of MSEs to the national income, the study shows that MSEs in Kenya contribute 12 per cent to 14 per cent of the national income.

Romign (1999) reviewed various technological assistance programmes implemented in different developing countries[66]. The study analysed why it is important to apply dynamic approach in designing technology support programmes for small enterprises in developing countries. The failure of early technology support programmes in developing countries was as a result of non commercialisation of the so-called appropriate technologies. Romign argues that the current globalisation pressure which the small enterprises in developing countries face require dynamic support approach. The competitiveness of the SEs in the region will depend on the ability of the small firms to acquire internal capability needed to make improvement in product quality and in production

66 The study excluded African small enterprises on the grounds of relatively high dominance of microenterprises.

processes in an ongoing basis. In this case, technology learning could be considered as the most effective method of supporting the small enterprise in the region. The implication here is that technological learning can be effective when there is effective linkage between large and small enterprises.

Beck, et al (2005) investigated the impact of business environment on SMEs and used a sample of 45 countries to explore the relationship between firm relative size, economic growth and poverty alleviation. The former concerns the degree at which laws, regulations, and levies impede firms' entry to and exist from market. The later focused on the relationship between SMEs development and economic growth, and the impact of SME growth and poverty alleviation. The empirical results revealed a strong positive association between SME development and economic growth. However, the contribution of SMEs to economic growth in Sub-Saharan Africa economies appeared to be very weak. On the assertion that SMEs exert special impact on the income of the poor was found to be weak. In other words, all enterprises (small, medium and large) play important role in poverty alleviation.

Currently, literature on SMEs in developing countries is focusing on global value chains. The rational is centred on how countries in the region can effectively be integrated in global economy. The analytical approaches focus on global networks that foster linkages, product and process upgrading. Nadvi (1995, p. 5) argues that inter-firm cooperation will not only induce growth but also will appropriately insert the SMEs in developing countries in the global value chains. On the other hand, integration of SMEs in the global value will depend on capability of the firms in the region to upgrade and generate continuous improvement in product and production processes (Kaplinsky and Readmann, 2001, p. 67; Humphrey and Schmitz, 2002, p. 5).

3.4 The political economic weaknesses in the promotion of SMEs in Africa

3.4.1 Market failure and small enterprises development problems

In the past, most governments in sub-Saharan Africa pursued protective industrialisation strategies by using high tariff and different non-tariff measures on imports. The measures generated turbulence in the market functions due to price distortions and reduced competition which supposes to provide information to economic actors (Söderbom and Teal, 2003, p. 29). The argument is that the smaller the degree of competition, the more limited information will be available, and less chances to develop new ideas hence market becomes less effective. The business environment in the region is characterised by information asymmetries. Consequently, access to simple credit or overdraft facilities requires cumbersome processes with high administrative costs. There are difficulties in scoring the probability of customers' default in the credit market. Hence, banks sustain high costs in verifying credibility or trustworthiness of potential small entrepreneurs. Therefore, credit facilities to finance working capital or loan to finance capital investment are often limited. Small entrepreneurs have to rely on informal financing through contributions from family members, friends or relatives (Fafchamps, 1994, p. 9; Uzor, 2003, p. 318). Furthermore, moral hazards have negative influence on labour productivity in the region in the sense that optimal efficiency of labour is rarely considered in labour contracts. Recruitments are often based on patronages that undermine firm efficiency and competitiveness (Fafchamps, 1994, p. 7).

Market failure in sub-Saharan Africa extends to pool of resources from stock market for project financing. The general weakness in Africa's stock market means that those small investors who wish to invest part of their savings in high return/high risk investments cannot invest (Fafchamps, 1994, p. 8). Existence of developed stock market could have minimised the problem of funding projects in the region. This argument leads to further investigation of a possible role of stock market in poverty reduction in Africa. Theoretically, if a small enterprise successfully raises fund from the stock market, it could mean that the credibility of the small enterprise as a corporate entity is positively valued by the public. Raising substantial fund in the stock market may result to increase in employment as production increases due to investment on better equipment or introduction of better quality raw material. Stock market is therefore very important for SMEs because it can serve not only as means of pooling financial resources but also as indicator for public assessment of SME performance. SMEs can also increase their competitive position by sourcing funds from stock market thereby keeping their profits as reserve. Development of stock market will enhance the rate of small enterprises transformation, entrepreneurship learning and competition in sub-Saharan Africa. Small enterprises in informal sector will appreciate the need to formalise in order to be qualified for joint venture activities. The relevance of joint venture and efficient entrepreneurial management will become significant feature in small enterprises. Information on market relevance will increase hence competition will intensify. This will not only induce market orientated capacity building in the system but also foster functional efficiency in other market institutions such as banks and insurance firms.

The failure of market in highly centralised and regularised economy has led to market friendly economic reform in most African countries. However, one assumption is clear, even if markets allocate resources efficiently; they are not the effective instruments for income distribution. Market friendly economic reforms require institutional support, investment in human capital, and complementary reform directed towards poverty reduction. In this context, a policy that encourages increased productivity in the form of investing in human capital development, reducing unguided registration barriers and multiple taxes imposed on small enterprises will help to increase the income of the majority of small producers. For example, harmonisation of taxation system will reduce disproportionate burden on small scale producers. Tax discrimination tends to reduce competitiveness of small scale producers and high cost of business registration often discourages entrepreneurial motivation. One could argue that there are remarkable differences between intervention and protection. For example, policies to make financial markets work better by making credit available for small enterprises and provision of better education, basic technology and infrastructure are necessary for general economic development. Protection in terms of very high tariffs raises prices, reduces domestic demand for protected good and at the same time provides no incentive for competition and exports.

3.4.2 Institutional failure and small enterprises development problems in Africa

The theories of institutions are embedded in three different traditions in economics. One is the old institutionalists' idea presented by Thorsten Veblen, John R, Commons among others. Their arguments are based on the assumption that institutions are less instrumental and more as settled habits of thought common to the generality of man (Veblen, 1919, p. 239). The second concept relates to the neoclassical viewpoint which argues that exchange arises spontaneously from the atomistic interaction of self-seeking individuals. Goods that traded in every market are assumed to be homogenous so that prices provide the only information needed to make the decisions on production and purchases. The third is the new institutionalists' concept represented by the work of Douglass North, Oliver Williamson and Ronald Coase that considered institutions as means of reducing transaction and information costs so that markets can operate with the kind of fluidity and efficiency projected in the neoclassical model.

Veblen's work played an important role in academic debate on the definition and theory of institution. In his early work, he considered the nature of economic organisation as an evolutionary economic life process that lacks certainty, direction or stability. This alienated him from the mainstream economics thinking of his time that described the economy as tending towards an ideal stationary state, subject to unceasingly balancing equilibrium that would ensure a beneficent condition of static equilibrium (Street, 1987, p. 1864). Veblen's early work was therefore characterised by scornful derision of the prevailing economic doctrine which earned him a statue no more than a social critic. In the course of time, some important elements concerning an alternative theory of social change emerged from his work. This spawned enquiries in different ideological viewpoints on what constitutes the term institution. Schotter (1981) view institutions as regularities agreed by members of a society which specify behaviours in specific recurrent situations. Williamson (1985, p. 15) consider firms, markets and relational contracting as economic institutions that are evolutional products of several organisational innovations. Institutions are social assets or liabilities because they govern human or corporate or political behaviour. In a competitive environment, institutions always provide solutions to problems related to transaction costs for organisations (Williamson 1985, p. 17). North (1991, p. 97) defines institutions as the humanly devised constraints that structure political economics and social interaction. In the course of time, human beings devised institutions to create order and reduce uncertainty in exchange. Hence, institutions consist of both informal and formal rules[67]. Institutions play an important role in economic growth by specifying and enforcing the property rights that may increase productivity. The productive gains from modern technology can be realised by effectively specifying and enforcing the property rights and reducing transactions (North, 1989, p. 1320-3)[68].

Markets need the support of other institutions to ensure confidence. For example, maintaining the rule of law and enforcement of contracts are measures aimed at reducing uncertainty, and the renegade of promises or defaults in the market (World Bank, 2003, pp. 38-9). Market institutions in the sub-Saharan Africa appear not only to be weak, but appear to be absent in rural areas. A weak market institution is detrimental to the poor since it limits access to production factors hence reduces rural employment and income generation. Developed legal and financial institutions support the market for economic growth and support poverty reduction in a way that under a zero uncertainty, economic actors can make effective productive decision. Chong and Calderón (2000) study revealed that weak institutional quality is positively related to income inequality in poor countries. If a country's institutional capability is high, its, economic performance will equally be high. Knack and Keefer (1995) showed that the measure of institutional quality is positively linked with economic performance.

67 Formal institutions are rule written into the law by government, rules codified and adopted by private institutions. While informal rules reflect unwritten codes of social conducts e.g. land inheritance norms and moneylenders using social networks to determine credit worthiness by reputation or a dense social network of informal constraints that facilitates local exchange in small-scale village trade. Generally, in any civil society, all public and private organisations are operating under public institution (North, 1991, p. 97).

68 This is a major problem in sub-Saharan Africa because high transaction and information costs in the regional market are associated with poor institutional development.

3.4.3 Good governance and small enterprises development

The nature of governance determines the standard of the economy and well being of the citizens. If governance structures and the system are poor, a successful development path cannot be achieved. Good governance is reflected on the effective management of the country's resources, equitable distribution of the resources, response to the needs of the citizens, adherence to public code of conduct by being transparent and accountable for all daily transactions of the business to the citizens. Good governance also signifies the ability of the government to recognise the importance of a social pact with its citizens, thereby protecting vulnerable, recognising women rights as well as the poor. Good governance implies government commitment to the rule of law provided by the constitution and respecting the freedom of judiciary (Gradstein, 2004, p. 516)[69]. Poor governance is related to selective distribution of resources in a manner of political patronage, poor management of the scarce resources, ineffective public institutions, corruption in public institutions, and neglect of the rule of law. In this respect, corruption has been identified as a major factor that affects private sector investment in sub-Sahara African countries in general and Nigeria in particular: Corruption is defined as the misuse of entrusted power for private gain. In manufacturing and service investment activities, investors tend to choose a country with low corruption index in order to avoid risks (Velde, 2001, p. 5). For example, bribery is regarded as informal taxation on investment which leads to poor performance of an enterprise[70]. This can be in the form of multiple taxes, high tax rates and harassments by local authorities as well as unguided procedures in business registration which hurt entrepreneurship (Tokman, 1989, p. 1073).

The relationship between good governance and Small Enterprises Development (SED) can be observed in four dimensions. First is the impact of macroeconomic stability on activities of small enterprises. Macroeconomic stability as a pure public good has positive impact on pattern of employment growth. In the period of general economic decline, the share of employment and sales in the existing SMEs often contracts and subsequently expands during the economic boom period (Liedholm and Mead, 1998, p. 69). Good governance in this context reflects the ability of the government to manage its macroeconomic variables. This is because creating a more dynamic economy can be an effective vehicle for fostering the growth of productive employment in small

69 See appendix 3.1 on leadership and development

70 In analysing the relationship between corruption and private investment, Everhart and Sumlinski (2001) described corruption such as bribery or over valuation of prices as a form of taxation on investment called "Corruption tax". It increases the cost investment as well as reduces motivation in business ventures.

enterprises[71]. Furthermore, promoting private sector development in terms of implementing policies that can strengthen the market functions is what good governance demands. The major point scored by Structural Adjustment Programme (SAP) in Africa was the introduction of basic discipline in macroeconomic management.

The second is that economic growth is a mechanism which can influence standard of living and eradicating poverty. This can be possible when opportunities and incentives are created for firms to invest productively, create jobs and expand (World Bank, 2005, p. 19)[72]. The link between good governance and SED is the policies aimed at promoting entrepreneurial competence and skills acquisition. Evidence shows that small enterprises with experienced, educated and trained personel often grows rapidly than those with less trained and educated personel (McPherson, 1996, p. 273-4). The capabilities of small entrepreneurs increase if policies are directed towards promoting investment in technical education and high educational attainment nation wide. Such measures will reduce deficiencies in human capital especially in technical skilled workforce (McPherson, 1996, p. 274).

The third dimension is that good governance has become a central issue in International Development Agencies' objectives. Government policies can create good environment for broad based growth and poverty reduction[73]. To avoid financing bad policies that can sustain elements of bad governance such as corrupt and incompetent government, it is imperative to attach specific conditions to Development Assistance (Aid). Resources should be directed to good policy measures that can produce positive return on development assistance as well as increasing the benefits of such policy (Devarajan, et al, 2001, p. 6)[74]. For example, reform processes aimed at promoting economic empowerment, the rule of law, institutional pluralism, and respect for human right at meso and micro level of governance should be considered as effective strategies to integrate the poor producers in the economic and in the political processes.

---

71 Liedholm and Mead, (1998) argue that the relationship between enterprises performance and the state of the economy are not easy to identify in enterprise level surveys, since respondents are not likely to recognize the state of the macro econmy as a key determinant of their own success.

72 Growth is not just associated with higher national and household income, but with better indicators of human development such as infant mortality, broader education, and longer life expectancy.

73 See Wohlmuth, 1999, pp. 26-43.

74 This argument reflects the relevance of political and economic reforms in terms of governance system, macroeconomic policies, structural policies, public and corporate management, and social inclusion.

The fourth dimension of good governance relates to investment conditions for SED. Investment climate is defined as the set of location specific factors that shape the opportunities and incentives for entrepreneurs to invest productively, create jobs, and expand wealth)[75]. Good investment conditions foster productive private investment, which is the engine of growth and poverty reduction. A good investment climate is not just centred on profit of a firm; but also for the interest of the society at large by contributing to poverty reduction (Pfeffermann, 2001, p. 44; World Bank, 2005, p. 24.

3.4.4 Mobilisation of domestic capital for the promotion of SMEs

Low level of investment in sub-Saharan Africa is a major policy concern in the region. The obvious reason is that domestic investment is the major source of GDP growth which has positive effect on standards of living of the people on the long run. The basic fact is that firms' investment demand and household savings supply determine the investment level of an economy. Since investment is highly volatile, its demand therefore may have great impact in short run economic fluctuation (Romer, 2006, p. 386). This suggests that rapid growth of domestic investment arises from the growth or mobilisation of domestic income. In this respect, economic development is measured not only by rising national income but also by increased capacity for self-sustained growth. Hence development is a process that involves the ability to add value (Helmboldt, et al, 1988, p. 343). Private sector therefore possesses the capacity to add value and private investment is the key factor for economic growth and development in Africa (Söderbom and Teal, 2002, p. 27).

In sub-Saharan Africa, the production units in private sector are predominantly found in the smallholder agriculture sector, small enterprises in informal sector that absorb the major share of employment in manufacturing, and in few large enterprises that provide substantial portion of GDP growth. The major policy failure in the region was limited opportunities for the growth of domestic private sector. Access to investment capital for modern firms in private sector in the region only came from the commercial bank lending. The domestic capital markets in the region are still very weak. The nature of uncertainty in the existing ones is such that the potential domestic investors have no guarantee to recover his or her equity stake at any desired time. Consequently, development of venture capital activities in the region has been forestalled (Helmboldt, et al, 1988, pp. 344-6). With the exception of South Africa, the private sectors have very limited access to financial resources in most countries in the sub-region.

75 Reducing the barriers to competition expands opportunities, spurs innovation, and ensures that the benefits of productivity improvements are shared with workers and consumers.

Table 3.1 shows the domestic credit flow to private sector expressed as a percentage of GDP in four selected countries in sub-Saharan Africa[76]. As indicated in Table 3.1, the domestic credit to private sector in South Africa increased from 81.0 per cent in 1990 to 160.8 per cent in 2006.

Table 3.1: Domestic credit to private sector in four selected countries in sub-Saharan Africa as % of GDP between 1990 and 2006

	Nigeria	Ghana	Mauritius	South Africa
1990	9.4	4.9	35.6	81.0
1995	7.8	5.2	48.7	130.6
1996	10.6	6.6	44.7	137.0
1997	8.2	8.2	50.5	135.0
1998	9.1	9.4	59.2	118.9
1999	13.8	12.0	58.5	136.3
2000	13.9	14.1	61.4	141.9
2001	17.8	14.1	62.7	148.5
2002	17.8	12.0	61.3	131.7
2003	15.7	11.8	59.3	142.1
2004	15.6	13.1	59.5	141.3
2005	14.9	15.5	76.7	143.5
2006	15.0	18.0	78.0	160.8

Source: The World Bank, World Development Indicators 1997, pp. 232-234; 1998, pp. 154-156; 1999, pp. 270-272; 2000, pp. 260-262; 2001, pp. 270-272; 2002, pp. 280-282; 2003, pp. 258-260; 2004, pp. 255-256; 2005, pp. 270-272; 2006, pp. 266-268; 2007, pp. 264-266; 2008, pp. 268-170

In Mauritius, the domestic credit to private sector increased from 35.6 per cent in 1990 to 78.0 per cent in 2006 relative to Nigeria and Ghana, thus indicating a percentage point increase of 42.4. The scenario is quite different, in respect to Nigeria and Ghana. The domestic credit to private sector in both countries is not only very low but also increases sluggishly with a percentage point increase of 5.6 and 13.1 respectively. The implication is that limited access to credit for firms could result to low aggregate investment levels which arguably will lead to aggregate shortfall in output growth.

In modern economic activities, economic growth depends on an efficient financial sector that can pool domestic savings and mobilise foreign capital for productive investments and international trade. Productive projects will be unexploited when some sets of financial institutions do not exist in the economy (Bekaert et al, 1995, p. 3). The capital market serves not only as means of ensuring liquidity and risk diversification in the economy but also as means of

76 Domestic credit to private sector reflects the degree of financial resources provided to the private sector through credit, loans and purchases of non-equity securities, and trade credits and other accounts receivable that established a claim for repayment (World Bank, 2002, p. 283).

acquiring information about firms and reducing transaction costs. Table 3.2 shows the position of capital market in four selected countries in sub-Saharan Africa. The Table shows that market capitalisation or capital market value in Nigeria grew from US$1,372 in 1990 to US$86,347 in 2007. The relative increase in overall size in stock market between 2005 and 2007 can be linked to the capitalisation of Nigerian commercial banks.

Market capitalisation in nominal value is relatively low in Ghana and Mauritius indicating that the domestic capital is poorly mobilised. High market capitalisation in South Africa suggests that the market is relatively large, less risky and diversified compare to Ghana, Mauritius and Nigeria. The market capitalisation expressed as a percentage of GDP shows the rate at which securities are traded in the capital market. It also reflects the size of the market and the liquidity position in the capital market.

Table 3.2: Capital market position in four selected countries in sub-Saharan African

	1990	1995	2000	2005	2006	2007
Nigeria						
Market capitalisation (mil. US$)	1,372	2,033	4,237	19,356	32,819	86,347
Market capitalisation as % of GDP	4.2	7.5	10.3	19.6	28.5	n.a
Turnover Ratio*	0.9	0.6	7.3	11.5	13.8	28.7
Size of listed domestic stocks	131	181	195	214	202	212
Ghana						
Market capitalisation (mil. US$)	76	1,680	502	1,661	1,729	2,380
Market capitalisation as % of GDP	1.1	26.6	9.7	12.8	25.0	n.a
Turnover Ratio	0.0	1.2	1.5	3.2	3.4	5.1
Size of listed domestic stocks	13	19	22	30	32	32
Mauritius						
Market capitalisation (mil. US$)	268	1,381	1,331	2, 617	3,598	5,666
Market capitalisation as % of GDP	10.1	35.2	38,7	41.6	56.7	n.a
Turnover Ratio	4.5	4.8	5.0	6.1	6.0	8.7
Size of listed domestic stocks	13	28	40	42	41	41
South Africa						
Market capitalisation (mil. US$)	137,540	280,426	204,952	565,408	715,025	833,548
Market capitalisation as % of GDP	128.9	206.2	254.2	236.0	280.2	n.a
Turnover Ratio	6.1	6.7	33.9	41.6	49.5	52.8
Size of listed domestic stocks	732	640	616	388	401	422

Key: n.a = not available at present year; * turnover ratio is the value of share traded as % of capitalisation

Source: World Bank, World Development Indicators, 1997, pp. 241-243; 2002, pp. 288-290; 2006, pp. 278-290; 2007, pp. 276-278; 2008, pp. 280-282

As shown in Table 3.2, in 2006, market capitalisation as a percentage of GDP recorded 280.2 per cent in South Africa, 56.7 per cent in Mauritius, 28.5 per cent in Nigeria and 25.0 per cent Ghana. This shows that securities can easily be bought and sold in South African capital market than in Mauritius, Nigeria or Ghana stock market. It also suggests that there is existence of effective institutions protecting investors in South Africa.

The turnover ratio which is the value of traded shares expressed as a percentage of GDP in Nigeria improved from 7.3 in 2000 to 28.7 in 2006 but relatively low compare to South Africa. The low turnover ratio in Ghana and Mauritius can be explained by high transaction costs and low liquidity existing in the market. Low number of local domestic companies listed in Ghana and Mauritius capital market suggests that the ability to mobilise capital and diversify risk in both countries will continue to be low. In general, SMEs in sub-Saharan Africa will benefit immensely if capital market is effectively promoted in the region.

At macro level, mobilisation of domestic investment capital depends on government policy. Government interest rate policy can reduce or increase domestic capital formation. It can reduce domestic capital formation by restricting domestic capital mobilisation efforts for investments. If government fixes the interest rate at the rate below the inflation level, the real value of bank deposits would decline and household incentives to save will be low. Three implications can emerge. First, such artificially low interest rate would create the demand for loans that cannot be met due to high inflation. Second, it could lead to crowding of small firms such that only the large borrowers can easily have access to loans. Third, the end effect is that accumulation of savings by banks will be limited. A higher level of accumulated savings would have forced banks to spread risks and increase lending by making profitable loans. Hence, the smaller businesses would have more access to loans (Helmboldt, et al, 1988, p. 345).

Savings and investments naturally play an important role in the development process and economic growth by determining the national capacity to invest and to produce which in turn has affect on economic growth. Low saving rates is one of the most serious constraints to sustainable economic growth. Romer (1986) and Lucas (1988) argue that higher savings and the related increase in capital accumulation can result to a permanent increase in growth rates. De Long and Summers (1992) provided empirical evidence that capital accumulation and savings are central for understanding growth differentials across countries. Furthermore the relationship between savings and investments can have significant implications on the economy. Low and declining saving rates can contribute to unsustainable current account deficits which in turn can lead to economic crisis.

Table 3.3 shows the relationship between gross domestic savings and gross domestic investment expressed as a proportion of GDP. The Table shows that the gap between domestic savings and gross domestic investment can be narrowed by foreign capital inflow such that disturbances in the current account balance can be reduced. The negative sign in the differences between Gross Domestic Savings (GDS) and Gross Domestic Investment (GDI) indicates that the proportion of investment satisfied by foreign capital. The positive sign suggests that there is surplus in domestic savings which supports country's outward FDI or has been reinvested in the economy. As shown in the Table, the ratio of gross domestic saving to GDP declined from 29 per cent in 1990 to 12 per cent in 1998. The ratio of gross domestic savings to GDP increased from 12 per cent in 1998 to 34 per cent in 2000 but declined to 17 per cent 2002. It increased also from 17 per cent 2002 to 34 per cent 2006. The GDI increased from 15 per cent in 1990 to 28 per cent in 2001 and fall to 22 per cent in 2006. The low savings rate in periods 1998-1999, and 2001-2001 suggest that Nigeria's gross domestic investment in the periods were strongly supported by foreign capital which is was highest in 1998[77].

Table 3.3 also revealed that Nigeria is a capital exporting country. This could mean that the country is actively engaged in financing development projects and/ or have reduced dependency on foreign aid. The problem SMEs face in Nigeria is not due to capital shortage in the country rather as a result of weak financial system that failed to channel financial resources effectively to private sectors. Furthermore, the recent privatisation efforts in the sub-Saharan Africa represent a shift in policy towards market economy aimed at mobilising domestic and foreign capital. The privatisation process a reflection of transfer of ownership from public to private.

Table 3.3: Nigeria's gross domestic savings (GDS) and gross domestic investment (GDI) as a % of GDP, 1990-2006

	1990	1997	1998	1999	2000	2001	2002	2003	2004	2005	2006
GDS	29	22	12	18	34	27	17	32	27	30	34
GDI	15	15	20	24	23	28	23	23	22	19	22
GDS-GDI	14	7	-8	-6	11	-1	-6	9	5	11	12

Source: The World Bank World Development Indicator 1999, p. 221; 2000, p. 215; 2001, p. 227; 2002, p. 237; 2003, p. 219; 2004, p. 215; 2005, p. 231; 2006, p. 223; 2007, p. 219; 2008, p. 227

The ownership was concentrated on friends and relatives of the politicians. Evidence from Sudan and Eriteria indicates that transparency issues and the method of privatisation have undermined the importance of the programme.

77 This is because increased FDI inflow usually supplements domestic savings in order to raise domestic investment rates, and accelerate income and employment growth as well (UNCTAD, 2006, p. 196).

This is linked partly to poor institutional and the legal framework required for the execution of the privatisation programme and weak stock market in both countries (Musa, 2000, pp. 93-94). Privatisation initiatives outside the stock market and in the weak economies of sub-Saharan African countries put firms in a position vulnerable when the owners lack corporate management experience. Mobilisation of domestic capital is not enough to stimulate economic growth. Other factors such as stimulating production by reallocating resources to improve productivity of population active labour force is also important (ILO, 1972). Moreover, removing some of the existing disincentive to private sector investment is important for sustainable development in sub-Saharan Africa (World Bank, 1984). These measures are not only aimed to support the efforts of domestic private investors but also will stimulate the external capital inflow. The obvious reason is that inflow of foreign capitals always acts as the major factor which can support the acceleration of economic development and ameliorating the commercial bank debt in developing countries (Moran and Pearson, 1990, p. 28).

3.5 Foreign direct investment (FDI) and Small Enterprises Development

3.5.1 FDI in economic development discourse

The increased call for foreign direct investment in SSA is intended to bring capital, technology, management skill within the region and improve linkages in international market. These resources are significantly lacking in the region and require urgent measures for industrial learning. The dependency theory argues that resources flow from poor and underdeveloped states to wealthy states.The wealthy states are enriched at the expense of the poor states. Capitalist development depends on the supper exploitation of labour. The main objective of multinational enterprises (MNEs) is to exploit economic surplus in terms of profits, interest, royalty payments and debt repayment from the developing countries. The argument further suggests that introduction of capital intensive investment by MNEs in the developing countries has worsened employment situation in the region so that governments have lost control of their economies. Hence, it is difficult for developing economies to industrialise under capitalist dispensation (Dos Santos, 1970, pp. 234-6). This argument was refuted by the success story in East Asia industrialisation process. The industrial success of Hong Kong in particular has explicitly shown that relying and learning from advanced capitalist nations is an important development technique (Deyo, 1970, p. 15).

FDI is defined as an investment involving a long-term relationship and reflecting a lasting interest and control by a resident entity in one economy (foreign direct investor or parent enterprise) in an enterprise resident in an economy other than that of the resident entity's (UNCTAD, 2004a, p. 345). FDI is grouped into traditional and new forms of foreign investment. The traditional form of FDI are the equity capital defined as foreign direct investor's purchase of shares and enterprise in a country other than its own; (b) Reinvestment of earning of the direct investor's share which is not distributed as dividends by the affiliates or earnings not remitted to the direct investor; (c) FDI can be in the form of intra-company loans or intra-company debt transactions. This can be through short-term or long-term borrowing and lending of funds between direct investors and affiliates enterprises in another country (UNCTAD, 2004a, p. 345). The new forms of FDI include: joint venture, licensing agreements, franchising, management contracts, turnkey contracts, product-in-hand, and production-sharing contract, risk service contracts and international sub-contracting[78]. The former implies whole or majority foreign ownership of the investment project while the latter implies partly whole or with majority local ownership in the investment project (Oman, 1984, p. 20). Multinational enterprises (MNEs) are the main actors in direct investments across boarders. They are increasingly seen as links binding states with one another and as having vast political, social, and economic influences both for the countries receiving the investments and for the state from which the investment originates. The rationale for special focus on FDI is its capability to generate externalities in form of technology transfer and learning. For domestic economy, it tends to generate crowd in effect in the sense that the local suppliers of raw materials or sub-products or spare parts can vertically be integrated in production system. The local supplier can learn quickly and take advantage of the technology

78 Technology comprises all knowledge embodied in physical assets and in the workers that are involved in organising and managing the production of goods and services in a particular environment. Technology determines the method and processes in which the natural resources and created assets are combined to produce outputs (Dunning, 1998, p. 287). Technology transfer refers to the formal method of transferring technological knowledge through the market processes to another country. The mechanism of technology transfer varies according to the agents and the type of technology (Stewart Jr, et al, 1987, p. 10). The transfer can be through FDI or contractual purchases in form of patent, licensing, contract management etc. Technology transfer through FDI is not only in terms of equipment but also tacit knowledge that can be transmitted to local workers and management through training. The workers in direct investment enterprises are trained on new skill or specific skills and the employees are trained in management methods and organisational patterns. This can be transmitted to the economy in general.

brought in by the foreign investor and improve its efficiency[79]. FDI will support subcontracting, transfer of best practices and upgrading of local SMEs if there is existing firm capacity, institutional capacity and skill labour force available. Increased foreign equity participation in local enterprises can also produce positive effect on productivity and accelerate technology diffusion[80]. Since the local small enterprises cannot finance research activities, they may benefit from the new technology brought in by the subsidiaries of MNEs by restructuring and improving the production system. The new technologies may stimulate national investment in research and development (R&D) in such new technologies (Artken and Harrison 1999, p. 606).

Table 3.4 shows that the share of SSA in global FDI inflow is significantly very low and has not been able to exceed 2 per cent. The share of SSA in FDI flow to developing countries is between 2.30 and 6.43 per cent which is significantly low in comparison with other developing regions. The value of SSA inward FDI performance index increased only from 0.89 between 2000 and 2002 to 1.28 per cent between 2001 and 2003 (UNCTAD, 2004b, p. 12)[81]. Table 3.4 also shows that FDI inflow in the region increased from 0.42 per cent in 2000 to 1.96 per cent in 2005. The increase in FDI inflow in the region in the period was a reflection of economic reform processes that lay emphasis on better investment climate, macroeconomic stability coupled with on going privatisation programme in the region (Lall and Kraemer-Mbula, 2005, p. 68). The implication is that increased FDI inflow in SSA will not only support the expansion of capital stock of the countries in the region but also will contribute to employment growth in the region.

---

79 This is a case of missing middle problem in African in dustrial structure in the sense that the domestic small enterprises are so weak to meet the standard or the requirement of the foreign investors as suppliers of inputs.

80 Technology diffusion or spillover is an informal or non-market intermediary whereby the productivity or efficiency gains are transmitted to host country's enterprises due to the presence of foreign firms (Blomström and Kokko, 1996, p. 3). In other words, it represents unintentional knowledge transfer from the foreign enterprises to the local enterprises. Such transfer occurs effectively through labour turnover because domestic employees can move from the foreign firm to a domestic firm or start running their own business. The economy will benefit generally whenever a foreign firm introduces new product or process into a domestic market. This is because the new product or process always comes with new technology, and with low information costs for adoption of the product or process engineering (Teece, 1977, p. 212).

81 Inward FDI performance Index is the measure of the host region's share in global FDI as a ratio of its share in Global GDP.

Table 3.4: FDI inflows in sub-Saharan Africa (SSA) in millions of US dollars and in percentage

	FDI Inflow			FDI in SSA as a % of Global FDI	FDI in SSA as a % Of Developing Countries
	World	DCs	SAA		
1992-97 (AAv.)	310,879	118,596	4,010	1.29	3.38
1998	690,905	194,055	6,209	0.90	3.20
1999	1,086,750	231,880	8,558	0.79	3.69
2000	1,387,953	252,459	5,810	0.42	2.30
2001	817,574	219,721	14,126	1.73	6.43
2002	678,751	152,612	8,149	1.20	5.17
2003	559,576	172,033	9,250	1.65	5.38
2004	710,755	275,032	11,294	1.59	4.11
2005	916,277	334,285	17,934	1.96	5.36

Key: A.Av. = Annual Averages; DCs= Developing Countries; SSA= sub-Saharan Africa
Source: UNCTAD, 2005b, pp. 367-8; 2006; p. 299

3.5.2 FDI and SME development

3.5.2.1 FDI and SME development through linkages

Investment made by multinational enterprises (MNEs) is more competitive than the local firms. On the other hand, the investment activities of the MNEs often create new business opportunities for specialised SMEs in the host countries. The new business opportunities include supply of raw materials and components, engaging in franchising activities, building technology partnership in the form of joint venture business activities and other related services. To meet the performance criteria required by MNEs for joint venture or subcontracting business activities, local SMEs have to upgrade their capabilities. In this case, the MNEs create the opportunities in terms of new business model for local SMEs to learn, copy and practice (UNCTAD, 1999, p. 198; Altenburg, 2003, p. 144). In recent times, corporate led initiatives in the form of Corporate Social Responsibility (CSR) or Corporate/SME partnership arrangements have become relevant in SME development programmes in developing countries (UNIDO, 2004, p. 6).

MNEs-SMEs partnership can be in the form of backward or forward linkages or technology partnership that can positively affect the performance of local SMEs. Each of the linkages or partnership arrangements can have different impact not only on the local SMEs but also on the entire economy of the host country. MNEs use SMEs as suppliers to source some of their inputs and components. Such backward linkages encourage sub-contracting of certain steps in production and dissemination of technical information, and serve as means of providing technical assistance. In some cases, sub-contracting arrangements provide the required reputation which serve as collateral for SMEs to raise credit and loans from commercial banks. In a nutshell, backward linkages are used to promote technological spillover (Altenburg, 2003, p. 144). The lucrative advantages associated with backward linkages pushed some governments in developing countries to strengthen local domestic suppliers with MNEs by imposing restriction in the form of local-content. Such restrictions are not within the market function. It often leads restructuring the entire production system thereby generating high cost. For example, brewery industry in Nigeria suffered high costs and many incurred losses or forced out of market due to government mandatory backward integration policy in the mid-1980s where maize was used to replace barley malt (Ogun, 1995, p. 271).

The MNEs forward Linkages comprise marketing outlets and the activities of industrial buyers. Local enterprises can benefit from forward linkages if MNEs concentrate in core areas in various stages of the value chains. In other words, MNEs can concentrate on what they have comparative advantage and outsource activities such as distribution and after sales services to local SMEs. The SMEs can use the brand name of MNEs and pay royalties for it. The advantage here is that local SMEs will not pay advertisement costs at the same time benefit from various training programmes provided by the MNEs (Altenburg, 2003, p. 144). The SMEs can use the training received and experience acquired in running and changing their business line. As equipment buyers, MNEs can offer after sales and advisory services on the use of the equipment purchased. This is an important aspect of technology transfer because the equipment manual always provides background information on how to use the equipment and how the workers can operate the equipment. MNEs-SMEs linkage formation depends on the ability of the local enterprises and the host country to exploit these linkages. The local SMEs must be in the position to meet the specified target of MNEs requirement. Government policies and government governance system must be favourable in order to stimulate the willingness of the MNEs to build a long-term relationship with the local SMEs. The determinants of such linkages are similar to "Altenburg's Linkage Triangle" illustrated in Figure 3.1.

Figure 3.1 describes the two inter-dependant forces that bind the MNEs and SMEs linkages in the form of MNEs corporate strategy and competitiveness of the local SMEs. The corporate strategy is a function of the company's motives and willingness to develop linkages. The former depends on the MNEs' economic objective such as resource seeking, market seeking or export oriented investment in the host country. The later is a reflection of cost of production that usually stimulates internalisation vs. outsourcing politics. The effectiveness of govern-ment policies determines the inflow of FDI and the competitiveness of the SMEs depends on their ability to meet quality standards. The MNEs-SMEs linkages in Africa can be in the form of partnership arrangements that allow corporate firms to make considerable financial investment at early stages of the partnership with the Under the partnership arrangement, Unilever first stipulated the quality standards, established the technology input necessary to achieve these quality standard requirements, and provided financial support to ensure the long-term growth of these SMEs. The selected local SMEs in turn gained not only from the transfer of technologies and improved capabilities, but also were able to diversify their businesses to other frontiers (UNIDO, 2004, p. 5). Sialkot surgical instrument cluster in Pakistan is also an example of FDI/Cluster related case study. International joint venture initiatives in the cluster which comprises several external service providers played an important role in quality upgrading required for quality assurance certification.SMEs. Such initial financial investment is deemed to reduce the SME capability gap problems and improve efficiency. The initial financial gestures during the partnership arrangement can be regarded as social benefit on the part of the corporate firms. The partnership agreement however changes as the capabilities of the SMEs improve such that subsequent financial commitments are viewed as commercial venture (UNIDO, 2004, p. 3).

Figure 3.1: Determinants of Linkage formation

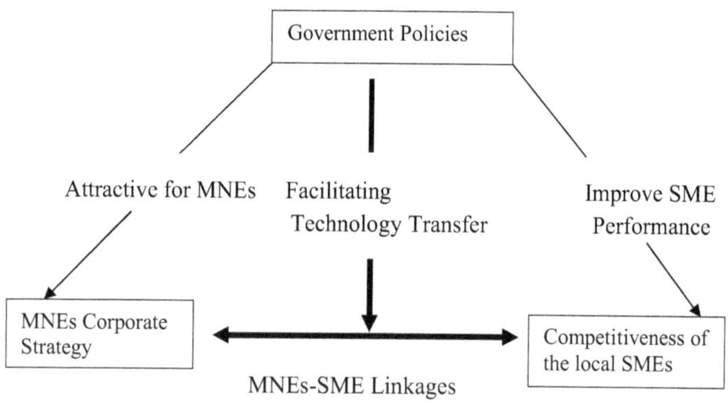

Source: Altenburg, 2003, p.167

As shown in Figure 3.2, a successful corporate partnership program can expand from general support to direct commercial link that include supply chain and distribution linkages. For example in the 1990s, Unilever selected some local SMEs in the supply of raw materials and manufacturing in Vietnam that are willing to learn and be able to implement new practices. Unilever worked closely with the SMEs and helped them to improve their capabilities. Firms in

Sialkot engaged foreign partners in technical services and know-how in quality and management training. The long term effect of the measure is the cultivation of quality–driven values at every stage in the production system (Nadvi, 1999, pp. 1613-4). Furthermore, as a result of joint venture agreement with Tuttlingen surgical instrument producers in Germany, Sialkot firms increased their economy of scope and scale by gaining access to European market. Tuttlingen producers provided technology and training that facilitated increased efficiency and increased quality standard. This facilitated sub-contracting of some parts of particular instrument to Sialkot firms (Nadvi and Halder, 2002, p. 6).

Corporate social responsibility (CSR) has also become relevant in recent times in the promotion of SME development. Corporate Social Responsibility (CSR) is a concept which explained the obligation the corporations should consider in the interests of their customers, employees, shareholders, communities and ecology. In this regards, CSR initiatives for the promotion of small scale enterprises can be through several channels such as microfinance, credit funds and capacity building programmes. In 1998, Shell Petroleum Development Corporation of Nigeria (SPDC) launched business development programme in order to promote micro, small and medium scale enterprises in Nigeria.

Figure 3.2: Forms of corporate partnerships for SME development

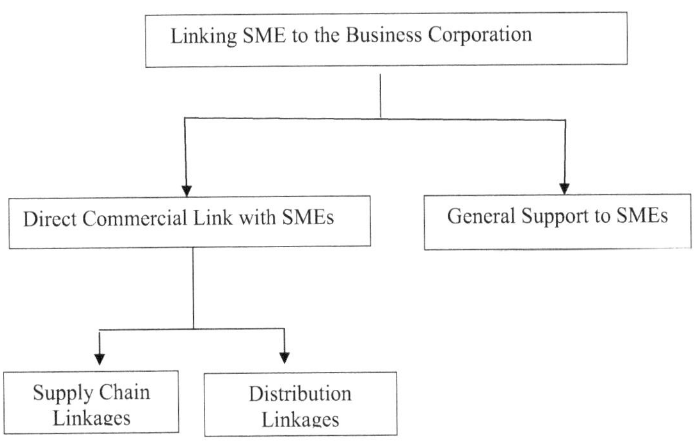

Source: UNIDO, 2004, p. 5

The business development projects comprise Micro credit; Livewire Nigeria Programme and Women Development programme. Micro credit facilities represents part of employment creation strategies aimed at grass root level. Livewire Nigeria Programme was a project designed to support youths' entrepreneurship development. The women development programme on the other hand was designed to serve as poverty reduction program and women empowerment measures (Shell Nigeria, 2006).

Deutsche Bank of Federal Republic of Germany created Microcredit Development Fund in order to support the emerging small scale entrepreneurs in developed and developing countries. The Bank provides low cost financing of 1-3 per cent rate loans to local microfinance institutions (MFIs). The Loans serve as collateral for the MFIs to obtain additional funds from the local financial institutions. This allows the MFIs to capitalise and grant micro loans to local and foreign small scale entrepreneurs (UNIDO, 2004, p. 38). Generally, government policies can shape and facilitate the intensity of these linkages for technology transfer. Hence, improving the factors that will enhance SME performance will not only strengthen their competitiveness but also their bargaining position in the formation of linkages for example in franchising and joint venture business arrangements.

3.5.2.2 FDI and SME development through franchising and joint ventures

Franchising is a special form of licensing in which one firm contract with another firm to operate a certain type of business under an established name according to specific rules. The owner of a standardised business (the franchiser) grants the right by contract to an entrepreneur (the franchisee) to establish similar business in exchange of franchise fees and obligation to adhere to strict quality standards. The franchisee acquires the right to use the franchiser's trademark and receives marketing support, detailed manual on how to operate the business, start-up assistance, staff training, equipment, raw material procurement, and regular visits by a representative of the franchiser (Henriques and Nelson, 1997, p. 23). This becomes foreign direct investment on the part of foreign investor when such relationship evolves a foreign and local firm. This definition explains explicitly several ways local SMEs can benefit from franchise business arrangements. It also shows different ways on how technology can bc transferred in the process. The training is a continuous process and the franchiser always monitors the entire outlet continuously in order to improve operations. Continues monitoring on franchise operators allows the franchiser to maintain quality standard and improvements which will add value to the franchise (Altenburg, 2003, p. 171).

A joint venture is an entity formed between two or more parties to undertake economic activity together. The parties agree to create a new entity by both contributing equity and share the revenues, expenses, and control of the enterprises. The concept of joint venture has developed in modern business but in such a diverse business activities no precise definition has emerged to represent or cover its legal meaning. The venture can be for specific project only, or continuing business relationship. This is in contrast to a strategic alliance, which involves no equity stake by the participants. A joint venture may be a corporation, limited liability company and partnership. When such cooperation exists between foreign firm and a local firm, it can then be regarded as foreign direct investment from the part of foreign partner (Sell, 1994, p. 13). Joint ventures can be initiated on the grounds of internal restructuring for effective management, competitive and strategic goal. Firms can cooperate on the ground to streamline internal organisation and specialise on core areas where they have best efficiency in order to spread costs and risks. They can enter into joint venture in order to increase the company's strength such that access to financial resources can be improved. The advantage here is that economies of scale and scope can be realised when productivity increased. When firms enter into joint venture agreement local firms can have access to new technologies and the opportunities to improve managerial practices which can in turn strengthen the competitive position of both firms in the partnership arrangements. Joint venture arrangement can serve as a strategic measure in the form of diversifying activities and improving synergies when firms have acquired new technology and improve skilled force (Altenburg, 2003, p. 172).

3.5.3 The determinants of FDI inflow

3.5.3.1 Economic Performance and Micro-determinants of FDI

The microeconomic determinants of FDI reflect Dunning's location-specific advantages which can favour location of business activities in a certain geographical location. The factors represent a country's production factors which can affect future profits and the costs to locate production at a specific location. One basic factor that determines the location of a business in a specific country is the level of the country's economic performance. The measure of economic performance of a country is the real per capita GDP and income per capita growth. GDP measures not only a country's economic output but shows the strength and size of the domestic market. The growth of the domestic market means that investors can recover quickly the sunk cost of investment and attain economies of scale as well (Nguyen, 2003, p. 34). The income per capita or GDP per capita therefore gives rough indicator of a nation's prosperity or the standard of living. Per capita income growth on the other hand shows how much each individual receives, in monetary terms of the yearly income that is generated in the economy through productive activities. It shows what each citizen would receive if the yearly income generated in the country from productive activities were equally shared among everyone. A country with persistent growth of GDP per capita in purchasing power parity expressed in USA dollar provides confidence signal to foreign investors as country with expanding profitable market. This gives a rough overview on how wealth or purchasing power of the citizens in the country is in terms of personal income and capability to buy[82]. These indicators underscore the business prospects and opportunities that drive foreign investors' motivation. Countries with high income per capita can have high rates of returns on investment and high business opportunities which often attracts FDI (Caves, 1996, p. 25).

The unit labour cost and the nature of skilled labour can influence the MNEs decision to invest in a particular country. For example, if the wages increase relative to cost of capital, there will be a tendency to substitute capital for labour which will result to unemployment trade-off. An export oriented FDI may be discouraged if the wage rise escalates in the sense that products for exports will be less competitive (Lucas, 1993, p. 401). If the skilled labour is very weak in the host country, it will be a problem for FDI seeking qualified personals and skilled labourers because the productivity and efficiency gain will be very low. Countries having relatively low labour cost with higher productivity are likely to attract more FDI for local production than countries with low labour cost with a lower productivity (Veugelers, 1991, p. 369). This suggests that FDI can impact poverty reduction only if the qualified and skilled workers are present in the country.

Government policies such as taxation and subsidies, foreign exchange restrictions, ownership policy and sectoral specific limitations and entry rules can derail the inflow of FDI to the host country. A policy that pursues even treatment and a competitive playing field tends to maximise the increase in productivity and income. Different forms of restrictions on foreign exchange scare the investors. Sometimes the investors are forced to reinvest their share of profits on the business or denied access to foreign exchange. Reinvestment of profit is a function of improved investment climate and competitive forces which serve as signal for a growing market. If remittance of profit is restricted, investors always resort to transfer pricing which is also not favourable to the host country (Agarwal et al, 1991, p. 32)[83].

---

82 This however does not indicate the distribution of income within the country because a small wealth class can increase the measured per-capita income far above that of majority of the population.

83 Transfer pricing means the action of a firm to exchange goods and services within the organisation at a price different from that at which it would trade those goods and services to an independent firm (Dunning, 1998, p. 512).

3.5.3.2 Macro management as determinants of FDI

The movement in the general price level is a major determinant of FDI inflow. High inflation or uncontrollable increase in the price level signifies instability in macroeconomic management of a country and creates uncertainty in the economy. The effect of high inflation is that it can discourage export oriented FDI because the relative costs of production in the host country has increased. Foreign investors can also be discouraged if the general price level falls deflate resulting to contraction in production activities and even result to firm closure (Razafimahefa, and Hamori, 2005, p. 2). A persistent growth of a host country's balance of payments deficits indicates that a country is consuming more than it can produce. To reduce the deficit, the government may be forced to borrow from central bank to finance the deficit which can result to inflation. In extreme cases, government can restrict capital movement and prevent transfer of profits to investors' country. In general, the consequences of accelerating inflation rates often result to increased opportunity cost of cash holding by households due to anticipated inflation or lead to misallocation of resources as a result of unexpected inflation (Knedlik, 2003, p. 116).

The strength of the host country's currency measured in terms of the exchange rate also determines the FDI inflow in the host country. Two relationships between FDI and exchange rates can be observed depending on the aims of the foreign investor. If the aim of the foreign investor is to serve the local market where trade and non-trade barriers constrain the market entry, FDI can substitute trade. An appreciation of the local currency will attract FDI as a result of increased consumers' purchasing power. If the FDI is for export oriented strategy, an appreciation of the local currency will reduce inward FDI in the sense that the costs of factors of production will automatically increase thus pushing the export prices high and making the FDI output less competitive (Bénassy-Quéré, et all, 2001, p. 180, Krugell, 2005, p. 57). The exchange rate also determines the value of repatriated profits and unstable exchange or deteriorating exchange rate can threaten the remittance of the profits (Lucas, 1993, p. 393).

Infrastructure is a major determinant of FDI inflow. Infrastructure represents quo de facto that drives the economic activities in the sense that every section of economy needs the infrastructure. It has potential payoff in terms of economic growth because it increases productivity and reduces costs of production therefore remain a major factor in attracting foreign investors (Wheelers and Mody, 1992, p. 69)[84]. This suggests that MNEs cannot effectively integrate their operations without adequate supply of infrastructure. Velde (2001, p. 6) argues that infrastructure and skills are basic factors which can help to absorb positive effects of FDI in the sense that local SMEs can easily capture knowledge spillovers and perform better as local suppliers.

Political instability is always a great concern to foreign investors because it leads to disruption of production activities, confiscation of properties and may threathen local and foreign personnel employed by MNEs. The consequences can also lead to change in policies especially in macroeconomic management or introduction of unfavourable regulatory measures (Lucas, 1993, p. 394). Investors are always concerned with nature of change in government policy, the attitude of opposition groups towards FDI, the likelihood of labour unrest, corruption tendencies and bureaucratic rigidity as well as the effectiveness of the local legal institutions in the investment decisions. These factors can increase uncertainty, costs and reduce profitability of investment (Krugell, 2005, pp. 58-9).

3.5.3.3 Human capital development as a determinant of FDI

Education enhances the productive capabilities of persons by helping them to choose more optimal bundles of factors which increase their allocation efficiency in the production (Ram, 1980, p. 366). Increased investments in skill enhancement will not only generate higher wages of the labour force, but will also raise the productivity level of the economy (Stockey, 1991, p. 588). Human Development (HD) has become one of the most important objectives of human activity because people want to expand their choices so that they can the lead lives they desire and value[85]. The Human Development Index (HDI) value in sub Sahara Africa still remains an issu to policymakers in the region. Though there has been improvement from 0.471 in 2000 to 0.515 in 2003, the value is

---

84 Infrastructure defined by UNCTAD as "an indispensable condition for complex integration strategies is the ability to link specialised affiliates in mutually supporting networks of activities through adequate infrastructure facilities, such facilities includes high quality telecommunication links and reliable transportation system" are determinant for FDI (UNCTAD, 1998, p. 114). Infrastructure consists of networks system that links different points or economic activities into an effective production system. Therefore, removing bottlenecks at certain points of the system can produce very high returns. Adequate supply of good through reliable infrastructure is a key factor for countries to compete internationally in trade (World Bank, 1994, p. 17).

85 HD is defined as enlarging people's choices in a way, which enable them to lead a longer and healthy life, being educated, having access to the resources needed for a decent standard of living and being able to participate in the life of one community. Enlarging human choices means building human capabilities that cover range of activities or things people can do or be (UNDP, 2002, p. 13).

still very low. The region also has the lowest educational index of 0.56, GDP index of 0.63 and longevity index of 0.35 compared with other developing regions (UNDP, 2006, p. 222). Consequently, it negatively impacts on inflow of FDI in the region.

The concept of human capital tried to explain why individual invest in education and training that activities improve future income and the effect of education on wages is reflected on productivity (Strober, 1990, p. 214). The theories of human capital also explain why some countries perform better economically while others remain stagnant. For example, United States, Japan and many European countries continue to experience higher growth in per capita income than developing countries as a result of differences in in investment in human capital. Becker (1993, p. 24) argues that high rate of economic performance in these countries is as a result of investment in scientific and technical knowledge that raised the productivity of labour and other inputs in production. He further argued that the successful economic performance in some countries in South East Asia illustrate the importance of human capital to growth. People with high educational qualification receive higher wages. Differences in growth rates differ across countries are due to differences in stocks of human capital. In new growth model, the growth of total factor productivity is modelled as a function of the level of education or human capital. While an educated labour force is better in creating, implementing, and adopting new technologies, thereby generating growth (Benhabib and Spiegel, 1994, p. 144).

Inflow of FDI requires effective skill labour force that can quickly understand and apply relatively advanced foreign technologies in production (Caves, 1999, p. 6). Human capital is the stock of skills, productive knowledge, and competence and attributes embodied in human beings. It comprises knowledge, talent and experience, which an individual possess (Behrman and Taubman, 1982, p. 474). The stock of human capital a country possesses may serve as an instrument for attracting other factors such as physical capital, which in turn can contribute immensely to per capita income growth. The inflow of FDI is a function of the stock of human capital the receiving country possesses.

3.5.3.4 FDI and SMEs in Nigeria's Economic Development

The role of FDI in Nigerian economy has been subject to empirical studies dating back to 1960s. Edozien's (1966) study showed how transfer of best practices by foreign investors through linkages pioneered entrepreneurial learning in modern management in Nigeria. Langley, (1968) also showed how external resources contributed to economic growth in Nigeria by supplementing domestic saving and financing import surpluses, which in turn facilitated domestic investment (Langley, 1968, pp. 153-4). The end effect according to Lnagley study was increased Nigeria's export volume to more than sixteen fold between 1900 and 1962. Langley (1968, p. 159) argues that a greater proportion of the profits recorded by the large foreign trading companies in Nigeria were also reinvested in the economy. Chete (1998) examined the determinants of foreign direct investment in Nigeria from 1962 to 1992 and reviewed various Nigerian policies that affected foreign direct investment in the observed period. The findings call for control of interest rate by stabilising the fiscal and monetary policies so that the inflation rate can be controlled. The exchange rate, inflation, tax burden, institutional and regulatory lapses, social problems and as well, political instability were found to be the traditional constraints that hinder FDI inflow in Nigeria.

Table 3.5 shows not only the inward stocks in millions of dollars but also the proportion of FDI to GDP growth and gross fixed capital formation in Nigeria. As shown in the table, the inward FDI stock increased rapidly from 2.4 billion of US dollars in 1980 to approximately 8.1 billion US dollars 1990. The trend shows an increase to 20.2 and 34.8 billion US dollar in 2000 and 2005 respectively. The increase is also reflected on the ratio of FDI to the GDP growth. The FDI inward stock as a percentage of GDP increased from 3.7 per cent in 1980 to 50 per cent in 1995 and declined to 35.1 per cent in 2005.

Table 3.5: Nigeria's FDI Inward stock in millions of US dollars as a % of GDP and GFCF

Year	1980	1985	1990	1995	2000	2005
Inward Stock millions of US dollars	2,405	4,417	8,072	14,065	20,184	34,805
FDI Inward Stock as a % of GDP	3.7	15.5	28.3	50.0	49.1	35.1

FDI inward stock as a % of Gross fix capital formation (GFCF)			
Year (Annual Averages)	1992-1997	1998-2000	2001-2005
Inward flows as a % of GFCF	28.1	15.3	42.9

Key: GFCF = Gross Fixed Capital Formation; GDP = Gross Domestic Product
Source: UNCTAD World Investment Report, 2003, p. 258, p. 263 and p. 281; 2004b, p. 391 and p. 403; 2005b, p. 316; 2006, p. 303 and p. 309

The proportion of inward flow to gross domestic investment declined from annual averages of 28.1 per cent between 1992 and 1997 to an annual average of 15.3 between 1998 and 2000 but increased rapidly to annual average of 42.9 per cent in the period between 2001 and 2005.

3.6 SMEs in Nigeria's economy

3.6.1 Review of some studies on Nigerian SMEs

The role of small enterprises in Nigerian economy has been documented dating to 1960s. In analysing the industrialisation process in Nigeria between 1945 and 1966, Kilby (1969) explained the dual nature of industrial production in Nigeria in terms of modern and semi-traditional industrial sector. The dualism explains the remarkable differences in characteristics exhibited by both sectors in terms of degree of specialisation, division of labour, technology and quality of raw material input. The small scale industries are dominated by unskilled producers of crude consumer goods, skilled artisan that produce simple but better quality products such as furniture, leather products, goldsmith, motor vehicle repairs etc. The relatively modern small scale industries are found in bakery, soft-drink bottling, singlet manufacturing. The rural industries consist of household cottage industries engaged in food processing, textiles, palm oil extraction, weaving, and metal products (Kilby 1969, pp. 17-19).

Berger (1975) evaluated the success of import substitution strategy between 1964 and 1972 in Nigeria. The study show that the structure of tariff protection for Nigeria's industry provided the import substitution firms a clear advantage over export oriented firms. Within the import substitution firms, those that use indigenous raw materials enjoy a higher effective rate of protection than those using imported raw materials (Berger, 1975, p. 48). The implication is that policy discrimination is always counter-productive in the sense that protected firms usually become redundant and weak to initiate or introduce new ideas. The study further revealed that Nigeria industrial policies from 1964 to 1972 failed to recognise the impact of small scale industries and export oriented industries in agricultural processing sub-sectors in the economy.

Nafziger (1977) investigated the significant of entrepreneurship in Nigeria economic growth especially the indigenous entrepreneurs in manufacturing sector. The author used footwear sub-sector as case study to illustrate the entrepreneurial activities in Nigeria, and at the same time analysed the significance of foreign investment in the sub-sector. The structure of the firms according to study suggests that 95.5 per cent of indigenous footwear firm are microenterprises with firm size between 1 to 5 employees. Employment record in the sampled 2,885 indigenous small and medium in footwear sub-sector was 8,115 with output value of £989,740.00 then. While employment recorded in sampled 9 foreign small and medium in footwear sub-sector was 1,103 with output value of £1,732,550.00 then. This suggests that foreign investment in the sub-sector has been playing an important role in the economy and in Nigerian footwear sub-sector in particular. The major constraints identified in the sub-sector are lack of technical and managerial competence. The constraints invariably stand out to be the major barrier to success in the indigenous enterprises.

Osoba (1991) provided analytical work on the importance of small-scale industries (SSI) in Nigeria economy and the impact of linkages in industrialisation process. The analysis was critical on the pattern of Nigeria's industrial development process which laid more emphasis on large-scale enterprises. The author argues that the Nigerian in development policies failed to achieve its desired objectives because agricultural processing was neglected. The pattern of industrial development failed to promote sectoral linkages. Osoba further argues that definition and classification of small scale industries in Nigeria is vague in the sense that definition often changes as policies evolve. Definition and classification also depend on the prevailing exchange rate. In general, Osoba explained that the major problem that hinders SSI development in Nigeria is lack of exposure. The SSI in Nigeria lacks inter and entra-sectoral linkages that offer opportunities for industrial learning (Osoba, 1991, p. 634).

Studies on Nigeria's informal sectors attracted the attention of some scholars within and outside the country in 1990s. Most of the literature focused on employment and income generation in the sector during the Structural Adjustment Programme (SAP). Willer (1996) showed the effects of the SAP on employment in large companies, small and medium scale manufacturing enterprises in the formal sector as well as the small enterprises in informal sector. The analysis revealed that employment crisis in Nigeria began in 1981 after the oil boom era. The trend dropped sharply in 1982 below the lowest level in 1977 and reached the lowest level in 1984. The empirical result also revealed that company closures in Nigeria cannot be entirely linked the effect of SAP. The rate of firm closure in Nigeria is not significantly high in relation to international comparison. The major factors that led to crisis in many large companies during the SAP were as a result of management inefficiency and external competitive pressure. Contrary to large private and state owned industries, the effects of SAP on employment in small and medium scale manufacturing industry according to the study was positive (Willer, 1996, p. 230). SMEs responded positively to the local demand during the economic crises when large state enterprises loss government support in terms of access to foreign exchange.

Dike (1997) investigated how small scale entrepreneurs in Nigeria managed to survive during economic recession and structural adjustment. The conceptual framework of the study provided an insight into the economy of Nigeria prior to structural adjustment and how informal sector evolved in the economy. The macro and sectoral policy environment that influenced these responses or the behaviour of the small entrepreneurs were also analysed. The policy environment includes among others, changes in exchange rate, reduction in tariff protection levels, deregulation of interest rate and privatisation and government budgetary cuts. The analysis was structured to reflect three phases namely the pre oil boom, the oil boom and the post oil boom eras. Three important arguments which emerged from the study were: in pre-oil boom era, low standard of workmanship and poor product quality contributed low demand for products from the informal sector. The expansion of informal sector during the oil boom era was due to massive rural-urban migration. This was followed by growth in consumer demand among the low income segment in the urban working class due to rise in normal incomes in the urban sector. The expansion of informal economy in post oil-boom era according to the author was due to declining purchasing power among the urban working middle income. Consequently, the demand for cheaper goods and services produced in the informal sector increased drastically. In general, entrepreneurs adopted different strategies namely: costs optimisation, diversification of investment, reliance on local inputs and linkages to formal and rural sectors. During the SAP period Networks were developed in order to pool resources and provide utilities and access roads to workshops. Social networks also serve as means to forge solidarity against undue harassment by local authorities.

Bwala's (1996) and Wauschkuhn's (1996) works was focused on the role of institutions and the self-help associations in the informal sector. Bwala revealed various public support programmes aimed at promoting informal sector enterprises in Nigeria. Some examples were drawn from regional and central government programmes which include among others an integrated self-employment scheme for school leavers and graduates in Oyo state, the back-to-land programme in Rivers state and the graduate farming scheme in Lagos state. The federal government programmes according to the author focused on the provision of rural infrastructure and skilled development. The Directorate for Foods, Roads and Rural Infrastructure (DFRRI) and National Directorate of Employment (NDE) were established to implement these programmes respecttively. Bwala however argued that these programmes were undermined due to poor staffing, under funding, and financial mismanagement.

Wauschkuhn (1996) on the other hand, made an explicit analysis of the associations in informal sector enterprises. Associations in informal sector enterprises according to Wauschkuhn are groups of self-organisations. The aims of the organisations are to improve their members' economic situation, their professional knowledge, and their political interests. The author analysed why and how associations in informal sector enterprises evolved in Nigeria. The effect of SAP was the major factor that led to formation of associations in informal sector enterprises. Firms in the formal sectors were forced to establish links with informal sector in order to substitute imports with local resources. The associations invariably become informal institutions forging cooperation with enterprises in formal sector, with other associations, government institutions and non-governmental organisations. Such linkages and cooperation helped the enterprises in the informal sector to find solutions to their production constraints and improve performance. The study however outlined the costs and benefits for belonging in an association. The costs include membership fees, time expended in the association and the risk of moving out of informality. The benefits include among others participation in various programmes initiated by the association in order to improve of craftsmanship and entrepreneurial skills. The associations serve as umbrella that protects members against undue harassment from the local authorities. They also provide informal social security by organising limited financial support to member who is in need.

Oladeji (1998) investigated the technology problem in Nigeria's small and medium scale enterprises. The study provided theoretical framework on the rationale and scope of government intervention in the control of technology vis-à-vis the role of market forces. The analytical framework started with critical overview on Nigeria's poor technological base in terms of absence of engineering industry, lack of design and tooling up capability. Oladeji argues that SMEs including those in informal sector failed to explore the advantages SAP provided due to weak technological base in Nigerian economy. During the SAP, there was increased gap between the demand for and supply of local products. In general, SAP played an important role in reshaping Nigeria's technology policy towards SMEs. The major government technology initiatives for SMEs according to the author were significantly influenced by the impact of SAP.

Recently, emphasis has shifted towards SME clusters in Nigeria. Bräutigam (1997) analysed the trajectories of SME development in Nnewi where social capital plays an important role in local industrial development. Nnewi as an emerging organised industrial cluster in Nigeria was the focus of Oyelaran-Onyeyinka (1997), whereby he examined some of the characteristics of the economic activities of enterprises in Nnewi. Oyelaran-Onyeyinka (2001) further made an empirical enquiry into the dynamics of cluster growth in Nigeria. In the study, Oyelaran-Onyeyinka provided detailed comparative analysis of Lagos and Nnewi manufacturing enterprises clusters. Akinbinu (2003) study focused on innovation networks in small and medium scale enterprises clusters in South-Western and Northern Nigeria.

The Central Bank of Nigeria made also some documentary report on the role of SMEs in Nigeria economy. The report focused on policy issues on finance and how to improve SME performance (Sule, 1986, Adebusuyi, 1997 and Olorunshola, 2003). In general, World Bank and UNIDO have been conducting series of survey on economic environment, activities and the performance of the manufacturing enterprises in Nigeria (World Bank, 2002; UNIDO, 2002). These studies however failed to provide an in-depth study on the problems SMEs in Nigeria face. Most of the studies focus only on supply side analysis with little emphasis on the demand side. The studies failed to show how to impact linkages between small and large firms which have not been exploited in Nigeria SME studies. In other words, most of the studies failed to examine the relationship between SME capabilities and linkages with large firms. They failed to provide the framework on how technology problems in Nigerian SMEs can be reduced or address the question regarding why "the Missing-link" in Nigeria industrial structure exist. The studies failed to answer some basic questions on why SMEs in Nigeria are isolated in the global economy. Based on these limitations, this study looks into the dynamic factors in industrialisation process and analyse how microeconomic interventions can enhance these factors in Africa with Nigeria as a case study. This study uses three SME strategic operation namely clustering, networking and innovation to investigate these limitations. The concluding argument focuses on the role of productive investment in the development of small and medium scale enterprises in Nigeria.

3.6.2 Definition of SME in Nigeria

Definition of SME is relative and varies according to a country's level of industrial development. For example, what could be termed medium scale enterprise in Nigeria based on capital formation and number of employees can be considered a small-scale enterprise in Germany. A small scale enterprise in Nigeria could be a medium scale enterprise in Niger Republic. Prior to 1992, different institutions adopted different definitions to reflect differences in policy or capital formation (Olorunshola, 2003, p. 35). Arthur Andersen, an accounting firm in Nigeria, uses sales turn over as parameter for classification of SMEs while some agencies focus more on number of employees or capital formation as an important factor (Table 3.6). Different parameters for classification of enterprises often create some problems for empirical research. It also indicates weak institutional integration in policy formulation for SME development. In 1992, Nigeria Council of Industry (NCI) operating under the Federal Ministry of Industry streamlined the definition of SMEs in Nigeria.

The small scale enterprise was defined as enterprise with fixed assets above N1.0 million and not more than N10.0 million, excluding land but including working capital. Medium scale enterprise was defined as enterprise with fixed assets not more than N40.0 million including working capital but excluding land. The 1996 NCI revised version defined small scale enterprises as those with total cost, including working capital but excluding cost of land above N1.0 million but not exceeding N40.0 million with labour size between 11 to 35 workers. While medium scale enterprise was defined as those with total cost, including working capital but excluding cost of land, above N40.0 million, but not exceeding N100.0 million, with labour size between 36 and 100. In 2001, the definition was further revised (Olorunshola, 2003, p .35).

Table 3.6: Definition of SMEs by Nigerian Institutions

	Assets excl. real estate (In million Naira/ Sector)			Annual Turnover (In million Naira/ Sector)			Number of Employees/Sector		
Institutions	Medium	Small	Micro	Medium	Small	Micro	Medium	Small	Micro
CBN	<150	<1		<150	<1		<100	<50	
NERFUND		<1							
NASSI		<40			<40			>3<35	
Ministry of Industry*	<200	<50					<300	<100	<10
NASME	<150	<50	<1	<500	<100	<10	<100	<50	<10
Arthur Andersen				<500	<50				

Key: the symbol < stand for less than; > stand for greater than. CBN = Central Bank of Nigeria; NERFUND= National Economic Reconstruction Fund; NASSI= Nigerian Association of Small-Scale Industrialist; NASME= Nigerian Association of Small and Medium Enterprises. * National Council of Industry under Ministry of Industry revises SME definition once a year

Source: World Bank, 2002 p. 138[86]

The small-scale enterprise was defined as those with a labour size between 11 to 100 workers or a total cost, not more than N50.0 million, including working capital but excluding cost of the land. While medium scale enterprise was defined as those with labour size between 101 to 300 workers or a total cost of over N50.0 million but not more than N200.00 million, including working capital but excluding cost of land (Olorunshola, 2003, p. 35; Udechukwu, 2003, p. 8). Fre-quent change in definition and classification is inline with Osoba (1991 p.633)'s argument that definition of SMEs in Nigeria is a function of exchange rate.

3.6.3 Structure and geographical distribution of Nigeria's industrial establishments

3.6.3.1 Distribution of Industries in Nigeria

Nigeria's private sector can respond quickly to an improved business environ-ment and can contribute immensely to the economic development and growth. Forrest, (1993. p. 92) implicitly revealed that some leading Nigerian firms such

86 World Bank= the World Bank Group, Regional Program on Enterprises Development, Africa Private Sector Department, Small and Medium Enterprises Department.

as IBRU and Odutula have achieved a scale of operation not possible in other sub-Saharan African countries outside South Africa. Table 3.7 indicates structure and geographical distribution of industrial establishment in Nigeria.

Table 3.7: Geographical distribution of Nigerian industrial establishment by size

Regions	Size	West	East	North-West	North-East	Total	% to Total Ind
Micro-Enterprises	5-9	30,188	12,862	5,895	6,745	55690	0.610
Small-scale Enterprises	10-49	10,016	8,167	2,975	2,524	23682	0.259
Medium-scale Enterprises	50-99	3,501	2,933	881	942	8257	0.090
Large scale Enterprises	100+	2,132	714	313	622	3781	0.041
		45,837	24,676	10,064	10833	91410	1.00
Total % of the Total		(0,501)	(0,27)	(0,110)	(0,119)		

Source: Nigeria Bureau of Statistics, 2006

Table 3.7 shows that 61 and 25.9 per cent of Nigeria's industrial establishments are in micro and small scale enterprises respectively. 86.9 per cent of the industrial establishment are small enterprises including those in informal and formal sectors. Only 9 per cent is in medium scale enterprises while 4 per cent represents large scale enterprises. The Table also indicates that about 50.1 per cent of Nigeria's industrial establishments are located in western part of the country while 27 and 22.9 per cent are located in Eastern and Northern Nigeria respectively. In western region, 65.8 of the enterprises are micro enterprises, 21.9 per cent and 7.6 per cent are small and medium scale enterprises respectively. 4.7 per cent of the industrial establishment are large scale enterprises. Lagos remains the industrial nucleus of Nigeria. Most of the small, medium and large scale enterprises are located in Ikeja, Apapa, Agege, and Isolo and in the neighbouring Sango Otta in Ogun state. The firms are engaged in diversified production especially in chemicals/paints, pharmaceuticals, wood/furniture, food/beverages, textile and paper/printing, metal fabrication and plastic products (Forrest, 1993 pp. 170-4). The industries produce extensively for local consumers and export to West African market (Onyeyinka, 2001).

In Eastern region, 52.1 per cent and 33.1 per cent of industrial establishment are micro and small enterprises respectively while 11.9 per cent and 2.9 per cent are medium and large scale enterprises respectively. The industrial areas in Eastern region comprise Aba, Nnewi, Onitsha and Port Harcourt with Enugu and Uyo being the new potential industrial cities[87]. In the 1960s, the major products in small manufacturing enterprises in Aba and Port Harcourt were shoe production, singlet, blacksmithing, welding and plastic pro-

87 Söderbom and Teal, 2002; World Bank 2002 and researcher's surveys 2001, 2003-4 and 2005.

ducts. After the civil war in 1970, SMEs in metal fabrication successfully copied the foreign technology in designing and fabricating of kernel crushers, Garri pro-cessors, baking machines and paper converters (Forrest, 1993 pp. 170-4). The small firms in the region have diversified production such as soap manufacturing, paper conversion/recycling with garment and shoe production concentrated in Aba. Nnewi industries consist of small and medium scale light engineering producing motor/motorcycle spar parts and metal fabrications. The small and medium enterprises in Enugu are mainly engaged in palm kernel extraction and furniture production (Uzor, 2004 and 2007). While the SMEs in Port Harcourt are mainly found in petroleum sector providing support services to large scale oil companies in the city. The impact of FDI in Port Harcourt is such that small and medium enterprises are engaged in subcontracting business with large oil companies.

In Northern Nigeria, 60.5 and 26.3 per cent of industrial establishment in the region are micro and small enterprises while 8.3 and 4.5 per cent are medium and large scale enterprises respectively. The industrial areas in northern Nigeria comprise Kano, Kaduna, Jos and Bauchi. The regional industrial activities started with trade in textiles, kola nuts, livestock, and grains. The SMEs are found in hides and skins, craft, garment and leather goods production. The modern industries are found discussion in food/beverages, textile, chemicals pharma-ceutical chemical/paints and leather production (Forest, 1993, World Bank 2002). Table 3.8 reveals the polar structure and unbalanced regional industrial distribution. The implication is that low ratio of medium scale enterprises in industrial activities created vacuum in industrial linkages. The medium scale enterprises usually serve as link between small and large enterprises. They strengthen the production capacity of small enterprises and support the large enterprises by providing the necessary inputs through subcontracting (Uzor, 2003).

The obvious reason for the promotion of SME in Nigeria is centred on its contribution in wealth creation and employment generation (NEEDS, 2004, p. 63). Nigeria economy was dominated by the state-owned enterprises with private sectors largely playing passive role. When the state owned enterprises collapsed in the 1980s, small enterprises played an important role in providing the basic needs, and served as safe net for retrenched workers in public service. Several surveys and research works have shown different contributions of small enterprises in Nigerian economy. Dike (1997, p. 13) revealed that in a sample of 100 small enterprises investigated, 28.2 per cent of the employees are hired and wage workers, 36.2 per cent of the workers are household members and relatives while 35.6 per cent are apprentices. Bräutigam (1997, p. 1075) showed that employment in SMEs in Nnewi Light engineering sub-sector increased from 1415 in 1991 to 1718 in 1994 by 21.4 per cent. Oyelaran-Oyeyinka (2004) showed that 42 per cent of small firms in Ikeja industrial cluster have a labour force between 1 to 49 and 58 per cent of medium scale enterprises employ about 50 to 99 workers (Oyelaran-Oyeyinka, 2004, p. 7). Meagher (2004, p. 22) cluster census showed that the total employment in Aba informal shoe and garment enterprises clusters is about 12,115 while Ilorin cloth weaving enterprises cluster engage about 10,374 workers. The contribution of SMEs in GDP growth has not be defined but on the aggregate level, SMEs employ about 60 per cent of labour force of the non-farm labour in Nigeria (Oyekanmi, 2003, p. 67).

3.6.3.2 Constraints surrounding Nigeria's small enterprises

3.6.3.2.1 Business Environment for SME development

Corruption has been identified as the major factor working against Nigeria's economic development. The basic fact in this context is that private sector depends on public sector for supply of services, maintenance of law and order, provision of basic amenities. Corruptive acts can induce distortions in economic activities and raise the cost of doing business. This is because firms of all kinds often asked to make additional unofficial payments in order to ensure a steady supply of public services (UNIDO, 2002a, p. 42).

Poor infrastructure development is also the central problem the firms face in Nigeria. The most outstanding is energy problems especially the inefficiency in energy supply. Despite government subsidies that cover over 69 per cent of production cost per KWH, the efficiency remains very low (World Bank, 2002, p. 13). The consumers are frustrated due to inaccurate billing system and poor services rendered by energy generating authority in Nigeria. Frequent power fluctuation raises costs of production measured in terms of cost of purchasing private generators and accessories, damage to equipment caused by power fluctuation, cost of gasoline and maintenance (Agboli and Ukaegbu, 2006, p. 22; Uzor, 2007).

Söderbom and Teal (2002) showed how poor infrastructure especially bad roads accounted for low productivity in the Nigerian enterprises. The study revealed that due to poor access roads, micro enterprises are often operating at the roadsides in order to reach their customers therefore putting themselves in tremendous road hazards. The study also showed that market infrastructure such as workshops, sites for business or marketplace are not adequately provided by the government. Telephone services often failed to function on the average of about 3 days per week in Nigerian cities. Hence firms are increasingly embracing mobile telephones with high cost but relatively reliable. Most firms invest in private bore holes water or rely on private water tankers supply therefore increasing the cost of production (UNIDO, 2002, pp. 37-42; Agboli and Ukaegbu, 2006, p. 22).

On micro-level, lack of trust in business transaction induced by the '419' is an advance fee fraud which has made business transactions in Nigeria to rely on cash payment and "face-to-face" contact[88]. An advance fee fraud coined as '419' is a confidence trick in which the target is persuaded to advance relatively small sums of money in the hope of realising a much large gain. The effect of the '419' has extended across international boundaries whereby the Nigerian entrepreneurs have lost reputation and have been isolated. The fee fraud has advanced into internet and has impeded Nigeria electronic mail (e-mail) output in the economy. Many legitimate Nigerian business e-mails increasingly failed to reach their targets. Most companies overseas treat all mail containing the words "Nigeria" and "Nigerian" or mail orignating from Nigeria as spam or even deleted. Moreover, management and employees in large and medium industries in Nigeria are locked in strained relations thereby leading to strict monitoring of employees. Hence the employees cannot apply innovative concepts due to strong management control systems. Foreign investors or potential business partners find it unsafe to share business information with a potential Nigerian entrepreneur. Foreign firms that planned to enter Nigerian market find it difficult to access or evaluate the business environment (World Bank, 2002a, p. 69).

3.6.3.2.2 Government

The institutional problems in Nigeria are reflected on the costs of doing business and uncertainty in the economy. Contract enforcement is a major institutional problem in Nigeria. The problem of Nigeria's legal system lies on enforcement mechanisms of commercial contracts. The ability to resolve commercial disputes quickly is a key element in private sector development. Enforcement of contracts and bureaucratic procedures has positive effects on economic efficiency. For example, it takes an average of 23 forms of procedures and 730 days to enforce a commercial contract (e.g. debt recovery) in Nigeria (World Bank, 2005, p. 279). In Ghana, with the same forms of procedures, it takes an average of 200 days to enforce commercial contract (World Bank, 2005, p. 279)[89]. One encouraging aspect of Nigeria's legal system is that it has high disclosure index value of 6 (World Bank, 2005, p. 279). This implies that even

88 419 is an advance fee fraud originated from a section of Nigeria panel code (World Bank, 2002).

89 Disclosure index measures the degree to which investors are protected through disclosure of ownership and financial information. The index value is between 0 and 10 with value 0 indicating high probability of investors loosing their assets and value 10 suggesting very high probability of assets recovery.

under a hostile economic environment, the investors are highly protected. The delays in contract enforcement were linked to several factors such as poor administrative capacity and low incentives for effective discharge of judicial proceedings. A stable legal and judicial system is very important not only in terms of resolving disputes among private parties, and litigation involving private sector and the government.

Poor governance increases the cost of doing business in the sense that arbitrary imposition of different forms of taxes or levies, different permit requirements, high cost of licensing tends to retard private sector motivation. Söderbom and Teal (2002) shows the unofficial payment made by firms in getting access to public services. The study indicates that for firms to get access to public service supply requires additional unofficial payments not only to the workers, but also to the respective team leaders. The amount of money paid depends on the nature of government services and public utility required. For example, connecting telephone line or electricity or water supply requires additional payment to workers, team leader or the manager. Such payments amount to 44 per cent of the total official costs of business transactions. To get government contract and tax clearance require additional unofficial payment of 34 and 23 per cent of total official payment respectively (Söderbom and Teal, 2002, p. 43). The transaction costs incur by the enterprises in trying to comply with and avoid complicated tax system are enormous. Small enterprises face psychological pressure due to different taxation system. The aggressive or violent methods of collecting taxes by the local authorities always lead to frustration. This tends to demoralise motivations in the entrepreneurship activities.

3.6.3.2.3 Access to Financial Capital and Limitations

Nigeria has a relatively long history of support programmes for SME development. In 1971, the Federal and State Government introduced Small scale Industries Credit Scheme (SSICS) with relatively more liberal conditions than in commercial banks. The credit scheme was later abandoned following allegation of mismanagement hence the Federal Government pulled out of SSICS. Subsequently, Nigerian Bank for Commerce and Industry (NBCI) was established in 1979. The reason for the establishment is to restore financial discipline and introduce efficient management prudence. The persistence of inefficiency and inadequate funding and political interference, paralysed the laudable objectives of the loan scheme (Inang and Ukpong, 1993, p. 258).

In 1970, Central Bank of Nigeria introduced several special credit guidelines for commercial banks towards channelling loans to small scale industries. The guideline stipulates that 10 per cent of total loans granted by the bank would be allocated to small scale enterprises. This was increased to 16 and 20 per cent in 1980 and 1990 respectively (Inang and Ukpong, 1993, p. 259; Anyanwu, 2003, p. 24). The rural banking programme was introduced in 1977 with the aim to reduce the problems associated with access to credit by rural farmers and none-farm operators. Commercial banks were therefore directed to open branches in rural areas in order to facilitate loan disbursement. A total of 756 rural branches of the major bank were established by 1989 (Inang and Ukpong, 1993, p. 259; Anyanwu, 2003, p. 24). In spite of these loan schemes initiated by various governments, access to finance remains one of the major problems in the sector.

When SAP was introduced in 1986, small enterprises find it difficult to raise investment loans and credit for working capital as a result of drastic depreciation of the local currency (Naira), and rising interest rate. Federal Government of Nigeria negotiated financial assistance from World Bank in 1987 in order to finance the US$418 million SME support project. In this respect, a loan package of US$270million was approved in 1989 representing 65 per cent of the total project costs (Olorunshola, 2003, p. 40). Supported by the World Bank and African Development Bank, the Federal Government of Nigeria set up the National Economic Reconstruction Fund (NERFUND) in 1990. This was designed to make fund available for SMEs at a moderate interest rate lower than the market rate and on medium/long-term bases (5 and 10 years). The scheme allowed easier access to foreign exchange. The cumbersome lending processes and conflicting objectives of the participating banks made the programme problematic and unworkable (Inang and Ukpong, 1993, p. 260; Anyanwu, 2003 pp. 24-25). African Development Bank also granted export stimulation loan (ESL) of US$2,709 million to Nigeria government for SMEs in Nigeria. The grant was a 20 years loan repayable with a concessionary interest rate of 7.3 per cent (Olorunshola, 2003, p. 40). The aim of the loan was to support SMEs in financing the acquisition of capital equipment required for better quality production in order to improve exports and diversification of the non-oil sector (Inang and Ukpong, 1993, p. 261). The International Finance Corporation (IFC) increased its interest in financing small and medium scale enterprise in order to support private sector development and economic growth in Nigeria. Five financial institutions received loans ranging from US$20.0 million to US$40.0 million to finance SME viable projects. Two companies received direct loans between US$0.5m and US$0.9m from the organisation (IFC, 2002)[90].

Informal microfinance has been the major source of raising fund by microenterprises. Informal microfinance originated as a result of the inability of the formal financial institutions to provide financial services to the urban and rural poor. The small enterprises in the informal sector cannot provide the

---

90 International Finance Corporation data sourced from internet

required collateral for loan security. The government sponsored credit schemes failed to provide grass root development financing. Hence the informal micro-finance flourished but at the expense of the poor due to high interest rate. The microfinance institutions (MFIs) emerged recently in Nigeria and are registered as non governmental organisation (NGOs). The principal source of funds for the organised microfinance institution in Nigeria are mainly from aid and grants from outside Nigeria with about 51.2 per cent from western countries (Anyanwu, 2004, p. 6). The major donor organizations to MFI in Nigeria are the UNDP, the Ford Foundation, the African Development Foundation, Community Development Foundation, Development and Peace of Canada, EZE of Germany and the Catholic Agency for International Development of The Netherlands (Anyanwu, 2004, p. 6). Collateral as lending security is not pronounced in MFIs operation system rather the lending rely on collective pledge of each group based on recognitions. Lending is done on a grouping system made up of 5 to 10 clients and each member is subjected to norms of business transactions. Interest rate in the MFIs is much higher than the bank interest rate because of the risks and absence of collateral involved (Anyanwu, 2004, p. 7). The average lending rate in MFIs was 32.0 per cent in 2003 while the average saving deposit rate was 7.5 per cent compared with 3.5 per cent in the formal banking sector (Anyanwu, 2004, p. 8). The ability to attract deposits from the poor is higher because the institutions are very close to low-income group and operates on a very low administrative cost with relatively higher savings rate than the banks. Despite high lending interest rates, repayment rate is higher in MFIs. Low incidence of default in loan grouping system is due to sanction mechanisms within each group. The sector has relatively low average loan size of N8,800 but high recovery rate of 92.5 per cent in 2003. Though the activities of MFIs are expanding, financial resources remain limited. 78.4 per cent of MFIs' lending is directed to commerce and women entrepreneurs (Anyanwu, 2004, pp. 8-9).

3.6.3.2.4 Capacity building and the need for capacity building programme for SME development

In expressing the ability of a country to follow sustainable development paths, United Nations Conference on Environment and Development (UNCED) Agenda 21 chapter 37 defines capacity building as follows: "Specifically, capacity building encompasses the country's human, scientific, technological, organisational, institutional, and resource capabilities. A fundamental goal of capacity building is to enhance the ability to evaluate and address the crucial questions related to policy choices and modes of implementation among development options, based on an understanding of environmental potentials and limits and of needs as perceived by the people of the country concerned"

(UNCED, 1992)[91]. Capacity building embraces human capital accumulation needed to sustain public and private sectors such that productivity of factor stocks is increase in order to be competitiveness internationally. It also implies improving the capacity of institutions for efficient service delivery and adapt to changing environment through learning (Wohlmuth, 2004, pp. 139-140). This includes constant improving human resources especially in technical and managerial skills so that workers can adapt to increasingly changing technology. In other words, the concept of capacity building captures the process of equipping individuals' capacity on new skills or ability to understand and interpret technical information that enables them to perform effectively.

The challenge in many developing countries is to combine the employment potential of SMEs to enhance their productivity (UNIDO, 2003, p. 3). Capacity building in SMEs is therefore very important and involves improving entrepreneurial skills especially managerial capability in order to increase entrepreneurs' ability to identify business opportunities. Due to size factor, SMEs have limited resources and access to finance, low economies of scale, high relative costs in accessing and utilising information technology, and deficiencies in entrepreneurial skills. They lack information on market opportunities and skills in dealing with customers and have limited knowledge in legal issues and bureaucratic processes especially in exports (Harvie, 2004, pfr. 14).

Human resource development for SMEs embraces educational reform that geared towards the needs of industries. The capacity building programmes is very important for enterprises upgrading and attracting foreign investment. Foreign capital needs to be complemented with high skilled labour. This requires education in science and mathematics as well as training aimed at the needs of the industry (Naudé and Krugell; 2004, p. 177). In the context of trade liberalisation, SMEs need to develop capacities to take advantage of opportunities arising from a more open regional market. For example, in a Knowledge-based economy, application of information and communication technology (ICT) can be a great lever for SMEs. This can be possible when the entrepreneurs and workers can have access or be able to understand these technologies (Harvie, 2004, p. 14). The new approach to technology capacity building in developing countries is through technology partnership in the form of strategic alliance. In this case, multinational companies can play an important role through strategic alliance that allows SMEs to gain access to technology that is within their level (van Dijk, 2003, p. 353). Many SMEs lack the knowledge on how to source finance or aware about programs available in comercial banks and government institutions regarding SME development programmes. How to increase the opportunities for access to capital can be an important catalyst for small enterprises development (IFC, 2005). This is

---

91 Capacity Building – Agenda 21's definition, chapter 37 UNCED, 1992.

particularly critical for small and microenterprises. Capacity building for microfinance entails how to make wider coverage of financial services to small entrepreneurs and at the same time, maintain a viable and sustainable microfinance institution such that a long-term financial and operational self-sustainable microfinance system can be guaranteed (Congo, 2004, p. 243).

3.7 Summary and Conclusion

This chapter has explained the relationship between small enterprises and economic development. The chapter started by explaining the genesis and theoretical conception on how small enterprises evolved in early times. The general contributions of SMEs to the economy in terms of job creation, economic growth, and their role in poverty reduction were examined. Why multilateral institutions and Development Agencies support SED were analysed. The deduction is that SMEs stand as the bedrock for private sector development and plays an important role in employment generation and poverty reduction. The political economic factor behind the weak SMEs in Africa is discussed. In other words, poor institutional development, markets failures, poor governance and weak FDI justify the need for intervention necessary for the growth of the sector. Financial intervention is necessary but not the sufficient instrument for SME development. An analysis of the role of FDI in stimulating the weak SME for economic growth and poverty reduction is explained. The chapter argued that technology transfers and technology diffusion can strengthen SMEs through FDI. With regard to the relationship between human capital and SMEs development the chapter argues that capacity building is an important factor for SME development in Nigeria. Apart from human development, upgrading the public and private institution in line with changing global economy is imperative.

The proceeding chapters tend to focus on theoretical and empirical evidences showing to what extent small firm clustering and networking have contributed to SME growth. How SMEs sustain competition in the growing globalisation pressure. The empirical analysis will also focus on the innovative capabilities in Nigerian small enterprise clusters.

Chapter 4: SME Clusters in Nigeria: Performance and Constraints

4.1 Introduction

The concept of small firm clustering has become prominent in the analysis of industrialisation and employment generation strategies in developing countries. The strategy has been intensified following economic restructuring in terms of liberalisation, globalisation of production, and downsizing the state participation in production activities. There is combination of factors that supports the promotion of small firm clustering in developing countries. Clustering explores the gains of economies of scale by facilitating specialisation and division of labour among small producers. The growth of clusters leads to emergence of suppliers of different kinds, specialised producer services and pool of technical skilled workers. The social relations among the producers in the cluster often promote deliberate actions for performance improvement (Schmitz, 1997, p. 4). Concentration of largely homogenous enterprises within relatively defined geographical area facilitates intervention as a result of similarity of needs. The rate of dissemination of best practices among a large number of beneficiaries and distribution of fixed costs arising from interventions are easier (Mitullah, 1996, p. 23). Clustering tends to generate economic governance that induce efficiency, cooperation, competition and innovative activities which facilitate the growth of small firms (Meagher, 2005, p. 1). Recently, arguments have shifted to small enterprises clustering as poverty reduction strategy in the sense that the features and dynamic process of cluster development have positive impact on poverty reduction (Nadvi and Barrientos, 2004, pp. 9-13). Hence, various research works are now integrating micro and macroeconomic level analysis as well as the experiences in European industrial districts to investigate and analyse enterprises cluster performance in developing countries.

Unlike clusters in East Asia and Latin America, African clusters have neither evolved nor maximised the gains associated with enterprise clustering. The poor performance of African clusters are linked to various factors including lack of strong ties of socio-cultural identity (Schmitz and Nadvi, 1999, p. 1506); failure of entrepreneurs to pursue risk minimising networks that can enhance performance (Bräutigam, 2003, p. 452); and inability to overcome ethnic divisions and link up with international business associates in order to enhance performance (Barr, 1999, p. 130-1). This study considers the capability gap and poor business environment as the major factors responsible for the weak performance of African SME clusters. The capability gap consists of external and internal constraints. The external environment such as poor infrastructure, neglect, and weak institutional support tend to crowd out the small enterprises. The internal environment is linked to poor human capital development especially in technical skill manpower, and weak technological frontiers such as access to modern equipment and poor managerial ability.

In line with various works on small enterprise clusters in developing countries, this study uses performance indicators to examine the capabilities of small and medium scale enterprise clusters in Nigeria. The chapter starts by reviewing literature on SME clusters in developed and developing countries, followed by theoretical framework, definitions, classification and determinant of cluster development path. The analysis also reflects the relevance of SME clustering to poverty reduction. The empirical analysis was designed in such a framework that allowed the author to gain insight into the performance SME clusters and their challenges in Nigeria. It also examined if there is a relationship between firm clustering and performance by comparing the performance of firms in cluster area and those located elsewhere. The chapter concludes with comparative analysis of the clusters investigated.

4.2 The theoretical framework on SME Clusters

4.2.1 Definitions

Literally, the term cluster has different connotations. In economic literature, a cluster can be defined in various forms. Porter (1990, p. 655) defined cluster as a group of firms engaged in similar or related activities within a national economy. Schmitz's (1992) definition of a cluster is centred on the impact of externalities using Marshallian (1890) approach on localised industries and their advantages. He defined a cluster as a group of enterprises belonging to the same sector and operating in close vicinity (Schmitz, 1992). Porter (1998, p. 78) further define clusters as geographically concentration of interconnected firms and institutions in a particular sector. The linkages existing between the firms are very important in strengthening competition. Clusters are sets of complementary firms (in production and service sectors) public, private and semi-public research and development institutions, which are interconnected by labour market and /or input-output and/or technological links. Clusters are highly competitive when these linkages are governed by the market mechanism and direct structures of single organisation (Steiner and Hartmann, 1998, p. 211). All the definitions with exception of Schmitz's approach provided real economic scenarios in industrialised countries. Adoption of definition depends on the environmental context in which the subject is applied. This paper adopts Schmitz's definition because geographical proximity appears to be important for African SME clusters and in Nigeria. This is because institutions governing economic exchanges are very weak in Nigeria. Physical infrastructures such as roads and telecommunication are poorly developed. Furthermore, face-to-face business transactions are much valued because of opportunistic behaviours common in Nigerian market. Therefore, perceived from Schmitz's background, Uzor (2004, p. 9) defined cluster as group of small firms operating in a defined geographic location, producing similar products or services, cooperating and competing with one another, learning from each other in order to overcome internal problems, setting common strategies to overcome external challenges, and reaching distance market through developed networks.

4.2.2 Terminologies and classification of the term enterprise clusters

The term "industrial district" and "cluster" are often interchangeable in context and application. Prominent in the districts are small and medium sized firms with close inter-firm collaboration and competition that derive from innovation. The main characteristics of industrial district are geographical proximity, sectoral specialisation, inter-firm division of labour, and cooperation among firms supported by local economic agents. These characteristics help to enhance local production and innovation capability which feature in European firm clustering (Rabellotti, 1995, p. 35). In Europe, socio-cultural identity is used to describe the characteristics of industrial district because it helped to facilitate trust supported by active self-help organisations as well as regional and municipal government interventions. Industrial district can be classified as a cluster but cluster is not necessarily an industrial district.

In other words, cluster can grow, mature and evolve into an industrial district[92]. The term cluster refers to sectoral and geographical concentration of firms. Such concentration allows small enterprises to benefit from external economies. In developing countries, clusters enjoy abundance of labour force with low wages that facilitate competition (Schmitz, 1999, p. 1629). However, clusters often face two contrasting growth paths namely a high road, characterised by innovation, quality improvement, functional flexibility and good working conditions (Sengenberger and Pyke, 1992, pp. 11-12). The low road which is synonymous with low prices, cheap input materials, labour flexibility and cheap labour (Sengenberger and Pyke, 1992 pp. 11-12). Some

---

92 These characteristics however differ from country to country. The Third Italy and Baden-Württemberg are two European clusters usually cited as reference in research work on clusters in developing countries (Schmitz, 1995, p. 537). "Third Italy" Idiomatic term applied to the proliferation of small-scale skilled production units associated particularly with recent developments in parts of the country, chiefly in the regions of the North East (Veneto, Friuli), Emilia and Central Italy (Tuscany, Marches). The economic development of the "Third Italy", based mainly on industrial districts, has been contrasted both with that of the North and with the backwardness of the South. (The European Foundation for the Improvement of Living and Working Conditions, October 2007).

clusters in East Asia, share aspects of high and low road growth path. A number of South Korean clusters operate under excess labour surplus but show signs of innovation and technological upgrading (Nadvi, 1995, p. 57).

In developing countries, clusters are grouped into three namely: informal clusters, organised clusters and innovative clusters (UNCTAD, 1998a, p. 4). Informal clusters are micro and small firms that have low level technology, low skilled workers as well as low barrier to entry. The combination of these factors results to rapid explosion in terms of increasing number of enterprises in the cluster. Informal clusters are also characterised by low managerial skill and poor product quality. They comprise large number of skilled and unskilled artisans with limitd knowledge on product standard and maintainance. An example of an informal cluster is Suame micro and small scale enterprises cluster in Ghana. Organised clusters are characterised by collective structuring in terms of sharing infrastructure services as well as cooperation and networking which tend to emerge among the member firms, example of such cluster are Sinos Valley, Brazil, Nnewi Light-Engineering cluster, Nigeria. Innovative clusters are knowledge intensive firms with capacity to undertake technology adaptations, innovative designs, new products and processes. They have the capacity to target niche market and improve quality. Such clusters are predominantly found in developed countries. The Indian software cluster, Bangalore has emerged as one of the growing innovative cluster in developing countries (UNCTAD, 1998a, pp. 4-6).

Classification of clusters also depends on the nature of their operations. Clusters are said to be diversified when there is strong vertical specialisation of individual enterprises in the cluster with broad specialisation in a specific sector (Pedersen, 1997, p. 23). A cluster is called subcontracting cluster when most enterprises are dependent and linked as subcontractor to one or few large enterprises. Clusters can also be described as distribution cluster when service related firms are located or clustered in a defined location such that transaction cost and other related inputs are shared at reduced costs. Such clusters are common in logistic branch where logistic firms are located close to one another in order to share common facilities for easy local and regional distribution of goods and services.

Clusters are heterogeneous and have distinctive characteristics across sectors. "Incipient" or "survival" clusters are terms used to capture the early stage of cluster development or industrialisation. Such clusters are usually located in poor areas, producing for local markets with simple technology and low skilled labour. Mature clusters are more advanced in terms of technology and skill. They often produce for global market but are vulnerable to global structural change (Schmitz and Nadvi, 1999, pp. 1505-09; Altenburg and Meyer-Stamer, 1999, p. 1695). Moreover, typologies of clusters show some polar structures in the form of dormant and dynamic characteristics. The dormant clusters show little or no growth in terms of transformation over time, they produce basic products for poor consumers and attract more employment (Sandee, 2002, p. 188). In Africa, explosion of employment in the sector is due to lack of access to better paid alternative employment. Such growth of small producers often leads to severe price competition which undermines firm existence at the same time lead to low wages. The dynamic clusters show stable inter-firm linkages and have the capability to break into national and international markets (Sandee, 2002, pp. 188-189).

4.2.3 Determinants of cluster growth-paths

4.2.3.1 Size of the market and nature of products

Domestic market and industrialisation processes appear to be correlated because the scale of product demand determines the growth rate of the producer. The size of market is reflected on the number of participants, its geographical spread as well as the level of purchasing power[93]. Rosenstein-Rodan (1943) reiterated the importance of domestic market in industrialisation process. According to Rosenstein-Rodan, if series of industries increase their production such that incomes are created and spent by workers in other sectors, markets will expand and industrialisation will be profitable (Rosenstein-Rodan, 1943, p. 206). The share of domestic demand and per capita income also play an important role in the growth of domestic industrial output[94]. Countries that have expanded domestic demand and high per capita income enjoy increase in domestic industrial output (Chenery et al, 1986, p. 156; Chenery and Syrquin, 1975, p. 78). Intensive export of manufactures will eventually begin only after the industry became established in the domestic market (Chenery and Syrquin, 1975, p. 101). Expanded domestic market is a major factor for cluster development. Export markets begin when the domestic market is close to saturation point and export growth is built through the experience gained from quality production in the local market (Cawthorne, 1995, p. 51).

In Africa, the impact of clustering is limited due to the low demand of their products caused by low per capita income. Relative growth in African clusters is due to positive changes in money income, because small enterprises can gain from such changes without increasing their own efficiency (Pedersen,

---

93 Industrialisation can be stalled when the domestic markets are limited, and when there is high cost of transaction and high barriers in world trade. Firms therefore cannot generate enough sales to adopt increasing returns of technologis profitable (Murphy et al, 1989, p. 1009).

94 "Clustering propagates successive layers of specialisation provided that the overall scale of demand grows" (Schmitz, 1997, p. 14).

1997, p. 26). Such growth is related to what Kaplinsky 2000, p. 120; Kaplinsky and Readman (2001 pp. 24-5) described as "immiserizing growth" because an increase in money income does not mean an increase in real income[95]. McCormick (1998, p. 6) further argues that the growth of African clusters are limited due to inter-regional restrictions on movement of goods and people which resulted to an underdeveloped distribution system in the region. The nature of cluster products has a direct relation to the cluster growth path. If the products are made from scrapes, the manufactured goods will be inferior in the sense that their demands will have an inverse relation as income increases. If also the products are perishable goods, it then requires storage and standardised quality control system which small firms in Africa in deed lack. Durability, reliability, conformance to specification and safety are considered to be the important part of product quality measures (Nadvi, 1999b, p. 1607).

4.2.3.2 The stock of economies of scale and scope

Access to market is an important factor for cluster development because reaching larger markets will not only induce proportionate increase in productivity but also will lead to increasing returns. Increasing returns are the by-product of economies of scale in the sense that an increase in all production inputs will result to a more than proportionate increase in output (Schmitz, 1997, p. 13). Economies of scale that support increasing returns are derived from several factors namely: firm's ability to reach larger markets; ability to acquire capital goods, ability to introduce effective managerial skills, and creation of division of labour in the production system (McCormick, 1998, p. 7). Clustering can propagate inter-firm division of labour such that one artisan can specialise in a specific assignment and allow another artisans to perform the rest. Economies of scope on the other hand arise due to the efficiency of the firm to engage in more than one activity successively. There are three kinds of economies of scope - concurrent scale economies, coordinative scale economies, and sharing of technical know-how and skilled workers (McCormick, 1998, p. 8). Concurrent scale economies are the economies gained by enterprises in diversifying their products with the least possible output costs (e.g. fabricating bakery ovens/palm kernel nut crackers). This aspect of economy is common in Nigerian machine makers (Oyeyinka-Oyelarin, 2001, p. 39). Generally, concurrent scale economies are still very weak in Africa. Coordinative scale economy is where an enterprise has the organisational ability to integrate factors of production in an effective production system. Sharing of technical know-how and skill workers are benefits gained by small enterprises clusters in developing countries because firms cannot

95 This describes a situation where there is increasing economic activity (more output, more employment) but falling economic returns (Kaplinsky, 2000, p. 120).

individually afford the costs of high technical skill workers or invest capital goods (Bräutigam, 1997, p. 1075).

4.2.3.3 The rate of upgrading

Upgrading is the process of changing the state or the nature of product quantitatively and qualitatively. It is the process of increasing the present state of the output in order to meet local demand and encourage producers for exports. Value chain and cluster approaches are the medium at which effective product and process upgrading can take place in order to maintain growth (Humphrey and Schmitz, 2002, p. 3). Value chain is defined as the process which is required to bring a product or service from the conception, through the intermediary phases of production, then delivery to the final consumers and finally disposed off after use (Kaplinsky, 2000, p. 121) . The relationship between value chains and upgrading are reflected on (a) identifying where the key problems in the entire production system lay, (b) the methods through which upgrading can occur. Upgrading can occur at each stages of the chain as shown in Figure 4.1. In reality, value chains are more complex than as illustrated above due to several linkages within each chain. Upgrading can be in different forms namely: process upgrading, product upgrading, functional upgrading and chain upgrading at each level of the value chains (Kaplinsky and Readman, 2001, p. 30)[96]. Humphrey and Schmitz, (2002) argue that focusing on the role of local linkages in generating competitive advantages in labour intensive export industries such as footwear and garments is not enough to stimulate upgrading, rather cross-border linkages in global production and distribution play an important role (Humphrey and Schmitz, 2002, pp. 1-2). Gereffi (1999, p. 39) argues that participation in global commodity chain is a necessary step towards industrial upgrading because such chains put the firms and economies on potentially dynamic learning curves.

96 Process upgrading occurs when the local producers improve effectively the internal working process of entire production system, maintain product quality, and increase the speed of response (Humphrey and Schmitz, 2000, p. 12). Product upgrading entails ability to introduce new products or improve old products (Kaplinsky and Readman, 2001, p. 30). This form of upgrading can be carried out through three underlining principles namely: product upgrading through learning by export, product upgrading through buyer and supplier investment strategies, and product upgrading through constant buyer and supplier exchange of ideas and knowledge (Humphrey and Schmitz, 2000, p. 12). Functional upgrading occurs when the productivity is increased by improving the quality of management skill and organisation of labour factor within the firm. This involves taking care of entire production processes, sourcing of inputs, designing, and sale of their own branded merchandise (Kaplinsky and Readman, 2001, p. 30; Humphrey and Schmitz, 2000, p. 13).

Figure 4.1: Simple illustration of value chain

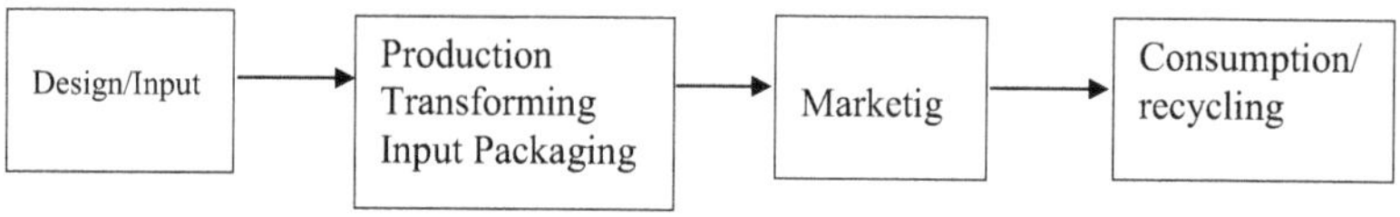

Source: Kaplinsky and Readman, 2001, p. 28

Clustering on the other hand facilitates upgrading easily in different forms; first learning by interaction is encouraged when local small firms are located in close vicinity. This is effective when there is an institutionalised network that encourages learning. The second form occurs when the cluster of small producers gain access to global buyers that set conditions for upgrading. The third option is when the cluster of small local producers is linked to core large firms located in the same vicinity. The second and third options are possible when firms in the cluster are willing to learn and/or have acquired the required skilled workers and technology.

4.2.3.4 The nature of collective efficiency existing in the cluster

Alfred Marshall (1890, p. 211) highlighted the economies gained as a result of agglomeration of small businesses of similar character in a particular locality. He referred such economies as external economies which are of importance for small firms. Krugman (1991) applied the Marshallian concept in identifying four reasons for localisation of industries[97]. Schmitz 1992 extended the concept by considering the factors that contribute to small firms' growth in the face of pervasive state and market failures in developing countries. In his thesis on Collective Efficiency (CE), Schmitz defined CE on the premise of external economies and joint action (Schmitz, 1995, p. 530)[98]. CE is the competitive advantage derived from local external economies and joint action. The former is incidental while the latter is consciously pursued. The combination of the two according Schmitz varies among clusters and over time (Schmitz, 1999, p. 1628). The instances of local collective efficiency underscore the importance of clustering in terms of the extent small firms can be efficient and competitive. Diffusion of technological know-how can easily be facilitated because business

---

97 Agglomeration of several enterprises in a geographical location employment to workers with specific skills and support the production of non-tradable specialised inputs as well as information spillovers (Krugman, 1991, pp. 484-5).

98 The economies arise due to unintended or incidental by products of some otherwise legitimate actions (Mishan, 1971, p. 2).

information flows rapidly between producers, and between producers and suppliers (Nadvi and Schmitz, 1994, p. 18). Firms can forge collective will in order to achieve some desired end (Schmitz, 1997, pp. 7-8).

Olson (1968) argues that the concept of joint action does not serve the interest of individual economic actors[99]. Social scientists have argued that people will be better off by acting cooperatively. Joint actions in this context are some deliberate and strategic actions that do not oppose market competition but rather are needed to sustain growth of small firms in the cluster. The actions are cooperative and jointly pursued such that an impeding constraint can be overcome or positive turning point of the cluster can be induced (Uzor, 2004, p. 15)[100]. Some empirical results have analysed the role of joint action in products quality standard upgrading in developing countries so that firm meet export conditions (Nadvi, 1995; Cawthorne, 1995, and Schmitz, 1995; Mitullah, 1996). In general, collective efficiency is possible when there is presence of dynamic growth externalities. Such externalities include human capital formation, mobility of skilled labour, networks for technology diffusion and increased interaction among firms (Stewart and Ghani, 1991, p. 571). The gains from collective efficiency can be achieved through a growing market (Pedersen, 1997, p. 26).

4.2.3.5 The nature of institutions supporting the cluster

Enterprises cluster is a composition of several small enterprises with an element of social interactions embedded in the system. The social interactions help to foster the development path of the enterprises in the cluster. This argument captures the concept of social capital which various traditional sociologists have tried to explain[101]. Some features of social capital such as trust, norms, and networks can improve efficiency in the society by supporting coordination of actions. Such features also help to form the milieu that generates economic governance in the clusters and linkages. These features over time develop

---

99 Die Vorstellung, dass Gruppen von Individuen so handeln, dass sie ihre gemeinsamen oder Gruppeninteressen erreichen, ist keineswegs eine logische Folge der Annahme, dass die Einzelnen in einer Gruppe rational ihre individuellen Interessen verfolgen, sondern ist im Gegenteil mit dieser Annahme unvereinbar“ (Olson, 1968, p. 2).

100 For more details see Axelrod, (1984); Coleman (1990), Burt, (1992) and Putnam, (1993)

101 The rational choice theorists regard social capital as an informational resource, emerging from interaction between rational agents that needed coordination for mutual benefits. Another argument considers social capital as ties and norms binding individuals within constituent elements of large organisations. The third argument explores the weaknesses of social capital literature which fail to recognise that solutions to modern social ills lie in re-establishing the mediating structures of local civic associations (Woolcock, 1998, p. 155).

spontaneously and are also fundamental at the early stages of cluster development because they helped to shape the growth path. Informal institutions such as norms of behaviour are embedded in organisations and are probably the most important source of stability in human interaction. They are extensions, elaborations, and qualifications of rules that have tenacious and survival ability and they are integral part of habitual behaviour (North, 1989, p. 1324). If there is a high level trust existing in the organisation, there will be greater likelihood of cooperative norms within the organisation. Cooperation becomes institute-ionalised when human interaction is regular hence mistrust is reduced.

In concrete terms, two characteristics tend to capture the concept of collective efficiency (CE), namely the passive and active CE. The passive CE comprises the cost advantages resulting from agglomeration effects such as pool of specialised workers, easy access to suppliers of inputs, dissemination of information and ideas. The active CE evolves only when there are concerted efforts aimed at generating them (Schmitz and Nadvi, 1999, p. 1505). Institut-ions are therefore very important for active CE to occur. Caniels and Romijn, (2003, p. 193) argue that inter-firm collaboration and networking rooted in a common culture are supported by common institutions. This is the driving force in boosting firm competitiveness in terms of CE approach. Moreover, as cluster mature and transactions become complex and across local boundaries, a stronger institutional framework that supports the effective function of the market becomes inevitable. Schmitz and Musyck (1994, p. 902) however warned that government or government-sponsored institutions cannot create industrial organisation which can allow competition on the basis of CE. Government-sponsored institutions can play an important role in helping the industry to expand after the private sector has established the basic concentration of industrial activities. In other words, economic institutions, legal institution, financial institutions and stable macroeconomic frameworks are needed for the growth of the cluster.

4.2.3.6 The role of the state

The gap in technical skill has been a major constraint in industrialisation efforts of African countries south of Sahara. The stock of technically skilled workers is an important factor for technology diffusion and competitiveness (Lall and Kraemer-Mbula, 2005, p. 49). Government intervention in cluster development programme is therefore necessary especially in human capital development. The intervention can be in the form of capacity building in managerial and technical skills.

At the macro level, the area of intervention is the stability of relative prices. Under stable exchange rate, firms that depend on foreign raw materials can predict the market, plan accurately and produce effectively. Under stable real interest rate, short and medium term loans can be borrowed with little or less uncertainty to meet investment strategies. Rabellotti (1999, p. 1583) shows how government macroeconomic measures in Guadalajara, Mexico footwear cluster induced a positive turning point. The structural reforms undertaken by Mexican government in the form of liberalisation helped small firms to enhance performance. In general, government specific actions such as provision of special credit lines for SMEs or provision of space in terms of site, building and workshops can support firms to increase productivity.

At Meso level, regulatory instruments such as import quota or prohibition, stringent measures to protect infant industries are found to be ineffective measure in industrialisation process. For example, if a regulation is imposed to protect local industry, it will remain unchanged for lengthy period of time. A drastic change in technological innovation will quickly reduce the effectiveness of such regulation (Lam and Lee, 1992, pp. 120-1). Moreover, protectionism always has less effect on entrepreneurial objects because firms always readjust strategies in order to explore opportunities where they have competitive advantages (Yu, 1993, p. 171). Many entrepreneurs in Africa lack technical skills and machinery to act competitively. Capability and capacity building in terms of technology and human skill development are fundamental instruments for small enterprises competitiveness and development strategy (Romijn, 1999, p. 13).

At micro level, the competitiveness of small enterprises depends on efficiency, quality; flexibility and responsiveness of the firms in the diverse volatile market (Meyer-Stamer, 1995, p. 144). The role of the state in this context is to enhance productivity through investment in quality standard system and skill training. For example, the quality assurance crises in Sialkot surgical instrument cluster, Pakistan was resolved through massive government intervention in quality standard. This was done by funding the establishment of new internationally recognised metal testing laboratory as well as providing technical training facilities in the cluster (Nadvi 1999b, p. 1611).

4.2.4 SME Clusters and Poverty Reduction

The relationship between small firm clustering and poverty reduction depends on the dynamic development processes or path in which the small enterprises in the cluster are embedded. The impact of the embeddedness can have influence on income and employment growth. The dynamic processes here refer to upgrading and linkages that can lead to the growth of the entire cluster. The growth of the cluster will in turn bring about changes in aggregate income and employment. The two plausible features of cluster that can have impact on poverty reduction are the agglomeration effects and joint action (Nadvi and Barrientos, 2004, p. 15). At incipient stages, the small firm clustering serve as safe net by engaging numerous artisans, unskilled labours or workers who are qualified but cannot find job in the formal sector. For example, small enterprises footwear cluster in Agra, India, comprising 5,000 enterprises employ about 60,000 workers (Knorringa, 1999, p. 1590). In Gararra garment cluster in Lima, Peru, there are about 6,384 registered SMEs with large number of them consisting microenterprises (Visser, 1999, pp. 1666-7). In Indonesian rural cottage industry cluster, there are 10,000 registered enterprises producing different products ranging from woven bamboo, food products to furniture. The enterprises are located in densely populated and poverty ridden areas (Weijland, 1999, p. 1518).

At mature stages, linkages are developed in the cluster such that direct and indirect employments are created and higher wages are paid to specialised labour. For example, the Torreon's apparel industrial cluster, Mexico, upgraded significantly by enhancing skills and capabilities, moving from simple assembly to full package production. Employment in the cluster increased from 12,000 in 1993 to 65, 000 in 1998 by 411.7 per cent. It also increased from 65,000 in 1998 to 75,000 in 2000 by 15.4 per cent (Bair and Gereffi 2001, p. 1889). Employment in footwear exporting cluster in Sinos Valley, Brazil rose from 27,000 in 1970 to 150,000 in 1990 and from 153,400 in 1991 to 170,500 in 1996 (Schmitz, 1998, p. 10 and p. 13).

The effect of small enterprises clustering on income can be measured in terms of workers' differential wage growth in firms in cluster areas and those located elsewhere. For example, the Italian experience shows that in the 1990s, salaries of both white and blue collar workers were higher in cluster settings than those outside the clusters (Nadvi and Barrientos, 2004, p. 17). At macro-level, the analysis can also be related to income differential of average government worker's wage level and wages of workers in the cluster. The wage level is considered in terms of relative wage which is the basis for accessing the impact of cluster. In developing countries, Schmitz (1995, p. 558) and Nadvi (1999a, p. 88) revealed that wage levels are low in Sinos Valley shoe and surgical instrument clusters but are better than average regional wage levels. Sandee (2002, p. 197) also shows that wage levels for skilled furniture craftsmen were significantly higher than average provincial wage levels. Similarly, in Gamarra garment cluster in Peru, the average monthly pay per worker was 30 per cent higher in the cluster than those located elsewhere in the city (Visser, 1999, p. 1559). Pro-poor cluster development programmes therefore demands integrated public and private sector initiatives supported by global actors.

4.2.5 Arguments against firm clustering

Clustering is a combination of sectoral and geographical concentration of enterprises which can leave a town or region vulnerable if there are structural changes in production and technology. Dominance of a particular industry in the cluster can make several enterprises vulnerable if there is break in ties or cooperation with the industry (Schmitz, 1995, p. 534). Some structural problems in the core firms can affect the small enterprises that depend on the core firms. In concrete terms, some firms may leave the cluster after acquiring capability and competence, hence producing structural problem in the entire cluster. If wrong networks are inserted, clustering can foster collaboration that can lead to compromising individual firm's efficiency which can undermine competition. Clustering tends to foster transparency which makes each firm vulnerable in terms of exposing business secrecy or encouraging free riders.

In developing countries, clusters comprise large number of artisans and craftsmen; politician can easily influence or use the leaders of the associations in the cluster. They can also manipulate the cluster brokers for political gains therefore making the entire system vulnerable. The key feature of small firm clustering is the emergence of social capital. The mainstream economists view social capital as an idealized fashion or where individuals act uniformly. Fostering trust with strong community ties can be difficult especially when enterprises are in direct competition with each other. For example, the relationship among firms in Torreon's cluster Mexico appears to be distance or even strained despite the fact that most of the major firms are owned by relatives. The fundamental reason for such development was attributed to the absence of private and public support institutions at early stages of the cluster development (Bair and Gereffi 2001, p. 1899). Moreover, as clusters mature, smaller producers are often squeezed out or become less autonomus in their ties with larger producers within the cluster. The implication is that small firms lose their own competitive strategies and their importance in the cluster (Schmitz, 1995, p. 547).

4.3 Literature review on SME Clusters in developed and developing countries

Literature on SME clusters in both developed and developing countries cover variety of theoretical analyses and empirical case studies. For obvious reasons, various authors use different approaches and methodologies in their analytical works because SME clusters are heterogeneous in nature, and level of development differs among regions and sectors. Moreover, investigations and analyses are however subject to authors' perspective. Some authors apply sociological approach, by investigating the relationship between social interactions and the growth of clusters. While others adopt anthropological approach in the sense that cultural and ethnical homogeneity has impact on cluster development. Neo-classical and new institutionalist literature respectively focus their analyses on the productivity growth and transaction costs effects of firm clustering. On regional perspective, literature in developed countries focuses on firms' productivity by analysing workers productivity, linkages and innovation milieu in firm clustering. In developing countries most literature borrowed the conceptual frameworks from Europe. The analyses are however centred on industrialisation development processes and employment generation strategies. There are remarkable differences in literature on cluster from South East Asia, South America and Africa. Most literature on South East Asia clusters provide evidence in respect to cluster transformations from incipient and assembling to advanced brand production in modern and traditional industrial sectors. Literature on Latin American clusters reveal that clusters in the region are found mainly in the traditional industrial sector. Generally, clusters in both regions have shown evidence of structural transformation and capability to compete in global market. Literature on African clusters show that clusters in Africa are still at incipient level, mostly in informal sector and have not been able to maximise the advantages associated with external economies for competitiveness. The enterprise clusters in Africa are concentrated in service sector such as automobile technicians, hairdressing and petty trading dominated by women. The manufacturing clusters in the region are predominant in the labour intensive wood/furniture, leather/footwear; garment and metal work. However, the light engineering cluster in Nnewi, Nigeria shows an example of organised cluster in Africa.

Generally, Porter's (1990) theory of competitiveness revived the cluster debate by providing the framework on how interdependence firms and institutions affect innovation and growth. In the 1990s, series of case studies on European industrial districts started to surface in economic development literature. Sengenberger's and Pyke's (1992) work was a compilation of case studies and policy perspectives on European industrial districts. In analysing the concept of industrial districts and local economic regeneration, Sengenberger and Pyke investigated the characteristics and the success of Italian industrial districts. The industrial districts comprise North Central and Eastern part of the country as well as the province of Emilia-Romagna. Their analyses revealed that firms' growth in the districts is not due to low cost of factors of production, rather a case of effective social and economic organisation in the region. Trigilia's (1992) contribution on development of Italian industrial districts focused on the impact of improved organisational synergies in terms of network formation. The organisational networks in the region were a reflection of integrated linkages across sectors and firm size with traditional firms playing an important role (Trigilia, 1992, p. 34). Benton (1992) focused on how proximity facilitated communication among firms in the same and related sectors in Spanish industrial districts. The proximity helped to create collective innovation process. The social ties in the cluster helped to foster competitive environment and cooperation among individuals and firms (Benton, 1992, p. 48). Schmitz's (1992) contribution on the impact of proximity focused on the success of the German industrial district in Baden-Württemberg. The analysis covered both the model and the factors which explain the growth of small firms in the region. In other words, the study showed how inter-firm cooperation and effective regional/local government policy facilitated the growth path of small and medium size firms in the region. Kristensen (1992) related the Italian industrial district phenomenon to cases of small firms' success in traditional garment-/knitting and furniture industries in Denmark. The study revealed a case of relocation of production to agricultural areas that induced drastic increase in proportion of employment in the region. In other words, employment change in the region reflected an increase in technical skilled workforce as well as increased proportion of unskilled women in industrial production in the 1970s and 1980s.

In later 1990s, literature on European industrial clusters comprises the contributions from different researchers on clusters and regional specialisation edited by Steiner (1998). In their contribution, Steiner and Hartman's (1998) showed why enterprise clusters are considered to be learning organisation. The authors used the concept of learning organisation to analyse the nature and development of industrial organisation in Upper Styria, Austria. They argued that clustering facilitates organisational learning in the sense that firms tend to expand their capacity continually which may lead to innovation and development of new technologies (Steiner and Hartman, 1998, pp. 212-213). The recent research works edited by Karlsson et al. (2005) also provided an in depth analysis on industrial clusters and networks. The analytical framework was structured to capture the global spectrum and greater understanding of cluster and network concepts. The work was grouped into four analytical procedures in the form of cluster and networks as a model, empirical evidences of clustering effects, country case studies as well as cluster policy analysis and strategies.

The European experience led to the appearance of bodies of literature on small firm clustering in developing countries. Some features of European industrial districts such as composition of small firms and the proximity factor were perceived by researchers in development economics as a model for promotion of industrialisation in developing countries. As policy recommend-dation for developing countries, Schmitz and Musyck (1994) analysed the role of formal public and private institutions at meso and micro level in enterprise cluster development. Their policy framework covers the supply and demand side. The former focused on access to credits, training infrastructure and institutional support. The latter focused on the importance of product quality upgrading and creation of new markets as measure for cluster growth. Schmitz (1995) study focused on the form of industrial organisation in which small firms cluster in common vicinity in order to gain efficiency which individual firms can rarely attain. The theoretical background of the study covered a brief explanation of the distinction between the old and new industrial development approaches. In the former, the author revisited the failed import substitution and industrial protection strategies in the developing countries. The latter relates to economic geography approach where proximity and sectoral concentration can produce gains of Marshallian economies. The proximity factor can lead to the emergence of joint actions that can foster growth (Schmitz (1995, pp. 530-6). He therefore used the European industrial district experience to analyse the industrial transformation in the Sinos Valley south of Brazil. Schmitz (1999) further investigated how the firms in Sinos Valley footwear cluster coped with the com-petitive pressure in the global markets. Three remarkable strategies emerged from the study. Wage contraction in labour intensive industries led to immisering growth. Intensive product and process upgrading helped the firms in the cluster to capture wider market and remain competitive. Firms in the cluster adopted just-in-time production system in terms of reliability and faster production in order to market quicker than their competitors.

Rabellotti (1997) compared the Mexican industrial organisation with Italian industrial districts. The effects of external economies and cooperation as well as linkages in the district were investigated in the study. His findings revealed how changes in the economic environment improved linkages in the form of strategic alliance of small firms. The alliances provided the framework for an effective supply of specific inputs to firms (Rabellotti, 1997, p. 58).

Visser (1997) also investigated the significance of spatial clustering by making a comparative study on the performance of small scale clothing industry in cluster area and those located elsewhere in Lima, Peru. His empirical evidence provided an insight into the effects of proximity on input prices. The effects include reduced search/matching costs, easy sharing of information on market conditions. The reduced transactions costs which led to downward pressure on the prices of inputs and final goods (Visser, 1997, pp. 80-1). Bair and Gereffi's (2001) study focused on the export-oriented apparel industry in Torreon, Mexico. The authors used the Industrial District and Global Commodity Chains (GCC) concepts to analyse the dynamics of industrial transformation in Torreon after North American Free Trade Association (NAFTA). Their findings revealed how firms in the cluster moved from a full-package production system that lacked the capacity for process upgrading to GCC that set conditions for quality upgrading. This subsequently led to an export and employment boom in the region. Altenburg and Meyer-Stamer (1999) used Latin America experience to develop the policy framework for the promotion of clusters in developing countries. The conceptual background of the policy framework focused on transaction costs reduction, collective efficiency and linkages.

In Asian clusters, Nadvi (1999a) investigated the development trajectories of SMEs in the Sialkot surgical instrument cluster, Pakistan. The study showed how specialised small and medium scale producers in the cluster are positioned to respond to rapidly changing demand driven-global market. The author used the concept of collective efficiency to explain the efficiency gain by small firms in the cluster which led to increased export market. The analyses also explained the joint initiative that helped to find solutions to product quality crises following increased international pressure on quality assurance.

Weijland (1999) provided empirical evidence on microenterprise clusters in rural Indonesia by analysing the benefits of clustering for small rural enterprises. The theoretical analysis covered among other things, the rural trading networks, location and organisation of the clusters. The factors which contributed to the success of rural enterprise clusters in Indonesia were analysed. A cross-sectional analysis was used to explain the performance of the clusters. As a result of heterogeneity factor and differences in cluster characteristics, the author recommended policy interventions which will reflect specific constraints across sectors[102]. Sandee (2002) investigated the impact of economic crisis on small enterprise clusters between 1997 and 1998 in Java, Indonesia. The conceptual framework focused on the impact of small industries on poverty reduction during the country's economic crisis. The findings revealed that firms which are actively involved in export performed better as a result of depreciation of the local currency (Rupiah) during the economic crises. The export boom led to increase in wage income in the cluster. However, the increase in price and production did not affect employment growth in the traditional roof tile cluster positively.

Krnorringa (1999) used international commodity chain approach to show how heterogeneous cluster evolved in Agra, India. The difference between the market channel approach and Global commodity Chain (GCC) approach was analyesed in the theoretical framework. The market channel illustrates the scenario where traders, producers and other relevant units are linked in the production and distribution of particular products to a specific market segment. The GCC explains how international manufacturers and traders incorporate producers from developing countries in the supply chain. The findings of the

102 For example, technology limitations and group targeting should be more appropriate for poverty reduction.

study suggest that the performance of the producers in cluster is significant related to the main markets channel of these producers.

Literature on African clusters is limited due to the low level of industrial development in the region. As a result of failed import-depended industrial development strategy pursued in the region, the research on African industrial production activities shifted to informal sector production activities in the late 1980s. The role played by small enterprises during period of Structural Adjustment Programme (SAP) period in the 1990s in terms responding to local demand during economic crises further intensified researchers' interest in informal sector activities. Subsequent empirical studies started to focus on the growth constraints, marginalisation claims and organisational structures of small producers in region.

In his work on clusters of enterprises within the system of production and distribution, Pedersen (1997) investigated the claims associated with collective efficiency and transaction costs. The analysis showed the processes of vertical, horizontal specialisation within and between sectors. Types of cluster in Africa were identified and analysed in Tanzania, Zimbabwe and Uganda showing for example, the structure of maize trading and milling industries. The study provided an insight into the limits of collective efficiency in African clusters which include among other factors, weak local market, limited vertical specialisation and collaboration, and slow expansion in non-local/export market.

McCormick (1997) focused on features and organisational structures of garment manufacturers in Nairobi, Kenya. She identified the weaknesses and prospects of the mini-manufactures in the garment cluster and further analysed the typology as well as firm distribution in the cluster. The study also provided information on how and why firms value their networks. McCormick argued that the entrepreneurs value their social and professional networks for effective business operations because of weak institutional support (McCormick, 1997, p. 125). McCormick and Ongile, (1997) further investigated the growth and barriers to growth among small and medium sized garment producers in Nairobi. Their empirical evidence focused on the problems related to capital and credit, technology and location. They further analysed the entrepreneurial character-rristics which cover gender and the educational level across firm type. Their findings revealed how weak product demand remains a general problem in the cluster and conclude by arguing that policies aimed at strengthening the economy will benefit the small producers in the cluster.

Mitullah (1996) examined the impact of collective efficiency on the Lake Victoria fishing cluster in Kenya. The conceptual framework of the study reflected the relationship between collective efficiency and the cluster growth. The study analysed the structure of fishing and marketing in the cluster which consist of four operational groups. The groups comprise the fishermen across national boundaries and various market distribution channels. The author also went further to analyse different challenges the fishermen face such as rapid decline in the volume of fish supply and quality control pressure from European Union. The study concludes by showing how lack of effective economic institutions within the cluster has limited the effectiveness of joint action, hence irrational actions of the fishermen remain a major problem in the cluster.

Oyeyinka-Oyelarin (2001) examined the "process and dynamics" of cluster growth in Nigeria, by making a comparative analysis on Lagos and Nnewi manufacturing clusters. The conceptual background of the study covered not only the various forms of inter-firm linkages in developing countries but also the dynamics of clusters in terms of product market demand. The analyses revealed different investment strategies, technological learning mechanisms and development of capabilities in the two clusters. The educational background of the entrepreneurs, the age of the firms and ownership as well as inter-firm linkages were analysed. The research findings indicate that both clusters have the potential to expand and grow but various constraints such as infrastructure, market size and type tend to limit the performance of the firms in the clusters.

Generally, most of the literature in developed and developing countries focus on empirical research works and case studies of individual clusters with little systematic comparative analytical work. Emphasis in the literature relates mainly on the gains from clustering but the counterfactual analysis in terms of comparing clusters with dispersed firms are relatively very few. This study therefore considers both empirical case study and comparative analysis approach to investigate cluster performance and capabilities in Nigeria.

4.4 Small scale enterprise clusters performance in Nigeria

4.4.1 Introduction

This sub-sector concerns the empirical data analyses of the small scale enterprises covered in the field survey. Different methodological approach was adopted in the study to reflect the heterogeneity of the SMEs. Different methodolical approach was adopted in order to provide insight into the specific constraints in each sub-sector. The analyses cover the origin and developmental background of each sub-sector. This is followed by the characteristics of the enterprises in each sub-sector. The characteristics reflected firm informality in terms of regulatory status and the nature of labour force in use. The empirical data analyses were designed to investigate the hypotheses, employment potential of the small enterprises, proximity as a factor in small firm performance, the competitive factors in terms of the level of human capital developpment, and the local technological capability. The comparative analysis of the five clusters was performed in order to identify not only the level and characteristics of each cluster but also the competitive lag of each cluster. The findings of the empirical work conclude the study.

4.4.2 Aba small scale footwear Enterprises Cluster

4.4.2.1 Introduction

The origin of Aba small scale shoe manufacturing enterprises is directly linked to Mbaise migrants to Aba city during the colonial era. Mbaise is a former colonial district in Eastern Nigeria located in present Imo state of Nigeria with high population density. The Mbaise shoe producers have little or no formal training in shoe production. Early account revealed that after observing the nature of footwear the European Missionaries wore; the people of Mbaise designed similar footwear made of wood; later with scrapes of syntactic materials and used tyres. Over time, the production changed to commercial venture as the demand increases across the region.

Early production was based on trial and error with simple hand tools and workshops located at the road sides and later in the market place. The new industrial sector created employment opportunity for the poor and rapid growing population[103]. The growth of Aba as commercial axis of Eastern Nigeria attracted the Mbaise shoe production artisans in 1930s. In the 1940s and 1950s, production started to reflect modern designs and product imitation from multinationals such as Bata in the 1960s. Between 1970 and 1975, Aba footwear industry witnessed a boom in the eastern region as a result of a combination of factors such as civil war and income effects. The end of the civil war created an opportunity for rapid increase in demand for locally made shoes in the region. Low income in the region then led to increased demand for cheap locally made footwear products. As a result of the boom, producers began to offer trade credits to traders who have developed trading networks across regional and national markets[104]. Skills later changed as national and regional markets expanded such that modern hand tools and materials were introduced in production activities. However, the Mbaise shoe producers lost the monopoly of the sector in middle of 1970s when other members of Ibo ethnic group and other

103 Interview with Chief I. O. Uwagwa, The founder/ Chairman Board of Trustees-Shoemakers Industrial Union Inc. on 18.05. 05 from 10 am to 1.00pm. Present at the discussion were Mr. FranSata Andagi!cis Apugo-Onyeagwara, Secretary of Assembly of Lines; Ikechukwu Aneme, Line Chairman Goodness Line; Edyson Njoku, Chairman of all the line Chairmen; Chief Patrick Uzoma, 1ST Market Committee Chairman Umuellegbu Industrial Market.

104 Interview with Francis Chukwu, the Chairman Power line shoemakers Association on 18. 05.05, Time 14pm-15.30pm.

neighbouring ethnic groups joined in the production activities. Presently, the footwear enterprises cluster in Aba is a composition of three main units namely: the Umuelem shoe industry, popularly known as "Bakassi" ladies shoe and bag production unit; the "Power Line" ladies shoe production unit and the "Shoe-Plaza" men shoe production unit. Meagher's (2004, p. 22) cluster census put the population of Aba informal shoe producers in the cluster at about 11,535 enterprises with approximately 27,223 workers and 19,610 seasonal workers. With respect to social composition, the sub-sector is dominated by male enterprises head due to the nature of production activities in shoe making that demands physical application. Women are employed as shoe tailors, and shoe dressers. Female enterprises heads are common in designing different stamps and trade marks as well as supply related activities such as marking papers and chemicals.

4.4.2.2 Methodology

The questions this subsection tends to examine are: Is there significant difference in firm performance in clustered small enterprises and those located elsewhere? To what extent external economies and joint action have explained small firm performance? Is there any positive correlation between employment change and increase in firms' sales volume? In this context, a comparative approach is adopted to analyse the differences in performance of enterprises in clustered area and those located elsewhere. In making the deductions, assumptions such as working days effect, price and boom period were considered. The analysis was classified into normal and seasonal production with the aim to generating the scenario where seasonal production became a proxy for boom period. Hence, changes in employment and variation in sales volume can be reflected in the analyses. The number of working days per week was used since the small scale enterprises do not keep records on costs and working hours which can make calculation of firms' productivity easier. Data on marketing processes, reflecting the number of items sold and discounts were not available hence data on discounts were not considered. Price range was determined, median price was taken as unit price and assumed to be constant. The average gross sales per month were calculated by multiplying the unit price by average production output. Hence, the arithmetic mean and standard deviation of output per worker and gross sales per worker were calculated. Thereafter, statistical tests on differences between two sample statistics were performed in order to determine if the differences in performance are significant. This allows the researcher to make inferences on the impact of clustering on small firms' performance. Furthermore; a linear correlation was performed using the product moment method to investigate if sales volume is correlated with employment intake[105].

4.4.2.3 Informality Characteristics

The legal status of the sampled firms appears to be the same and predominantly sole proprietorships. As shown in Table 4.1, all the firms sampled were not officially registered and failed to meet the annual tax obligations as well as keeping of daily records. 43 per cent of enterprises in the cluster pay wages above the minimum wage. Disaggregate data show that 55 per cent of the firms in shoemaker unit met minimum wage requirement. 44 and 40 per cent of enterprises in shoe tailoring and smoothing respectively met minimum wage requirement.

Table 4.1: Some regulatory indicators as informality characteristics

Some Formality Indicators	Shoe maker	Shoe Tailor	Smoothing	Stamping	All Invest. Sample
Sample size	24	5	4	3	36
Percentage of Firm Officially Registered	0.0	0.0	0.0	0.0	0.0
Percentage of Firms that met Tax obligations/ Keeping of account	0.0	0.0	0.0	0.0	0.0
Percentage of Firms that met Minimum Wage Requirements	0.55	0.44	0.4	0.0	0.43
Percentage of firms Operating within Local Government Regulations	0 .833	0.80	0.75	0.0	0.75

Source: Author's field survey

The local government regulations are mainly the business premises registration, payment of environmental levy, and other miscellaneous dues. These payments are made through the central union; hence 75 per cent of the sampled enterprises in the cluster operate within these regulations. The type of labour force is shown in Table 4.2 with 1.5 as the average number of apprentices in the firms located in the cluster area. 1.4 and 1.2 represent the average number of regularly paid workers and seasonal workers respectively. 47.2 per cent of the firms operate only without workers and apprentices. The table also shows that 50 per cent of enterprises in shoemaker production unit did not employ workers. Shoe tailors hire more temporary workers at the peak of the season than other production units. On the average, firms use more apprentice than paid workers. The survey reveals that firms in Aba footwear cluster operate a 7 days working day and more than 18 hours working period per day.

105 All calculations are found in appendix 4.1 to 4.12

Table 4.2: Some labour force indicators as informality characteristics

	Shoe maker	Shoe Tailor	Smoothing	Stamping	All Invest. sample
Sample size	24.00	5.00	4.00	3.00	36.00
Average No of Regular Paid Workers	0.70	1.50	0.00	0.00	1.40
Average No of Apprentices	1.20	1.00	0.00	0.00	1.50
Average No of Seasonal Workers	1.25	2.50	1.20	0.00	1.20
Firms with out Workers (in %)	50.00	20.00	25.00	100.00	47.20
Average No of Unpaid Workers	0.20	0.00	0.00	0.00	0.140

Source: Author's field survey

4.4.2.4 Competitive factors

The debates on the link between education and economic growth are based on the externalities generated by an improved educational level. Such improved educational level is reflected on the increased stock of human capital that favours economic growth (World Bank, 2002, p. 39). Table 4.3 shows a deve-loppment problem where educational level of enterprises heads is weaker than workers.

Table 4.3: Educational background in percentage of enterprises heads and workers

	Primary Education	Secondary Education	Post Secondary Education	Vocational Training
Enterprises Heads	71.40	12.50	4.20	7.10
Enterprises Workers	32.30	67.60	0.00	0.00

Source: Author's field survey

Table 4.3 indicates that 71.4 per cent of the enterprise heads have primary education only as against 32.3 per cent of the workers. 67.6 per cent of the workers have secondary education as against the 12.5 per cent of the entre-preneurs. Over the sample, only 4.2 and 7.1 per cent of the entrepreneurs have post secondary education and vocational training respectively. In pre-SAP era, shoemaking as a profession was regarded as survival occupation for poor people. Hence, most entrepreneurs have only primary school leaving certify-cates. Despite the production structure that represents a model of different specialised micro enterprises forged into a production process (Figure, 4.2), the firms in the cluster have limitations due to weak human capital development especially the enterprise heads.

The emergence of different small scale firms in the area represents a classical agglomeration effect[106]. Agglomeration of large number of small scale shoemakers in a defined geographical location attracted other support enterprises in the area. At the centre of production and transactions is the shoemaker who performs the designing works, cutting activities, sub-contracting other activities, control the quality and couple the parts[107]. Shoemaker's production unit is however less mechanised. The production activities are performed manually with hand tools. The shoe tailors and smoothing units are semi-mechanised part of the production in the cluster. Sewing machines with different designing mechanisms are used to sew and design the shoe tops and floors.

Figure 4.2: Production Structure in Aba small scale footwear enterprise Cluster

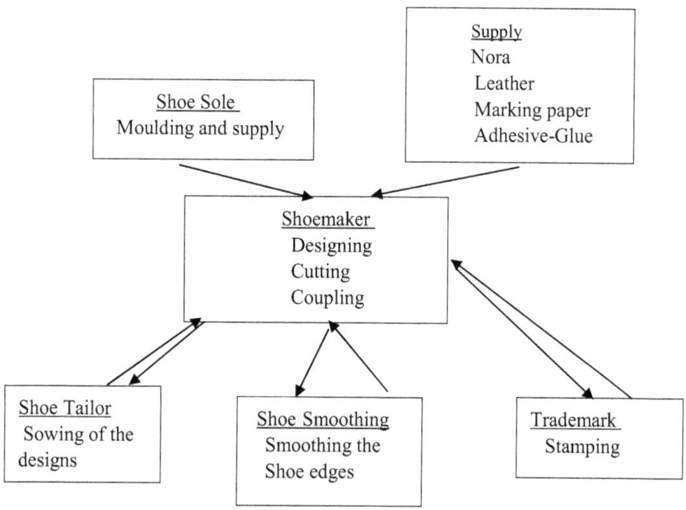

Source: Based on Author's field survey

The smoothing of the soles is done by grafting or filing machines operated with generator. One remarkable problem in the smoothing unit is the health hazard

106 For example, pool of market for workers with specific skills (Krugman, 1991, pp. 484-5). Agglomeration facilitates easy meeting of buyers and sellers (McCormick, 1998, p. 9). It also facilitates rapid flow of technical information between producers, traders and suppliers (Nadvi and Schmitz, 1994, p. 18). Pooling of efficiency and competitiveness (Schmitz, 1997, p. 7).

107 One basic advantage of such linkage is; producers who cannot bear the cost of equipment for entire production process can concentrate on a particular stage and subcontract other stages to other entrepreneurs (Schmitz, 1999, p. 1505).

due to limited space in the workshop, pollution from saw particles and smokes from the generator. Other related factories such as shoe soles are located close to the cluster such that the factory can make special designs at the request of the shoemakers as well as supplying variety of shoe soles to retail-traders in the cluster. Inter-firm linkages in the cluster depend on the specific needs of each firm and the nature of equipment the cooperating firm possesses. The two common inter-firm relationships identified in the cluster are the trader-producer and producer-producer relationships (Table 4.4). Trader–producer relation covers information sharing and granting of trade credit. Granting of trade credits depend on the degree of trustworthiness. Traders on the other hand source the required input materials across Europe and Asia at the same time market the products across local and African regional markets[108].

Table 4.4: Inter-firm relationship identified in the cluster

Characteristics (Pure Horizontal)	Actors	Characteristics (Semi-Vertical)	Actors
Sharing of Equipment	Producer-Producer	Supply of materials	Trader-Producer
Sharing of Market Information	Trader-Producer	Supply of Shoe Soles	Producer-Producer or Trader-Producer
Informal sub-contracting	Producer-Producer	-------------	--------------

Source: Author's field survey

The producer–producer relationship is the informal sub-contracting arrangements that are governed by institutionalised norms of cooperation. Inter-firm transactions are performed at the preparatory rather than at assembly stage of production hence classified as horizontal cooperation. Since most producers lack the basic equipment due to lack of finance. They rely on equipment sharing or borrowing that helps to sustain the production activities[109]. The supply of materials and shoe soles are classified as semi-vertical because they are not made at different stages in production line rather during coupling of the shoes.

4.4.2.5 Firm Performances in Clustered and Dispersed Aba Small Scale Footwear Enterprises

Firm performance can be measured in terms of output per worker linked with specialisation of labour and the investment strategy that maximises productivity. The Aba small scale footwear cluster is labour-intensive comprising large

108 This form trader-producer linkage tends to reduce the search and transaction costs for the producers and facilitates information on market trend (Bräutigam, 1997, p. 1074).

109 Such horizontal cooperation helps small firms improve performance and overcoming obstacles (UNIDO, 2001, p. 18).

number of artisans with low financial base. There is no existing product quality standard or quality bench mark therefore the quality of goods is assumed to be the same[110]. The only information about the product quality is the price range. This can give wrong quality signal if the labour cost is high or as a result of asymmetric information where the producers set high price in disguise of offering high quality. The price ranges between N170 to N3, 500 (US$1.4 to US$28) in clustered enterprises and N200 to N3,500 (US$1.6 to US$28) for dispersed enterprises (see appendix 4.2). This suggests that the product range in the cluster and dispersed cover the poor but not the "very poor" segment of the population[111]. The standard profit margins are not calculated due to lack of dataor records on profit related information (an indicator of informality)[112]. Table 4.5 shows the mean output per worker in the clustered and dispersed enterprises.

Table 4.5: Mean monthly output per worker in footwear enterprises

Mean normal monthly output per worker			Mean seasonal monthly output per worker		
	Mean	S.D		Mean	S.D
Clustered Ent.	1008.56	707.82	Clustered Ent.	1039.17	692.32
Dispersed Ent.	571.86	342.84	Dispersed Ent.	683.45	54638
% differences in mean output	76.4		% differences in mean output	52.1	
Sample Size=36			Sample Size=36		

Source: Author's field survey, calculations by the author (see appendix 4.1, 4.1a 4.2 and 4.2a)

The question is, which factors contribute to or explain the differences in performance of enterprises in the cluster better relative to others located elsewhere? Three empirical considerations namely: output per worker, enterprises employment potential and average sales per worker were used to analyse the differences in the two production scenarios. As shown in the table, there are differences in mean output per worker in both normal and seasonal production periods. In normal production period, the difference in mean output per worker between firms in clustered and those located elsewhere is 76.4 per cent. During

110 The was confirmed by Mr Francis Chukwu, Chairman Power line Shoemakers association who argued that weak quality of adhesives of international standard, poor mechanised system of shoe coupling and poor training in terms of updating entrepreneurial knowledge in shoe industry have contributed to low firm performance in terms of international standard (18.05.05: Time, 14pm to 15.30pm).

111 The "very poor" in this contest, refer to the population living under the expenditure of US$1 per day.

112 See Daniels and Mead, 1998, p. 5 for the factors that hinder data collection in small enterprises related economic activities in developing countries -

the boom period, the mean output difference is 52.1 per cent. Since the technological application in the firms is the same. The survey shows that there is no evidence of joint action that could possibly enhance production or reduce costs in the cluster. The only information available here is the horizontal cooperation that entails sharing of tools. This cannot effectively explain the impact of clustering on small enterprises better. The second option is to examine the differences in enterprise employment potential (EEP) in both production scenarios.

As shown in Table 4.6, EEP is simply derived by dividing the arithmetic mean of total labour intake by total number of firms in the investigative sample and multiply the result by 100. Table 4.6 shows that during normal production, there is a 1.319 percentage point difference of EEP between enterprises in the cluster and those located elsewhere. During the boom period, there is a percentage point difference of 1.85.

Table 4.6: Enterprises employment potential (EEP) in the footwear

Indicators		Normal	Seasonal
	Clustered Enterprises	5.40	8.72
EEP (in %)	Dispersed Enterprises	4.09	6.87
	Percentage point difference	1.32	1.85

Source: Author's field survey, calculation by author (see appendix 4.1; 4.3)

This suggests that small enterprises have capacity to generate create employment (hypothesis A)[113]. This also suggests that under a favourable economic environment or during economic growth period, employment intake in small enterprise footwear cluster will increase by 1.85 per cent than those located elsewhere. However, difference in EEP is not sufficient to explain the impact of clustering on small enterprises with respect to employment creation and firm performance. The third option is to investigate if the relatively high sales recorded by enterprises in cluster are due to relatively higher productivity per worker. In other words, there could be internal and external factors which influence higher productivity in the cluster area than those located elsewhere. To investigate this, significant test analyses on the differences between the mean monthly sales per worker in both production scenarios was performed (Appendix 4.5). A sample of 36 enterprises in stratum A (Cluster) and 36 enterprises in stratum B (Dispersed) are subjected to significant testing. The aim is to investigate if the difference in performance indicator (gross sales per worker) is statistically significant.

113 Hypothesis A: There is positive correlation between SME growth and employment creation (chapter 1, page 7).

As shown in Table 4.7, difference in the mean monthly sales per worker in stratum A (cluster) and stratum B (dispersed) during the normal and seasonal production periods are statistically significant at 5 per cent. During the normal production period, the mean sales per worker in cluster area are higher than those enterprise located elsewhere by a margin of 118,138.5 (35%). During the seasonal period, the difference in the mean monthly sales per work is 106,493.84 (26.48%). Since all enterprises in the sample are within micro and small enterprises category, the location effects therefore overrule the size effects. The difference in mean monthly sales per worker can be explained by several factors attributed to spatial clustering which reduces cost (hypothesis B)[114].

Table 4.7: Mean monthly sales per worker in footwear enterprises

Mean normalmonthly sales per worker				
Sample Size=36	Mean	S.D	t-test	Prob. Value
Clustered Ent.	455242.7	27361.635	2.287	0.05
Dispersed Ent	337104.2	136244.818		
Mean seasonalmonthly sales per worker				
Sample Size=36	Mean	S.D	t-test	Prob. Value
Clustered Ent.	508641.6	2303362.42	2.178	0.05
Dispersed Ent.	402147.76	175019.224		

Source: Author's field survey; calculations by the author (see Appendix 4.2-4.6)

The cost saving factors in the cluster arises from reduced search costs, workshop costs, transport costs as well as matching of inputs such as labour and material. The impact of reduced cost is reflected on the low unit cost which makes firms in the cluster to enjoy market advantage of economies of scales. Higher sales per worker in the cluster areas can be linked to the impact of externalities and concentration of demand due to relatively high density of similar activities. In this case, information about market conditions such as price changes and new knowledge on product demands are quickly generated, hence firms can quickly respond to such changes. Concentration of firms and service providers in the cluster help reduce diseconomies of scale and scope in the sense that each small production unit (shoe tailors, shoe smoothing units, shoe makers and stamping) are structured to respond to customers needs and timing in order to improve sales turnover. This means that there is likelihood that few unsold items will be recorded in the cluster areas[115].

114 Hypothesis B: Proximity enhances the economic performance of small enterprises (chapter 1, page 7).

115 The extent to which the profitability of the firms in the cluster is affected by product price and volume remains an open question.

The fourth investigation concerns the relationship between the employment intake and sales volume. Table 4.8 shows the values of the correlation coefficient of the sales volume and employment intake in small enterprises. The value shows a high positive correlation during the normal production. With standard error estimate of 0.9706, there are 70 per cent chances that an increase in sales volume during the normal production period more workers will be employed. Hence the number of workers employed during normal production period is closely associated with sales volume of the enterprise. At 1.2684 standard error estimate, there are 80.6 per cent chances that employment intake will increase during peak periods and falls thereafter[116]. This suggests that under favourable macroeconomic environment, creation of new market and skill development the potential of small enterprises as means of job creation would be enhanced (hypothesis A).

Table 4.8: Correlation between the sales volume and enterprises employment intake

Clustered Enterprises	Normal	Seasonal
Correlation coefficient of sales volume and employment intake (r^2)	0.70 0.9706*	0.806 1.2684*

Note: * = are the standard error estimates for employment intake
Source: Author's field survey, calculation by the author (see appendix 4.5 and 4.6)

In terms of income generation, researchers have tried to explore empirically the role of small enterprises in poverty reduction[117]. Table 4.9 shows the average monthly cash earnings by labour type expressed in US Dollar at official exchange rate as at December 2007. The average monthly wage earning is US$96.49 in clustered shoemakers as against US$85.58 for those operating elsewhere. The monthly wage earnings in shoe tailor, smoothing and stamping units are US$69.86, US$77.91 and US$39.73 respectively. The highest total average monthly cash earning of US$146.63 was recorded in clustered shoemaker production unit. This is followed by shoe smoothing with average total monthly cash earnings of US$125.12. The shoemakers operating outside the cluster recorded total average monthly cash earning of US$119.79 lower that those in the cluster with US$146.63. While the total monthly cash earnings in shoe tailor and shoe stamping units averaged US$117.3 and US$75.54 respectively.

---

116 This supports Liedholm and Mead (1998) argument that during the boom period, employment in small enterprises tend to grow and fall subsequently.

117 An overview of income generating potential of small enterprises can be checked in the following literatures: Sengenbergen and Pyke, 1992; Maldonado, 1995; Daniels and Mead, 1998,).

Table 4.9: Mean monthly cash earnings of entrepreneurs/workers in Aba small scale footwear enterprises cluster (in US$)

	Shoemaker (Cluster)	Shoemaker (Dispersed)	Shoe tailor	Smoothing	Stamping
Enterprises Heads					
Wages	136.47	98.514	155.04	109.82	39.73
Std	*(32.06)*	(25.35)	*(30.64)*	*(22.38)*	*(4.61)*
Paid skilled workers					
Wages	46.99	43.80	42.64	na	na
Std	*(8.84)*	(3.78)	*(6.33)*		
Allowance	26.32	24.74	29.84	na	na
Std	*(5.37)*	(4,7)	*(5.43)*		
Bonus	na				
Std	na				
Paid unskilled workers					
Wages	33.59	34.88	32.95	30.04	na
Std	*(2.24)*	(5.48)	(2.74)	*(4.11)*	
Allowance	18.81	21.71	21.71	23.88	na
Std	*(2.5)*	(5.91)	(6.14)	*(3.07)*	
Bonus	na	na	na	na	
Std	na	na	na	na	
Apprentices					
Wages	na			na	na
Std	na			na	na
Allowance	46.40	47.21	48.19	48.84	35.81
Std	*(5.43)*	(6.23)	*(3.57)*	*(4.60)*	*(4.60)*
Bonus	12.4	10.34	8.53	10.85	na
Std	*(1.60)*	(1.79)	*(1.55)*	*(2.19)*	na
Average monthly cash earnings in all					
Wages	96.49	85.58	69.86	77.91	39.73
Std	(55.90)	(33.04)	(58.76)	(46.52)	*(4.61)*
Allowance	37.74	23.87	38.91	36.36	35.81
Std	(12.26)	(4.16)	(12.19)	(14.76)	*(4.60)*
Bonus	12.4	10.34	8.53	10.85	na
Std	*(1.60)*	(1.79)	*(1.55)*	*(2.19)*	na
Total Average monthly cash earnings	146.63	119.79	117.3	125.12	75.54

Note: Workers wages were computed on the bases of weekly wage payment to workers, daily feeding allowances and weekend pocket money. Enterprises Heads' income were calculated based on personal out-of-pocket weekly expenses, monthly expenditure on housing, family maintenance upkeep etc. plus average monthly savings. The Naira - US$ exchange ratewa taken at US$1 to N129.00 at 30.12. 2007

Source: Based on Author's field survey (see appendix 4.8 for calculation of wages, allowances and Bonus in Naira).

The Table also indicates that with exception of stamping, the total cash earnings in the cluster are higher than those located elsewhere. The low values of standard deviations indicate that wages, allowances and bonus are closely dispersed. Thus, suggesting that earnings in small enterprises sector fall within the same income bracket. The apprentices are not wages earners but their daily allowances and weekend bonus are more than the wages of skilled workers. The implication is that small scale entrepreneurs in footwear industry that make use of more apprentices indirectly bear more costs than those with paid skilled or unskilled workers. The table generally indicates that the wages of the workers are below the minimum wage for the private sector which stands at US$50 (or N5500) per month, and unskilled workers have comparatively much lower earnings.

4.4.2.6 Constraints faced by Aba Small Scale Footwear Enterprises Cluster

The major constraints faced by the firms in the cluster face are not only related to business uncertainty in Nigerian economy but specific problems that retard their economic activities. Asked to mention the major problems that constraints their economic activities. Constraints specific to individual firms were reported and were ranked according to order of highest severity.

Figure 4.3: Distribution of interviewees' perceptions to their major constraints in Aba small scale footwear enterprises cluster in % of sample size

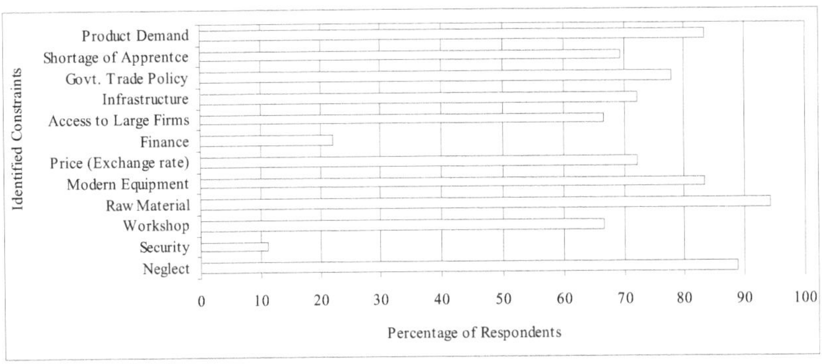

Key: Govt. = Government

Source: Author's field survey, (derived from data in Appendix 4.9)

Over the sample, 94.4 per cent of interviewees reported shortage of raw materials as the major factors that retard production in the cluster. Price due to exchange rate fluctuations and government trade policy are the two factors tied to shortage of raw materials in the cluster. Through experience, the interviewees maintained that appreciation of Naira against foreign currency reduces the prices of import but have a negative impact on their export market. However, exchange rate instability tends to affect production negatively because traders increase the price of imported raw materials arbitrarily on the pretence of exchange rate situation. Moreover, government use different methods such as high tariffs and levies on imported leather and other related raw materials without designing measures to improve the quality of local manufactured leather. 88.9 per cent of the respondents used the word 'neglect' to reflect on government attitude and passive nature of the local authorities with regards their contribution to the economy. The interviewees recognised the need for skilled development and constant upgrading of knowledge. Hence shortage of apprentices and low skilled workers affects the cluster negatively. Other factors that amount to neglect are poor state of infrastructure. For example, 100 per cent of energy supply to cluster is private provision, access roads are in dilapidated conditions; workshops are crowded such that production activities are impeded. 83.3 per cent of respondents linked poor quality of their products to lack of modern equipment. Security and finance are considered to be part the problems the enterprises face in the cluster but are ranked lowest. Only 22.2 per cent of the respondents see finance as a major problem while 11.1 per cent consider loss of product due to theft and robbery as social problem in the economy. Internal security system was developed through the organisational structure in the cluster.

4.4.2.7 Remarks

This study revealed some characteristics of spatial clustering with evidence of specialisation and inter-firm linkages that form the basis for sub-contracting. Despite absence of formal institution in the cluster, inter-firm linkages helped to minimise uncertainty and reduction of production costs. However, enforcement of quality and technical standards in production process is not possible due to lack of formal institutional support[118]. There is no trace of joint action initiatives hence the concept of collective efficiency for growth strategy has been undermined. The local authorities are busy collecting different forms of levies without providing services. At the time of the survey, Aba city had the worst infrastructure in the region. The only external support to the cluster is the recent

118 For example, Standard Organisation of Nigeria (SON) has not be able to come up with concrete measures to support quality improvement in order to have access to wider market (Interview with Mr Francis Chukwu, Chairman Power line Shoemakers association 18.05.05: Time, 14pm to 15.30pm).

UNIDO initiatives that tend to provide advisory services on quality related problems and small enterprises empowerment in Aba[119].

Five factors which led to the growth of Aba footwear enterprises cluster are the civil war, oil boom, changes in nominal and real income, structural adjustment effect and liberalisation policy. At the end of civil war in Eastern region, demand for domestic footwear products increased due to low wages in early 1970s. The demand for locally made footwear was relatively high as a result of low income. The oil boom of mid 1970s and subsequent increase in wages by government civil service wage review commission (known as "Udoji Award") pushed the demand for higher quality foreign made footwear products from Italy, Spain and Brazil high. Consequently, the demand for locally made footwear declined during the period. The implementation of Structural Adjustment Programme (SAP) created a contraction in real income hence the demand for locally made footwear increased again and demand for foreign products also drastically declined. The sector also witnessed increased number of new entry of entrepreneurs as Nigerian unemployment crisis sharpened during the SAP. Liberalisation on the other hand created competitive scenario such that producers have to introduce strategies to contain the pressure of cheap products from China and Dubai.

4.4.3 Aba small and medium scale garment enterprises cluster

4.4.3.1 Introduction

Garment manufacturing in Aba is directly linked to migrants from Bende communities and has history that spanned from colonial time. Bende is a colonial district in Eastern region of Nigeria located in present North-Eastern part of Abia State. The cluster formation in Aba town began as migrants with specialised skill in weaving and tailoring expanded in the area settled by Bende indigenes. The workshops were located within the residents of the entrepreneurs which later formed the nucleus of the cluster (Meagher, 2005, p. 8)[120]. Unlike shoe production, garment production is relatively capital intensive and require special skills. Vocational training in weaving and sewing initiated by early missionaries for women in the Bende provided the background skill development in tailoring. Initial capital for industrialisation was raised through early trading activities on textile and second-hand clothes. Over time, trading-networks were developed which became the distribution channel of the manu-

---

119 Interview with Mr Amah, UNIDO Cluster National Expert on 17 06 05, between 2.30-3.50.

120 This is a collaboration between author's field survey and interview with Mr Divine Heat, Secretary of Aba garment producers cooperative union on 14.05.05, 12.30-14pm

factured products. There is division of functions among the Bende entrepreneurs such that traders provide business related information, supply of raw materials and credits to the producers.

4.4.3.2 Methodology

The empirical analysis is based on the assumption that competitiveness of small enterprises is a function of capital stock and level of technological application within the firm (Lall, 2001, p. 1509)[121]. Four indicators were used to analyse the local competitiveness of garment producers. They include level of education of enterprise heads and workers, skill of workforce, nature and age of technology in use. The nature of technology in use is classified into those operating with second hand machines only, new machines only and those with mixture of new and old machines. The analysis is focused on the relationship between quality of skill workforce, technology and competitiveness in the local market. The technology root in the firm is assumed to be zero since all equipment is externally imported.

4.4.3.3 Informality characteristics

Table 4.10 shows that firms in the cluster neither met the annual tax obligations nor paid the minimum wage level of 5,500 Naira stipulated for private sector in Nigeria. Unlike the footwear cluster, 18.8 per cent of the firms are officially registered. 67 per cent of the firms in the sample operate under the local government regulation by paying all levies prescribed by the local authority.

Table 4.10: Regulatory indicators as informality characteristics

Some Informality indicators	In Percentage
Percentage of Firm Officially Registered	18.80
Percentage of Firms that met Tax obligations/ Keeping of account	0.00
Percentage of Firms that met Minimum Wage Requirements	0,00
Percentage of firms Operating within Local Government Regulations	67.00

Source: Author's field survey

121 The capital stock includes level of education, workforce skills and attitude, and managerial talent. Other forms of capital stock are the quality of legal interventions, regulatory practices governing business as well as social capital that contribute to the quality of overall capital stock. Technology includes the technological knowledge embedded in nation's scientific and technological institutions as well as those rooted in the firm (Lall, 2001, p. 1509). In this study we considered two aspects of capital stocks namely educational level, the skill of the workforce and the regulatory practices.

Table 4.11 shows that the average number of regular paid workers in the cluster including the skilled and unskilled workers is 3.2. The average number of apprentices and unpaid workers such as family members is 2.1 and 0.6 respectively. 12 per cent of the firms in the sample are without unpaid or paid workers. This indicates high incidence of sole proprietorship and indivisibility of functions[122]. Average number of seasonal workers of 1.1 is recorded in the sub-sector.

Table 4.11: Labour force indicators as informality characteristics

Indicators	Value
Average No of Regular Paid Workers	3.2
Average No of Apprentices	2.1
Average No of Seasonal Workers	1.1
Firms without Workers (in %)	12.0
Average No of Unpaid Workers per firm	0.6

Source: Author's field survey

4.4.3.4 Competitive Factors in Aba small and medium scale garment enterprises cluster

Competitiveness has become common slogan in the policy discourse in many African countries. However, little attention is given to underlying factors that support competition. Economists define competitiveness in different form. The first is based on macroeconomic framework in terms of real exchange rate, full employment, and persistent current account position. The measure of competitiveness in this context is the relative price/or cost indices expressed in some common currency (Boltho, 1996, p. 3). The second definition is based on the structural factors affecting medium to long term economic performance such as productivity, innovation, skills in terms of human capital stock (Fagerberg, 1996). The latter can be referred to what (Lall and Kraemer-Mbula, 2005, pp. 55-56) considered as competitive laxity in Africa which form the basis of this study. As shown in Table 4.12, the education of heads of enterprise did not change significantly in comparison to the firm size. 59.7 per cent of workers and enterprise heads in the total sample had primary education while 39.4 per cent had secondary education.

122 This leads to the argument that 'non-specialisation is a form of insurances when costs and uncertainties of transacting are high (North 1990, p. 34).

Table 4.12: Education Level of enterprises heads and workers expressed in percentage of sample number across firm size

Sample Object	Sample No	Primary Education	Secondary Education	Post Secondary Education	Skilled Tailors
Enterprises Heads		No. (%)	No. (%)	No. (%)	No. (%)
Micro	24	10 (0.357)	12 (0.536)	2 (0.12)	18 (0.75)
Small	3	1 (0.333)	2 (0.667)	na	2 (0.667)
Medium	1	1 (1.0)	na	na	
Manager					
Micro	24	10 (0.5)	14 (0.583)	na	15 (0.625)
Small	3	na	3 (1.0)	na	2 (0.667)
Medium	1	na	1 (1.0)	na	
All workers including					
Manager	74	46 (0.622)	28 (0.378)	na	38 (0.514)
Micro	37	25 (0.676)	12 (0.48)	na	21 (0.568)
Small	54	39 (0.722)	15 (0.278)	na	33 (0.611)
Medium					
Sample Total	221	132(0.597)	87 (0.393)	2 (0.01)	
Total skilled Tailors including managers and Enterprises heads	129	85(0.644)* (0.385)**	44 (0.506)* (0. 199)**	na	129 (0.535)

Key: * = Expressed as percentage of total number of those that had primary or secondary education;
** = expressed as percentage of sample total

Source: Author's own field survey

Only 1 per cent of enterprise heads in micro enterprises had education beyond secondary school. The Table also shows that 75 and 66.7 per cent of enterprises heads in micro and small enterprises respectively had vocational training in tailoring. Over the sample, 53.5 per cent of the workers and enterprise heads are trained tailors. The scenario however portrayed a different picture when the educational level of skilled tailors including the enterprise heads and workers are considered. The total number of skilled tailors (including enterprises heads and managers) expressed as a percentage of total number of those that had primary education and secondary (basic education) is 64.4 and 50.6 per cent respectively. When expressed as percentage of total sample, 38.5 per cent of the skilled tailor had primary education while only 19.9 per cent received secondary education.

Table 4.13 shows the nature of technology in use in the cluster. According to the survey, 25 per cent of micro enterprises started with new machines. 14 per cent of the firms in the sample started with mixture of new and second-hand machines while 60.7 per cent use second hand machines only[123].

123 The second-hand machines are quite obsolete. Equipment age is determined by the date of purchase plus the 10 years depreciation period of the origin.

Table 4.13: Nature of technology

Sample size	Micro (24)	Small (3)	Medium (1)	All (in %)
No. of firms started with new machines only	7	na	na	0.25
Average No of firms with mixture of new/secondhand machines	3	1	na	0.14
Average No of firms with Second hand machines only	14	2	1	0.607

Source: Author's own field survey

As shown in Table 4.14, the minimum average age of the equipments in the sampled firms is 8.50 while the maximum average age is 20.50. Table 4.14 shows that the mean age of the equipment in the cluster is 15.083 while the mean age of the firm is 13.482[124]. This suggests that the firms have little or limited access to modern technology.

Table 4.14: The mean age of equipment

Mini.	Max.	Mean	Std	Std Error
8.5 0	20.50	15.083	3,299	1.615

Source: Author's field survey

4.4.3.5 Average monthly cash earnings in Aba small and medium scale garment enterprises cluster

Table 4.15 highlights the income situation in Aba garment cluster expressed in US$. There are no differences in wage earnings in micro and small enterprises in the cluster. However, income becomes higher as firm move up to medium size. Over the sample, the average cash earnings in garment cluster are below the minimum wage of US$50 for private sector. The use of more apprentices is high in garment industry. The production cost is relatively low in garment enterprises because firms make use of more apprentices (i.e. unpaid workers with low allowances or bonus) than paid workers. This is relatively low in garment than the footwear industry because most of the applentices come from their respective homes.

124 The low standard deviation implies that the age of the equipment is clustered around the mean.

Table 4.15: Average monthly wage earnings of entrepreneurs/workers in Aba small and medium scale garment enterprises (in US$)

	Micro	Small	Medium
Average wage earning of enterprises heads	77.52	77.52	116.27
Paid skilled workers	31.01	31.01	34.88
Paid unskilled workers	23.26	23.26	27.13
Apprentices allowance	7.75	7.75	na
Average cash earnings	34.89	34.89	44.57

Note: Workers wages were computed on the basis of monthly wage payment to workers, Enterprises Heads income was calculated based on personal out-of-pocket weekly expenses, monthly expenditure on housing, family maintenance upkeep plus average monthly savings. The Naira equivalent of US$ is based on exchange rate of US$1 to N129.00 at 30 12.07.

Source: Author's field survey

4.4.3.6 Factors Affecting the Growth of Aba Small and Medium Scale Garment Enterprises Cluster

The growth of Aba small and medium scale garment enterprises cluster is not only affected by internal constraints but also due to several external problems facing the sub-sector. The responses from interviewers on the factors that hinder production activities indicate common problems that are divergent in perception. Figure 4.4 shows that 89 per cent of the entrepreneurs interviewed linked the problem of infrastructure to the case of neglect by the authorities. The dilapidated nature of the access roads and frequent power failure are often cited as examples. More than 96.4 per cent of the interviewees gave government trade policy as the reason for shortage of raw materials. The respondents argued that import restrictions on foreign inputs have paralysed the production activities in Nigeria's apparel industry. Most of the local textile industries have been forced out of production due to low quality of products that can no longer compete in current Nigeria's fashion industry. The interviewees were asked if liberalisation measures have any effect on their firm performance. Three factors which affect productivity emerged. 92.9 per cent of the interviewees insist that the nature of old technology applied hinder production. The respondents argued that since their financial strength cannot afford modern technology, they have to rely on old second-hand equipment. 89.3 per cent of the interviewees considered shortage of skilled workers and educational level of the skill workers as major challenge. They acknowledged that the sub-sector is competitive and required creative designers that can go along with fashion trend. 85.7 per cent of the entrepreneurs interviewed linked poor local demand of their products to price and quality. They argued their products were created as an alternative since those consumers that cannot afford foreign products resort to locally produced ones. 71.4 per cent of the interviewees insist that product upgrading in the cluster is limited partly due to financial constraints to acquire modern equipment and partly due to present a low level of skilled workforce.

Figure 4.4: Distribution of interviewees' perceptions to their major constraints in Aba small scale garment enterprises cluster in % of sample size

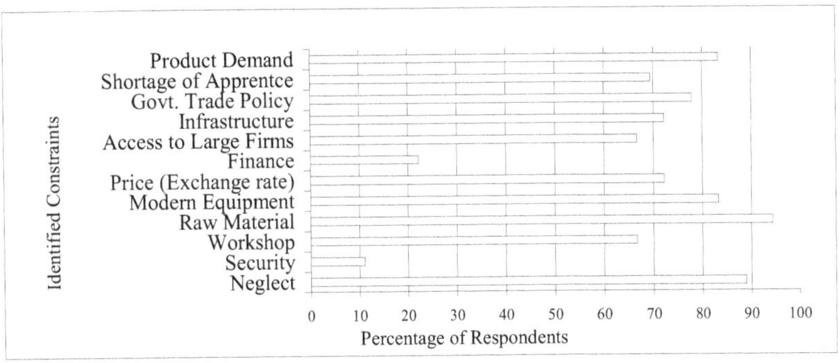

Key: Govt. = Government
Source: Author's field survey, (derived from data in Appendix 4.9)

4.4.3.7 Remarks

Two forms of production activities were identified in the cluster namely: Direct market supply and production by order. In the former, the producers supply their products directly to the market through their trading networks. In the latter, agents were used to get contracts for production of school uniform for academic education institutions and organisations. Unlike footwear, the garment enterprises have been unable to enhance strategies to sustain the liberalisation pressure. According to the interviewees, the external factors affecting the sub-sector negatively include increased imports of finished products from Asia, change in test of domestic consumers, government partial prohibition of imported textiles and high demand for second-hand clothes. In general, the garment enterprises failed to identify market niches effectively and cannot maintain the quality standard to accommodate the changing consumer test. Poor business environment and weak inter-firm relations undermine entrepreneurship efforts in the sub-sector. The internal constraints identified in the sub-sector are low skill workers and technology problem. The firms use obsolete machines which have high energy consumption rate. Unlike footwear enterprises cluster, the networks in garment enterprises cluster are not innovative enough in finding solutions to the market changes so that economies of scale can be achieved. The cluster has not managed to forge collective action in order to improve quality, to facilitate access to large external markets.

4.4.4 Enugu Small Scale Wood and Furniture Enterprises Cluster

4.4.4.1 Introduction

In Enugu, there are several units of small wood and furniture enterprises clusters located in different parts of the city[125]. The history of modern wood and furniture enterprises in the area is linked to the return of retrenched wartime soldiers after the Second World War. Soldiers that received vocational training in modern handicrafts during the British colonial Military service formed the Enugu carpenter's union in 1946. The objectives of the union are; to commercialise their newly acquired knowledge during the military service; to promote woodwork handicrafts; to transfer their newly acquired knowledge to younger generation through informal vocational training. The historical development and the economic activities of two clusters namely Ogui and Asata carpenters union were analysed investigated in the author's previous work on cluster in 2001 and were also revisited in field survey of 2003/4 and 2005.

4.4.4.2 Methodology

The question this sub-sector tends to answer is; are Enugu small scale wood and furniture enterprises clusters exploiting the advantages of scale economies after 60 years of existence? The analysis starts with brief discussion on the structure of firms and their informality characteristics related to regulatory and the nature of labour in the production. Following this is the evaluation of the competitive factors of the enterprises in terms of educational level of workers and enterprises heads as well as technologies in the production. Inter-firm relationships and linkages in the cluster are also investigated. The constraints that hinder growth in the sub-sector and how enterprises in the cluster tried to sustain production over some decades without institutional support are also examined.

4.4.4.3 Sample structure

The firm structure indicates three major production units, that is; sawmill enterprises unit, wood construction unit, and upholstery/office furniture manufacturing unit. As indicated in Table 4.16, 91.3 per cent of the firms in the cluster are micro while 8.7 percent are small enterprises by definition. Over the sample, internal organisation revealed an unorganised production system typical

---

125 see Uzor, 2004

of the informal sector with workshops divided proportionately but over crowded.

Table 4.16: Structure of sampled enterprises in Enugu small scale wood and furniture enterprises cluster

Sector	Sawmill	Furniture		Total
		Wood Const	Upholstery	
Micro Enterprises	3	6	12	21 (0.913)
Small Enterprises	1	na	1	2 (0.087)
Medium Enterprises.	na	na	na	na
Total	4	6	13	23

Source: Author's field survey

4.4.4.4 Informality Characteristics

As shown in Table, 4.17, only 4.3 percent of the sampled enterprises are officially registered. None of the enterprises in the cluster met the tax obligations or maintained formal business records. The Table shows that 82.6 per cent of the firms pay wages above official minimum wage of US$50.00 for private sector and 30.4 per cent of the firms operate under stipulated government regulation by paying the various local government levies.

Table 4.17: Some regulatory indicators as informality characteristics

Indicators	Sawmills	Furniture		% of All
		Wood Const.	Upholstery	
Percentage of Firm Officially Registered	0.25	0.00	0.00	0.043
Percentage of Firms that met Tax obligations/ Keeping of account	0.00	0.00	0.00	0.00
Percentage of Firms that met Minimum Wage Requirements	0.75	0.833	0.845	0.826
Percentage of firms Operating within Local Government Regulations	0.25	0.333	0.307	0.304

Key: Wood Const. = Wood Construction

Source: Author's field survey

The type of labour force in the cluster is shown in the table 4.18. The average number of paid workers (skilled and unskilled) is 1.6 while the apprentices working in the cluster per enterprise averaged 2.5. Enterprises without paid and unpaid workers averaged 4 per cent. This suggests that wood and furniture enterprises unit make use of more apprentices. On the other hand, no family members and seasonal workers were identified in the cluster.

Table 4.18: Labour force indicators as informality characteristics

Indicators	Value
Average No of Regular Paid Workers	1.6
Average No of Apprentices	2.5
Average No of Seasonal Workers	0.0
Firms without Workers (in %)	0.4
Average No of Unpaid Workers	0.0

Source: Author's field survey

4.4.4.5 Linkages in Enugu small scale wood and furniture enterprises clusters

Figure 4.5 shows a relatively dense inter-firm relationship in the cluster. Sawmill and wood construction enterprises units play the role of middle link between the timber dealers and the furniture makers. The timber dealers are the suppliers of major woods. They source wood across the forest regions of Nigeria, saw the timber into planks and transport them to Enugu timber market[126].

Figure 4.5: Linkages in the Enugu small scale wood and furniture enterprises cluster

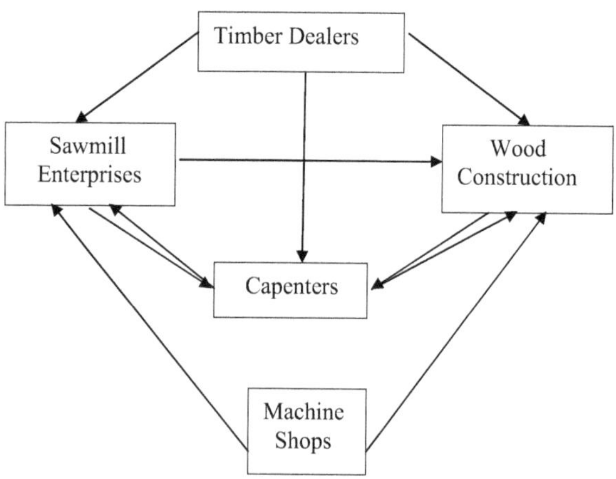

Source: Author's field survey

Timber dealers are classified into timber trading merchants and timber sawmill/trading merchants diversifying either milling and trading on woods or

126 The forest regions comprises Nsukka, Benue Cross-River and Delta regions

only on milling[127]. The wood construction enterprises are responsible for shaping the wood according to specifications designed by the capenters. The machine shops in the cluster on the other hand, provide the basic technology for sawmill and wood construction units. The technologies/equipment is the saw blades, curving machines and cutting machines. They also offer equipment maintenance services especially repair of old imported second hand mechines. As shown in table 4.19 above, the entire system indicates a value chain framework in the sense that each or group of entrepreneur(s) specialise in different activities and offer different products ranging from sourcing of wood, service delivery to manufacturing of the end products.

Table 4.19: Specialisation in Enugu small scale wood and furniture enterprises cluster

Enterprises Units	Specialisation	
	Activities	Products
Timber Dealers	Sourcing of woods. Wholesale/ retail sale of Wooden planks	Wooden raw materials
Sawmill	Cutting of wood ploughs to planks of different sizes	Services
Wood Construction	Construction of product according to designs.	Services
Wooden Furniture	Designing and Manufacturing	Upholstery furniture seats, wardrobes, beds, bedside-tables, shelves, door and window Frames, school seats, school tables and office cabinets

Sources: Own field survey

4.4.4.6 Competitive factors in Enugu small scale wood construction and furniture enterprises clusters

Carpentry is a traditional industry that requires basic technical skills such as standards in measurement and accuracy as well as wood treatment. Table 4.20 shows that 23.1 and 16.7 per cent of enterprise heads in small scale furniture and wood construction received formal technical training respectively. 5.5 and 11.1 per cent of workers in furniture and wood construction received formal technical training. Over the sample, only 8.5 per cent of enterprise heads and workers had formal technical training in wood and furniture. The implication is that when 91.5 per cent of the work force lacks formal technical knowledge, production efficiency in terms of standard and product quality will be low. In this context, the study supports Lall and Kraemer-Mbula, (2005, p. 56) argued that very low

127 Diversification however depends on the financial strength of the entrepreneur.

intensity of technical skill contributes to negative outcome of Africa's industrial development efforts[128]. Over the sample, 62.7 and 27.1 percent of enterprises heads and workers attended primary and secondary school respectively while only 1.7 went beyond secondary school level. This also suggests that entrepreneurial managerial skill will be very low in the sub-sector.

Table 4.20: Educational Level of enterprises heads and workers expressed in percentage of sample number across firm size

Branch	Sample No.	Primary only	up to Secondary	Post-Secondary	Vocational/ Technical
Sawmill					
Enterprises Heads	4	0.25	0.25	0.50	na
Workers	22	0.727	0.273	na	na
Wood construction					
Enterprises Heads	6	0.50	0.333	na	0.167
Workers	18	0.667	0.222	na	0.111
Furniture					
Enterprises Heads	13	0.538	0.231	na	0.231
Workers	55	0.636	0.291	na	0.055
Total Sample	118	0.627	0.271	0.017	0.085

Key: value in decimal multiply by 100

Source: Own field survey

The nature and level of technological application in the subsector are shown in Table 4.21. As shown in the Table, there is absence of the new or modern equipment. Technology application in the cluster comprises old second-hand machines and locally constructed sawmill machines. The locally constructed machines are powered by refurbished old electric motors. The fluctuation in energy supply often results to break down of entire production system. The upholstery production unit make use of basic hand tools and spraying machines.

Table 4.21: Nature and level of Technology

Branch	New/modern	Second Hand	Import/ Local machines
Sawmills	Obsolete	Very high	Imported and locally constructed
Wood Construction	Absence	Very high	Imported and locally constructed
Upholstery	Low level hand tools	Very high	Imported

Sources: Author's field survey

128 Africa's intensity of technical skill generation creation lay between 0.01 and 0.17 per cent. Intensity skill generation creation is technical tertiary enrolments expressed as a percentage of the population of the country (Lall & Kraemer-Mbula, 2005, pp. 56-58). Available data shows that the number of researchers in R&D per million people in Nigeria between 1990 and 2001 is 15 (UNDP, 2004a, p. 182).

As shown in Table 4.22, inter-firm relationship in the furniture makers is mainly in the form of sharing tools, information and knowledge sharing in furniture designs as well as sharing of transportation costs of woods from forest region. There is no evidence of vertical cooperation in the cluster. The bilateral actions among firms are focused only on costs reduction while multilateral action exists only between the firms and the Government technical collage, Enugu. The cooperation is related only to technical advice on new production system but not commercially oriented. The enterprises in the cluster offer students positions for practical work in wood and furniture.

Table 4.22: Inter-firms relationships and Forms of joint action in Enugu small scale furniture enterprises cluster

Type of Cooperation	Horizontal	Vertical
	- Sharing of hand tools - sharing information and knowledge on designs - sharing transport costs -Sharing central saw machines	None
Type of joint Action	Bilateral	Multilateral
	- Joint sourcing and purchase of woods from forest region and - joint purchase Planks at reduced unit costs and cost transportation	Weak

Sources: Own field survey

4.4.4.7 Constraints in Enugu small scale wood construction and furniture enterprises Clusters

There are several factors that constrain the growth of Enugu small scale wood and furniture enterprises cluster. According to survey, 95.6 per cent of the interviewees linked the major constraints in the cluster to lack of skilled workforce. The technical skilled training in the cluster is based on informal apprenticeship system. The survey shows that production depends on household demand because government direct procurement has declined over decades. The implication is that macroeconomic strategy should aim at stimulating income growth in the sub-sectoral through government intervention[129]. 91.3 per cent of the interviewees also argue that infrastructure especially access road, energy supply and workshop are major limitation to production. The trans-portation of wooden planks requires good access roads, the sawmill needs constant energy

129 Survey revealed that irregular and none payment of public workers' salary have reduced household demand for furniture products. The decline of direct government procurement was an indication of bad governance in the sense that the normal public contract awarding procedure through tender boarder has become invalid.

supply to work at full capacity and the workshops are so narrow for such labour intensive and bulky production activities. 69.6 per cent of the interviewees acknowledged that finance is a problem due to constraints related to access to credits and loans for investment.

Figure 4.6: Distribution of respondents' perceptions to their major constraints in Enugu small scale wood construction and furniture enterprises clusters

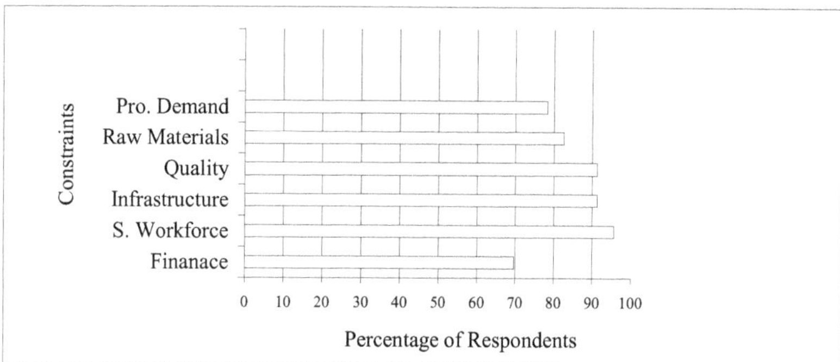

Key: Pro. Demand = Product Demand, S. Workforce = Skilled Workforce
Sources: Author's field survey (derived from data in Appendix, 4.12)

4.4.4.8 Remarks

The major limitations identified in the cluster include the neglect of forestry department in the value chains. An efficient wood and furniture cluster starts with effective forestry department that is responsible for reforestation and control of deforestation activities. This is very weak in the region as a result weak environmental law and institutions responsible for environmental protection. The entrepreneurs are ignorant of social costs of the wood and furniture industry in the economy. Hence there is no identified action programme among the users of natural resources with regards to sustainability of the ecosystem[130]. Integration of forestry development unit in wood and furniture value chains process is fundamental in order to avoid the break down of the ecosystem. Forestry is an important public good hence the need for private-public partnership in the development wood/furniture industrial cluster. There is weak government policy on wood related technology development or promoting the

130 The average annual deforestation increased from 0.7 percent in 1980-1990 to 0.9 in 1990-1995 and to 2.6 percent in 1990-2000. The total annual deforestation is estimated at about 400,000 ha as against reforestation of about a 1,043 ha (CBN, 2002, p. 153). This has negative consequences not only on Nigeria's wood and furniture industry, but also on the entire ecosystem.

sector in order to improve quality. The survey shows that skill development in the sub-sector is very weak. In Enugu region, only one technical college is functional and those established by NGOs in the early 1960s have been converted to normal secondary school due to poor funding. Firms lack access to modern equipment in order to improve standard. Most of the technological application in the sub-sector is old second-hand machines or locally constructed machines with high energy consumptions. The enterprises in the cluster have not been able to improve quality to international (ISO) standard in order to penetrate markets beyond the national boundary. Access to modern machines can enhance technology diffusion in the sector and increase production of better quality.

4.4.5 Nnewi small and medium scale light engineering enterprises cluster

4.4.5.1 Introduction

Light engineering industry is a diverse group of firms in a number of distinctive sectors such as low-tech items like casting, forgings and fasteners, to the highly sophisticated micro processors based on process control equipment and diagnostic medical instruments. The products covered under the light engine-eering industry are largely used as input to the capital goods industry. The demand for this sector depends on the demand of the capital goods industry[131].

The impact of social networks in development path of Nnewi light engineering cluster have cut the attention of researchers on African economic development in recent times. The cluster has been classified as the only organised cluster in Africa (UNCTAD, 1998, p. 6). Economic specialisation especially in motor spare parts has led to evolutionary process of social groupings, trust, trading norms and network formation. Such non state economic governance is imperative due to problems created by market and institutional failure especially in area of search and transaction costs (Bräutigam, 1997; Uzor, 2004). Despite numerous research attention given to Nnewi light engineering enterprises cluster in recent times. Unlike other clusters in Latin America and South East Asia, the cluster has not been able to forge into global market due to obvious reasons. This sub-section therefore examines the extent of the dynamic factors in the cluster and why the small firms in the cluster have not been able to forge linkages with large firms in the region.

131 Internet Source:Light Engineering Sector: http//dipp.nic.in/industry/content industries-/LIGHT sourced on 12 06.07 Time 21:49

4.4.5.2 Methodology

In this sub-section, the sample is grouped into manufacturing and service units. Under the manufacturing, the industrial spring manufacturing, foundry and metal fabrication/welding were investigated. The service sector comprises the machine shops and the automobile technicians. The spring production covers light industrial and automobile springs while foundry includes moulding of household utensils, motorcycle crouches, pedals and other motor-cycles related parts.

Table 4.23: Structure of sampled enterprises in Nnewi small and medium scale Light Engineering cluster

	Manufacturing			Services		
Sector	Spring	Foundry	Fabrication & Welding	Machine Shops	Automobile Technicians	Total
Micro Enterprises	2	2	2		6	12 (0.667)
Small Enterprises		1	2	1		4 (0.22)
Medium Enterprises		1		1		2 (0.11)
Total	2	4	4	2	6	18

Source: Author's field survey

The welding and fabrication are small scale producers that fabricate metal products for building and industrial usage. The machine shops are the engine-eering workshops that provide maintenance services for small and medium scale industries. The automobile technicians provide repair services for personal and commercial vehicles. The empirical analysis therefore focuses on the level of human capital, technology and the nature of raw materials applied in production. Table 4.23 indicates that 66.7 per cent of the firms are micro enterprises while 22 and 11 per cent of the enterprises are small and medium scale respectively.

4.4.5.3 Informality characteristics

As shown in Table 4.24, all firms in the spring manufacturing and automobile technicians represent a classical case of informal sector. Individually, they are not officially registered, no daily records of business activities, and fail to maintain tax obligations as well as not able to comply with all local regulatory obligations. The Table further indicates that machine shops are officially registered as corporate firms with 50 percent of them meeting tax obligations and minimum wage requirement. However, most of the firms have problems with local authority in terms of meeting the numerous local government regula-tions.

Table 4.24: Some regulatory indicators as informality characteristics

Indicators	*Manufacturing*			*Services*	
	Springs	Foundry	Fabr. & Welding	Machine Shop	Automobile Technicians
Percentage of firm officially registered	0.00	0.25	0.00	1.00	0.16
Percentage of firms that met tax obligations/ keeping of account	0.00	0.25	0.00	0.50	0.00
Percentage of Firms that met Minimum wage requirements	0.00	0.25	0.00	0.50	0.00
Percentage of firms operating within local government regulations	0.00	0.75	0.75	0.00	0.00

Key: Fabr. = Fabrication
Source: Author's field survey

Table 4.25 shows the type of labour force applied in the production. The average number of regular paid workers (skilled and unskilled) is 4.2. The apprentices averaged 1.6 and only 6 per cent of the firms are without workers and apprentices. There is no record indicating seasonal workers or unpaid workers.

Table 4.25: Labour force indicators as informality characteristics

Indicators	Value
Average No of regular paid workers	4.2
Average No of apprentices	1.6
Average No of seasonal workers	0
Firms without workers (in %)	0.06
Average No of unpaid workers	0

Source: Author's field survey

4.4.5.4 Competitive factors in Nnewi small and medium scale light engineering cluster

Lall, and Kraemer-Mbula, (2005, p. 22) argue that the skill base of a firm determines the technological learning path of the firm. In other words, the level and form of educational attainment of entrepreneurs and workers plays an important role in firm's production. Table 4.26 shows the problem in Nnewi light engineering cluster in terms of deficiency in technical knowledge per branch. Over the sample, only 4.3 per cent of the enterprise heads and workers have formal technical education. The springs and foundry manufacturing operate with workers and entrepreneurs without technical educational background. The machine shops recorded the highest number of enterprise heads with formal technical training.

Table 4.26: Educational level of the enterprises heads and workers expressed in percentage

Branch	Sample Size	Primary	Secondary	Post Secondary	Vocational/ Technical
Spring Manufacturing					
Enterprises Heads	2	0.50	0.50	0.00	0.00
Workers	8	0.625	0.375		
Foundry					
Enterprises Heads	4	0.25	0.75	0.25	0.00
Workers	43	0.302	0.698	0.00	0.00
Fabrication and Welding					
Enterprises	4	0.25	0.50	0.00	0.25
Workers	34	0.382	0. 529		0.088
Machine Shops					
Enterprises Heads	2	0.00	0.00	0.50	0.50
Workers	28	0.143	0.857	0.036	0.036
Automobile Technicians					
Enterprises Heads	6	0.50	0.333	0.00	0.167
Workers	9	0.778	0.222	0.00	0.00
Total Sample	140	0.336	0.60	0.022	0.042

Source: Own field survey

Table 4.26 also shows that 33.6 and 60 per cent of enterprise heads and workers attained primary and secondary school education respectively. Only 2.2 per cent had been educated beyond secondary school level. According to the sample, concentration of workers with primary education is relatively high in automobile technicians and spring manufacturers. The quality of a product depends not only on the nature of technological application but most importantly on the nature of raw materials used in producing the product. Many studies have shown that Africa's competitive dilemma rest not only on human capital but also on poor management, poor infrastructure, and lack of access to raw materials (Gerry, 1978, p. 1158; Schmitz, 1982, p. 439; Hansohm, 1992). These factors made it impossible for SMEs to develop supply linkages with large firms in the region

Table 4.27 shows that the use of scrape metal as raw material is relatively high in foundry and fabrication firms. The spring products are mainly made of scrape metal with low resistant quality and command less value relative to products with original raw materials. Table 4.27 reveal that technology in the cluster is a combination of old imported and locally fabricated machines. The small scale spring manufacturers and metal fabrication use only self constructed machines while the machine shops operate with imported but old second-hand machines[132]. The foundries visited operate with small furnaces of about 50 to 70kg capacity. The furnaces are used to convert scrap metal into aluminium ingots according to specification. Small firms like Aninna industries in Ichi town close to Nnewi is focusing on quality improvement by undertaking reconstruction and standardisation of some imported motorcycle parts from China.

Table 4.27: Nature of raw materials and technology in use

	Nature of Raw materials			Technology		
Branch	Scraps	New	Import/Local	Second Hand	New	Import/Locally constructed
Spring	Very High	na	local	na	na	Locally constructed only
Foundry	High	Limited	Import &Local	na	na	Imported/ Locally constructed
Fabrication and Welding	High	Limited	Local	na		Locally constructed only
Machine Shops	na	na		old	na	Imported

Source: Author's field survey

In 1990, some technology institutions started to provide basic services in terms of improving the capacity gap in Nnewi. Assisted by government of Germany, the Metallurgical Training Institute (MTI) was established in 1980 in Onitsha. The main focus of institute is to offer training programmes to personel in the metallurgical and allied industries in Nigeria. The Institute now offer short term courses in relevant to the needs of the Nnewi light engineering development programme. The courses include welding of ferrous and non-ferrous metals, design and analysis of electric motor controls, rewinding and repair of electrical machines, maintenance of hydraulically operated heavy duty equipment and machining processes. Nnewi Technology Business Incubator Centre (TBIC) was established in 1998 and operates under the Federal Ministry of Science and Technology. The objective of TBIC is to provide support services to the start-up firms and advisory services for new businesses engaged in value-added technology related activities. This is aimed at enhancing Nigeria's indigenous potential for economic growth. The centre however lacks the technical staff for such stereo-typed objectives. There is no evidence of formal collaboration with

132 The technologies include the centre lathe turning that performs basic operations such as turning, facing and some single point tread turning. Others are the milling machines of different kinds, small drill presses and large radial drilling machines; crankshaft regrinding machines; cylinder boring machines, surface grinding machines and smaller machines such as lathe tool grinder and powered hacksaws as well as electrical welding sets.

technical colleges needed in such technology business incubator programme[133]. Inadequate funding remains a major constraint in the centre hence limiting the pace of development of activities in the centre. The NEDDEC was established in 1999 with the mandate among other things, to improve the engineering designing capacity and dissemination of such capacity to Nigerian SMEs.

Figure 4.7: Linkages and Distribution Network in Nnewi Light Engineering Cluster

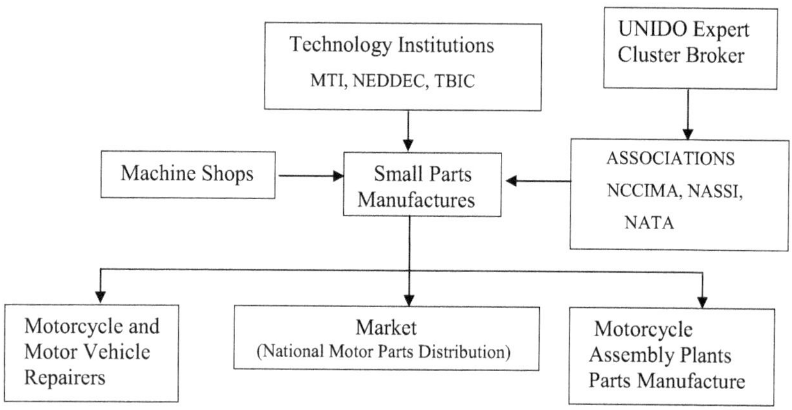

Key: MTI= Metallurgical Training Institute; NEDDEC = National Engineering Design Development Centre; UNIDO = United Nation Industrial Development Organisation; TBIC= Technology Business Incubators Centre; NACCIMA= Nigerian Chambers of Commerce Industry Mines and Agriculture; NASSI= Nigerian Association of Small Scale Industrialists; NATA = Nigerian Automobile Technicians Association

Source: Author's field survey

The institute tries to enhance production standard in terms of staff training in designing and technical drawing. Five main areas of focus include industrial and engineering design, rapid prototyping, and production systems, integrated manufacturing systems and capacity building in terms of human development[134]. The role of UNIDO Cluster Broker at the time of the field survey was an

133 Observing the activities in the centre shows a clear contradiction of stereotyped objectives and reality. The workshops are very small with poor lighting and ventilation. They are typical of informal sector with working system in disorder and failed to follow systematic working procedure.

134 Implementing top down programme objectives in a dual economic system where informal producers are more than formal producers is difficult. It requires a mechanism that can first put the entire system into an interactive learning process, and as well identification of the specific branch that can comparative advantage over other branches in the light engineering sector.

advisory function to the associations such as NCCIMA, NASSI and NATA in the cluster. NACCIMA's services to the cluster are commercial oriented. They include finding solutions to import related problems; mediation in controversial issues such as local government multiple taxation as well as lobbying for infrastructure development. Members of NACCIMA include manufacturers and traders in medium and large scale enterprises. One of the major achievements of the chamber is formation of large, medium and small scale entrepreneurs in an interactive framework in the form Local Economic Forum (LEF)[135]. The LEF provides a platform for exchange of business ideas, entrepreneurship experiences and learning by example within the cluster.

The NASSI and NATA are associations representing the interest of micro and small enterprises. At the time of the field work, the NASSI has not been able to develop articulated programme for its members due to leadership squables. NASSI problem is a case of large number of small producers in different sectors that lack cohesive goal. Formulation of development programme always results to conflict of individual interest that undermines collective interest[136]. NATA on the other hand seems to be more organised and over time has developed organisational structure based on zoning system.The association is divided into ten zones each with independent governing body but under one central executive council and constitution. NATA play an important role in the cluster by providing economic governance to its members. The association organises welfare programme, training programme for members as well as mediation on internal/external conflicts. The association also serves as a medium for information exchange on product quality to large and small scale motor parts manufacturers by using their products as sample test[137].

4.4.5.5 Constraints Identified in the Cluster

Figure 4.8 shows six major constraints identified in the cluster. 94 per cent of the interviewees consider neglect, technological problem and technical workforce as three major problem areas of the cluster. Neglect in this context ranges from the problem of infrastructure especially, access roads, energy supply and other utilities to local government multiple taxation. Cost of production in Nnewi manufacturing tends to be high as a result of poor infrastrure development. Firms sustained substantial costs in energy supply by purchasing and

135 Interview with the President of NACCIMA, Nnewi Branch, Chief C. Nzewi on 20.03.05, from 10an to 11.30.pm.

136 Interview with UNIDO cluster Broker in Nnewi Professor Chukwujekwu on 07. 04. 05 from 12pm to 1.30pm.

137 Interview and discussion with executive committee of NATA on 1 May 2005, from 1pm to 2.30 pm. Present meeting are: Chairman Mr. Francis Nwagbala the General Secretary of the Association and the representatives of the ten zones.

maintaining private electric generating plants for production. 84.9 per cent of the interviewees in the cluster view multiple-taxation as a problem. According to the interviewees, non-rationalised taxation system always have induced indirect corruption tendencies in the sense that firms are forced to make some unauthorised gestures in order to influence tax reductions.

Figure 4.8: Distribution of respondents' perceptions to their constraints in Nnewi light engineering cluster in % of sample size

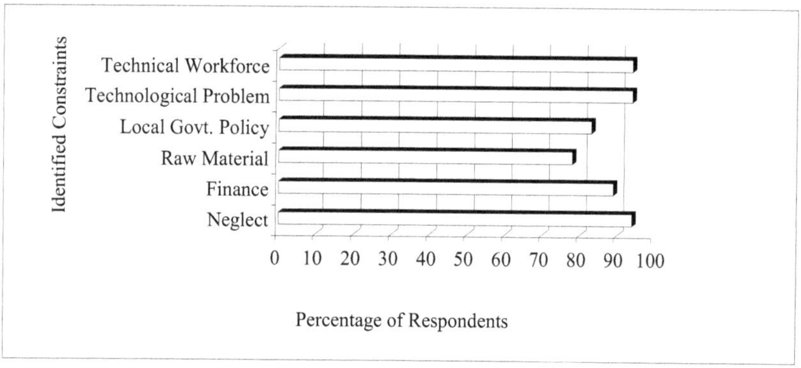

Source: Own field survey (derived from data in appendix, 4.13)

On technical skill workforce, entrepreneurs argue that most of the school leavers have poor technical background. They consider job-on-training as expensive because workers are horridly trained and the lack the capability to be flexible in production. The major problems facing the NATA include among others, high rate of apprenticeship dropout, i.e. high rate of non-completion of the training programme by the apprentice; high rate of workshop mobility due to forced evacuation and lack of modern equipments to dictate faults in new automobile models with sophisticated electronic gadgets during maintenance services. 89 per cent of the entrepreneurs in the cluster view finance as major problem in their production activities. Due to low financial base, investment in original raw material and purchase of the required modern equipment is limited.

4.4.5.6 Remarks

One basic factor identified in the cluster is the location. Unlike automobile technicians, the small scale manufacturing firms are scattered in different parts of Nnewi town. Despite formal support from technology institutions and

NACCIMA initiatives, the cluster lacks the capacity to forge into modern inter-firm linkages. Most firms' productions are for direct supply to local and African sub-regional markets. Business uncertainty and transformation costs are very high due to poor infrastructure especially the energy supply. The small enterprises tend to survive by taking advantage of low income in the region and producing low quality products. Majority of the firms in the cluster are predominantly locally owned with limited technology cooperation from Taiwan. The training programmes in the cluster are non-market oriented because the entrepreneurs have not been able to appreciate the importance of knowledge upgrading in the world of competitive market. One general characteristic in the cluster is high entrepreneurship spirit based on imitation and competition. The working environment is very poor and typical of informal sector with workshops unorganised and very narrow. Institutional support failed to focus effectively on basic factors such as technical skill development, workshop organisation and product quality measures.

4.4.6 Enugu small scale palm kernel extraction enterprises cluster

4.4.6.1 Introduction

Oil palm production and exportation in Nigeria has a relatively long history dating back to the pre-colonial era. In 1834, about 14,000 tonnes of palm oil, valued about £ 33 to £ 34 per ton, were exported from the Niger Delta to England (Helleiner, 1966, pp. 97-8). Correspondingly, the share of Nigeria's palm kernels exports increased from 45.5 per cent of world exports in 1938 to 58.1 in 1961. The share of Nigeria's oil palm export increased from 29.4 per cent of world exports in 1937 to 32.6 per cent in 1959 (Kilby, 1969, p. 141). Nigeria continued to be the world leading producer and exporter of oil palm products between 1961 and 1965 with an average annual output of 43 per cent of global production. However, by 1997, Nigeria accounted for only 7 per cent of world production (Kajisa et al, 1997). The average share of palm produce to total non-oil exports has been on a downward spiral from 9.8 per cent in 1970-1974 to 3.9 per cent in 1975-1979 and an alarming 1.7 per cent in 1995-1999 (Aigbokhan, 2001, p. 8). The trend dwindled from the 1970s onwards as indicated in Figure 4.9 due to a combination of factors including the civil war; oil boom effect, and unfavourable agricultural policies (Forrest, 1993). The export of palm kernel and palm oil together increased from 200,000 tonnes in 1900 to 450,000 tonnes in 1954, accounting for about 25 per cent of Nigeria's exports value then.

Figure 4.9: Annual output of palm oil and palm kernel (1970-2002) in thousand tonnes

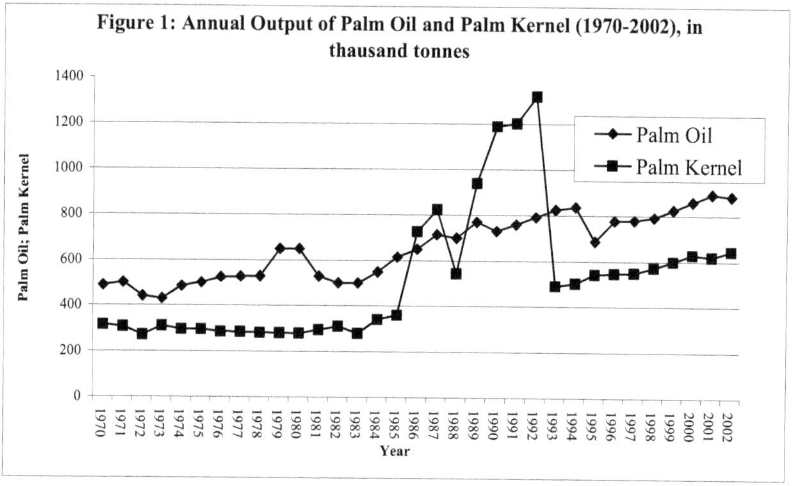

Source: Central Bank of Nigeria, 2003, p. 120.

Figure 4.9 shows that between 1970 and 2002, there was a progressive but low marginal annual increase in oil palm production. The output has a mean annual capacity of 654.91 tons and standard deviation of 145.04 tons within the period. Palm kernel production on the other hand, experienced a negative trend between 1970 and 1985; with the turning points in 1986 showing very high marginal annual increase of 102 per cent and in 1992 with the highest production output of 1,321 tonnes. This was the period of Structural Adjustment Programmes (SAP) that favoured agricultural production and rural economy in Nigeria (Adubi and Okunmadewa, 1999, p. 10). The trend changed drastically in 1993 with annual marginal decreases of 62.9 per cent and a relatively low output level. Between 1970 and 2002 palm kernel industry has a mean annual output of 522.24 with standard deviation of 290.93. Despite current low production output that fail to meet local demand and export chances, oil palm is arguably still an important segment in Nigerian economy, providing rural and urban income, employment opportunities and industrial inputs.

4.4.6.2 Methodology

Two approaches were adopted in this sub-section. First is the investigation of backward and forward linkages in the cluster. The aim is to examine the extent of rural and urban economic relationships in Enugu. In the backward linkages, the sources of palm kernel to the cluster and the volume of palm kernel supplied per week were investigated. For forward linkages, the volume of output per week and the channel of distribution of palm kernel oil (PKO) were considered. This helped to generate the parameters needed for the evaluation of firm performance in the cluster and those operating elswhere. The parameters include weekly output projections based on the rate of supply of palm kernel, the real output of PKO per worker and the output shortfall. The second approach concerns firm competitive factors in terms of human capital and the nature of technology. The effect of proximity with respect to reduction of output shortfall was investigated. The impact of local technology on the output volume per worker was also investigated. In the former, the aggregate mean monthly output per worker in clustered enterprise and those located elsewhere were compared. Statistical test of significant on differences between mean monthly output per worker in clustered and dispersed enterprises were performed. This was followed by examination of the relationship between local technology and output per worker. The price of raw material (palm kernel) is considered to be the same since all supplies came from rural economy of the same income basket. Technology is also considered to be the same because all sampled firms use locally constructed machines. A vocational training centre for PKO production in Enugu was visited in order to examine the kind of training and services offered by the centre.

The field survey in Enugu city was divided into three zones or strata such that investigative enterprises were selected randomly in each zone or stratum. Table 4.28 shows the distribution of firms across the strata. The firm structure revealed that 73 per cent of the firms are micro enterprises and 27 per cent fall into small scale category. The average age of the enterprises sampled is 13 years. 95 per cent of enterprises are sole proprietorship, while only 5 per cent are joint-ventures.

Table 4.28: Sampled structure of Enugu palm kernel extraction enterprises cluster

	Zone 1	Zone2	Zone 3	
Sector	Abakpa/Emene	Ogbete/Railway	Agbani/ Uwani	Total
Micro Enterprises (1-9)	2	3	3	8 (0.727)
Small Enterprises (10-49)		2	1	3 (0.273)
Medium Enterprises (50-99)	na	na	na	na
Total	2	5	4	11

Source: Author's field survey

4.4.6.3 Informality characteristics

Table 4.29 shows that 82 per cent of the firms are officially incorporated. 91 per cent of the firms claimed to have met tax obligation but investigation shows that only one firm in the sample has managed to keep accounting and administrative records. The table also indicates that all the firms met minimum wage requirement of US$50.00 stipulated for private enterprises. 82 per cent of the interviewees operate within the stipulated local government regulations in terms of paying different forms of levies.

Table 4.29: Some regulatory indicators as informality characteristics

Indicators	PKO Enterprise
Percentage of firm officially registered	0.82
Percentage of firms that met tax obligations/ keeping of account	0.91
Percentage of firms that met minimum wage requirements	1.00
Percentage of firms operating within local government regulations	0.82

Source*:* Author's field survey

Table 4.30 shows that firms in the sample operate with paid regular workers and apprentices only. The regular paid workers are mixture of skilled and unskilled labour. The classification of skilled workers is based on training and experience in PKO extraction methods. Skilled workers are those workers that received vocational training on PKO extraction system either through the Volunteers Service Agency (VSA) or by in-house-training processes.[138] Apprentices are those undergoing in house-training and the students who are on practical training

Table 4.30: Labour force indicators as informality characteristics

Indicators	Value
Average No of Regular Paid Workers	4.2
Average No of Apprentices	0.45
Average No of Seasonal Workers	0
Firms without Workers (in %)	0
Average No of Unpaid Workers	0

Source: Author's field survey

138 In 1987, the regional government in Enugu established VSA for training of prospective entrepreneurs and workers in PKO extracting business as youth unemployment reduction strategy. An average of six volunteers is trained annually. The one-year training course covers a range of activities such as cost management, machine operating, techniques and processes involved in the palm kernel drying before extraction.

4.4.6.4 The competitive factors in Enugu small scale PKO extraction enterprises

Table 4.31 indicates that enterprises heads in the cluster have relatively high education qualifications. 72.7 per cent of them have education above secondary school while 27.3 per cent of them pass through formal technical training. The entrepreneurs have varied experience in technical and managerial knowledge. 57 per cent of the entrepreneurs interviewed have educational background in engineering but lack experience in production management in the sense that raw- and production materials are left in a disorganised manner. Among the male entrepreneurs, there is mixture of mechanical and agricultural engineers competing alongside with those that have business and economic background.

Table 4.31: Educational level of enterprises heads and workers expressed in percentage

	Sample No.	Primary	Secondary	Post Secondary	Formal Vocational
Enterprises Heads	11	na	na	0.727	0.273
Workers	65	0.462	0.538	na	na
% of the total	76	0.395	0.461	0.105	0.039

Source: Author's field survey

The female entrepreneurs are mostly ex-primary/secondry school teachers with National Certification of Education (NCE) qualification. Others are trained agricultural extension officers who have experience in PKO industry. The Table also show that 46.2 per cent of the workers have primary education while 53.8 per cent of them had formal education up to secondary school level.

Figure 4.10 illustrates the backward/forward linkages in Enugu small scale PKO extraction enterprises. The economic activities are grouped into three zones; the palm kernels supply zone; the PKO extraction zone, and vegetable oil refinery zone. The supply system in the palm kernel sub-sector is an embodiment of agents, dealers and rural small holder farmers. The palm kernel supply zones comprise Abakaliki, Nkanu and Udi/Eziagu. 85 per cent of the kernels processed in Enugu are supplied from rural communities in Abakaliki and Nkanu zones while the rest supply came from the Udi/Eziagu areas.

Figure 4.10: Territorial input-output structure in palm kernel economy in South-Eastern Nigeria

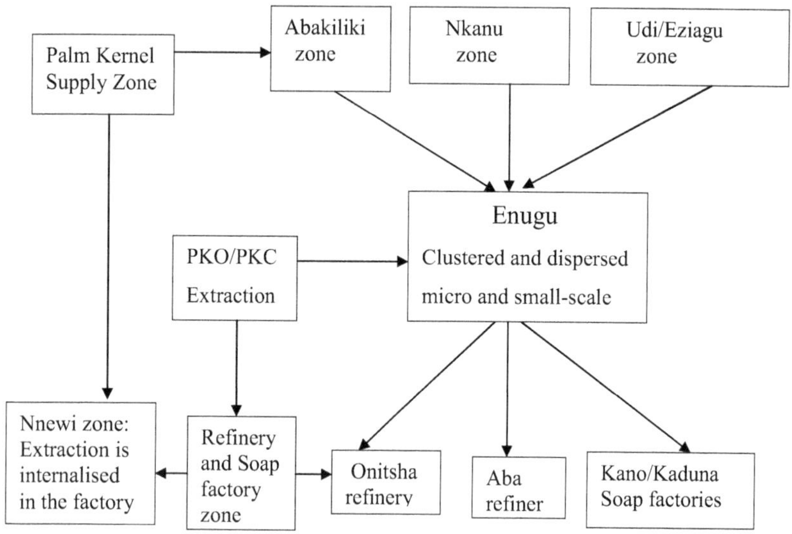

Source: Author's field surve

On the average, 3 tonnes of kernels per week are processed by each enterprise in the PKO enterprises cluster, while in dispersed enterprises an average of 2tonnes of kernels per week are been processed. The refineries in the South-Eastern region consist of 10 medium scale and 3 large scale enterprises located in three industrial and commercial towns of Aba, Nnewi and Onitsha.

4.4.6.5 Small firm performance in Enugu small scale PKO extraction industries

Table 4.32 shows the mean monthly production output per worker in clustered and dispersed small scale PKO extraction enterprises. The mean monthly projected outputs per worker for clustered and dispersed enterprises are 10.60 and 10.09 tones respectively. The mean monthly realised output per worker is 7.56 tones for clustered enterprises and 5.78 tones for enterprises located elsewhere. This indicates a mean monthly output shortfall per worker of 3.05 and 4.31 tones in clustered and dispersed enterprises respectively. The empirical result shows that difference in output shortfall in clustered area and those located elsewhere is statistically significant at $p < 0.05$. The average monthly output per worker for firms in cluster area is significantly higher than those operating elsewhere. If the relatively high palm kernel supply in the cluster area leads to relatively large output volume, then there could be other explanatory factors that contributed to higher productivity in cluster areas. The factors could be first, joint action initiatives by firms in the cluster that resulted to minimal output shortfall; second, efficient technological application by firms in the cluster areas that tend to increase output per worker and reduce the output shortfall per worker as well. The implication is that it becomes difficult to distinquish which of the two factors explain output performance of the firms in cluster area better.

Table 4.32: The aggregate mean monthly output per worker in clustered and dispersed in Enugu small scale PKO extraction enterprises (in Tonnes)

Cluster PKO Enterprises			Dispersed PKO Enterprises			t-test value
MMO per worker (Projected)	MMO per worker (realised)	MMO Shortfall per worker	MMO per worker (Projected)	MMO per worker (realised)	MMO Shortfall per worker	2.90 Prob. value
10.60 (0.91)	7.56 (0.68)	3.05 (0.84)	10.09 (1.26)	5.78 (0.72)	4.31 (1.36)	1.96

Note: Output shortfall is the difference between the monthly projected output and monthly real output (in tonnes); the figures in the bracket are the standard deviation.
Key: MMO = Mean Monthly Output; PKO = Palm Kernel Oil
Source: Author's field survey; calculations are shown in appendix 4.14-4.20.

The survey reveals that firms in the region assumed to transform products and function collectively such that exclusion and constraints are reduced. One can argue that several small producers are placed in a position to initiate joint action in order to meet a particular target. For example, two or more enterprises often undertake joint supply of PKO in order to meet the requirements of the refineries resulting to increased supply contract. In the event of a machine break down, one can move the kernels to another firm's production unit and continue production. The engineers in the cluster provide free machine maintenance services. Moreover, the frequency of business transactions between palm kernel dealers or agents and enterprises in the cluster is higher. This is because probability of selling palm kernel to any of the enterprises in the cluster is higher. The entrepreneurs in the cluster apply rotational production system in order to reduce the rate of power failure in the cluster. To maintain a relative constant power supply to the cluster, there was an established agreement among the enterprises in the cluster with the authorities of NEPA on energy sharing system in form of rotational production arrangement[139]. The second step is to investigate the impact of local technology on the production output per worker. The challenging fact in this sub-sector is high dependence on local technology. The firms operate mostly with local fabricated machines produced from refurbished electric motors with low resistance capacity. Investments are channelled either towards upgrading the capacity of extracting machine or towards additional purchasing of two important machines- the expeller and the toaster (dryer).

Table 4.33: Mean of major equipment (expeller and toaster) in use by firms

Cluster	Mean No. of Expeller	Mean No.of Toaster	Mean Equipment
Equipment at Start-up	1.27	0.64	1.96
Additional Equipment	2.09	1.55	3.64
Dispersed			
Equipment at Start-up	1.18	0.55	1.73
Additional Equipment	1.00	0.73	1.73

Source: Author's field survey

Table 4.33 reveals that the investment behaviour of the entrepreneurs in the sub-sector. The mean number of expeller and dryer machines at start-up is 1.27 and 0.64 respectively. This implies that some of the entrepreneurs started with more than one expeller machine, while some started without dryer machine. The mean number of additional equipment after five years of start-up is 2.09 and 1.55 for expeller and dryer respectively. This indicates that some of the entrepreneurs in cluster area introduced more than two expeller machines and more than one toaster machine after 5 years of production life. In dispersed enter-prises, the mean number of equipment did not change after 5 years of production life suggesting that enterprises in the cluster area have higher propensity to invest. The empirical results as shown in Table 4.34 suggest that the relationship between technology in use and output per worker are not correlated. In other words, the technology employed by firms has little or no effect on production efficiency. The negative correlation value in cluster area suggests that despite minimal output shortfall, investment in local technology which did not underscore efficiency. In the production, one can observe the frequency of machine breakdown and time spent in assembling, adjusting and coupling the entire machine system. The machines are working in a single calibrated system of compressing and separating. The production depends on the sun intensity for drying of the kernel hence there must be constant study of weather condition.

139 Rotational production system in this context is a system where a group of enterprises produce at particular time schedule as result of production constraint such as limited energy supply.

Table 4.34: Correlation values of technology and production output per worker

	Cluster	Dispersed
Mean total of major equipment after 5 years	5.55	3.45
Correlation values	-0.046	0.049

Source: Author's field survey

4.4.6.6 Constraints identified in PKO extraction enterprises

Six major constraints were identified in small scale PKO extraction industry in Enugu as shown in Figure 4.11. They include energy problem, technology problem, and multiple taxation, shortage of finance, government policy and the declining rate of palm kernel supply. Over the sample, 91 per cent of the interviewees consider poor energy supply, technology and raw material (palm kernel) as the major constraints in the sub-sector. PKO extractions require high-energy consumption and most of the small firms cannot afford the cost of heavy generating plants. Therefore they have to depend on public energy supply for production. The average power failures range from 4 to 5 hours per day and 1 to 3 days per week. The frequent power failures often produce chain reactions in the production system. Productions are interrupted within those periods hence supply of palm kernel by dealers is reduced. Consequently, supply of PKO to refineries is also delayed therefore leading to output shortfall in vegetable oil production. The entrepreneurs acknowledged that technology is a general problem in the sub-sector. 55 per cent of them opted for foreign machines with an integrated dryer system in order to increase the rate of extraction. They argue that since the technical knowledge is already available, adaptation of the foreign machines in their production system will be much easier. 45 per cent of the interviewees based their argument on the grounds of financial constraints because most small scale industrialists have low financial base to purchase modern machines. The declining rate of palm kernel supply according to the interviewees is partly due to seasonal variation. They also argue that governments at national and regional levels have not done enough to expand the palm kernel industry or encourage private sector initiatives in the development oil palm industry.

Figure 4.11: Distribution of respondents' perceptions to their major constraints in Enugu PKO enterprises clusters in % sample size

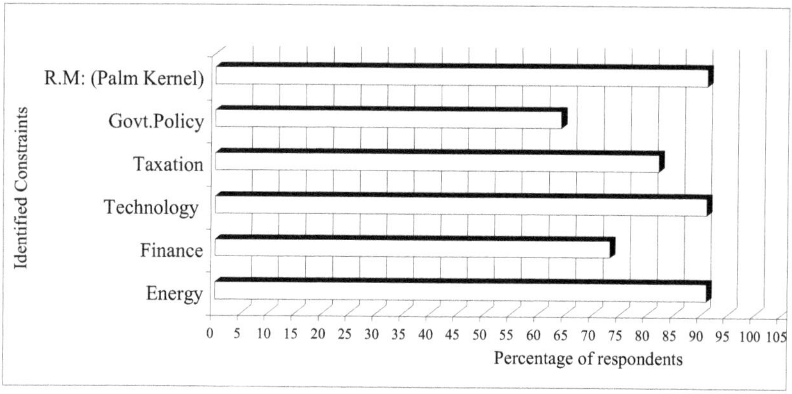

Key: R, M = Raw Materials
Source: Author's field survey derived from appendix 4.21

Appendix 4.23 shows different types of levies the small enterprises in PKO extraction industry pay annually. The interviewees argue that produce tax and local government business permit levies amounts to tax duplication. Business premises tax is arguably an unjustified payment because firms pay monthly rents to landlords for the workshops. The interviewees also argue that there is a systematic indirect subvention politics in favor of entrepreneurs operating in government established industrial estates. Entrepreneurs operating in government owned workshops enjoy exemptions from business premises tax and reduced workshop rent. In this context, Levy, 1991 argues that tax discrimination reduces competition among the small enterprises and entrepreneurship spirit. Uneven enforcement of regulatory obligations can create discontinuities and high tax obligations such as tax duplications can induce disproportionate burden on business operations (Levy, 1991, p. 20).

Recent government polices, such as the tree planting programme and the rural development programme have tried to expand the oil palm sector production in Nigeria. The aims are to meet domestic demand for oil palm products for food and industrial usages, to generate employment and improve rural quality of life and income. In contrast, the neglect of the rural areas in terms of poor road networks, poor rural market development and lack of financial incentives tend to work against this avowed goal. Consequently, the oil palm sector is not responding to government policies. Moreover, market orientated economic reforms always induce uncertainty at the beginning. Such reforms however provide the opportunity for economic improvement through learning and competition. The PKO extraction enterprises are subjected to stiff competition as a result of trade liberalisation in Nigeria. This has posed challenges to local entrepreneurs to adapt and improve their entrepreneurship skills as well as for government to provide an enabling environment for competition. Many entrepreneurs lack technical skills and machinery to act competitively. Capability and capacity building in terms of technology and human skill development are fundamental instruments for small enterprises competitiveness and development strategy (Romijn, 1999, p. 13). Unfortunately, these policies have been neglected in Nigeria.

Lack of finance is also one of major factor that affects the development of small enterprises in the sub-sector adversely. Like other small scale enterprises, this problem is accentuated by the inherent constraints associated with smallness. The enterprises experience poor capitalisation due to unwillingness of the entrepreneurs to allow external participation since they fear to loose control over their businesses. 0.05 per cent of the enterprises interviewed were joint ventures, suggesting that the pool of resources is small. The size factor also discourages banks to grant loans hence firms continue to rely on informal sources of finance. Despite various special credit schemes approved for small enterprises development by the previous Nigerian government, the World Bank and the African Development Bank, small enterprises in PKO extraction still lack access to credit facilities to expand investment[140]. The Small and Medium Scale Industries Equity Investments Scheme (SMIEIS) introduced by the Central Bank of Nigeria has remained an ineffective instrument in addressing small enterprises' financial constraints. This is because the conditionality and modalities of the scheme are beyond the premise of small enterprises[141].

140 The successive loan schemes include the Small-Scale Industrial Scheme (1971), the Agricultural Credit Guarantee Scheme (1973), Nigeria Agricultural and Co-operative Bank (1973), Nigerian Bank for Commerce and Industry (1973), Small and Medium scale Enterprises Loan Scheme (1992), National Economic Reconstruction Fund (1994), Family Economic Advancement Program (1997), World Bank SME Loan Scheme I (1973-1989) and World Bank Loan Scheme II (1989).

141 For the eligibility of the fund, a prospective small enterprise must be registered as a limited liability company with the Corporate Affairs Commission and must comply with all relevant regulations of the Companies and Allied Matters Act (1990) such as filing of annual returns, including audited financial statement. The scheme promotes exclusion since small enterprises that cannot afford the cost of incorporation will not have access to the fund.

4.4.6.7 Remarks

Small scale farmers continue to dominate the production structure in the Nigerian oil palm industry. To upgrade the production output of PKO in Nigeria requires the collaboration of the private and the public sector. First step is to identify how land holdings can be consolidated in order to induce private initiative to invest in medium-scale palm plantation. Smallholder farming in the oil palm sector is necessary and should be strengthened through medium scale palm plantation to meet the local demand as well as to exploit export chances. Increased participation of private firms in medium scale plantation would also be desirable since development efforts of large scale plantation failed in the past. Large scale plantations are usually owned by the government and are poorly managed. These large scale projects involve huge capital outlays and can also result to conflicts in agrarian land. To this end, the Nigerian Land Use Decree of 1978 has to be reformed such that access to land can be attractive for private sector investment in rural areas.

Second step is to identify how local and national technology policy can positively influence private sector investment in small scale PKO extraction enterprises. Nigerian technology policy has not been able to address the basic technologies that are fundamental for small-scale enterprise developments (Oladeji; 1998, p. 128). Despite the importance of the PKO industry for Nigeria's socio-economic development, the Science and Technology (S&T) policy has not placed the sub-sector on priority list. Government intervention would however be important in order to improve production efficiency and technology application in the sub-sector. This could be done by encouraging private investment in new technology on PKO extraction. It could also foster cooperation between local S&T institutions such as RMRDC, IDC, PRODA and SEDI with foreign research institutions. Capacity building has to be intensified in these institutions so that research works can be promoted. The empirical result revealed that private collective actions play an important role in small firm survival in Africa. Clustering provide the organisational structure that facilitates such actions.

4.4.7 Comparative Analysis of the clusters

4.4.7.1 Comparative analysis of the clusters

Table 4.35 revealed some remarkable differences among the regional sectoral clusters. These differences underscore the level, characteristics and weaknesses typical in African sectoral clusters. Aba footwear enterprises cluster is classified as an active cluster because the small and micro enterprises have developed strategies to overcome competitive pressure penetrate distance markets, and at the same time operate informally. There are evidences of agglomeration effects such as rapid labour migration and increased different service suppliers to the shoemakers in the cluster. There is evidence of division of labour and linkages among the enterprises in the cluster. The shoemakers tend to specialise in the core production unit such as designing and coupling of the shoes and subsequently sub-contract other activities to shoe tailors, shoe smoothing and stamping. There is evidence of easy dissemination of new ideas in modern shoe designing and production in the footwear cluster. Concentration of firms in a define location allows easy dissemination of new ideas through learning by observation. The small enterprises in the cluster compete in terms of introducing new designs in the market and cooperate in meeting the production target through subcontracting production. The cluster has developed common strategies to overcome external competition and access to distance markets. This is through different cost reduction strategies which have positive effect on economies of scale. However, the informality effect in the cluster is such that quality standard is not observed or controlled effectively hence firms compete by concentrating on low product quality. The working conditions and standard are also not observed in the cluster.

The PKO extraction enterprises cluster in Enugu is classified as semi-active in the sense that firms in the cluster have been able to establish grass root backward and forward linkages that can promote growth and local value chains. There is evidence of labour migration to cluster and suppliers' services to the cluster. Joint actions were undertaken in order to reduce energy and transportation costs. There is evidence of cooperation among the entrepreneurs on machine maintenance services and supply of PKO to refineries. The production is labour-intensive and production shortfall is a reflection of the weak technology, low supply of kernels and poor infrastructure. However, the sector has shown the impact of linkages between urban and rural economy in the production system.

The wood construction and furniture are classified as dormant clusters because they have not been able to upgrade in terms of quality or penetrating national market. The firms in the cluster have not been able to develop strategies to gain economies of scale. Despite its dormant nature, there is evidence of joint action in the provision of infrastructure. Firms share information on new furniture designs, share hand tools, and sub-contract activities when there is high production order. There is absence of institutional support and no linkages with the forestry department as well as limited cooperation with technical institutions hence the gains of clustering have been limited. The garment enterprises cluster in Aba is classified as dormant cluster in the sense that the cluster has not be able to develop strategies in order to over come the trade liberalisation effect.

Firms have not improved quality in order to attract external buyers. Production are internalised with limited division of labour hence there is diseconomies of scale. There is evidence of joint action in terms of raising funds for working capital through cooperative initiatives.

Table 4.35: The level, characteristics and weaknesses of the clusters by sub-Sector and location

Cluster Level	Sectoral Cluster	Location	Characteristics	Weaknesses	Remarks
Active	Footwear	Aba	The cluster has partlyovercome competitive pressure. There is presence of linkages within the cluster that promotes growth.	No established linkages with large multi-national shoe companies. Absence of institutional support.	The firms are taking the advantage of low income in the regionby producing according to income level.
Semi-Active	PKO Extraction	Enugu	Has established grassroots' production system for industrial linkages	High output shortfall due to poor technology limitations	There is evidence of local supply chain which can be upgraded to a global value chain.
Dormant	Wood & Furniture Garment	Enugu Aba	Have not been able to overcome the competitive pressure and lacked the capacity to upgrade	Low product quality and absence of institutional support and low technology	The role of forestry department in the cluster is not defined. Garment producers have failed to identify niche market
Informal	Footwear Wood & Furniture Garment	Aba Enugu Aba	High degree of informality indicator.	Technological weakness	Absence of Institutional support
Organised (formal & informal)	Light Engineering	Nnewi	Formation of organised social interaction that foster cooperation and solution to problems arising from state and institutional failure.	Firms are scattered in different parts of Nnewi town such that learning process and linkages are limited	Limited branch or sectoral specialisation. Firms producing low sub-standard products due to income in the local and sub-African regional market.

Source: Author's field survey

The networks are relatively close hence competition and creation of new ideas are relatively weak. Nnewi Light engineering small cluster comprise formal and informal production units. The cluster is organised in the sense that private organised associations such as local manufacturers association, local Nigerian Chambers of Commerce Industry Mines and Agriculture, and other associations play dominant role in organisational structure of the cluster. The social interaction in the cluster provided the platform for problem solving in terms of technology and raw material sourcing. This tends to reduce search costs and access to information regarding market conditions. The gains from externalities cannot be exploited because inter-firm linkages are weak.

There is evidence of weak technological capability in the various clusters investigated. Capacity to engage in process and product upgrading is very weak in the clusters, hence policy intervention in necessary. Most importantly the entrepreneurs in the clusters show relatively high degree of entrepreneurship in terms of risks taking in new ventures but state and institutional supports are very low.

4.4.7.2 Competitiveness problems across the clusters by sector

Table 4.36 indicates that in every sector, technical skill remains very weak. The percentage of workers and enterprise heads across the sectors with formal technical knowledge and skill training are between 8.5 and 3.9 per cent. Firms will continue to experience managerial problem because education level of enterprise heads is not beyond primary school level.

Table 4.36: Level and nature of Human Development by sector (%)

Sector	Educational level of EH and Workers			
	PE	SE	PS	TE
Footwear	71.4	14.3	7.1	7.1
Garment	59.7	39.3	1.0	na
Wood Construction & Furniture	62.7	27.1	1.7	8.5
Light Engineering	33.6	60.0	2.2	4.2
PKO Extraction	39.5	46.1	10.5	3.9

Key: PE = Primary Education; SE= Secondary Education; TE= Technical Education

Source: Author's field survey

The nature of technology and raw material in use is an important firm competitive factor. Table 4.37 shows the level of technological base and linkages in the clusters. The Table indicates that hand tools are the major equipment in the footwear enterprise clusters. This suggests that the sub-sector has low technological base which needs to be upgraded. The linkages in footwear enterprises are informal sub-contracting with traders acting as suppliers and providing major information about the market. The equipment in garment enterprises is mainly old and out dated. The entrepreneurs cannot afford the cost of modern equipment due to low financial base. The linkages are relatively low in the sub-sector hence there is high degree of internalisation. The technological application in PKO, light engineering and wood construction are limited to locally constructed machines. The furniture makers and footwear also operate mainly with hand tools. The institutional linkages which can support local innovation system are relatively present in Nnewi light engineering cluster but lack effective coordination. There is relatively high incidence of backward and forward linkages in PKO extraction enterprises cluster.

Table 4.37: The level of technology and linkages in clusters by sub-sector

Sector	Nature of Technology	Nature of Linkages
Footwear	Local hand tools and labour intensive production	Informal sub-contracting. Evidence of Trader-producer and producer-producer relationship Absence of institutional support.
Garment	Old and out dated technology.	Very low linkages with high degree of internalisation of production.
Wood & Furniture	Locally constructed light engineering combined with obsolete foreign second hand machines, application of hand tools	There is evidence of inter-linkages but weak. The Forestry Department are not integrated in the process
Light Engineering	Technology is limited to locally constructed machines and imported old second hand machines	There is evidence of some basic interactions with technical institutions for technical support
PKO Extraction	Locally constructed light engineering technology with low resistance capacity	Relatively high incidence of backward and forward linkages.

Source: Author's field survey

4.5 Summary and Conclusion

This section provided the empirical works on the impact of clustering in small scale enterprise in Nigeria. The empirical analyses show some conventional results that are typical of agglomeration effects such as availability of labour force, market creation and linkages which tend to enhance small firm performance. The results indicate that employment creation and income generation by small scale industries in cluster area is higher during normal economic activities and during the boom period. Footwear and PKO extraction enterprise cluster provided some evidences of proximity effects. This is effective through co-operation and linkages that led to cost reduction. The study revealed that each sub-sector has specific constraints. This implies that policy solutions require different intervention measures that can reflect on each constraint in order to avoid exclusion. Generally, firm performance depends on the nature of education level of the workforce, technology frontiers and the macroeconomic environment. There is no evidence suggesting that small scale industries in the region have the capacity to compete. The empirical outcome suggests that skilled workforce required for modern production is very weak. The technological base such as equipment and physical infrastructure is also weak. Firms tend to experience immersiering growth as a result of a low income level in local and African regional markets by producing low quality products without expanding their capabilities. The findings suggest that informality characteristics tend to over shadow the impact of small scale manufacturing in Nigeria. As a result government tend to neglect the contributions of the small enterprise to economy in terms of income generation and job creation. The basic finding is that the small firms in cluster area tend to add values in terms of product transformation. The preceding chapter looks into the extent non-state economic governance (social networks) have contributed to SME performance in Nigeria is subject to investigation in the proceeding chapter. In this case, the role of networks in supporting performance of firms, access to external market and promote innovative activity of the small enterprises is also looked into in the next section.

Chapter 5: Networks in Small and Medium Scale Enterprises in Nigeria

5.1 Introduction

This chapter investigates how African SMEs operate in spite of unstable political and macroeconomic conditions in the region. Political instability in the region has generated uncertainty and created high risks in business transactions. The pressure generated by economic reforms in the form of SAP and trade liberalisation has also forced small enterprises in formal and informal sector in the region to restructure their strategies. The scenario has also produced a growing entry of new entrepreneurs and increased need for information, technology, new markets and partners in order to remain in production. Since the state lacks the capacity to provide functional institutional services for the development of the market in the region, entrepreneurs in the region have to rely on their personal contacts (networks) in order to improve performance and reduce risks.

The analytical approach of the study is borrowed from the concept of embeddedness which helped to capture the role social networks play in economic development. In his article, Granovetter (1985, p. 504) argue that economic behaviour is embedded in networks of inter-personal relations. Intra-firm activities or the input of workers depend on the nature of personal relationship among workers, and personal relationship between workers and their superiors (Granovetter, 1995, p. 35). Macaulay (1963, p. 63) argues that personal relationships across different business units have influence on firm performance and exert pressure on conformity to expectations. The assumption is that if an entrepreneur is a socially embedded person, to what extent can he/her use his/her networks under the prevailing economic environment to increase performance? The argument is that networks can enhance performance but performance is a function of commitment which in turn is the primary obligation of an entrepreneur and the state (Macaulay, 1963, p. 63; Nijkamp, 2003, p. 401). Hence, the proposition contends that African enterprise networks lack the commitment to undertake risks and expand business across borders or enhance performance for firm growth. In line with this argument, this chapter looks into the nature of small enterprise networks in Nigeria and seek to investigate how the networks impact on firm performance. The chapter is divided into six sub-sections. The next is the theoretical framework which covers the definitions, forms, functions and problems of the networks. The literature is classified into ethnic entrepreneurship literatures and comparative institutionalist literature. The empirical analysis looks into the structure of the networks in terms of personal relationships and organisational aspects of the networks. The analysis also shows the extent in which firms have penetrated their national and African regional markets; the impact of contacts the entrepreneurs make on their business activities.

5.2 Theoretical Conception

5.2.1 Definitions

The term network is used to describe the observed pattern of relationship individuals and organisations build to their advantage. The central issues on the analyses of networks are the nature of personal and organisational interactions (Nohria, 1995, p. 1). Networks can be defined as a configuration of different entities with common social structure, facilitating actions among the actors and within the structure. The actors can be personal or corporate firms (Coleman, 1988, p. 598)[142]. Personal networks focus on entrepreneur as a social agent while the organisational networks focus on the functional structure of the enterprise (Brüderl and Preisendörfer, 1998, p. 214). A broader concept is related to new institutional economic frameworks based on formalised institutional relationships and structures of government which constitute social and political environment that foster social capital (Grootaert, 1998, p. 3). Social capital refers to networks of civil engagements with associated norms that have effect on the productivity of individuals, organisation and community. A social network can also be defined as a set of persons or organisations linked by a set of social relationships of a specified type (Laumann, et al, 1978, p. 458).

Networks and trust are sources of social capital and have become important in development studies. The voluntary and spontaneous cooperation existing within a given community depends on the stock of inherited social capital in the community. This can be in the form of norms of reciprocity or networks of civic engagement (Putnam, 1993, p. 167). In this case, social capital can have direct effect on macroeconomic outcome and support economic development in the sense that it facilitates co-ordination of actions (Woolcock 1998, p. 156; Grootaert, 1998, p. 7). Meagher (2006, p. 554) argues that social capital as factor in Africa's economic development is a function of good governance. If the social capital is devoid of state discriminatory interventions and regulations its role can be maximised[143].

---

142 The concept of externalities is reflected in this definition in the sense that a firm's action can be harmful or useful to another firm. The definition incorporates the horizontal and vertical relationships, and as well individual firm behaviour.

143 This is in line with Grootaert, (1998, p. 7) argument which states that "the differences in per capita income across countries can also be explained by differences in institution, social capital and public policy. These factors determine the returns a country can extract from other capital"

Trust as a social capital can be referred to what Hirschman, (1984, p. 95) described as input or resources in the form of public morality. The supply of moral resources increase in value when they are frequently used in transactions and depreciates when they are not applied (Hirschman, 1984, p. 93)[144]. Economic exchange will not take place normally without a certain measure of trust which involves share of expectations (McCormick, 1998, p. 8). Trust can be viewed as certainty when devoid of fraudulent actions. In this context, Humphery and Schmitz, (1986, p. 35) define trust in terms of agents engaging in transactions with the belief that others will not act opportunistically when given the chance. Trust is also manifested when the possible damage in transaction is greater than the advantage the agents seek. It can also manifest as a result of the existing cooperation among a set of actors such that the more it is displayed in transactions, the greater is its mutual confidence (Sabel, 1992, p. 219). Transactions and exchange can break down when the value of trustworthiness is not perceived accurately by economic actors (Barr, 2000, p. 9). Therefore, trust possesses considerable value that has direct impact in reducing various forms of monitoring. Monitoring business transactions usually involves considerable direct costs as well as indirect costs in terms of generating distrust or uncertainty in business community (Ottari, 1994, p. 532).

5.2.2 Forms of Networks

It is often desirable to distinguish between personal networks and organisational networks when conducting empirical work on entrepreneurship and networks. The economic actions of entrepreneurs are inherently enmeshed in social relations of one configuration or another (embeddedness), and development is essentially brought about by a change in the kind of embeddedness (Granovetter, 1985, p. 504). This captures Schumpeterian view that an entrepreneur is an organiser of economic change and is always seeking for new combinations while destroying the existing constellations in a creative manner. An entrepreneur undertakes risks and can reduce high risks by involving in local or broader industrial networks (Nijkamp, 2003, p. 401). Woolcock (1998, p. 167) extended this argument on the ground that all forms of exchange are inherently embedded in social relationships. Embeddedness itself could take several distinctive forms (social ties, cultural practices and political contexts). However, many benefits gained by embeddedness in a given network were indeed not without corresponding costs. This is because a business strategy requires investment in social communication, informal bonds, training and education. It also requires time and efforts in order to build up and operate effectively in the networks (Nijkamp, 2003, p. 401). Networks require also public intervention in

144 This is the major problem in African leadership and administrative system that have very low moral resources in terms of commitment.

the sense that norms of cooperation and networks of civic engagement among ordinary citizens can be promoted by public agencies and used for development purpose (Evans, 1996, p. 1119).

Networks in terms of enterprise relations can be defined as a selected set of multiple autonomous organisations which interact directly or indirectly based on one or more alliance agreement between them. The aim of this form of networks is to gain competitive advantage for individual organisation involved and some times for the entire network (de Man, 2004, p. 4). The position of the organisation in its network determines its ability to compete in the network. The nature of network surrounding a company also determines the company's ability to control information, knowledge and financial flow (Duysters, et al, 1999, p. 182). The importance of networks is reflected on the network effects. A network effect is the impact of belonging to networks or alliances on organisation and the effects can be positive or negative. For example, ties can generate considerable amount of business for firms when connected with alliance. The alliance can however constrain firms in making choices at the same time subject to the strategic choices of the firms thus become dependent on their relation with partners (Duysters, et al 1999, p. 184). These constellations lead to the development and study of network economy. The network economy is an enterprise-based system of developing and marketing goods and services in which a substantial amount of business activity is conducted in the alliances between multiple firms. This suggests that networks can be found in all sectors and can exist at every stage of value chain (de Man, 2004, p. 7).

Networks can be classified according to spatial ranges in terms of regional (sub-national) and global. The analyses of regional networks tend to reflect not only the importance of geographical proximity but also the interactions in network structure. This comprises local private and public economic actors which have developed regional collective policies in terms of sharing of knowledge or competencies within a local framework (Rallet and Torre, 1998, p. 49). The limit of the local or regional networks in implementing policies depends on the support by local or regional institutions. The functionality of local or regional networks is also subject to the nature of development and their objectives. Local networks can develop spontaneously or can be created by public bodies (institutional local networks). Spontaneous local networks are grouping of local actors around one or several joint economic projects according to non-market form of organisation. The aim is based on common interest in the production of a good and in sharing of a technique, or in the search for information needed by all the members. The institutional local networks are the structures created by public bodies in order to support firms (Rallet and Torre, 1998, p. 49). Rallet and Torre argue that when the spontaneous local networks do not exist or are poorly developed, policies should aim at creating or promote them through incentives. In other words, the local authorities should also promote linkages among institutional networks and spontaneous networks of economic actors. National networks include the national socio-political environment that enables norms to shape the social structure and institutions that have an important effect on the pattern of economic development (Grootaert, 1998, p. 3). Global networks reflect not only the increasing forms of global decision making in resolving global problems but also the structure by which the multinational corporation engages in international business.

5.2.3 Network structures

In general, networks have become an important socio-economic infrastructure for risk reduction and enterprise performance enhancement. They are considered to be the medium for solving or resolving local, regional, national and global problems. Network structure refers to the pattern by which partners tend to stick together. Networks born out of bilateral alliances and ties are said to be redundant if the actors or firms in the networks are not linked to others (Figure, 5.1). Coleman (1990) argues that collective action is easier in redundant ties because such ties always create coherent groups with strong interdependencies. This kind of network is similar to the case where the main contractor is surrounded by several suppliers. All the initiatives and communication activities concerning the project are carried out by the main contractor (Figure, 5.1a). The suppliers can also sub-contract part of their activities to a third party (Figure, 5.1b). This form of network is of particular importance to SMEs and MNEs relationship in the sense that MNEs can concentrate in the core segment of the production and sub-contract the rest to SMEs.

Figure 5:1: Redundant Network Structure

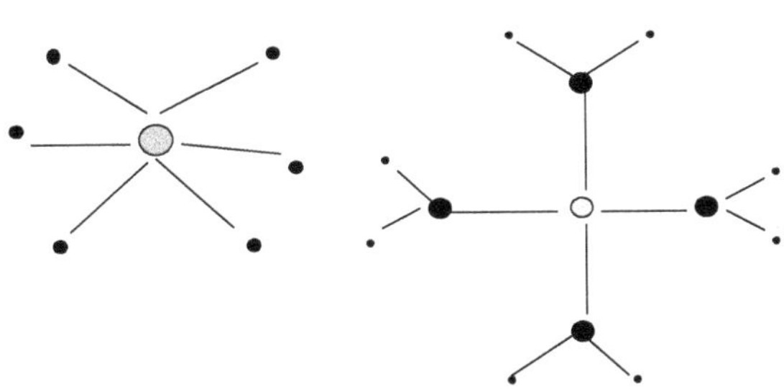

5.1a 5.1b

Source: Steiner and Hartmann, 1998, p. 218; de Man, 2004, p. 79

In a non-redundant networks, the extent at which partners stick together in groups and in relationships with other partners can result to simple or complex web-like network structure (Figure, 5.2). This form of networks can also be described as clustering in the sense that all partners are connected in one multi-partner alliance structure. Steiner and Hartmann (1998, p. 18) argue that all members in the web-like network structure may act in a given project as supplier of knowledge for system solutions. If one firm has a new project, the other network members are invited to participate in the project. A simple web-like network structure is common in the air line industry where all members are being connected to one multipartner alliance (de Man, 2004, p. 79). This form of network is very important to SMEs in the sense that they can be integrated in producing services or production of spare parts needed in an industry.

Figure 5.2: Simple and Complex – Web like network structure

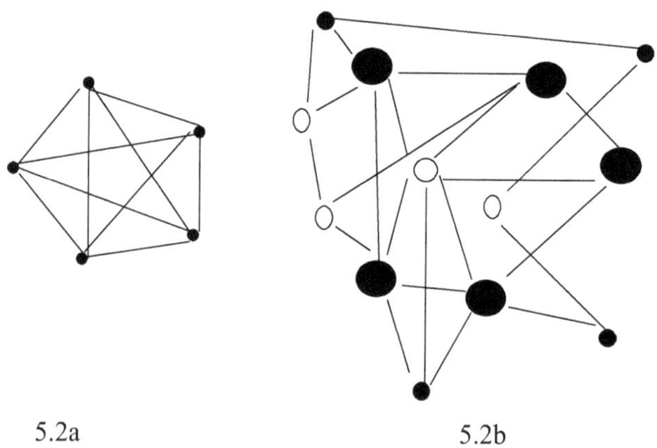

Source: Steiner and Hartmann, 1998, p. 218; de Man, 2004, p. 79

5.2.4 Functions of networks

Micro-level functions of network refer to generation of information which serves as valuable input needed to reduce search costs. Search costs are costs associated with identifying matching partners, sources of raw materials and technology as well as new market opportunities (Burt, 1995, pp. 61-2; Barr, 1998, p. 122). In complex situations, networks support the corporate bodies and managers to streamline information accurately and timely according to their specific needs. Networks induce discipline or serve as watch dogs in such a way that information is filtered and passed around the agents in a mutual and in opposite directions (Burt, 1995, p. 62). Technical information needed in production can be generated from engineers in the networks and raw materials and equipment can be sourced.

Entrepreneurs in developing countries find it difficult to score the performance capability of other entrepreneur due to high incidence of underperformance. Firms in the region always renege from agreements under the pretence of financial or technical handicap, consequently leading to malfeasance. Barr (2000, p. 3) argues that if entrepreneurs often use unavoidable circumstances as reasons for underperformance there is tendency that agreements can be reneged at will. Under such circumstances, networks can help to reduce uncertainty by helping to filter information about such situation and the integrity of others. In this respect, entrepreneurs' performance problem can be distinguished between malfeasance and unavoidable underperformance in contract agreement. Sanctions can be applied in order to enforce agreement or reduce malfeasance. Networking can enable other groups or individuals not party to the contract agreement impose sanctions too (Barr, 2000, p.3). In this case, Granovetter, (1995) argues that even when enterprises have access to formal legal systems, they often prefer to use their networks to enforce contract discipline.

In developed countries, networks often help firms to induce discipline in terms of conformity to quality specifications. For example, consider a system where small firms are lucked in a production of a certain good at specific time and in accordance to defined specifications. Each firm is expected to perform according to specification and deliver at specified time schedule. The chances of securing future contracts therefore depend on performance in previous contracts. Macaulay (1963) used the term 'commitment' to explain why networks serve as instrument for pressure to conformity. He argues that firms are committed to perform better under non-contractual arrangements in order to establish good will for future contracts. The degree of commitment in present assignment reflects on the quality of present outcome which will serve as benchmark for future contracts.

Moreover, networks can also provide the framework for informal credit and insurance arrangements. Udry (1994) and Lyon (2000) provided an insight into the impact of networks in terms of creating and guiding credit relationships in rural Nigeria and Ghana respectively. Udry (1994, p. 496) argues that risks in credit transactions in Nigeria's informal credit and insurance markets are reduced due to free flow of information between borrowers and lenders. Past information about characters of parties in the transaction can easily be traced. In Ghana, farmer–trader relationship helped to reduce uncertainty and income fluctuations of rural tomato farmers. The relationship provided a scenario where supply to traders is guaranteed during crop scarcity and traders guarantee to buy during output glut. Such relationship helped the tomato farmers secure credit from traders when banks reduced credit facilities to farmer in Ghana as a result of low repayment rates (Lyon, 2000, pp. 668-9). Chamlee's (1993, p. 81) study also revealed that most large investment activities by small and micro enterprise in Ghana are financed through indigenous informal arrangements. The loans, according to Chamlee, though being relatively small, are effectively utilised.

At meso-level, networks serve as economic institution that can help to sort out the problems or costs in transacting businesses and protection of property rights. Williamson (1985, p. 17) argues that the main purpose of economic institution of capitalism is to reduce transaction costs. Transaction costs are costs of running the economic system (Arrows, 1969, p. 48). The costs of running an economic system are high when the modes of economic organisation are not standardised and interpreted. Such costs include the costs of drafting, negotiating and safeguarding agreements as well as costs of enforcing commitments and restoring of integrity in transactions (Williamson, 1985, pp. 19-20). Networks can reduce transaction costs by helping in enforcing contract discipline in economic transactions thereby preventing the costs of litigation arising from breach of agreement. This reveals the importance of embeddedness because customs, norms, habits etc, in which transactions are embedded, can play an important role in reducing the cost of transactions (Williamson 1985, p. 22). Networks also create the framework for assets specification in investments and protection of property rights. Such rights include right to use the asset, the right to appropriate returns from the asset, and the right to change the form and/or substance of an asset (Furuborn and Pejovich, 1974, p. 4).

At macro-level, networks promote efficient market outcomes by sharing information, improving collective decision and aligning individual incentives with group objectives. The impact of networks can be explained by GDP in the sense that corruption, intensity of political discrimination, misallocation of public funds, exclusion or low participation in decision making always leads to weak economic outcomes. Networks may help improve governmental performance and the quality of economic policies through the nature, level and character of political participation (Knack and Keefer, 1997, p. 1254). Networks contribute to poverty alleviation through sharing of information or educating the poor on how to overcome problems relating to income fluctuations and credit constraints. For example, the cooperative farmers associations always share resources in the case of harvest failure. Rotational savings mechanisms provide the framework for raising investment funds. Generally, donor agencies operate effectively when there is local network formation in poverty alleviation projects (Grootaert, 1998, pp. 4-5). This section therefore tries to analyse the extent to which social networks have contributed in SME performance in Nigeria. The section also examines the commitment of entrepreneurs, institutions and the state in promoting good business environment in Nigeria.

5.2.5 Networks and Economic Development

Networks have been receiving attention of researchers in development economic in recent times. In market economy for example; it is assumed that the state is responsible for the establishment of the stable framework necessary for economic development and growth. Such framework includes among others the institutional arrangements that support private sector development. The weak institutions in sub-Saharan African countries have brought the concept of common set of values and norms needed for development. The effectiveness of the market can be impeded if the market operates without embedded common set of values and norms in a larger institutional framework (Egbert, 2003, p. 305). Society and firms are negatively affected directly or indirectly if a nation lacks the moral discipline in management of the economy. Firms on the other hand face uncertainty and suffer losses if policy changes frequently or become unfavourable.

Civic associations promotes efficient market outcomes by sharing information, aligning individual incentives with group objectives, and improving collective decision making (Grootaert, 1998, pp. 6-7). This triggers the question whether personal network is useful in entrepreneurship and economic development? The first consideration is that personal networks are embedded in entrepreneurship activities and serve as resources to entrepreneurs (Brüderl and Preisendörf, 1998, p. 215). Personal contacts play an important role during the business formation. Entrepreneurs need to mobilise support through exchange of ideas and discussions of specific business matters with friends and relations. Contacts may open the possibility to broaden the financial base of a new firm. For example, informal credits received from relatives or friends are helpful during business formation. Personal networks provide an alternative solution when the formal institutions are very weak or when the small producers could not have access to credits. The formal legal system in the region is some how complicated and expensive for the producers hence personal contacts and membership in business associations help the poor to find solution to business problems. Networking has played an important role in enhancing workers' productivity and economic growth in small manufacturing enterprises in Asia and European industrial district (Barr, 1998, p. 1). The proponents of social networks in Africa base their argument on the grounds that pervasive state failure and weak market institutions have contributed to poor economic performance in the region. Hence, personal contact plays an important role in reducing uncertainty and enhancing performance (Fafchamps, 1996, p. 428).

Arguments against networks always centre on costs of belonging, restrictions, discrimination against non-members and encouragement of free riders in the system (Woolcock, 1998, p. 165; Egbert, 2003, p. 293). Mainstream economics often reject the ties based on kinship, friendship and community in economic relations because they tend to undermine competition. In this case, Burt (1995, p. 84) argues that competition is a matter of securing productive relationships.

5.3 Review of literatures on SME networks in developed and developing countries

Literature on small enterprises networks focuses the analysis on the importance of networks especially in dissemination of information on new technology and source of inputs. Social networks often serve as medium for raising finance, identifying the credibility of potential partner thereby reducing transaction costs, fostering collective action and division of labour among enterprises. In his work on civic traditions in modern Italy, Putnam 1993 showed how fundamental networks are to entrepreneurs and the society at large. For example, informal savings institutions around the world have shown the role of rotational credit associations as source of loan or credit for business financing (Putnam 1993, p. 167). Putnam (1963) explicitly analysed the functions and benefits of social networks to entrepreneurs. The analyses covered how networks support reduction of opportunism in the sense that individuals tried to avoid cost of defecting such as sanction in business relations. Information about the entrepreneurs' reputation or past potential partner activities is easily available due to dense interaction in social networks. Networks provide informal solutions to mutual problems (Putnam, 1993, pp. 173-4). In this case, Putman stressed the importance of good governance and supports the view that organised private sector associations should be linked to government structure so that the benefits of social networks can be realised (Putnam, 1993, p. 175).

Macaulay (1963) argues that entrepreneurs rely on their networks to reduce asymmetric information. Even when enterprises have access to formal legal system, they often use their networks to enforce conformity to expectations in order to ensure contract discipline and commitment. Organisations and large firms use their networks to streamline and select information that supports competition. The basic assumption here is that networks must allow unilateral decision taken in order to ensure competitiveness (Macaulay, 1963, p. 63).

Recent literature on networks focuses on case studies and providing evidences revealing the importance of social networks to manufacturing sectors in developing countries. Fafchamps (1996) study revealed how networks provided institutional solutions to the problems related to contract enforcement which enables business to develop and firms gain access to trade credit. The fragmentation of the economy into networks led to improved efficiency in timing in service delivery where traders play the intermediary functions. However, the trade-off in such scenario gives rise to plethora of commercial intermediaries which invariably raises the production costs of small producers in

Africa. In this respect, Fafchamps argues that even when networks try to provide solutions to contract enforcement problem in developing countries it is accompanied with costs. Hence, efforts should be directed towards improving the enforcement of commercial laws in order to increase efficiency and reduce costs. For example, where there is efficient financial institution, producers can make orders or deliveries of goods and services on short-term deferred payments. In so doing, the costs of trade intermediaries and monitoring can be reduced (Fafchamps, 1996, p. 445).

Bräutigam (1997) argues that even in the event of pervasive state institutional failures, informal institutions and family ties have fostered the growth of entrepreneurial activities in Nnewi light engineering cluster. The social network that emerged in the cluster helped to find solutions to problem of high transaction costs for new manufacturers. Family ties and participation in different social associations helped to generate information needed for business decisions. This helped to reduce search costs that usually lead to principal agent problems of monitoring and enforcement. The social networks facilitated horizontal cooperation among firms in terms of sharing of special skilled workers and equipments. Risks are reduced and trust was enhanced such that information is easily shared among entrepreneurs on source of raw materials and technological partner or reliable equipment. Distribution networks developed during trading activities were used effectively in marketing manufactured products (Bräutigam, 1997, p. 1074).

Barr (1998) provided empirical evidence on the link between enterprise performance and functional diversity of social networks in Africa. The study focused not only on the levels of network activities but also on the types of networks in which enterprises belonged. The question is wheather the contacts entrepreneurs make enhance enterprises performance and reduce uncertainty. In other words, can networks be considered as performance enhancing and uncertainty reducing institution? Barr argues that differences in network functions tend to explain the diversity of networks. For example, networks that reduce uncertainty by providing high degree of information are different from networks that focus on transaction costs. Uncertainty reducing networks enhances performance indirectly by increasing the levels of information for investment strategies. Informal credit arrangements are aimed to reduce financial constraints since transaction costs of borrowing in the bank tend to be higher for small enterprises (Barr, 1998, p. 4).

Hussain (2000) provided theoretical explanation on the importance of linkages for SME development. The linkages can create opportunities for transformation from microenterprise to SME and from SME to large firm. This is because such linkages according to Hussain will help to facilitate efficiency and product upgrading to internationally acceptable standards. The author's argument is based on advantages created by rapidly changing global economic environment which African SMEs can exploit through networking. The first advantage according to Hussain is that under the WTO, new markets are being created and the existing ones are opening up due to liberalisation such that better export opportunities are now increasingly opening than before. The second is that the globalisation process has made non-price competition increasingly important. SMEs in Africa have to focus on non-price elements such as product quality upgrading, to international standard, and as well timing in product delivery. This suggests that emphasis should focus on how to improve technology capabilities through formation of joint ventures with large foreign firms.This could contribute to performance improvement through learning-by-doing (Hussain, 2000, p. 4).

Barr (2000) further investigated collective action and bilateral interaction in entrepreneurial networks in Africa. The theoretical framework of the study reflected the functions of the networks and characteristics of different network activities. Networks facilitate information inflow thereby reducing search costs in identifying new markets, in finding trading partners, in sourcing inputs and in establishing fair prices. Moreover transaction costs can be reduced through networking by enforcing and improving contract discipline especially in African market with problem of information asymmetries. The study provided analytical differences between networks and collusion. Bar argues that networks do not emerge as collective action or represent collective action which is collusion. Networks rather provide the cooperation necessary for collective action to function. This is by facilitating information necessary to reduce common constraints. Such information may relate to the conducts of other entrepreneurs in order to avoid or reduce risks associated with transactions. In such a situation, entrepreneurs can use the information available to distinguish between mal-feasance and unavoidable under performance (Barr, 2000).

Nijkamp (2003) used the Schumpeterian view to analyse the importance of networking in business development in the sense that an entrepreneur is seeking for new combinations while destroying in a creative way the existing constellations. The risk-taking behaviour of an entrepreneur can be ameliorated by externalising some of the risks through participation in local or broader industrial networks. Nijkamp however warned that networking as business strategy is not a "manner from heaven" rather requires investment in social communication, informal bonds, training and education. To build up and participate effectively in networks requires time and efforts (Nijkamp, 2003, p. 401). To this end, one can argue that the problem associated with African social networks is lack of commitment on the part of entrepreneurs to engage in learning in order to improve performance. Another problem is lack of government commitment to invest in network capacity building so that Schumpeter entrepreneurs can effectively emerge in the region.

Meagher (2006) analysed the social networks in Nigeria's informal small scale manufacturing enterprises and provided theoretical inductions on why African social networks failed to diversify and enhance performance in the context of regional and global economic activities. The underling weaknesses of Africa networks according to the study are due to inherent constraints related to discriminatory state regulatory system. This is supported by lack of the ability of entrepreneurs to develop economically effective networks, and the embedded corruptive system in the political institutions as well as dysfunctional cultural values existing in the region (Meagher, 2006, pp. 554-5). The study specifically investigated the institutional capacities of the small enterprises networks in Nigeria and the linkages in each networks. The findings suggest that the economic potential of small firms in Africa have been eroded by liberalisation pressures and political opportunism that offer no solutions to the growth constraints of small producers hence the small firms engage in survival strategies (Meagher, 2006, p. 579).

5.4 Networks in small and medium scale enterprises in Nigeria: Empirical Evidence

5.4.1 Methodology

Different approaches were considered in the empirical analyses on the impact of networks in small enterprises economic activities. The first approach is the analysis that focuses on the structure of the networks and the density of interactions in the networks. This provides the insight on the extent the contacts the entrepreneurs made have reduced costs, risks or promote firms' performance. In this context, the entrepreneurs were asked to explain why they belong to associations and how they perceive the contact they make in the associations? Family ties were not considered. Rather a broader investigation was conducted in order to analyse the nature of the interaction. Questions were also directed on how they market their products. The second approach is the analysis that focused on network functions. This helped the researcher to understand the behavioural patterns of entrepreneurs in terms of openness and trust. Barr (1998, p. 24) argues that if the members keep secrets about themselves, they will also find it difficult to access information that may enhance their firm performance. Information is considered to be an important element in knowledge spillover and performance enhancement.

The surveys contain a wide range of data about small scale manufacturing enterprises. In evaluating the pattern of the responses, the study did not apply econometrics techniques rather the responses were presented in cross-tabulations showing the data and the related outcome from the responses. The analysis did not include some areas of network composition such as gender, ethnic and kin group dimensions due to the scope and time constraints. Sub-sectoral comparative analysis was however made in order to show the impact of networks on small enterprises by sub-sectors and firm sizes for policy recommendation.

5.4.2 The structure of business related associations the entrepreneurs belong

Entrepreneurs require social activities and interactions in order to make effective decision because they are the organisers and coordinators of resources (Brüderl and Preisendörfer, 1998, p. 214). Such social interactions serve as means of accessing business information for decision making. Table 5.1 shows the distribution of entrepreneurs according to the association they belong by sub-sector.

Table 5.1: The structure of entrepreneurs belonging to business related associations 100 % by sub-sector and size.

Sub-sector	No of Sample	Subsectoral Association -NATA, Shoemakers Association (by 100%)	Business Association -NASSI, MAN, NCCIMA (by 100%)	Professional Association - Nigeria Association Engineers (by 100%)	Non-membership in any association (by 100%)	% of Resp. Actually Member in Association (by 100%)
Footwear	68	1.00	0.09	na	na	1.0
Micro Ent.	68	1.00	0.09	na	na	1.0
Small Ent	na	na	na	na	na	na
Medium	na	na	na	na	na	na
Garments	28	0.71	0.46	na	0.04	0.96
Micro Ent.	24	0.61	0.43	na	0.04	0.82
Small Ent	3	0.07	0.03	na	na	0.11
Medium	1	0.03	na		na	0.03
Woods & furniture	39	0.92	0.15	na	0.08	0.92
Micro Ent.	21	0.82	0.10	na	0.05	0.82
Small Ent	3	0.10	0.05	na	0.03	0.10
Medium	na	na	na	na	na	na
Light engineering	18	0.33	0.67	0.11	0.11	0.89
Micro Ent.	12	0.33	0.39	na	0.06	0.61
Small Ent	4	na	0.17	0.06	0.06	0.17
Medium	2	na	0.11	0.06	na	0.11
PKO Extraction	22	0.95	0.50	0.64	0.05	0.95
Micro Ent.	9	0.73	0.45	0.55	0.05	0.68
Small Ent	2	0.22	0.05	0.09	na	0.27
Medium	na	na	na	na	na	na
Network density	175	0.86	0.27	0.09	0.04	0.96

Note: 1.00 = 100 per cent
Source: Author's field survey

As indicated in Table 5.1, 86 per cent of sampled entrepreneurs belong to sub-sectoral association while 27 and 9 are members in business and professional association respectively. This suggests that small entrepreneurs value their sub-sectoral more than business and professional associations. Sub-sectoral association is an association formed by members of a handicraft group (in informal sector or in formal cooperative union) with the aim to serve the interest of their members. Business association such as chambers of commerce and industry is the umbrella which covers different branches of business units in small, medium and large scale enterprises. The professional association is an association of specialised academic discipline such as engineers, medical doctors etc. Table 5.1 also revealed that 100 and 95 per cent of interviewees in footwear and PKO belong to sub-sectoral association while only 9 and 50 per cent respectively are members in business association. The Table also shows that 92 and 71 per cent of interviewees in wood/furniture and garment enterprises respectively belong to sub-sectoral association as against 15 and 46 per cent respectively are members in business associations. The density of networks is such that 96 per cent of interviewees belong to one or more associations while only 4 per cent reported not to belong to any association. This suggests that membership in an association is voluntary. It also indicates that entrepreneurs are not restricted to one particular association. Remarkably, the findings suggest that entrepreneurs with low educational qualification tend to relay more on their sub-sectors associations. In PKO extraction enterprises, more than 50 per cent of entrepreneurs in micro and small enterprises are members in a professional association.

Memberships in non-business related associations such as religious community, town union, or state voluntary organisation can serve as means of establishing business relations. For example, the Age-Grade system among the Igbo groups in Eastern Nigeria serves as means of promoting competition and personal achievement among ones peers. Such associations are embedded in a hierarchy of stages according to age groups (Forrest, 1994, p. 178). Membership in town unions also serves as the framework for community development and granting of trade credit and assessment of trade networks across local and regional markets (Meagher, 2004, p. 8). As shown in the Table 5.2, 88 to 100 per cent of the sampled entrepreneurs belong to their respective town union. Table 5.2 shows that between 79 and 95 per cent of the sampled entrepreneurs belong to a religious association. Membership in state voluntary organisation is less important to entrepreneurs while 5 to 12 per cent of the entrepreneurs do not belong to any association.

Table 5.2: The structure of entrepreneurs belonging to non-business related Associations by sub-sector

Sector	Sample Size	Town Union, Age grade Association	Religious group	State voluntary organisation (e.g. Red Cross)	Not belonging to any group
Footwear	68	0.88	0.79	0.03	0.12
Garments	28	0.96	0.92	0.04	0.05
Woods and furniture	39	1.00	0.95	na	0.05
Light engineering	18	1.00	0.89	na	na
PKO Extraction	22	0.95	0.91	0.05	na
The total frequency	175	0.94	0.87	0.02	0.06

Note: 1 = 100 per cent
Source: Author's field survey

The intensity of membership in an association could be linked to weak institution of economic governance. As a result of weak institutional support, entrepreneurs have to find strategies to resolve their business related problems. Such economic scenario is similar to what Northrup (1978) described as "Trade without Rulers".

Table 5.3 shows how individual entrepreneurs perceive their networks. Several questions were asked and discussions were held to ascertain if membership in an association is useful or not in all aspects of business activities. Investigation revealed that interviewees perceive their networks differently according to the sub-sector. In general, 60 per cent of all interviewees consider the contacts they make in the association as useful in both business and social activities. Entrepreneurs value their networks not only for business purposes but also for other social issues like welfare. 90 per cent of the entrepreneurs in the PKO extraction industry perceive their networks as useful in all areas of their business. In general, the interviewees were asked to explain the role the association body plays for their business activities. They were also asked to explain the nature benefits they have received from or rendered to any member in the association. This is to understand if networking is directed towards resolving business related problems only or a combination of business problems and social security. They were also asked to name which areas they found their networks useful. As shown in the Table 5.3, 60 per cent of the entrepreneurs consider membership in the associations as useful to all areas of their business, 43 per cent reported to have received financial support from a member while 34 per cent reported to have given financial assistance to a member in the association. The Table also shows that 13 per cent of the interviewees have received technical assistance from other firms such as maintenance services of local fabricated machines. 14 per cent in the interviewees reported to have had some technical training in terms of seminar and workshops organised by the association body.

In terms of sub-sectoral comparisons, Table 5.3 indicates that 90 and 75 per cent of the interviewees in PKO and light engineering respectively consider membership in the associations as useful to all areas of their business. 67 and 56 of the interviewees in garment and wood/furniture enterprises respectively consider membership in the associations as useful to all areas of their business and 48 per cent of the footwear enterprises. In terms of mutual support, entrepreneurs were asked whether they have given financial assistance to any of their members in the association. The responses in Table 5.3 show that 86 and 66 per cent of the interviewees in PKO and light engineering enterprises claimed to have received financial help from some of their members in the association. In wood/furniture and footwear enterprises, 36 and 32 per cent of the interviewees claimed to receive financial assistance from their members as against 30 per cent in garment. 76 and 38 per cent of the interviews in PKO, light engineering and footwear enterprises respectively claimed to have given financial assistance to members as against 33 and 14 per cent of interviewees in garment and wood/furniture enterprises. 38 per cent of the interviewees in PKO enterprises claimed to have received technical assistance from their members as against 25 per cent in Light engineering, 30 per cent in footwear and 6 per cent in wood/furniture enterprises. The entrepreneurs were asked whether the association body has rendered assistance in sourcing funds and technical matters. The responses as shown in Table 5.3 indicate that 44 per cent of interviewees in garment sub-sector received financial assistance through their cooperative funds managed by the association body. 56 per cent of interviewees in Light engineering claimed to have sourced technical assistance through association body as against 4 per cent footwear enterprise. The zero response in PKO and wood and furniture enterprises signifies weak performance of the association body in terms of rendering assistance in securing financial assistance[145].

When asked if the contacts they make in non-business related associations are relevant to their business activities, 50 per cent of the interviewees consider membership in non-business association as relevant to all areas of their business. The high percentage value in footwear and garment sub-sectors suggests that the town union and religion play a significant role in entrepreneurship activities in the sub-sectors. Information about the market and some assistance relating to their business activities can be indirectly derived during discussions after church services or town union meetings. However; this does not imply that town union or religious bodies provide direct assistance rather they create an interactive forum for discussions among members.

145 Funding small scale enterprises through cooperative system has been part of objectives of central bank Nigeria but the survey indicates that funding has been limited.

Table 5.3: Perception of entrepreneurs to the association they belonged with their business by sub-sector

A Membership in sub-sectoral, business and professional associations						
	Footwear	Garment	Wood & Furniture	Light Engineering	PKO	All
Sample size	68	27	36	16	21	168
Proportion of interviewees that						
a) perceived the contact they make in the association as very useful to all areas of their business.	0.48	0.67	0.56	0.75	0.90	0.60
b) received financial support from any member of the association.	0.32	0.30	0.36	0.66	0.86	0.43
c) have given financial support to any or some members in the association.	0.38	0.33	0.14	0.38	0.76	0.34
d) have received technical assistance from any member of the association	0.10	0.0	0.06	0.25	0.38	0.13
e) have received financial/ technical assistance or market information from the association body.	0.04	0.44	0.00	0.56	0.0	0.14
B Membership in non-business related associations						
	Footwear	Garment	Wood & Furniture	Light Engineering	PKO	All
Sample size	68	27	36	16	21	168
Proportion of interviewees that						
a) perceive the contact they make in the association as very useful to all areas of their business	0.79	0.74	0.06	0.31	0.14	0.50
b) have received financial, technical or market information from any member of the association.	0.38	0.44	0.03	0.19	0.05	0.25

Source: Author's field survey

Table 5.4 reveals how the responses are translated according to firm size. It shows why small enterprises are likely to value personal contacts and why micro credits from donor organisation are very important for microenterprise[146]. As shown in Table 5.4 line 1, 85 and 75 per cent of the interviewees in micro and small enterprises respectively consider the contacts they make in business related associations to be very useful in all areas of their businesses. All the entrepreneurs in medium scale enterprises perceived the contacts they make in association to be useful in their businesses. In terms of mutual assistance to members, Table 5.4 line 2, 75 per cent of the interviewees in small scale enterprises reported to have received financial assistance from some members in the association as against 67 and 39 per cent in medium and micro enterprises.

Table 5.4: Perception of entrepreneurs to the association they belong by firm size

A Membership in sub-sectoral, business and professional associations in 100 %				
	1-9	10-49	50-99	All
Sample Size	149	16	3	168
Proportion of interviewees that				
a) perceive the contact they make in the association as very useful to all areas of their business.	0.85	0.75	1.00	0.60
b) have received financial support from any member of the association.	0.39	0.75	0.67	0.43
c) have given financial support to any or some members in the association.	0.30	0.88	1.00	0.34
d) have received technical assistance from any member of the association	0.03	0.88	0.67	0.13
e) have received financial/technical assistance or market information from the association body.	0.07	0.75	0.67	0.14
B Membership in non-business related associations				
	1-9	10-49	50-99	All
Sample size	149	16	3	168
Proportion of interviewees that				
a) perceive the contact they make in the association as very useful to all areas oftheir business	0.49	0.56	0.67	0.50
b) have received financial, technical or market information from any member of the association.	0.23	0.43	0.33	0.25

Note: 1.00 = 100 per cent
Source: Author's field survey

Table 5.4 line 3 shows that all the interviewees in medium scale enterprises reported to have given financial assistance in one form and another to a member

146 This is based on the argument that small enterprises face many constraints related to infrastructure and have little state support in terms access to information and finances.

in their association as against 88 and 30 per cent in small and micro enterprises respectively. In Table 5.4 line 4, 88 per cent of the interviewees in small scale enterprises claimed to have rendered technical assistance to one or more members in their respective associations as against 67 and 3 per cent in medium and micro enterprises respectively. In evaluating the performance of the association bodies according to firm size, 75 per cent interviewees in small scale enterprises reported to have received financial assistance through the support of the association body while 67 and 7 per cent of the interviewees claimed to have received technical or financial support through the association body.

Table 5.4 also shows the relationship between firm's size and membership in non-business association. 67 per cent of entrepreneurs in medium scale enterprises value the contacts they make in non-business related associations as very important in all aspect of their businesses as against 56 and 49 per cent in small and micro enterprises respectively (Table 5.4, line 6). In terms of benefits from non-business association, 43 per cent of the interviewees in small enterprises reported to have received financial assistance from members in non-business related association they belonged to as against 33 and 23 per cent in medium and micro enterprises (Table 5.4, line7). This suggests that there is need to increase microfinance programmes through government agencies, NGOs and donor assistance programmes. The aforementioned networks are personal networks which the entrepreneurs as social agents are embedded.

Table 5.5 shows the structure of the organisational networks of micro small and medium enterprises by sector. The Table explains how firms are linked in production and their marketing outlets. Four types of linkages were identified, namely the input and output structures, linkages with large firms, and institutions. The analysis provides an insight into the impact of network structure on economic activities of the SMEs. As indicated in Table 5.5, 52 per cent of all sampled enterprises source their raw materials through independent entrepreneurs, in most cases the traders. 42 per cent of the firms depend on other firms for the supply of components while the 35 per cent of the firms sub-contract the activities to other firms. There is evidence of high degree of backward and forward supply linkages in PKO sub-sector with 91 per cent of the enterprises making supplies to large firms. Table 5.5 also indicates that outside PKO extraction enterprises, 89 to 100 per cent of the small enterprises in the sub-sectors channel their output through an informal marketing system. Firms market their products either directly to consumers or to traders without keeping records[147]. The PKO producers have developed formal linkages with

147 Informal marketing channel often aimed at convincing people to try out or keep using particular products or services by planning their marketing strategies and performance. In informal marking system, sales are directed towards ultimate consumer through traders or cooperatives.

medium and large vegetable oil refineries and soup industries such that orders can be made on regular basis depending on the market demand.

Government and public institutions procurement has become a major source of promoting small producers. ILO (1972) emphasised on the need for government and public institutions to procure from small producers in the formal and informal sectors in order to increase productivity and as well stimulate employment creation. Supply linkages with institutions were identified in footwear, garment and furniture enterprises. 23 per cent of the sampled enterprises in men shoe production unit claimed to produce for Nigeria Military, Nigerian Navy, and Police forces. 11 per cent of the sampled enterprises in the garment industry have at one time been involved with education institutions especially the nursery, primary and secondary school by supplying uniform and sportswear. 5 per cent of interviewees in wood and furniture industries have some times engaged with government institutions and supplies to education institutions.

Table 5.5: The structure of the organisational networks in the sub-sectors

Sector	Footwear	Garments	Woods & furniture	Light engineering	PKO Extraction	All
Sample size	68	28	39	18	22	175
Input Networks						
Supply of materials	0.82	0.68	0.15	na	0.73	0.52
Supply of components	0.88	na		0.44	na	0.42
Backward contracting	0.88	0.04	na	na	na	0.35
Output Networks						
Formal marketing	0.01	na	0.03	0.11	0.91	0.14
Informal marketing	0.97	1.00	0.97	0.89	0.09	0.86
Large firms	na	na	na	0.17	0.91	0.13
Institutions	0.23	0.11	0.05	na	na	0.12

Source: Author's field survey

This is translated in Table 5.6 indicating that less than 15 per cent of the sampled small enterprises have linkages with institutions and organisation firms. Table 5.6 also shows that 58 per cent of micro enterprises engage independent agent in sourcing their raw materials as against 33 and 1 per cent in medium and small enterprises. 42 per cent of micro enterprises source the components of their production equipment through agents while 33 per cent in medium scale enterprises reported using agents in sourcing machine components. 39 and 5 per cent of entrepreneurs in micro and small enterprises sectors reported to have engaged in sub-contracting their production activities. 14 and 15 per cent of sampled micro and small enterprises market their product formally using sales agents or supply to organised market outlet as against 33 per cent in medium scale enterprises. Hence, 89 per cent of the enterprises market their products informally through traders or direct to the market as against 67 and 65 per cent in medium and small enterprises.

Table 5.6: The structure of organisational networks by firm size

Sector	1-9	10-49	50-99	All
Sample size	152	20	3	175
Input Networks				
Supply of Materials	0.58	0.1	0.33	0.52
Supply of Components	0.42	na	0.33	0.42
Backward sub-contracting	0.39	0.05	na	0.35
Output Networks				
Formal Marketing	0.14	0.15	0.33	0.14
Informal Marketing	0.89	0.65	0.67	0.86
large firms	0.14	0.1	na	0.13
Institutions	0.14	na	na	0.12

Source: Author's field survey

The entrepreneurs were asked to explain where they market their products or the market channels of their products. As shown in Table 5.7, 87 per cent of the products are sold in the local markets, 67 per cent are sold within the country (i.e. national markets) while 28 per cent export their products within sub-regional African markets. In decomposing the analysis according to sub-sectors, Table 5.7 shows that 99 and 88 per cent of the output in footwear enterprises are sold in the local and national markets respectively while 66 per cent are exported to African regional markets. 100 and 71 per cent of outputs in garment enterprises are sold in the local and national markets respectively as against 7 per cent export to African sub-regional markets.

Table 5.7: Distribution networks of SMEs by sub-sector

Sector	Footwear	Garments	Woods & Furniture	Light Engineering	PKO	All
Sample size	68	28	39	16	22	175
Local Market	0.99	1.00	1.00	1.00	0.09	0.87
National Market	0.88	0.71	0.05	0.88	1.00	0.67
African regional Market	0.66	0.07	0.03	0.06	0.00	0.28

Note: 1.00= 100 per cent
Source: Author's field survey

Table 5.7 also shows that 100 per cent of the outputs in wood/furniture and light engineering enterprises are sold in the local markets while 5 and 88 per cent are sold in the national market respectively. The exports activities in wood/furniture and light engineering enterprises to African regional market recorded only 3 and 6 per cent respectively. In contrast to other sub-sectors, 9 per cent of outputs in

PKO extraction enterprises are supplied to local firms but no export was recorded in the PKO. Table 5.7 further reveals the export potential of footwear subsector. It also shows that footwear enterprises have developed export strategy which is extremely lacking in other sub-sectors.

Table 5.8 shows the distributive networks in the Aba footwear enterprises cluster across African sub-regional markets. To determine the marketing networks of the footwear producers, the interviewees were asked to mention country of origin of their African customers. The frequency of customers' visit was determined as shown in appendix 5.9. Nine major countries from west to east coast of Africa were identified. Cameroon remains the major trading country of Nigeria's footwear export.

Table 5.8: African regional distribution networks of Aba footwear small scale industries (in average No. and % of yearly order)

Countries	Ladies-Shoes (Sample Size = 16)	Men-Shoes (Sample Size = 8)	Total No of yearly orders	% of annual total orders by country
Cameroon	24	24	48	0.38
Ghana	12	6	18	0.14
Gabon	12	4	16	0.13
Togo	12	4	16	0.13
Benin.Rep.	6	4	10	0.08
Congo	4	3	7	0.06
Angola	2	2	5	0.04
Ivory coast	2	2	4	0.03
Malawi	1	1	2	0.02
Total	75	50	126	1.00

Key: Av. = Average; No. = Number; Yr. = Yearly
Source: Author's field survey (see Appendix 5.9)

As shown in Table 5.8, the average total number of yearly orders from Cameroon is 48. This indicates that 38 per cent of total orders from African countries originate from Cameroon. The Table shows that export to Ghana amounts to 14 per, Togo and Gabon recording 13 per cent while export to Malawi is the lowest with 2 per cent of the total export. This is translated in Figure 5.3 showing the average annual frequency of orders expressed in percentage from different countries in African sub-region. It also shows the increased trading activities among the Anglo and Franco phone countries. This can be linked to reduced restrictions on movement of goods and people induced by regionalisation processes and liberalisation of the market in sub-Saharan African countries. Moreover, the survey revealed that increased Chinese presence in region has also induced product competition in the sub-sector hence small firms have developed different strategies to remain competitive in the local and African regional markets.

Figure 5.3: African regional customers' annual order by country in %

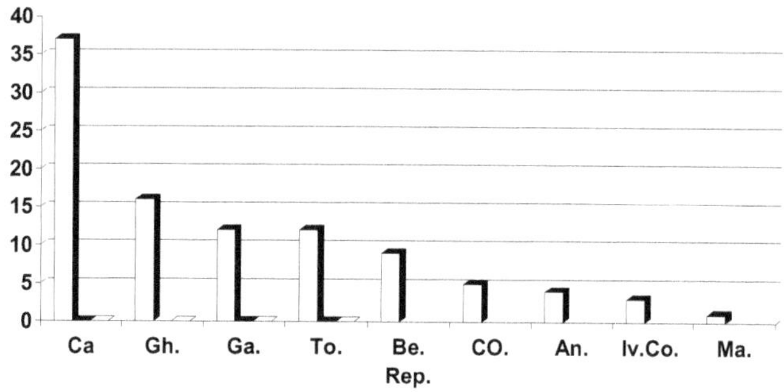

Key: Ca= Cameron; Gh. = Ghana; Ga = Gabon; To. = Togo; Be. = Benin- Republic; Co. = Congo; An. = Angola; Iv.Co. = Ivory Coast; Ma, = Malawi
Source: Derived from Table 5.8

The interviewees were also asked to explain the methods of distributing their products. The responses revealed that there are different methods of product marketing. As shown in Table 5.9, 63 per cent of the sampled enterprises produce by order. 13 per cent of the sampled enterprises make supplies direct to the market and 57 per cent produce on specification in terms of specific designs to customers while 16 per cent supply to firms. When asked to explain how their products reach the final consumers, 4 per cent of the interviewees reported using informal methods by displaying samples, giving out business cards or through informal marketing agents[148]. 41 per cent of the sampled enterprises supply to individual and households while 77 per cent supply to traders.

At sub-sectoral level, 95 and 88 per cent of productions in PKO and foot-wear are carried out on customers' order. 33 and 29 per cent of the enterprises in light engineering and garment channel their products direct to the market. This suggests that some firms rent shops in the local markets in order to have direct sales outlet. When asked to explain how their customers make request, 79, 57 and 46 per cent of enterprises in footwear, garment and furniture enterprises respectively reported that their customers come with specific designs from catalogues or sample design with specifications. In terms of direct supply to firms, 100 per cent of enterprises in PKO extraction make direct supply to firms and individuals while 100 per cent of the enterprises in footwear deal with trader as against 91 and 83 per cent in PKO and light engineering respectively.

148 An informal marketing agent often uses a sample design to look for customers.

Table 5.9: Methods of distributing products

Sector	Footwear	Garment	Wood & Furniture	Light Engineering	PKO Extraction	All
Sample size	68	28	39	18	22	175
Supply by order	0.88	0.54	0.08	0.67	0.95	0.63
Supply direct to market	0.00	0.29	0.15	0.33	0.09	0.13
Producing by Specification	0.79	0.57	0.46	0.61	0.00	0.57
Producing for firms	0.00	0.00	0.00	0.33	1.00	0.16
Use of informal methods or marketing agents	0.04	0.18	0.00	0.00	0.00	0.04
Use of formal advertisement	0.00	0.00	0.00	0.00	0.00	0.00
Individuals and household	0.16	0.75	0.46	0.00	1.00	0.41
Traders	1.00	0.79	0.23	0.83	0.91	0.77

Source: Author's field survey

5.4.3 Network functions and their effect on firm performance

The analyses of networks structure helped to develop the working definition of the respective networks. It also helped to reduce ambiguities due to heterogeneity in sub-sectoral activities. The interviewees were further asked to remember the contacts they maintain in their respective networks and how they value the contacts. This is to ascertain if the networks have direct relevance to entrepreneurs' business activities. During discussions, five functions of networking namely: information, protection, credits and loan, government policy and guarantee of social welfare were identified. The interviewees were asked to give reasons why they join association. As shown in Table 5.10, information about business partners (90%), new market (86%) technical issues (78%) and sources of raw materials (73%) are the major reasons for joining association. Majority of the interviewees value their networks as means of reducing search costs associated with product and input markets. Such information according to the interviewees is very important for firm performance. Furthermore, 92 per cent of the interviewees reported welfare while 90 per cent consider protection from undue harassment from local authorities as the major reasons for membership in an association. Table 5.10 further shows that 49 per cent of entrepreneurs consider understanding government policy and how to deal with local authorities as important reasons for membership in an association. 33 and 14 per cent respectively consider access to credits and loans, and reaching out for subcontracting as part of the reasons for belonging in an association. The findings therefore suggest that belonging in an association help small entrepreneurs in finding solutions to internal and external problems concerning their business activities.

Table 5.10: Assessment of network functions by sub-sector

Sector	Footwear	Garments	Wood & Furniture	Light engineering	PKO extraction	All
Sample size	68	28	39	18	22	175
The proportion of entrepreneurs in the sub-sector who view the contact they make in their networks as						
- source of technical information	0.91	0.57	0.67	0.67	0.45	0.78
- source of information for raw materials	0.66	0.64	0.69	0.89	0.95	0.73
- source of information for new market	0.91	0.86	0.77	0.94	0.82	0.86
- source of information for the assessment of trade partners	0.96	0.79	0.82	1.00	0.91	0.90
- means of reaching out for sub-contracting	0.00	0.00	0.10	0.17	0.77	0.14
- means of protection	0.97	0.93	0.87	0.61	0.95	0.90
- means ofaccessing credits and loans	0.18	0.86	0.31	0.33	0.14	0.33
-how to deal with government func-tionaries and policy	0.15	0.57	0.69	0.94	0.91	0.49
-means of contact and social welfare	0.97	0.96	1.00	0.50	0.95	0.92

Note: 1 = 100
Source: Author's field survey

In small enterprises, 82 and 80 per cent of the entrepreneurs consider information concerning technology and assessment of new partners as reasons for joining an association. 75 and 70 per cent of the entrepreneurs consider information about raw materials and new market as very important to them. 91 per cent of the entrepreneurs in microenterprises consider membership in an association as means of getting information about a potential business partner while 89 per cent microenterprises consider membership in an association as means of sourcing information about potential new markets. 76 per cent of entrepreneurs in microenterprises consider information about raw materials as very important for their business while 72 per cent view access to new market an important reason for joining an association. Table 5.11 shows the assessment of network functions by firm size. As shown in the table, 100 per cent of the entrepreneurs in medium scale enterprises consider information concerning technology, access to raw materials or about new markets as well as assessment of new partners as major reasons for joining an association.

Table 5.11: Assessment of network functions by firm size

Sector	Micro Enterprises	Small Enterprises	Medium Enterprises	All
Sample size	152	20	3	175
The proportion of entrepreneurs in the sub-sector who view their networks as				
- means to source technical information	0.76	0.82	1.00	0.78
- means to source information for raw materials	0.72	0.75	1.00	0.73
- means to source information for new market	0.89	0.70	1.00	0.86
- means to source information for the assessment of trading partners	0.91	0.80	1.00	0.90
- means to reaching out for sub-contracting business	0.12	0.25	0.33	0.14
- means to protection	0.93	0.70	0.67	0.90
- means to access credits and loans	0.34	0.45	1.00	0.36
- means to understand how to handle business issues with government functionaries and policy	0.45	0.75	1.00	0.49
- means of contact and social welfare	0.95	0.70	0.67	0.92

Source: Author's field survey

Table 5.11 above further indicates that 93 per cent of interviewees in microenterprises consider protection against undue harassment from local authorises while 95 per cent of interviewees in microenterprises consider welfare and solidarity support during personal problem as the most important reasons of membership in an association. 75 and 70 of the interviewees in small enterprises reported understanding government policies and how to handle business issues with the authorities as the reasons for joining associations. 100 per cent of the interviewees in medium scale enterprises consider how to get access to loans and credits as very important for them in their respective networks as against 45 and 34 per cent in small and microenterprises respectively. In a nutshell, business related information including government policies and access to loans and credits are the major challenges facing the medium scale enterprises. The small enterprises consider technology, business partners, raw materials and government policies as their major concern. While micro enterprises consider welfare, protection, access to trading partners, access to new markets and technology as their major business concern.

Table 5.12 shows how entrepreneurs value their networks in terms of protecting business interest. Questions were directed specifically on the measures that tend to reduce risks and increase performance. When asked to explain how they protect their interest, Table 5.12 suggested that all enterprises except PKO collect cash deposits before production as a measure of security and source of working capital.

Table 5.12: Networks as risk reduction instrument by sub-sector

Sector	Footwear	Garments	Wood & Furniture	Light Engineering	PKO Extraction	All
Sample size	68	28	39	18	22	175
The proportion of entrepreneurs who view their networks as means of reducing business risks by:						
-assessment and making joint purchases or supplies	0.76	0.25	0.74	1.00	1.00	0.64
-assessment and monitoring of trade credits	0.82	0.79	0.51	0.73	0.72	0.58
-enforcement of conformity to business relations	0.25	0.11	0.10	0.23	0.23	0.19
Proportion of Entre-preneurs who view their networks as means of protecting business interest by						
-accepting some cash deposit before production	1.00	1.00	1.00	1.00	0.09	0.87
-accepting all payment before production	0.03	0.04	0.03	0.06	0.0	0.03
-accepting personal Guarantees in offering trade credit	0.15	0.07	0.08	0.11	--	0.10

Source: Author's field survey

When asked to explain how they ensure quality or fulfil agreements made, the values in Table 5.12, line 3 indicate that commitment to improve standard is very weak across sub-sectors. 19 per cent of the sampled entrepreneurs value their networks as means of ensuring conformity to agreements[149]. When asked whether they had problem with trade credit offered to their customers, Table 5.12, line 2 shows that monitoring trade credit is effective in footwear and garment enterprises but relatively weak in wood/furniture enterprises. Table 5.12, line 1 indicates that access to raw materials and making joint supplies are relatively stronger in PKO and light engineering sub-sectors but relatively weak in garment enterprises. In general, accepting cash deposit is the obvious method of reducing risks and avoids conflicts as a result of default in payment.

Table 5.13 shows how risk reduction is reflected across firm size. The Table indicates that the frequency of cash deposit before production and monitoring trade credit are relatively high in micro and small enterprises respectively. Assessment and making of purchases or supplies is relatively stronger in medium and microenterprises than in small enterprises.

Table 5.13: Risk reduction Networks by firm size

Sector	Micro Ent	Small Ent.	Medium Ent	All
Sample size	152	20	3	175
The proportion of entrepreneurs that value the contact they make in their networks as means of protecting Business interest by				
-assessment and making joint supplies or purchases	0.64	0.60	0.67	0.64
-assessment and monitoring of trade credits	0.59	0.70	0.33	0.58
-enforcement of conformity to business relations	0.18	0.20	0.33	0.19
The proportion of entrepreneurs that protect their business interest by				
-accept cash some deposit before production	0.93	0.45	0.33	0.87
-accepting all payment before production	0.02	0.05	0.33	0.03
-accepting personal guarantees in offering trade credit	0.07	0.30	0.33	0.10

Source: Author's field survey

On the average, enforcement of conformity to business relations and accepting all payment before production are relatively weak across sectors irrespective of the firm size. 33 and 30 per cent of entrepreneurs interviewed in medium and small scale enterprises demand guarantees when establishing business relationship with new customers. Generally the findings suggest that through personal interactions, entrepreneurs can have access to valuable information which can contribute in reducing costs and enhancing performance. The findings also suggest that association serve as an umbrella to protect the small enterprises and provide informal social welfare services to their members which individual

149 This indicates high rate of under performance which often leads to high risks, uncertainty and increased cost. The implication here is that orders placed by customers cannot be met in line with market demand.

firms alone cannot guarantee. The findings also indicate that constraints the firms face differ according to sub-sector and size. Hence, social networks help in the reduction of internal and external constraints small enterprises in Nigeria face (hypothesis c). Conflicts usually arise in business relations in different forms but the common conflicts identified in the survey are under performance, delay in payment and refusal to honour payment. The survey revealed that conflicts often arise when there is refusal to honour payment due to underperformance.

Table 5.14 shows that 83 per cent of all sampled enterprises have experienced problems with their business partners during the past year. In this case, 88 per cent of the entrepreneurs that had conflict with customers resolved them without a third party. 21 per cent consulted a third party and 11 per cent turned to the association body in finding solutions to trade related problem while 1 per cent used formal processes.

Table 5.14: Conflict management by sub-sector

Sector	Footwear	Garments	Wood & Furniture	Light Engineering	PKO	All
Sample size	68	28	39	18	22	175
The ratio of the entrepreneurs who have experienced problems with their business partners during the past year	0.85	0.86	0.82	0.78	0.82	0.83
The ratio of the entrepreneurs who resolve their problem with customers themselves without third a party	0.89	0.83	0.81	0.87	0.91	0.88
-with intervention of a third party.	0.13	0.18	0.18	0.56	0.27	0.21
- by formal legal system	na	na	na	0.06		0.01
- by evolving police	na	na	na	na	na	na
- by association body	0.16	0.07	0.13	na	0.05	0.11

Source: Author's field survey

This suggests that weak legal institution in Nigeria forced entrepreneurs to apply informal methods of resolving business conflicts. It also suggests that judicial process is costly in terms of time and money when resolving simple business conflicts. Hence; entrepreneurs resort to alternative means in resolving trade related conflicts. At sub-sectoral level, Table 5.14 shows that business related problems is relatively high in garment and footwear enterprises. The ratio of entrepreneurs who resolve their problems with customers without third party is relatively high in PKO extraction and footwear enterprises. Table 5.14 also shows that 56 per cent of the interviewees in light engineering call in a third party in resolving trade related conflicts. In general, the low rate of consulting the association body or the police in resolving business related conflicts across sectors suggests that firms often exhaust all forms of measures in conflict management before looking for external help.

5.4.4 Comparative analysis of Networks effects

The survey findings also indicate that sub-sectoral associations are more important to entrepreneurs than business and professional associations. This suggests that the sub-sectoral associations are in a better position to understand their needs, problems and help to find solutions. It also suggests that firms in the same problem group interact more than those outside the group. As shown in Table 5.15, there is a relationship between the educational level of the entrepreneurs and membership in an association. Entrepreneurs with relatively higher educational attainment (Light engineering and PKO) have the highest membership record in business and professional associations.

Table 5.15: Sub-sectoral comparison of the network effects by sub-sectors

	Sectoral Comparison					
Network Structure	Footwear	Garment	Wood/ Furniture	Light Engineering	PKO	ALL
Membership in Sectoral Association	1.00	0.71	0.91	0.33	0.95	0.86
Membership in Business Association	0.09	0.46	0.15	0.67	0.50	0.27
Membership in Professional Association	na	na	na	0.11	0.64	0.09
Membership in Non-business Association	0.88	0.95	0.95	1.00	1.00	0.94
Educational Level of the Respondents (EH)	Footwear	Garment	Wood/ Furniture	Light Engineering	PKO	
Primary Education	0.714	0.597	0.627	0.336	0.395	
Secondary Education	0.143	0.393	0.271	0.600	0.461	
Post Secondary	0.071	0.010	0.017	0.220	0.105	
Vocational Training	0.071	NA	0.085	0.420	0.089	

Note: 1= 100
Key: EH = Enterprises Head; NA = Not Available
Source: Author's field survey

The entrepreneurs in footwear, garment and wood/furniture with relatively low educational attainment have the highest membership in sub-sectoral association.

This is a reflection of Brüderl and Preisendörfer (1998) network compensation hypothesis[150]. In general, 94 per cent of the interviewees belong to non-business related associations. Table 5.15 also indicates that networking is more diversified in PKO extraction and Light engineering sub-sectors than other sectors.

Table 5.16: Forms of networks by sub-sector and their effects

Sub-Sectors	Type of Networks	Major networks effects
Footwear	Personal Networks	Information on design, new markets, trade partners protection and welfare
	Organisational Networks	High input supply linkages, Informal marketing system, No evidence of linkages with large firms but have developed customer relationship with Nigerian Police and the Military.
Garments	Personal Networks	Mainly for welfare, information for new market, business protection, access to credit through existing cooperative association fund
	Organisational Networks	Supply of materials, Informal marketing and supplies to educational institutions
Woods & furniture	Personal Networks Organisational Networks	Welfare oriented networks, as means of finding trade partners, raw materials, and new markets. Informal supply and marketing system
Light Engineering	Personal Networks	Information about trade partners, new market, and raw material, understanding govt policies.
	Organisational Networks	Depends largely on informal marketing and supply of components
PKO Extraction	Personal Networks Organisational Networks	Welfare, protection, locating source of raw material, trade partners and new markets. Relative semi formal marketing and linkages with larger firms.
All Sectors	Personal Networks	Relatively Strong: personal contact aids solution due to lack of institutional support and poor infrastructure
	Organisational Networks	Relatively very weak: the organised linkages are very weak and are informal in nature.

Source: Author's field survey

Table 5.16 shows the forms of networks and their effects on firms' performance by sub-sector. The Table indicates a higher density of personal interaction than organisational linkages. This is arguably due to size effect on one hand, and lack of structural institutionalisation on the other. Hence, small entrepreneurs have to organise their production and marketing activities in line with their networking capabilities. In this context, Egbert (2003, p. 291) argues that small enterprises networks are part of the measures the entrepreneurs apply during

150 The hypothesis suggests that "business founders with a less favorable human capital profile and with restricted financial resources try harder to activate their social ties and receive more support out of their networks" (Brüderl and Preisendörfer, 1998, p. 218).

establishment and maintenance of business activities. Table 5.16 also shows that information and social welfare are the most valuable functions generated by personal networks because personal networks involve direct contacts. The social welfare serves as informal social security during business crisis or ill health and family related problems. The organisational networks in the region are informal supply of materials and marketing of products by traders[151]. PKO extraction enterprises have managed to establish informal linkage based on market demand with the medium, large firms and the rural peasants. Vertical sub-contracting and specialised division of labour that are usually associated with the organisational networks exists at low level in the footwear sub-sector.

The findings reveal that networks investigated are exclusive in the sense that it lowers transaction costs for those enterprises in the network structure. The implication is that inefficient enterprises or those that produce low quality products enjoy network protection and remain in the market because income is very low in the region. Furthermore, local competitors are driven out of the market. This can substantially impede development and growth of small enterprises in Nigeria. If the degree of exclusion is high, innovative activity of the enterprises will be affected negatively. Consequently, the basic function of networks as innovation milieu will be marred. In general, personal networks are vital to small enterprises but the value attached to personal networks tends to decrease as firms gains in economy of scales and scope. Hence, the need for stable and functional formal institution is imperative.

5.5 Summary and Conclusions

This chapter provides an in-depth analysis on the forms and the structure of networks. This gives insight into the differences between personal and organisational networks, and how networks can facilitate linkages between SMEs and MNEs. The empirical analyses of the network functions are classified in terms of micro, meso and macro-level functions. Micro level functions reflect the cost reduction effects and performance enhancement. The meso-level functions focus on how networks serve as economic institutions for the protection of property rights and reducing the cost of transacting business. Macro-level analysis concerns with the aggregate outcome due to improve collective decision making and governmental performance translated into GDP

151 Organisational networks indicate the number of intermediaries or steps necessary to make the contact. In a limiting case, it shows whether an organisation or firm is in fact completely isolated. The network indicate very clearly where new services or communication lines are necessary, or where there are already too many. This could take the form of an information map indicating the ease with which information from certain points could be obtained when starting from others which are very weak in Nigerian enterprises networks.

growth. The relationships between networks and economic development were also analysed. This is followed by the review of literature on small scale enterprises networks in developed and developing countries.

The empirical evidence focused on micro level analysis of the networks in small scale enterprises in Nigeria. The analyses were grouped into how entrepreneurs value the contacts they make and their impact on business performance. The study also investigated the nature of organisational networks among the enterprises and how network functions are translated in business performance. The findings indicate that firms value their sub-sectoral associations than the professional and business association such NASSI, MAN or NCCIMA. This is because problems related to business are easier to resolve at sub-sectoral association level. The findings also show that belonging to non-business related associations such as town union and religious association are relevant in business. This however does not imply that town union or religious bodies provide direct assistance to business activities. They serve as a forum for interaction that gives room for business discussion and information flow. There is evidence of backward and forward linkages in footwear and PKO sub-sectors. The PKO producers have developed informal linkages with medium and large scale vegetable oil refineries and soap industries as well as rural farmers. Informal distribution channels are used in product marketing within the local and across African sub-regional market. Government and institutional procurement were identified in the survey. The findings also indicates that networks serve as means of reducing search costs associated with inputs and protection against opportunists. Cash deposit before production is the measure designed for risks reduction in producer-trader economic transaction.

Generally, there is no evidence suggesting that networks investigated are knowledge networks or facilitate product quality upgrading. The chapter has shown how small scale producers in Africa continue to thrive for progress in spite of poor institutional infrastructure, unstable political and macroeconomic conditions common in the region. The chapter also provided empirical evidences on impact of networks on small enterprises economic activities in terms of reducing risks, conflict management and access to distance markets. The findings also provided answers to some basic questions concerning African small enterprises networks (African networks are mere welfare supporting strategy but weak in risks reduction?). The major problem identified in this analysis is the inability of the networks to expand beyond African sub-regional boundaries or linkages with large firms. The second weakness is the dominance of social networks as against strong inter-firm linkages. This shows that networks investigated cannot enhance performance effectively. It also suggests that networks are only horizontal networks not knowledge networks hence national and local systems of innovation will remain underdeveloped.

Chapter 6: Innovation in Nigerian Small and Medium scale Enterprises

6.1 Introduction

Innovation refers to the process of bringing new ideas into use (Kanter, 1983, p. 20). Such process is considered very important for small enterprises to become competitive. In principle, innovation is a macro-phenomenon in the sense that it is an activity that creates economic growth (Schumpeter, 1934, p. 68). Innovation theories offer insight into how the innovation process takes place at individual enterprises level. They also explain the relationship between micro and macro innovation processes. Micro level analyses focuses on who generate or which factors generate innovation. Macro level analysis explains how innovation spread through society (Sundbo, 1998, pp. 1-2). Innovation is assumed to be the major factor responsible for most growth when an economic boom begins in a period of depression. Schumpeter (1934, p. 65) argues that economic growth is a function of entrepreneurship because entrepreneurs continue the process of innovation.

Discussions about innovation in small enterprises in developing countries have different roots dating back to 1970s and can be linked to appropriate technology (AT) movement. In the 1980s, emphases were shifted to technological capability but recently the role of clustering and networking in promoting innovation in small enterprises in developing countries has become critical. Innovation as a concept at firm-level in Africa has been controversial due to the level of industrial development in the region. Many factors such as poor economic governance, low level of human capital development and poor market development have contributed to pessimistic view about innovation in the region. Van Dijk (2003, p. 345) cautioned that innovation is not the major challenge small enterprises in Africa face rather the acquisition of technology capabilities or the capability to innovate. Despite these arguments, World Bank has been encouraging innovation at firm level in the Africa in order to promote economic growth (Aubert, 2004, p. 5).

This chapter analyses the mechanisms through which small enterprises in Africa acquire local technological capability and bring it to use. The study considers among others the capability of local enterprises to adapt and develop technology. In this respect, the analyses focuses on how the small enterprises respond to changes in demand, explore new markets, and respond to competition. The chapter is organised into seven sub-sections. The next section reviews the theory of innovation with different definitions and conceptual in respect to small enterprises reflecting African contest as well. This is followed by literature review which focuses on the origin and the nature of innovation in small enterprises in developing countries. The empirical analysis covers investigation into the innovative activities of small enterprises and the relationship between innovation and poverty reduction. Four assumptions were considered namely the rate at which the small producers adopt new technologies, the degree of market liberalisation, the education level of enterprise heads and workers, and institutional incentives the small producers face. These assumptions provided the framework for the econometric analysis whereby the output is modelled against explanatory variables. The chapter concludes with remarks and policy perspectives.

6.2 Theoretical concepts

6.2.1 Definitions and theoretical explanation of innovation

Schumpeter (34, pp. 65-66) defined innovation as introduction of new elements or a combination of old elements in industrial organisation. The main emphasis here is introduction of new idea or invention of new element. This conceptualisation has been expanded to include the application of existing ideas in new ways or in new fields. Innovation is also referred to as a process of solving problems which can be enhanced through learning, searching and exploring or through social exchange (Lundvall, 1992, p. 8; Landry, et al, 2001, p. 3). In recent times, attention has shifted from national innovation system to regional innovation system. Regional innovation system is defined as a set of economic, political and institutional relationships that generate a collective learning process leading to rapid diffusion of knowledge and practice. Innovation at regional level is very important in the sense that proximity provides the framework for face-to-face interaction which facilitates learning and the growth of specialised knowledge (Wolfe, 2002, p. 5). Furthermore, globalisation has also intensified actions for learning and innovation among local economic actors due to the emergence of networks of suppliers and buyers (Wolfe, 2002, p. 4).

Innovation is synonymous with technological change because both emphasis practical use of a new productive technique. However, a distinction is always made between product and process innovation. Product innovation refers to changes in the nature of output while process innovation concerns with changes in the amount, combination, quality or types of inputs required in producing the same output. In most cases, product and process innovation do occur simultaneously. However, product innovation can take place without changes in the production process. Innovation at firm level is the outcome of cumulative process in the sense that technologies used today have influence on learning process and accumulation of experiences. Generally, the factors which condition the innovative processes change over time (van Dijk, 2003, pp. 355-6). In the 1980s, the idea of technology capability becomes prominent in development economic research circle especially researchers in informal sector. Capability is defined as the information and skills as well as technical, managerial and institutional framework which allows productive enterprises to utilise equipment efficiently. For example, entrepreneurs and workers should possess the prerequisite in terms of skills required to manage and interpret technological information and operate modern machinery. It is imperative to upgrade these skills in order to enhance productivity and respond effectively to changes to incentives and grow overtime. Biggs et al (1995, p. 1) argue that the concept of technological capabilities is centred on new growth theories which focuses on technology and human capital are engines for economic growth. In this respect, Romijn (1999, p. 12) argues that acquiring technology capabilities is a function of internal capacity of firms to make independent and unique contribution to local technical progress. In developing countries, small producers should develop the ability to adapt new machines, develop product design or acquire manufacturing techniques which are invented elsewhere (Romijn, 1999, p. 17). For example, innovation in small enterprises in developing countries can be seen as the ability to use different raw materials or optimal use of raw materials. Innovation can also be the capability to introduce new methods of reducing energy, improving the product quality or introducing a new ways of financing and managing small businesses (van Dijk and Sandee, 2002, p. 4).

The components of innovation are learning, clustering, and managing the innovation process. Learning relates to the knowledge economies built on knowledge, creative capacity and connections. They are knowledge, skills and competencies and attributes embodied in individuals that facilitate the creation of personal, social and economic well being (OECD, 2001, p. 18). OECD (2001, p. 11) classifies knowledge into know-what, know-why, knowhow and know-who[152]. Entrepreneurship know-how begins with the internal organisation of a micro-unit and the ability to understand how the micro unit functions; how it interacts with others and how each unit understands the game played by other units (Uzor, 2003, p. 316). Tacit knowledge is another important aspect of knowledge. Tacit knowledge is non-codified knowledge derived from experiences and mutual learning through monitoring a relationship or participation in relevant networks. Tacit knowledge is required to help customize products and services, and adapt to rapidly changing situations (Jarboe, 2001, p. 7).

Cluster is regarded as component of innovation in the sense that clusters support the exchange of knowledge, skills and as well serve as efficient means

152 Know that or what is the knowledge of facts, relationships and theories acquired through formal education. Know-why is knowledge about principles and provides explanation about factual information. Know-how represents the skills required to carry out definite actions or the ability to perform the appropriate actions in order to achieve a desired result. Know-who entails the ability to cooperate and communicate with different kinds of people and experts (OECD, 2001, p. 15).

of knowledge management (Jarboe, 2001, p. 8). This is because geographical proximity involving people, enterprises and institutions serve as an efficient means of transferring and accumulating personal knowledge (Jarboe, 2001, p. 8). In developed economies, clusters can be seen as a reflection of modern innovation due to increasing interaction of interdependent highly skilled actors. They often involve many innovative firms that are driving growth and development (Torjman and Leviten-Reid, 2003, p. 8). Clustering serves as innovative milieu and is very important for micro, small and medium enterprises in developing countries because they cannot innovate on their own. (van Dijk, 2003, p. 354). By clustering, strategies can easily be designed and implemented in order to improve local capability gap for technology development and adaptation. New possibilities such as partnership and new forms of cooperation between enterprises can be promoted. This can be in the form of policy incentives necessary to encourage cooperation among developed and developing countries or between TNCs and local SMEs for technological learning (van Dijk, 2003, p. 355).

Managing innovation process is an important component of innovation because of many generic factors that usually accompany innovation process. The factors are: a) creating a vision that sets out the objectives innovation process seeks to achieve; b) identifying assets needed for the innovation process to take place. Such assets includes workforce skills, knowledge and research developpment, creativity in financial capital etc.; c) framing opportunities and challenges based on solid understanding of the local economy; d) developing action plan which encourages investment in developing new area; e) mobilising the factors needed for implementation of innovation process which often requires collaboration across boundaries; f) monitoring and assessing performance at individual firm and regional level (Torjman and Leviten-Reid, 2003, pp. 9-13). International co-operation is very important in creating the enabling environment for innovative activities in developing countries. The first step is to understand the processes involved in innovation process. This is followed by a build up of innovative trend in order to stimulate imitation and adaptation such that local technological capabilities and support institutions can be strengthened. Furthermore, promotion of clusters and networks that support local linkages for learning and diffusion processes in innovation can be developed (van Dijk, 2003, pp. 355-6).

6.2.2 Innovation in small enterprises and poverty alleviation

The aim here is to explore if the objectives of innovation in small enterprises relate to the goals of poverty alleviation. The goals of poverty alleviation are to engage the poor in productive activity; to increase the household income of the productive poor; to reduce the capability gap of the poor producers by improving his/her knowledge. In general, poverty reduction implies the ability to improve the capability of poor producers. Improving the capability in this context means improving the speed at which the small producers and workers can adopt new technology. This is an important measure of increasing productivity and reduction of unit cost. Two major factors can influence positively the speed of technology adaptation. One is the degree at which openness affects access to new technology and economic growth. The other is the impact of good institutions and qualities of governance that support skill development such that the benefits from globalisation can be derived.

The impact of innovation in small enterprises with respect to poverty alleviation can be classified into two namely direct and indirect effects. Direct effects are the benefits captured by the producers who implement changes which can lead to higher profits. For example, introduction of new technology will induce productive increase which can improve small producers' income when the marginal cost of producing one unit of output is reduced. In other words, those producers who adapt new technology earlier will earn higher profits than late adapters (Berdegué and Escobar, 2002, p. 2). The late adopters or non-adopters may negatively be affected when costs and prices are already determined by the new adopters. If the economy is protected, there will be higher premium for early adopters because access to inputs and information will be limited. If the market is liberalised, many producers will try to adapt the new technology afterwards thereby pushing the output growth higher with possible reduction of output prices (Berdegué and Escobar, 2002, p. 2; Thomas and Slater, 2006, p. 283).

Indirect effects of technological innovation on poverty reduction are the benefits passed on to others by the producers who actually implement changes. These effects can take one or more several forms; first is increased productivity and low output prices due to technical change; second is generation of employment as a result of increased output per unit costs. This can result to increased wage rates depending on the conditions of the labour market; the third is the broad-based economic growth through production and consumption linkages with other sectors in the economy (Berdegué and Escobar, 2002, p. 3). The net impact of direct and indirect effects of innovation on poverty largely depends on the following factor; firstly, the tradable status of the product; secondly, the position of the household in the market as net buyer or net seller of the product; thirdly, the position of the enterprises (i.e. early, late or non-adopter) as adopter of the technology (Berdegué and Escobar, 2002, p. 3).

By clustering, entrepreneurs can be in a better position to exchange knowledge, ideas and skills which tend to improve the production gap. This can serve as means of diffusing knowledge, sharing knowledge, transferring and building knowledge. Clustering tends to impact on different types of labour force. For example, a cluster which has upgraded substantially will generate demand for new jobs and new skills (Bair and Gereffi, 2001, pp. 1889). Cluster growth trajectories leads to differentiated outcomes in the sense that local linkages often give way to external linkages which enhances growth and poverty reduction (Nadvi and Barrientos, 2004, p. 26). Value chain framework also provides a basis for mapping local and external ties. In cluster analysis, mapping can help identify poverty groups within a cluster such as small producers who lack assets or capacity, or poorly remunerated casual wage labourers. Poor groups may also have a particular gender, ethnic or religious composition that restricts access to the means that can enhance their position (IDS, 2004, p. 1). This implies that assessment should identify ways which stakeholders and poor groups in the clusters can be monitored and evaluated (IDS, 2004, p .2).

6.2.3 Factors influencing innovative milieu in Africa

Factors influencing innovative milieu can be classified into macro, meso and micro. The macro factors explain the role of science and technology policies, and the national systems of innovation in promoting innovation and innovation diffusion. van Dijk (2003, p. 340) argues that beside stable macroeconomic conditions and other factors such as improved transport conditions around the region, potential for niche market, use of different marketing techniques and part of national network can contribute to the innovative milieu for micro and small enterprises in Africa. This is because stable and credible macroeconomic policies tend to remove the bias in favour of specific enterprises (public vs. private or domestic vs. foreign). Development of human capital plays an important role in technology diffusion. For example, if the educational system fails to provide the right skills and specializations that industry demands, the problem of asymmetric information between technology suppliers and users may arise: Hence the users of technology will lack the awareness and capability to master and assimilate new technologies (UNCTAD, 1995, p. 10)[153]. In concrete terms, innovation adaptation in smallscale enterprises does not necessarily lead to an upgrading of their technology capability rather the innovative mentality of the entrepreneur and the skill level of the workers are important factors for technological capability and competitiveness of the SMEs (van Dijk, 2003, p. 341).

153 The concept of national systems of innovation was coined by the neo-schumpeteriar-ans. The conceptual framework stems from the investigation on what may occur for innovation to take place. The concept often of stresses the synergy effects of all the institutions active in the field of innovation. Freeman (1987, pp. 98-100) used the term mental capital or intellectual or intangible capital to illustrate how development of an education and training system is capable of putting the whole system of acquiring and disseminating world technology into on regular and systemic basis.

Meso-policies are concerned with the development of technology partnerships at the level of specific industries, regions and institutions. The policies usually define the nature of technology, learning processes and technology requirements for specific industries (UNCTAD, 1995, pp. 11-12). This is because industrial activities do not operate in a "vacuum" hence the role of intermediary organisations such as business support systems (BSS) are very important. Furthermore, clusters and networks serve as innovative milieu for small enterprises in industrial and developing countries. Both scenarios facilitate collective efficiency in terms of external economies and collaborations. Collaborations among small enterprises can be horizontally or vertically. Such collaborations are the basic characteristics of small enterprises clusters and networks (UNIDO, 2001, p. 7). Clustering makes intervention more effective in the sense that international development institution, government agencies and NGOs can effectively design and implement innovation adaptation program that can facilitate technological learning and diffusion processes (van Dijk, 2003, p. 346).

The micro-level factor underscores the outcome of cumulative process at firm level. Innovation at firm level is a cumulative process in the sense that the capabilities are built overtime and conditions which influence innovation changes also overtime as well (van Dijk, 2003, p. 351). Researchers therefore investigate how these capabilities are built up overtime and which factors influence the process and how the process can be reinforced (van Dijk, 2003, p. 357). The important factors that facilitate innovative activities of small enterprises are cooperation and linkages. Horizontal and vertical cooperation among SMEs enterprises facilitates learning and performance improvement (UNIDO, 2001, p. 18). Linkages between large international enterprises and local small enterprises have influence on local small enterprises capability building and innovative activities (Altenburg, 2003, p. 144).

In general, technology development demands huge capital outlay and available skilled workers. Parrilli (2002, p. 145) argues that measuring innovative activities is very difficult in Africa because of low capital, limited skilled work force and low investment in R&D in the region. Innovation can be defined as imitation or adaptation of successful experience and models because it costs less and easier to reproduce (Parrilli, 2002, p. 146). Pissarides (1997, pp. 22-23) argues that successful imitation with low labour cost arguably have increased industrial competitiveness in some developing countries.

6.3 Review of literature on innovation in SME in developing countries

Promotion of technological development and innovation in small enterprises in developing countries and Africa in particular has occupied the attention of researchers and policy makers since early 1970s[154]. Schumacher, (1974) used the phrase "Small is Beautiful" to analyse the importance of small producers in developing countries and analysed the conditions under which they operate. Schumacher looked into the relationship between poverty and low technological capability. The poverty in developing countries according to Schumacher is as a result of low productivity. He argues that the output of the poor especially in rural areas failed to lead them out of poverty misery and their productivity is exceedingly low. Lack of capital to investment modern technology arguably is the main reason for low productivity. Schumacher argued that policy objectives should concentrate on development of specific technology that can support productivity growth in the region (Schumacher, 1974, p. 144). Schumacher argues that such technology must be cheap, more productive than indigenous technology and should be in line with the economic environment in the developing countries (Schumacher, 1974, pp. 150-1). The implication of AT initiative is that specific technology should be chosen and promoted for micro and small enterprises in developing countries (Schumacher (1974, pp. 155-6)[155].

Evans and Adler (1979) further provided a logical discourse on the role of appropriate technology in economic development. They argued that AT seeks to optimise solutions, by using capabilities that is sensitive to environment and culture. Hence, factor endowment in developing countries should be considered in selecting the AT. The basic argument that supports the promotion of AT is its characteristics that are compatible with production structure in developing countries. The characteristics include among others low cost technology; the technology is manageable and can responsive to country's needs. However, there are some basic limitations of AT in development strategy. The limits are such that some particular elements of the country's productive structure can be maximized at the expense investment alternatives (Evans and Adler, 1979, p. 46). AT can also lead to low capital utilisation and poor labour utilisation. Hence the ability to to meet the domestic and export market demand will be limited. It also limits technological learning because industrial productions are dispersed in different rural areas. It can have negative effects on general economic performance because it can foster poor infrastructure and ineffective government policy (Evans and Adler, 1979, pp. 52-56). This suggests that AT appears to be inappropriate in contemporary technology dynamism.

Ngahu (1995) analysed factors that influence technology choices at the enterprise level and the constraints small scale enterprises face in making

154 The proponents of appropriate technology were critical on the technology policies in developing countries in the 1970s. The policy based on setting choices between capital and labour or large and small scale industrial development strategies.

155 This implies that technology choices should reflect product quality as well as technique. Such choices must be defined relative to the society's time- specific endowment and its time specific objectives (Ranis, 1979, p. 23).

decisions on the choice of technology. Choice of technology according to Ngahu has important implications for productivity growth in an industry because the use of technology is always tied to firm's objective. Technology choice assumes to depend on access to information on alternative technologies in technology market. The ability to evaluate the alternatives is based on pre-selected criteria for a particular technology to meet specified needs, the ability to identify and recognise opportunities in different technologies. The gap in knowledge, skills, or resources tends to hinder effective choice of technology at the enterprise level in Africa. To choose a technology according to Ngahu, one must be able to assess the demand for the firm's products, estimate the rate of change in the market that may call for change in technology, gather information about alternative technologies, and estimate the potential return on investment for each alternative. In this context, many small scale entrepreneurs in Africa lack the education, training, management experience, needed to respond to technology issues. Ngahu also argues that lack of access to credit affects technology choice by limiting the number of alternatives that can be considered. Many SEs usually opt for an inappropriate technology due to low capital base. In this case, the national policy, regulatory environment and lending conditions play an important role in technology decisions at enterprise level. The major problem is the poor living conditions of small producers which force many small-business owners to draw more money from their businesses to satisfy household needs. This has negative impact on investment for business expansion[156].

Stewart (1987) used two contrasting views to analyse the concept of AT. The first is based on welfare economic approach which defines AT as a set of techniques for making optimum use of available resources in a given environment. The second approach is based on sociological background that defines AT with specific sets of characteristics. The characteristics defining AT include "more labour-using, less capital-using, less skill-using, use of local materials and resources, and smaller in scale. On this note, Ranis (1979, p. 29) argues that appropriateness has to be identified in the contest of the best

156 The lessons from appropriate technology initiates are the dominance of technology development initiative from the public sector. There were difficulties in technology diffusion due to non-commercialisation of technology outcome. There was knowledge gap between the researchers and users of technology especially the poor producers. This is because there were little or no collaboration efforts between the producers and the users of the AT (Romijn, 1999, p. 7). Beyond this, Romijn (1999, p. 8) argues that other factors such as poor utilisation of the incentives or assistance by the small producers and absence of weak market often leads to disappointing outcome of technology support programmes for small producers. She further explains that social factors in terms of poor communication, educational gap and class differences between producers and users of AT contributed to the failure of the programme. In general, the policy makers failed to integrate the promotion of their SEs sectors within the broader framework of their industrialisation strategies and objectives.

techniques available and the extent to which private search for appropriateness coincides with or deviate from social appropriateness

Choice of technology was revisited in van Dijk's (2002) analyses on innovation and small enterprise development in sub-Saharan Africa. The author used the experience in developed economy to review the circumstances in which technologies are made known, made available and made attractive for small scale enterprises. He argues that technology capacity is often developed from below and builds on to the level of skills the workers possess. The producers of technology normally consider the training capacity available in the country and the support institutions for technology adaptation and innovation diffusion. His emphasis is on the need to shift policy from transfer of technology approach to promotion of local capacity for adaptation of technology. According to van Dijk, this can be possible through increased development cooperation, building of technology partnership with research institutes and active involvement of the private firms.

Romijn (1999) reviewed various technological assistance programmes implemented in different developing countries. The study intensively analysed the importance of dynamic approach in designing technology support programmes for small enterprises. The author argument is based on the pressure induced by globalisation; hence the article outlined the failure of early technology support programmes. The early technology support programmes according to the author, only focused on development of technology that could not be commercialised. Romijn argues that competitiveness of the SEs depends on the ability to acquire internal capability needed to make improvement in product quality and process organisation. Technological learning is likely to be the most effective method of supporting the small enterprise in the region. This can be effective when producers have the opportunity to interact with each other and with other actors in the economy.

In early 1990s, the concept of flexible specialisation (FS) became prominent among researchers in economic geography. FS is used to explain the success of industries in Italy, Japan and Germany which places emphasis on craftsmanship, multipurpose equipment, industrial district and networks of innovative enterprises. The concept explains how firms interact with other firms and how firms use their technologies in competitive environment. The key elements in FS concept are technology and division of labour. The flexibility is such that firms tend to position their production system in a continuous alertness. They explore the strategy that supports competition and collaboration as well as actions that focus on advantages of subcontracting relations

(Pedersen, et al 1994, p. 7)[157]. In general, FS stresses the importance of clusters and networks for innovative activities because both tend to create innovative milieu (van, Dijk, 2003, p. 342).

In this respect, Camagni (1991, p. 5) argues that since clusters and networks reflects economic of space; they provide the local milieu that serves as the generator of innovative behaviour. Both tend to encourage collective learning that enhance local creativity, and local technology capability building. Camagni (1991, p. 5) and van Dijk (2003, p. 344) argued that cooperation among enterprises produce new ideas and new ways of doing things, proximity therefore can enhance innovative activities that can improve economics of scale of small enterprises. For example, information from traders is useful for product design, and business support programmes can create new knowledge. Small enterprises can learn easily by imitation and observation. When small enterprises are clustered in a define location, producers in the cluster are better positioned to have comparative advantage in innovative activities in terms of sharing costs and information (van Dijk, 2003, pp. 344-5).

Parrilli (2002) used the concept of flexible specialisation (FS) to analyse the innovative activity in small furniture industry in Nicaragua. The analysis started with the identification of the problems associated with innovation and competitiveness in furniture industry. The most predominant problem according to Parrilli is the level of industrial development which consists of mainly handicraft with low productivity, low mechanisation and use of family labour. Parrilli argues that a more systematic approach is required in addressing the issue of innovation in the developing region. Strategy should focus towards a high road development path and this is can occur only through an innovative path that ensures high product quality and targets better market (Parrilli, 2002, p. 144).

Qualmann (2002) investigated the responses of small and medium sized enterprises to external shocks. The conceptual approach of the study is based on the assumption that small and medium sized enterprises are often assumed to adjust quickly to sudden structural changes than the larger firms. In the study, the response of SMEs to sharp devaluation of the CFA Franc in Senegal in 1996 was investigated. The findings revealed that small enterprises react quite diversely to adjustment measures. Majority of the enterprises according to the

---

157 The interrelated characteristics of flexible specialisation in dynamic enterprise sector are: entrepreneur's innovative mentality, multipurpose characteristics of technology usually applied by trained personal, inter-firm cooperation often in the form of sub-contracting, clustering of micro and small enterprises, networking of micro and small enterprises specialisation and proven flexibility (van Dijk, 2002, p. 128). The interplay of these characteristics often leads to a collective efficiency for the enterprises in the clusters (Schmitz, 1992).

study to a large extent, show defensive reactions rather than dynamic or innovative approach in terms of introducing new products or processes.

Oladeji (1998) investigated technology problem in Nigeria small and medium scale enterprises. The study provided theoretical framework that questioned the rationale of government control of technology vis-ã-vis the role of market forces. The author argues that the small enterprises in formal and informal sector could have effectively explored the advantages provided during the SAP in terms of meeting local demand if technological base was at hand. The basic impact of SAP on technology development was shaping Nigeria technology policy towards SMEs. Government technology initiatives for SMEs during SAP implementation were significantly influenced by the effects of the SAP.

Aubert (2004) provided a conceptual framework for promotion of innovation in developing countries. The motivation of the paper stems from the argument that economic reforms such as privatisation, liberalisation, and deregulation policies have limitations in sustaining growth. Hence, creation of technology and its diffusion is considered to be the engine for economic development. The author argues that promotion of technology in developing countries should be a gradual process[158]. The process should take into account country's specificities including their conditions of governance (Aubert, 2004, p. 7). The governance quality has influence on business environment and innovation performance. For example, communication infrastructures are needed for easy flow of information and transportation[159]. According to the author there are many public institutions competing in the promotion of enterprises in developing countries. In such a multiple support system, it is difficult to establish efficient system for the promotion of innovation in the region (Aubert, 2004, pp. 9-10).

158 Technological change often occur in different forms and stages, for example, introducetion of new technology, imitating a particular technology, adopting the technology to local circumstances or developing the technology further by local producers (van Dijk, 2003, p. 338). This requires gradual process that encourages learning.

159 For example, a bureaucratic climate which forces an entrepreneur to obtain a hundreds of authorizations to establish his/her enterprise is a problem (Aubert, 2004, p. 9). A business environment that promotes tax discrimination discourages competition among the enterprises which is also a problem for the growth of enterprises (Uzor, 2007, p. 287).

6.4 Empirical analysis of innovative activities in small enterprises in Nigeria

6.4.1 Methodology

This study is not intended to measure the innovativeness of small enterprises rather attempts to provide an insight into how small enterprises compete and survive in an open economy in Africa. The study tries to examine if innovative activity in small enterprises is consistent with theory innovation in the mainstream literature. The study did not consider the traditional measure of innovative activity in terms of the measure of input such as R&D in the innovative process due to the level of industrial development in the country. Innovative activity as a proxy measure of innovative output such as patented inventions was also not considered. The measure of innovative activity considered in this study is the impact of creativity in terms of number of product design introduced in the market. This is because the chances of a small firm to survive and be successful are becoming over-dependent on creativity (Heunks, 1998, p. 264).

The questions are, is innovative activity in small enterprises in Africa a survival or growth oriented strategy? To what extent has innovative activity in small enterprises contributed to firms' productivity growth? It is paramount to be careful when formulating the hypotheses concerning innovation in African small firms. Evidence shows that firms use local fabricated machines, hand tools and low quality inputs. The hypothesis in this context tries to focus on how small enterprises survive despite low product quality and weak technology in a competitive market. In this case, can one view innovative activity in small enterprises in Africa as survival or growth strategy?

Based on these questions, the hypotheses were formulated as follows: "innovative activity in small enterprises in Africa is a survival strategy"[160]. To investigate this, two factors "price and quality" were considered in investigating the innovative activities in African small enterprises using shoemakers in Aba as an example. This provided insight on how small enterprises compete and the cost of competition in terms of staying in the market. The second hypothesis is "innovative activity in small enterprises in Africa has implicit relationship to the goals of poverty alleviation". Since the study is not investigating the innovative firms in the sample population, the idea is to use some variables to investigate the firms' productivity growth. Regression analysis is therefore used to model the relationship between output growth and nature of technology, labour, level of education of entrepreneurs and workers, incentives, and government trade

160 This similar to modified Schumpeterian hypothesis that the relative innovative advantage of large and small firms is determined by the extent to which a market is characterised by imperfect competition (Acs and Audrescht, 1978, p. 573).

policy in two subsectors. The central idea here is to show that innovative activity in small enterprise is a combination of factors that influence productivity growth. The anticipated productivity growth can lead to transformation effect on small enterprises and transmission effect on the economy in general. To investigate the innovative activities of small enterprises, it is necessary to ascertain or evaluate the nature of incentives available for innovative activity.

6.4.2 The incentives small enterprises face

Incentives for small enterprises are market based policy packages that tend to enhance productivity; raise quality standards; help in generating additional employment or boost small firm competitiveness. Such incentives can be in different forms but are collectively applied in order to promote the growth of small firm. In other words, one cannot apply one incentive package and leave others because incentives for small enterprises development are a combination of policy matrix. Moreover, good investment environment act as incentive for foreign direct investment which can have positive influence on local small enterprises development as well. Fiscal incentives in the form of exemptions from permit fees, building permit fees, taxes and other fees and charges imposed by authorities can stimulate small and large firms productivity alike (Velde, 2001, pp. 6-11; Agboli and Ukaegbu, 2006, pp. 9-13). However, tax exemptions should not be discriminatory otherwise it becomes an indirect subsidy which normally hampers competition (Uzor, 2007, p. 287).

Figure 6.1: Forms of taxation experienced in PKO extraction

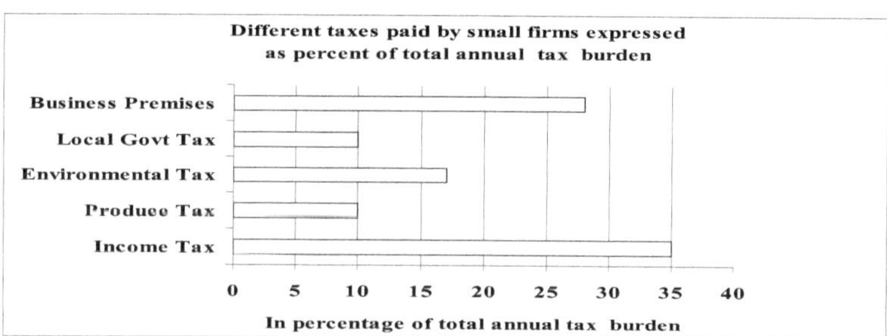

Source: Appendix 6.7

Non-fiscal incentive such as skill development through capacity building programme and infrastructure will upgrade small entrepreneurs' knowledge in a competitive market economy but will also support performance (Velde, 2001, p. 6). In general, the growth of small enterprise depends on an efficient regulatory system. The business environment plays an important role in small enterprise development. An uneven enforcement of regulatory obligations can create discontinuities. High tax obligations such as tax duplications can induce a disproportionate burden on business operation (Levy, 1991, p. 20). For example, Figure 6.1 shows different types of tax expressed as percentage of total annual tax burden and levies the small enterprises in PKO extraction industry have to pay annually. It is arguable that produce tax and local government business permit levy represents a case of tax duplication that tends to discourage small producers and investors.

Table 6.1 represents the support which the sampled enterprises received from government. The Table however did not suggest that all the enterprises did receive a particular support programme rather it indicates the number of support programme that reached its target. Despite numerous government financial assistance programmes designed for small enterprise, only in wood/furniture sub-sector did report government financial assistance. In light engineering cluster, two technical assistance programmes were reported to have been received from UNIDO and NEDDEC.

Table 6.1: The number of support received by sub-sector

Incentives	Footwear	Garments	Wood & furniture	Light Engineering	PKO extraction
financial Assistance	na	na	1	na	na
Non-fiscal (training programmes)	1	2	1	2	na
Technical Assistance	na	na	na	2	na

Source: Own field survey

The interviewees were further asked about their perceptions on government support programmes. As shown in Table 6.2, 3 percent of the interviewees see government support programmes as adequate but blamed the poor performance on the implementation. One reason is that the policymakers have little or no knowledge/expertise on how to evaluate the problems small producers face. This suggests that there is large social gap between the policymakers, implementing agencies and the target groups. In general, 90 percent of the respondents see government support programmes as inadequate. This is largely because the impact of numerous government support programmes failed to reach the target. In this respect, 61 per cent of interviewees perceive government programmes as too political while 81 per cent view the programmes as influenced by politics hence 94 per cent see government support programme as not really reflecting the realities small producers face. The interviewees were asked why they are marginalised from the programmes. 44 per cent named inconsistency due to incoherent multiple programmes and multiple institutions. 74 per cent claimed that frequent change in policy and short term nature of the programmes leads to confusion in the system. The Table also suggests that micro enterprises view government programmes with discontent with 95 per cent view government as not reflecting the reality while 92 per cent maintain that support programmes are not inadequate. These responses provided an insight on how small entrepreneurs perceive capacity building needs.

Table 6.2: Firms' assessment of government incentives by firm size

Sector	Micro Enterprises	Small Enterprises	Medium Enterprises	All
Sample size	152	20	3	175
The proportion of entrepreneurs in the sub-sector who view government support initiatives as				
adequate	0.20	0.10	na	0.03
Inadequate	0.92	0.75	0.67	0.90
too political	0.60	0.65	1.00	0.61
only politics	0.82	0.75	0.67	0.81
not reflecting the reality	0.95	0.90	0.67	0.94
Inconsistent	0.43	0.55	0.33	0.44
short term measures only	0.78	0.44	0.67	0.74

Source: See Appendix 6.4

Table 6.3 presents the overview of capacity building programmes needed by small enterprises. The interviewees were asked to name the assistance programme they consider important in order to improve performance. Technology assistance and training programmes ranked highest. However, the demand for capacity building programme differs across sub-sector. For example, PKO extraction enterprises consider how to improve their technological capability and access to finance as their major need while wood and furniture consider training and technology as their major capacity needs.

Table 6.3: Capacity building assessment needs by sub-sector

Sub-sector	Footwear	Garments	Wood & furniture	Light engineering	PKO extraction	All
Sample size	68	28	39	18	22	175
Securing financial assistance	0.66	0.89	0.51	0.83	0.95	0.72
Business support services	0.88	0.71	0.72	0.78	0.95	0.82
Training Program	0.96	0.96	0.95	0.94	0.45	0.89
Technology assessment	0.93	0.89	0.90	0.89	1.00	0.92

Source: See Appendix 6.5

Garment enterprises consider training, technology and finance as very important in the sub-sector. In terms of firm size, Table 6.4 indicates that micro and small enterprises value training programmes more than the medium scale enterprises while small and medium enterprises view technology assistance more important than micro enterprises. The lesson here is; when designing capacity building programme for SMEs, heterogeneity factor and the degree of capacity gap have to be recognised.

Table 6.4: Capacity building assessment needs by firm size

	Micro	Small	Medium	All
Sample size	152	20	3	175
Securing financial Assistance	0.70	0.90	0.67	0.72
Business support services	0.82	0.80	1.00	0.82
Training Program	0.89	0.95	0.33	0.89
Technology assessment	0.97	1.00	1.00	0.92

Source: See Appendix 6.6

6.4.3 Innovative activity in footwear small scale enterprises in Nigeria as survival strategy

In competitive viewpoint, small firms' survival is often determined by risks taking, flexibility and creativity. This can be in the form of selecting the most appropriate strategy and technology or by maintaining a persistence quality assurance that can influence a particular market segment. It is difficult to see how small entrepreneurs can survive in an economy with little or no institutional incentive. In this study, the interviewees were asked to explain how they compete in the local markets. The answers were peculiar and consistent with the problems firms face in terms of ability to remain in the market. The response revealed that their major competitive instrument is the ability to introduce as many designs as possible in the market. In other words, the probability of remaining in the market depends on number of successful designs that capture a given market (local or regional). The interviewees were further asked to explain how many designs they introduced in the market and how many are successful in a year. This is because innovation can be defined as successful implementtation of a creation (Henuks and Roos, 1992, p. 6). They were also asked to give an estimate of the cost of introducing new design. The question helped the researcher to estimate the value of total cost of new product design introduced and the total cost of design successful in the market. The difference between the total cost of new product design introduced in the market and the total cost of successful design in the market represents the value of investment individual firm have to forego in order to stay in the market (sunk costs).

Table 6.5: Calculation of average number of successful designs in the market in clustered Aba micro and small footwear enterprises (in N)

Sample No.	Row 1	Row 2	Row 3	Row 4	Row 5	Row 6
1	100	15.00	200.00	20,000.00	3,000.00	17,000.00
2	120	17.50	150.00	18,000.00	2,625.00	15,375.00
3	110	17.50	175.00	19,250.00	3,062.50	16,187.50
4	100	10.00	225.00	22,500.00	2,250.00	20,250.00
5	80	15.00	175.00	14,000.00	2,625.00	11,375.00
6	90	7.50	250.00	22,500.00	1,875.00	20,625.00
7	100	10.00	275.00	27,500.00	2,750.00	24,750.00
8	110	12.50	175.00	19,250.00	2,187.50	17,062.50
9	120	17.50	275.00	33,000.00	4,812.50	28,187,50
10	110	15.00	225,00	24,750.00	3,375.00	21,375.00
11	5*	5.00	1,100.00	5,500.00	5,500.00	0.00
12	10*	8.00	1,200.00	12,000.00	9,600.00	2,400.00
13	4*	4.00	2,000.00	8,000.00	8,000.00	0.00
14	6*	5.00	1,500.00	9,000.00	7,500.00	1,500,00
15	4*	4.00	1,500.00	6,000.00	6,000.00	0.00
16	80	12.50	225.00	18,000.00	2,812.50	15,187.50
17	85	12.50	175.00	14,875.00	2,187.50	12,687.50
18	4*	4.00	2,500.00	10,000.00	10,000.00	0.00
19	90	10.00	175.00	15,750.00	1,750.00	14,000.00
20	110	15.00	260.00	28,600.00	3,900.00	24,700.00
21	100	12.50	200.00	20,000.00	2,500.00	17,500.00
22	110	15.00	225.00	24,750.00	3,375.00	21,375.00
23	5*	5.00	2,500.00	15,000.00	12,500.00	2,500.00
24	4*	4.00	2,250.00	9,000.00	9,000.00	0.00
25	120	15.00	200.00	24,000.00	3,000.00	21,000.00
26	110	17.50	175.00	19,250.00	3,062.50	16,187.50
27	100	15.00	250.00	25,000.00	3,750.00	21,250.00
28	4*	4.00	2,000.00	8,000.00	8,000.00	0.00
29	5*	5.00	1,500.00	7,500.00	7,500.00	0.00
30	6*	4.00	2,000.00	12,000.00	8,000.00	4,000.00
31	10	8.00	1,750.00	17,500.00	14,000.00	3,500.00
32	110	15.00	250.00	27,500.00	3,750.00	23,750.00
33	100	12.00	200.00	20,000.00	2,400.00	17,600.00
34	90	9.00	200.00	18,000.00	1,800.00	16,200.00
35	80	7.50	200.00	16,000.00	1,500.00	14.500.00
36	6*	5.00	2,000.00	12,000.00	10,000.00	2,000.00
				TCSD = 623975.00		
	2308/36 = 64.11	371/36 =10.31		ATCSD = 623975.00/36 = 17,332.64		

Note: The values in asterisk are for men shoes; TCS = Total Costs of Successful Designs; ATCSD = Average Total Costs of Successful Designs; N = Naira; Survival Cost = Total cost of new design introduced by firm. Row 1 = No. of design introduced in the market yearly; Row 2 = No. of successful designs in the market yearly; Row 3 = Cost of design introduced by firm; Row 4 = Survival Cost; Row 5 = Total cost of successful designs by firm; Row 6 = Sunk Costs

Source: Own field work (See Appendix 6.1)

Table 6.6: Calculation of average number of successful in dispersed Aba micro and small footwear enterprises (in N)

Sample No.	Row 1	Row 2	Row 3	Row 4	Row 5	Row 6
1	50	7.50	150.00	7500.00	1,125.00	8,375.00
2	60	8.00	175.00	10,500.00	1,400.00	9,100.00
3	40	6.50	155.00	6,200.00	1,007.50	5,192.50
4	70	8.00	225.00	15,750.00	1,800.00	13,950.00
5	40	6.00	250.00	10,000.00	1,500.00	8,500.00
6	60	8.00	250.00	15,000.00	2,000.00	13,000.00
7	70	10.00	350.00	24,500.00	3,500.00	21,000.00
8	3*	3.00	1,500.00	4,500.00	4,500.00	0.00
9	5*	4.00	2,500.00	12,500.00	10,000.00	2,500.00
10	90	12.50	175.00	15,750.00	2,187.50	13,562.50
11	70	7.50	225.00	15,750.00	1,687.50	14,062.50
12	60	12.50	250.00	15,000.00	3,125.00	1,1875.00
13	60	7.5 0	150.00	9,000.00	1,125.00	7,875.00
14	5*	4.00	2,000.00	10,000.00	8,000.00	2,000.00
15	4*	4.0 0	175.00	7,000.00	7,000.00	0.00
16	3*	3.0 0	225.00	6,750.00	6,750.00	0.00
17	5*	4.00	2,500.00	12,500.00	10,000.00	2,500.00
18	70	12.50	250.00	17,500.00	3,125.00	14,375.00
19	60	7.50	180.00	10,800.00	1,350.00	9,450.00
20	5*	15.00	205.00	16,400.00	3,075.00	13,325.00
21	50	7.50	250.00	12,500.00	1,875.00	10,625.00
22	60	3.00	2,250.00	6,750.00	6,750.00	0.00
23	3*	3.00	2,000.00	6,000.00	6,000.00	0.00
24	3*	12.50	275.00	9,250.00	3,437.50	15,812.50
25	80	22.50	350.00	28,000.00	7,312.50	20,687.50
26	60	12.50	250.00	15,000.00	3,125.00	11,875.00
27	70	15.00	205.00	14,350.00	3,075.00	11,275.00
28	70	15.00	250.00	17,500.00	3,750.00	13,750.00
29	60	12.50	275.00	16,500.00	3,437.50	13,062.50
30	40	7.50	205.00	8,200.00	1,537.50	6,662.50
31	60	10.00	200.00	12,000.00	2,000.00	10,000.00
32	70	15.00	225.00	15,750.00	3,375.00	12,375.00
33	60	7.50	275.00	16,500.00	2,062.50	14,437.50
34	4*	3.00	2,900.00	11,600.00	8,700.00	2,900.00
35	3*	3.00	2,000.00	6,000.00	6,000.00	0.00
36	4*	4.00	1,750.00	7,000.00	7,000.00	0.00
				TCS = 445,800.00		
	1417/36 =39.36	300.5/36 =8.35		ATCS = 445,800/36 =12,383.33		

Note : The values in asterisk are for men shoes. TCS = Total Costs of Successful Designs; ATCSD = Average Total Costs of Successful Designs; N = Naira; Survival Cost = Total cost of new design introduced by firm

Source: Own field work (See Appendix 6.2)

Table 6.5 and Table 6.6 reveal how small shoemakers survive in Nigeria and African regional markets. The Tables show the average total costs of designs introduced and the average costs of successful designs in the market. The 2nd row of the Table shows the number of designs introduced by each shoemaker in the sample in a year. The 3rd row shows the average number of successful design by each shoemaker in the sample in a year. New designs can originate from shoemaker's creativity or samples from catalogues. In most cases, traders act as source of information for new designs. The higher the number of successful design, the higher the probability of the shoemaker to be competitive and remain in the market. The 4th row shows the average cost of new design while 5th row represents the total cost of new design introduced by each shoemaker. The total cost of new designs introduced can be described as survival cost because the probability of an enterprise to remain in the market depends on the number successful designs in the market. Hence, the 6th row shows the total cost of successful designs in the market. The argument is, if the number of designs introduced in the market is low, the chances of staying in the market will depend on the quality of the product. If the product quality is low, the enterprise must introduce as many designs as possible in order to increase the share of successful design in the market and cover the sunk costs. Otherwise the enterprise will be forced out of the market. The 7th row relates the total investment costs (sunk costs) the shoemakers have to invest in order to remain in the market. Low sunk cost indicates that average number of successful design in the market is relatively high hence there will be increase in firm's revenue and profit. The argument here is that shoemakers can compete effectively in the local market, if the cost of successful design is equal to the total cost of designs introduced in the market. Hence there will be zero sunk costs, increased profitability and income which will have positive impact on poverty reduction.

As shown in Table 6.5 and 6.6 above, the average total survival cost in shoe production in the cluster area is N17,332.64 while the average total survival cost in dispersed enterprises is N12,383.64. This implies that enterprises in cluster area shoemakers sustain higher survival cost than enterprises located elsewhere due to higher volume of transactions in the cluster area. This suggests that the differences in mean sales per worker in clustered and dispersed enterprises as shown in Table 4.7 (Page 152 above) can also be explained by the differences in average number of successful designs in market. The policy implication here is that institutional measures are urgently needed such that commercial banks can open credit line between N15,000.00 to N20,000.00 as overdraft for shoemakers in cluster area in order to offset high survival costs. A credit line between N10,000.00 and N15,000.00 should be opened for shoe makers in operating elsewhere.

Table 6.7: Calculation of survival cost and successful in Aba Micro and Small Footwear Enterprises (in Naira)

Sample No.	Row 1	Row 2	Row 3	Row 4	Row 5	Row 6
1	100	15.0	200.00	20,000.00	3,000.00	17,000.00
2	120	17.5	150.00	18,000.00	2,625.00	15,375.00
3	110	17.5	175.00	19,250.00	3,062.50	16,187.50
4	100	10.0	225.00	22,500.00	2,250.00	20,250.00
5	80	15.0	175.00	14,000.00	2,625.00	11,375.00
6	90	7.5	250.00	22,500.00	1,875.00	20,625.00
7	100	10.0	275.00	27,500.00	2,750.00	24,750.00
8	110	12.5	175.00	19,250.00	2,187.50	17,062.50
9	120	17.5	275.00	33,000.00	4,812.50	28,187,50
10	110	15.0	225,00	24,750.00	3,375.00	21,375.00
11	5*	5.0	1,100.00	5,500.00	5,500.00	0.00
12	10*	8.0	1,200.00	12,000.00	9,600.00	2,400.00
13	4*	4.0	2,000.00	8,000.00	8,000.00	0.00
14	6*	5.0	1,500.00	9,000.00	7,500.00	1,500,00
15	4*	4.0	1,500.00	6,000.00	6,000.00	0.00
16	80	12.5	225.00	18,000.00	2,812.50	15,187.50
17	85	12.5	175.00	14,875.00	2,187.50	12,687.50
18	4*	4.0	2,500.00	10,000.00	10,000.00	0.00
19	90	10.0	175.00	15,750.00	1,750.00	14,000.00
20	110	15.0	260.00	28,600.00	3,900.00	24,700.00
21	100	12.5	200.00	20,000.00	2,500.00	17,500.00
22	110	15.0	225.00	24,750.00	3,375.00	21,375.00
23	5*	5.0	2,500.00	15,000.00	12,500.00	2,500.00
24	4*	4.0	2,250.00	9,000.00	9,000.00	0.00
25	120	15.0	200.00	24,000.00	3,000.00	21,000.00
26	110	17.5	175.00	19,250.00	3,062.50	16,187.50
27	100	15.0	250.00	25,000.00	3,750.00	21,250.00
28	4*	4.0	2,000.00	8,000.00	8,000.00	0.00
29	5*	5.0	1,500.00	7,500.00	7,500.00	0.00
30	6*	4.0	2,000.00	12,000.00	8,000.00	4,000.00
31	10	8.0	1,750.00	17,500.00	14,000.00	3,500.00
32	110	15.0	250.00	27,500.00	3,750.00	23,750.00
33	100	12.0	200.00	20,000.00	2,400.00	17,600.00
34	90	9.0	200.00	18,000.00	1,800.00	16,200.00
35	80	7.5	200.00	16,000.00	1,500.00	14.500.00
36	6*	5.0	2,000.00	12,000.00	10,000.00	2,000.00
37	50	7.5	150.00	7,500.00	1,125.00	8,375.00
38	60	8.0	175.00	10,500.00	1,400.00	9,100.00
39	40	6.5	155.00	6,200.00	1,007.50	5,192.50
40	70	8.0	225.00	15,750.00	1,800.00	13,950.00
41	40	6.0	250.00	10,000.00	1,500.00	8,500.00
42	60	8.0	250.00	15,000.00	2,000.00	13,000.00
43	70	10.0	350.00	24,500.00	3,500.00	21,000.00
44	3*	3.0	1,500.00	45,00.00	4,500.00	0.00
45	5*	4.0	2,500.00	12,500.00	10,000.00	2,500.00
46	90	12.5	175.00	15,750.00	2,187.50	13,562.50

Source: Own field work (See Appendix 6.1 and 6.2)

Table 6.7: continues

Sample No.	Row 1	Row 2	Row 3	Row 4	Row 5	Row 6
47	70	7.5	225.00	15,750.00	1,687.50	14,062.50
48	60	12.5	250.00	15000.00	3,125.00	11,875.00
49	60	7.5	150.00	9000.00	1,125.00	7,875.00
50	5*	4.0	2,000.00	10000.00	8,000.00	2,000.00
51	4*	4.0	175.00	7000.00	7,000.00	0.00
52	3*	3.0	225.00	6750.00	6,750.00	0.00
53	5*	4.0	2,500.00	12500.00	10,000.00	2,500.00
54	70	12.5	250.00	17500.00	3,125.00	14,375.00
55	60	7.5	180.00	10800.00	1,350.00	9,450.00
56	5*	15.0	205.00	16400.00	3,075.00	13,325.00
57	50	7.5	250.00	12500.00	1,875.00	10,625.00
58	60	3.0	2,250.00	6750.00	6,750.00	0.00
59	3*	3.0	2,000.00	6000.00	6,000.00	0.00
60	3*	12.5	275.00	9250.00	3,437.50	5,812.50
61	80	22.5	350.00	28000.00	7,312.50	20,687.50
62	60	12.5	250.00	15000.00	3,125.00	11,875.00
63	70	15.0	205.00	14350.00	3,075.00	11,275.00
64	70	15.0	250.00	17500.00	3,750.00	13,750.00
65	60	12.5	275.00	16500.00	3,437.50	13,062.50
66	40	7.5	205.00	8200.00	1,537.50	6,662.50
67	60	10.0	200.00	12000.00	2,000.00	10,000.00
68	70	15.0	225.00	15750.00	3,375.00	12,375.00
69	60	7.5	275.00	16500.00	2,062.50	14,437.50
70	4*	3.0	2,900.00	11600.00	8,700.00	2,900.00
71	3*	3.0	2,000.00	6000.00	6,000.00	0.00
72	4*	4.0	1,750.00	7000.00	7,000.00	0.00
	Av= 51.74	Av = 9.32		ATCS=1,079,775.00		

Source: Own field work (See Appendix 6.1 and 6.2)

As shown in Table 6.7 above, the total cost of survival in the sampled small enterprises in the sub-sector is N1,079,775.00. The empirical analysis in chapter 4 indicates that despite high informality characteristics, Aba footwear enterprises cluster represents an active small enterprises cluster. Policy recommendation here is that, if the small and micro enterprises can formalise and enter into partnership ventures with local or foreign large enterprises, institutional incentive in terms of access to loans and credit are imperative. The commercial banks can open credit line between N1.00 million and N1.5million for shoemakers for the purchase of new equipment and working capital. Further research problem is how to reduce the suck costs and increase the number of successful designs in the cluster. Arguably, suck cost can be reduced if entrepreneurs can invest in other frontiers such skilled workers and high quality input Figures 6.2 shows graphical illustration of the relationship between the three set of costs namely the total costs of the designs introduced in the market, total costs of successful designs and the sunk costs[161]. The sharp slope in the graph shows the extreme values between men and ladies shoe production units. The Figure 6.2 shows that total cost of introducing new sample design and the sunk cost are relatively close to each other. A high sunk cost suggests that the shoemakers are competing in the market under a high investment costs. Low sunk cost suggests that the revenue and income of the shoemakers will be higher[162]. Furthermore, if the total cost of introducing a new design (survival costs) and the sunk costs are very close, it suggests that firms are surviving in the market based on a least possible advantage such as low price and low quality. On the other hand, if the sunk costs are very low, the firms are therefore surviving in the market based on a combination of different factors or advantages. The factors include using high quality inputs, improved workers productivity or access to better market.

Figure 6.2: The survival costs in sampled Aba footwear enterprises cluster by all firms

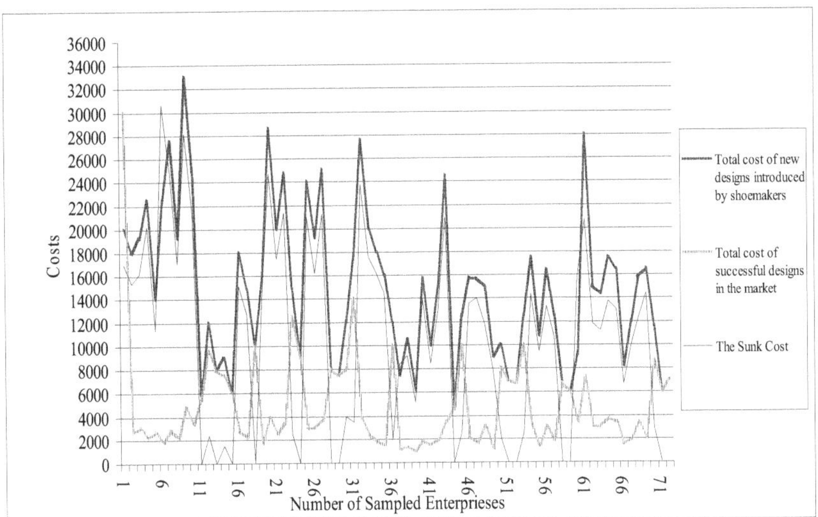

Source: From Table 6.7

To capture the relationship between the sunk cost and survival cost clearly, Figure 6.2 is decomposed into ladies and men shoe production units. As shown

161 The analysis considered the enterprises in the cluster and those located elsewhere. The enterprises are classified into men and ladies shoe production units for analytical purposes.

162 The steep fall or rise in the both trend lines signifies the case of extreme values in the general sample.

in Figure 6.3, the cost of staying in the market by sample of ladies shoe production unit is very high because the total value of successful design in the market is very low. In ladies shoe production unit, the cost of new design is relatively low due to low input price hence the quality is very inferior. Figure 6.3 also shows that the survival costs and the sunk costs are very close to each other. This suggests that small firms are operating under very high costs with low profits in order to remain in the market. To maintain annual profitable sales volume, small enterprises in ladies shoe production unit must introduce many designs regardless of quality. The basic idea is such that the probability of increasing the market share depends on the frequency of successful design. The implication here is that income elasticity effect can induce crisis in the ladies production unit. In other words, a positive change in household's aggregate real income will lead to negative shift in demand curve of ladies shoes away towards imports. If the real wage increases, consumers demand will shift to products with higher quality hence the producers in ladies shoe production unit will lose the market share. Consequently, there will be unemployment in the cluster which can undermine poverty reduction.

Figure 6.3: The cost of staying in the market in sampled Aba ladies shoe production unit of the footwear cluster a by firm

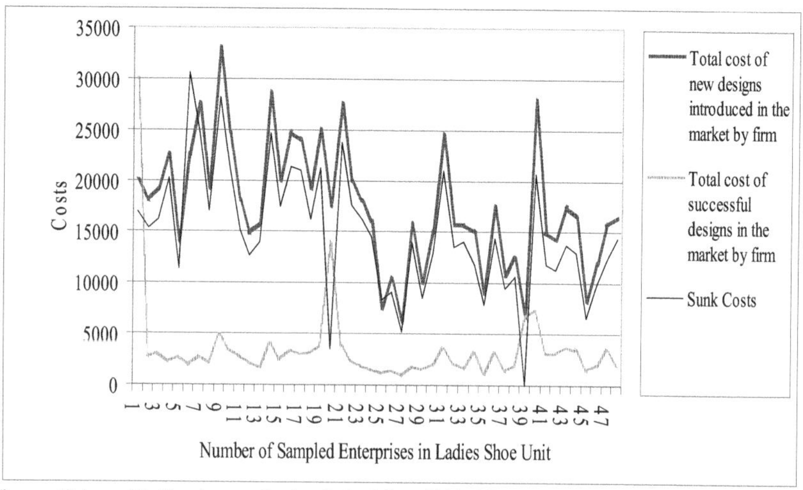

Source: Values of Ladies shoe production derived from Table 6.7

Figure 6.4 shows that in men shoe production unit, total cost of introducing new design and total value of successful design introduced in the market are very close and the sunk cost are relatively very low. This suggests that the difference between the sunk costs and survival costs are converging to zero. The implication here is that contrary to ladies shoe production unit, the competitive advantage in men shoe production unit depends on other factors outside good quality designs. Lower sunk cost in men shoe production unit can be explained by several factors. First, the production strategy in the men shoe production unit tend to focus on relatively higher quality at moderate price in order to be competitive in the local and African regional market. The second factor is ability to identify niche market which seeks to target the Nigerian Army, Nigerian Navy and the Police. The third is the ability to comply with specifications and develop a scenario of quality consciousness along the production system.

Figure 6.4: The cost of staying in the market in sampled Aba men shoe production unit of the footwear cluster by firm

Source: Values of men shoe production derived from Table 6.7

Figure 6.5 shows the source of information for new design by firm. It also explains the role of networking as source of information for innovative activities. As shown in Figure 6.5, the major source of information for new design came from traders. Traders provide information about market conditions to the producers and bring special designs and as well provide the initial capital for the realisation of the new designs. Some enterprises in the cluster run more than one workshops in order to maintain secrecy. One workshop is specifically used for production of special designs for customers or for producing own special designs. The second workshop is located in the cluster in order to reach a wider market. Figure 6.5 also shows that more than 60 per cent of the new designs introduced in the market in a year are through imitation of other firms' original designs and personal creativity. Since most of the firms are in close vicinity, it suggests that agglomeration can occur in the sense that information; ideas and knowledge are easily circulated among the enterprises in close vicinity. Concentration in a close vicinity facilitates imitation is through copying of a standard designs from foreign catalogues.

Figure 6.5: Firms source of information for new design in percentage

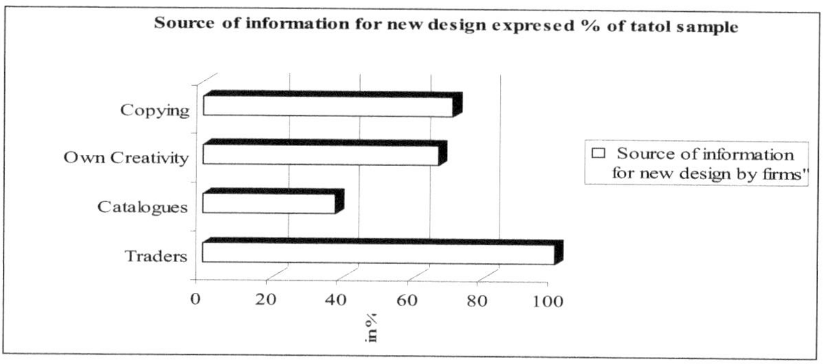

Source: Own fieldwork

6.4.4 The innovative activity and the growth of small enterprises

This subsection tries to relate innovative activities in the small enterprises with poverty alleviation goals. In this analysis, new growth model is used to examine the extent at which technology, the level of human capital, the incentives small producers face, and government trade policy have influenced the productivity in the small enterprises. The basic reason is that the study of innovation in small enterprises covers not only the micro- level factors but also the macro and meso-level factors. This sub-section starts with a brief review of endogenous model in order to understand why policy support for small cluster development in Nigeria can foster sectoral growth and as well serve as poverty alleviation strategy.

6.4.4.1 Endogenous growth model and small enterprises development

The new growth theory laid much emphasis on endogenous source of growth by showing how technological innovation and human capital accumulation in a selected economic sector can raise the growth rate of an economy (Mayer, 1996, p. 1). The theory provided the analytical framework which shows the sources of growth in production activities which are linked to externalities created by investments in human capital and technology. It also shows how new technology introduced in production can create learning-by-doing advantages such as skill upgrading (Mayer, 1996, p. 2). Endogenous growth model put forward by Romer (1986) is expressed as:

$$Y_i = F(K_i, L_i, k) = K_i b L_i^{(1-\beta)} k^n \tag{1}$$

model suggests that "N" firms are assumed to be sufficiently large, and all firms are identical. $\beta = 0$ or 1, the total stock of knowledge increase

such that $k = NK_j$

Given that N is large; each firm takes the aggregate capital stock or stock of knowledge as given. In this case, increasing returns are external to the firm. On the other hand, if all firms increase their kj, the total stock of knowledge will increase such that all firms will benefit (Veraga, 1991, p. 17). The capital accumulated can therefore generate endogenous growth since there are increasing returns to scale in the production function. Increasing returns however is not a sufficient condition for positive endogenous growth in the long run. There must be constant return to factors at firm level that can lead to capital accumulation and the corresponding endogenous growth (Romer, 1986, p. 1013)[163]. Romer (1986, p. 1015) argues that output per person can grow without limit in the sense that the rate of investment does not decline over time as capital accumulates because the marginal productivity of the factor is not decreasing. The model therefore suggests that growth function of technological progress also depends on the stock of human capital. Hence, increasing returns in human-capital will produce endogenous growth which is translated to growth of an economy (Vergara, 1991, p. 20)[164]. In this context, the effect of growth can be classified into two. One is transformation effect that is reflected on firm growth in terms of achieving economy of scale and scope. The second is transmission effect that is reflected on general economy such as GDP growth, poverty reduction and export chances. The central argument is that accumulation of physical capital and human capital will generate endogenous growth. In this context, Romer (1990, p. S75) argues that human capital is an important driver

163 In this case, $\beta + n \geq 1$ is needed such that $\beta + n = 1$, growth will be constant in the long run. On the other hand, if $\beta + n > 1$, growth will be explosive (Vergara, 1991, p. 18 quoted from Sala-i-Martin, 1989).

164 The endogenous growth models explicitly introduce imperfect competition, increasing returns, and admit, by preventing the marginal product of capital from falling, the possibility of differences in country growth rates, and lack of convergence of per capita incomes. This suggests that endogenous growth can produce two effects (Felipe, J. 1997, p. 1).

of technological change and as well the basic determinant of long term growth. Lucas (1988, p. 23) also argues that spillover effect which increases the level of technology is derived from investment in human capital. While Kumar (2003, p. 590) argues that technological progress reflects the effects of new intermediate goods introduced in the production.

New growth theory implicitly shows that there are two types of investment costs associated with innovation. The invention cost that covers creation of new technology, and adoption costs associated with creation of human capital required for the use of new technology. Adoption costs have a direct component in the form of investment outlays for schooling, on-the-training and indirect cost in the form of forgone output. This implies that analysis of endogenous growth model can be distinguished according to emphasis on invention or adoption costs (Mayer, 1996, p. 7). In this context, the policy option for sub-Saharan Africa countries in the contest of new growth model is the balance between invention costs and adoption costs. Capability for invention demands on accumulation of human capital that involves huge capital outlay. This happened to be limited in the sub-Saharan Africa. Policy option should be directed towards adoption cost which involves increasing investment on schooling and skill training.

6.4.4.2 Model and Data Specification

Based on the above analogue, this study adopts the production function similar to new growth model as shown in equation 2. In the model, Technology and human capital are considered to be endogenously given. Technology is the stocks of quasi-fixed capital (major equipment) in production while skilled and unskilled labour represents the nature of human capital employed in production. The school year is introduced in the production function because the number of years spent in schooling has influence on workers productivity. Market based incentives is introduced in the model because such incentives can have different effects on productivity growth. This is because motivation increases learning process and competition which can result to direct effect on product and process upgrading, and can induce sectoral growth as well. Openness is de facto competitiveness and usually underscores the degree of trade reform in a country. Openness is important because it can induce direct impact on the rate at which producers have access to foreign inputs such as raw materials and new machines. In general, the analysis is aimed at establishing if the theory of openness, education, access to new technology and incentive are consistent with productivity growth

Yi = F(K, L, SCH, INC, SDESN, OP) (2)

Where Y = Output, Y is the commodity output in tons considered as dependent variables.

K = Stock of quasi-fixed capital (major equipment)

L = labour breaking into L1 and L2 where L1 = skilled Labour and L2 = unskilled Labour

INC = Market based incentives small producers receive

SCH = Year of Schooling

SDESN = the number of successful designs which represents innovation variable or the nature of equipment

OP = Openness

ki = accumulated knowledge in respect to R&D or patent which is not known or given, the only information about accumulated knowledge is different types of design introduced and locally constructed machines.

The analysis is restricted to PKO and Footwear due to lack of basic information regarding innovation in other sub-sectors. The sample data cover the small and micro enterprises in clustered and dispersed areas. The data generated was subjected to regression analyses in order to understand the behaviour of the explanatory variables with respect to output. The study assumes that investment in human capital will foster technology adoption; liberalisation (openness) will induce competition, and have influence on access to new technology and productivity growth in all sectors. Furthermore, output growth depends on the technological adoption based on the nature of available labour in terms of skilled and unskilled labour. In this case, years of schooling plays an important role in the sense that skills acquisition is a function of years invested in acquiring skills. In general, increased productivity is subject to market incentives that foster harmonisation of taxation system, access to better inputs, knowledge upgrading and better business environment. Four functional forms were therefore tested in order to determine which models best explains the productivity growth of small scale enterprise in Nigeria.

First is to consider linear regression model (3) which shows for example that an extra increase in number of K will produce a corresponding increase in units of output. In other words, how change in unit of output is explained by the unit change of the coefficients of independent variables.

$$Y_i = a_0 + b_1 K_i + b_2 L_{i1} + b_3 L_{i2} + b_4 SCH_i + b_5 INC_i + b_6 SDSEN_i + b_7 OP_i + u_i \quad \text{----------3}$$

Where a_0 is constant, op and INC are dummy variables for openness and incentives respectively, while u_i represents the error terms. The problem here is that the results can be inconclusive because there could be evidence of non linearity of variables.

The second consideration is to investigate if there is proportional change in output Y for a given proportional change in explanatory variables. This takes care of non-linearity nature of parameters and variables. This is defined as:

$$\log Y_i = a_0 + b_1 \log K_i + b_2 \log L_{i1} + b_3 \log L_{i2} + b_4 \log SCH_i + b_5 \log INC_i + b_6 \log SDSEN_i + b_7 \log OP_i + u_i \quad (4)$$

The equation considers the elasticity of Y with respect to explanatory variables and is defined as proportional change in output Y for a given proportional change in explanatory variables (K, L1, L2, SCH, ICN and OP).
For example, if Y is the output and K is the stock of capital.

$$\text{elasticity}\, y = \frac{dY/Y}{dK/K} = \text{output elasticity of stock of capital}$$

The marginal change in output can be explained by marginal change in the independent variables and may be express as.

$$\text{elasticity}\, y = \frac{dY/dk}{Y/K} \quad (4a)$$

Equation 4a can be interpreted as the marginal propensity to produce the commodity PKO or Footwear and will depend on the propensity to invest in equipment for production activities.

Similarly,

$$\text{elasticity}\, y = \frac{dY/dL}{Y/L} \quad (4b)$$

Equation 4b suggests that the marginal propensity to produce the commodity PKO or Footwear will also depend on the propensity to invest in labour for the productivity growth.

Similarly,

$$\text{elasticity}\, y = \frac{dY/dSCH}{Y/SCH} \quad (4c)$$

Equation 4c explains to what extent educational attainment of workers and entrepreneurs can influence output? In other words, the marginal propensity to produce PKO or Footwear will depend on the marginal increase in workers' and entrepreneurs' educational profile.

Similarly,

$$\text{elasticity}\, y = \frac{dY/dINC}{Y/INC} \quad (4d)$$

Equation 4d suggests that marginal propensity to produce PKO or Footwear will depend on the propensity to improve the business environment and condition necessary to enhance productivity growth.

Similarly

$$elasticity y = \frac{dY/dSDESN}{Y/SDESN} \quad (4e)$$

Equation 4e suggests that marginal propensity to increase sales volume and profit depends on the propensity to introduce successful designs in the market. For PKO; the propensity to improve output depends on the propensity to apply modern technology or innovate in terms of restructuring the new technology for efficient adaptation for local production.

Similarly,

$$elasticity y = \frac{dY/dOP}{Y/OP} \quad (4f)$$

Equation 4f indicates that marginal propensity to produce the PKO or Footwear will depend on the propensity to improve trade policies that favour competitiveness and output growth.

The third is to consider the extent every extra stock of capital accumulated can increase the output volume by a certain proportion?

$$\log Y_i = a_0 + b_1 K_i + b_2 L_{i1} + b_3 L_{i2} + b_4 SCH_i + b_5 INC_i + b_6 SDSEN_i + b_7 OP_i + u_i \quad (5)$$

Equation 5 shows that proportional change in output per unit change in K, L1, L2, SCH, ICN and OP is valid only when value of coefficient is small, otherwise it may be more complex to explain when the value of coefficient is large (Dougherty, 2002 p158).

The fourth consideration is whether output Y has a constant proportional growth rate as units of the independent variables increases.

$$Y_i = a_0 + b_1 \log K_i + b_2 \log L_{i1} + b_3 \log L_{i2} + b_4 \log SCH_i + b_5 \log INC_i + b_6 \log SDSEN_i + b_7 \log OP_i + u_i \quad (6)$$

6.4.4.3 Descriptive analysis

Table 6.8 shows the mean and standard deviation of dependent and independent variable. The mean number of years of schooling is very low in both sub-sectors with the value of 10.0412 and 6.8042 in PKO and Footwear respectively. The low education profile suggests that the managerial capabilities of the entrepreneurs will be low and therefore influence productivity to become low. This supports Daniels and Mead, 1998, p. 63 argument that low education level of small enterprise heads and workers limits entreprenurship development in Africa. Table 6.8 also shows that on the average, more than one labour are employed in PKO sub-sector while the average number of skill workers in the footwear enterprises is less one. The implication is that unskilled labours are mainly employed in both sub-sectors. There is no evidence of government incentive reported in PKO while the mean number of government support reported in Footwear sub-sector is less than 1.

Table 6.8: Summary Statistics

	PKO		Footwear	
Variables	Mean	Std. Deviation	Mean	Std. Deviation
Output in Tons	6.8029	1.03125	2026.39	1636.82
Equipment	4.7451	1.45387	2.4583	0.50176
Schooling	10.0412	0.86998	6.8042	1.49020
Skilled labour	1.1981	0.40098	0.1528	0.36230
Unskilled labour	5.0392	1.38507	1.5417	0.42767
Incentives	0.0000	0.00000	0.2361	0.49647
Openness		0.50254	0.5833	0.48093
S.design	0.0980	0.30033	na	na

Note: S.design = Successful design, Sample size = 51 for PKO and 72 for footwear
Source: Calculation by Author

This means that small enterprises receive little or no attention from the state and institutions. Openness can be measured in terms of the ratio of capital import to GDP. In other words, the value of capital goods import (adjusted by PPP investment prices) is expressed to GDP. The argument here is that openness stimulates growth by increasing capital import (Kumar, 2003, p. 602). In this model, the measure of openness reflects the degree of competitiveness and the trade policy reforms as it affects the small producers. The value falls between 0 and 1. If the value is 0, it implies that the economy is operating under a highly restricted or closed economic environment. If the value is 1, it shows that the economy is operating under absolute liberalised and highly competitive economic environment. The interviewees were asked to explain how the trade policy reform has affected their economic activities. As shown in Table 6.8, the values 0.50254 and 0.5833 of openness in PKO and Footwear respectively. This suggests that the firms are operating under a relatively moderate open economy.

6.4.4.4 Pearson linear correlation of output and the explanatory variables.

As shown in Table 6.9, the correlation coefficient (CC) of equipment (0.665) in PKO is positive and significant at 1 percent level. This suggests that equipment is contributing to the productivity growth in PKO sub-sector. The correlation coefficient (CC) of equipment (-0.135) in Footwear is negative and not significant.

Table 6.9: Pearson linear correlation of output in PKO and footwear enterprises

Sub-Sector	Equip.	Sch	Skilled Labour	Unskilled Labour	Inc	Op	Special. design	Sample Size
PKO	0.665	-0.134	-0.300	0.108	na	0.154	-0.88	
Output	*(0.001)**	*(0.174)*	*(0.417)*	*(0.226)*	na	*(0.269)*	*(0.272)*	51
Footwear	-0.135	-0.071	-0.190	0.348	0.252	-0.121	0.551	
Output	*(0.125)*	*(0.278)*	*(0.056)*	*(0.0021)***	*(0.241)*	*(0.317)*	(0.001)*	72

Note: in parentheses are t-statistics; * indicate 1 percent; ** indicates 5 percent and *** indicates 10 percent levels of significant. Equip. = Equipment; Sch= Schooling; Inc= Incentives; Op. = Openness.

Source: Author's own calculation

The low and negative value of CC of equipment in Footwear explains the poor nature of equipment (hand tools) used in production. It shows that equipments are not contributing effectively in the productivity growth. This suggests that the producers have to work extensively longer hours in order to meet the output target. The value of CC schooling in PKO and Footwear are negative and not significant. This implies that the types of education and years of schooling confer on workers are not significantly related to their occupation. It is arguable that the educational system is not in line with the economic system. The relationship between skilled labour and output is negative and not significant in PKO and Footwear. This suggests that most of the labour employed in these sub-sectors is unskilled and the level of entrepreneurship development is still low. It also indicates that even when new technology is introduced, firms have to spend extra investment capital in training the workers for the application of the technology. On the other hand, the skilled labour is negatively correlated with output in both sub-sectors. The negative correlation coefficient suggests that skilled labour is not valued in Nigeria's small manufacturing enterprises activities hence policies are not directed effectively towards skills enhancement and acquisition. The implication here is that the ability of youths to engage in self-employment in the productive sectors will be limited. It also suggests that labour force employed in the production sector is not compatible with job hence many workers may leave the sub-sectors when there are better alternatives. The low values in the unskilled labour suggest that unskilled labour force has no influence in output growth. The implication here is that with current level of technological application in the sub-sector, the quality of the products will be below international standard and cannot compete in international market. In general, it shows that Nigeria's labour market is poorly developed to face the challenges in the globalisation process. The CC value of market incentive in footwear is positive but not significant. This suggests that there is need for institutional support so that firms can respond to market changes effectively.

Invariably, the CC value of openness in PKO is positive but very low. This suggests the liberalisation has no negative impact on firms' activities, however, due to low capital base; the firms cannot tap the opportunities associated with liberalisation of the market in terms of access to foreign technology for efficient production. The negative value of CC in openness of footwear indicates that the sub-sector is vulnerable to liberalisation in the sense that higher quality products produced elsewhere can induce crises in the sub-sector. Hence, the need for institutional incentive that targets quality upgrading is imperative. In general, descriptive analysis only shows how the output is directly related to the explanatory variable but failed to show the influence of these explanatory variables on output.

6.4.4.5 Result of Regression Analysis

Table 6.10 shows the result of regression analysis of the output in the production functions of PKO and Footwear sub-sectors. The log linear function is selected as equation best fit in PKO because it has the highest adjusted square value of 0.555 with F-value significant at 1 per cent. Table 6.10 shows that constants (Proxy for outcome of technology adoption) and equipment are significant determinants of PKO output. The constant is positive and significant at 1 percent, indicating that technology can influence the output in PKO positively. If new technology is applied in production, an increased productivity in one firm will influence other entrepreneurs to introduce new technology in the production. In other words, PKO producers who introduce new technology will gain more than non-adopter, and earlier adopters will gain more economies of scale than late adopters. Producers who introduce new technology will be better of than non- and late adopters (Berdegué and Escobar's, 2002, p. 2).

Equipment is positive and significant at 1 per cent. This suggests that output PKO responds positively to increase in equipment hence capitalisation of the sub-sector is very important. On the other hand, the nature of the equipment has impact on the marginal increase in the rate of output. The marginal increase in the rate of output depends not only on the nature of equipment but also on other factors such as energy and raw material supply. It also depends on the ability of the workers to handle equipments efficiently. The impact of increased marginal rate of output can positively affect poverty reduction by increasing employment opportunities. It will also have positive effect on income of the entrepreneurs and workers only if there is relatively higher productivity growth. The argument here is that local technology is inefficient hence output can neither meet local demand nor explore the changes in export market. Firms will not enjoy the economies of scale and as well not be able to meet export market demand. In a nutshell, using local technology only will discourage technology learning and improvement of ideas[165]. The value of CC in years of schooling is negative and significant at 1 per cent. This suggests that the type of education received in schools may not be directly related to PKO production. It also implies that firms will allocate extra investment fond for training of workers on how to handle new technology in PKO extraction. The negative sign in education in PKO suggests that the higher the educational level of the PKO workers have, the more the tendency to abandon PKO production for more lucrative jobs. Hence, learning on the job can be an effective means of training workers in the sub-sector. It also raises the question on the kind of incentive necessary to motivate and retain the labour force in the sub-sector. Argueably, accumulation of human capital depends on the ability to acquire and retain skill labour in the system. The negative values in unskilled labour suggest that employment in the sub-sector does not require specific unskilled or special knowledge. It also indicates that labour market is vulnerable in the sense that labour migration will be high.

Openness is a proxy to liberalisation policy and was introduced in the equation as a dummy variable. This helps to ascertain the extent at which trade reform has influenced the output. Since the influence of trade reform on output cannot be quantified, yes or no answer to questions were used in scoring the influence of trade reform on the interviewees' business activities. The value of openness dummy variable in PKO production function is positive in all the models but not significant. The positive value suggests that openness can influence access to modern machines but firms have not been able to exploit the opportunities due to low capital base. It also suggests that firms in PKO extraction can compete in the local market and even export, if access to new technology improves.

Absence of incentive suggests that firms are surviving without government intervention or surviving under harsh business environment. In this case, how to improve productivity growth in the PKO sub-sector will be the basic policy objective. The innovation variable in PKO reflects the nature of the equipment in production. The interviewees were asked to explain the nature of machines in production (for example new machines, second hand or locally made machines). They were also asked to describe the nature of reconstruction

165 Effective innovative activity similar to Sverrisson, (1997, pp. 174-5) argument could occur if the imported new machine is modified to local adaptation for efficient production. It can also be in the form modifying the local input suit the new machine.

made on the new or second machines in order to adapt to local production. Since the nature of the machine cannot be quantified, the 'yes' or 'no' answer was used. 'Yes' is assigned to the innovation if the machines are new machines or reconstruction of the machine for adaptation in local production effectively otherwise 'no'.

Table 6.10: Output regression in PKO enterprises

PKO				
Var.	Linear	Log-linear	Semi-log	Expo.
Cons.	8.793	2.852	2.253	14.320
	*(7.139)**	*(6.699)**	*(11.635)**	*(5.061)**
Equip	0.806	0.794	0.803	0.788
	*(7.554)**	*(7.917)**	*(7.490)**	*(7.929)**
SCH	-0.386	-0.383	-0.368	-0.403
	*(-3.630)**	*(-3.767)**	(-3.440)*	*(-4.002)**
L1	-0.081	0.409	-0.071	0.625
	(-3.630)	*(0.696)*	(0.675)	*(1.074))*
L2	0.031	-0.365	0.055	-0.610
	(0.310)	*(-0.365)*	*(0.549)*	*(-0.1.053)*
INC	na	na	na	na
OP	0.040	*0.071*	0.039	0.720
	(0.403)	*(0.752)*	*(0.397)*	*(0.773)*
SDESGN	*-0.45*	*-0.79*	*-058*	*-0.074*
	(-0.442)	*(-0.783)*	*(-0.560)*	*(-0.745)*
F-Value	10.540*	11.395*	10.259*	10.301*
R	0.768	0.780	0.764	0.795
R^2	0.590	0.608	0.586	0.601
R (adj.)	0.534	0.555	0.526	0.550
Durbin-Watson	1.731	1.823	1.762	1.818
Sample size			51	

Key: = Constant; Equip = Equipment; SCH. = Year of Schooling; L1 = Skilled Labour; L2= Unskilled Labour; INC. = Incentives; OP = Openness. SDESGN = Successful Design

Note: Values in parentheses are t-statistics. * indicate 1 percent; ** indicates 5 percent and *** indicates 10 percent levels of significant.

Source: Author's own calculation

The negative value in SDESIGN suggests that there is no innovative activity in the PKO production. The locally constructed machines are inefficient hence there is high incidence of output shortfall. Log linear function is selected as the equation best fit in footwear production function because of its highest adjusted square value of 0.403 with F-value signifycant at 1 per cent. The log linear relation therefore suggests that additional increase in equipment will increase the output by -15.5 per cent. It also implies that since the equipment are mainly hand tools, additional increase in equipment can produce diminishing returns. The value of education is negative and significant at 10 percent level. This suggests that weak educational attainment has positive effect on firm performance. This can also imply that the level of educational attainment is not related to the industrial need. Hence development of the appropriate skill for modern technology is imperative. Entrepreneurs and the workers will be better off if there is increased investment in skill development that is compatible with new technology introduced in the production.

Table 6.10a: Output regression in Footwear enterprises

Footwear				
Var.	Linear	Log	Semi-log	Expo.
Cons.	162.727	7.061	*7.548*	92.217
	(0.118)	(4.690)*	*(0.7.157)**	(0.046)
Equip	0.043	-0.155	-0.161	0.041
	(0.409)	(-1.590)	*(-1.627)*	(0.139)
SCH	0.948	-0.163	-0161	-0.116
	(0.347)	(-1.670)***	*(-1.640)*	(-1.090)
L1	-0.148	-0.163	.149	-0.182
	(-1323)	(-0.163)	*(-1.406)*	(-1.600)
L2	0.152	0.030	0.012	na
	*(1.319)***	(0.288)	*(.0.108)*	na
INC	0.168	0.087	0.069	0.142
	*(1.506)****	(0.895)	*(.697)*	(1.373)
OP	0.060	-0.050	-0.059	-0.016
	(0.556)	(-0.501)	*(-0.57))*	(0.898)
SDESGN	*0.505*	0.565	*0.553*	0.503
	(4.552)	(5.595)*	*(5.277)**	(4.566)*
F-Value	5.557	7.842*	7.346	5.719
R	0.615	0.678	0.667	.588
R^2	0.378	0.462	0.446	0.346
R (adj.)	0.378	0.403	0.385	0.285
Durbin-Watson	1.264	1.307	1.283	1.246
Sampl size		72		

Key: = Constant; Equip = Equipment; SCH. = Year of Schooling; L1 = Skilled Labour; L2= Unskilled Labour; INC. = Incentives; OP = Openness. SDESGN = Successful Design

Note: Values in parentheses are t-statistics. * indicate 1 percent; ** indicates 5 percent and *** indicates 10 percent levels of significant.

Source: Author's own calculation

The value of skilled labour is negative but has no significant influence on output. It suggests that the quality of the products will remain low hence firms can only produce for local and African regional market. The value of unskilled labour is positive but not significant suggesting that the enterprises employ mainly unskilled labour and apprentices. The value of incentive is positive but not significant indicating the need for institutional support. The negative value in openness suggests that firms are sensitive to competition. Hence, there is the need for policy support in order to improve performance. Design is positive and significant at 1 percent level suggesting that innovative activities of the shoemakers contribute to the survival and competitiveness of the micro and small footwear enterprises in the local market.

6.4.4.6 The Lead Equation and Results

Table 6.10 shows that firms in different sub-sectors have different constraints and respond differently to a given production function hence the lead equation tend to be different.

Log Y = 2.852+ 0.794Equip – 0.383SCH + 0.409L1 – 0.365L2 +0INC + 0.71OP - 0.79SDESIN -- (7)

In PKO, Log linear equation shows the high values in F^2 and F-value function. It explains relatively better the total variation of dependent variable with independent variables. The table shows that with the highest R^2 value of 0.555, the log-linear has the F-value of 11.395 and significant at one per cent. This suggests that without government support, 55 per cent change in output is explained by the nature of the equipment, the nature of the labor, year of schooling and the government trade policy.

Log Y = 7.061- 0.155Equip – 0.163SCH – 0.1635L1 + 0.30L2 + 0.087INC – 0.050OP 0.565SDESIN-- (8)

In footwear, linear equation shows high values in R^2 and F-value function. It suggests that relatively better variation of the dependent variable with the independent variables. With highest F-value of 7.061 and adjusted R^2 of 0.403 suggests that 7.061 per cent change in output the equation is explained by the nature of equipment, the nature of labour incentives the small entrepreneurs receive and government trade policy. In the equation, unskilled labour and incentive have significant relationship with the output. This suggests that output in the footwear can be increased by increasing number of unskilled labour but the negative sign implies that product quality will remain a problem. The implication is that incentive which targets skill development and access to modern equipment will enhance productivity and will support poverty reduction.

6.5 Summary and conclusion

This chapter has provided analytical work on how small enterprises survive in Nigerian market. It started with theoretical analysis on innovation and innovative activities in small enterprises. The theoretical analyses suggest that innovation is analysed in different levels namely the macro, meso and micro levels. The macro factors explain the role of science and technology policies and national systems of innovation in promoting innovation and innovation diffusion. The impact of stable macroeconomic conditions such as price level, labour market conditions and educational system was analysed. Meso-level analysis is concerned with policies that support development of technology partnership, policies that define the nature of technology, and the learning process in specific industry. The micro-factors underscore the outcome of cumulative learning process and capability building at firm level. Hence, co-operation and linkages play an important role in facilitating innovation in small enterprises. The theoretical analyses of the relationship between innovation in small enterprises and poverty reduction focused on how the goals of innovative activities in small enterprises are related to the goals of poverty alleviation. In this case, the effect of productivity growth on poverty reduction is linked to access to modern technology, the nature of labour, the incentives the small producers face, and the nature of the country's trade policy. The literature review focused on different conceptual approaches starting from appropriate technology movement, the concept of technology capability to the impact of clusters and networks.

The empirical analyses show how small enterprises survive in an open market on one hand and the analysis of the factors that explain the variation in output in footwear and PKO enterprises on the other. The first concerns with the cost of introducing new product design and the number of design realised in the market. This helps the research to determine the value of forgone investment (sunk costs) in order to remain in the market. The second investigates how dependent variable (output) is explained by the independent variables (techno-logy, years of schooling, skilled labour, unskilled, incentives and the openness). Two sub-sectors were examined and the outcome of the empirical evidences indicate that small firms are surviving by the use of unskilled labour, low technology under little or no government support.

This study therefore suggests that policy interventions should focus on how to improve small enterprises' access to new and modern equipment. The negative value of year of schooling, skill and unskilled labour suggests that that sub-sectors is labour-intensive. It also implies that skill development is neglected in Nigeria's industrial policy initiatives. Hence, there is urgent need for change in policy strategy that focuses on appropriate skill development and capitalisation of the small enterprises in order to increase productivity. In PKO, the central problem is poor technology and declining rate of palm kernel production. Firms in the PKO sub-sector face the challenges of meeting the local demand and export opportunities due to weak technology. Increasing the palm kernel production through the support of medium scale palm plantation could be an important strategy. Externalities can be induced if there are linkages with external buyers such as large transnational corporations which will provide the milieu for product quantity and quality upgrading in both sub-sectors. Getting access to international commodity supply chains will not only increase output volume but also will force the local small firms to improve the product quality to meet international standard. Technological improvement can be effective through linkages with transnational firms such that productivity increase and access to international market can be feasible. This requires creating the conditions necessary for large international firms to invest in Nigeria favourably. Investment in human capital in terms of skill development and partnership building can induce technology learning and technology transfer. In general, the regression helped to appreciate the influence of openness in terms of access to capital goods and increased competition. This will help the small enterprises to reduce the capability gap and as well reduce the high investment costs in order to compete effectively in the local and wider markets.

Chapter 7: The Synthesis of the Study

7.1 Introduction

Several studies on small enterprises development in Africa have shown the patterns of growth among small enterprises in sub-Saharan African (Mead, 1994); the role and impact of SMEs on economic growth and poverty alleviation in the sub-region (Kings, 1998); the level of income generation in small enterprises in Kenya (Daniel and Mead; 1998); how indigenous small and medium enterprises perceive their business environment (Levy, 1991); the nature of knowledge networks and technological capabilities in the African manufacturing clusters (Oyelaran-Oyeyinka, 2003); business environment and entrepreneurial activity in Nigeria (Agboli and Ukaegbu, 2006) etc. Arguably, these studies show the importance of SMEs in African economies.

This study goes further by first looking into the SME development trajectories in Africa. It also explores the possible dynamic path through which SMEs in the region can be promoted and growth can be sustained in the region. There is a combination of factors such as investment in technology, human capital developmet and policy environment which drives SME development. To analyse this, the study adopted a comparative approach in investigating different dimensions of SME operational structures. The first approach concerns the impact of spatial clustering on SMEs. The competitive factors such as the level of human capital development, the technological applications and linkages existing in five sub-sectors were investigated. The second approach fouces on how SMEs in the region operate in spite of weak institutional development, unstable political and macroeconomic conditions. In this context, the social networks in which the entrepreneurs are embedded and organisational networks of the SMEs were investigated. In the third approach, study looked into the innovative activities of the small enterprises. The aims here are to investigate how small firms compete in an open economy and to explore if the objectives of innovation in small enterprises relate to the goals of poverty alleviation.

The findings revealed some conventional results similar to previous studies on African SMEs in terms of employment creation, and income generation. The characteristics of small enterprises investigated are similar to previous findings which include among others, high degree of informality, dominance of micro and small enterprises, low education background of enterprises heads and workers, poor book-keeping and accounting system, poor technological application and etc. Three unique findings emerged from the study; firstly, the study revealed that small enterprises cluster with high degree of informality characteristics can be active and as well be competitive in local market by using different marketing strategies to overcome external competitive pressure; secondly, regionalisation processes and liberalisation of the market in sub-Saharan African countries have increased trading networks across the borders of Anglo and Franco phone countries in African sub-regional market; thirdly, innovative activity in small enterprises in sub-Saharan Africa is a survival strategy in an open economy. The empirical findings also revealed several weaknesses and limitations of SMEs similar to the findings of previous studies in Africa. The limitations include among others, low skilled labour force, weak technological base and absence of linkages with large firms especially in traditional manufacturing industries (garment, footwear and wood/furniture).

This section therefore presents theoretical analysis of the role of investment in bridging these gaps and shows how investment can impact transformation in small and medium scale enterprise clusters and Nigerian SMEs in general. The analysis starts by introducing the "Investment and SME Development (ISMED) model". The model shows why and how investment relates to SME development. It also shows how investment can positively impact enterprises cluster development in Nigeria. The influence of networks SME development was also included in the model. In general, the ISMED model shows how investment can enhance SME compatibilities in terms of human and physical in order increase aggregate efficiency. The aggregate effects of investment can be measured in terms of transformation and transmission effects on enterprises and on the economy in general.

7.2 Investment and SME Development (ISMED) Model

7.2.1 The motivation of the ISMED model

This study started by highlighting the major controversies surrounding African SMEs. Different empirial findings have come up with the arguement that SMEs in sub-Saharan Africa countries possess the potential to create employment and generate income. The counter claims suggest that SMEs in Africa cannot sustain employment creation and that they tend to generate low income. While some argue that SMEs in Africa are isolated and lack the potential individually to improve performance or sustain competition (the missing link). In general, the economic globalisation literature argues that the capabilities of SMEs in Africa are very weak and lack the potential to play their role in economic development and in the ongoing globalisation process.

The empirical findings of this study revealed that SMEs in Nigeria possess the potential to create employment and generate income. However, the employment created cannot be sustained. The incomes generated across the sectors are below monthly wage of US$50 stipulated for private sector in Nigeria. There are evidences of high degree of unskilled and unpaid labour in production. This suggests that with low skilled workers and low wages, productivity will be very low. There is also evidence of underemployment in terms of underutilisation of labour in the sense that qualified workers were engaged in low-wage job. The implication is that workers could leave their jobs suddenly when there are better alternatives. Three empirical outcomes explained the factors leading to absence of linkages. The first is the capability gap reflecting low technological capacity and low human capital development. The second is poor domestic investment reflecting low capital base which resulted to low quality of input and outputs. The third factor is poor institutional development and poor policy environment in which SMEs operate. This is reflected on the structure of networks and why FDI inflow is weak in manufacturing sector. These factors arguably justify the claims of the globalisation literature that Africa SMEs (excluding South Africa) are very weak and lack the potential to play their role in economic development. It also justifies the claims that SMEs in Nigeria cannot sustain employment hence the ISMED model tries to provide an interactive solution to these weaknesses.

7.2.2 The ISMED Model

The ISMED model seeks to confront the following problems; one, how technological disadvantages in the SMEs can be reduced in order to foster linkages with large firms; two, how the institutional and policy environment can be strengthened in order to improve the capabilities of the SMEs. The ISMED model is a simple interactive process based on the outcome of the empirical study showing the processes on how domestic investment supported by FDI can stimulate capability upgrading in SMEs. Figure 7 illustrates how the three SME operational structures namely clustering, innovation and networking are linked in the model. It also shows the interdependencies in the operational structures which require different policy approach. The upper segment of the model represents the impact of investment which invariably depends on policy environment. The assumption here is that SME growth is path dependent which invariably is a function of domestic investment. Hence, FDI inflow can stimulate SMEs growth if there is an improvement in domestic investment. The lower segment of the model represents the outcome of the model. Since SMEs represents 95 per cent of Nigeria's industrial structure, growth in SMEs sector in terms of size and capacity will have multiplier effect on the entire economy.

The model is built under the concept of new growth theory which shows the relationship between stock of knowledge and firms growth. It also shows that human and physical capital accumulations are the important variables which explain differences in growth rate across countries. The ISMD model therefore shows how domestic investment and FDI backed by effective policies can contribute in the reduction of the capability gap in the SMEs. In this context, the model explains the conditions under which firms and institutions can create wealth or economic growth in Nigeria. The conditions which are responsible for mobilisation of domestic investment are stipulated in the model. The conditions cover the physical and social infrastructure existing in a specific location of a country.

Figure 7.1: Investment and SME development (ISMED) Model

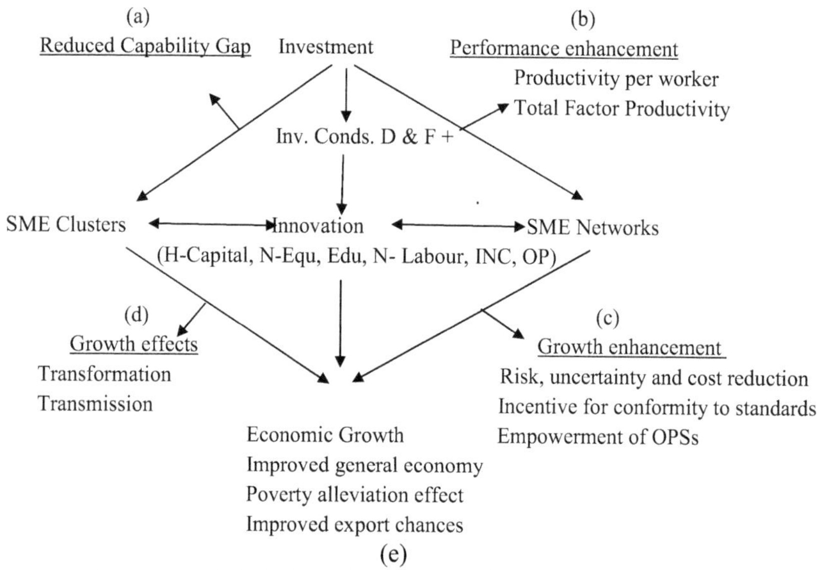

Key: D & F = Domestic and Foreign Direct Investment; Inv. Conds. = Investment Conditions; H-Capital = Human Capital; N- Equ. = Nature of Equipment; Edu. = Education; N-Labour = Nature of Labour; INC. = Incentives; OP = Openness; OPSs = Organised Private Sectors

Source: Author's own compilation based on the research outcome

An important aspect of the model is role of openness and incentives in technological learning and firm performance. In this respect, two important propositions are referred to. The first is that relative international prices can be reflected on the international marginal rate of transformation. This can be equated with domestic prices for an efficient allocation of resources. Resource allocation can affect growth positively especially in developing countries through an increased efficiency of investment in imported capital goods. This will therefore promote the ability to expand at a constant rate rather than at diminishing returns in longer period through access to larger market as Berg and Krueger (2008, p. 176) suggested. The second preposition is that institutions provide the incentive structures that make human environment effective. This is because the human environment sets the rules for interactions and induces motivations that facilitate firms to create wealth (Dunning and Zhang, 2007, p.

2). This suggests that social networks are important factors but not sufficiently enough in supporting market development. Openness stands as productive incentive for access to technology.

a) Investment and capability gap eduction

The empirical results of this study revealed high incidence of poor technology, low skill labour force weak institutional and physical infrastructure. This suggests that the SMEs in Nigeria lack the capacity to improve capabilities individually. The financial base of the firms is very weak hence the firms cannot invest in modern technology or hire skilled workers. This supports UNCTAD, (2007a, p. 7) report which revealed among others; low technological capabilities, underdeveloped skilled workforce needed in modern production, are lacking in the region. Effective market institutions which could have supported technology acquisition and diffusion are the major problems firms face in the region. These factors arguably explain the increasing marginalization of sub-African region in the globalisation process. Thus, there is an urgent need for new policy measures that focuses on reducing the capability gap problems. Reducing the deficiencies in infrastructure, human and physical capital, and improving the macroeconomic policies is absolutely important in order to ensure effective resources allocation for investment. Technological progress will not occur without an improvement in these factors (UNCTAD, 2007a, p. 5).

In this respect, the investment strategies adopted by the government and local firms can produce synergy not only to encompass MNCs investment criteria but also induce structural transformation in the economy. In this case, upgrading domestic knowledge system is very important because it supports the creation, accumulation, use and sharing of knowledge. Experience has also shown that linkages with MNCs facilitate innovation through learning and imitations (Kim, 1997). The intensity of the linkages and increased technology learning always generate a competitive environment. In this context, building up capability and efficiency requires active learning of individuals and organisations taken part in the process of innovation. The efficiency of these learning activities depends on economic, political and social infrastructures. Furthermore, Li and Liu, (2005, p. 404) study revealed that technological gap has resulted to poor interaction between the FDI and local firms in developing countries. This suggests that investment in factors which can enhance productivity growth will produce a business environment compatible to foreign firms' interest (e.g. in the area of sub-contracting or joint venture activities). Positive effect of FDI is such that the local firms may try to upgrade their technology in order to be qualified for sub-contracting activities with large firms (Michie, 2001, p. 3). Oyelaran-Oyeyinka (2007, p. 225) argues that since Africa is in an early industrialisation process and the SMEs are highly imitative innovators, to catch up with the trend, investment will compell the local firms to explicitly modify the process and product which can lead to learning and competitive trajectory.

Furthermore, domestic investment and FDI play an important role in generating the much needed Information and Communication Technology (ICT) for the reduction of capability gap in the African economy. This is because ICT can link the technological learning process with governance system at the same time showing how transformation process in each case evolves (Juma und Yee-Cheong, 2005, pp. 48-9). ICT has also a direct impact on the efforts to improve people's lives through better information flows and communication which enhances economic growth by improving firm productivity (Juma und Yee-Cheong, 2005, pp. 48-9). Moreover, knowledge has become increasingly important in recent times due to rapid increase in technological advancement therefore has created pressure for workers to upgrade their skills constantly (Yusuf, et al, 2003, p. 216). This suggests that ICT can play an important role in the learning dynamics by widening the opportunities for individuals who would like to further their learning when such infrastructure is provided (Yusuf, et al, 2003, p. 218).

The implications of reduced capability gap in Nigeria and Africa at large are such that SMEs will not only gain by upgrading the quality of output and capacity but also can diversify their production to other frontier. An improve product quality may lead to increased export possibilities or offer the possible channels for integration of the Nigerian SMEs into the global value chains.

b) Investment and performance enhancement

Performance enhancement can be observed in two forms in ISMED model. First is the improved productivity of workers and the second is the growth in Total Factor Productivity (TFP). Investment in performance enhancement can be considered as the basic measure that supports long term sustainability of small and medium scale enterprises and the economy in general. The empirical findings of the study indicate that human capital is low, skill labour force is weak, physical infrastructure and markets are relatively weak. The growth in output per worker is associated with the accumulation of physical capital, human capital and technological change (Baier et al, 2002, p. 29). Policies targeting the expansion of skill and physical infrastructure development in Nigeria will attract FDI inflow and foster transfer of technology effectively. Effective technology transfer depends on the nature of the technology that is in line with the level of skill labour available (Michie, 2001, p. 5). For example, transfer of technology was effective in Thailand because the majority of the FDI inflow to Thailand is low and medium technology industry that does not require relatively very high skilled labour (Michie, 2001, p. 5).

Furthermore, the plausible factors that determine the efficiency of labour include education per worker, knowledge, economic, political, and social systems. Education is the only factor that has a scale of measurement in terms of years of schooling. For example, some differences in the efficiency of labour across time and countries can be explained by differences in the average years of schooling per worker (Benhabib and Spiegel, 1994, p. 144). Investment in education is therefore deemed at upgrading the output per worker in a competitive environment. However, education alone is not the overwhelming factor that determines efficiency of labour. Knowledge is also an important factor in explaining differences in efficiency of labour over time because some knowledge is scientific, technical and tacit. In this context, learning mechanism of different kinds are significant determinants of productivity in Africa (World Bank 2002, p. 21). Performance enhancement depends on economic policy, political environment, and social system. These are the basic factors that determine total factor productivity of an economy.

In general, TFP measures the improvement and efficiency in terms of quality aspects of labour and capital. In other words, it is the measure that relates output to all inputs in the production process (Söderborn and Teal, 2002, p. 24). Productivity development in SMEs is also interrelated with wage and non-wage working conditions. There is relationship between higher income, firm growth and increased efficiency. For example, some efficient SMEs in Malaysia compete extensively with large companies by focusing on high product quality. Entrepreneurs in SME sector invested strongly on acquiring new technology and know-how through licensing, joint ventures and exports. This is supported by different capacity building programmes designed to cover training and implementtation of national human resource development policies (World Bank, 1997a). As SMEs in Nigeria continue to face intense international competition as result of liberalisation and globalisation efforts, they must upgrade and improve standards by investing in modern equipments. Government should as well focus on improving the enabling environment and reforming the education systems.

c) Investment and institutions in growth enhancement

Uncertainty is the relevant variable in investment decision process because investment demands time and involves costs during planning and implemention. Firms consider all available information and the uncertainty associated with the information during their decision making process. If investment expenditures are irreversible, there will be an option to postpone investment when uncertainty persists. This allows the decision makers to obtain further information about the future market conditions (Butzen et al, 2002, p. 2). However, the option to postpone investment has its own price in terms of opportunity cost of investing today. Hence, firms will only invest when the net present value of the investment project covers the value of opportunity cost of postponing investment. This is because cost increases with uncertainty and irreversibility increases the cost associated with investment. According to the real option theory, uncertainty and irreversibility tend to deter current investment, and as well delay investment projects (Butzen et al, 2002. pp. 1-3). The role of network in this context is such that uncertainty can be reduced when network ties are created by coherent groups with strong interdependencies. Entrepreneurs can then streamline information accurately and timely according to their specific needs. This is only effective when market and the economy are small. As the market expands and the economy deepens, institutional stability comes into play in reducing uncertainty (World Bank, 2002a, pp. 179).

In an economy with stable institutions, transaction cost arising from the cost of coordinating and formalisation of business ventures can be effectively reduced. Transaction costs are not only the costs of coordinating increasingly complex interdependent groups in an economy but also the costs of enforcing agreements and making credible commitments across time and space (North, 1990, p. 27). For example, imperfect enforcement of property rights is arguably has negative effect on the economy. It may be part of the causes of growth failures in developing countries as put forward by Zak (2001). Insecurity in property rights drives investment opportunities away such that the economy can be reduced to rent-seeking phenomenon. In such a phenomenon, there is tendency that the majority of the population are exposed to the risk of being caught in a poverty trap because investment is not directed to productive sector. This is highly plausible even when government policy to enforce property rights is optimal (Zak, 2001, p. 11). This argument also suggests that effective legal instrument is the major instrument for protecting investment. Countries with poorer investor protection mechanisms have smaller and narrower financial markets relative to the size of the economy. Individuals in these countries trade less in financial markets and the value of publicly traded securities is always lower; and the overall number of market participants is also lower (La Porta et al. 1997, p. 1149). Hence, there is a need for effective market institution necessary to protect investment and enhance growth in the economy.

On this note, the role of the state in the economy has become a central discussion in the development paradigm since 1997. Using the words of the World Bank Development Report 1997- "the state is central to economic and social development, not as a direct provider of growth but as a partner, catalyst, and facilitator (World Bank, 1997b, p. 1). The central issue here is that in economic development, there is a need for participation of groups, non-governmental organisation (NGOs) and other private actors in the economy. According to Hartwig (1999, p. 57), "one hand no fit tie bundles"- this means that you cannot tie a bundle with one hand only. In development policy and practice, self-help activities are predominant in poverty alleviation. This is because an individual or group can design and implement its own strategy effectively in order to improve his/her situation or the situation of the group members (Cullison, 1993, p. 6). This brings to focus the capability of the state in performing such functions. This is referred to the ability of the state to undertake and promote collective actions effectively. This entails ability of the state to use its available resources effectively in providing such services. This demands an improvement in public institutions that facilitate the effective rules and restrain as well as checking corruptive actions in the system (World Bank, 1997b, p. 3). For example, social policy is very important for success of the any economic reform hence the state should concentrate in service financing, guidance and monitoring of the economy (Cornia, 1998, p. 33).

In this respect, empowerment is a central issue in development economic discourse because it fosters decentralisation of functions; it allows civil liberty, fosters the stability of democracy and creates checks and balances as well as promoting collective actions for private sector development. In this case, empowerment of the organised private sectors (OPSs) is very important in industrialisation process. This is because the central objective of the organisations is to serve the interest of the firms in the organisation. OPSs have an inbuilt self-adjusting mechanism directed towards efficiency and profitability in the sense that they have two headed structures. One made up of unpaid politically elected management structure and the other paid full-time administrative staffs (Krief, 2007, p. 174). The functions of the OPSs goes beyond serving the interest of their members but include reinforcing business community's commitment to the society, and as well foster cooperation with related national and foreign actors. They also provide advisory services to government because they understand the problems firms face. They lobby as and when required in formulation and execution of business and industry related policies (Krief, 2007, p. 174). OPSs also provide an up-to-date information services to business, government and the community at large. For example, through networking, national chambers of commerce and industry can be linked with local and international sectoral organisations. The linkages will provide small entrepreneurs the opportunity to learn how small and medium enterprises in developed countries run their businesses. They can also learn how government policies in developed countries help to promote the growth and development of SMEs. This will at the same time support the promotion of trade and investment across borders[166].

166 The Country Reports presented by the participants to the CACCI Chamber Operations Course held on November 18-30, 2007 in Taiwan.

d) Growth effects

In general, the above analyses indicate that 'a', 'b' and 'c' are the determinants of d and e. The empirical findings of this study revealed the capability problem in Nigeria SMEs. There is evidence of weak or absence of linkages between SMEs and Large companies in manufacturing. There is also evidence of poor infrastructure and institutional development. The quality of input materials and output products are very poor in order to support modern production linkages. The level of skilled development is very low. Hence, the ISMED model seek to improve 'a', 'b' and 'c' in order to realise d and e in Nigeria. In other words, if the outcome in 'a', 'b' and 'c' are significantly positive then'd' and 'e' can be strengthened otherwise the outcome in d and e will be weak. As shown in Figure 7.2 Growth effects are the transformation and transmission processes which firms and the economy will experience as a result of the investment strategies adopted by the state and firms. In general, transformation in terms of structure is often analysed as a shift in economic structure from agriculture to industrial production. The transformation process is seen as an inevitable outcome that is associated with rapid growth (Cook, 2006, p. 57). Transformation effect shows the extent at which private investment impact economic growth. It could be regarded as an important variable in the structural transformation process in Africa (Sackey, 2007, p. 6). In this context, it is the changes in the internal production process that allow individual small enterprises to achieve economies of scale and scope. It is also referred as the growth process in term of change in size structure or scale experienced overtime by the micro and small enterprises. This argument reflects Anderson's (1982, p. 917) observation in respect to enterprises development in Africa, where transformation in size and capability remain static. In this respect, one can then argue that small firm's growth is a function of policy and investment in new technology. Policy in this case covers not only the macroeconomic policy but also government trade policy that recognises the importance of openness and incentives. The outcome of effective policy is the long run positive changes in employment and productivity over time can be the long run outcome of the effective policy.

The measure of transformation effect can be classified in two forms namely increase in employment share and the degree of externalities. Employment shares are the parameter used to define SMEs. Every country has its own threshold in scaling the firm size. Transformation in this context suggests that if the threshold increases overtime due to technological changes, then the share of SMEs in total employment generation increases too. The degree of externalities is a reflection of changes in economies of scale and scope the small firm enjoy due to increase in productivity. Low productivity trap in Africa is linked to relatively smallness of firm size and domestic markets that failed to exploit economies of scale hence there is slow growth in the region

(Collier and Gunning, 1999, p. 9). In the light of this, there is positive association between the incidence of investment in new machinery and the growth of SME. Economies of scale and scope would increase if there is increased investment in new machinery and linkages among small and large firms in the region (Sackey, 2007, p. 15).

Figure 7.2: The Outcome of the ISMED-Model

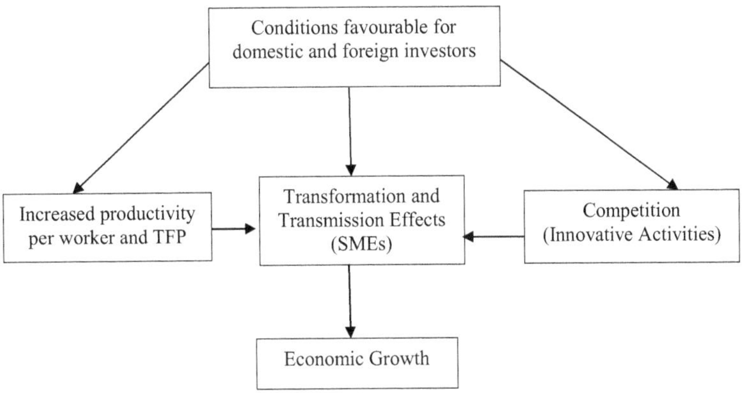

Source: Author's model based on the research work

Firms investing in new machinery, relative to non-investing firms, are more likely to be recording net additions to employment. SMEs currently using faster communication methods in interacting with their clients and suppliers tend to be associated with an increased probability of having net additions to employment. Such firms are likely to minimize delays in dealing with suppliers and clients and therefore less loss of potential revenues from sales. Hence, growth in sales is more likely to induce more employment than otherwise (Sackey, 2007, p. 17). Policy measures tailored towards access to new technology and skilled development will be the effective policy that promotes development and economic growth in Africa.

Transmission effects include among others the externalities generated by the investment during transformation process. For example, SME which can adopter new technology earlier will gain more economies of scale than the late adopters. The non-adopters will be forced out of the system as a result of the new competitive force or they may be forced to adopt through incentives. This will invariably generate a scenario of industrial learning by imitation such that a generation of new adopters will emerge in the process. In general, the system will be skewed into a dynamic economic development trajectory that can be sustainable over time. In this case, since industrial structure in Africa is relatively small in size, industrial policy that focused on access to technology, skill development will affect the growth rate of per capita income positively. This suggests that upgrading the capabilities of SMEs will generate such transmission effect in the economy. Government investment in the social and physical infrastructure will support the investment efforts of the SMEs in uplifting the economy.

e) Economic Growth

Productivity growth is the important determinant of long-run economic performance in terms of GDP while accumulation of machinery is a prime determinant of national rates of productivity growth (De Long and Summers, 1995, p. 1). High rate of investment in equipment is regarded as the key cause of rapid economic growth (De Long and Summers, 1992, p. 38)[167]. The most plausible positive effect of externalities is learning-by-doing that increases workers' skills and organizations' capacities to handle technologies. In this case, technological accumulation is very important and capital market plays an important role in financing the accumulation process. The more developed the local financial markets, the easier it is for credit constrained entrepreneurs to start their own firms expand and acquire varieties of intermediate goods. If the local financial markets are effectively developed, an increase in the number of varieties of intermediate goods will produce positive spillovers in the final goods sector (Alfaro et al, 2007, p. 3). This suggests that the growth of domestic investment depends the level at which the domestic stock market has been developed. A developed stock market serves as signal to domestic and foreign investors and as well, provides the framework for linkages in international capital markets. There are four plausible effects of capital market on local SMEs. Firms are required to improve their managerial capabilities by hiring qualified workers when listing for public shares. Firms can improve their human and capital stock through capitalisation. Firms can acquire good will and reputation hence joint venture initiatives between local and foreign partners can be facilitated easily.

The general effect of the investment strategies is reflected on the improved value added to the GDP growth. GDP growth has explicit impact on aggregate employment and income changes in the sense that firms employ more workers during the boom period as shown in the empirical results. Investment in education and capacity building leads to better income such that workers are open for alternatives and opportunities. This study shows that educational quail-

167 For example, if government strategy targets productivity growth of three percent per year, then the income per worker will increase eight fold over a lifetime and the income itself will also double if annual growth is one percent (De Long and Summers, 1992, p. 19).

fications of the workers are very low, technical knowledge is low in Nigeria. The aim to invest is to upgrade the output in terms of quantity and quality. This will facilitate increase in the country's export share of non-natural resource. The linkages established with international firms will open opportunities for international sub-contracting and integration of the local firms in global value chain.

7.3 Decomposition of the empirical results and the ISMED -Model

7.3.1 Capability factor

This sub-section presents the results of the empirical analyses as they relate to the ISMED–Model discussed above. The sub-section provides an insight into the position of small enterprises in Nigeria and the measures to be adopted for the promotion of SMEs in the region. It helps also to formulate the policy recommendation for SME development in Nigeria and Africa in general in the preceding chapter.

7.3.1.1 Investment in Social Infrastructures

Social investment consists of public expenditure on education, health and environmental protection. The degree of expenditure on social environment explains the extent government is committed to human capital development and environmental protection. Such investment is deemed to enhance better social environment that supports economic development. For example, the percentage of GNP allocated to education always explains the extent government resources have been translated to educational outcome. Basic education for schoollaged children is an overriding priority of any national development policy because access to basic education is the foundation for poverty eradication. This study revealed the weaknesses in Nigeria's public expenditure on education which declined from 6.4 per cent in 1980 to 0.76 per cent in 2000 (see Table 2.25). The decline in education outcome can be linked to poor budget allocation. The low productivity is reflected on the poor educational level of enterprise heads and workers' across the sampled (see Table 4.36). The weakness in technical education as indicated in Table 4.36 suggests that domestic and foreign investors have to commit some part of investment fund on extra training of workers. In most cases, local firms lack the will to investment on workers training because the probability of losing the worker thereafter is very high. Low level of human capital stock will affect FDI negatively because high costs and low productivity. In this respect, Cullison (1993. p. 32) argues that government spending on education and labour training will have significant effects on future economic growth and investment on education, civilian safety, and labour training will directly affect human capital positively.

The level of human capital development in a given plays an role on foreign direct investment discisions of large firms (Bloom and Canning, 2000, p. 2). For example, workers' health condition plays an important role in economic development because healthy individuals are more efficient at assimilating knowledge and exhibit higher productivity levels (Bloom and Canning, 2000, p. 2). Increased better health condition raises life expectancy and increased life expectancy contributes to the demand for education and increase in domestic saving which invariably has direct positive impact on economic growth (Bloom and Canning, 2000, p. 5). This suggests that workers' productivity and efficiency is a function of the workers' health condition. Aggregate economic growth would therefore depend on government policy in terms of resource allocation to health care. Hence, government investment in health care is an important aspect of national policy objective. The annual per head expenditure on health by government in Nigeria was only 3.00 US$ in 2001 (Table 2.20). The implication here is that workers' input would be low due to high rate of absenteeism caused by frequent sickness. It is therefore arguable that low government expenditure on health care and high rate of illness would lead to higher private out of pocket expenditure on health care. This will also lead to exclusion of the very poor in terms of access to better health care services.

Environment is the public good that provides the basis for sustainable development and growth in an economy. The growing economic expansion can have negative consequences on the environment in the sense that natural resources can be irreparably damaged. This argument is based on the concepts that more output requires more inputs such that the natural resources can easily be depleted. More output means more emissions and wastes hence the environment could exceed the absorptive capacity of the biosphere (Galeotti, 2003, p. 2). In this context, deforestation in Nigeria is increasing rapidly on the annual average rate of 2.6 per cent since 1990 (Table 2.27). The research findings reveal that forestry department is not integrated in the production networks in wood and furniture enterprises cluster in Nigeria. An efficient wood and furniture industry starts with an effective forestry department that is responsible for the control of deforestation and reforestation programme as well. Government and entrepreneurs have not recognised the impact of social costs of wood and furniture industry in the economy. They have not been able to provide or identify action programmes for the sustainability of the ecosystem in terms of effective reforestation programmes. Integration of forestry department unit in wood and furniture value chain process is very fundamental in order to avoid the break down of the ecosystem. Furthermore, the emission of organic water pollutants per day has increased by 30127 kg since 1990 (Table 2.27). Government has not designed effective policy that encourages private sector investment in the production and protection of public goods especially in water resource management.

7.3.1.2 Investment in physical capital

In general, improvement in longevity is the basis for people to save for their retirement and savings means more disposable fond for increased investment. If there is increased investment in capital goods, trained workers will have more access to capital equipment and improve productivity resulting to rise in economies of scale and income (Bloom and Canning, 2000, p. 2). Investment in physical capital will influence the stock of human and physical capital positively. This is the problem in less developed economies with low human capital stock because growth will be retarded due to weak absorptive capacity (Romer, 1986, pp. 1034-5). Consequently, the externalities of knowledge impacted by FDI will be limited. In general, investment in new equipment is regarded as fixed asset with fixed costs and can be used over time with little or no additional costs. Hence, the weak per capita output in Africa is due to low accumulation of knowledge and physical capital.

In the case of Nigeria, technological application in small enterprises is rudimentary and dominated by local hand tool and locally constructed equipments made of scraps. Weak technological application here is not really due to the level of human development. For example even in PKO sub-sector where the entrepreneurs have relatively higher educational qualification, firms' investments are mainly on weak locally made machines. There is evidence of high incidence of output shortfall due to frequent machine. In garment enterprises 60.7 per cent of the production machines are old second hand machines. Due to low capital base common in the sub-sector cannot invest in the modern technology. Even when the finance is made available, poor energy supply will make investtment in modern machines unprofitable.

Bräutigam (1997, p. 1075) and Uzor (2004, p. 24) showed how networking provided the opportunity for technology sourcing, improved method of production, increased rate of wage employment in Nnewi SMEs clusters. However, technology is a major problem in micro enterprises in Nnewi spare part manufacturers. Weak technological input and poor human capital development in Nigeria's production system can be linked to the growth problem in Nigeria's manufacturing sector. GDP growth in Nigeria has no corresponding increase in productivity growth rather as a increa result of in export value of natural resources. Capacity utilisation in local and foreign firms in is 49.00 and 56.21 per cent respectively (World Bank, 2002b, p. 29).

7.3.2 Performance enhancement factor

7.3.2.1 Productivity per worker enhancement

This analysis has shown how increased domestic and foreign investment can induce technological change in the economy. Technological change provides the incentive for continued capital accumulation. Capital accumulation and technological change account for much of the increase in workers' output per hour. There are three plausible interventions that support accumulation of capital and technological change. The first is the innovative actions taken by Schumpeter's entrepreneurs who respond to market incentives[168]. The second is government intervention in science and technology for advancement and adaptation of technological change. The third is the economic reform process that allows the Schumpeter's entrepreneur who responds to market incentives to have access to new technology developed elsewhere.

This study revealed how small enterprises compensate technological deficiency through longer working hours and days. The major problems identified in the empirical analysis are those associated with weak technology, linkages and access to market. The percentage of workers and enterprise heads across the sectors with formal technical knowledge and skill training are between 8.5 and 3.9 per cent. Even when the firms in the cluster areas experience higher production output than the firms in dispersed areas, technological spill over are weak due to the nature equipment. Government efforts to improve productivity growth through incentives are very weak. The study shows that the total average monthly cash earnings are below US$50.00 stipulated for private sector loan. With rapid increase in inflation and out of pocket private expenditure on health care, the productivity per worker will invariably be low. Direct consequences are significant reduction in economic productivity via reduced FDI and weak technology diffusion (World Bank, 2002b, p. 22). The study shows that high tax obligation in terms of tax duplication increases disproportionate burden on business operations. The degree of tax distortion also affects productivity growth negatively. Tax discrimination tends to discourage competition among firms.

Institutional linkages are very weak hence diffusion of knowledge and dissemination of information is very limited. The small firms cannot embark on research and development ventures or invest in new technology due to poor capital base and lack of access to finance. Due to lack of access to credits, most

---

168 Growing interest in the study of technological change over the last decade has led to a resurgence of interest in Schumpeter's concept of the entrepreneur. In Schumpeter's theory, the entrepreneur is responsible for introducing change into a commercially organized economic system. An innovation in this environment is not an automatic adjustment, but a break with the past (Bruce, 2000).

of the SMEs investigated have limited working capital therefore depend on customers' cash deposit before production. In some cases, working capital is being financed through informal credit institutions with very high interest rates. Networks are not knowledge based networks rather personal interactions among entrepreneurs.

7.3.2.2 Openness and Trade

Researchers in international trade are often confronted with the question on the extent protectionism has affected the movement of goods, investment, labour and capital across borders. This covers for example, the impact of import quota on local consumers in terms of increase in price above world market price or the welfare gains of removing import quota. The questions also reflect the impact of financial market liberalisation on exchange and interest rates. These and other hypothetical framework often leads to the analysis of the relation between openness and trade in economic growth in developing countries. More open and outward economies persistently outperform countries with restricted trade and investment regimes. Policies directed towards foreign trade can be viewed as a major factor that promotes growth and convergence in developing countries. Openness and per-capita-income growth can strongly be correlated. Frankel and Romer (1996, pp. 13-15) analysis suggests that a large amount of growth in Hong Kong is explained by openness. In most cases, the contribution of openness to growth is due to trade that follows gravity model[169]. For example, openness to trade helped to stimulate investment and schooling. Hence, investment and schooling became the dominant factor for growth in the region (Frankel and Romer, 1996, p. 15).

With respect to Nigeria, there are contradicting arguments on the impact of trade reform on the economy. Tariff reduction resulting from multilateral and regional integration in Economic Community of West African State (ECOWAS) has raised uncertainty in textile and manufacturing enterprises (Ogujiuba, et al, 2004, p. 19). On the other hand, Olusi and Folorunso (2005, p. 13) argue that openness would encourage investment and full integrate into global economies if Nigeria wants to achieve accelerated growth and development. This can only be possible by removing all barriers to trade and liberalise all the sectors of the economy. These arguments bring to focus the relationship between the rate of protection in terms of effective and nominal tariff rates. The uncertainty in Nigeria's economy is not related to economic integration rather a problem of policy inefficacy that failed to effectively restructure the economy towards

169 The gravity model of trade predicts bilateral trade flows based on the economic sizes of countries (often using GDP). The model is used to evaluate the impact of treaties and alliance on trade. It can be used to test the effectiveness of trade agreements and organizations such as NAFTA and the WTO.

export. Foreign trade policies require dynamic strategy based on Heckcheter-Ohlin's factor endowment. Diversification of the economy away from dependence on natural resources would have been an important Nigeria's foreign trade strategy (Uzor, 2007a, p. 1; Wohlmuth et al, 2007). As opposed to the strategy that focuses on narrow effective and nominal tariff rate politics, diversification of economy would have increased Nigeria's export base. In this case, economic growth is a function of the variables such as accumulation of savings, physical accumulation in terms of domestic and foreign investment, and accumulation of knowledge (Wohlmuth, 1999, p. 77; Ogujiuba, et al, 2004, p. 19; Uzor, 2007b, p. 442).

The empirical result of this study that reveals some sectors are sensitive to openness and require effective policy support while in some sectors, openness has no negative impact. One the other side, liberalisation only cannot influence TFP growth. TFP growth requires the economic policy that recognises the importance of investment in new technology, schooling for knowledge accumulation and improved political environment that favours investment. For examples, PKO sub-sector need to be capitalised in order to increase output and investment should not only focus on modern machines but also upgrading the oil palm industry in Nigeria. There is the need for government to increase investment in cotton production for local consumption and exports. Garment industry should increase membership in their cooperative union beyond ethnic boundaries in order to capitalise the union. Strategies in the sub-sector should include how to improve skills and access to modern machines in the sector. There is the need for intensive capacity building on social costs on consumption in wood and furniture sub-sector in Nigeria. In general, the Nigerian government's increase in skill trading and the trade policies should exploit the means for small enterprises to improve access to modern equipments especial small and medium technology.

7.3.2.3 The political governance and performance enhancement

The impact of effective governance on economic development as shown in appendix 3 underscores the role of political governance in enhancing economic performance. Effective governance is not only the ability to understand public policy, respect for civil liberty, sensitive to corruptive actions but also the ability to understand the role of private sector in the economy. Three issues are recognised here, first is the development of political and policy-making institutions that can negotiate and respond to shocks. Second is the capacity of political systems that can sustain popular democracy. The third is the capacity of institutions to rework dysfunctional economic arrangements (Hall and Jones, 1999, p. 84). In this case, Hall and Jones (1999, p. 84) argue that differences in capital accumulation, productivity growth and output per worker across countries are driven by differences in institutions and government policies called social infrastructure. The social infrastructure determines the economic environment within which individuals can accumulate skills, and firms can accumulate capital and produce efficiently. Social infrastructure is the institutions and government policies that provide the incentives for individuals and firms in an economy. On the other side, an environment with weak social infrastructure can foster predatory behaviour such as rent-seeking and corruption (Hall and Jones, 1999, p. 95). Poor social infrastructure can be correlated with output per worker in the sense that a country with corrupt government official, severe impediments to trade, poor contract enforcement and government interference in production cannot achieve high level of output per worker (Hall and Jones, 1999, p. 86). These indicators can impede motivation to workers input and encourage price distortion in the economic system. A country can achieve high levels of output per worker in the long-run if the country can achieve high rates of investment in physical and human capital driven by social infrastructure (Hall and Jones, 1999, pp. 113-4).

Nigerian economy has followed unstable development path arising from ethnic conflicts in the 1960s, unprecedented civil war that lasted for nearly three years, two decades of frequent military intervention in the governance. The consequences of political instability are reflected on frequent policy reversal, distortions in governance and market system which created space for flamboyant budget spending. However, recent capitalisation in the banking sector in Nigeria has brought about not only relatively stability in the country's financial institutions. It has also reduced drastically the exchange rate premium in the informal foreign exchange rate market. Capitalisation has also brought innovation in banking and financial instruments such that liquidity and banking transactions have become relatively more flexible. However, high bank interest rate that has emerged is a major concern to large and small investors alike. Interest rates are not harmonised and fall within the range of 23 to 27 per cent (CBN, 2006). Apart from that, additional loan management interest rate of 3 percent is charged, making a total interest rate of approximately 30 per cent. High interest rate is a market disincentive to private firms in the sense that lending will be restricted only on short term basis and to large sum borrowers. It often leads to high inflation since the lending price is passed on to the consumers.

The problem firms' face in respect to access to credit in Africa prompted Singh (1999) to question the rational of investing the scarce resources on stock market development at the current stage of African development. In this context, Singh (1999, p. 361) argues that it is a waste of scare resources to develop stock market that serves the interest of a small number of urban corporation. Efforts should be directed towards development of the banking system that can meet the savings and investment needs of vast producers in agricultural sector. In contrast to Singh (1999) view, high bank interest rate in Nigeria suggests that vast majority of small farmers and entrepreneurs cannot benefit from the bank capitalisation efforts due to high cost of borrowing. A functional stock market has its own distinctive advantage in an economy in the sense that it creates liquidity in the economy and makes diversification of risks possible, and as well provides the platform for medium scale enterprises to capitalise their asset base. In general, it plays an important role in the stabilisation of the banking sector and opens the window for local firms to have access to foreign capital. An important issue that emerged from Singh's argument is development of effective Microfinance Institutions (MFIs) of all kinds in formal, semi-formal and informal sector. The MFIs arguably would bridge the liquidity problem by providing soft loans and credits to small producers in urban areas and the majority of farmers in the rural areas.

7.3.3 Growth enhancement factor

7.3.3.1 Risk and uncertainty reduction

Firm performance can be influenced by different factors but entrepreneurs respond to uncertainty by increasing their source of information through networking activities. Personal networks serve as a response to environmental uncertainty that can hinder firm performance (Sawyer, et al, 2003, p. 274). The analyses of network activities show that networks serve as means of maintaining conformity to expectations (Macaulay, 1963, p. 63), diversifying risks (Nijkamp, 2003, p. 401), reducing of opportunism (Putnam, 1963, p. 173), and influence firm performance positively by reducing costs (Barr, 1995, p. 15). Network structure explains the pattern by which alliances tend to stick together while diversity of entrepreneurs' networks plays a greater impact on outcomes. In general, the analysis of the networks functions provides an insight on how risks, uncertainty and malfeasance are reduced. It further explains how networks serve as means of reducing costs of transacting business and provides the framework for assets specification in investment and protection of property rights. These characteristics and functions suggest that networks can be treated as productive input. This depends on how effective information and knowledge is disseminated within the network structure (Barr, 1995, p. 15).

This study shows the patterns of alliances the small entrepreneurs in Nigeria tried to embrace in order to reduce risks and perform their entrepreneurial activities in the absence of institutional support. It shows diversified membership in sub-sectoral, business, professional and nonbusiness related associations. The lesson here is social networks promotes competition due to openness and non-restrictive membership in networks. The diversity of the networks increases the degree of information dissemination. However, unlike knowledge networks, information generated is not scientific or codified. However, entrepreneurs perceive their networks to be very important because the business environment is very volatile and source of information is limited to the number and nature of contact made. How the entrepreneurs perceive their networks vary according to sectors and firm size. Personal networks are more prominent due to the level of industrial development. Organisational network in terms of linkages with large firms is very weak. Hence, the entrepreneurship networks investigated can be classified as horizontal or learning networks. Weak institutional support as identified in the study raises some questions on the sustainability of the industrial growth in Nigeria. Social networks failed to explain or specify the extents risks and costs identified can be reduced. Social networks cannot specify how effective international industrial linkages and business transactions can be arranged or organised. Weak institutional framework creates uncertainty in business environment for both domestic and foreign investors alike. Even when social networks create the framework for property rights, it always fails to provide the standardised specifics in terms of protecting property rights and enforcement of contracts. In the current globalisation of the markets and integration of economic activities, social network is only effective at the local business activities but not effective in international joint venture and franchising activities for growth enhancement. The study further shows the extent small enterprises distributive networks have evolved in the national and African regional markets. The movement of business across regional borders have increased due to liberalisation in recent time in Africa.

7.3.3.2 Capacity building

In recent times, global development community has turned to result oriented paradigm. International intervention in capacity building is such that development assistance focuses more on effective capacity building. In this context, capacity building programme must specify the objective in terms of what to be focused on. It must identify the subject in terms of whom or the constituency to be targeted. In pursuing the goals, demand and supply led-strategies are employed in shaping the incentives that promotes skill development. The capacity building programmes explores how incentives can be used to promote the utilization and retention of skills developed (Nair, 2003, p. 3). In concrete terms, demand-led approach inculcates evaluation culture based on transparency and programmes that targets poverty reduction. It also encourages participatory approaches that cover the citizen's rights to demand for results and government's ability to respond to this demand (Nair, 2003, p. 2). The supply-led approach focuses on the role of human, institutional, financial and physical infrastructure in nurturing capacity building. These approaches emphasis not only the measures aimed at skill acquisition but also how to retain and utilise the skill acquired.

IFC and UNIDO have been designing various programmes to support SME development in Africa and developing countries in general. The IFC focuses on three strategic areas in Nigeria namely development businesses and projects in key sectors, diversification of portfolio in financial markets and increase financial products and advisory services. An International Development Assistance (IDA) fund of US$32 million was approved in 2004 for Nigeria to strengthen financial and non-financial institutions that supports small business. This is to support small entrepreneurs so they can operate effectively and sustainable deliver commercially-based services in the market. IFC is expected to invest in some of the private sector participants in the project (World Bank, 2004)[170]. In recent times, emphases have shifted to innovative projects that can enhance access to ICT and improving the capacity of business association in order to strengthen the competitiveness of SMEs in Africa (UNIDO, 2007)[171]. In general, both institutions support capacity building that is designed to encourage programmes that aimed at strengthening FDI and promotion of SME partnership with MNCs. In addition, human resource development is the main focus of UNIDO cluster development programme in developing countries. The organisation tries to create awareness on the principles of clustering and networking by providing training programmes for cluster development agents in developing countries (UNIDO, 2001).

In this regard, this study has explicitly argued that capacity building programmes for SMEs have not been effective in Nigeria. The skill development programmes are not only weak but have no institutional backing in Nigeria. The study shows that demand for capacity building programmes are very high and differ in types according to sub-sector and size. Each sub-sector has no capacity to formulate and implement its own programme. The challenge here is how to design appropriate capacity building programmes that reflect sub-sectoral specific problems. In the survey, government assisted programmes failed to integrate the private sector organisations effectively in capacity building designing.

7.4 Remarks

This chapter focussed on the relationship between investment and SME development. It provided an insight on how investment can lead to general economic upgrading in Nigeria. The empirical analyses showed not only the weaknesses in Nigerian small enterprises but also provided an insight on the position of Nigerian SMEs and their ability to compete in the on going globalisation

170 World Bank Press Release No: 2004/205/AFR

171 UNIDO Support to NEPAD Period of Report: July 2006 to June 2007.

(hypothesis d)[172]. The theory of openness has been controversial in economic development circle. The general consensus is that restriction can be counter-productive in terms of access to capital goods needed for economic upgrading. The concept of new growth theory introduced in the model explained the impact of externalities generated by new technological application in the economy. This suggests that technological learning in Nigeria is visible only when there is effective policy that recognises the importance of access to modern technology. Since investment expenditure is irreversible, measures regarding uncertainties are crucial to domestic and foreign investors. Thus, social networks only are not sufficient to reduce uncertainty in an unstable and developing economy that needs foreign assistance in technology transfer. Hence, developed and stable market institution is crucial in confidence building for investors.

The various approaches in development economic literature focus on the role of investment promotion agencies, the impact of macroeconomic stability, fiscal incentives as well as business environment as important factors in boosting FDI inflow. This study laid emphasis on productivity and small enterprises growth enhancement factors as well as social and physical infra-structure. The analysis revealed various distinctive advantages and weaknesses of small enterprises clusters, advantages and weaknesses of social networks and how small enterprises sustain competition in an open economy. Low technological application and skill development as shown in the case studies suggest that small firms in Nigeria cannot effectively compete under the current globalisation pressure. It also suggests that small enterprises in Nigeria are isolated and lack the capability to forge linkages with large firms. The technological gap is too wide to sustain business relation among local SMEs and foreign MNCs. There is therefore an urgent need for effective policy adjust-ment that focuses on reducing the capability gap in Nigerian SMEs and Africa in general.

---

172 For hypothsis'd' see page, 5 above.

Chapter 8: Industrial Policies and SME Development in Nigeria

8.1 Introduction

Industrial policies or microeconomic interventions are pursued on the assumptions that an effective set of microeconomic policies will address specifically the problems associated with market failures (Rodríguez-Clare, 2005, p. 4). Nigerian microeconomic interventions are characterised by policy shifts and reversals. The industrial policy objectives and strategies in Nigeria are often subject to either modifications or neglect or even total abandonment. The policies are influenced by debates about intentions, the extent and nature of government interventions. This often leads to controversy over what should be exclusive for the public sector and what the private sector is capable of doing (Dauda, 1993, p. 74). In this context, Ohiorhenuan, (1989, p. 145) described Nigeria's industrial policies as highly pervasive because the state is more directly involved in economic processes thereby circumscribing the autonomy of the private economic agents. The controversies are based on different ideological backgrounds and its often questioned whether the previous policies have responded adequately to the changing nature of world economy. This argument occurs frequently when the programmes initiated failed to produce significant positive results. Dauda (1993, p. 84) argues that the misery index i.e. unemployment and inflation, are often used in assessing the impact and implications of various industrial policies in Nigeria. It is thus very important to analyse industrial policy sequentially or holistically to have clear insight on policy failures and successes. In line with Ikpeze (1991) and Dauda (1993) holistic approach, this chapter classifies and reviews Nigerian industrial policies in the period between 1900 and 2007. The analyses provide the background framework for policy recommendations based on the research findings.

8.2 Review of Nigerian Industrial and Technological Policies

8.2.1 Nigerian Industrial Policies from 1900 to 1954

Nigerian industrial policy analysts have provided an unbalanced account of British colonial administration's industrial policies in Nigeria. Part of the literature suggests that pattern of industrial development during colonial era was on the basis of imperialism in the sense that British colonial policy tended to undermine private sector development in Nigeria. The analyses however failed short of recognising that promotion of modern trade and commerce in Nigeria started actively between 1900 and 1954. This was possible through the provision of infrastructural amenities in the hinterland which gave rise to movement of people and goods across regions. During that period, the framework that fashioned the guarantee of law and order in the Nigeria was established (Dauda, 1993, p. 75). Most critics also failed to recognize that industrial development often starts from grassroots. There were relatively high risks for private investment at early stage of Nigeria's development. Moreover, financing industrial development depends on budget allocation to oversee development department and British national interests. In this case, budget allocation must go through parliamentary debates that always put questions on return on investment. Dauda (1993, p. 75) argues that between 1900 and 1954 the colonial administration refrained from active participation in productive activities. This was as a result of the British tradition of *laissez-faire* and a rather negative attitude to a central economic planning system.

Specifically, under British colonial administration, promotion of industrial development was entrusted on two agencies: the Nigeria Local Development Board (NLDB) and the Department of Commerce and Industry (DCI) (Ikpeze, 1991, p. 585). The functions of the NLDB were to promote and develop rural crafts and industries; promote industrial development that focused on the development of products from Nigeria. NLDB was also charged with the responsibility for setting the modalities for Research and Development (R&D) in processing industries and other matters concerning industrial development as approved by the Governor-in-Council. The DCI on the other hand was responsible for overseeing and promoting local trade and industrial development (Ikpeze, 1991, p. 586). Three implications incidentally emerged from these policy specifications. Firstly, the policy specifications suggested that industrial development should start from the grassroots. Secondly, the policies targeted grassroots development by emphasizing on small scale processing and handicraft industries in rural areas. Thirdly, efforts were directed on the promotion of trade and commerce at the early stage of Nigeria's history. However, Ikpeze (1991, p. 586) questioned the effectiveness of the policy in the sense that about £22 million was budgeted for industrial development in the planed period, only £6 million was spent. One would also argue that even during colonial administration, government's direct involvement in industrial development appeared to be ineffective in Nigeria.

In general, it can be concluded that during the colonial administration between 1990 and 1954, industrial development in Nigeria was influenced by the following factors: provision of physical infrastructure characterised by construction of access roads and construction of rail tracts to the hinterland which gave rise to rapid movement of people and goods across regions; creation of regional and provincial administrative authorities that allowed decentralisation of administrative functions and establishment of institutional framework for industrial development (Asiodu, 1967, p. 161)[173]. Dauda (1993, p.7 5) argues that the colonial government used the available local resources and funds to promote the enabling environment for private commercial activities. Ikpeze (1991, p. 586) argues that government interventions in industrial development in Nigeria is not a new phenomenon. It became popular at the end of the World War II with 182 companies registered between 1935 and 1946.

8.2.2 Nigerian Industrial Policies from 1954 to 1958

Between 1954 and 1958, the regional governments and legislative councils were established. In preparation for independence, the central government subsequently established the basic institutions such as central bank and national regulatory bodies for international trade, finance, and foreign exchange (Dauda, 1993, p. 76). However, the policy initiatives concerning social economic matters then were concentrated in the hands of the regional government. The regional governments became actively involved in industrial and commercial activities by using surpluses accumulated from agricultural commodities to fund their respective industrial development projects (Ohiorhenuan, 1989, p. 147, Forrest, 1993, p. 21). The central government was very weak in terms of policy implementtation. During that period, each region had foreign offices in different countries while the federal government had none (Dauda, 1993, p. 76). The regional governments pursued different foreign policy interest that sometimes contradicts national foreign policy goals.

However, three major statutes were used to advance industrial development programmes during that period namely; *the Industrial Development (Import Duty Relief) Act of 1957; the Industrial Development (Income Tax Relief) Act of 1958, and the Customs Duties (Dumping and Subsidised Goods) Act of 1958* (Ikpeze, 1991, p. 587). Under the Import Duties Relief Act, a firm could be granted concessionary rates of duty on imported raw materials and tax breaks for importation of industrial capital goods. In some cases, the relief can be to the extent of 100 per cent. The industrial Income Tax Relief Act was aimed at offsetting investment costs against profits during the tax holiday period. The Act was effective as it provided relief for foreign companies operating in Nigeria by granting them pioneer status with tax holidays for a period of five years. This was also extended to the shareholders of the pioneer firms so that the dividends accrued to them were exempted from taxes during the tax holiday period (Aremu, 2003, p. 50). Under the Customs Duties (Dumping and Subsidised Goods) Act, the government could charge additional

173 Institutional framework is such as legislative instrument for example Aid to Pioneer Industries Ordinance of 1952 aiming at providing incentives for industrial development in Nigeria was created (Asiodu, 1967, p. 161).

duties on specific imported goods, when there is clear evidence of dumping or government subsidy in the country of origin. The government can also grant duty drawbacks or refunds of duty paid on materials imported and used in the manufacture goods for exports (Asiodu, 1967, p. 166).

The above Industrial Development Acts attracted criticism for lack of specifications in terms of industries that are qualified for pioneer status for tax relief during tax holiday (Asiodu, 1967, p. 163). The implication of the non specification is that all newly established enterprises were automatically qualified for pioneer status regardless of national interest or needs. Moreover, the Acts were also considered to be the corner stone that laid the foundation for import substitution programmes with little or no articulated industrial strategy (Ohiorhenuan, 1989, p. 146). The Acts provided the framework for increased foreign investment in Nigerian industrial sector. On the other hand, the Acts failed to recognise the importance of human capital development and development of local inputs (Ogbuagu, 1983, p. 244). In general, export promotion and import substitution strategies were the two basic strategies that emerged during the colonial administration. This led to rapid increase in number of registered industrial establishments from 182 companies recorded between 1935 and 1946 to about 1,027 companies between 1946 and 1958 with 15 per cent of them being medium/large scale enterprises (Usoro, 1977). The import substitution was intensively pursued immediately after independence in Nigeria.

8.2.3 Nigerian Industrial Policies from 1958 to 1972

Government participation in promoting industrial development became more visible between 1958 and 1972. The theoretical assumption backing government intentions was that the private sector was very weak hence government had to engage in proper industrial planning and programming for public sector development.The government considered such measures to be necessary in order to encourage the private sector to channel their investment strategies towards areas of greater priority (Asiodu, 1967, p. 162). In the late 1950s and early 1960s, government intervention became much vivid such that industrialisation programmes were directly linked to general economic development and growth. To achieve this, funds were made available for government to participate directly in industrial development activities. Besides the direct intervention, indirect measures were also pursued. The measures were in the form of guaranteeing foreign loans for new industrial projects or rendering special assistance like providing industrial estates and public utilities to public industries (Asiodu, 1967, p. 162). To strengthen their participation in industrial development activities, the government later integrated industrial development policies in the National Development Plan (NDP). Under the NDP framework, the government pursued regulated industrial development activities which were based on open-door-policy (Dauda, 1993, p. 76). In the first NDP of 1962-1968, about 14 per cent of public investment was directed to industrial development (Asiodu, 1967, p. 162).

However, the debate about nationalisation of businesses resurfaced in Nigerian political discussions during parliamentary debate on Petroleum Profit Tax Bill in 1959. In November 1961, the tune of the debate changed from "Nigerianisation" to "Nationalisation" in order to reduce the level of foreign influence and control of the economy[174]. In the political circle, the resentment on foreign dominance in the country's economy especially in extractive and secondary industries, commerce, small scale distributive trade and shipping sectors became very high (Ogbuagu, 1983, p. 247). Consequently, government started gradually to introduce measures to reduce foreign dominance of the economic activities. The first formal step taken to promote indigenisation of businesses after the independence was the establishment of the Immigration Act of 1962. The Act excluded the foreigners who wished to participate in trade already served by Nigerians. The Act also specified the ratio of Nigerians to non-Nigerians employed in foreign firms. This was followed by the creation of an Expatriate Quota Allocation Board in 1966. The board was charged to ensure greater indigenous participation in the control, development and management of certain economic resources of Nigeria.

The second step was the promulgation of the *Companies Decree* of 1968 that provided the formalities for incorporation of foreign companies in Nigeria[175]. The aims of the decree were to bring local subsidiaries of foreign firms under the control of the Federal government and later to secure the participation of Nigerians in such businesses. The decree also made it illegal for a company to render financial assistance to any person in the polity to help in the purchase of its shares or shares of its holding company (Ogbuagu, 1983, p. 248). In 1971, skill acquisition programme was introduced for the first time in Nigeria's industrial development programmes. The decree establishing Industrial Training Fund was promulgated in 1971 with the aim to encourage the acquisition skills in industries. The decree also recognised the need to train and supply the capable manpower needed in Nigeria's growing economy.

The success of the first industrial development plan was measured according to the number of industrial establishment and employment generated.

174 'Nigerianisation' in this context implies increasing the ratio of Nigerians in foreign firms' management position and "nationalisation" implies increasing the ratio of equity share of foreign firms to Nigerian.

175 The Companies Decree of 1968 stated that every foreign company "...shall in respect of its operation in Nigeria be deemed to have been incorporated under the decree as a separate entity from the company incorporated outside Nigeria in whose name a place of business in Nigerian was established, and company so deemed to have been incorporated in Nigeria shall have as part of its name (unless already therein) the word Nigeria".

Berger (1975) argues that between 1964 and 1972, import substitution strategy implicitly succeeded in Nigeria. Economic indicators at the period suggest that number of industrial establishments grew at average annual rate of 12.1 per cent. The number of employees in industrial sector increased at the annual average rate of 12.6 per cent. Between 1964 and 1972, the annual average growth rate of wage bill and the gross domestic output increased by 17.9 per cent and 16.4 per cent respectively. While the gross value added of industrial sector grew at the rate of 18.7 per cent. Following massive criticisms on government's poor implementation of first NDP, the call for Nigerianisation of Nigerian business become intensive in 1970. These events arguably led to the birth of Nigerian Enterprises Promotion Decree of 1972 and the second NDP of 1970-1974.

8.2.4 Nigerian Industrial Policies from 1972 to 1985

The major Nigeria industrial policy initiative 12 years after attaining independence was the Nigerian Enterprises Promotion (NEP) Decree of 1972 "Indigenisation Decree". The objectives of the policy were to create an economically independent country with increased opportunities for indigenous Nigerian businessmen; to ensure greater retention of profits accruing from the economic sector; and to encourage further foreign investment in the sophisticated area of intermediate and capital goods production. NEP created two categories of business enterprises known as schedules 1 and 2. Schedule 1 contained the list of enterprises which were exclusively reserved for Nigerians. Schedule 2 contained businesses which foreigners could engage in but under certain conditions, for example, the size of the business, and the ratio of indigenous share of participation. Under the decree, foreigners lost the right to own business in Nigeria. One remarkable argument in favour of the indigenous decree was that the idea of *imperialism* became off the Table in Nigeria's political and economic discussions, hence Nigerians could account for their own political and economic destiny. Soyode, (1989, p. 195) argues that governments all over the world adopted nationalisation as a strategy to support local control of their economy after attending political independence. The policy of indigenisation therefore should be seen as complement to political sovereignty.

The indigenisation decree of 1972 failed to meet its desired objective in terms of reducing foreign dominance in Nigeria's economy. The members in Chambers of Commerce and Industry, and the Manufactures Association of Nigeria continued to push for more participation of Nigerians in the country's businesses. The decree was seen to be very weak and was modified in 1977 such that the classes of enterprises that fall in each schedule were reviewed. Changes were made in equity share participation between Nigerians and foreigners in any business venture (Ogbuagu, 1983, pp. 252-3). The 1977 revision however did not improve the situation; instead it turned out to be a failure. According to

Ikpeze (1991, p. 593), the policy tried to use a single instrument to achieve three distinctive objectives, that is, indigenisation, diversification and 'Nigerianisation' of management simultaneously. Dauda (1993, p. 77) argues that the actions were not simply based on nationalistic ideology rather a reflection of economic situation then[176]. Aremu (2003, p. 56) argues that in the 1970s, policymakers failed to understand that foreign investors rarely wish to invest in country where they have no effective voice and control over their capital. Consequently, the policy explicitly exposed Nigerian weaknesses in terms of business environment. Such policy according to Aremu should not be a priority option in a country that was in serious need of FDI. One can also argue that policymakers then, pursued a short sighted economic development strategy that failed to recognise the importance of entrepreneurial learning in Nigeria's development path. The neglect of learning process created vacuum in Nigeria's entrepreneurship development. Hence, the trade off between the NEP policy and property right was massive loss of foreign direct investment in manufacturing sector in Nigeria.

The central policy issues of the second NDP were the promotion of regional development, diversifying the industrial sector, increasing manufacturing value-added, increasing employment opportunities and promoting of manufacturing exports. The priority areas of industrial policy in the second NDP drastically shifted to capital intensive industries. The areas include among others agro-allied, chemical and petro-chemical, textile industries. Investment in integrated iron and steal complex, motor assembly plants and other import substitution industries were intensively pursued. Consequently, Nigeria's industrial policy gradually shifted from open door policy to increased government dominance in production activities (Ohiorhenuan, 1989, p. 148). In order to sustain the NEP policy and protect its new industries, the government introduced different types of import restrictions. Between 1973 and 1982, Nigeria witnessed rapid industrial expansion with compound growth rate of manufacturing sector, which rose by 9.5 per cent and a GDP growth rate of 2.3 per cent. The impact of NEP and government active involvement in production activities were such that about 600 public enterprises (PEs) at the federal level and about 900 smaller PEs at the state and local levels were established. The share of employment, value added and gross fixed capital formation of public enterprises generally exceeded those of other African countries. By 1997, estimated 1,500 public enterprises accounted for about 57 per cent of aggregate fixed capital investment and about 66 per cent of formal sector employment in Nigeria (Jerome, 2008, p. 4). In 1982, the symptoms of economic down turn started to emerge as access to foreign exchange became persistently difficult. Firms could no longer import spare parts and the required raw materials hence

176 As Dauda (1993, p. 77) put it - "The 1970s were a period in which Nigeria felt it can be able to use its *petropower* to establish its economic power".

industrial capacity utilisation began to drop. The expected gains from industrialisation such as employment generation, acquisition of skills and development of local technological capability became a total flop (Ikpeze, 1991, p. 593).

8.2.5 Nigerian Industrial Policies from 1985 to 1988

The Economic Stabilization Acts of 1982 and 1983 failed to rescue Nigeria's ailing economy. After a national debate in 1986, a structural adjustment program (SAP) was launched in July 1986 in order to restore confidence in the economy. A new economic and industrial development path based on market principles was adopted. Critically, the SAP was a reversal of second NDP with specific policy instruments. The measures were aimed at rolling back the public sector and shrinking government involvement in production through privatisation. On economic front, deregulation and liberalisation of the market were simultaneously introduced. The Second-Tier Foreign Exchange Market was created in order to enhance foreign currency, facilitate imports and exports. The tariff structure was simplified, privatisation of public enterprises, and promotion of small scale enterprises as well as rationalization of institutions for industrial development were also implemented (Ikpeze, 1991, p. 596).

One major argument in favour of the new policy was reduction of the potential conflicts arising from bureaucratic powers. The rise in bureaucratic power can be measured in terms of rapid increase in Federal government employees[177]. Prior to 1970, National Economic Council (NEC) and Joint Planning committee (JPC) were the two intergovernmental organs responsible for the formulation of industrial development plan. In 1970, both were replaced by Supreme Military Council and the Joint Planning Board respectively. The two organs continued to function until 1988 when an independent National Planning Commission (NPC) was established as part of civil service reform (Dauda, 1993, p. 80)[178].

The privatisation and commercialisation decree No. 25 of 1988 was promulgated with an autonomous NPC established to oversee the implementtation of the program. The policy objective was to restructure the economy towards fiscal-balance and economic growth in order to enhance efficiency

177 The Federal government employees increased by 54.21 per cent from 196,068 in 1979 to 302,349 in 1985.

178 Change of the structure is not the real problem that confronts Nigerian policy initiatives rather functionality and effectiveness. As Dauda (1980, p. 80) put it, the non-Nigerian members left the planning scene shortly after the launching of the first NDP. They were however not replaced by Nigerians of the same number with the same educational level and quality.

through privatisation and commercialisation[179]. A 13-member committee known as Technical Committee on Privatisation and Commercialisation (TCPC) was created for the implementation of the programme (Onah, 1991, pp. 619-23). The committee succeeded in privatizing about 34 firms across several sectors through public floatation (Mahmoud, 2004, p. 1). The persistent economic downturn in Nigeria forced the government to make further review of NEP in 1989. The two schedules were reduced to a single schedule in NEP Act No. 54 of 1989. Foreigners were no longer restricted to the proportion of shareholdings in their investment (Aremu, 2003, p. 59). The recent appraisal of the programme suggests that appropriateness or accountability of the regulatory framework raises questions and suspicion about the effectiveness of the programme. The implementation lacks political leadership, allegation of corruption and lack of adherence to a transparent process (Ariyo and Jerome, 2005, p. 344)[180].

8.2.6 Nigerian Industrial Policies from 1988 to 1999

The failure of the previous microeconomic policy and the persistent economic down turns forced the government to review the NEP Act of 1977 in 1989. The two schedules in NEP were reduced to a single schedule in NEP Act No. 54, of 1989. Under the Act, a foreigner can own an enterprise classified in the single schedule if the level of capitalization is not less than N20 million. This implies that foreigners were no longer restricted to the proportion of shareholdings in their investment. It also suggested that the foreigners could identify and invest in areas and sectors in Nigerian economy that have higher returns on their capital and with maximum incentives (Aramu, 2003, p. 59). Subsequently, the Companies and Allied Matters Act (CAMA) was promulgated in 1990. The CAMA became the principal law regulating the incorporation of businesses in Nigeria. Under section 54 of the Act, foreign investors intending to transact business in Nigeria are mandated to take all the necessary steps required to incorporate their companies[181]. The significant aspect of the Act was the establishment of Corporate Affairs Commission. Contrary to the old system which was problematic due to its centralised and organisational structure, the

179 The terms privatisation means disinvestments (partially or fully) of government equity interest in wholly or partially state owned enterprises. Commercialisation implies retaining government ownership but improving performance and reducing or eliminating subsidies and subventions (Wilson, 1990, p. 12 quoted in Onah, 1991, p. 621).

180 However, the economy witnessed a drastic policy reversal in 1988 that eroded the gains of the reform which consequently injected uncertainty in the economy.

181 However, foreign companies invited by the Federal Government, foreign government-owned companies engaged solely on export promotion activities. Foreign engineering consultant and technical experts were exempted from incorporation subject to the approval of the Council of Ministers (Aremu, 2003, p. 60).

new Corporate Affairs Commission was decentralised with an office in each State of the Federation. The decentralisation of functions helped to reduce the cost of registration and made the registration processes less cumbersome (Ekwere, 1993, p. 52).

In 1995, the Exchange Control Act of 1984 was repealed and was replaced by foreign exchange Decree No. 17 of 1995[182]. As a result of persistent pressure from organised private sector, an Autonomous Foreign Exchange Market (AFEM) was created. This made it possible for individuals or corporate bodies to invest in any Nigerian enterprises or securities. According to the Acts, foreign investors can bring in foreign currency in Nigeria only through an authorized dealer. In other words, the modalities for capital importation for foreign investors were deregulated and simplified[183]. Furthermore, the Nigerian Investment Promotion Commission (NIPC) was established. The main objective is to market Nigeria's investment environment to foreign entrepreneurs. The Act establishing the Investment and Securities was as signed into law in 1999. The reform was aimed at deregulating the Nigerian capital market as well support inflow of FDI in the country. The major reform in this case was the harmonisation of Capital Gains Tax Act, the Venture Capital (incentives) Act and the NIPC Act which are often conflicting and overlapping in terms of jurisdiction (Aremu, 2003, pp. 63-4). Generally, industrial activities during the period suffered serious set back due to political instability and civil unrest following human right abuse by the military dictatorship. The expected gains from the reform in terms of private sector development and FDI in manufacturing sector could not be achieved.

8.2.7 Nigerian Industrial Policies from 1999 to 2007

Nigeria departed from its past pervasive state intervention policies to a new path that tried to embrace free market capitalism. The policy initiatives were embedded in the new policy framework called the "National Economic Empowerment and Development Strategy" (NEEDS) launched in 2004[184]. The NEEDS policy document explicitly recognised economic growth as the basic instrument for poverty reduction. To stimulate economic growth, promotion of private sector development became the central objective of the NEEDS policy

182 The Exchange Control Act of 1984 was the principal legislation regulating foreign currency related transactions in Nigeria.

183 Nigeria Foreign Exchange: Deregulation and Guidelines. www.nigeria-law.org/-Foreign Sourced on 22.03.10.

184 A critical view of the policy framework shows that NEEDS is a revised SAP that aimed at reforming government institutions by encouraging effective budgetary implementation, fighting corruption, promoting accountability and transparency (NEEDS, 2004, p. 12). The basic difference between the NEEDS and SAP is that NEEDS is a locally groomed concept with a neo-liberal background.

package. The key elements of the strategy focused on privatisation of public enterprises, deregulation and liberalisation, investment in infrastructure for development. The policy also targeted specific sectors such as agriculture, industry/SMEs, services, oil and gas, and solid minerals. The policy document also recognised the importance of small and medium scale enterprises (SMEs) in economy in terms of employment generation and wealth creation. Enterprises clusters were also regarded as a key strategy in Nigerian industrial development in the policy document (NEEDS, 2004, p. 7). In 2002, the government launched Small and Medium Industry Equity Investment Scheme (SMIEIS). Under the scheme, commercial banks were mandated to set aside 10 per cent of pre-tax profits for equity investments in SMEs[185]. Equity investment could be in the form of cash injection and/or conversion of existing debts with additional funds as loan by the banks (World Bank, 2002. p.16; Oyekanmi, 2004, p. 66). By September 2008, a total of about N26 billion had been distributed to SMEs. Firms in Lagos state received about 56.02 per cent of the total sum followed by Ogun and Abuja FCT with 7.83 and 3.01 per cent respectively. 43.07 per cent of total disbursement went to the manufacturing, 22.29 per cent the service sector and 13.55 per cent went to Agro-allied industries (CBN- SMEEIS table 1 and 2, 2008).

Furthermore, telecommunication was actively privatised which led to rapid increase mobile phone and internet revolution in the country. The state owned industries were completely privatised coupled with massive campaign for foreign direct investment. The energy sector was partially deregulated in order to allow public and private partnership investment. This was followed by the establishment of Small and Medium Enterprises Development Agency of Nigeria (SMEDAN) through the parliamentary process. The agency was assigned to promote, facilitate and coordinate all government policies on SMEs (NEEDS, 2004, p. 80). The implication is that policies on SMEs in Nigeria are now macroeconomic issue and centralised with unified mechanism. This is against flexibility and effectiveness which implementation of SME policies demands. Furthermore, a new national policy on Micro Small and Medium scale Enterprises (MSMEs) was launched in March 2008. The fundamental objectives of the policy according to the report are, to provide an overall framework of action as a guide for well focused, harmonious and coordinated programming by all actors. According to the document, the objective cover among others, evaluation and monitoring of stakeholders activities. The major technical problem of the policy is lack of clarity and functional objectivity. In academic circle, it is very difficult to understand whether the package represents a "policy document" or an "institutional structure". The former is concern with the application of specific economic and political instruments in order to achieve specific objective or objectives. While the latter focuses on information flow,

185 NEEDS documents were created in march 2004, pp. 78-83.

coordination, monitoring, evaluation and documentation of the problems the SMEs face. If the objective of SMEDAN is to combine both, then there will be a problem. SME policy implementation requires sequential scheduling, targeting and costing with evaluation mechanism that involves different actors and independent monitoring agencies.

8.3 Nigerian Technology Development

The essence of technology politics is to validate the conditions necessary for *Pareto optimality* which the market often cannot perform. The problems with technology are that it is not homogeneous and its information is limited. The producers are very few relative to buyers and changes rapidly overtime. The externalities generated by technology usage are not in line with the concept of *Pareto optimality*. The characteristic of technology is such that benefits arising form spillover effects and the corresponding divergence between private and social returns made it impossible for market to dictate the technology politics. Thus, the exclusive reliance on competitive pressures of the market to determine the allocation mechanism will result in some social underinvestment in technology (Oladeji, 1998, p. 126). In analysing Nigerian technology policies, two approaches namely direct and indirect have to be considered. Direct approach is a reflection of government policy instruments that are aimed at supporting research and development. In other words, a reflection on the extent to which policy interventions has resulted to *Pareto improvement*. The indirect approach on the other hand focuses on the impact of industrial houses with regards to technology transfer and diffusion. In other words, to what extent the import substitution industries or FDI have contributed to technological change in the country.

The genesis of Nigerian technology policy can be linked to the establishment of a botanical research centre in Lagos by Sir Claude McDonald in 1893 and the establishment of cotton experimental workshop called "Moor Plantation" in Ibadan in 1899. In 1912, the colonial government established Department of Agriculture in the southern and northern protectorates in order to create institutional framework to strengthen the agricultural research and extension (Obiaga, 1992, p. 15). The British colonial technology policies focused mainly on how to enhance the productivity of raw materials such as cocoa, palm oil, rubber etc needed for their home industries. This led to plethora of agricultural research institutes Nigeria. The aim was to improve agricultural sector and increase the production of cash crops for exports (Obiaga, 1992, p. 19). Industrial research started in Nigeria in 1959 when the Department of Commerce and industry in Oshodi, Lagos was refurbished with laboratory equipment, industrial workshops and subsequently converted to Federal Institute for Industrial Research.

Table 8.1: Summary of Industrial and Technology Policy Initiatives (1900-2007)

Periods	Major Industrial policy Initiatives	MajorTechnology Policy Initiatives	Policy Evaluation	
			Successes	Failures
1900-1954	-Provision of physical infrastructure -Establishment of Institutional Frame work for Industrial Development -Creating institutions (NLDB and DCI) for thepromotion of Industrial development	-Establishment of Institutional Framework for agricultural research.	-Nnational integration through communication -Using available local resources for enabling environment for private commercial activities. -Policies targeting grass roots development -Promoting Small scale processing and handicraft industries in rural areas	-Government investment in education was very weak hence the NGOs provided education extensively.
1954 - 1958	Import Duty Relief Act of 1957, Income Tax Relief Act of 1958, Dumpling and Subsidies Goods Act of 1958	No major technology policy initiative	Establishment of Legislative process for industrial development -Rapid expansion of industrial establishment in the country	Promotion of SMEs was neglected -foundation for import substituting industrial programme was laid for the promotion of Import
1958-1972	- Active government participation in industrial develop-ment under NDP framework began to emerge. - Nigerianisation and nationalsiation process of the economy began -Promulgation of NEP Decree of 1972	Establishment of -FIIR Oshodi (1959), NCST, IRCN & PRODA in Enugu (1971)	Investment in Technological infrastructure andincreased national awareness on modern technology	Increasing uncertainty in Nigeria's industrialisation process
1972 - 1985	-Policy shift from open- door policy to government dominance in production activities. - Foreign Exchange - Control Act No.	NBTE and NSTDA	Expansion of access roads and infrastructure Increased local participation in industrialisation process	Investment climate deteriorated Vacuum in industrial learning

Source*:* Own Compilation based on the research findings

Table 8.1: (Conted.)

Periods	Major Industrial Policy Initiative	Major Technology Policy Initiatives	Policy	
			Successes	Failures
1985-1988	-Implementation of SAP - Second Tier Foreign exchange Market - Privatisation and Commercialisation Decree No. 25 of 1988; Creation of Independent NPC	Raw Materials Research and Development Council Decree (Now Act) No.39 of 1987	Integration of micro and small enterprises in the country in Nigerian Industrial policy.	Policy reversal which led to increased uncertainty and socio-economic breakdown
1988-1999	-Revised NEP act of 1989; Promulgation of Companies and Allied Matters Decree Acts No.1; 1990 Act; Foreign Exchange Decree No. 17 of 1995 (AFEM); NIPC and Harmonised Capital Gains Tax Act	No major technology policy	Dominance of Micro and small enterprises in informal sector	Economic Crises with lowest industrial Capacity Utilisation
1999-2007	- New sector specific Policy (NEEDS) -SMEDAN and SMIEIS -Capital Market Development - Capitalisation of the Commercial Banks	No major technology Policy	-Emphasis on PSD, Stability in banking sector and improved capital market -Recognition of SMEs as major factor in economic development	-High unemployment and poverty incidence -SME development path, Industrial and technology policies are jet to be defined.

Source: Own Compilation based on the research findings

In 1971, Industrial Research Council of Nigeria (IRCN) was established and was charged with coordinating all industrial research activities in the country. In the same year, the then East Central State Government of Nigeria also set up the Project Development Agency (PRODA) which was integrated into national industrial research institution in 1976 (Obiaga, 1992, p. 15; Makanjuola, 1992, pp. 296-7). Most importantly Nigeria's membership in United Nations after the independence helped to promote the development of science and technology in the country[186]. For example, Nigerian Council of Science and Technology (NCST) was established in1969 through the technical support from UNESCO. The major achievement of NCST was specification of policy priorities for

186 Nigerian participation in the UN Conferences on The Application of Science and Technology for the Benefits of Developing Countries in 1963 and the subsequent 1964 UNESCO International Conference on Research and Training in Africa influenced Nigeria's initiatives on Science and Technology Policy (Obiaga 1992, p. 20).

scientific research and development for the country. Subsequently, the National Board on Technical Education (NBTE) was established in 1977 (Makanjuola, 1992, p. 302). However, NBTE was replaced by Decree No. 5 of 1977 establishing National Science and Technology Development Agency (NSTDA). The NSTDA was placed under the office of Chief of Staff Supreme Headquarters which was responsible for the allocation of research grants to universities and other tertiary institutions for projects of national interest (Obiaga, 1992, p. 21).

Indirect approach focuses on how regulations on business establishment in Nigeria would effectively influence transfer of technology. Indirect approach also covers the impact of joint venture or franchise agreements, trade marks, patents and designs on local technological capability development. In this case, transfer of technology or national technology capability depends on the ability of the public institutions to influence or enhance technology transfer. Indirect approach tries to explain whether public institutions have the appropriate skills needed to analyse and implement technology transfer. Technology transfer is not a goodwill gesture because technology producers regardless of where they are located need commercial returns for their efforts (Maya, 2002, p. 5). This means that the expected gains from imported technology cannot be fruitful if the skilled manpower and infrastructure are not adequately at hand.

In general, Table 8.1 above shows the summary of Nigeria industrial and technology policy initiatives from 1900 to 2007. The policy evaluation provides an insight into the policy successes and failures in each period with respect to SME development. The table shows that grass root industrial policy took place between 1900 and 1954, 1985 and 1988. Nigeria policy on SME development in the period 1999 and 2007 is not concrete or defined; hence evaluating the policy impact will be difficult.

8.4 Lessons from Nigerian industrial and technology policies

The analyses of Nigerian past industrial and technological policies provided an insight on why the overall economy failed to perform. The failure is attributed to the fact that the policies did not reflect the realities at the grassroots. Most of the policy design and implementation followed a top-down approach. Lessons derived from the past policies initiatives in Nigeria can be summarized as follows.

On attaining independence, Nigeria's economic policy drifted from grassroots development strategy to rapid expansion of urban economy (Kilby, 1969, p. 81). The strategy did not provide the required absorptive capacity for the increasing urban unemployment. Consequently, there was drastic increase in informal sector economy in urban cities and rapid decline in rural labour force. At early stage of the country's development, government intervention policies did not primarily focus on promoting technical and handicraft education which are crucial for industrial sector development. Nigeria industrial policy failed to link educational system and human capital development for industrial needs (Ikpeze, 1991, p. 609). Skill development which is the basic element in any industrial policy framework was neglected. This should have allowed individuals to enhance their talents and engage in a meaningful self-employment. It would have served as incentive for firms to invest on capital goods for productive growth because the level of skill manpower serves as a magnet for FDI.

The timing of indigenisation policy at early stage of self governance was a major policy failure in Nigeria (Aremu, 2003, p. 56). The 1960s and 1970s were the period when the country's technological capability and managerial know-how were at their lowest level. The policy ended up in creating uncertainty in business environment, mistrust for FDI inflow and vacuum in terms of entrepreneurship learning.

The past policies failed to identify niches or recognise the impact of sectoral and sub-sectoral linkages in industrial development (Osoba, 1991, pp. 636-9). One basic argument in favour of industrial linkages is their transmission mechanism which tends to improve economic upgrading and learning (Osoba, 1991, pp. 636-9; Uzor, 2008). For example, industrialisation based on agricultural development would have been the basic policy in Nigeria. Such policy would have played an important role in promoting the growth of micro and small scale enterprises in agricultural processing industries through linkages.

Linkages between large, medium and small enterprises were neglected hence the need to include capability building in policy options were left out (Uzor, 2008). Industrial policy that aimed towards exports was not effectively pursued in the sense that incentives for quality upgrading and linkages with global buyers were not regarded as a major policy in Nigeria.

One important lesson from World Bank and IMF imposed economic reform on Nigeria (i.e. SAP) was recognition small enterprises in Nigerian economy. Consequently, this led to institutions and programmes aimed at supporting micro and SMEs in Nigeria (Osoba, 1991, p. 637). Despite the importance of the small scale industry in Nigeria's socio-economic development, Nigerian technology policies did not aggressively tackle basic technology issues that are of vital importance to small scale industries. The Science and Technology (S&T) policy has not been effectively designed to recognises the problems in the SMEs (Oladeji, 1998, p. 126).

The analysis of Nigerian technology policies shows a rapid growth in sciences and technology institutions. However, there is no evidence of technology output; there is no direct linkage between producers of technology and the users of technology. This can be attributed to poor commercialisation of technological outcome.

The analyses also shows that Nigeria has been able to create modern science and technology institution but has failed to effectively link the institutions into an interactive process that can forge national innovation system. In other words, there is no clear policy objective aimed at fostering cooperation among local S&T institutions. There is no clear incentive that supports linkages of local research institutes with foreign research institutions.

This study revealed that local technology producers in informal sector are users of their own developed technology. These technologies are weak in the sense that as the economy deepens, markets expand and competition escalates, local technology alone cannot effectively sustain competitive pressure in an open economy. The study also shows that capacity building programmes for institutions and organisations supporting small enterprises development at regional and local levels are not effectively promoted. This is very important for SME development because such incentive serve as knowledge upgrading. The previous policies also failed to recognise the impact of information asymmetry and free rider problems that are pervasive in Nigerian credit markets. SMEs will continue to face severe financial problems due to poor access to credit and loans for investment capital.

The previous Nigerian industrial policies are dominated by laws which often change as government changes. Policy implementation are highly centralised and dominated by multiple government institutions and agencies. This often led to conflicts of interest and poor outcomes. Moreover, implementtation of industrial policies is subjected to political consideration based on federal character and ethnic origin. The consequences are such that location of firm is based on political considerations.

A close look at all the industrial policies suggests that most micro- and small entrepreneurs lack the skills and capability to understand or interpret government policies. This makes them ignorant of government intentions and objectives. In some cases, even when policies are of good intent, there is always suspicion due to low level of educational background and poor information on policy issues. There is no articulated role of Organised Private Sectors (OPSs) in policy implementation due to government dominance in industrial development efforts. The OPSs play passive role and also lack the required empowerment for active role in Nigeria's industrial development initiatives. This has immensely contributed to most industrial policy failures in Nigeria. In other words, the government interventionism gave no room for an active role of OPSs in industrial development efforts. This makes the OPSs and firms functionally ineffective in responding to government policy objectives. It also makes the policies to be vulnerable because changes in government leads to policy reversals that often produce distortions and uncertainty in the economy. The OPSs are in the position to eliminate some of the major constraints that can hinder rapid development and growth of their industries (Osoba, 1991, p. 642).

The consequences of the policy failures are reflected on the poor performance of Nigeria's manufacturing sector. The small enterprises are very weak and isolated due to technological capabilities. They cannot effectively compete in the local market or be integrated in the global production networks due to capability problems and poor access to modern equipment.

In general, as Ikpeze, Soludo and Elekwa (2004, p. 341) put it; *Nigeria's industrial policies, objectives and strategies are often subject to either modifications, or neglect or even total abandonment. In other words, industrial policies and practices are pursued on an ad.hoc basis and in a most uncoordinated manner. This major shortcomings explains the reason for the most concentration of Nigeria's industries in major cities like Lagos, Kano, Ibadan and Port Harcourt; the centre of political power of the ruling elites. This partly explains why industrial location is not solely a function of reasoned entrepreneurship planning and decisions, since political considerations are often given under weight.* On this note, the experiences from Nigeria's previous policy initiatives raise some questions whether Nigerian SMEs can sustain employment or generate the income which can lift the population out of the poverty threshold? There is a vacuum in terms of missing-link between large and small enterprises and between sectors. There is absence of dynamic policy that aimed at improving SME capabilities so that the local firms can be integrated in the global value chains.

8.5 The Dynamic Policy for SME Development in Nigeria

To address these issues, this study presents two approaches. First are the policy measures which focused on Clusters, networks and innovation. The measures were aimed at promoting productivity at grassroots' level, encourage inter-dependencies and learning. It is designed to highlight the general and sector specific measures. The second approach is the analysis of a policy matrix that outlines the strategic implementation of the policies at local, regional and federal levels.

8.5.1 Policy on Promoting SMEs Clusters in Nigeria

8.5.1.1 General Policies on Promoting SME Clusters in Nigeria

Territorial concentration and linkages are the two major characteristics associated with SME clusters. Policy support for small enterprises cluster development should consider the impact of territorial concentration (Pietrobelli and Rabellotti, 2004, p. 49). The policy support should as well recognise the role of socio-cultural factors on entrepreneurs. In general, policies promoting cluster development must first identify the cultural norms and social cohesion existing in the cluster. Socio-cultural identity of the entrepreneurs explains how social interactions can generate social capital in the cluster development. It is imperative to recognise the impact of agglomeration effects such as employment growth, market expansion and support institutions on small enterprises growth. Government intervention measures should also reflect on how to enhance productivity growth in the cluster; improve infrastructure conditions; strengthen the incentives for support institutions to improve delivery of services. As clusters mature, policies should shift to the conditions that will attract large firms to cluster and influence linkages both horizontally and vertically.

Figure 8 for example, shows three policy areas that are aimed at promoting SME development. One is the policy that focuses on development of the competitive factors. The second is the policy that promotes networks while the third is the policy that promotes linkages with large firms. The intersection in the two policy areas represents the cluster development policy objectives. The intersection suggests that there are some overlapping policy instruments from the two policy areas that highlight cluster development objectives. The central argument of the cluster proponents is that clustering fosters collective efficiency that facilitates the growth of small enterprises.

Collective efficiency comprises the external economies and joint action which firms and institutions tend to pursue in order to strengthen small enterprises competitiveness (Schmitz, 1995; Schmitz, 1997 and Nadvi, 1999). In this context, Pietrobelli and Rabellotti, (2004, p. 49) argue that a well articulated cluster development policy should therefore focus on promoting collective efficiency. This means that policies aiming at enhancing collective efficiency tend to target development of local competitive factors and fostering of linkages (Pietrobelli and Rabellotti, 2004, p. 49). To enhance collective efficiency in small enterprise clusters in Nigeria, first, resources should be directed to measures that enhance local competitive factors such a human development, access to new technology, promotion of technology partnership and the linkages among firms and institution[187]. The second step is the selection mechanisms of the clusters that would be promoted. To achieve this, three criteria to be considered in selecting the clusters to be promoted are: impact, costs and comparative adventage in terms of local circumstances. The Policy should consider how to measure the impact of the policy intervention. It should provide the mechanism impact assessment for periodical evaluation.

Cluster development often involves huge financial outlay and time for learning process. Since financial resources are limited, measures should focus on result oriented strategy that demands targeting and efficient management. Promotion of cluster should be based on local comparative advantage. Sectors

187 Pedersen (1997, p. 5) argues that the problem with collective efficiency in African clusters is not only due to weak local market but also as a result of limited vertical specialisation, collaboration among economic actors and poor human development

that have growth potential based on local comparative advantage should be targeted.

Figure 8: Policy Diagram for SME and Small Enterprises Cluster Development

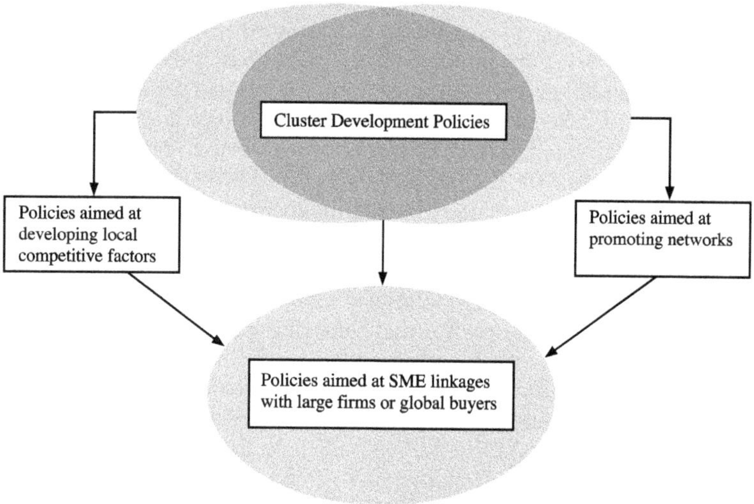

Source: Pietrobelli and Rabellotti (2004, p. 49) concept for Latin America but extended to include linkages with large firms by the author.

To effectively implement cluster development policies, there is the need to decentralise functions that include local financial autonomy (Pietrobelli and Rabellotti, 2004, p .50). Cluster policies must be initiated locally and from the grassroots. The policies must be separated from general SME development programme. For example, cluster development in Nigeria has been integrated in the new policy on Micro Small and Medium Enterprises (MSME). Integrating SME development policy and SME cluster development will not only generate confusion but will also create false expectations (Pietrobelli and Rabellotti, 2004, p. 50). This is because cluster policies follow evolutionary trends. Moreover, policies on cluster must recognise the role of value chains and linkages which are very crucial in cluster development.

8.5.1.2 Specific policies for Promotion of SME Clusters in Nigeria

The necessary and sufficient conditions for local economic development are the provision of the basic education, human resources improvement and development of the local endowments. The major problem that emerged from this study is high degree of competitive lag across the sample and sub-sectors.

Nigerian educational policy should be reformed to reflect industrial needs. For example, the education level of small enterprise heads and workers in the sample is very low. Most regrettably is the low level of technical education and skill acquisition the workers possess. Policies should be directed to technical knowledge and should be promoted from the grassroots level. Development of technical knowledge is not a spontaneous phenomenon, it follows an evolutionary trend. Technical colleges and vocational training institutes should as a matter of urgency be established and equipped in all local government area of Nigeria. The technical school curriculum needs to be redesigned in order to reflect practical works at grassroots. Training of workers by firms and agencies such as Industrial Training Fund (ITF) can be productive only when the educational system provides the formal training needed for industrial capabilities.

Clusters must be strongly linked with local universities and polytechnics to allow upgrading of knowledge through training and research. The universities and polytechnics should develop cluster related curriculum with emphasis on dynamic factors. Such measure will offer the students the opportunity to carry out practical works in the local firms. It will also help to establish legitimacy and recognition of the clusters for international cooperation or interventions.

The cluster must be linked to local credit institutions for easy access to short term credits. Credit is necessary not for all small enterprises but for those enterprises seeking to expand or innovate. The Loan Guarantee Consortia of Modena in the Emilia-Romagna region, Italy is an example of local credit initiative that provide credit to small and medium scale enterprises. The local consortia include 3,500 small and medium scale enterprises which provide mutual credit guarantees. The mutual credit is generated through membership fees and supplemented by the municipal, regional and national government. The application for loan is vetted by specialised subcommittees and the consortium's board (Schmitz and Musyck, 1994, p. 892). In Badan-Württenberg, Germany, the local banks serve as source of credit for small and medium scale enterprise while self-help institutions facilitate access to finance for innovative ventures by providing credit guarantees (Schmitz and Musyck, 1994, p. 892).

Policy measures also should include the establishment of skill centre in the cluster. In this context, the skilled centre should serve as centre for knowledge development and knowledge transfer that are peculiar to the cluster. The skill centre should collaborate with institutions and universities. The naure of programmes offered in the skill centre should be inter-disciplinary to cover cluster management, environmental issues and marketing strategies among others. Since training of workers in the cluster is done through informal apprentice system, programmes in the skill centre should be standardised. The success of Sinos Vallay, Brazil is linked to the emergence of freelance designers, technical and financial consultants and specialised transport services within the cluster. Three centres provide specialised training and technical services for shoe and leather industry in the cluster. The sub-sectoral and business associations in the cluster should be integrated in the cluster development process. They are placed in better position to understand the problems the enterprises face and how policy can be shaped to solve the challenges. The role of the OPSs should be moved from a supportive role to an active and functional role. For example, in Sinos Vallay, Brasil, there are six specialised industrial associations and two professional associations supporting the cluster. This underscores the importance of cooperation and collective approach in problem solving (Schmitz (1995, p. 544).

Cluster development policies must reflect measures that facilitate external connections or linkages to world market. In this case, effective supporting institutions are important in order to facilitate cooperation and collaboration among firms in the cluster (Bair and Gereffi, 2001, p. 1899). Measures on how to exploit niches and diversification by targeting sub-contracting, and establishing joint venture relationship with external buyers are neceasary. The policy measures must also include ways to reduce technology problems, supporting learning by observation through sponsoring cluster stakeholders' to participate in international conferences and trade fairs.

The capacity building programmes for the entrepreneurs in clusters should be intensified. Such programmes should include ways to improve job quality, product quality, process upgrading which are crucial for cluster growth. It is also imperative to constantly improve the capabilities of business associations and employers of organisations supporting the cluster because they facilitate and promote collective efficiency. For example, capacity building on product quality measures in the Sialkot surgical instrument cluster in Pakistan helped to find solution to quality crises in the cluster (Nadvi, 199a).

Policy for cluster development in Nigeria should effectively identify the value chains in which the SMEs are involved and their mode of governance. This will help intensify interactions within the local value chains and exploit the opportunities offered by the chains such as upgrading and improving performance effectively. The most effective means of strengthening interactions is to tie incentives to the commitment to cooperate. For example, to facilitate interactions within the value chains, there is the need to inject consultants or brokers in the system in order to facilitate interactions between parties.

8.5.2 Policy on SME Networks in Nigeria.

8.5.2.1 General Policy Measures on SME Networks in Nigeria

Policies supporting network development are aimed at enhancing trust between firms and reducing uncertainty in business environment. The instrument often used in enhancing trust are promotion of social capital, linkages, reduction of free riders, reducing cost of transacting business and malfeasance.

Social capital as an intangible asset or input is in the form of public morality and serves an important instrument that promotes social-economic growth. Such an intangible asset is very crucial in promoting cooperation among economic actors. The more moral resources are displayed in transactions, the greater is the mutual confidence. However, public morality depends on political environment in terms of governance structure and system. Policies aimed at promoting social capital should recognise the need for transparency, democracy, empowerment, civil liberty and human rights. For example, a corrupt political system tends to pollute the business environment in terms of mistrust. Policy reversal often generates uncertainty, increases costs in terms of price distortions hence malfeasance is promoted in the system. Policies for the promotion of networks are indirect methods of stimulating and upgrading the entire economic system.

Promoting networks implies initiating projects that aimed at encouraging interactions or relationships between firms and individuals. It includes measures that foster learning networks such as improving standards, or networks that focus on reducing transaction costs, or establishing technical assistance partnerships. The UNIDO (2000) network policy concept is used in promoting small enterprises networks. The concept focuses on specialised technical assistance that can facilitate linkages. The UNIDO concept explains that financial incentive is not the effective means of forging participation or promoting cooperation in learning networks. Special experts such as trained network brokers are rather more important in promoting cooperation. Network brokers can be trained and experienced personals with good technical skills or established institutions which can facilitate actions or development programmes. The Network brokers must possess the required credibility before the local actors. They must be highly independent from local lobbies. In general, they should not be influenced by other vested interests (Pietrobelli and Rabellotti, 2004, p. 53).

Policies promoting small enterprise networks should aim at performance enhancement in terms of reducing the circumstances that lead to under performance. Mechanisms that can strengthen interactions and enforcement of agreements are considered to be crucial for small enterprises. Small entrepreneurs individually have weak bargaining power and lack the financial resources to engage formal legal processes. Thus strengthening the legal system in order to protect poor producers is an essential instrument in entrepreneurship development. Though firms use their networks to enforce contract discipline but development of legal system is the only sufficient measure to install confidence in business transactions in an economy. Furthermore, information pooling centre is very important for firms in order to have easy access to information about previous performance or character of a new customer. This will generate positive effect by reducing cost of transacting business.

8.5.2.2 Sector Specific Measures on SME Networks in Nigeria

Designing policies for SME networks is a complex field because it is difficult to measure the impact of social networks quantitatively despite potential advent-ages networks offer. In formulating sector specific policy design for SME networks in Nigeria, the followings measures must be considered:

Targeting interdependent and coherent groups should be primary focus of the policy support for SME networks in Nigeria. Local production system depends on interdependences at the territorial, functional and sectoral levels. The expansion of enterprises in Tiruppur cluster India was due to increased labour productivity which sustained raise in wages (Cawthrone, 1995). For example, palm kernel oil (PKO) production depends on supply of palm kernels and market demand in soap factories and vegetable oil refinery. Strengthening productivity in each group will help to upgrade outputs in the sub-sector.

Networks comprise personal and organisational interactions in which individuals, firms and institutions are put in an interactive process. Targeting groups in this context implies exploiting the opportunities that will allow them to develop joint projects and complement each other to overcome common problems. In other words, targeting each group will enhance collective efficiency and facilitate firms' rate of penetrating market beyond their individual capability. For example, policies aimed at fostering collaboration between forestry department and firms in wood and furniture industry will help to support reforestation efforts and increase output. Policies supporting SME networks in Nigeria should focus on measures that will increase the capacity to learn and capacity to innovate. Network characteristics such as information filtering, knowledge diffusion and structural flexibility are of peculiar importance for innovation and technological change. Promotion of networks should reflect on how to facilitate technology transfer. This could be possible through linking SMEs with large MNCs and through linking the national innovation systems with Global innovation system.

Like linkages in South East Asia and Japan, policies should focus on how firms in Nigeria can exploit historical advantages and establish linkages with firms in EU. The advantage of such scenario is such that firms are embedded in business networks that span national borders will develop positive attitudes towards liberalization (Bräutigam, 1999, pp. 19-20).

Strengthening the commercial regulations and legal institutions will serve as a basic instrument for protection of property rights and contractual relationships. This study revealed that enterprises rely mainly on norms and informal sanctions which are not effective as market deepens and cross border transactions increases. Effective institutional mechanisms which are transparent and functional in terms of specifying and protecting investments are conditions for good business for local and foreign investors. Moreover, rationalising the taxation system will enable the firms to take risks and readily invest in the domestic economy.

The role of stock exchange in SME development has not been effectively promoted and exploited in Nigeria. Nigerian stock market should be expended and upgraded. The state government in conjunction with state chambers of commerce and industry should establish its own local stock exchange. This will aid public listing of SMEs in the local stock markets. It will also create opportunities for greater specialisation and capitalisation of SMEs. Such opportunities include among others investment in modern technology and improvement of managerial techniques. Such kind of evolution serves as an efficient means of raising capital by building a reputation without relying on social networks. For example, in India, the Securities and Exchange Board of India (SEBI) approved an exclusive stock exchange for SMEs by providing alternative private equities and some venture capital fund for SMEs. In the context of Nigeria, the basic role of local (state) stock market would have been to facilitate the Small and Medium Industry Equity Investment Scheme (SMIEIS) so that it can achieve its desired objectives by reaching wider areas (geographically and sectorally).

8.5.3 Policy on Innovation and SMEs Capability Development in Nigeria

Policies on innovation can be viewed in different levels of the economy. It can be at the macroeconomic level that focuses on price of inputs such as capital and labour. They can also be directed to microeconomic level such as entrepreneur's perception (attitude) on innovation, and the conditions that affect enterprise's innovative activity or on how exposure affects innovative activities. At meso level, innovation policies focus on how the cluster and network characteristics foster technological and social innovation. At the micro level, this study shows how the small enterprises perceive innovation as survival strategy and how government policies conditions in terms of openness and incentive can influence productivity.

Promotion of innovation depends upon the resources and capabilities available in the country, the level of the country's development, and the nature of governance in the country. In general, innovation climate such as educational attainment, the business environment and the information infrastructure dictate the innovative activity in the country (Aubert, 2004, pp. 7-8). The fundamental principle behind promoting innovation is to encourage upgrading processes. Upgrading is a function of innovation systems which in turn depends on the innovation climate in the system[188]. To upgrade for example requires research community linked to local labour market with technological support services and infrastructure as well (Aubert, 2004, p. 10). Peculiar to Nigeria is that technological support services and infrastructure to research communities are very limited.

Nigeria industrial sector is dominated by micro and small enterprises operating in the informal economy with few large foreign firms co-exists in isolation. Policies should focus on how capability gap in micro and small enterprises can be narrowed so that linkages with large firms can be feasible. At macro and meso levels, two approaches need to be considered in targeting local technological capability. The first approach is to identify the sectors with very weak institutional capabilities. Policy on innovation should focus on investment in basic technology infrastructure such as improving communication, data storage system and access to ICT network institutions etc. The policy should define means of promoting practical demonstration of new ideas at grassroots that reflects basic innovation. This however, demands reform in education system at all levels that encourage technical knowledge. The second approach is to identify the sectors with relatively stronger institutional capabilities. In this case, policies should therefore focus on development of articulated entrepreneurial culture that based on the advantages each sector possesses. This is an important approach that will foster the national innovation system. Policies aimed at promoting the national innovation system (NIS) will invariably exploit the role of science and technology in the promotion of innovation and its diffusion in the society[189]. Interaction among these units may be technical, commercial, legal, social and financial as much as the goal of the interaction may be development, protection, financing or regulation of new science and technology (Niosi et al, 1996, p. 139). The concept of NIS rests on the premise that understanding the linkages among the institutions, especially how they relate to each other as elements of a collective system of knowledge creation, diffusion and use, is a crucial instrument to improving a country's innovative performance (OECD, 1997, p. 9). The institutions include both 'things that pattern behaviour' like norms, rules and laws (such as patent systems and technical standard). It also includes 'formal structure with an explicit purpose' such as firms, industrial R&D laboratories, universities, and public R&D institutes (Edquist, 1997, p. 26). In this context, to achieve a sustainable NIS in

188 The innovation system is defined as the set of organisations (firms, universities, public laboratories, etc.) and the linkages through which innovation processes develop. The roots of the innovation systems (IS) concepts are based on the Neo-Schumpeterian economics, emphasising innovation and entrepreneurship.

189 NIS can be defined as the network of institutions in the public and private sectors whose activities and interactions initiate, import, modify and diffuse new technologies (Freeman, 1987).

Nigeria, there is a need to promote linkages among local institutions and forge technology partnership across countries. It can be in the form of promoting international joint research projects, linkages with other research institutes in developed countries as well as reaching out for technical assistance from donor agencies.

Promotion of innovation without better welfare conditions is counter-productive in the sense that improving the welfare conditions of the citizens is a means of improving innovative thinking. NIS can be effective when issues regarding the health care and food security are effectively integrated in the national innovation policy. For instance, increased agriculture productivity will not only serve as means of providing food for non-agricultural labour force. It will serve as means of sustaining the entire economy. A good health care system will reduce the infant mortality rates and serve as an incentive for productivity growth.

Mesoeconomic policy for innovation should first identify the factors that promote cluster development and factors that influence entrepreneurs' success. Policy on innovation often aims at promoting technology capability building so that collective efficiency can be enhanced. Formulating innovation policy appears to be easy but implementation is often difficult especially in large country like Nigeria with numerous institutions. To implement innovation policy, policymakers must consider the institutional capacities in various institutions involve and availability of funds as well as the coordination mechanism (van Dijk, 2003, p. 355). At cluster level, technology centres and incubators are the most popular economic and technological support instruments for the promotion of innovation and innovation diffusion in the cluster. Incubators create favourable environment for start-ups especially for innovative and technology oriented-firms, reducing fixed costs and sharing services (Pietrobelli and Rabellotti, 2004, p. 56). Nigeria has established technology and business Incubators for start-ups. The major problems the centres face are inadequate funding and poor staffing. The staffs lack the required experience and exposure on how to run the centres and facilitate technology diffusion. In general, the incubators are not effectively linked to local institutions or international technology partners that can allow sharing of experiences and exchange of new knowledge.

At micro level, the first basic policy strategy is to consider how to facilitate competitive activities because competition drives innovation. Competitiveness requires improvement in product quality, marketing, organisation, and logistics and so on. For small and medium enterprises, development of competitive industries in Nigeria will help to create the environment that can induce learning, linkages and promote value chains in the system. Policy must also identify ways of forging partnership with local small firms and MNCs. This will encourage learning and technology transfer among firms. Local small firms and MNCs partnership formation should not be initiated through legislative agreement rather a mutual process that allowed identification of the level and conditions which partnership can be more effective for both firms.

Since cluster and network provide innovative milieu, it will be easier to foster collaboration among small firms and subcontractors. The collaboration helps find ways to stimulate and develop local technological capability for the small and medium scale enterprises development (UNCTAD, 1998). Apart from encouraging inter-firm cooperations, policies should extensively reflect measures that could enable small enterprises to have access to modern technology. Trade policies should recognise the negative impact of high tariff on imports especially on capital goods. Access to new technology often creates externalities in terms of creating new knowledge and productivity growth (Berdegué and Escobar, 2002, p. 2).

8.5.4 Policy Matrix for SME Development in Nigeria

Table 8 shows a policy matrix representing the issues, policy areas and actions. The policy issue comprises not only the policy objectives and current status of the target area but also the classification of actions in general and sector specific areas. The policy issue also covers measures responsible for policy evaluation with respect to time limits, costs, implementation and monitoring agencies. Furthermore, the policy issue should specify the area of intervention and responsibilities in central, regional and local governments. It also covers the level where the global community can intervene. The policy areas and actions describe the major policy measures directed at specifying the operational actions for SME cluster development, measures aimed at facilitating networking and innovative activities. The Policy objectives are the concrete measures defined according to the policy areas and provide the measures for evaluation. For example policy objective on social capital for cluster development needs be different from policy objective aimed at facilitating networking and innovative activities. The objectives of the policy measures should define the aims to be accomplished and explicitly linked to growth or poverty reduction. It should also be as specific as possible so that the potential positive outcome of the policy measure can be appreciated. The current status of the policy area needs be recognised when formulating the policy. For examples, policy for incipient cluster should be different from policy for organised cluster.

There should be difference in the policy actions promoting knowledge networks and the policy actions promoting resource networks. It is important because policy targeting always serve as baseline for monitoring the outcomes. Priority actions must show a clear clarification on how the actions will impact outcomes. Cost estimates of policy actions require specifition including adequate information and policy guidance on cost determinants. In projecting the cost of the policy actions, simple costing model program should reflect unit cost estimates.

Table 8.2: Policy Matrix for SME and SME Cluster Development in Nigeria

Policy Issue		Policy Areas and Actions		
		Clusters	Networks	Innovation
Policy Objectives		Promoting - Collective efficiency, Social Capital; Linkages & Investment	Promoting-Social Capital, Linkages, Strengthen formal institutions	Promoting – Investment, Social Capital, Local Technological capability building
Current Status		Incipient/Informal Organised Clusters	Personal- Strong Organisational – weak Knowledge Network – not present	As a survival Strategy
Priority Actions	General	Identifying the Agglomeration Effects -Education Reform that linked to productivity growth	Social Capital Commercial Law Contract enforcement Protection of property rights	Promoting innovation climate -Improving the welfare conditions of the citizens -building institutional capability
	Specifics	Targeting sectors with growth Potential, Promoting: TechnicalEducation, Skill development, Linkages, Microfinance	Targeting collaboration among coherent groups. Promoting: - Linkages -Partnership with large firms-Local stock exchange	Promoting: -Product and Process upgrading, -Skill development, -Microfinancing, -Local stock exchange
Implementation Schedule		Time frame :Dynamic; Specific project with specified time frame	Dynamic Depending on the project	Dynamic Depending on the project
Implementation Agencies		PSOs, or Associations in the Cluster with Ministry of Labour and Education and a Research Institute Ministry of Industry and Ministry of Environment	Ministry of Justice, Labour and Industry PSOs A research institute	Science and technology institutions Research Institutes Ministry of Industry
Costing		Cost estimates of programs and actions must be as specific aspossible	Cost estimates of programs and actions must be as specific as possible	Cost estimates of programs and actions must be as specific as possible

Key: Agglom. = Agglomeration; PSOs = Private Sector Organisations; NIS = National Innovation System; LIS = Local Innovation System; Fed. = Federal

Source: Complied by the author based on research outcome

Table 8.2: Continues

Policy Issue		Policy Areas and Actions Clusters	Networks	Innovation
Monitoring		A Research Institute, Cluster Brokers	A Research Institute, Network Brokers	A Research Institutes Network/Cluster Brokers
Levels/Areas of Intervention by the government	Local	-Skill Development - Vocational Educational	Social Capital Social Infrastructure	Skill Development
	State	- Identifying Agglom. Effects -Promoting cluster development projects - Skill development - Technical education	Promoting Transparency Reducing Corruption through Checks and Balances, Promoting Democracy	Local technological capability building -Technical Education -Adult Education Promoting partnership of Promoting LIS
	Fed.	Education reform Funding cluster development projects	Social Infrastructure Promoting Civil Liberty Promoting Checks and Balances	Promoting: Local technological capability building, NIS Promoting- Skill Development, Small and large firms Linkages
Donor Agencies		Providing Technical Suppor; t echnical & Financial Assistance in Cluster Development Targeting the Meso–Level	Targeting Meso-level Supporting Democracy	-Promoting partnership in small and large firms -promoting collabor-ations in international research works

Key: Agglom. = Agglomeration; PSOs = Private Sector Organisations; NIS = National Innovation System; LIS = Local Innovation System; Fed. = Federal

Source: Complied by the author based on research outcome

The responsible agencies should identify each priority action, and identify the responsibility of each level of government. Furthermore, there should be a time frame and deadlines for each priority actions to be completed so that outcomes can be observed and evaluated. At each stage of implementtation, concrete benchmarks have to be established. Outcomes have to be linked to poverty reduction or growth with a specified monitoring mechanism. Finally, an important aspect of accomplishing a strategy is the mobilisation of own and donor resources for program implementation. Policy implementation is not possible without clearly identifying sources of funding. Therefore, it is important to achieve a degree of inter-sector coordination to determine all available resources.

Chapter 9: General Conclusion

9.1 The Resume of the Research Concept

Fundamentally, this study departed from the traditional static supply side approach in SMEs analyses to an investigation the dynamic factors of industrial develop-ment that focuses on a combination of supply and demand side approach. This study focused on Nigeria in verifying various claims and counter-claims from literature that SMEs in Africa possess the potential to create employment and generate income; that African SMEs cannot sustain employment creation because they tend to generate low income; and that African SMEs are isolated and lack the potential individually to improve performance or sustain competition; SMEs in Africa are very weak and lack the capability to play their role in the ongoing globalisation. To investigate these claims, the study developed different analytical and empirical approaches that reflect not only the impact of proximity but also the influence of networks in SMEs' business activities. Finally, the study examined how small enterprises in Nigeria compete in an open market economy.

The investigations were necessary because of the deteriorating economic situation of large segment of Nigerian population. Moreover, the socio-economic structural changes in Nigeria have led to increased employment generation and income earning in micro and small scale enterprises in Nigeria. Hence, the motivation of the study was to look into the following prevailing questions: Can micro small and medium scale enterprises in Nigeria sustain employment? If yes, can the income generated in the sector be significantly substantial in reducing poverty? If yes, can the sector compete in an open market economy? These questions led to the designing of the research structure in terms of clusters, networks and innovation in small enterprises. This allowed the researcher to investigate the proximity factor, the structure of the networks and innovative activity of the small enterprises in Nigeria. This chapter will highlight the conclusions drawn from the empirical data analyses, and then seek to discuss the challenges and prospects of the SMEs in Nigeria and sub-Saharan Africa in general.

9.2 The Empirical Conclusion

9.2.1 SME Clusters in Nigeria

The findings revealed that the characteristics of enterprise clusters in Nigeria are similar to literature accounts of enterprise clusters in developing countries. There are incipient clusters with high degree of informality characteristics and dormant clusters identified in some sub-sectors such as garment and wood/-

furniture enterprises that cannot compete. The findings also revealed that despite high degree of informality, some small enterprise clusters as indicated in the Aba footwear and PKO enterprises can as well be competitive in the local market and reach distant markets through organised trade networks. The empirical data show that there are some conventional evidences typical of agglomeration effects in enterprise cluster investigated. The analyses revealed that the concentration of firms in similar production and in a defined location generated labour migration to these areas. Migration of unskilled labour to the cluster is very high compare to skilled labour force. The findings also revealed that employment is higher in the cluster areas during normal and seasonal production period than in the small enterprises located elsewhere. For example in footwear, enterprises employment potential is relatively high in clustered areas than in the dispersed areas. The pool of unskilled workers in the specific sector provided cheap labour such that with reduced labour cost enterprises in the clusters enjoy low unit cost of production than those located elsewhere. Since majority of the labour forces fall within the class of low skilled labour with low educational background, the positive effect of agglomeration in terms of externalities is limited. The findings show that there is no evidence which suggests that higher productivity recorded in the cluster areas is due to higher technological capabilities. The reduction in unit cost can be related to proximity effects which appeared to reduce costs.

The findings also unvail cases of collective efficiency identified in some clusters. Adam smith's division of labour and flexible specialisation were identified in PKO, footwear and wood/furniture clusters with linkages strengthening competition amongst the small enterprises. While internalisation of production activities is strong in the garment enterprises hence the productivity tends to very low. The independent suppliers provide the raw materials or components helped to reduce search costs in footwear and PKO enterprise clusters. The traders who sell to distant national and regional markets footwear enterprises often provide funds for working capital and inform the producers about designs and market conditions. The findings also show that individual firms join forces in business associations in enforcing local governance in the clusters. The relatively high shared information between trader and producer in the cluster helped to support small enterprises flexibility in the cluster. However, there is no evidence of technological spillover or diffusion due to the nature of technology in use.

The study also revealed that the degree of joint action of local producers differ according to sub-sectors. There are three factors identified that inspire joint actions among the producers in the cluster. Joint action of producers is relatively high in cluster with ethnic origin. This is common in garment enterprises cluster where entrepreneurs are dominated by people from old Bende district of eastern region of Nigeria and in light engineering enterprises cluster with producers mainly from Nnewi locality. Entrepreneurs in Aba garment enterprises cluster support each other financially through cooperative initiatives. Joint action is relatively high within highly educated entrepreneurs. This is evidenced in PKO producers with higher educational qualification with rationalisation of production among firms in order to reduce high energy consumption. The firms in PKO undertake joint supply of PKO to refineries and engineers in the cluster provide free technical services to their fellow producers in the cluster. The market forces also tend to drive joint action initiate among producers in order to reduce costs. This is evidenced in wood/furniture enterprises cluster where firms in joint financing transportation of woods.

The study indicates that despite the production structure that represents a model of different microenterprises forged into a production process, competitive factors such as human capital development, linkages, technological capability and firms' financial base are very weak in the clusters investigated. This suggests that the enterprises will continue to experience poor product quality due to weak technology and lack of access to required raw materials. There is evidence of linkages in the across sub-sectors in the clusters but the degree of linkages differ across sub-sectors. In PKO enterprises, there is relatively high incidence of backward and forward linkages production while production is highly internalised in the garment sub-sector. It implies that different policy measures must be applied to different sub-sectors based on the specific problems. For example, government interventions in PKO should aim at strengthening value chains in the sub-sectors for increased volume for export. Interventions in garment enterprises cluster should focus on capacity building programmes aimed at promoting local and international linkages.

9.2.2 SME Networks in Nigeria

Some studies of small enterprise networks in developing countries have provided different analytical evidences on why African small enterprise networks are not risk taking networks or cannot enhance performance. This study looked into wider dimension of small enterprises networks in small enterprises in Nigeria. The study also examined the extent to which the contact small entrepreneurs maintain have explained the characteristics of small enterprise networks. The study further looked into the structure of the networks and investigated the extent to which the networks have contributed to small enterprises performance. The analyses of networks were grouped according to sub-sector and size. The findings generally indicate that entrepreneurs in Nigeria like others elsewhere are social agents. As social agents they perceive the contact they make in business related associations very useful to all areas of their businesses. However, entrepreneurs value the contact they make differently. Hence, policy interventions promoting networks should recognise the heterogeneous factors in SMEs. For example, in microenterprises the contacts entrepreneurs make have no positive effect on technical upgrading in their business. Entrepreneurs in micro sector receive or offer relatively little financial assistance to members than those in small and medium scale enterprises. This explains why microfinance and technological capacity building programmes are very important for micro and small enterprises in Nigeria. In order to improve access to investment capital for small and medium in Nigeria, efforts should be directed to the expansion of stock exchange at state levels which can invariably support mobilisation of local capital for productive use.

The findings also indicate that there is evidence of organisational networks in terms of input and output networks as well as weak linkages with large firms and institutions. Poor linkages with large firms validate missing link arguments of Fafchamps (1994, p.3) and Wohlmuth (1990, p. 7) in African industrialisation efforts. Linkage will be very difficult due to low technological capability and poor product quality in the local small enterprises. As ILO (1972) suggested, public procurement is another aspect of government direct intervention that supports the growth of small enterprises in Nigeria. The findings indicate that procurement by public institutions helped to stimulate product quality upgrading in men shoe production unit in Aba footwear enterprises cluster. The enterprises that supply military shoes to Nigerian Armed forces and special shoes to Nigeria special police unit (Nigerian Mobile Police Force) face intensive quality standard measures. This helped the entrepreneurs to develop quality consciousness at every stage of production. This is an important measure that can be extended to other sectors in order to stimulate quality consciousness in small enterprise production system.

Furthermore, the study shows that social interactions helped entrepreneurs to gather business information easily, reaching out for contract, understand how to deal with government, solicit credits and loans as well as protecting their business and resolving business conflicts. The findings indicate that network functions not only serve as means of providing social welfare for members and access to information but also helped small enterprises to reaching national and sub-regional markets. For example, through their developed distributive networks, Aba footwear has expanded show export across the west coast to east coast of sub-Saharan African countries. This was aided by trade liberalisation regimes in sub-Saharan African countries that have encouraged trade relations across countries in the sub-region. Evidence also shows that networking has helped small enterprises in the clusters investigated to resolve conflicts between entrepreneurs and customers and relatively find solutions to their problems where the state support failed.

The study also revealed that at micro-level, network functions serve as informal institutions that guide exchange where the formal institution appears to be very weak. Douglas North's argument explicitly recognised the importance of the rule of law as means of guiding interactions and exchange among economic actors locally and internationally. Informal networks can strengthen business trust and values among local actors. In some cases, such informal institutional arrangement often violates human civil rights and induces exclusion. The financial costs and time spent in maintaining the membership in the network can run above benefits derived in belonging to networks. This suggests that policies aimed at promoting social networks should also include measures on how to strengthen the formal institutions. This will help to maintain the credibility of the market and effectively enforce contractual agreements, protect local and foreign investors' property rights so that the costs of transacting business can effectively be reduced.

9.2.3 Innovative Activities in Small Enterprises in Nigeria

Early studies on innovation in African small enterprises were focused on issues regarding productivity and technology choices in rural economy and later to technology learning. The recent concept tends to centre on the impact of capability building that reflects adaptation and diffusion of technology in developing countries. The findings show that innovative activities in small entr-prises in Nigeria are in line with some elements of Schumpeter ideas on entrepreneurship and innovation. In order to be competitive in the local market, some entrepreneurs are risks takers by creating and introducing different designs at a high survival costs. Some entrepreneurs are quality conscious and exploiting niches at low survival costs. Lack of access to modern equipment and invest-ment capital forced some entrepreneurs to use low quality materials and their creative talent to produce their own local technology. However, there are limitations innovative activities in small enterprises in Nigeria due to several factors.

Small firms survive in the market by producing low quality commodities due to low income while some cannot expand as a result of absence of linkages with large firms. In other words, the innovative activity is limited due to weak product market. Small enterprises cannot upgrade or lack the capability to initiate upgrading process or link with large due to capability gap problems. Poor incentives such as opportunities for capacity building can limit knowledge upgrading. Multiple taxation system in Nigeria tends to reduce motivation to take risks or embark on innovative activity. In other hand, entrepreneurs' perception on innovation can influence innovative activity. Entrepreneurs that invest in capacity building programmes have the chance to open their doors for new knowledge and high road development path.

In general, the research findings show that Nigeria's trade policy can influence innovative activity of the small enterprises in Nigeria. The trade reform generated competition such that local firms tried to adjust strategies and develop new competitive path. On the other hand, government failed to design incentives that can allow the small to rip the benefits of the trade policy reform or create opportunities for private sector organisations to take active role in industrial development programmes. As neo-Schumpeterian argue that innovation goes beyond creating research institutes or erecting laboratories, Nigerian government should design measures that can induce cooperation among the institute. This will not only streamline the research activities in the country but also help to generate synergy effects which national systems of innovation are all about.

9.3 Challenges and Prospects

In general, this study showed that the road map out of poverty for Nigeria should be built on the dynamism of entrepreneurs in the country. As ILO (2005) argues *...changing the policy paradigm to recognize that employment, and the promotion of enterprises that create jobs, is the most effective route to poverty eradication.* This study explicitly argued that entrepreneurship dynamism in Nigeria depends on the extent at which Nigerian government can provide political and overall macroeconomic stability; the extent at which government at all levels can provide the basic public goods such as education, health care and physical infrastructure. Furthermore, the policy analyses explicitly showed how government dominance in economic activities led to unprecedented missallocation and wasteful spending of scare resources. The analyses also revealed that Nigeria has not been able to develop articulated industrial policy model that reflects the reality at the grassroots. Like other African countries, Nigeria has experimented different forms of development strategies ranging from ideologically dominated development movement to developmental state intervention strategy that produced negative outcomes[190].

This study has provided a model that focuses on restructuring and strengthening the small and medium scale enterprises in Nigeria and Africa in general. The central argument is that improved domestic investment supported by FDI inflow will stimulate SME development in Nigeria through linkages. Domestic investment is fundamental in the sense that improved capabilities of the local SMEs will serve as means of improving linkages with large foreign firms. Hence, the model seeks to analyse how inter-firm and sectoral linkages can lead to SME development and economic growth. The conditions necessary for realisation of the model include among others government intensive invest-

190 The ideological development path in Nigeria then was such that the regional government in Western Nigeria pursued a socialist ideological development strategies thinking. The regional government in Eastern Nigeria followed a neo-liberal ideological path while the regional government in Northern Nigeria positioned itself with strong feudal capitalism.

ment in human capital accumulation, technological accumulation, infrastructure development and security. In doing this, government should also continue to expand and diversify the county's foreign reserve base. This is possible by maintaining conservative fiscal policy that avoids wasteful spending. Government should fundamentally ensure that effective a legal framework exists because relying on social networks could be counter productive to competition as economy expands. Moreover, government cannot act alone as the economy expands and the globalisation pressure increases. Therefore, empowerment of independent local business organisations is very crucial. In addition, empowering the local chambers of commerce and industry, business and sub-sectoral associations will not only facilitate flexibility but induce efficiency in the implementation of Nigeria's industrial policy.

South Korea is a homogeneous state which successfully applied developmental state strategy. South Korean success was partly due to human capital accumulation and developed private sector. Heterogeneity of the society in terms of ethnic diversity, poor human capital development and weak private sector contributed to the failure of various developmental state strategies applied in Nigeria and sub-Saharan Africa in general. Ethnicity provides the framework which directs government's policy choices in Nigeria and other countries in sub-Saharan Africa. Consequently, this has led to poor industrial policy outcome and marginalisation of the region from global income. It has also fuelled corruption and civil conflicts in the distribution of resources. In this context, as Bräutigam (1999, p. 21) argues, the challenge for the Nigeria and African government in terms of ethnic equity is to promote growth while at the same time promoting greater inclusion in the rewards of growth.

In general, this study has opened several new research frontiers on how SMEs in Nigeria and sub-Saharan African countries can effectively play their role in poverty reduction and effectively be integrated into the global economy.

Abbreviations

ACGS	Agricultural Credit Guarantee Scheme
AD	After Death of Christ
ADA	Accelerated Development Area
ADB	African Development Bank
ADP	Agricultural Development Programme
AFEM	Autonomous Foreign Exchange Market
AG	Action Group
AIDS	Acquired Immune Deficiency Syndromes
AOA	Agreement on Agriculture
AT	Appropriate Technology
BC	Before Christ
BHSS	Basic Health Services Scheme
BLP	Better Life Programme
BPE	Basic Primary Education
BSS	Business Support Services
CAMA	Companies Allied Matters Act
CB	Capacity Building
CBI	Capacity Building Index
CBN	Central Bank of Nigeria
CC	Correlation Coefficient
CE	Collective Efficiency
CFA	The Central Africa CFA Franc (Currency)
CSR	Corporate Social Responsibility
DAC	Development Association Committee
DCI	Department of Commerce and Industry
DFRRI	Directorate for Foods, Roads and Rural Infrastructure
EAP	Economic Active Population
ECA	Economic Commission for Africa
ECOWAS	Economic Community for West African States
EEP	Enterprises Employment Potential
EFA	Education for All
ESL	Export Stimulation Loan
EU	European Union
FAO	Food and Agriculture Organisation
FBS	Federal Bureau of Statistics

FCT	Federal Capital Territory
FDI	Foreign Direct Investment
FEAP	Family Economic Advancement Programme
FEPA	Federal Environmental Protection Agency
FOS	Federal Office of Statistics
FS	Flexible Specialization
FSP	Family Support Programme
GCC	Global Commodity Chains
GDI	Gross Domestic Investment
GDP	Gross Domestic Product
GDS	Gross Domestic Savings
GFCF	Gross Fix Capital Formation
GNI	Gross National Income
GNP	Gross National Product
HD	Human Development
HDI	Human Development Index
HIV	Human Immune Virus
HPI	Human Poverty Index
IBRD	International Bank for Reconstruction and Development
ICT	Information and Communication Technology
IDA	International Development Association
IDC	Industrial Development Council
IDS	Institute for Development Studies
IFC	International Finance Corporation
IFS	International Finance System
ILO	International Labour Organisation
IMF	International Monetary Fund
IRCN	Industrial Research Council of Nigeria
IRR	Internal Rate of Return
ISI	Import Substitution Industrialisation
ISMED	Investment and SME Development
ISO	International Standard Organisation
JPB	Joint Planning Board
JPC	Joint Planning Committee
KwH	Kilometre wax per Hour
LDCs	Least Developing Countries

LEF	Local Economic Forum
LGAs	Local Government Areas
LIS	Local Innovation System
LSAs	Location-Specific-Advantages
MAN	Manufacturers Association of Nigeria
MCU	Manufacturing Capacity Utilisation
MDGs	Millennium Development Goals
MES	Minimum Efficiency Scale
MFIs	Microfinance Institutions
MFN	Most Favoured Nation
MNCs	Multinational Corporations
MNEs	Multinational Enterprises
MSEs	Micro and Small Scale Enterprises
MSMEs	Micro Small and Medium scale Enterprises
MTI	Metallurgical Training Institute
N	Naira (Nigerian Currency)
NACCIMA	Nigerian Chambers of Commerce Industry Mines and Agriculture
NAFTA	North American Free Trade Agreement
NAP	National Action Programme
NAPEPs	National Poverty Eradication Programmes
NASME	National Association of Small and Medium Scale Enterprises
NASSI	National Association of Small Scale Industrialists
NBCI	Nigeria Bank for Commerce and Industry
NBSCI	Nigerian Bank for Commerce and Industry
NBTE	National Board of Technical Education
NC	Numerically Controlled
NCE	National Certificate of Education
NCI	Nigeria Council of Industry
NCNC	National Convention of Nigerian Congress
NCST	Nigerian Council of Science and Technology
NDE	National Directorate of Employment
NDP	National Development Plan
NEC	National Economic Council
NEDDEC	National Engineering Design Development Centre
NEEDS	National Economic Empowerment and Development Strategy
NEP	Nigerian Enterprises Promotion
NEPA	National Electric Power Supply
NERFUND	National Economic Reconstruction Fund
NGOs	Non-Governmental Organisation

NICs	New Industrialising Countries
NIGEP	Nigerian Guinea Worm Eradication Programme
NIPC	Nigerian Investment Promotion Commission
NIS	National Innovation System
NISER	Nigerian Institute for Social and Economic Research
NLDB	Nigerian Local Development Board
NMES	Nigerian Manufacturing Enterprises Survey
NPC	National Planning Commission
NPC	Nigeria People Congress
NOAS	National Open Apprenticeship Scheme
NSTDA	National Science and Technology Agency
ODA	Official Development Aid
OECD	Organisation for Economic Cooperation and Development
OER	Official Exchange Rate
OLS	Ordinary Least Square
OPEC	Oil Producing and Exporting Countries
OPS	Organised Private Sector
PAP	Poverty Alleviation Programme
PEs	Public Enterprises
PKO	Palm Kernel Oil
PPP	Purchasing Power Parity
PPPs	Public-Private Partnerships
PQLI	Physical Quality of Life Index
PRODA	Project Development Agency
PSD	Private Sector Development
PTF	Petroleum Trust Fund
R&D	Research and Development
REER	Real Effective Exchange Rate
RMRDC	Raw Material Research and Development Council
RPED	Regional Programme on Enterprises Development
SAP	Structural Adjustment Programme
SDRs	Special Drawing Rights
SEs	Small Enterprises
SED	Small Enterprises Development
SEDI	Scientific Equipment Development Institute
SMEs	Small and Medium scale Enterprises
SMEDAN	Small and Medium Enterprises Development Agency of Nigeria

SMIEIS	Small and Medium Scale Industries Equity Investments Scheme
SON	Standard Organisation of Nigeria
SPDC	Shell Petroleum Development Corporation
SSA	Sub-Saharan Africa
SSI	Small Scale Industry
SSICS	Small Scale Industries Credit Scheme
S&T	Science and Technology
TBIC	Technology Business Incubators Centre;
TCPC	Technical Committee on Privatisation and Commercialisation
TFP	Total Factor Productivity
TNCs	Transnational Corporations
TOA	Total Official Aid
UBE	Universal Basic Education
UNCED	United Nations Conference on Environmental Development
UNCTAD	United Nations Conference on Trade and Development
UNDP	United Nation Development Programme
UNESCO	United Nation Education and Scientific Organization
UNIDO	United Nations Industrial Development Organisation
UNICEF	United Nations Information Cultural and Education Fund
UNEP	United Nations Environment Programme
UPE	Universal Primary Education Programme
VSA	Volunteers Service Agency
WDI	World Development Indicators
WHO	World Health Organisation
WTO	World Trade Organisation

References

Acs, Z. J. & Audrescht, D. B. (1978). Innovation, Market Structure, and Firm Size. In: The Review of Economic Statistics, Vol. 69, No. 4, pp. 567-574.

Acs, Z J. & Audretsch, D. (1990). Innovation in Small Firms. The MIT Press, Cambridge, Massachusetts, London.

Adebusuyi, B. S. (1997). Performance Evaluation of Small-Medium Enterprises (SMEs). In: Nigeria Bullion, Vol. 21, No. 4, The Central Bank of Nigeria.

Adubi, A. A. & Okunmadewa, F. (1999). Price, exchange rate volatility and Nigeria's agricultural trade flows: A dynamic analysis. In: AERC Research Paper 87, Nairobi.

Agarwal, J. P. (1991). Foreign Direct Investment in Developing Countries. The Case of Germany, Institute für Weltwirschaft an der Universität Kiel, Kieler Studien, 288, Kiel, Germany.

Agboli, M. Ukaegbu, C. C. (2006). Business environment and entrepreneurial activity in Nigeria: implications for industrial development. In: Journal of Modern African Studies, Vol. 44, No. 1, pp. 1-30.

Aigbokhan, B. (2001). Resuscitating Agricultural Production (Cocoa, Cotton, Groundnuts, Palm oil, Rubber, etc.) For Export. Paper Presented at the 10th annual Conference of zonal research units of central bank of Nigeria, On the theme Resource Endowment, Growth and Macro-economic Management in Nigeria, held in Owerri, June pp. 4-8.

Akanji, O. O. (2002). Micro-Finance as a strategy of for Poverty Reduction. In: CBN Economic & Financial Review, Vol. 39, No. 4. The Central Bank of Nigeria.

Ake, C. (1985). The Nigerian State: Antinomies of a periphery formation, In: Cluade Ake (ed.): Political Economy of Nigeria. Longman, London and Lagos, pp. 9-32.

Alfaro, L., Chanda, A. Kalemli-Ozcan S. & Sayek, S. (2007). How Does Foreign Direct Investment Promote Economic Growth? Exploring the Effects of Financial Markets on Linkages. Departmental Working Paper from Department of Economics, Louisiana State University www.people.hbs.edu/lalfaro/fdiandlinkages.pdf Sourced on 10.07.08.

Altenburg, T. & Meyer-Stamer, J. (1999). How to promote clusters, Policy experience from Latin America. In: World Development, Vol. 27, Issue 9, pp. 1693-1713.

Altenburg, T. (2003). Transnational Corporations and the Potential for Developing Complementary SMEs in Developing Countries. In: Robert Kappel, Utz Dornberger, Michaeler Meier an Ute Rietdorf (Eds.) Klein- und Mittelunternehmen in Entwicklungsländern. Die Herausforderungen der Globalisierung. D; Hamburg, pp. 143- 182.

Anderson, D. (1982). Small Industry in developing countries: A discussion of issues. In: World Development, Vol. 10, No. 11, pp. 913-948.

Anyanwu, C. M. (2003). The Role of Central Bank of Nigeria in Enterprises Financing. In: Central Bank of Nigeria Seminar on Small and Medium Industries Equity Investmentnts Scheme (SMIEIS) Publication. CBN Training Centre, Lagos No. 4, pp. 20-32.

Anyanwu, C. M. (2004). Microfinance Institutions in Nigeria: Policy, Practice and Potentials.Paper Presented at the G24 Workshop on "Constraints to Growth in Sub Saharan Africa. Pretoreia, South Africa, Novermber 29-30, 2004.

Aremu, J. A. (2003). An Overview of Foreign Private Investment in Nigeria. In: O.J. Nnanna and C.M. Okafor (eds.). Foreign Private Investment in Nigeria. Proceedings of the Twelfth annual Conference of the Regional Research Units Research Department, CBN 01.09.03 -5.09-03 Kaduna, Nigeria, pp. 39-66.

Ariyo, A. and Jerome, A. (2005). Privatisation in Africa: Lessons from the Ghanaian and Nigerian Experience. In: Wohlmuth, K.; Gutowski, A.; Knedlik, Tobias; Meyn, M.; Ngogang, *S.:* African Development Perspectives Yearbook: Private and Public Sectors: Towards a Balance, in: Wohlmuth, K.; Gutowski, A.; Knedlik, T.; Meyn, M.; Ngogang, S. (eds.), African Development Perspectives Yearbook: Private and Public Sectors: Towards a Balance, LIT, Münster, Hamburg, London 200 pp. 325-350.

Artken, B. & Harrison, A. E. (1999). Do Domestic Firms Benefit from Direct Foreign Investment? Evidence from Venezuela. In: American Economic Review, Vol. 89, pp. 605-618.

Asiodu, P. C. (1967). Industrial Policy and Incentives in Nigeria; Nigerian Institute of Social and Economic Research, Ibadan. NISER Reprint Series No. 44.

Aubert, Jean-Eric (2004). Promotion of Innovation in Developing Countries: A Conceptual Framework World Bank Institute. Paris.

Axelrod, R. (1984). The Evolution of Cooperation. Basic Books, New York.

Baier, S. L., Dwyer, Jr., G. P. & Tamura, R. (2002). How Important Are Capital And Total Factor Productivity for Economic Growth? www.vanderbilt.edu/Econ/faculty/Crucini/tamura.pdf Accessed on 07.07.08 Time 16.30.

Bair J. & Gereffi, G. (2001). Local Clusters in Global Chains: The Causes and sequences of Export Dynamism in Torreon's Blue Jeans Industry. In: World Development, Vol. 29, No. 11, pp. 1885-1903.

Barr, A. M. (1995). The Missing Factor: Entrepreneurial Networks, Enterprises and Economic Growth in Ghana:WPS/95-11 Centre for the Study of African Economies, University of Oxford

Barr, A (1998). Enterprise Performance and the Functional Diversity of Social Capital. Working Paper Series 98-1. Centre for the Study of African Economics. Institute for Economics and Statistics, University of Oxford.

Barr, A. (1999). Do SMEs Networks for growth. In: K. King and S. McGrath (Eds.). Enterprise in Africa: Between poverty and growth, London, Intermediate Technology Publications, pp. 121-131.

Barr, A. (2000). Collective Action and Bilateral Interaction in Ghanaian Entrepreneurial Networks. Working Papers No. 182, UNU World Institute for Development Economics Research, Helsinki.

Basdan, G. T. (1966). Niger Ibos: A Description of the Primitive Life, Customs And Animistic Beliefs etc of the Ibo people of Nigeria. Frank Cass & Co. Ltd.

Bayer, K. (1994). Co-operative small-firm networks as factors in regional development. Occasional paper No. 48, European Free Trade Association affairs department.

Bazan, A. & Schmitz, H. (2000). Social Capital and Export Growth: An Industrial Community in Southern Brazil, IDS Discussion Paper No. 361, IDS Sussex.

Beck, T. Demirgüc-Kunt, A. & Levine, R.(2005). SMEs, Growth, and Poverty. Working Paper 11224, National Bureau of Economic Research, Cambridge.

Becker, G. (1993). Human capital: A theoretical and empirical analysis with special references to education. USA: The University of Chicago Press.

Bekaert, G., Garcia, M. G. P. & Harvey, C. R. (1995). The role of Capital Markets in Economic Growth. Departmento De Economia PUC-RIO; TEXTO;PARA DISCUSSÃO No. 324.

Bénassy-Quéré, A., Fontagné, L .& Lahrèeche-Révll, A. (2001). Exchange-Rate Strategies in the Competition for Attracting Foreign Direct Investment, In: Journal of Japanese and International Economies, Vol. 15, pp. 178-198.

Benton, L. (1992). The emergence of industrial districts in Spain: Industrial restructuring and diverging regional responses. In: F. Pyke and W. Sengenberger (eds.). Industrial district and local economic regeneration, ILO, International Labour Studies. Geneva, pp. 34-48.

Behrman, J & Taubman, P. (1982). Human Capital. In: D. Greenwald (ed.), Encyclopaedia of Economics, McGraw-Hill Book Company, USA, pp. 474-476

Benhabib, J. and Spiegel, M. (1994). The role of human capital in economic development: evidence from aggregate cross-country data. In: Journal of Monetary Economics Vol. 34, pp. 134-173.

Berdegué, J. A. & Escobar, G. (2002). Rural Diversity, Agricultural Innovation Policies and Poverty Reduction. Network Paper No. 122, ODI, Agricultural Research & Extension Network.

Berger, M. (1975). Industrialisation Policies in Nigeria. Weltiforum Verlag, München

Berg, A. & Krueger, A. (2008). Trade, Growth and Poverty - A Selected Survey. In: Paul Collier and Jan Willem Gunning (eds.): Globalisation and Poverty. Edward Elgar Publishing Limited, Cheltenham, UK and Massachusetts, USA.

Beyer, J. & Knight, J. (1989). The role of occupation in the determination of wages, In: Oxford Economic Papers, Vol. 41, issue 1, pp. 595-618.

Biggs Tyler et al, (1995). Technological Capabilities and Learning in Africa Enterprises, World Bank Technical Paper No. 288, Africa Technical Department Series.

Bigsten, A., Collier, P., Dercon, S., Gauthier, B., Gunning, J. W., Isaksson, A. Oduro, A, Oostendorp, R., Pattilo, C., Söderbom, M., Sylvin, M., Teal F., & Zeufack, A. (1999). Investment in Africa's Manufacturing Sector: A Four Country Panel Data Analysis. In: Oxford Bulletin of Economics and Statistics, Vol. 61, Issue 4, pp. 489-512.

Biobaku, S. O.(1973). Sources of Yoruba History, Clarendon Press. Oxford. Blomström, M. & Kokko, A. (1996). How Foreign Investment Affects Host Countries. In: Policy Research Working Paper 1745: The World Bank, International Economics Department, International Trade Division, Washington D.C.

Bloom, David E.& David Canning (2000)."The Health and Wealth of Nations," In: Science, Vol. 287, pp. 1207-1208.

Boehm, U. (1996). Human resource development in African small and micro-enterprises: the role of Apprenticeship. In: Wohlmuth, K. Bass, H. H. Kappel R.; Wauschkuhn M., Regional perspectives on Labour and employment, Africa Development Perspectives Yearbook, yea Book Lit Münster/Hamburg, Vol. 5, pp. 319-333.

Boltho, A. (1996). The assessment: International Competitiveness. In: Oxford Review of Economic Policy, Vol. 12; Issue 3, pp. 1-16.

BPE report, (2006). Shell Nigeria, www.shell.com, under community involvement: Business Development.

Brannen, J. (1992). Combining qualitative and quantitative approaches: an overview. In: Julia Brennen (ed.). Mixing Methods: Qualitative and Quantitative Research. Avebury, Aldershot, Brookfirld USA etc., pp. 3- 37.

Bräutigam. D. (1997). Substituting for State: institutions and industrial development in Eastern Nigeria: In: World Development, Vol. 25, No. 7, pp. 1963-1980.

Bräutigam, D. (1999). Local entrepreneurs, networks and linkages to the global economy in Southeast Asia and Africa Chr. Michelsen Institute Development Studies and Human Rights Working Paper, No. 2.
Bräutigam, D. (2003).Close encounters: Chinese business Networks as Industrial Catalysts in Sub-Saharan Africa, In: African Affairs. Vol. 102 Issue 408, pp.447-467.
Brock, W. A. & Evans, D. S. (1986). The Economics of Small Businesses, Their Role and Regulation in the U.S.A Economy. New York. Holmes and Mier.
Bruce, M. (2000). Schumpeter's entrepreneurs and common's sovereign authority. In: Journal of Economic Issues, September 2000.
Brüderl, J. & Preisendörfer, P. (1998). Network Support and the Success of Newly Founded Business . In: Journal of Small Business Economics. Vol. 10, No. 3, pp. 213-223.
Bulmer, M. (1983). General Introduction. In: Martin Bulmer and Donald P. Warwick (eds.): Social Research in Developing Countries: Survey and Censuses in the Third World. John Wiley & Sons Limited. Chichester. New York, etc. pp.3-24.
Bureau of Public Enterprises; (2006). Nigeria: www.bpeng.org/10/0317731265-632b.asp Accessed on 03.03.2006. 20.13.
Burgess, R. G. (1982). Elements of Sampling in Field Research. In: Robert G. Burgess (ed.): Field Research: a Source book and Field Manual: George Allen & Unwin, London, Boston , Sydney, pp. 75-78.
Burns, A. (1969). History of Nigeria. George Allen and Unwin Ltd. London.
Burt, R. S. (1995). The Social Structure of Competition. In: Nohria, N. and Ecclces, R. (eds.); Networks and Organisations: Structure, Form and action. Harvard Business School Press, Boston, Massachusetts; pp. 57-91.
Burt, R. S. (1992). The Social Structure of Competition. In: Nohria, N. & Eccles, R. G: Networks and Organisation: Structure, Form, and Action, Harvard Business School Press: Boston, MA pp. 57-91.
Butzen, P. Fuss, C. & Philip V. (2002). The Impact of Uncertainty on Investment Plans. BB, Working Paper No. 24.
Bwala, A. B. (1996). Institutional Activities for the Enhancement of Nigeria's Informal Sector Employment. In: Karl Wohlmuth, Hans H. Bass, Robert Kappel and Markus Wauschkuhn (eds.): Regional Perspectives on Labour and Employment. African Development Perspective Yearbook, Vol. 5, pp. 245-250.

Camagni, R., (1991) Local Milieu, Uncertainty and Innovation Networks: Towards a New Dynamic Theory of Economic Space. In: Camagni (ed.), pp. 121-145.

Caniels, M.C. J.& Romijn, H. J. (2003). SME Clusters, Acquisition of Technological Capabilities and Development: Concepts, Practice and Policy Lessons. In: Journal of Industry, Competition and Trade, Vol. 3, No. 3, pp. 187-210.
Caves, R E. (1996). Multinational Enterprises and Economic Analysis 2nd Ed. Cambridge: Cambridge University Press.
Cawthorne, P. (1995)."Of Networks and Markets: The Rise and Fall of a South Indian Town: Tirrupur's Cotton Knitwear Industry" In: World Development. Vol. 23, No 1, pp. 43-56.
CBN, (2002). Selected Social Indicator of Nigeria. Central Bank of Nigeria Annual Report & Statement of Accounts for the Year Ended 31st December 2003. The Central Bank of Nigeria, Abuja
CBN, (2003a). Statistical Bulletin, Financial Statistics Statbull. Vol. 13 part. A 12-31 The Central Bank of Nigeria, Abuja
CBN (2003). Statistical Bulletin–Price Statistics: In: Statbull. Vol., 13 part C. The Central Bank of Nigeria.
CBN, (2004), Statistical Bulletin, Financial Statistics Statbull., Vol. 14 part. C 12-32 The Central Bank of Nigeria, Abuja.
CBN, (2004). Nigeria: Major Economic, Financial and Banking Indicators. Research Department; September 2004, The Central Bank of Nigeria, Abuja
CBN (2005). Central Bank of Nigeria Annual Report for the year ended 31st : The Central Bank of Nigeria. P.. 175.
CBN (2006). Statistical Bulletin, Financial Statistics Statbull. Vol. 17, The Central Bank of Nigeria, Abuja.
CBN (2007). Statistical Bulletin, Financial Statistics Statbull. Vol. 18. The Central Bank of Nigeria, Abuja.
Chamlee, E. (1993). Indigenous African Institutions and Economic Development, In: Cato Journal, Vol. 13, No. 1, pp. 79-99.
Chenery, H. B. & Syrquin, M. (1975). Patterns of Development: 1950-1970, Oxford: Oxford University Press.
Chenery H. B, Robinson, S. and Syrquin, M. (1986). Industrialisation and Growth: a comparative Study, Oxford; Oxford University Press.
Chenery, H., Montek, S. A. Bell, C. L. G., Duloy, J. H. & Jolly, R. (1974). Redistribution with Growth, Oxford University Press, London.
Chete, L. N. (1998). Determinants of Foreign Direct Investment in Nigeria: An Error Correction Specification. In: The Nigerian Economic Society, Vol. 40, No. 1, pp. 1-17
Chong, A. & Calderón, C. (2000). Institutional Quality and Income Distribution. Economic Development and Cultural Change. Vol. 48, No. 4, pp. 761-786.

Coleman, J. S. (1965). Nigeria: Background to Nationalism. University of California Press, Berkeley and Los Angeles.

Coleman, J. S. (1990). The Foundations of Social Theory. Cambridge (Mass.). The BelknapPress.

Cointreau-Levine, S. (1994). "Private sector participation in municipal waste services in developing countries, Volume 1: the formal sector", World Bank Urban Management Programme Discussion Paper 13, Washington D. C.

Cointreau-Levine, S. & Coad, A. (2000). Guidance Pack Private sector participation in municipal solid waste management SKAT 2000Swiss Centre for Development Cooperation in Technology and Management, St. Gallen, Switzerland.

Collier, P. & Gunning, J. W. (1999). Why Has Africa Grown Slowly? In: Journal of Economics Perspectives. Vol. 13, issue 3, pp.3-22.

Congo, Y. (2004). Provision of Sustainable Microfinancial Services to the Poor in very Poor Economies. Evidence from Burkina Faso. In: Karl Wohlmuth, Achim Gutowski, Tobias Knedilk, Mareike Meyn, Samuel Ngogang (Eds). Private and Public Sector Towards a Balance. African Development Perspectives Yearbook, Lit Münster. Vol. 10, pp. 161-181.

Cook, S. (2006). "Structural Change, growth and Poverty Reduction in Asia: Pathways to Inclusive Development". In: Development Policy Review. Vol. 24, No. 1, pp. 51-80.

Cornia, G. A. (1998). Adjustment with a Human Face: Ten Countries Case Studies, Vol.II, Oxford University Press, Oxford co-edited with R. Jolly and F. Stewart

Country Report Asia Pacific, (2007). CACCI, In: Journal of Commerce and Industry. Vol. 2.

Cullison, W. E. (1993). Public Investment and Economic Growth. In: Federal Reserve Bank of Richmond Economic Quarterly, Vol. 79, Issue 4 ttps://www.richmondfed.net/publications/economic_research/economic_quarterly/pdfs/fall1993/cullison.pd

Daniels, L. & Mead, D. C. (1998). The Contribution of Small Enterprises to Household and National Income in Kenya. In: Economic Development Cultural Change. Vol. 47, Issue 1, pp. 45-71.

Danju, D. & Weiss, J. (1997). Manufacturing Performance during Adjustment: Evidence from Nigeria. In: Development Policy Review, Vol. 15, Issue 4, pp. 357-369.

Dasgupta, P. (1988). Trust as commodity, in: Diego Cambetta (ed) marking and breaking cooperative relations, Basil Blackwell, Oxford UK, pp. 49-72.

Dauda, B. (1993). Industrial Policy and The Nigeria Bureaucracy, 1900-1988. In: Elizabeth Eldredge, Toyin Falola, Paul Lovejoy, Donna Maier, and Ann O'Hear (Eds.); African Economic History, Vol. 21, pp. 73-96.

De Long, J. B & Summers, L. H. (1992). Equipment Investment and Economic Growth: How Strong Is the Nexus? www.j-bradford-delong.net/pdf_files/-Brookings_Equipment.pdf Sourced on 10.07.08.

De Long, J. B & Summers, L. H. (1995). Equipment Investment and Economic Growth: www.j-bradford-delong.net/pdf_files/QJE_Equipment. Sourced on 10.07.08.

De Man, A. (2004). The Network Economy: Strategy, Structure and Management. Cheltenham [u.a] : Elgar.

De Soto, H. (1989). The other Path: the Invisible Revolution in the Third World. New York: Harper & Row.

Devarajan, S, Dollar, D. & Holmgren, T. (2001). Overview: In: Shantayanan Devarajan, David, R. Dollar, and Torgny Holmgren (Eds.): Aid & Reform in Africa. The World Bank/IBRD. Washington D.C, pp. 1-41.

Deyo, F. C. (1970). The Political Economy of the New Asian Industrialism: Introduction. In: Frederic C. Deyo (Ed.): The Political Economies of the New Asian Industrialism: pp. 11-12, Cornell University Press, ITHACA and London.

Dike, E. (1997). Structural Adjustment and Small-Scale Industrial Entrepreneurs in South-Eastern Nigeria. UNRISD DP 81.

Dike, V (2008). The state of education in Nigeria and the health of the nation. Available on the internet at www.africaeconomicanalysis.org/

Dillman, B. (2000). State and Private Sector in Algeria: The politics of Rent-Seeking and Failed Development, Boulder, Westview Press.

Dixion, N. (1995). The Organisational Learning Cycle: How we can learn collectively, McGraw-hill, Ottawa.

Dollar, D. & Kraay, A. (2001). Trade, Growth, and Poverty. In: Finance and Development, Vol. 38, No.3.

Dos Santos, T. (1970). The Structure of Dependence. In: The American Economic Review, Vol. 60, No. 2, pp. 231-236.

Dougherty, C. (2002). Introduction to Econometrics, 2nd Edition, Oxford University Press, Oxford New York.

Dunning, J. H. (1988). The eclectic Paradigm of International Production: A Restatement and Some Possible Extensions. In: Journal of International Busines Studies, pp.1-32.

Dunning, J. H. (1998). Multinational Enterprise and the Global Economy, Addison-Wesley, Essex, England.

Dunning J. & Zhang, F. (2007). Foreign Direct Investment and the Locational Competitiveness of Countries UNCTAD, Palais des Nations, Geneva.

Duysters, G., de Man, A. P. & Wildeman, L. (1999). A network approach to alliance management. European Management Journal, 17, 2.

Edozien, E . C. (1966). Linkages, Direct Foreign Investment and Nigeria's Economic Development. Department of Economics, University of Ibadan.

Edquist, C. (1997). Systems of Innovation: Technologies, Institutions and Organisations, Pinter Publishers.

Egbert, H. (2003). Networking and Entrepreneurial Success: A case Study from Tanga, Tanzania. In: Karl Wohlmuth, Achim Gutowski, Tobias Knedlik, Mareike Meyn and Sunita Pitamber (eds.): Afrcan Entrepreneurship and Private Sector Development. African Development Perspectives Yearbook. Vol. 9, pp. 291-309.

Ekpo, A. (1986). Food Dependency and the Nigerian Economy: An ex-post analysis, 1960-80. Nigerian. In: Journal of Economic and Social Studies, 28, 2 July.

Ekwere, F. N. (1993). Some Aspects of the Nigerian Company and Allied Matters Decree, 1990 as They Affect Investors. In: Journal of African Law. Vol. 37, No. 1 pp. 52.

Evans, D.D. & Adler, L. N. (1979). Appropriate Technology for Development. Denver Institute, University of Denver. Boulder, Colo: Westview Pr.

Everhart, S. S. & Sumlinski, M. A. (2001). Trends in Private Investment in Developing Countries Statistics for 1970-2000 and the Quality of Public Investment. International Finance Corporation Discussion Paper No. 44. The World Bank Washington, D. C.

Fafchamps, M. (1994). Industrial Structure and Micro Enterprises in Africa. Journal of Development Areas. Vol. 29, No. 1, pp. 1-30.

Fafchamps, M. (1996). The Enforcement of Commercial Contracts in Ghana. In: World Development. Vol. 24, No. 3, pp. 427-448.

Fage, J.D. (1969). A History of West Africa. An Introductory Survey. The fourth edition of An Introduction to the History of West Africa. Cambridge University Press.

Fagerberg; J. (1996). Technology and Competitiveness. In: Oxford Review of Economic Policy, Vol. 12, No. 3, pp. 39-51.

FAO (1966). Agricultural Development in Nigeria 1965-1980 Food and Agriculture Organisation of The United Nations. Rome.

Federal Bureau of Statistics (2004). Nigeria Federal Office of Statistics Register of Establishment.

Federal Bureau of Statistics (2006). Nigeria Federal Office of Statistics Register of Establishment.

Federal Bureau of Statistics (2007). Nigeria Federal Office of Statistics Register of Establishment.

Felipe, J. (1997). Total Factor Productivity Growth in East Asia: A Critical Survey. EDRC REPORT SERIES NO. 65. Economics and Development Resource Centre. Asian Development Bank, Manila, Philippines.

Fields, G. S., Cichello, P .I., Freije, S., Menendez, M., & Newhouse, D., (2003). Escaping from poverty: Household Income Dynamics in Indonesia, South Africa, Spain, and Venezuela. In: Gary S. Fields and Guy Pfeffermann (eds.): Pathways out of Poverty: Private firms and Economic Mobility in Developing Countries. Kluwer Academic Publishers, pp. 13-34.

Folorunso, B. A & Olusi, J. O. (2005). Effect of Globalisation on Economic Growth in Nigeria. In: European Journal of Economics, Finance and Administrative Sciences, Vol 2, No 1, pp. 5-16.

Forrest, T. (1993). Politics and Economic Development in Nigeria: In: African Modernisation and Development Series.Westview Press, Boulder, San Francisco, Oxford.

Forrest, T. (1994). The advance of African Capital: the growth of Nigerian private enterprise, a paper presented to the workshop on Alternative Development Strategies in Africa. Queen Elizabeth House, University of Oxford, pp. 11-13 December.

Frankel, J. A., Romer, D. Cyrus T. (1996) Trade and Growth in East Asian Countries: Cause and Efffect? NBER Working Paper No. 5732.

Freeman, C. (1987), Technology and Economic Performance: Lessons from Japan, Pinter, London.

Furubotn, E. & Pejovich, S. (1974). Introduction. The New Property Rights Literature. In: E. Furubotn, S. Pejovich (Eds.): The Economics of Property Rights, Cambridge, Mass., (Ballinger Pub. Co.), pp. 1 - 9.

Galeotti, M. (2003). Environment and Economic Growth: Is Technical Change the Key to Decoupling? CLIM – Climate Change Modelling and Policy.

Gelb, A. H. (1986). Adjustment to Windfall Gains: a Comparative Analysis of Oil Exporting Countries. In: P. J. Neary and S. van Wijnbergen (eds.): Natural Resources and the Macroeconomy. Oxford. Basil Blackwell.

Gereffi, G. (1999). International Trade and Industrial Upgrading in the Apparel Commodity Chain, In: Journal of International Economics. Vol. 48, No, 1, pp. 261-264.

Gerry, C. (1978). Petty production and capitalists production in Dakar, the crises of selfemployment . In: World Development, Vol. 9/10, pp. 1147-1158.

Goltzsche, M. (1976). Gesellschaft und Politik bei den Ibo um 1900: Peter Lang Frankfurt/M. Herbert Lang Bern.

Gradstein, M. (2004). Governance and Growth. In: Journal of Development Economics, Vol. 73, issue 2, pp 505-518.

Granovetter, M. (1985). Economic Action and Social Structure: the Problem of Embeddedness. In: American Journal of Sociology, Vol. 91, Issue, 3, pp. 481-510.

Granovetter, M. (1995). Problems of Explanation in Economic Sociolog. In: Nohria, N. and Ecclces, R. (eds.); Networks and Organisations: Structure, Form AND action. Harvard Business School Press, Boston, Massachusetts, pp. 25-56.

Grootaert, C. (1998). Social capital: The missing link? Social Capital Initiative Working Paper No. 3.Washington, DC: World Bank.

Gutkind, P. C. W. (1967). Orientation and research methods in African Urban Studies. In: D. G. Jongman and P. C. W. Gutkind (eds.): Anthropologists in the field. Royal VanGorcum Ltd, pp. 133- 169.

Hall, Robert, and Jones, Chad (1999), "Why Do Some Country Produce so Much More Output Per Worker than Others?", In: Quarterly Journal of Economics. Vol. 114, pp. 83-116.

Hansohm, D. (1992). Small Industry Development in Africa- Lessons from Sudan Bremer Afrika-Studien Bd. 2 Lit Verlage Hamburg, Münster.

Hart, K. (1970). Small Scale Entrepreneurs in Ghana and Development Planning. In: Journal of Developing Studies. Vol. 6, No. 4, pp. 104-120.

Hartwig, E. (1999). "One hand no fit tie bundle" – You can't tie a bundle with one hand only. Economic Self-Help Activities- A Base for Self-Organisation. In: Karl Wohlmuth, Elke Grawert, Markus Wauschkuhn and Achim Gutowscki (eds). African Development Perspectives Yearbook. Lit Verlage Hamburg, Münster. Vol. 7, pp 44-57.

Harvie, C. (2004). East Asian SME Capacity Building, Competitiveness and Market Opportunities in a Global Economy. University of Wollongong Economic Working Paper Series. WP 04-16.

Helleiner, G. K. (1966). Peasant Agriculture, Government, and Economic growth in Nigeria. Homewood, Illinois: Richard Irwin; INC.

Helmboldt, N. E., West, T. & Hardy, B. H. (1988). Private Investment and African Economic Policy. In: Robert J. Berg and Jennifer S. Whitaker (Eds.): Strategies for African Development, A Study for the Committee on African Development Strategies, Sponsored by the Council of Foreign Relations and the Overseas Development Council, pp 331-357, University of California Press, Berkeley, Los Angeles, London.

Henriques, M. & Nelson, R. E. (1997). Using franchise to promote small enterprise development. In: Small Enterprise Development. Vol. 8, No.1, pp. 23-31.

Henry, G. (1990). Practical Sampling. Applied Social Research Methods Series. Vol. 21. Sage Publications; Newbury Park, London, New Delhi.

Henuks , F. J. & Roos, H. (1992). Entrepreneurs in a Changing Business Cultural Context. In J.J.J van Dijck and A. A. I. G. Wentink (eds.). Transnational Business in Europe, Economic and Social Perspectives Tilburg: Tilburg University Press, pp. 4-13.

Herbst, J. & Soludo, C. C. (2001). Aid & Reform in Africa: Lessons from Ten Countries. In: Devarajan, S., Dollar, D. & Holmgren (eds): The World Bank . Washington, D.C, pp. 647-678.

Heunks, F. J. (1998). Innovation, Creativity and Success. In: Small Business Economics, Vol. 10, pp. 263-272.

Hinchcliffe, K. (2002). Public Expenditures on Education in Nigeria: Issues, Estimates and Some Implications. In: African Region Human Development Working Paper Series, World Bank, he World Bank /IBRD; Washington D.C.

Hirschman, A. (1984). Against Parsimony. In: Economic and Philosophy, Vol. 1, pp. 7-21.

Humphrey; J. & Schmitz, H. (2000). Governance and Upgrading: Linking Induustrial Cluster and Global Value Chain Research, Brighton, IDS Working Paper, 120.

Humphrey, J. & Schmitz, H. (2002). How does inserting in global value chains affect upgrading in industrial clusters? IDS, University of Sussex, Brighton BNI 9Re, UK.

Hussain N. M. (2000). Linkages between SMEs and Large Industries for Increased Markets and Trade: An African Perspective, Economic Research Papers No. 53. The African Development Bank Abidjan 01Côte d'Ivoire.

IDS Policy Briefing (2004). Small Firm Clusters; Working to Reduce Poverty, Issue 21, May 2004.

IFC, (2002). International Finance Corporation Project in Nigeria: Finance in Nigeria www.nigeriabusinessinfo.com/ifcfinance-nigeria 2002. Accessed on 12.05.2006 22:35.

IFC, (2005). IFC SME – Capacity Building Facility Themes. Small and Medium Enterprises Development. http//www.ifc.org/ifcext/sme.nsf/Content/CB-Themes Accessed on 29.05.2006.

Ikpeze, N. I. (1991). New Industrial Policies and Perspectives for Manufacturing in Nigeria. In: In: Karl Wohlmuth, Peter Oesterdiekhoff, Robert Kappel. Dirk Hansohm, Barbara Worch, Hans H. Bass, Elke Grawert, Gaby Zdunnek, Jutta Franz, Marlene Conrad and Klaudia, Kleine (eds.): Industrialisation based on Agricultural Development, African Development Perspectives Yearbook. Vol. 2, Muster/Hamburg, Lit, pp. 585-608.

Ikpeze, N. I., Soludo, C. C. and N. N. Elekwa (2004). Nigeria: The political Economy of the Policy Process, Policy Choice and Implementation. In: Charles C, Soludo, Osita Ogbu and Ha-Joon, Chang (eds.). The Politics of Trade and Industrial Policy in Africa: Forced Consensus? International Development Research Centre. Nairobi, Ottawa etc. pp. 341-365.

ILO, (1972). Employment, Income and Equity: A Strategy for Increasing Productive Employment in Kenya, Geneva.

ILO, (1990). Role of Small Scale Industries and Non-Farm Employment, ILO Technology and Employment Branch, Geneva.

ILO, (2005). Jobs and the millennium generation: Working out of poverty. World of Working Magazine No. 55, December, 2005, Geneva.

ILO (2007). Employment and unemployment – Overview and topics - Statistics and databases - What we do: www.ilo.org/global/What_we_do/Statistics/-topics/Employment/langen/index.

IMF, (1995). International Financial Statistics Yearbook, International Monetary Fund, Washington D.C.

IMF, (1997). International Financial Statistics Yearbook, International Monetary Fund, Washington D.C.

IMF, (1999). International Financial Statistics Yearbook, International Monetary Fund, Washington D.C.

IMF, (2001). International Financial Statistics Yearbook, International Monetary Fund, Washington D.C.

IMF, (2002). International Financial Statistics Yearbook, International Monetary Fund, Washington D.C.

IMF, (2003). International Financial Statistics Yearbook, International Monetary Fund, Washington D.C.

IMF, (2004). International Financial Statistics Yearbook, International Monetary Fund, Washington D.C.

IMF, (2005, Dec.). International Financial Statistics Yearbook, International Monetary Fund, Washington D.C.

IMF, (2006, Feb.). International Financial Statistics Yearbook, International Monetary Fund, Washington D.C.

IMF, (2007). International Financial Statistics Yearbook, International Monetary Fund, Washington D.C.

IMF, (2008, Oct.). International Financial Statistics Yearbook, International Monetary Fund, Washington D.C.

Inang, E.E. & Ukpong, G. E. (1993). A Review of Small-Scale Enterprises Credit Delivery Strategies in Nigeria. CBN Economic and Financial Review, Vol. 30, No.4, pp. 249-278.

Jarboe, P. J. (2001). Knowledge Management as an Economic Development Strategy. U.S. Economic Development Administration, Athena Alliance, Washington D.C.

Jerome, A, (2008). Privatization and Enterprise Performance in Nigeria: Case Study of Some Privatized Enterprises. AERC Research Paper 175 African Economic Research Consortium, Nairobi.

Johnson, A. C., Johnson, M. B. & Buse, R. C. (1987). Econometrics: Basic and applied. Macmillan Publishing Company, New York and Collier Macmillan Publishers London.

Juma C, & Yee-Cheong, L. (2005). Innovation: Applying Knowledge in Development UN Millennium Project Task Force on Science, Technology, and Innovation London.

Kajisa, K., Maredia, M. & Boughton, D . (1997). Transformation Versus Stagnation in the Oil Palm Industry: A Comparison Between Malaysia and Nigeria, Staff Paper 97-5 Department of Agricultural Economics Michigan State University East Lansing; Michigan 48824.

Kandori, M. (1992). Social Norms and Community Enforcement; Review of Economic Studies, Vol. 59, pp. 63-80.

Kanter, R. M. (1983). The Change Masters. Corporate Entrepreneurs at Work. GEORGE ALLEN & UNWIN; London, Boson and Sydney.

Kaplinsky, R. (2000). Globalisation and Unequalisation: What can be learned from value chain analysis? In: The Journal of Development Studies. Vol. 37, No. 2, pp. 117-146.

Kaplinsky, R. & Readman. J. (2000). Globalization and Upgrading: What Can (and cannot) be Learned fromInternational Trade Statistics in the Wood Furniture Sector? Mimeo, Brighton, Centre for Research in Innovation Management, University of Brighton and Institute of development Studies, University of Sussex.

Kaplinsky, R. (2001). Learning Networks in the South African Auto Components Industry. Innovation News.

Kaplinsky, R., and J. Readman. (2001). How Can SME Producers Serve Global Markets and Sustain Income Growth? Mimeo, Brighton: University of Brighton and University of Sussex. www.ids.ac.uk/ids/global/valchn.html

Kaplinsky, R. & Readman, J. (2001). Integrating SMEs in global value chains, Towards Partnership for Development. *UNIDO ,Vienna.*

Karlsson, C., &. Westin, L. (1994). Patterns of a Network Economy- An Introduction, in: Johansson, B,; Karlsson, C. & Westin, L. (Eds.): Patterns of a Network Economy, Berlin: Springer-Verlag.

Karlsson, C. & Johansson, B. (2005). Industrial Cluster and Inter-Firm Networks. Edward Elgar publishers: Cheltenham, UK. Northampham, M.A, USA.

Katz, M: Bartsch, U. Malothra, H, & Cuc. M. (2004). Lifting the Oil Curse: Improving Petroleum Revenue Management in Sub-Saharan Africa. International Monetary Fund, Washington D.C.

Kilby, P. (1969). Industrialization in an open Economy: Nigeria 1945-1966. Cambridge at the University Press.

Kilby, P. (1983). The role of Alien Entrepreneurs in Economic Development. In: American Economic Review, Vol. 73, No. 1, pp. 107-111.

Kim, L. (1997). Imitation to Innovation: The Dynamics of Korea's Technological Learning. Boston, Mass. Harvard Business School Press.

Kings, K. (1998). Rethinking small enterprises development: between poverty and growth. Research and Policy issues in Kenya's Small Scale and Jua Kali. www.cespi.it/STOCCHIERO/COOPecASS/KING.pdf

Knack, S. & Keefer, P. (1995). Institutions and Economic performance: Cross-Country Tests Using Alternative Institutional Measures. In: Economics and Politics Vol. 7, No. pp. 207-208.

Knack, S. & Kneefer. P. (1997). Does Social Capital Have Economic Payoff? A Cross-Country Investigation. In: Quarterly Journal of Economics. Vol. 112, No. 4, pp. 1251-1288.

Knedlik, T. (2003). Monetary Policy and Private Sector Development. The case of South Africa. In: Karl Wohlmuth, Achim Gutowski, Tobias Knedlik, Mareike Meyn and Sunita Pitamber (Eds.): African Entrepreneurship and Private Sector Development. African Development Perspectives Yearbook. Vol. 9, pp. 115-138.

Knorringa, P. (1999). "Agra. An Old Cluster Facing the New Competition". In: World Development. Vol. 27, No. 9, pp. 1587-1604.

Kranton, R. E. (1996). Reciprocal Exchange: A self-sustaining System. In: American Economic Review, Vol. 86, pp. 830-851.

Krief, N. (2007). Rebuilding the Identity of Chambers of Commerce and Industry: Reinforcing Legitimacy and effectiveness. In: Anthony F. Buono and Henri Savall (eds.), Socio-Economic Intervention in Organisations: The Intervener-researcher and the SEAM approach to organisational analysis. IAP ISBN 1593116225, p. 171-174.

Kristensen, P. H. (1992). Industrial districts in West Jutland, Denmark. In: F. Pyke and W. Sengenberger (Eds.). Industrial district and local economic regeneration. ILO, International Labour Studies. Geneva, pp. 88-122.

Krugman, P. (1991). Increasing Returns and Economic Geography. In: Journal of Political Economy. Vol. 99, No. 3, pp. 483-499.

Krugell, W. (2005). The Determinant of Foreign Direct Investment in Africa. In: Bernard M. Gilroy, Thomas, Gries and Willem, A, Naudé (Eds.), Multinational Enterprises, Foreign Direct Investment and Growth in Africa. South African Perspectives, pp. 49-71, Physica-Verlag, Heidelberg.

Kumar, K. B. (2003). Education and Technology Adaptation in Small Open Economy: Theory and Evidence. In: Macroeconomic Dynamics. Vol. 7, pp. 586-617.

Lall, S. & Kraemer-Mbula, E. (2005). Industrial Competitiveness in Africa. Lessons from East Africa. ITDG Publishing: Schumacher Centre for Technology and Development, Bourton Hall, Bourton-on-Dunsmore. Warwickshire CV239QZ, UK.

Lall, S. (2001). Competitiveness Indices and Developing Countries: An Economic Evaluation of the Global Competitiveness Report. In: World Development. Vol. 29, No. 9, pp. 1501-1525.

Lam, D. Kin-Kong & Lee, I (1992). Guerrilla Capitalism and the limits of statist theory:compaing the Chinese NICs, In C. Clark and S. Chan eds, The Evolving Pasific Basin in Global Political Economy, London: Lynne Rienner, pp. 107-24.

Landry, R., Amara, N. & Lamari, M. (2001). Does Social Capital Determine Innovation? To What Extent? Paper presented at the 4th International Conference on Technology Policy and Innovation, Curitiba, Brazil, August 28-31, 2000

Langley, K. M. (1968). The External resource factor in Nigeria's economic development. Nigerian Journal of Economic and Social Studies. Vol. 10, No 2, pp. 191-203.

La Porta, R., F. Lopez-de Sil, Shleifer, A. & R. Vishny (1997). Legal determinants of external Finance. In: Journal of Finance. Vol. 52, pp. 1131-50.

Laumann, E. O., Galskeiwicz, L. & Marsden, P. V. (1978). Community Structure as Interorganizational Linkages. In: Annual Review of Sociology. Vol. 4, pp. 455-48 Leach, E. R. (1967). An anthropologist's reflections on a social survey. In: D. G. Jongman and P. C. W. Gutkind (Eds.): Anthropologists in the field. Royal VanGorcum Ltd, pp. 75-88.

Levy, B. (1991). Obstacle to Developing Small and Medium Sized Enterprises: An Empirical Assessment, Working paper 558, Washington, D. C, The World Bank.

Levy, P. S. & Lemeshow, S. (1999). Sampling of Populations. Methods and Applications, Third Edition, Wilsey Series in Probability and Statistics. John Wiley & Sons INC. New York. Chichester etc.

Li, X. & Liu, X. (2005). Foreign Direct Investment and Economic Growth: An Increasingly Endogenous Relationship. In: World Development. Vol. 33, No, 3, pp. 393-407.

Liedholm, C &. Mead, D. C. (1998). The Dynamics of Micro and Small Enterprises in Developing Countries. In: World Development, Vol. 26, No. 1, pp. 61-74.

Livingstone, I. (1996). Small Scale Industry and Employment Creation in Africa. In: Wohlmuth, K et al (Eds). Active Labour and Employment Policies in Africa; African Development Perspectives Yearbook, Vol. IV. Lit Verlag- Münster, Hamburg, pp. 251-267.

Lucas, R. E. Jr. (1988). On the mechanics of economic development. In: Journal of Monetary Economics. Vol. 22, Issue 1 pp. 3-42. 2.

Lucas, R. C. (1993). On the determinants of foreign direct investment: Evidence from east and south-east Asia. In: World Development. Vol. 21, No. 3 pp. 391-406.

Lundvall, B.A. (1992) National Systems of Innovation: Towards a Theory of Innovation and Interactive Learning, London, Pinter

Lyon, F. (2000). Trust, Networks and Norms: The Creation of Social Capital in Agricultural Economies in Ghana. In: World Development. Vol. 28, No. 4, pp. 66681.

Macaulay, S. (1963). Non-contractual relations in business: A preliminary study. In: American Sociological Review. Vol. 28, pp. 55-69.

Mahmoud, D. (2004): Privatization and Poverty Reduction in Nigeria www.odi.org.uk/events/nigeria_2004/mahmoud web paper.pdf

Makanjuola, G. A. (1992). Industrial Technology. In: Muyiwa Awe and A. F. Oluwole (Eds). Nigeria since Independence: the First Twenty-Five Years. Science and Technology, Vol. XI, pp. 293-310.

Maldonado, C. (1995): The Informal Sector: Legalisation or Laissez-faire? In: ILO, International Labour Review. Vol. 134, Issue 6, pp. 705-728.

Marshall, A. (1890. Principles of Economics, London, Macmillian. Mauro, P. (1995). Corruption and Growth. In: The Quarterly Journal of Economics, August pp. 681-712.

Maya, S. (2002). Capacity Building for Technology Transfer in the African Context: Priorities and Strategies United Nations Framework Convention on Climate Change (UNFCC) Mayer, J. (1996). Implications of new trade and endogenous growth theories for diversification policies of commodity-dependent countries. UNCTAD/-OSG/DP/122

McCormick, D. & Pedersen, P. O. (1996). Small Enterprises: Flexibility and Networking in an African Context. Longhorn, Kenya, pp 301-314.

McCormick, D. (1997). Industrial District or Garment Ghetto? Nairo's Mini-Manufacturing, In: M. P. van Dijk, & R. Rabellotti (eds.). Enterprise Clusters and Networks in Developing Countries, Frank Cass, London, pp. 109-130.

McCormick, D. & Ongile, G. (1997). Growth and Barriers to Growth Among Nairobi's Small and Medium-Sized Garment Producers. In: World Development, Vol, 25, No.7, pp. 1095-1100.

McCormick, D. (1998). Enterprise Cluster in Africa: On the way to Industrialisation? IDS Discussion Paper 366, Sussex: IDS.

McPherson, M. A. (1996). Growth of micro and small enterprises in southern Africa. In: Journal of Development Economics. Vol. 48, pp. 253-277.

Mead, D. C. (1994). The Contribution of Small Enterprises to Employment Growth in Southern and Eastern Africa. In: World Development, Vol. 22, No. 12, pp. 1881-1894.

Mead, D.C. (1998). MSEs tackle poverty and growth but in differing proportions. Paper presented at the conference Enterprise in Africa: Between Poverty and Growth, Centre for African Studies, University of Edinburgh, 26–27 May.

Mead, D.C & Liedholm, C. (1998). The dynamics of micro and small enterprises in developing countries. World Development, 26: 61–74.

Meagher, K. (2004). History Matters: Institutional Legacies, Economic Change and Social Networks in Aba's Shoe and Garment Clusters. Centre for Research and Development (CRD), Kano, Nigeria.

Meagher, K. (2005). Social Networks and Economic Ungovernance in African Small Firm Clusters. Queen Elizabeth House, Paper for the QEH 50th Birthday Conference. www.qeh.ox.ac.uk/pdf/qehconf/meagher.pdf source on 23 sept. 2006

Meagher, K. (2006). Social capital, social liabilities, and political capital: Social networks and informal manufacturing in Nigeria. In: African Affairs. Vol. 105 Issue 421, pp. 553-582.

Meek, C. K. (1925). A Sudanese Kingdom. An Ethnographical Study of The Jukun-Speaking Peoples of Nigeria. Negro Universities Press, New York

Meyer-Stamer, J. (1995). Micro-Level Innovations and Competitiveness. World Development, Vol. 23, No. 1, pp. 143-148

Michie, J. (2001). The Impact of Foreign Direct Investment on Human Capital Enhancement in Developing Countries. A Report for the OECD

Mishan, E. J. (1971). The Post war Literature on Externalities: An Interpretative Essay. In: Journal of Economic Literature. Vol. 9, pp. 1-28.

Mitullah, W. V. (1996). Lake Victoria's Nile Perch Fish Cluster: Institutions, Politics and Joint Action, Brighton IDS Working Paper 87.

Moran, T. H. & Pearson, C. S. (1990). Do TRIPS trip up Foreign Direct Investment? An International Business Diplomacy Perspective. In: Cynthia Day Wallace (ed.) Foreign Direct Investment in the 1990s: A new climate inn the third World. Martinus Nijhoff Publishers, Dordorecht, Boston and London pp. 28-60.

Murphy, Kevin M. & Finis Welch (1989). "Recent Trends in Real wages: Evidence from Household Data, " Program in Applied Econometrics Discussion Paper No. 24. University of California, Los Angeles,

Murphy, J. T. (2002). Networks, Trust, and Innovation in Tanzania's manufacturing sector, In: World Development. Vol. 30, No. 4, pp. 591-619.

Musa, E. A. (2000). Privatisation in Africa: The experience of Sudan and Eriteria with an introduction by Eckhard Dittrich: Privatisation- Lessions from Africa. Profession Wissenschaftsedition im Rainer Hampp Verlag, München and Mreing.

Nadvi, K. (1995). Industrial Clusters and Networks: Case Studies of SME Growth and Innovation. Paper commissioned by the Small and Medium Industries Branch UNIDO Small and Medium enterprises programme.

Nadvi, K. (1999). Collective Efficiency and Collective Failure: The Response of the Siakot Surgical Instrument Cluster to Global Quality Pressure. In: World Development, Vol. 27, No.9, pp. 1605-1626.

Nadvi, K. & Halder, G. (2002). Local clusters in global value chains: exploring dynamic linkages between Germany and Pakistan. IDS Working Paper 152, Brighton, Institute of Development Studies, Sussex.

Nadvi, K. & Schmitz, H. (1994). Industrial Cluster in Less Developed Countries: Review of experience and research agenda. Discussion Paper, No 339, Institute of Development Studies, University of Sussex, Brighton.

Nadvi, K. (1995). Industrial Clusters and Networks: Case Studies of SME Growth and Innovation. Paper commissioned by the Small and Medium Industries Branch UNIDO Small and Medium enterprises programme.

Nadiv, K. (1999a). The cutting Edge: Collective Efficiency and International Competitiveness. In: Oxford Development Studies, Vol., 27, No. 1, pp. 81-107.

Nadvi, K. (1999b). Collective Efficiency and Collective Failure: The Response of the Siakot Surgical Instrument Cluster to Global Quality Pressure. In: World Development. Vol. 27, No.9, pp. 1605-1626.

Nadvi. K., & Barrientos, S. (2004). Industrial Clusters and Poverty Reduction: Towards a methodology for poverty and social impact assessment of cluster development initiatives. UNDO Vienna, Austria.

Nafziger, E. W. (1969). The effect of the Nigerian Extended family on Entrepreneurial Activity. In: Economic Development and Cultural Change, Vol. 18, No. 1, pp. 25-33

Nafziger, W. E. (1977). African Capitalism: A Case Study in Nigerian Entrepreneurship.Hoover Institution Press, Stanford, California.

Nair, G. G. (2003). Nurturing Capacity in Developing. From Consensus to Practice Capacity Enhancement Briefs Number 1 The World Bank Institute

NAP, (1997). National Action Programme to Combat Desertification Report; Federal Ministry of Environment, Nigeria.

Naudé, W. & Krugell, W. (2004). Human Resource Development and FDI in Africa. In: Karl Wohlmuth, Achim Gutowski, Tobias Knedilk, Mareike Meyn, Samuel Ngogang (Eds). Private and Public Sector Towards a Balance. African Development Perspectives Yearbook, Lit Münster. Vol. 10, pp. 161-181.

NEEDS, (2004). Nigeria: National Economic Empowerment and Development Strategy, The NEEDs Secretariat, National Planning Commission, Federal Secretariat, Abuja.

Ngahu, C. (1995). Choice of Technology in Small Scale Enterprises. In. Ogbo, O. M., Oyeyinka, B. O. & Mlawa, H. M. (eds). Technology Policy and Practice in Africa. IDRC Books. Nguyen, Thi

Nguyen, P. H. (2003). Foreign Direct Investment and its Contributions to Economic Growth and Poverty Reduction in Vietnam (1986-2001) Peter Lang, Frankfurt am Main s, Berlin, Bern, Bruxelles. New York,

Nijkamp, P. (2003). Entrepreneurship in Modern Network Economy. In: M. W. Danson (Ed.): Debates and Surveys. Regional Studies. Vol. 374 pp. 395-405. www.taylorandfrancis.metapross.com

Niosi, J. et al, (1996). Flexible Innovation : Technological Alliances in Canadian Industry, McGill.

Nnadozie, E. (2002). African Indigenous Entrepreneurship, Determinants of Resurgence and Growth of Igbo Entrepreneurship during the Post-Biafra Period. In: Journal of African Business. Vol. 3. No. 1, pp. 49-80.

Nnadozie, E. (2003). Overview of African Development. In: Emmanuel Nnadozie (Ed.): African Economic Development. Academic Press, Amsterdam, Boston. London etc. pp. 152-154.

Nohria, N. (1995). Introduction. In: Nitin Nohria and Robert G. Eccles (Eds.). Networks and Organisation: structure, form, and action. Harvard Business School Press. Boston, Mass, pp. (1- 22).

North, D. C. (1989). Institutions and Economic Growt: An Historical Introduction. In: World Development. Vol. 17, Issue 9, pp. 1319-1332.

North, D.C. (1990). Institutions, Institutional Change and economic performance, Cambridge: Cambridge University Press.

North, D. C. (1991). Institutions. In: Journal of Economic Perspectives. Vol. 5, No. 1 pp. 97-112.

Northrup, D. (1978). Trade without Rulers: Pre-Colonial Economic Development in South-Eastern Nigeria. Oxford: Clarendon.

Obadan, M. I. (1996). Analytical Framework for Poverty Reduction: Issue of Economic Growth versus other Strategies in Poverty Alleviation in Nigeria, Nigerian Economic Society (NES), Ibadan.

Obadan, M. I. (2002). Poverty Reduction in Nigeria: The Way Forward. In: CBN Economic and Financial Review, Vol. 39 No. 4.

Obiaga, T. I. (1992). Science and Technology Policy for Nigeria: In Muyiwa Awe and A. F. Oluwole (eds). Nigeria Since Independence: the First Twenty-Five Years. Science and Technology Vol. XI pp 14-29.

Okowa, W. (1985). Public Policy and rural-urban distribution of income in Nigeria. In: Claude Ake (ed.): Poltical Economy of Nigeria. Longman London and Lagos.

OECD, (1997). National Innovation System, Paris: OECD Publications.

OECD, (2001). The Well-Being of Nations: The Role of Human and Social Capital. Paris.

Ogbuagu, C. S. A. (1982). The Nigerian Indigenization Policy: Nationalism or Pragmatism? In: African Affairs. Vol. 82, No. 327, pp. 241-266.

Ogu, V. I. (2000). Nigeria Private sector participation and municipal waste management in Benin City, Nigeria. In: Environment and Urbanization. Vol., 12, No 2, pp. 113-117.

Ogujiuba, K. K., Oji, G. O. & Adenuga, A. (2004). Is "Trade" Openness Valid for Nigeria's? Long-Run Growth: A Cointegration Approach? www.ideas.repec.org/p/wpa/wuwpit/0412009.html

Ogun, O. (1995). Nigeria. In: Samuel M. Wangwe (ed.). Exporting Africa: Technology. Trade and Industrialisation in Sub-Saharan Africa. UNU/-INTECH. Institute for New Technologies. Routledge, London and New York, pp. 244-295.

Ohiorhenuan, F. E. (1989). The State and Economic Development in Nigeria Under Military Rule, 1966-79: In Tekena N. Tamuno and J. A. Atanda (eds.); Nigeria Since Independence: The First Twenty-Five Years Vol. IV Government and Public Policy pp. 141-151.

Oladeji, S. I. (1998). Technology policy and the development of small and medium scale enterprises in contemporary Nigeria. In: Technovation, Vol. 18, Issue 2, pp. 125-132.

Olaloku, F. A. (1979). Introduction: A Profile of the Nigerian Economy. In: Olaloku, F. A (ed.): Structure of the Nigerian Economy, The Macmillan Press Ltd. and University of Lagos Press, pp 1-9. Oman, C. (1984). New forms of international investment in developing countries. Development Centre Studies, OECD Paris.

Olorunshola, J. O. (2003). Problems and Prospects of Small and Medium-Scale Industries in Nigeria. In: Seminar on Small and Medium Industries Equity Investments Scheme (SMIEIS). The Central Bank of Nigeria, Central Bank of Nigeria Training Centre, Lagos, publication, No. 4, pp. 34-49.

Olson, M., (1968). The Logic of Collective Action, Cambridge, Mass, Harvard University Press.

Oman, C. (1984). New forms of international investment in developing countries. Development Centre Studies, OECD Paris.

Onah, F. E. (1991). Privatisation and Commercialisation – The Nigerian Experience. In: Karl Wohlmuth, Peter Oesterdiekhoff, Robert Kappel. Dirk Hansohm, Barbara Worch, Hans H. Bass, Elke Grawert, Gaby Zdunnek, Jutta Franz, Marlene Conrad and Klaudia, Kleine (eds.): Industrialisation based on Agricultural Development, African Development Perspectives Yearbook, Münster/Hamburg, Lit. Vol. 2 pp. 619-631.

Oni, B. (1999). The Nigerian University Today and the Challenges of the Twenty First Century. IWIM Working Paper Nr. 60

Onibokun, A. G. & Kumuyi, A. (1996). Urban Poverty in Nigeria. Centre for African Settlement Studies and Development (CASSAD). Publishers, Lagos, Nigeria.

Osoba, A. M. (1991). The Missing Middle- New Chances and Programmes of Developing the small-scale Industries in Nigeria. In: Karl Wohlmuth, Peter Oesterdiekhoff, Robert Kappel. Dirk Hansohm, Barbara Worch, Hans H. Bass, Elke Grawert, Gaby Zdunnek, Jutta Franz, Marlene Conrad and Klaudia, Kleine (eds.): Industrialisation based on Agricultural Development, African Development Perspectives Yearbook, Münster/-Hamburg, Lit. Vol. 2, pp. 529-546.

Ottari, G. D. (1994). Trust, interlinking transactions and Credit in the industrial district. In: Cambridge Journal of Economics, Vol. 18, pp. 529-546.

Oyekanmi, R. (2003). Concepts of Equity Financing and its implication for SMIEIS. In: Seminar on Small and Medium Industries Equity Investments Scheme (SMIEIS). The Central Bank of Nigeria, Central Bank of Nigeria Training Centre. Lagos, Publication, No. 4, pp. 66-84.

Oyelaran-Oyeyinka, B. (1997). Technological Learning in African Industry: A Study of Engineering Firms in Nigeria. In: Science and Public Policy, Vol. 24, No.5, pp. 309-318.

Oyelaran-Oyeyinka, B. (2001). Networks and Linkages in African Manufacturing Cluster: A Nigerian Case Study. The United Nations University, Discussion paper series

Oyelaran-Oyeyinka, B. (2004). Networking, Technical Changes and Industrialisation: The case of Small and Medium Firms in Nigeria. African Technology Policy Studies Network (ATPS). Nairobi, Kenya.

Oyelaran-Oyeyinka, B. (2007). Technological Learning in African Industry: A Study of Engineering Firms in Nigeria. In Science and Public Policy. Vol. 24, No.5, pp. 309-318.

Oxford policy management (2004), Nigeria: Economic Growth Analysis, June.

Parrilli, M. D. (2002). Innovation and competitiveness within the small furniture industry in Nicaragu. In: Meine Peter van Dijk and Henry Sandee (Eds.): Innovation and Small Enterprises in the Third World. Edward Elgar Cheltenham, UK. Northhamption MA. USA.

Pedersen, P. O., Sverrison, A. & van, M. P. Dijk (1994). Flexible Specialisation: The Dynamics of Small-Scale Industries in the South. Intermediate Technology Publications, London.
Pedersen, P. O. (1997). Clusters of Enterprises within Systems of Production and Distribution: Collective Efficiency and Transaction costs. In: M. P. van Dijk, & R. Rabellotti (Eds.): Enterprise Clusters and Networks in Developing Countries, pp (11-29). Frank Cass, London.
Pfeffermann, G. (2001). Poverty Reduction in Developing Countries: The Role of Private Enterprises. In: Finance and Development, vol. 38, No. 2 pp 42-45.
Pietrobelli, C. and R. Rabellotti (2004), Upgrading in Clusters and Value Chains in Latinamerica: The Role of Policies (Sustainable Department Best Practices Series). New York: Inter-American Development Bank.
Pissarides, C. (1997). Learning by trading and the returns to human capital in developing countries. In: The World Bank Economic Review Vol. 11, pp. 17–32.
Porter, M. (1990). The Competitive Advantage of Nations, New York, The Free Press.
Porter, M. (1998). The Clusters and the new Economic of Competition. In: Harvard Business Review, Nov.-Dec., p. 77-90.
Powell, J. W. (2003). Cluster Development Programme in Eastern Nigeria. Business Linkages and Enterprises Support Services Component. Nnewi Light Engineering enterprises cluster. United Nations Industrial Development Organisation Vienna.
Putnam, R. D. (1993). Making democracy work: civic traditions in modern Italy. Princeton University Press, Princeton New Jersey.

Qualmann, R. (2002). Why do(n't) they innovate? Explaining diverse SME adjustment strategies after an external shock. In: M. P. van Dijk, & R. Rabellotti (Eds.): Enterprise Clusters and Networks in Developing Countries, pp (166-186). Frank Cass, London.

Rabellotti, R. (1995). Is there an "industrial district model"? Footwear districts in Italy and Mexico compared. In: World Development. Vol, 23, issue 1, pp. 29-41.
Rabellotti, R. (1997). Footwear Industrial Districts in Italy and Mexico. In: M. P. van Dijk & R. Rabellotti (Eds.): Enterprise Clusters and Networks in Developing Countries, Frank Cass, London, pp. 30-60.
Rabellotti, R. (1999). Recovery of a Mexican Cluster: Devaluation Bonanza or Collective Efficiency? In: World Development. Vol. 27, No. 9, pp, 1571-1585.

Rallet, A. & Torre, A. (1998). On Geography and Technology. Proximity Relations in Localised Innovation Networks. In: M. Steiner (ed.) Clusters and Regional Specialisation: On Geography, Technology, and Networks. European research in regional science, Vol. 8, pp. 41-56.

Ram, R. (1980). Role of education in production: A slightly new approach, In: The Quarterly Journal of Economics. Vol. 95, pp. 365-373.

Ranis, G. (1979). Appropriate Technology: Obstacles and Opportunities. In: Samuel M. Rosenblatt (ed.). Technology and Economic Development: A realistic Perspective. Westview Press/Boulder, Colorado, pp. 23-58.

Razafimahefa, I & Hamori, S. (2005). An Emperical Analysis of FDI Competitiveness in Sub-Saharan Africa and Developing Countries. In: Economics Bulletin, Vol. 6, No. 20, pp. 1-8.

Reichardt, C. S. & Cook, T. D. (1979). Beyond Qualitative Versus Quantitative Methods. In: Thomas D. Cook and Charles S. Reichardt (Eds.): Quantitative and Qualitative Methods in Evaluation Research. Sage Research Progress Series in Evaluation. Vol. 1, pp. 7- 32.

Rodríguez-Clare, A. (2005) Coordination Failures, Clusters and Microeconomic Interventions. Inter-American Development Bank Working Paper No.544.

Romer, P. M. (1986). Increasing Returns and Long-Run Growth. In: Journal of Political Economy. Vol. 94, Issue 5, pp.1002-1037.

Romer, P.M. (1990). Endogenous Technological Change. In: Journal of Political EconomyVol. 98, No. S5: pp. S71-S102.

Romer, P.M. (1993) 'Implementing a National Technology Strategy with Self-organising Industry Investment Boards. In: Brooking Papers on Economic Activity, Vol.2, pp. 345–390.

Romer, D. (2006). Advanced Macroeconomics 3rd Edition McGraw-Hill Inc. New York

Romijn, H. (1999). Technology Support for Small Industries in Developing Countries: From Supply Push to Eightfold-C, Development Studies Working Papers University of Oxford.

Romijn, H.A. (1999): Acquisition of technological capabilities in small firms in developing countries, London: Macmillan.

Rosenfeld, S. (2002). Creating Smart Systems: A Guide to Cluster Strategies in Less Favoured Regions. Mimeo. Regional Technology Strategies Carrborto, North Carolina, USA, for the EC.

Rosenstein-Rodan, P. N. (1943). Problems of Industrialisation of Eastern and South-Eastern Europe. In: The Economic Journal, Vol. 53, No. 210/211, pp. 202-211.

Rushbrook, P., Pugh, M. & Banco, M. (1999). Solid waste landfills in middle- and lower- income countries: A Technical guide to planning, design, and operation. World Bank Technical Paper, No. 426, Washington, D. C.

Sabel, C. F. (1992). Studied trust: Building new forms of Co-operation in a volatile economy. In: Frank Pyke & Werner Sengenberger, (Eds): Industrial districts and local economic regeneration. ILO Publications, (International Institute for Labour), pp. 213-250.

Sackey, H. A. (2007). Private Investment for Structural Transformation and Growth in Africa: Where do Small and Medium-Sized Enterprises Stand?

Sandee, H. (2002). The impact of the crisis on small-scale enterprises in Java, findings from selected case studies. In: M. P., van Dijk, and H. Sandee (Eds.). Innovation and small enterprises in the Third World, pp. 187-222 Edward Elgar, Cheltenham, UK Northampton MA; USA.

Sawyerr, O. O., McGee, J. & Peterson, M. (2003). Perceived Uncertainty and Firm Performance in SMEs: The Role of Personal Networking Activities In: International Small Business Journal. Vol. 21, 3, pp. 269–290.

Schmitz. H. (1982). Growth Constraints on Small-Scale Manufacturing in Developing: a critical review. In: World Development, Vol. 10, No. 6, pp. 429-450.

Schmitz, H. (1992). Industrial districts: Model and reality in Baden-Württemberg, Germany. In: F. Pyke and W. Sengenberger (Eds.). Industrial district and local economic regeneration,In: ILO, International Labour Studies. Geneva pp. 87-121.

Schmitz, H. & Musyck, B. (1994). Industrial Districts in Europe: Policy Lessons for Developing Countries? In: World Development. Vol. 22, No. 6, pp. 889-910.

Schmitz, H. (1995). Collective Efficiency: Growth Path for Small-Scale Industry. In: journal of Development Studies. Vol. 31. Nov. No.4, pp. 529-566.

Schmitz, H. (1997). Collective Efficiency and increasing returns. In: IDS working paper 50, IDS, Sussex.

Schmitz, H. (1998). Responding to Global Competitive Pressure: Local Co-operation and Upgrading in the Sinos Valley, Braszil, IDS Working Paper 82.

Schmitz, H. (1999). Global Competition and Local Cooperation: Success and Failure in the Sinos Valley, Brazil. In: World Development. Vol. 27, No. 9, pp. 1627-1650.

Schmitz, H. & Nadiv, K. (1999). Clustering and Industrialisation: Introduction: In: World Development, Vol. 27, No. 9, pp. 1503-1514.

Schumacher, E.F. (1974). Small is Beautiful: A Study of Economics as if People Mattered. Sphere Books Ltd. 30/32 Gray's Inn Road, LondonWCIX8JL.

Schumpeter, J. (1934). The theory of economic development: an inquiry into profit, capital, interest, and the business cycles. Cambridge, Mass, Harvard University Press.

Schumpeter, J. A. (1968). The Theory of Economic Development: An Inquiry into Profit, Capital, Credit, Interest, and the Business Cycle. Harvard University Press, Cambridge, Massachusetts.

Schneider-Barthold, W. (2001). Das Beschäftigiungspotential des Klein-gewerbes, fuer eine menschenorientierte Entwicklungspolitik". E&Z jg. 42.2001.11, pp. 331-333.

Schotter, A (1981). The Economic Theory of Social Institutions. Cambridge: Cambridge University Press.

Sell, A. (1991). "Einführung in die internationalen Wirtschaftsbeziehungen" De-Gruyer-Lehrbuch ISBN 3-11-012887-X.

Sengenberger, W. & Pyke, F. (1992). Industrial districts and local economic regeneration: Research and Policy issues. In: F. Pyke and W. Sengenberger (eds.). Industrial district and local economic regeneration. International Labour Studies. Geneva. pp. 1-29.

Sethuraman, S. V. (1977). The Urban Informal Sector in Africa: In: ILO, International Labour Review. Vol. 116, No. 3, pp. 343-352.

Shell Nigeria, www.shell.com, under community involvement: Business Development.

Sieber, S. D. (1982). The Integration of Fieldwork and Survey Methods. In: Robert G. Burgess (ed.): Field Research: A Sourcebook and Field Manual. George Allen & Unwin, London, Boston , Sydney, pp. 176-188.

Sik, E. (1966). The History of Black Africa Volume, Akadémiai Kiadó, Budapeast

Singh, A. (1999). Should Africa Promote Stock Market Capitalism? In: Journal of International Development, Vol. 11, pp. 343-365.

Sofo, C. A. & Ali-Akpajiak, Toni.Pyke (2003). Measuring Poverty in Nigeria. In: Oxfam, Working paper series, June.

Söderbom M. & Teal, F. (2002). The Performance of Nigerian Manufacturing Firms: Report on the Nigerian Manufacturing Enterprise Survey 2001, CSAE; University of Oxford, UK.

Söderbom, M. Teal, F. (2003). How can policy towards Manufacturing in Africa Reduce Poverty. In: Karl Wohlmuth, Achim Gutowski, Tobias Knedlik, Mareike, Meyn, Sunita Pitamber, African Enterpreneurship and Private Sector Development. Lit Münster Vol. 9, pp. 29-52.

Soyode, A. (1989). Indigenization: In: Tekena N. Tamuno and J. A. Atanda (Eds.): Nigeria Since Independence: The First Twenty-Five Years Government and Public Policy, Vol. IV, pp. 191-208.

Staley, E. & Morse, R. (1965). Modern Small-Scale Industry for Developing Countries. McGraw-Hall.

Steiner, M. (1998). Clusters and Regional Specialisation – On Geography, Technology and Networks. European Research in Regional Science, Vol. 8.

Steiner, M. & Hartmann, C. (1998). Learning with Clusters. A case study of Upper Styria. In: Steiner, M. (Ed.): Clusters and Regional Specialisation – On geography, Technology and Networks, European Research in Regional Science. Vol. 8, pp. 211-225.

Stewart, F. (1977). Technology and Underdevelopment. London: Macmillan.

Stewart Jr. C. T. & Nihei, Y. (1987). Technology Transfer and Human Factors. D. C. Heath and Company/Lexington, Massachusetts/Toronto.

Street, J. H. (1987). The Institutionalist Theory of Economic Development. In: Journal of Economic Issues. Vol. XXI; No. 4, pp. 1860- 1887.

Strober, M. (1990). Human Capital Theory: implications for HR managers. Industrial Relations, Vol. 29, pp. 214-239.

Stockey, N. (1991). Human capital, product quality and growth. In: Quarterly Journal of Economics, Vol. 106, pp. 587-616.

Sule, E. I.K. (1986). Small Scale Industries in Nigeria: Concepts, Appraisal of Government Policies and Suggested Solutions to identified problems. In: Economic and Financial Review. The Central Bank of Nigeria. Vol. 24, No. 4.

Sundbo, J. (1998). The theory of innovation: entrepreneurs, technology and strategy. Edward Elga Cheltenham.

Sverrisson, A. (1997). Enterprise Networks and Technological Change: Aspects of Light Engineering and Metal Working in Accra. In: Meine Pieter van Dijk and Roberta Rabellotti (eds.), Enterprise Clusters and Networks in Developing Countries. EADI: Book Series 20. FRANK CASS. LONDON.

Talbot, D. A. (1969). Women's Mysteries of a primitive people: The Ibibios of Southern Nigeria. Frank Cass & Co. LTD.

Teece, D. J. (1997). Profiting from technological innovation: Implications for Integration, Collaboration, Licensing and Public Policy. In: David, J. Teece (Ed.): The Competitive Challenge, Strategies for Industrial Innovation and Renewal. Ballinger Publishing Company, Cambridge, Massachusetts, pp. 185-219.

Te Velde, D. W. (2002). Foreign Direct Investment for Development: Policy Challenges for Sub-Saharan African Countries. Overseas Development Institute.

Thomas, G. & Slater, R. (2006). Innovation, agricultural growth and poverty reduction. In: International Journal of Technology and Globalisation, Vol.2, Nos.3/4. pp.278-288.

Tokman, V. E. (1989). Policies for a Heterogeneous Informal Sector in Latin America. In: World Development. Vol. 12, No. 7 pp.1067-1076

Tomori, S. (1979). Agriculture, Forestry and Fishing. In: Olaloku, F. A (Ed.): Structure of the Nigerian Economy. The Macmillan Press Ltd. and University of Lagos Press pp. 10-33.

Torjman, S. & Leviten-Reid, E. (2003). Innovation and Poverty Reduction. Caledon Institute of Social Policy, Ottawa, Ontario, Canada. ISBN 1-55382-068

Trade Policy Review (2005). ww.wexpot.com/profiledwn/Africa/Nigeria.Trade. Profile.pdf. Sourced on 15.03.2009 time 19: 30.

Trigilia, C. (1992). Italian industrial districts: Neither myth nor interlude. In: F. Pyke and W. Sengenberger (Eds.). Industrial district and local economic regeneration,. International Labour Studies. Geneva, pp. 33-47.

Udechukwu, F. N. (2003). Survey of Small and Medium Scale Industries and Their Potentials in Nigeria. In: Seminar on Small and Medium Industries Equity Investments Scheme (SMIEIS). The Central Bank of Nigeria, Central Bank of Nigeria Training Centre. Lagos, Publication, No. 4, pp. 6-18.

Udry, C. (1994). Credit Market: An Empirical Investigation in Northern Nigeria. In: Review of Economic Studies. Vol. 61, pp. 494-526.

UNCED, (1992). Earth Summit Agenda 21, chapter 37: National Mechanism and International Cooperation For Capacity- building in Developing Countries. http://habitat.igc.org/agenda21/a21-37.htm accessed on 12.05.2006, 16:04.

UNCTAD (1995). Technological capacity building and technology partnership. Report of the Workshop on Selected cooperation Aspects for Technological Capacity Building in Developing Countries, Geneva: UNCTAD.

UNCTAD, (1995). Transnational Corporations and Competitiveness. United Nations Conference on Trade and Development. United Nations, New York and Geneva.

UNCTAD, (1998). Transnational Corporations, Employment and the Work place. World Investment Report. United Nations Conference on Trade and Development, United Nations, New York and Geneva.

UNCTAD, (1998a). Promoting and Sustaining SMEs Clusters and Networks for Development. Issues paper by the UNCTAD Secretariat, UNCTAD, Geneva.

UNCTAD (1998b). Report of the expert meeting on the impact of government policy and government/private action in stimulating inter-firm partnerships regarding technology, production and marketing, with particular emphasis on North-South and South-South linkages in promoting technological transfers (know-how, management expertise) and trade for SME development , Geneva: UNCTAD.

UNCTAD, (1999). Foreign Direct Investment and the Challenge of Development World Investment Report. United Nations Conference on Trade and Development, United Nations, New York and Geneva.

UNCTAD, (2000). Enhancing the Competitiveness of SMEs through Linkages. Mimeo. Geneva.

UNCTAD, (2003). FDI Policies for Development: National and International Perspectives. World Investment Report. United Nations Conference on Trade and Development United Nations, New York and Geneva.

UNCTAD, (2004). The Shift Towards Services. World Investment Report. United Nations Conference on Trade and Development, United Nations, New York and Geneva.

UNCTAD, (2004a). Development and Globalisation: Facts and Figures. United Nations Conference on Trade and Development. United Nations, New York and Geneva.

UNCTAD, (2005a). Economic Development in Africa, Rethinking the Role of Foreign Direct Investment. United Nations Conference on Trade and Development, United Nation, New York and Geneva.

UNCTAD, (2005b). Transnational Corporation and Internationalization of R&D. United Nations Conference on Trade and Development, United Nations, New York and Geneva.

UNCTAD, (2006). FDI from Developing and Transition Economies: Implications for Development. World Investment Report. United Nations Conference on Trade and Development, United Nations, New York and Geneva.

UNCTAD, (2007a). The Least Developed Countries Report 2007. Geneva.

UNCTAD, (2007b). Reduce poverty by narrowing technology gap, UNCTAD'S Least Developed Countries report 2007. www.unis.unvienna.org/unis/pressrels/2007/unisous001.html

UNDP, (2002) United Nations Development Programme, Human Development Report Lagos. Nigeria.

UNDP, (2003). United Nations Development Programme, Human Development Report Lagos. Nigeria.

UNDP, (2004). Cultural Liberty in Today's Diverse World. The United Nations Development Programme, New York, USA.

UNDP, (2004). United Nations Development Programme; Human Development Report 2004 Geneva, Switzerland.

UNDP, (2004a): National Millennium Development Goals Report, 2004 Lagos Nigeria.

UNDP, (2005). Human Development Report: International Cooperation at a crossroads. Aids, Trade and Society in an Unequal World. The United Nations Development Programme, New York.

UNDP, (2006). Human Development Report: International Cooperation at a crossroads. Aids, Trade and Society in an Unequal World. The United Nations Development Programme, New York.

UNDP, (1998). United Nations Development Programme, Nigeria Human Development Report, Lagos.

UNDP, (2007/08). Fighting climate change: Human solidarity in a divided World. The United Nations Development Programme, New York, USA

UNESCO, (2010). UNESCO Institute for Statistics. Science and Technology (S&T) data update. Posted on 2010.08.26. 5pm.

UNIDO, (2000). Partnership Programme: Joining Hands with Business to Promote Industrial Development Capacity Building for Private Sector Development in Africa Private Sector Vienna Austria.

UNIDO, (2001). Development of Clusters and Networks of SMEs, The UNIDO Programme, private sector development branch, UNIDO,Vienna, Austria.

UNIDO, (2002). Foreign Direct investor Perceptions in Sub-Saharan Africa, UNIDO Pilot Survey in Ethiopia , Nigeria, Uganda, Republic of Tanzania. UNIDO, Vienna.

UNIDO, (2002). Industrial Development Report 2002-03. Vienna: United Nations.Vargas, M.A. 2001 Local Systems of Innovation in Developing Countries: A Study of Technological Learning in Local Productive Arrangements in Brazil. Paper presented at the DRUID Winter Conference, Aalborg, 16-18 January www.druid.dk.

UNIDO, (2003). Capacity-building for business information networking . The UNIDO Support Programme. SME Branch, United Nations Industrial Development Organisation, Vienna.

UNIDO, (2004). Partnership for Small Enterprise Development. A joint UNIDO and UNDP Production, prepared by Deloitte.

UNIDO, (2007). UNIDO Support to NEPAD Period of Report: July 2006 to June 2007, www.un.org/africa/osaa/reports/2007 sourced on 07.09.08 Time 12.51.

United Nations, (2003). The United Nations Statistical Yearbook, Forty-eighth issue, New York United Nations (2005) The United Nations Statistical Yearbook, Forty-ninth issue, New York

Usoro, E. J. (1977). Government Policies, Politics and Industrial Development Strategy in Nigeria, 1947-1974. In: Teriba, O. and Kayode, M. O. (Eds.), Industrial Development in Nigeria: Patterns, Problem and Prospects, Ibadan University Press.

Uzor, O. O. (2003). Networks and Entrepreneurship Development in Nigeria. In: Karl Wohlmuth, Achim Gutowski, Tobias Knedlik, Mareike Meyn and Sunita Pitamber (Eds.): African Entrepreneurship and Private Sector Development. African Development Perspectives Yearbook. Vol. 9, pp. 311-336.

Uzor, O. O. (2004). Small and Medium Scale Enterprises Cluster Development in South-Eastern Region of Nigeria. IWIM, working paper No. 86.

Uzor, O. O. (2007). 'Oil Palm Production in Nigeria and the Improved Export Chances: The need for Upgrading'. In: Karl Wohlmuth, Mareike Meyn, Tobias Knedilk, Achim Gutowiski, Afeikhena, Jerome, Chicot Eboue, Touna Mama, Alexandre Schoname (Eds.): Africa- Commodity Dependence, Resource Curse and Export Diversification. African Development Perspectives Yearbook, Lit Verlag, Münster, Hamburg. Vol. 12, pp. 273-294.

Uzor, O. O. (2007a). Is Africa really the Loser from Globalisation? The Case of Nigeria. In: H. H. Bass, T. Knedlik, M. Meyn, and M. Wiegand-Kottisch (Eds.), Economic Systems in a Changing World Economy, pp. 429-445.

Uzor, O. O. (2008). Promoting Small and Medium scale Enterprises in Sub-Saharan Africa. The role of Investment and Linkages with Transnational Corperations (TNCs). Paper presented at the 12th General Conference of European Association of Development Institutions (EADI), Working Group 13, 24-28 June 2008, Geneva.

Van Dijk, M. P. (2002). Innovation and small enterprises development examples from Burkina Faso, Ghana and Zimbabwe. In:.Edward Elgar Cheltenham, UK. Northhamption MA. USA.

Van Dijk, M. P. & Sandee, H. (2002). Innovation and small enterprises development in developing countries. In: Meine Peter van Dijk and Henry Sandee (Eds.): Innovation and Small Enterprises in the Third World. Edward Elgar Cheltenham, UK. Northhamption MA. USA.

Van Dijk, M. P. (2003). Innovation and Micro and Small Enterprise Development in Africa. Examples from Burkina Faso, Ghana and Zimbabwe. In: Karl Wohlmuth, Achim Gutowski, Tobias Knedlik, Mareike Meyn and Sunita Pitamber (Eds.): African Entrepreneurship and Private Sector Development. African Development Perspectives Yearbook. Vol. 9, pp. 337-.358.

Veblen, T. (1919). "The place of Science in Modern Civilization and Constitution and other Essays". New York, Huebsch

Vergara, R. (1991). New Growth Models : Literature Review and Elements for a Development Strategy. In: Estudios Publicos, 43.

Veugelers, R. (1991). Locational determinants and the ranking of host countries. An empirical assessment. In: Kyklos. Vol. 44, No. 3, pp. 363-382.

Visser, E. (1997). Significant of Spatial Clustering: External Economics in the Peruvian Small-Scale Clothing Industry. In: M. P. van Dijk, & R. Rabellotti (eds.): Enterprise Clusters and Networks in Developing Countries, Frank Cass, London, pp. 61-92.

Visser, E. (1999). A comparison of Clustered and Dispersed Firms in the Small-Scale Clothing Industry of Lima. In: World Development. Vol. 27, Issue 9 pp. 1553-1570

Warwick, D. P. (1983). On Methodological Integration in Social Research. In: Martin Bulmer and Donald P. Warwick (eds.): Social Research in Developing Countries: Survey and Censuses in the Third World. John Wiley & Sons Limited. Chichester. New York, etc. pp. 275-297.

Watksins, K. (2000). The Oxfam Education Report, Oxfam Great Britain in association with Oxfam International.

Watts, M. & Lubeck, P. (1983). The popular Classes and The Oil Boom: A Political Economy of Rural and Urban Poverty: In: William I. Zartman (Ed.): The Political Economy of Nigeria, Praeger Publishers, pp. 105-144.

Wauschkuhn, M. (1996). Associations in the Informal Sector: Examples from Nigeria. In: Karl Wohlmuth, Hans H. Bass, Robert Kappel and Markus Wauschkuhn (Eds.): Regional Perspectives on Labour and Employment. African Development Perspectives Yearbook, Vol. 5, pp. 335-352.

Weijland, H. (1999). Microenterprise Cluster in Rural Indonesia: Industrial Seedbed and Policy Target. In: World Development. Vol. 27, No. 9, pp, 1515-1530.

Wheeler, D. & Mody, A. (1992). International investment location decisions: The case of U.S. firms. In: Journal of International Economics. Vol. 33, pp 57-76.

WHO, (2000). The World Health Report, Health Systems: Improving Performance World Health Organisation: Geneva, Switzerland.

WHO, (2002). The World Health Report,Reducing Risks, Promoting Healthy life, World Health Organisation: Geneva, Switzerland.

WHO, (2003). The World Health Report Shaping the Feature, World Health Organisation: Geneva, Switzerland.

Willer, H. (1996). Small and Medium Scale Industries in Nigeria: Employment effects of SAP and Personnel Policies: In: Karl Wohlmuth, Hans H. Bass, Robert Kappel and Markus Wauschkuhn (Eds.): Regional Perspectives on Labour and Employment. African Development Perspectives Yearbook. Vol. 5, pp 213-230.

Williamson, O. (1985). Economic Institution of Capitalism, New York: Free Press

Wohlmuth, K. (1991). Industrialisation based on Agricultural Development. An Introduction. In: Karl Wohlmuth, Peter Oesterdiekhoff, Robert Kappel. Dirk Hansohm, Barbara Worch, Hans H. Bass, Elke Grawert, Gaby Zdunnek, Jutta Franz, Marlene Conrad and Klaudia, Kleine (eds.): Industrialisation based on Agricultural Development, African Development Perspectives Yearbook, Vol. 2 Münster/Hamburg, Lit, pp. 3-29.

Wohlmuth, K. (1999). Global Competition and Asian Economic Development – some Neo-Schumpeterian Approaches and their Relevance, in: Berichte aus dem Weltwirtschaftlichen Colloquium der Unversität Bremen, Nr. 63.

Wohlmuth, K. (2004). Capacity Building and Private Sector Development: An Introduction. In: Karl Wohlmuth, Achim Gutowski, Tobias Knedilk, Mareike Meyn, Samuel Ngogang (Eds), Private and Public Sectors-Towards a Balance. African Development Perspectives Yearbook, Lit Münster. Vol. 10, pp. 161-181.

Wohlmuth et al, (2007). Africa Commodity Dependence, Resource Curse and Export Diversification. Karl Wohlmuth, Mareike Meyn, Tobias Knedlik, Achim Gutowski, Afeikhena, Jerome, Chicot Eboue, Touna Mama, Alexandre Schoname (Eds.), African Development Perspectives Yearbook, Lit Verlag, Muester, Hamburg, Vol. 12.

Wolfe, D. (2002). Social Capital and Cluster Development in Learning Regions. In: J. A. Holbrook & D. Wolfe (Eds.), Knowledge, Clusters and Regional Innovation: Economic Development in Canada Montreal and Kingston, London, Ithaca: School of Policy Studies, Queens University, pp. 11-38.

Woodcock, M. (1998). Social capital and economic development: Toward a theoretical synthesis and policy framework. In: Journal of Theory and Society. Vol. 27, No. 2, pp. 151-208.

World Bank, (1995a). Nigeria. A diagnostic review of the small and medium enterprise sector. Industrial and Energy Division. West Central Africa Department, World Bank, Washington D. C: The IBRD/The Work Bank.

World Bank, (1997). World Development Indicators. The World Bank/IBRD; Washington D.C

World Bank, (1998). World Development Indicators, The World Bank /IBRD; Washington D.C

World Bank, (1999). World Development Indicators, The World Bank /IBRD; Washington D.C

World Bank, (2000). World Development Indicators, The World Bank/IBRD; Washington D.C

World Bank, (2001). World Development Indicators. The World Bank /IBRD; Washington D.C

World Bank, (2002). World Development Indicators, The World Bank /IBRD; Washington D.C

World Bank,(2003). World Development Indicators, The World Bank /IBRD; Washington D.C
World Bank, (2004). World Development Indicators, The World Bank /IBRD; Washington D.C
World Bank, (2005). World Development Indicators, The World Bank /IBRD; Washington D.C
World Bank, (2006). World Development Indicators, The World Bank /IBRD; Washington D.C
World Bank, (2007). World Development Indicators, The World Bank /IBRD; Washington D.C
World Bank, (2008). World Development Indicators, The World Bank/IBRD; Washington D.C
World Bank, (1981). World Development Report, The World Bank /IBRD; Washington D.C
World Bank, (1982). World Development Report, The World Bank /IBRD; Washington D.C
World Bank, (1984). World Development Report, The World Bank /IBRD; Washington D.C
World Bank, (1987). World Development Report, The World Bank /IBRD; Washington D.C
World Bank, (1990). World Development Report, The World Bank /IBRD; Washington D.C
World Bank, (1992). World Development Report, Development and Environment The World Bank /IBRD; Washington D.C.
World Bank, (1993). World Development Report, Investing in Health. The World Bank /IBRD; Washington D.C.
World Bank, (1994). Infrastructure for Development. World Development Report The World Bank, Washington D. C.: The BRD/The World Bank
World Bank, (1995). World Development Report, Workers in an Integrating World. The World Bank /IBRD. Washington D.C
World Bank, (1996). World Development Report, From Plan to Market. The World Bank /IBRD; Washington D.C
World Bank, (1997). "Social capital: the missing link?" in cxpanding the Measures of Wealth: Indicators of Environmental Sustainable Development. The World Bank/IBRD; Washington, D. C.
World Bank (1997a). A World Bank Country Study: Malaysia—Enterprise Training, Technology, and Productivity, Washington, D.C.: IBRD/World Bank.
World Bank (1997b). World Development Report. The State in a Changing World. The World Bank /IBRD; Washington D.C

World Bank, (2000). The SME Capacity Building Facility. In: SME FACTS World Bank Group Small and Medium Enterprises Initiatives. Vol. 1, No.5. The World Bank, Washington D.C.: The IBRD/The World Bank

World Bank, (2000/01). World Development Report, Attacking Poverty. The World Bank /IBRD; Washington D.C

World Bank, (2002). World Development Report, Building Institutions for Markets. The World Bank /IBRD; Washington D.C. World Bank, World Bank Development Data, Summary of Education Profile, www.devdata.worldbank.org/edstats/SummaryEducationProfiles/Co Accessed 01 April 2006

World Bank, (2002a). Results of the Nigeria Firm Survey - Regional Program on Enterprises Development African Region The World Bank, Washington D.C.: The IBRD/The World Bank.

World Bank, (2003). Sustainable Development in a Dynamic World. World Development Report. The World Bank, Washington D.C.: The IBRD/-The World Bank

World Bank, (2004). World Development Report, Making Service Work for Poor People. The World Bank /IBRD; Washington D.C

World Bank, (2005). A Better Investment Climate for Everyone. World Development Report, The World Bank, Washington D.C.: The IBRD/The World Bank.

World Bank, (2006). World Development Report, Equity and Development. The World Bank/IBRD; Washington D.C.

World Bank, (2008). World Development Report: Agriculture for Development. The World Bank/IBRD; Washington D.C.

Yu, T. Fu-Lai, (1993). Entrepreneurship and Economic Development in Hong Kong. Routledge, London and New York

Yusuf, et al, (2003). Innovative East Asia: The Future of Growth. The World Bank Washington, D. C. A Co-publication of the World Bank and Oxford University Press

Zabel, M., Schneider, R. Wagner, T., Adegbie, A., de Cries, U, & Kolonic, S. (2001). Quaternary Climatic changes in Central Africa as inferred from ternigeous input to the Niger. In: Quat Res, Vol. 56, pp. 207-217.

Zak, P. J. (2001). Institutions, Property Rights, and Growth. The Gruter Institute Working Papers on Law, Economics, and Evolutionary Biology, Vol. 2, Issue 1 Article 2.

Zartman, W. & Schatz, S. (1983). Introduction. In: Zartman W. I. (Ed.): The Political Economy of Nigeria, Praeger Publishers, pp. 1-24.

Zelditch, M. Jr, (1982). Some Methodological Problems of Field Studies. In: Robert G. Burgess (Ed.): Field Research: A Sourcebook and Field Manual. George Allen & Unwin, London, Boston , Sydney, pp. 168-175.

Appendix

Appendix 1: Map of Nigeria

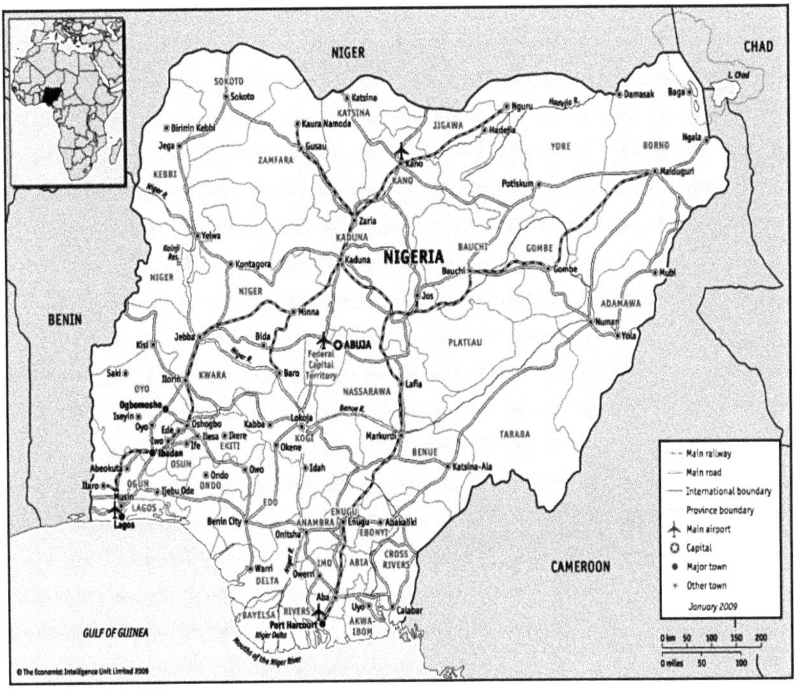

Source: The Economist: Country Profile - Main report: January 1st 2009

Appendix 2: Map of Research Area

Source: Derived fron Appendix 1by the Author

Appendix 3: Governance and Development

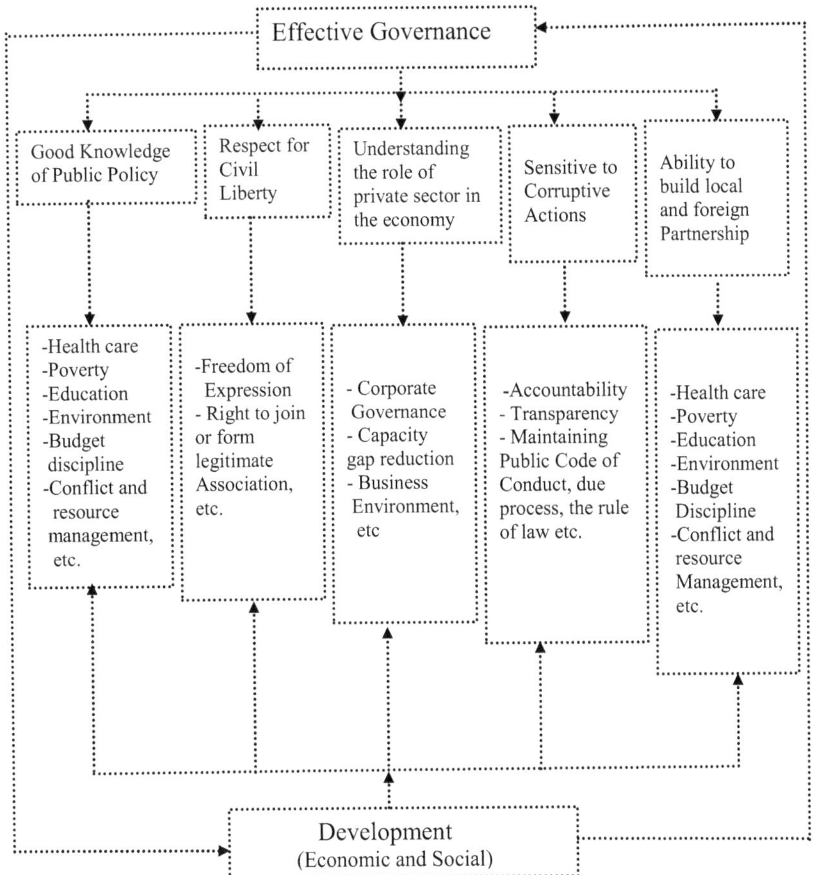

Source: Author's compilation from different literature on Development Studies

Appendix 4: Evalutation of Cluster Performance

Appendix 4.1: Calculation of arithmetic mean for monthly production output per worker and enterprises employment potential (EEP) in Clustered small scale footwear industry

Sample No.	No. of Labour (Xi)	NMPO in pairs (Yi)	NMPO per Worker in pairs (Y_1i)	No. of Labour (Xi′)	SPO in pairs (Yi′)	SPO per Worker in Pairs (Y_2i)
1	3	5,000	1,666.67	4	7,000	1,750.00
2	2	2,500	1,250.00	2	3,400	1,700.00
3	3	7,000	2,333.33	5	12, 000	2,400.00
4	2	200*	100.00	2	280	140.00
5	3	250*	83.33	5	1,200	240.00
6	2	2,800	1400.00	3	4,000	1,333.33
7	1	130*	130.00	2	300	150.00
8	1	100*	100.00	3	380	126.67
9	1	1,500	1,500.00	2	2,600	1,300.00
10	2	2,400	1,200.00	3	3,800	1,266.67
11	1	80*	80.00	2	220	110.00
12	3	4,800	1,600.00	5	8,200	1,640.00
13	1	1,000	1,000.00	2	2,500	1,250.00
14	2	2,500	1,250.00	3	3,800	1,266.67
15	1	1,400	1,400.00	2	2,300	1,150.00
16	1	1,200	1.200.00	2	2,300	1,150.00
17	2	2,000	1,000.00	3	3,500	1,166.67
18	1	110*	110.00	2	260	130.00
19	1	90*	90.00	2	220	110.00
20	3	4500	1,500.00	4	5,500	1,375.00
21	1	1400	1,400.00	2	2,500	1,250.00
22	1	1500	1,500.00	2	2,800	1,400.00
23	2	2400	1,200.00	3	5,000	1,666.67
24	1	100*	100.00	2	240	120.00
25	3	5000	1,666.67	4	7500	1,875.00
26	2	2800	1,400.00	3	4500	1,500.00
27	1	130*	130.00	2	280	140.00
28	3	250*	83.33	4	380	95.00
29	4	4500	1,125.00	6	7500	1,250.00
30	3	5000	1,666.67	6	8500	1,416.67
31	4	7500	1,875.00	5	8500	1,700.00
32	1	110*	110.00	2	300	150.00

Note: NMPO per worker (Yi') = NMPO (Yi)/No. of Labour (Xi); SMPO per worker (Yi'²) = SMPO (Yi²)/No. of Labour(XI') EEP= Arithmetic mean of total labour intake divided by total number investigative sample multiply by 100.

Key: * =Data for men shoes; EEP = Enterprises Employment Potential; NMO = Normal Monthly Production Output; SMPO= Seasonal Monthly Production Output; AM= Arithmetic Mean; TL= Total Labour; OP=Output;

Source: Author's field survey; Calculation by the Author

Appendix 4:1 Continues

	No. of Labour (Xi)	NMPO in pairs (Yi)	NMPO per Worker in pairs (Y_1i)	No. of Labour (Xi′)	SPO in pairs (Yi′)	SPO per Worker in Pairs (Y_2i)
33	2	200*	100.00	3	350	116.67
34	1	1400	1,400.00	3	4500	1,500.00
35	3	7000	2,333.33	5	9500	1,900.00
36	2	2500	1,250.00	3	4800	1,600.00
Total	70	81,350.00	36,308.33	113	130,880.00	37,410.02
AM of TL&OP	$\bar{X}=\frac{1}{n}\sum_{i=1}^{n}Xi$ =70/36 = 1.9444		$\bar{Y}=\frac{1}{n}\sum_{i=1}^{n}Y_1i$	$\bar{X}'=\frac{1}{n}\sum_{i=1}^{n}Xi'$ = 113/36 = 3.1389		$\bar{Y}=\frac{1}{n}\sum_{i=1}^{n}Y_2i$
AM of OP per Worker			=36308.33.00/36 = 1008.5647			= 37,410.02/36 = 1039.1672
EEP	1.9444/36 *100 =5.4011%			3.1389/36 *100 = 8.7192%		

Note: NMPO per worker (Yi') = NMPO (Yi)/No. of Labour (Xi); SMPO per worker (Yi'²) = SMPO (Yi²)/No. of Labour (XI') EEP= Arithmetic mean of total labour intake divided by total number investigative sample multiply by 100.

Source: Own field survey; Calculation by the Author

Appendix 4.1a: Calculation of Standard Deviation (SD) of the production output per worker in clustered small scale footwear industry

SD for normal monthly production output per worker

$$\sigma_X^2 = \frac{1}{n}\sum_{i=1}^{n}(Y_{1i} - \bar{Y})^2 \qquad \sigma_X = \sqrt{\frac{1}{n}\sum_{i=1}^{n}(Y_{1i} - \bar{Y})^2}$$

$$\sigma_X = \sqrt{\frac{1}{36}\sum_{i=1}^{36}(Y_{1i} - 1008.5647)^2}$$

= 707.8123

SD for seasonal monthly production output per worker

$$\sigma_X = \sqrt{\frac{1}{n}\sum_{i=1}^{n}(Y_{1i} - \bar{Y})^2} \quad \sigma_X = \sqrt{\frac{1}{36}\sum_{i=1}^{36}(Y_{1i} - 1039.1672)^2}$$

= 692.32480

Appendix 4.2: Calculation of arithmetic mean for the gross sales per worker in Clustered small scale footwear industry

Sample No.	Price Range (Po)	Mid Price Range (Pi)	NMGS per worker (Zi)	SMGS per worker (Zi')
1	200-600	400	666,668.00	700,000.00
2	170-350	260	325,000.00	442,000.00
3	200-700	450	1,049,998.50	1,080,000.00
4	2,200-3,000*	2,600	260,000.00	364,000.00
5	900-1,200*	1,050	87,496.50	252,000.00
6	250-500	375	525,000.00	499,987.50
7	950-2,500*	1,725	224,250.00	525,000.00
8	2,000-3,500*	2,750	275,000.00	348,342.50
9	250-500	375	562,500.00	487,500.00
10	200-600	400	480,000.00	506,668.00
11	900-1,500*	1,200	96,000.00	132,000.00
12	180-400	290	464,000.00	475,600.00
13	250-700	475	475,000.00	593,750.00
14	200-600	400	500,000.00	506,668.00
15	200-700	450	630,000.00	517,500.00
16	250-600	425	510,000.00	488,780.00
17	250-650	450	450,000.00	525,000.50
18	1,500-2,500*	2,000	220,000.00	260,000.00
19	1,800-2,000*	1,900	171,000.00	209,000.00
20	170-400	285	427,500.00	391,875.00
21	170-350	260	364,000.00	325,000.00
22	180-300	240	360,000.00	336,000.00
23	170-400	285	342,000.00	475,000.95
24	2,400-3,500*	2,950	295,000.00	354,000.00
25	300-600	450	75001.50	843750.00
26	200-600	400	560000.00	600000.00
27	1,500-3,500	2500	325000.00	385000.00
28	2,500-3,000	2750	229157.50	261250.00
29	350-750	550	618750.00	687500.00
30	250-500	375	625001.50	531251.25
31	350-800	550	1031250.00	935000.00
32	2500-3000	250	247500.00	337500.00

Note:

$$\text{NMGS per worker}(z) = \text{Av.Price}(P_i) \times \text{NMPO per worker}(Y_{1i})$$

$$\text{SMGS per worker}(z_i') = \text{Av.Price}(P_i) \times \text{SMPO per worker}(Y_{2i})$$

Key : * =Data for men shoes Med Price= median Price Rang; NMGS = Normal Monthly Gross Sales; SMGS= Seasonal Monthly Gross Sales; AMGNS = Average Normal Monthly Gross Sales; ASMGS= Average Seasonal Monthly Gross Sales; Min. = Minimum; Maxi. = Maximum.

Source: Author's field survey; Calculation by the Author

Appendix 4.2: Continues

Sample No.	Price Range (Po)	Mid Price Range (Pi)	NMGS per worker (Zi)	SMGS per worker (Zi')
33	1500-3500	2500	250000.00	291675.00
34	400-600	500	700000.00	750000.00
35	450-700	575	1341664.75	1092500.00
36	400-600	500	625000.00	800000.00
Total			16388738.00	18311078.07
ANMGS Per Worker			$\bar{Z}_1 = \frac{1}{n}\sum_{i=1}^{n} Zi$ = 16388738.25/36 = 455242.7	$\bar{Z}_1' = \frac{1}{n}\sum_{i=1}^{n} Zi'$
ASMGS Per Worker				= 18311078.07/36 =508641.6
Price Range		Min.= 170 Max.= 3,500		

Note:

$$\text{NMGS per worker}(z) = \text{Av.Price}(P_i) \times \text{NMPO per worker}(Y_{1i})$$

$$\text{SMGS per worker}(z_i') = \text{Av.Price}(P_i) \times \text{SMPO per worker}(Y_{2i})$$

Key: * = Data for men shoes Med Price= median Price Rang; NMGS = Normal Monthly Gross Sales;

SMGS= Seasonal Monthly Gross Sales; AMGNS = Average Normal Monthly Gross Sales; ASMGS= Average Seasonal Monthly Gross Sales; Min. = Minimum; Maxi. = Maximum.

Source: Author's field survey; Calculation by the Author

Appendix 4.2a: Calculation Standard Deviation (SD) of the monthly sales per worker

SD for normal monthly production output per worker :

$$\sigma_X^2 = \frac{1}{n}\sum_{i=1}^{n}(Z_{1i} - \bar{Z}_1)^2$$

$$\sigma_X = \sqrt{\frac{1}{n}\sum_{i=1}^{n}(Z_{1i} - \bar{Z}_1)^2}$$

$$\sigma_X = \sqrt{\frac{1}{36}\sum_{i=1}^{36}(Z_{1i} - 455242.7)^2}$$

$$= 273611.635$$

SD for seasonal monthly production output per worker

$$\sigma_X^2 = \frac{1}{n}\sum_{i=1}^{n}(Z_{1i} - \bar{Z}_1)^2$$

$$\sigma_X = \sqrt{\frac{1}{n}\sum_{i=1}^{n}(Z_{1i} - \bar{Z}_1)^2}$$

$$\sigma_X = \sqrt{\frac{1}{36}\sum_{i=1}^{36}(Z_{1i} - 508641.6)^2}$$

$$= 230363.418$$

Appendix 4.3: Calculation of arithmetic mean for monthly production output per worker and enterprises employment potential (EEP) in dispersed small scale footwear industry

Sample No.	No. of Labour (Xi)	NMPO (Yi)	NMPO per worker (Y_1i)	No. of Labour (Xi')	SMPO (Yi')	SMPO per Worker (Y_2i)
1	1	800	800	1	900	900
2	1	750	750	2	1,600	800
3	2	1,500	750	3	2,700	900
4	1	850	850	3	3,000	1,000
5	1	700	700	2	1,500	750
6	3	3,500	1,166.67	5	6,300	1,260
7	2	1,800	900	3	3,700	1,233.33
8	1	900	900	1	1,100	1,100
9	1	850	850	2	2,400	1,200
10	1	700	700	2	1,700	850
11	2	150*	75*	3	360*	120*
12	1	60*	60*	2	150*	75*
13	1	70*	70*	2	120*	100*
14	1	60*	60*	2	200*	80*
15	1	70*	70*	1	100*	100*
16	2	1,600	800	3	2,800	933.33
17	1	850	850	2	1,800	900
18	2	180*	90*	2	200*	100
19	2	1,700	850	2	2,200	1,100
20	1	800	800	2	1,400	700
21	1	750	750	1	900	900
22	2	1,600	800	3	2,800	933
23	1	70*	70*	2	200*	100*
24	2	150*	75*	3	360*	100*
25	2	1,400	700	3	2500	833.33
26	1	900	900	1	900	900
27	2	1,500	750	3	2,500	833.33
28	1	800	800	2	1,500	750
29	1	75	75	2	160*	80
30	3	3,000	1,000	5	6,500	1,300
31	1	60	60	2	150*	75
32	1	70	70	2	120*	60

Note: NMPO per worker (Yi') = NMPO (Yi)/No. of Labour (Xi) SMPO per worker (Yi'^{2}) = SMPO (Yi^2)/No. of Labour (Xi')

Key: *= Data for men shoes; EEP = Enterprises Employment Potential; NMPO = Normal Monthly Production Output; SMPO= Seasonal Monthly Production Output; AM= Arithmetic Mean; TL= Total Labour; OP=Output;

Source: Author's field survey; Calculation by the Author

Appendix 4.3: Continues

33	2	150	75	3	220*	73.33
34	1	900	900	3	2500	833.33
35	2	1500	750	4	5000	1250
36	2	1800	900	5	7000	1400
Total			20766.67			24623.31
AM of TL &OP	$\bar{X}=\frac{1}{n}\sum_{i=1}^{n}Xi$ = 53/36 = 1.472			$\bar{X}'=\frac{1}{n}\sum_{i=1}^{n}Xi'$ = 89/36 =2.472		
AM of OP per Worker			$\bar{Y}=\frac{1}{n}\sum_{i=1}^{n}Yi'$ = 20766.67/36 = 576.8519			$\bar{Y}'=\frac{1}{n}\sum_{i=1}^{n}Y_2i'$ = 24623.31/36 = 683.9808
EEP	1.472/36 x100 =4.09%			2.472/36 x 100 = 6.87		

Note: NMPO per worker (Yi') = NMPO (Yi)/No. of Labour (Xi) SMPO per worker (Yi'²) = SMPO (Yi²)/No. of Labour (Xi')

Key: *= Data for men shoes; EEP = Enterprises Employment Potential; NMPO = Normal Monthly Production Output; SMPO= Seasonal Monthly Production Output; AM= Arithmetic Mean; TL= Total Labour; OP=Output;

Source: Author's field survey; Calculation by the Author

Appendix 4.3a: Calculation of Standard Deviation (SD) for the monthly production output in dispersed small scale footwear Industry

$$\sigma_X^2 = \frac{1}{n}\sum_{i=1}^{n}(Y_{1i} - \bar{Y}_1)^2$$

$$\sigma_X = \sqrt{\frac{1}{n}\sum_{i=1}^{n}(Y_{1i} - \bar{Y}_1)^2}$$

$$\sigma_X = \sqrt{\frac{1}{36}\sum_{i=1}^{36}(Y_{1i} - 576.8516)^2}$$

$$= 342.84$$

SD for seasonal monthly production output per worker

$$\sigma_X^2 = \frac{1}{n}\sum_{i=1}^{n}(Y_{1i} - \bar{Y}_1)^2$$

$$\sigma_X = \sqrt{\frac{1}{n}\sum_{i=1}^{n}(Y_{1i} - \bar{Y}_1)^2}$$

$$\sigma_X = \sqrt{\frac{1}{36}\sum_{i=1}^{36}(Y_{1i} - 683.98)^2}$$

$$= 546.38$$

Appendix 4.4: Calculation of the arithmetic mean for gross sales per worker in dispersed small scale footwear industry

Sample No.	Price Range (P_0)	Av price (P_i)	NMGS per worker (Z_i)	SMGS per worker (Z_i')
1	250-750	500	400,000	450,000
2	200-700	450	337,500	360,000
3	300-850	575	431,250	517,500
4	400-700	550	467,500	550,000
5	300-650	475	332,500	356,250
6	200-850	525	612,501.75	661,500
7	300-750	525	472,500	647,498.25
8	400-700	550	495,000	605,000
9	350-700	525	446,250	630,000
10	400-600	500	350,000	425,000
11	1,500-3,000	2,250*	168,750	270,000
12	1,500-2,000	1,750*	105,000	131,250
13	2,000-2,500	2,250*	157,500	225,000
14	2,500-3,000	2,750*	165,000	220,000
15	2,200-3,000	2,600*	182,000	260,000
16	250-700	475	380,000	443,331.75
17	200-750	475	403,750	427,500
18	2,000-3,500	2,750*	247,500	275,000
19	200-750	475	403,750	522,500
20	200-800	500	400,000	350,000
21	300-700	500	375,000	450,000
22	250-700	475	380,000	443,331.75
23	1,500-2,000	1,750*	122,500	175,000
24	1,500-2,500	2,000*	150,000	180,000
25	200-700	450	315,000	374,998.50
26	250-750	500	450,000	450,000
27	300-850	575	431,250	479,164.75
28	250-750	500	400,000	375,000
29	1,500-3,500	2,500	187,500	200,000
30	400-700	550	550,000	715,000
31	1,500-2,500	2,000	120,000	150,000
32	2,000-3,500	2,750	192,500	165,000

Note:

$$\text{NMGS per worker}(z) = \text{Av.Price}(P_i) \times \text{NMPO per worker}(Y_{1i})$$

$$\text{SMGS per worker}(z_i') = \text{Av.Price}(P_i) \times \text{SMPO per worker}(Y_{2i})$$

Key: * = Data for men shoes Av. Price= Average Price; NMGS = Normal Monthly Gross Sales; SMGS = Seasonal Monthly Gross Sales; AMGNS = Average Normal Monthly Gross Sales; AMGSS= Average Monthly Gross Seasonal Sales

Source: Author's field survey; Calculation by the Author

Appendix 4.4: Continues

Sample No.	Price Range (P_0)	Av price (P_i)	NMGS per worker (Z_i)	SMGS per worker (Z_i')
33	2500-3000	2750	206250	201657.5
34	250-700	475	427500	395831
35	200-800	500	375000	625000
36	300-800	550	495000	770000
Total			12,135,751.75	14,477319.45
AMGNS Per Worker			$\bar{Z}_2 = \frac{1}{n}\sum_{i=1}^{n} Zi$ = 36 =337104.2	
ASMGS Per Worker				$\bar{Z}_2' = \frac{1}{n}\sum_{i=1}^{n} Zi'$ 14477319.45 /36 = 402147.7625
Price Range		Min.= 200 Max.= 3,500		

Note:

$$NMGS\ per\ worker\ (z) = Av.Price\ (P_i)\ x\ NMPO\ per\ worker\ (Y_{1i})$$

$$SMGS\ per\ worker\ (z_i') = Av.Price\ (P_i)\ x\ SMPO\ per\ worker\ (Y_{2i})$$

Source: Author's field survey; Calculation by the Author

Appendix 4.4a: Calculation of Standard Deviation (SD) for the monthly gross sales per worker in dispersed small scale footwear industry

SD for normal monthly sales per worker

$$\sigma_X^2 = \frac{1}{n}\sum_{i=1}^{n}(Z_i - \bar{Z}_2)^2$$

$$x = \frac{1}{n}\sqrt{\sum_{i=1}^{n}(Z_i - \bar{Z}_2)^2} \qquad \sigma_X = \frac{1}{n}\sqrt{\sum_{i=1}^{36}(Z_i - 337104.2)^2}$$

$= \quad 136244.818$

SD for seasonal monthly sales per worker

$$\sigma_X = \frac{1}{n}\sqrt{\sum_{i=1}^{n}(Z_i - \overline{Z}_2)^2} \quad \sigma_X = \frac{1}{n}\sqrt{\sum_{i=1}^{36}(Z_i - 402147.7625)^2}$$

$= 175019.224$

Appendix 4.5: Statistical test of significances of difference between two sample means

This is a problem of differences between two sample statistics such that a sample of 36 enterprises in stratum A (Cluster) and 36 enterprises in stratum B (Dispersed) are subjected to testing in order to investigate if the difference in performance indicator (gross sales per worker) is statistically significant.

Normal Sales per worker		Seasonal Sales per worker	
Stratum A	Stratum B	Stratum A	Stratum B
$n_1 = 36$	$n_2 = 36$	$n_1' = 36$	$n_2' = 36$
$\overline{Z}_1 = 455242.7$	$\overline{Z}_2 = 337104.2$	$\overline{Z}_1'' = 508641.6$	$\overline{Z}_2'' = 402147.7625$
$S_1 = 273611.635$	$S_2 = 136244818$	$S_1' = 230363.418$	$S_2' = 175019224$

The aim here is to verify if the two samples are drawn from the sample population. It is also a case where a sample mean of a 'control' group is compared with the "experimental" group (Kaplan, 1966). We apply the z formula such that

$$Z = \frac{\text{The difference between the mean of the first Sample}(\overline{x}_1)\text{ and the second Sample}(\overline{x}_2)}{\text{The Standard error of the difference of the means}(\sigma_{X_1} - \sigma_{X_2})}$$

Where $(\sigma_{X_1} - \sigma_{X2}) = \sqrt{\frac{S_1^2}{n_1 - 1} + \frac{S_2^2}{n_2 - 1}}$

This is based on the theorem: - The standard error of the difference between the mean of two independent random variables is equal to the square root of the sum of their variances.

$$Z = \frac{(\bar{x}_1 - \bar{x}_2) - (\mu_1 - \mu_2)}{\sqrt{\frac{s_i^2}{n_1 - 1} + \frac{s_i^2}{n_2 - 1}}}$$

$H_0, \mu_1 = \mu_2$), hence, $(\mu_1 - \mu_2) = 0$

Therefore

$$Z = \frac{(\bar{x}_1 - \bar{x}_2)}{\sqrt{\frac{s_i^2}{n_1 - 1} + \frac{s_i^2}{n_2 - 1}}}$$

n-1 = degree of freedom.

Solution:
The Null hypothesis (*H0*):
No significant difference exists between the average gross sales per worker in Stratum A and average gross sales per worker in Stratum B
The Alternative Hypothesis (*H1*):
A significant difference exists between the average gross sales per worker in Stratum A and average gross sales per worker in Stratum B
The level of significant is taken to be at 5 per cent. This is equivalent to a probability value of 1.96.
Decision rule: we reject *Ho*: if $|z| < -1.96$ or > 1.96
we accept H1 otherwise

Case 1: The z value for normal sales per worker

$$Z = \frac{\bar{Z}_1 - \bar{Z}_2}{\sqrt{\frac{s_1^2}{n_1 - 1} + \frac{s_2^2}{n_2 - 1}}}$$

$$= \frac{455242.7 - 337104.2}{\sqrt{\frac{273611.6^2}{36-1} + \frac{136244.8^2}{36-1}}}$$

$$= \frac{118138.5}{2138951647 + 530361300.8}$$

$$= \frac{118138.5}{51665.39}$$

$$= 2.287 > 1.96$$

Since 2.287is greater than 1.96, therefore, weeject the null hypothesis and accepthe alternative hypothesis that there is significant difference betwen the average gross sales per worker in stratm A and average gross sales per worker in stratumB. The difference between $\bar{Z}_1$ and $\bar{Z}_2$ is not due merely to chance rather as a result of several factors

Case 2: The z value for seasonal sales per worker

$$Z = \frac{\bar{Z}_1' - \bar{Z}_2'}{\sqrt{\frac{s_1^{\ 2}}{n_1 - 1} + \frac{s_2^{\ 2}}{n_2 - 1}}}$$
$$= \frac{508641.6 - 402147.8}{\sqrt{\frac{230363.4^2}{36-1} + \frac{175019.2^2}{36-1}}}$$
$$= \frac{106493.8}{1516208459 + 875192010.5}$$
$$= \frac{106493.8}{48901.95}$$
$$= 2.178 > 1.96$$

We also reject the Null hypothesis as the average gross sales per worker in stratum B became weaker during the boom period.

Appendix 4.6: Distribution of respondents' perceptions to their major constraints in Aba small scale footwear enterprises cluster in % of sample size

Ranking of Constraints	Identified Constraints (Sample size =36)	No. Firms	% of Respondents to Sample size
2	Neglect	32	0.889
11	Security	4	0.111
7	Workshop	24	0.667
1	Raw materials	34	0.944
3	Modern Equipment	30	0.833
5	Price (exchange rate)	26	0.722
10	Finance	8	0.222
7	Access to Large firms	24	0.667
5	Infrastructure	26	0.722
4	Government trade policy	28	0.778
9	Shortage of Apprentice	25	0.694
3	Product Demand	30	0.833

Note: the survey covered enterprises heads in show maker, shoe tailor, smoothing and stamping
Source: Author's field survey

Appendix 4.7: Average monthly wage earnings of entrepreneurs/workers in Aba Small and Medium Scale garment enterprises (in US$)

	Micro	Small	Medium
Average firm size	4.1	13.3	55
Average wage earning of enterprises heads	10,000	10,000	15,000
Paid skilled workers	4,000	4,000	4,500
Paid unskilled workers	3,000	3,000	3,500
Apprentices Allowance	1,000	1,000	

Source: Author's field survey

Appendix 4.8: Distribution of respondents' perceptions to their major constraints in Aba small and medium scale garment enterprises cluster in % of sample size

Ranking of Constraints	Identified Constraints (Sample size =28)	No. of firms	% of Respondents to sample size
3	Neglect	25	0.893
1	Raw materials	27	0.964
3	Workers	25	0.893
6	Finance	20	0.714
2	Equipment	26	0.929
5	Product Demand	24	0.857

Source: Author's field survey

Appendix 4.9: Distribution of respondents' perceptions to their major constraints in Enugu small scale wood construction and furniture enterprises clusters

Rank	Constraints	No. of firms	% of Respondents to sample size
7	Finance	16	0.696
1	Skill workforce	22	0.956
3	Infrastructure	21	0.913
3	Quality	21	0.913
2	Raw Materials	19	0.826
6	Product Demand	18	0.783
	Total sample	23	1.00

Source: Author's field survey

Appendix 4.10: Distribution of respondents' perceptions to their major constraints in Nnewi Light engineering cluster in % of sample size

Rank	*Constraints*	*No. of firms*	*% of Respondents to sample size*
1	Neglect	17	0.944
4	Finance	16	0.889
6	Raw Materials	14	0.78
1	Technology problem	17	0.944
1	Technical workforce	17	0.944
5	Local government policy	15	0.833
	Number of Sample	18	

Source: Author's field survey

Appendix 4.11: The aggregate mean monthly output per worker in clustered Small scale Palm Kernel Oil (PKO) Extraction industry (in Tonnes)

No. of Worker (Incl. EH)	MMO (Projected)	MMO per worker (Projected)	MMO (Realised)	MMO per worker (Realised)	MMO Shortfall per worker
4	10*4 = 40	40/4 = 10.00	7*4 = 28	28/4 = 7.00	10.00-7.00=3.00
6	16*4 = 64	64/6 = 10.67	13*4 = 52	52/6 = 8.67	10.67-8.67 =2.00
8	20*4= 80	80/8 = 10.00	14*4 = 56	56/8 = 7.00	10.00-7.00 =3.00
7	20*4 = 80	80/7 = 11.43	13*4 = 52	52//7 = 7.43	11.43-7.43 =4.00
13	40*4 =140	140/13 = 10.77	25*4 =100	100/13 = 7.69	10.77-7.69 =3.08
6	15*4 = 60	60/6 = 10.00	10*4 = 40	40/6 = 6.67	10.00-6.67 =3.33
5	15*4 = 60	60/5 = 12.00	11* 4 = 44	44/5 = 8.80	12.00-8.80 =3.20
11	25*4 =100	100/11 = 9.09	20*4 = 80	80/11 =7.27	9.09-7.27 =1.82
6	16*4 = 64	64/6 = 10.67	12*4 = 48	48/6 = 8.00	10.67-8.00 =2.67
5	15*4 = 60	60/5 = 12.00	9*4 = 36	36/5 = 7.20	12.00-7.20 =4.80
6	15*4 = 60	60/6 = 10.00	11*4 = 44	44/6 =7.33	10.00-7.33 =2.67
Total 77	808	116.63	580	83.06	33.57
AM 7	73.45	10.60	52.73	7.56	3.05
SD. 2.72	26.91	0.91	20.54	0.68	0.84

Note: Monthly output is derived from weekly production output multiply by 4; the projected output is based on the weekly order from refinery and soap making factories (formal and informal). MMO shortfall per worker is the projected MMO per worker minus realised MMO per worker. MMO per worker (projected) is derived from MMO (projected) divided by the number of workers including the Enterprises Heads

Key: MMO = Mean Monthly Output; Incl. EH = Including Enterprises Heads; PKO = Palm Kernel Oil; AM = Aggregate Mean: SD = Standard Deviation

Source: Author's field survey

Appendix 4.11a: Computation of Standard Deviation (SD) for monthly production output per worker in clustered sample scale PKO extraction industry.

SD for montly production output per worker:

$$\sigma_X^2 = \frac{1}{n}\sum_{i=1}^{n}(Yi-\bar{Y})^2$$

$$\sigma_X = \sqrt{\frac{1}{n}\sum_{i=1}^{n}(Yi'-\bar{Y})^2}$$

$$\sigma_X = \sqrt{\frac{1}{11}\sum_{i=1}^{11}(Yi'-7.56)^2}$$

$$= 0.68$$

SD for monthly production output Shortfall per worker:

$$\sigma_X = \sqrt{\frac{1}{11}\sum_{i=1}^{11}(Yi^2-\bar{Y}')^2}$$

$$= \sqrt{\frac{1}{11}\sum_{i=1}^{11}(Yi^2-3.05)^2}$$

$$= 0.84$$

Appendix 4.12: The aggregate mean monthly output per worker in dispersed small scale PKO Extraction industry (in Tonnes)

No. of Worker (Incl. EH)	MMO (Projected)	MMO per worker (Projected)	MMO (Realised)	MMO per worker (Realised)	MMO Shortfall per worker
4	10*4 =40	40/4 = 10.00	6*4 =24	24/4 = 6.00	10.00-6.00 = 4.00
11	30*4 =120	120/11= 10.91	15*4 =60	60/11=5.45	10.91-5.45 = 5.46
5	12*4 =48	48/5 = 9.60	7*4 = 28	28/5 = 5.60	9.60-5.60 = 4.00
3	8*4 =32	32/3 =10.67	5.5*4 =22	22/3 = 7.33	10.67-7.33 = 3.34
8	25*4 =100	100/8 = 12.50	10*4 =40	40/8 = 5.00	12.50-5.00 = 7.50
4	9*4 = 36	36/4 = 9.00	6*4 =24	24/4 = 6.00	9.00-6.00 = 3.00
9	20*4 =80	80/9 = 8.89	12*4=48	48/9 = 5.33	8.89-5.33 = 3.56
4	10*4 =40	40/4 =10.00	6.5*4=26	26/4 = 6.50	10.00-6.50 = 3.50
6	12*4 =48	48/6 =8.00	7*4 =28	28/6 = 4.67	8.00-4.67 = 3.33
7	20*4 =80	80/7 =11.43	10*4=40	40/7 = 5.71	11.43-5.71 = 5.72
5	10*4 =40	40/4 =10.00	5.5*4=30	30/5 = 6.00	10.00-6.00= 4.00
Total = 66	664	111	370.00	63.59	47.41
AM = 6	60.36	10.09	33.64	5.78	4.31
SD = 2.49	29.74	1,26	11.99	0.72	1.36

Key: MMO= Mean Monthly Output; Ent. = Enterprises; PKO= Palm Kernel Oil; AM. = ibid

Source: Author's field survey

Appendix 4.12a: Computation of Standard Deviation (SD) for monthly production output per worker in dispersed small scale PKO Extraction industry

SD for monthly production output per worker:

$$\sigma_X^2 = \frac{1}{n}\sum_{i=1}^{n}(Yi' - \bar{Y})^2$$

$$\sigma_X = \sqrt{\frac{1}{n}\sum_{i=1}^{n}(Yi' - \bar{Y})^2}$$

$$\sigma_X = \sqrt{\frac{1}{11}\sum_{i=1}^{11}(Yi' - 5.78)^2}$$

$$= .72$$

SD for production output Shortfall per worker:

$$\sigma_X = \sqrt{\frac{1}{11}\sum_{i=1}^{11}(Yi^2 - \bar{Y}')^2}$$

$$= \sqrt{\frac{1}{11}\sum_{i=1}^{11}(Yi^2 - 4.31)^2}$$

$$= 1.36$$

Appendix 4.13: Statistical test of significance for the indicator of firm performance Hypothesis

This is also a case of differences between two sample statistics with equal sample size such that a sample 1 in stratum A (Cluster) and sample 2 in stratum B (Dispersed) are subject to testing if the differences in shortfall is significant.

Monthly Output short fall per Worker

Stratum A	Stratum B
$n'_1 = 11$	$n'_2 = 11$
$\bar{z}'_1 = 3.05$	$\bar{z}'_2 = 4.31$
$S'_1 = 0.84$	$S'_2 = 1.36$

The z formula is applied in this case:

$$Z = \frac{\text{The difference between the mean of the first Sample}(\bar{x}_1)\text{ and the second Sample}(\bar{x}_2)}{\text{The Standard error of the difference of the means}(\sigma_{x_1} - \sigma_{x_2})}$$

Where $$(\sigma_{X_1} - \sigma_{X2}) = \sqrt{\frac{S_1^2}{n_1 - 1} + \frac{S_2^2}{n_2 - 1}}$$

This is based on the theorem: - The standard error of the difference between the mean of two independent random variables is equal to the square root of the sum of their variances.

$$Z = \frac{(\bar{x}_1 - \bar{x}_2) - (\mu_1 - \mu_2)}{\sqrt{\frac{s_i^2}{n_1 - 1} + \frac{s_i^2}{n_2 - 1}}}$$

Null hypothesis:-

$H_0, \mu_1 = \mu_2$), hence, $(\mu_1 - \mu_2) = 0$

Therefore

$$Z = \frac{(\overline{x}_1 - \overline{x}_2)}{\sqrt{\frac{s_i^2}{n_1 - 1} + \frac{s_i^2}{n_2 - 1}}}$$

Case 3:

The Null hypothesis (*H0*):

No significant difference exists between the mean monthly output shortfall per worker in Stratum A and Stratum B

The Alternative Hypothesis (*H1*):

A significant difference exists between the mean monthly output shortfall per worker in Stratum A and Stratum B

The level of significant is taken to be at 5 per cent. This is equivalent to a probability value of 1.96.

Decision rule: we accept *Ho*: if $\pm |z| < 1.96$

We reject H1 otherwise

The z value for monthly production output shortfall per worker

$$Z = \frac{\overline{Z}'_1 - \overline{Z}'_2}{\sqrt{\frac{s_1^2}{n_1 - 1} + \frac{s_2^2}{n_2 - 1}}}$$

$$= \frac{3.05 - 4.31}{\sqrt{\frac{0.84^2}{11-1} + \frac{1.36^2}{11-1}}}$$

$$= \frac{-1.26}{0.071 + 0.185}$$

$$= \frac{-1.26}{0.506}$$

$$= 2.49 > 1.96$$

We reject the null hypothesis and accept alternative that there is significant difference in output shortfall per worker in stratum A and B.

Appendix 4.14: Computation of mean No. of major start up and additional investment introduced (Expeller and Toaster) in clustered small scale PKO extraction industry

No. of Sample	No of Major Equipment at Start-up			No. of Additional. Major Equipment introduced			Total No. of Major Equipment.
	Expeller	Toaster	Total	Expeller	Toaster	Total	Expeller/Toaster
1	1	1	2	2	1	3	5
2	1	0	1	2	2	4	5
3	2	0	2	2	1	3	5
4	1	1	2	2	2	4	6
5	1	0	1	1	2	3	4
6	2	1	3	1	2	3	6
7	1	0	1	2	1	3	4
8	1	1	2	3	2	5	7
9	1	1	2	1	1	2	4
10	1	1	2	4	2	6	8
11	2	1	3	3	1	4	7
Total	14	7	21	23	17	40	61 (1.91)
Mean	1.27	0.64	1.91	2.09	1.55	3.64	5.55

Source: Author's field survey

Appendix 4.15: Computation of Correlation coefficient of the relationship between major investment and Out put per worker in clustered enterprises

Sample No.	X_2	Y_2	$\bar{X}=5.55$ $x_2=X_2-\bar{X}$	$Y=7.56$ $y_2=Y_2-\bar{Y}$	x_2y_2	x_2^2	y_2^2
1	5	7.00	-0.55	-0.56	0.308	0.303	0.314
2	5	8.67	-0.55	1.11	-0.611	0.303	1.232
3	5	7.00	-0.55	-0.55	0.303	0.303	0.303
4	6	7.43	0.45	-0.13	-0.059	0.203	0.017
5	4	7.69	-1.55	0.13	-0.202	2.403	0.017
6	6	6.67	0.45	-0.89	-0.401	0.203	0.792
7	4	8.80	-1.55	1.24	-1.922	2.403	1.538
8	7	7.27	1.45	-0.29	-0.421	2.103	0.081
9	4	8.00	-1.55	0.44	-0.682	2.403	0.194
10	8	7.20	2.45	-0.36	-0.882	6.003	0.130
11	7	7.33	1.45	-0.23	-0.334	2.103	0.053
Total					-4.06	18.73	4.67

Source: Author's field survey

Case 4: Calculation of coefficient of correlation (r) for major investment and output per worker in clustered small scale PKO extraction industry.

$$r_2 = \frac{\Sigma x_2 y_2}{\sqrt{\Sigma\left(x_2^{\,2}\right)\left(\Sigma y_2^{\,2}\right)}}$$

$$= \frac{-4.06}{\sqrt{(18.73)^2(4.67)^2}}$$

$$= \frac{-4.06}{\sqrt{(350.81)(21.81)}}$$

$$= \frac{-4.06}{\sqrt{7650.78}}$$

$$= \frac{-4.06}{87.47}$$

$$= -0.046$$

Appendix 4.16: Computation of mean No. of major start up and additional investment introduced (Expeller and Toaster) in dispersed enterprises

No. of Sample	No of Major Equipment at Start-up			No. of Additional. Major Equipment introduced			Total No of Major Equipment
	Expeller	Toaster	Total	Expeller	Toaster	Total	Expeller &Toaster
1	1	0	1	1	1	2	3
2	1	0	1	1	1	2	3
3	1	0	1	1	1	2	3
4	1	1	2	1	1	1	3
5	1	1	2	1	0	1	3
6	1	0	2	1	1	2	4
7	1	1	2	1	0	1	3
8	2	1	3	1	1	2	5
9	1	1	2	1	0	1	3
10	2	1	3	1	1	3	5
11	1	0	1	1	1	2	3
Total	13	6	19	11	8	19	38 (1.00)
Mean	1.18	0.55	1.73	1.00	0.73	1.73	

Source: Author's field survey

Appendix 4.17: Computation of Correlation coefficient of the relationship between Major investment and Out put per worker in dispersed enterprises

Sample No.	X_2	Y_2	$\bar{X} = 3.46$ $x_2 = X_2 - \bar{X}$	$\bar{Y} = 5.78$ $y_2 = Y_2 - \bar{Y}$	x_2y_2	x_2^2	y_2^2
1	3	6.00	-0.45	0.22	-0.099	0.203	0.048
2	3	5.45	-0.45	-0.33	0.149	0.203	0.109
3	3	5.60	-0.45	-0.18	0.081	0.203	0.032
4	3	7.33	-0.45	1.55	-0.698	0.203	2.403
5	3	5.00	-0.45	-0.78	0.351	0.203	0.608
6	4	6.00	0.55	0.22	0.121	0.303	0.048
7	3	5.33	-0.45	-0.45	0.203	0.203	0.203
8	5	6.50	1.55	0.72	1.116	2.403	0.518
9	3	4.67	-0.45	-1.11	0.500	0.203	1.232
10	5	5.71	1.55	0.07	0.109	2.403	0.005
11	3	6.00	-0.45	0.22	-0.099	0.203	0.048
Total	38				1.73	6.73	5.25

Source: Author's field survey

Case 5: Calculation of coefficient of correlation (r) for major investment and output per worker in small scale dispersed PKO extraction industry.

Appendix 4.18: Distribution of respondents' perceptions to their major constraints in Enugu PKO enterprises clusters in % sample size

Rank	Major Constraints	No. of firms.	% of Respondentsto Sample size
1	Energy	10	0.91
5	Finance	8	0.73
1	Technology	10	0.91
4	Taxation	9	0.82
6	Government policy	7	0.64
1	Raw material (Palm Kernel)	10	0. 91

Source: Author's field survey

Appendix 4.19: Taxation scene in PKO extraction enterprises

Forms of Taxes	Average Amount Paid annually	Percentage of the Total
Income Tax	N5,966.70	0.347
Produce Tax	N1,700.00	0.098
Environment Tax	N3,000.00	0.174
Local Govt Permit	N1,750.00	0.102
Business Premises	N4,800.00	0.279
Total	N17,216.70	1.00

Source: Author's field survey

Appendix 5 Evaluation of Enterprise Networks

Appendix 5.1: The structure of entrepreneurs belonging to sub-sectoral association, business association, and professional association expressed in % of the sub-sectoral and total sample size.

Sub-sector	No of Sample	Subsectoral Association E.g. NATA, Shoemakers Association	Business Association E.g. NASSI, MAN, NCCIMA	Professional Association E.g. Nigeria Association Engineers	Not a Member in any association	% of Resp. Actually Member in Association
Footwear	68	68	6	-----	-----	68
Micro Ent	68	68	6	----	-----	68
Small Ent	---	---	---	----	-----	---
Medium	----	---	----	----	-----	---
Garments	28	20	13	----	1	27
Micro Ent	24	17	12	---	1	23
Small Ent	3	2	1	---	---	3
Medium	1	1	---		---	1
Woods & furniture	39	36	6	----	3	36
Micro Ent	21	32	4	---	2	32
Small Ent	3	4	2	---	1	4
Medium	---	----	---	---	---	---
Light Eng	18	6	12	2	2	16
Micro Ent	12	6	8	----	1	11
Small Ent	4	---	3	1	1	3
Medium	2	---	2	1	----	2
PKO	22	21	11	14	1	21
Micro Ent	9	16	10	12	1	15
Small Ent	2	5 ---	1	2	---	6
Medium	--		---	---	---	---
Total Freq.	175	151	48	16	8	168

Source: Author's field survey

Appendix 5.2: The structure of entrepreneurs belonging to association outside the sub-sectoral association, business association, and professional association expressed in % of the sub-sectoral and total sample size.

Sector	Sample size	Town Union, Age grade Association	Religious group	State voluntary organisation	Not belonging to any group
Footwear	68	60	54	2	8
Garments	28	27	26	1	1
Woods and furniture	39	39	37	-----	2
Light engineering	18	18	16	-----	---
PKO Extraction	22	21	20	1	----
The total frequency	175	165	153	4	11

Source: Author's field survey

Appendix 5.3: Perception of entrepreneurs to the association they belong with their business by sector

A	Membership in sub-sectoral, business and professional associations					
Sector	Footwear	Garment	W&F	Light Eng.	PKO	All
Sample size	68	28	39	18	22	175
-Proportion of respondents that perceive he contact they make in the association as very useful to all areas of their business.	31	18	20	12	19	100
- The proportion of respondents that have received financial support from any member of the association.	22	8	13	11	18	72
- The proportion of respondents that have given financial support to any or some members in the ssociation.	26	9	5	6	16	62
- The proportion of respondents that have received technical assistance from any member of the association	7	0	2	4	8	21
- The proportion of the respondents that have received commercial assistance from any member of the association.	28	4	0	2	1	35
-The proportion of the respondents that have received commercial or technical assistance organised by the association body.	3	12	0	9	0	24
B	Membership in associations outside their sub-sectoral, business and professional associations					
	Footwear	Garment	W&F	Light Eng.	PKO	All
- Proportion of respondents that perceive the contact they make in the association as very useful to all areas of their business	54	20	2	5	3	84
- The proportion of the respondents that have received financial or technical assistance organised by the association body.	26	12	1	3	1	42

Key: W&F = Wood and Funiture; light Eng. = Light Engineering
Source: Author's field survey

Appendix 5.4: Perception of entrepreneurs to the association they belong in by firm size

A Membership in sub-sectoral, business and professional associations	1-9	10-49	50-99	All
Sample Size	149	16	3	168
- Proportion of respondents that perceive the contact they make in the association as very useful to all areas of their business.	85	12	3	100
- The proportion of respondents that have received support from any member of the association.	58	12	2	72
- The proportion of respondents that have given support to any or some members in the association.	45	14	3	62
-The proportion of respondents that have received technical assistance from any member of the association	1	18	2	21
- The proportion of the respondents that have received commercial assistance from any member of theassociation.	26	8	1	35
- The proportion of the respondents that have received commercial or technical assistance organised by the association body.	10	12	2	24
B Membership in associations outside their sub-sectoral, business and professional associations	1-9	10-49	50-99	All
- Proportion of respondents that perceive the contact they make in the association as very useful to all areas of their business	73	9	2	84
- The proportion of the respondents that have received commercial or technical assistance organised by the Association body.	34	7	1	42

Source: Author's field survey

Appendix 5.5: Institutionalised networks in the sub-sectors

	Footwear	Garments	W & F	Light eng:	PKO	All
Sample size	68	28	39	18	22	175
Input Networks						
Supply of materials	56	19	6	na	16	91
Supply of components	60	na	na	8	na	74
Backward contracting	60	1	na	na	na	61
Output Networks						
Formal marketing	62	na	1	2	20	25
channel	66	28	38	16	2	150
Informal marketing						
channel						
Large firms	na	na	na	3	20	23
Institutions	16	3	2	na	na	21

Source: Author's field survey

Appendix 5.6: Institutionalised networks by firm size

Sector	1-9	10-49	50-99	All
Sample size	152	20	3	175
Input Networks				
Supply of Materials	88	2	1	101
Supply of Components	73	na	1	74
Backward sub-contracting	60	1	na	61
Output Networks				
Formal Marketing Channel	21	3	1	25
Informal Marketing Channel	135	13	2	150
large firms	21	2	na	na
Institutions	21	na	na	21

Source: Author's field survey

Appendix 5.7: Distribution networks of SMEs by sub-sector

	Footwear	Garments	W&F	Light Eng.	PKO	All
Sample Size	68	28	39	16	22	175
Local Market	67	28	39	16	2	152
National Market	60	20	2	14	22	118
African regional Market	45	2	1	1	na	49

Source: Author's field survey

Appendix 5.8: Methods of effecting distributions of products

Sector	Footwear	Garment	W&F	Light Eng.	PKO	All
Supply by order	60	15	3	12	21	111
Supply direct to market		8	6	6	2	22
Producing by sample/ Specification	54	16	18	11		99
Producing for firms				6	22	28
Use of informal marketing agents	3	5				7
Use of formal advertisement	na	na				
Individuals and household	11	21	18		22	72
Traders	68	22	9	15	20	134

Source: Author's field survey

Appendix 5.9: Derivation of Average number of sales order of African regional customers by country in Aba shoe cluster

	Frequency of order		
Countries	Ladies Shoe	Men's Shoe	Bags
Cameroon	2 x 1months	2 x 1month	1 x 3months
Ghana	1 x 1month	1x 2months	1 x 3months
Gabon	1 x 1month	1 x 3months	1 x 6months
Togo	1 x 1month	1 x 3months	1 x 6months
Benin Republic	1 x 2months	1 x 3months	1 x 6months
Congo	1 x 3months	1 x 4months	na
Angola	1 x 6months	1 x 6months	1 x 6months
Ivory Coast	1 x 6months	1 x 6months	na
Malawi	1 x 1year	1 x 1year	na

Source: Author's field survey

Appendix 5.10: Export Distribution Networks (derived from appendix 1a)

	Ladies Shoes	Men-Shoes	Bags	Total	% of total
Cameron	24	24	4	52	0.37
Ghana	12	6	4	22	0.16
Gabon	12	4	2	18	0.12
Togo	12	4	2	18	0.12
Benin. R ep.	6	4	2	12	0.09
Congo	4	3	0	7	0.05
Angola	2	2	2	6	0.04
Ivory coast	2	2	0	4	0.03
Malawi	1	1	0	2	0.01
Total	75	50	16	141	1.00
% of Total	0.53	0.35	0.11	1.00	

Source: Author's field survey

Appendix 5.11: Network functions assessment by sub-sector

Sector Sample size	Footwear	Garments	Wood & furniture	Light engineering	PKO extraction	All
The proportion of entrepreneurs in the sub-sector who view the contact they make in their networks as						
- source of information for access to technology	62	16	26	14	18	136
- source of information for raw materials	45	18	27	16	21	127
- source of information for access to new market	62	24	30	17	18	151
- source of information for trade partners	65	22	32	18	20	157
- means of reaching out for sub-contracting	na	na	4	3	17	24
- means of protection	66	26	34	11	21	158
- means of accessing credits and loans	12	24	12	6	3	57
- for understanding how to deal with government functionaries and policy	10	16	27	17	20	86
-as contact and social welfare	66	27	39	9	21	161

Source: Author's field survey

Appendix 5.12: Network functions assessment by firm size

	Micro Enterprises	Small Enterprises	Medium Enterprises	All
The proportion of entrepreneurs in the sub-sector who view their networks as source of information				
-for access to technology	115	18	3	136
-for raw materials	109	15	3	127
-for accessing new market	136	14	3	151
-for assessment of trading partners	138	16	3	157
- for reaching out for sub-contracting business	18	5	1	24
- means of protection	142	14	2	158
- means of accessing credits and loans	51	9	3	63
- for understanding how to handle business issues with government functionaries and policy	68	15	3	86
-as contact and social welfare	145	14	2	161

Source: Author's field survey

Appendix 5.13: Networks and risk/uncertainty reduction by sub-sector

	Footwear	Garments	W&F	Light Eng.	PKO	All
The proportion of entrepreneurs who view their networks as means of reducing business risks by						
-assessment and making joint purchases	52	7	29	2	22	112
-assessment and monitoring of trade credits	56	22	20	12	16	102
-enforcement of conformity to business relations	17	3	4	3	5	33
Proportion of entrepreneurs who view their networks as means of protecting business interest by						
-accepting some cash deposit before production	68	28	39	16	2	153
-accepting all payment before production	2	1	1		na	5
- accepting personal guarantees in offering trade credit	10	2	3	2	na	17

Source: Author's field survey

Appendix.5.14: Networks and Risk/uncertainty reduction by firm size

	Micro enterprises	Small Enterprises	Medium Enterprises	All
The proportion of entrepreneurs that value the contactthey make in their networks as means of protectingBusiness interest by....				
- assessment and making joint	98	12	2	112
-assessment and monitoring of trade credits	90	14	1	102
-enforcement of conformity to business relations	28	4	1	33
The proportion of entrepreneurs that protect theirbusiness interest by				
-accept cash some deposit before production	141	9	3	153
-accepting all payment before production	3	1	1	5
-accepting personal guarantees in offering trade credit	10	6	1	17

Source: Author's field survey

Appendix 5.15: Networks and conflict management assessment by sub-sector

	Footwear	Garments	W&F	Light Eng.	PKO	All
The ratio of the entrepreneurs who have experienced problems with their business partners during the past year	58	24	32	14	18	146
The ratio of the entrepreneurs who resolve their problem with customer themselves without third a party	38	17	22	12	11	108
-with intervention of a third party.	9	5	7	10	6	37
- by formal legal system	na	na		1		1
- by evolving police	na	na				
- by association body	11	2	5	na	1	19

Source: Author's field survey

Appendix.5.16: Conflict management network assessment by firm size

	Micro enterprises	Small Enterprises	Medium Enterprises	All
The ratio of the entrepreneurs who have experienced problems with their business partners during the past year	130	14	3	146
The ratio of the entrepreneurs who resolve their problem with customer themselves without third a party	94	12	2	100
-with intervention of a third party.	34	3	na	37
- by formal legal system	na	na	1	1
- by evolving police	na	na	na	na
- by association body	11	8	na	19

Source: Author's field survey

Appendix 6: Evaluation of Innovativity Activities in SMEs

Appendix 6.1: Calculation of average number of new and successful product designs introduced in the market by Clustered Footwear (in Naira)

No	No. of design Introduced in the market yearly	No. of successful designs in the market yearly	Cost of introducing a new design by firm	Survival Costs	Total cost of design successful designs by firm	Forgone Investment Costs
1	100	10-20 = 15.0	100-300 = 200	20,000.00	3,000.00	17,000.00
2	120	15-20 = 17.5	100-200 = 150	18,000.00	2,625.00	15,375.00
3	110	10-15 = 17.5	100-250 = 175	19,250.00	3,062.50	16,187.50
4	100	5-15 = 10.0	200-250 = 225	22,500.00	2,250.00	20,250.00
5	80	10-20 = 15.0	150-200 = 175	14,000.00	2,625.00	11,375.00
6	90	5-10 = 7.5	200-300 = 250	22,500.00	1,875.00	20,625.00
7	100	5-15 = 10.0	200-350 = 275	27,500.00	2,750.00	24,750.00
8	110	10-15 = 12.5	150-200 = 175	19,250.00	2,187.50	17,062.50
9	120	15-20 = 17.5	250-300 = 275	33,000.00	4,812.50	28,187,50
10	110	10-20 = 15.0	200-250 = 225	24,750.00	3,375.00	21,375.00
11	5*	5.0	800-1400 = 100	5,500.00	5,500.00	0.00
12	10*	8.0	900-1500 = 200	12,000.00	9,600.00	2,400.00
13	4*	4.0	2,000	8,000.00	8,000.00	0.00
14	6*	5.0	1000-2000 = 1,500	9,000.00	7,500.00	1,500,00
15	4*	4.0	1,500	6,000.00	6,000.00	0.00
16	80	10-15 =12.5	200-250 = 225	18,000.00	2,812.50	15,187.50
17	85	10-15 = 12.5	150-200 = 175	14,875.00	2,187.50	12,687.50
18	4*	4.0	2500	10,000.00	10,000.00	0.00
19	90	5-15 = 10.0	150-200 = 175	15,750.00	1,750.00	14,000.00
20	110	15-20 = 15.0	220-300 = 260	28,600.00	3,900.00	24,700.00
21	100	10-15 = 12.5	150-250 = 200	20,000.00	2,500.00	17,500.00
22	110	15-20 = 15.0	200-250 = 225	24,750.00	3,375.00	21,375.00
23	5*	5.0	2,500	15,000.00	2,500.00	2,500.00
24	4*	4.0	2000-2500 = 2,250	9,000.00	9,000.00	0.00
25	120	10-20 = 15.0	100-300 = 200	24,000.00	3,000.00	21,000.00
26	110	15-20 =17.50	150-200 = 175	19,250.00	3062.50	16,187.50
27	100	10-20 = 15.0	200-300 = 250	25,000.00	3750.00	21,250.00
28	4*	4.0	2000	8,000.00	8000.00	0.00
29	5*	5.0	1000-2000=1500	7,500.00	7500.00	0.00
30	6*	4.0	2000	12,000.00	8000.00	4,000.00
31	10	8.0	1500-2000=1750	17,500.00	14000.00	3,500.00
32	110	10-20 =15.0	200-300 = 250	27,500.00	3750.00	23,750.00
33	100	8-16 = 12.0	2000	20,000.00	2400.00	17,600.00
34	90	5-10 = 9.0	150-250 = 200	18,000.00	1800.00	16,200.00
35	80	5-10 = 7.5	100-300 = 200	16,000.00	1500.00	14.500.00
36	6*	5.0	2,000	12,000.00	10000.00	2,000.00
37				ATCS		

Key: * = the number designs introduced by sampled enterprises in the men shoe production unit.

Source: Author's field survey:

Appendix 6.2: Calculation of average number of new and successful product designs introduced in the market by dispersed footwear (in Naira)

No.	No. of design introduced in the market yearly	No. of successful designs in the market yearly	Cost of introducing new design by firm	Survival Costs	Total cost of design successful designs by firm	Sunk Costs
1	50	5-10 = 7.5	100-200 = 150	7,500.00.0 0	1125.00	8375.00
2	60	6-10 = 8.0	100-250 = 175	10,500.00	1400.00	9100.00
3	40	5-8 = 6.5	110-200 = 155	6,200.00	1007.50	5192.50
4	70	6-10 = 8.0	200-250 = 225	15,750.00	1800.00	13950.00
5	40	4-8 = 6.0	200-300 = 250	10000.00	1500.00	8500.00
6	60	6-12 = 8.0	200-300 = 250	15000.00	2000.00	13000.00
7	70	5-15 = 10.0	300-400 = 350	24500.00	3500.00	21000.00
8	3*	3	1,000-3000=1500	4500.00	4500.00	0.00
9	5*	4	2,500	12500.00	10000.00	2500.00
10	90	10-15 =12.5	150-200 = 175	15750.00	2187.50	13562.50
11	70	5-10 = 7.5	200-250 = 225	15750.00	1687.50	14062.50
12	60	10-15 =12.5	200-300 = 250	15000.00	3125.00	11875.00
13	60	5-10 = 7.5	100 -200= 150	9000.00	1125.00	7875.00
14	5*	4	2,000	10000.00	8000.00	2000.00
15	4*	4	1,500-2000= 175	7000.00	7000.00	0.00
16	3*	3	2,000-2500 = 225	6750.00	6750.00	0.00
17	5*	4	2,500	12500.00	10000.00	2500.00
18	70	10-15 =12.5	200-300 = 250	17500.00	3125.00	14375.00
19	60	5-10 = 7.5	110-250 = 180	10800.00	1350.00	9450.00
20	5*	10-20 =15.0	110-300 = 205	16400.00	3075.00	13325.00
21	50	5-10 = 7.5	200-300 = 250	12500.00	1875.00	10625.00
22	60	3	2,000-2500 = 2250	6750.00	6750.00	0.00
23	3*	3	2,000	6000.00	6000.00	0.00
24	3*	10-15 =12.5	250-300 = 275	19250.00	3437.50	15812.50
25	80	20-25 =22.5	300-350 = 350	28000.00	7312.50	20687.50
26	60	10-15 =12.5	200-300 = 250	15000.00	3125.00	11875.00
27	70	10-20 =15.0	110-300 = 205	14350.00	3075.00	11275.00
28	70	10-20 =15.0	200-300 = 250	17500.00	3750.00	13750.00
29	60	10-15 =12.5	250-300 = 275	16500.00	3437.50	13062.50
30	40	5-10 = 7.5	110-300 = 205	8200.00	1537.50	6662.50
31	60	5-15 = 10.0	100-300 = 200	12000.00	2000.00	10000.00
32	70	10-20 =15.0	150-300 = 225	15750.00	3375.00	12375.00
33	60	5-10 = 7.5	200-350 = 275	16500.00	2062.50	14437.50
34	4*	3	1,800-2000 = 2900	11600.00	8700.00	2900.00
35	3*	3	2,000	6000.00	6000.00	0.00
36	4*	4	1,500-2000= 1750	7000.00	7000.00	0.00
37				ATCS	ATC	

Key: * = the number designs introduced by sampled enterprises in the men shoe production unit.; N= Naira

Source: Author's field work.

Appendix 6.3: Derivation of firms' source of information for new design (in %)

Source of Information	Sample size (24)	% of the Total Sample
Traders	24	100.00
Catalogue	9	37.50
Own creativity	16	66.70
Copying	17	70.80

Source: Author's field survey

Appendix 6.4: Calculation of firm investment on local machines in PKO enterprises

No. of Firms	X_2	Y_2	$X = 4.5$ $x_2 = X_2 - \bar{X}$	$Y = 6.36$ $y_2 = Y_2 - \bar{Y}$	$x_2 y_2$	x_2^2	y_2^2
1	5	7.00	0.5	0.64	0.32	0,25	0,4096
2	5	8.67	0.5	2.31	1.16	0,25	5,3361
3	5	7.00	0.5	0.64	0.32	0,25	0,4096
4	6	7.43	1.5	1.07	1.61	2,25	1,1449
5	4	7.69	-0.5	1.33	-0.67	0,25	1,7689
6	6	6.67	1.5	0.31	0.47	2,25	0,0961
7	4	8.80	-0.5	2.41	-1.21	0,25	5,8081
8	7	7.27	2.5	0.91	2.28	6,25	0,8281
9	4	8.00	-0.5	1.64	-0.82	0,25	2,6896
10	8	7.20	3.5	0.84	2.94	12,25	0,7056
11	7	7.33	2.5	0.97	2.43	6,25	0,9409
12	3	6.00	-1.5	-0.36	0.54	2,25	0,1296
13	3	5.45	-1.5	-0.91	1.37	2,25	0,8281
14	3	5.60	-1.5	-0.76	1.14	2,25	0,5776
15	3	7.33	-1.5	0.97	-1.46	2,25	0,9409
16	3	5.00	-1.5	-1.36	2.04	2,25	1,8496
17	4	6.00	-0.5	-0.36	0.18	0,25	0,1296
18	3	5.33	-1.5	-1.03	1.55	2,25	1,0609
19	5	6.50	0.5	0.14	0.07	0,25	0,0196
20	3	4.67	-1.5	-1.69	2.54	2,25	2,8561
21	5	5.71	0.5	-0.65	-0.33	0,25	0,4225
22	3	6.00	-1.5	-0.36	0.54	2,25	0,1296
mean	4.5	6.36			16.99	47.25	29.08

Source: Author's field Survey

Appendix 6.5: Firms' perception of government support by sub-sector

Sector	Footwear	Garments	Wood & furniture	Light engineering	PKO extraction	All
Sample size	68	28	39	18	22	175
The proportion of entrepreneurs in the sub-sector who view government support initiatives as						
adequate	2	1	2	na	na	5
inadequate	60	24	36	17	20	157
too political	48	18	14	12	15	107
only politics	58	20	30	14	20	142
not reflecting the reality	65	26	37	16	21	165
inconsistent	24	15	14	14	10	77
short term measures only	44	20	31	16	18	129

Source: Author's field survey.

Appendix 6.6: Firms' assessment of government incentives by firm size

	Micro Enterprises	Small Enterprises	Medium Enterprises	All
Sample size	152	20	3	175
Proportion of entrepreneurs in the sub-sector who view government support initiatives as				
adequate	3	2	na	5
inadequate	140	15	2	157
too political	91	13	3	107
only politics	125	15	2	142
not reflecting the reality	145	18	2	165
inconsistent	65	11	1	77
short term measures only	119	8	2	129

Source: Author's field survey

Appendix 6.7: Capacity building assessment need by sub-sector

Sub-sector	Footwear	Garments	Wood & furniture	Light engineering	PKO extraction	All
Sample size	68	28	39	18	22	161
Securing financial assistance	45	25	20	15	21	126
Business support services	60	20	28	14	21	143
Training Program	65	27	37	17	10	156
Technology assessment	63	25	35	16	22	161

Source: Author's field survey

Appendix 6.8: Capacity building assessment need by firm size

	Micro	Small	Medium	All
Sample size	152	20	3	175
Securing financial assistance	106	18	2	126
Business support services	124	16	3	143
Training Program	136	19	1	156
Technology assessment	148	20	3	161

Source: Author's field survey

Appendix 6.9: Forms of Taxation in PKO extraction enterprises

Forms of Taxes	Average amount paid annually	In percentage of total taxation
Income Tax	N5,966.70	35%
Produce Tax	N1,700.00	10%
Environment Tax	N3,000.00	17%
Local Govt Permit	N1,750.00	10%
Business Premises	N4,800.00	28%
Total	N1,7216.70	1.00

Key: N = Nigeria Currency Naira

Source: Author's field survey

Appendix 6.10: Mean year of schooling of enterprises head and workers in PKO extraction enterprises

No. of Ent.	No. of Workers/ETH	Pri.	Sec.	Post Sec.	Voca. Skill	AV. Yrs of Schl.
1	6	2*6= 12	3*11=33	1*15=15		60/6 =10.0
2	5	2*6= 12	2*11=22	1*15=15		38/5 =7.6
3	9	2*6= 12	5*11=55	1*15=15	1*11=11	93/9 =10.33
4	5	2*6= 12	2*11=22	1*15=15		49/9 =9.9
5	7	2*6= 12	4*11=44	1*15=15		71/7 =10.1
6	8	3*6=18	4*11=44	1*15=15	1*11 =11	86/8 =10.8
7	4	3*6=18	--------	1*14=14		32/4 = 8.0
8	6	2*6= 12	3*11=33	1*16=16	1*11 =11	72/6 =12.0
9	7	2*6= 12	2*11=22	1*16=16		50/7= 7.1
10	6	2*6= 12	3*11=33	1*16=16		61/6= 10.2
11	4	2*6= 12	1*11=11	1*16=16		39/4= 9.8
12	6	2*6= 12	3*11=33	1*14=14		59/6 =9,8
13	4	2*6= 12	3*11=33	1*15=15		60/6= 10.0
14	6	3*6=18	4*11=44	1*14=14	1*11 =11	78/9 =8.7
15	6	2*6= 12	3*11=33	1*14=14		59/6 = 9.8
16	9	3*6=18	3*11=33	1*15=15		66/6 =11.0
17	6	2*6= 12	2*11=22	1*16=16		50/5 =10.0
18	6	3*6=18	3*11=33	1*16=16		67/7= 9.6
19	5	2*6= 12	2*11=22	1*16=16		50/5 = 10.0
20	5	3*6=18	1*11=11	1*16=16		45/5 = 9.0
21	9	3*6=18	4*11=44	1*16=16	1*11 =11	89/9= 9.9
22	6	2*6= 12	3*11=33	1*16=16		61/6 = 10.2
23	5	3*18=18	1*11=11	1*16=16		45/5 = 9.0
24	6	3*18=18	2*11=22	1*15=15		55/6 = 9.2
25	9	3*18=18	5*11=55	1*16=16		89/6 = 9.9
26	4	1*6 = 6	2*11=22	1*16=16		44/4 = 11.0
27	8	3*18=18	3*11=33	1*16=16	1*11 = 11	78/8 = 9.8
28	7	2*6 = 12	4*11=44	1*16=16		72/7 = 10.3
29	8	3*18=18	4*11=44	1*16=16		78/8 = 9.8
30	4	1*6 = 6	2*11=22	1*15=15		43/4 = 10.8
31	6	2*6 = 12	2*11=22	1*16=16	1*11 = 11	61/6 = 10.2
32	5	2*6 = 12	2*11=22	1*16=16		50/5 = 10.0
33	7	2*6 = 12	4*11=44	1*16=16		72/7 = 10.3
34	6	1*6 = 6	4*11=44	1*15=15		65/6 = 10.8
35	6	2*6 = 12	3*11=33	1*16=16		61/6 = 10.2
36	7	2*6 = 12	4*11=44	1*15=15		71/ 7 =10.1
37	5	1*6 = 6	3*11=33	1*16=16		55/5 = 11.0
38	5	1*6 = 6	3*11=33	1*16=16		55/5 = 11.0
39	9	3*18=18	4*11=44	1*16=16	1*11 = 11	89/9 = 9.90
40	6	1*6 = 6	4*11=44	1*15=15		65/6 = 10.8

Source: Author's field survey

Appendix 6.10: Continues.

No of Ent.	No. of Workers/ ETH	Pri.	Sec.	Post Sec.	Voca. Skill	AV. Yrs of Schl.
41	5	2*6 = 12	2*11=22	1*16=16		50/5 = 10.0
42	6	1*6 = 6	4*11=44	1*16=16		66/6 = 11.0
43	6	2*6 = 12	3*11=33	1*16=16		61/6 = 10.2
44	7	2*6 = 12	3*11=33	1*16=16	1*11 = 11	72/7 = 10.3
45	6	2*6 = 12	3*11=33	1*15=15		60/6 =10.0
46	7	2*6 = 12	4*11=44	1*16=16		72/7 = 10.3
47	4	1*6 = 6	2*11=22	1*16=16		44/4 = 11.0
48	6	1*6 = 6	3*11=33	1*15=15	1*11 = 11	65/6 = 10.8
49	6	1*6 = 6	4*11=44	1*15=15		65/6 = 10.8
50	8	3*18=18	3*11=33	1*16=16	1*11 = 11	78/8 = 9.80
51	5	2*6 = 12	2*11=22	1*16=16		50/5 = 10.0

Source: Author's field survey

Appendix 6.11: Average year of schooling of enterprises head and workers in Aba footwear enterprises

No. of Ent.	No. of Workers/ ETH	Pri.	Sec.	Post Sec.	Voca. Skill	AV. Yrs of Schl.
1	3	3*6= 18				6
2	2	1*6= 6	1* 11= 11			17/2= 8.5
3	3	3*6= 18				6
4	2	1* 6= 6			1*11= 11	17/2= 8.5
5	3	3*6 = 18				6
6	2	2* 6= 12				6
7	1	1*6 = 6				6
8	1	1*6 = 6				6
9	1	1*6 = 6				6
10	2	2* 6= 12				6
11	1	1*6 = 6				6
12	3	2* 6= 12		1*13=13		25/3=8.33
13	1	1*6 = 6				6
14	2	1*6 = 6				6
15	1	1*6 = 6				6
16	1		1* 11= 11			11
17	2	1*6 = 6			1*11= 11	1572=8.5
18	1	1*6 = 6				6
19	1	1*6 = 6				6
20	3	3*6= 18				6
21	1		1* 11= 11			11
22	1	1*6 = 6				6
23	2	2* 6= 12				6
24	1	1*6 = 6				6
25	1	1*6 = 6				6
26	1	1*6 = 6				6
27	2	1*6 = 6	1* 11= 11			17/2=8.5
28	1	1*6 = 6				6
29	1	1*6 = 6				6
30	3	2* 6= 12	1* 11= 11			23/3=7.7
31	2	2* 6= 12				6
32	1	1*6 = 6				6
33	2	1*6 = 6	1* 11= 11			17/2= 8.5
34	1	1*6 = 6				6
35	2	1*6 = 6			1*11= 11	17/2 = 8.5
36	1	1*6 = 6				6
37	1	1*6 = 6				6
38	1	1*6 = 6				6
39	1		1* 11= 11			11
40	2	2* 6= 12				6
41	1	1*6 = 6				6
42	2	1*6 = 6			1*11=11	17/2= 8.5
43	2	2* 6= 12				6
44	1	1*6 = 6				6
45	1		1* 11= 11			11

Source: Author's field survey

Appendix 6.11: Continues

No. of Ent.	No. of Workers/ ETH	Pri.	Sec.	Post Sec.	Voca. Skill	AV. Yrs of Schl.
46	2	2* 6= 12				6
47	1	1*6 = 6				6
48	2	1*6 = 6				6
49	1	1*6 = 6				6
50	3	3*6 = 18				6
51	1	---	1*11			11
52	2	2*6 = 12				6
53	1	1*6 = 6				6
54	3	3*6 = 12	1*11			23/3 = 7.7
55	1	1*6= 6				6
56	1	1*6 = 6				6
57	2	2*6 = 12				12/2 = 6
58	3	2*6 = 12	1*11 = 11			23/3 = 7.7
59	1	1*6 = 6				6
60	1	1*6				6
61	2	1*6			1*11	17/2 = 8.5
62	3	2*6 = 12			1*11	23/3 = 7.7
63	1	1*6 = 6				6
64	1	1*6 = 6				6
65	1		1*11 = 11			11
66	3	1*6				6
67	1	1*6 = 6				6
68	3	2*6 = 12			1*11 = 11	23/3 = 7.7
69	1	1*6 = 6				6
70	1	1*6 = 6				6
71	2	2*6 = 12				6
72	2	2*6 = 12				6

Source: Author's field surve

Questionnaire and Interview Structure

Personal interview by questionnaire with entrepreneurs, workers, heads of association and institutions supporting SMEs

SECTION A: Characteristics of the Enterprises

i) What are you producing? ---------------------------------
ii) What kinds of items do you produce? ----------------------
iii) Please Name them

----
iv) What kind of skill training did you receive before starting this business?

Market
Where do you sell your products?
Local ----------------------------
National-------------------------
Other Areas, and name countries ---------

Regulatory Environment
i) Did you register your business by the government authority?
ii) If yes, how much was the cost of registering your business? -------------------
---
iii) How much tax do you pay on the average annually? -----------------------
iv) Which other kinds of levies do you pay to local authorities?
Please name them?

----
vi) How much? --
----
vii) What are the most frustrating aspect(s) of the taxation system?
a) Different methods of collecting taxes b) Multiple tax system c) High tax rate
vi) Why? ---

Employment structure

i) What kinds of labour force do engage in production?

Type of labour	Number
Skilled/Paid labour	
Unskilled/ paid labour	
Unpaid labour	
Apprentice labour	
Short term hired labour	
Subcontracting	

i) How many people are working with you at present? Ans............
ii) How many people do you employ during…:
Normal production Ans -------
Seasonal production Ans.------
v) When is your normal and seasonal period? -----

Income generation structure

i) What is the monthly income of employees/profit of the enterprises?

Income group		Min	Max.
Entrepreneur			
Workers	Skilled		
	Trainees		
	Unskilled		
Profit			

Section B: Networks

Membership in Business Related Association

i) Which of the following association(s) do you belong to?
a) NASSI
b) NASME'
c) Local manufacturers association
d) Local chambers of commerce and industry
e) Professional organisation

i) Does the contact in you make in the association very useful to all areas of your business?---
----
----

ii) What kind of assistance have you received from the association body?

----

iii) Name the services have you received from any member in the association?
----

iv) Name the services you have given to any member in the association(s) you belong to?

Membership in non-business related Association

Do you belong to any non-business related association?.
Membership any in religious organisation
Christian--------------------
Islam----------------------
Government Voluntary organisation-----------
Town Union----------------
Age grade -------------

i) If yes, does the contact you make in the association very useful to all areas of your business?
----

ii) What kind of training have you received from the association body?

----

iii) Name the services you have received from a member in the association?

----

iv) Name the services you have given to any member of the association?

Values of the Networks the entrepreneurs

i) What do you consider as very important in the business- related association you belonged?
ii) Is the association very important? If yes, why

Conflict Resolution

i) Have you had problem or some problems with your customers in the past one year?

What led to the problem?

----

ii) How did you resolve the problems ?
Without any third party -------------------------------------
With the help of a member in your association-------------------
With the help of the association's body--------------------------- -----
Engage the police or court process-------------------------

Protection of business interest

How do you protect the interest of your business? E.g.
Trade credit to your customers

Ensure quality

How do you make purchases or supplies?

How do you market your products?
a) Direct to market
b) Through special agents
c) Advertisement
d) Traders

What kind of business relationship do you have with other SMEs in your locality?
a) Supply of materials
b) Supply of products
c) Subcontracting
d) Maintenance of equipment
e) No relationship
What kind of business relationship do you have with large firms?
a) supply of materials

b) Supply of products
c) Subcontracting
d) Maintenance of equipment
e) No relationship
What kind of business relationship do you have with government institutions or large marketing firms?

Please name the institutions you have done business with?

Section C General Business Environment

Energy

i) How often do you experience power interruption by national electric power authority
(NEPA)?
a) one or more hours in a week b) one or more days in a week
c) week long d) over a month
ii) How much do you pay monthly to NEPA? ---
iii) What kind of alternative energy supply do you have?
a) Generating plant---------------------------b) Solar energy-------------------------
iv) How much do you spent monthly for the alternative energy supply? --------------
a) hourly b) every daily c) for a weakly d) months

Water Supply

i) How often do you experience water shortage?
a) one or mores hours in a week b) one or more days in a week
c) week long d) over a month
ii) How much do you spend monthly on water supply? ---------------
iii) What kind of alternative water supply do have?
a) Bore-hole b) water tanks supply c) collected rain water
iv) How much do you spend for the alternative water supply? -----------------

Finance

i) How did you raise the initial capital to start your business?

----
ii) How much was the initial capital? --------------------------
----
----
iii) You have experienced cash shortages in the course of running the daily business, how did you resolve the problem.

----
iv) When you bought additional equipment for production, how did you raise the fund.

----
v) How much money did your relative or friend invest in this business? Ans.---

vi) How much have you borrowed from the bank?

----
vii) How much financial assistance did you received from government assisted programmes?

----
viii) How much did you get from NGOs assisted programmes?

----
ix) How much did a partner invest in business?

Section D Output Performance and Price

Sales Turnover

i) On the average, how many units of the product do you produce per day?-------
----
ii) On the average, how many units are produced per month? ----------------------
----
iii) How many workers are engaged per production? ------------------------------
iv) How many skilled workers are engaged per production unit? ------------------

Price

i) What is the price of each item of your product? -------------
ii) What is the least price of your product? ------------

iii) What is highest price of your product? --------------------.

Section E Capabilities of the Enterprises

Kinds of Equipment

i) What kind of equipment is employed in production?
(a) New foreign equipment
(b) Second hand foreign equipment
c) Locally constructed equipment
ii) What was the cost of initial equipment in the production? --------------------
iii) What was cost of additional equipment in the production? --------------------

Entrepreneurs and Educational Workers Qualification[191]

At what level did you attend in schooling?

Workers	Type of Training				
Entrepreneur	Pri. Sch	Sec. Sch	Voc/T	Poly tech	University
Manager					
Skilled/paid workers					
Unskilled/ paid worker					
Unpaid worker					
Apprentice worker					
Subcontractors					

Key: Pri Sch = Primary School, Sec. Sch = Secondary School; Voc/T = Vocational/Technical School; Poly.Tech. = Polytechic

Competition

Do imports have any effect on your product? Yes -------- No ----------
If yes, How? -----------------
If No, Why? -----------

How do you withstand the market pressure due to government trade reform?
a) Producing at lowest cost
b) Introducing new designs

191 Workers capability is determined by the relationship between employment structure and the type of training received per worker

c) Introduce many designs
d) Maintaining product quality
e) Producing for special group
How much does it cost you to introduce one in the market?

Please explain the cost of each input for the new design

On the average how many designs do you introduce in the market annually?

How many designs are successful in the market?

Where did you get the ideas of the new designs?
a) Traders
b) Catalogues
c) From other producers
d) Your own ideas

Section F Institutional Support

Institutions and associations supporting small enterprises

Heads of institutions or associations supporting small enterprises development
(1) Features of the institution
i) What is your position in this institution or association? ------------------------
ii) How long have you been on this position? --
iii) Have you worked in a similar position elsewhere? if yes please name it-------
----

Services offered by the association or institution to SMEs

i) What kind of services do you offer to the enterprises? --------------------------
----
----

ii) Name the services you have rendered to members or to enterprises for the past one year
----
----

i) What kind of support did your association get from the central and local authorities?

-----

ii) What other local organisation or association have worked with you on specific project?--
----

iii) Which foreign organisation or institutions have supported your institution or association? for SME promotion in the past?

----

vi) What was the nature of the support? a) Technical (b) financial (c) advisory (d) training

vii) How long did the cooperation last? Ans. ---
----

viii) Why did the cooperation stopped?

----

ix) Which foreign organisation is supporting your association at present?

x) What is the nature of the support?

a) Technical b) financial c) advisory c) training

xi) Where is your source of information on the new trend on enterprises promotion
----
----

xii) How do you inform your members or the entrepreneurs on the new trend in business management?

----

xiii) How many workers in your association have received basic training on entrepreneurship development?

Workers	Area of Training		
	Accounting records only	Investment planning only	General business planning
Junior staffs			
Middle staffs			
Senior staffs			

Financing the SMEs

i) In what form did your institution or association tried to resolve the financial problem the Small enterprises face?

----

ii) How many entrepreneurs have received the government loan-scheme through the association?

Name of the Loan-Scheme	Period	No. of Entrepr. Received	Recovered Amount

iii) What factors led to the recovered loan?

----

iv) What factors led to non recovery of the loan?

----

v) How many enterprises have received loan from the bank through your association?

Type of loan	Period	No. of Entrepr Received	Recovered	Amount

vi) What factors lead to the recovered loan?

----

vii) What factors lead to non recovery of the loan?

----

www.ingramcontent.com/pod-product-compliance
Ingram Content Group UK Ltd.
Pitfield, Milton Keynes, MK11 3LW, UK
UKHW021847100926
8556IPUK00020B/1104

9 783631 603581